CW00918030

From Weimar to Auschwitz

From Weimar
to Auschwitz

Essays in German History

HANS MOMMSEN

Translated by Philip O'Connor

Polity Press

This edition copyright © Hans Mommsen 1991
Introduction to this edition copyright © Polity Press 1991

First published 1991 by Polity Press
in association with Basil Blackwell

Editorial office:
Polity Press, 65 Bridge Street,
Cambridge CB2 1UR, UK

Marketing and production:
Basil Blackwell Ltd
108 Cowley Road, Oxford OX4 1JF, UK

ISBN 0 7456 0557 5

British Library Cataloguing in Publication Data
A CIP catalogue record for this book is available from the British Library.

Typeset in 10 on 12 pt Ehrhardt
by Photo·graphics, Honiton, Devon
Printed in Great Britain by T. J. Press, Padstow
Printed on acid-free paper.

Contents

Acknowledgements		vii
List of Abbreviations		ix
Introduction		1
1	The Decline of the Bürgertum in Late Nineteenth- and Early Twentieth-Century Germany	11
2	Generational Conflict and Youth Rebellion in the Weimar Republic	28
3	Social Democracy on the Defensive: *The Immobility of the SPD and the Rise of National Socialism*	39
4	Class War or Co-determination: *On the Control of Economic Power in the Weimar Republic*	62
5	State and Bureaucracy in the Brüning Era	79
6	Heinrich Brüning as Chancellor: *The Failure of a Politically Isolated Strategy*	119
7	National Socialism: *Continuity and Change*	141
8	Hitler's Position in the Nazi System	163
9	20 July 1944 and the German Labour Movement	189
10	German Society and the Resistance to Hitler	208
11	The Realization of the Unthinkable: *The 'Final Solution of the Jewish Question' in the Third Reich*	224
12	Hannah Arendt and the Eichmann Trial	254
Notes		279
Glossary		354
Index		357

Acknowledgements

Chapter 1 is translated from 'Die Auflösung des Bürgertums seit dem späten 19. und 20. Jahrhundert', in Jürgen Kocka (ed.), *Bürger und Bürgerlichkeit im 19. Jahrhundert*, Göttingen: Vandenhoeck & Ruprecht, 1987. Copyright Vandenhoeck & Ruprecht 1987.

Chapter 2 is translated from 'Generationskonflikt und Jugendrevolte in der Weimarer Republik', in Thomas Koebner et al. (eds); *Mit uns zieht die neue Zeit; Der Mythos Jugend*, Frankfurt a.M.: Suhrkamp, 1985, pp. 50–67. Copyright Suhrkamp Verlag 1985.

Chapter 3 is translated from 'Die Sozialdemokratie in der Defensive: Der Immobilismus der SPD und der Aufstieg des Nationalsozialismus', in Hans Mommsen (ed.), *Sozialdemokratie zwischen Klassenbewegung und Volkspartei*, Frankfurt a.M.: Athenäum Fischer, 1974, pp. 106–33. Copyright Athenäum Fischer 1974.

Chapter 4 is translated from *Klassenkampf oder Mitbestimmung. Zum Problem der Kontrolle wirtschaftlicher Macht in der Weimarer Republik*, Frankfurt a.M.: Otto-Brenner-Stiftung, 1978. Copyright Otto-Brenner-Stiftung 1978.

Chapter 5 is translated from 'Staat und Bürokratie in der Ära Brüning', in Gotthard Jasper (ed.), *Tradition und Reform in der deutschen Politik. Gedenkschrift für Waldemar Besson*, Frankfurt a.M., Berlin and Vienna: Ullstein/Propyläen, 1976, pp. 81–137. Copyright Ullstein/Propyläen 1976.

Chapter 6 is translated from 'Heinrich Brünings Politik als Reichskanzler. Das Scheitern eines politischen Alleinganges', in Karl Holl (ed.), *Wirtschaftskrise und liberale Demokratie. Das Ende der Weimarer Republik und die gegenwärtige Situation*, Göttingen: Vandenhoeck & Ruprecht, 1978, pp. 16–45. Copyright Vandenhoeck & Ruprecht 1978.

Chapter 7 is reprinted from 'National Socialism: Continuity and Change', in Walter Laqueur (ed.), *Fascism: A Reader's Guide*, Harmondsworth: Gower, 1979, pp. 151–92. Copyright Gower Press 1979.

Chapter 8 is translated from 'Hitlers Stellung im nationalsozialistischen Herrschaftssystem', in Gerhard Hirschfeld and Lothar Kettenacker (eds), *Der 'Führerstaat'. Mythos und Realität. Studien zur Struktur und Politik des Dritten Reiches*, Stuttgart: Klett-Cotta, 1981, pp. 43–72. Copyright Klett-Cotta 1981.

Chapter 9 is translated from 'Der 20. Juli und die deutsche Arbeiterbewegung', Berlin: Gedenkstätte Deutscher Widerstand, 1985. Copyright Gedenkstätte Deutscher Widerstand 1985.

Chapter 10 is translated from 'Der Widerstand gegen Hitler und die deutsche Gesellschaft', in Jurgen Schmädeke and Peter Steinbach (eds), *Der Widerstand gegen den Nationalsozialismus. Die deutsche Gesellschaft und der Widerstand gegen Hitler*, Munich: Piper, 1985, pp. 3–23. Copyright R. Piper Verlag 1985.

Chapter 11 is reprinted from 'The Realization of the Unthinkable: The "Final Solution of the Jewish Question" in the Third Reich', in Gerhard Hirschfeld (ed.), *The Policies of Genocide: Jews and Soviet Prisoners of War in Nazi Germany*, London, Boston and Sydney: Allen & Unwin, 1986. Copyright German Historical Institute 1986. First published in German as 'Die Realisierung des Utopischen: die "Endlösung der Judenfrage" im Dritten Reich', in *Geschichte und Gesellschaft*, 9 (1983), Göttingen: Vandenhoeck & Ruprecht, 1983, pp. 381–420.

Chapter 12 is translated from 'Hannah Arendt und der Prozess gegen Adolf Eichmann'. Introduction to Hannah Arendt, *Eichmann in Jerusalem*, new edition, Munich: Piper, 1986, pp. I–XXXVII. Copyright R. Piper Verlag 1986.

Abbreviations

ADB	Allgemeiner Deutscher Beamtenbund	General Federation of German Civil Servants
ADGB	Allgemeiner Deutscher Gewerkschaftsbund	General Federation of German Trade Unions
AfA	Allgemeiner freier Angestellten-Bund	General Federation of (white-collar) Employees
APO	Ausserparlamentarische Opposition	Extra-Parliamentary Opposition
AVI	Arbeitsgemeinschaft der Eisenverarbeitendenindustrie	Working Association of the Iron Processing Industry
CDU/CSU	Christlich-Demokratische Union/Christlich-Soziale Union	Christian Democratic Union/Christian Social Union
DAF	Deutsche Arbeitsfront	German Labour Front
DAP	Deutsche Arbeiterpartei	German Workers' Party
DBB	Deutscher Beamtenbund	German Federation of Civil Servants
DDP	Deutsche Demokratische Partei	German Democratic Party
DHV	Deutscher Handelsgehilfenverband	German National Association of Commercial Employees
DNVP	Deutsch-Nationale Volkspartei	German National People's Party

DVP	Deutsche Volkspartei	German People's Party
Gestapo	Geheime Staatspolizei	Secret State Police
ISK	Internationaler Sozialistischer Kampfbund	International Socialist Fighting League
KJVD	Kommunistischer Jugendverband Deutschlands	German Communist Youth Association
KPD	Kommunistische Partei Deutschlands	Communist Party of Germany
KPO	Kommunistische Partei – Opposition	Communist Party Opposition
MSPD	Mehrheits-Sozialdemokratische Partei Deutschlands	Majority Social Democratic Party of Germany
NSBO	Nationalsozialistische Betriebszellenorganisation	National Socialist Factory-Cell Organization
NSDAP	Nationalsozialistische Deutsche Arbeiterpartei	National Socialist German Workers' Party (Nazi Party)
OHL	Oberste Heeresleitung	Army Supreme Command
OKH	Oberkommando des Heeres	Army High Command
OKW	Oberkommando der Wehrmacht	Armed Forces Supreme Command
RdI	Reichsverband der deutschen Industrie	Reich Federation of German Industry
RGO	Revolutionäre Gewerkschaftsopposition	(Communist) Revolutionary Trade Union Opposition
RhB	Reichsbund höherer Beamten	German Federation of Higher Civil Servants
RM	Reichsmark	(unit of currency)
RSHA	Reichssicherheitshauptamt	Reich Security Head Office
SA	Sturmabteilung	Storm troopers
SAJ	Sozialistische Arbeiterjugend	Socialist Working-Class Youth (youth wing of the SPD)

SAPD	Sozialistische Arbeiterpartei Deutschlands	Socialist Workers' Party of Germany
SD	Sicherheitsdienst der SS	SS Security Service
Sopade	Sozialdemokratische Partei Deutschlands	(Émigré SPD executive, 1933–45)
SPD	Sozialdemokratische Partei Deutschlands	Social Democratic Party of Germany
SPÖ	Sozialistische Partei Österreichs	Socialist Party of Austria
SS	Schutzstaffel	Defence unit
USPD	Unabhängige Sozialdemokratische Partei Deutschlands	Independent Social Democratic Party of Germany
VdA	Vereinigung deutscher Arbeitgeberverbände	Federation of German Employers' Associations
WTB	Woytinsky/Tarnow/Baade Plan	(ADGB work creation plan)
ZAG	Zentralarbeitsgemeinschaft	Central Working Association (of employers and unions)

Introduction

The selection of essays on German history published here spans the period from the late Wilhelmine empire to the Nazi epoch. The essays were written in different contexts and examine from a number of different perspectives the problem of how the relatively hopeful beginnings of a German democracy in 1918–19 ended finally in the catastrophe of Auschwitz. The name Auschwitz symbolizes the almost inconceivable crimes committed by the Nazi regime against the European Jews. But it also represents the 'destruction of politics' which occurred under Nazism; the process by which the system of balancing divergent societal interests, however imperfect, was replaced by a rampage of ruthless violence, unparalleled brutality and the destruction of large areas of Europe in the senseless continuation of a war which from the start Hitler could not have won. The period under review is characterized fundamentally by the events of the Holocaust. On the one hand, the Holocaust was the product of deeply rooted ideological delusions. But it also increasingly served as a psychological compensation in a system where the pipe dreams of the 'thousand-year Reich' were shattered by stark realities which Hitler's repeated avowal of unbending will-power could not change.

The political right essentially opted for the fatal path which was to lead to political, military and moral catastrophe when the system established by the Paris Treaties appeared to have put an end for ever to the hegemony of the German Reich in Europe. The innate weaknesses of the Weimar Republic at the time of its establishment were, contrary to what many analysts believed, due least of all to the foreign policy burdens which Germany had to bear as a result of the territorial and material losses she suffered and the reparations imposed on her. The new border with Poland was regarded by all political tendencies in Germany as untenable. It certainly provided an effective launching pad for those parties and institutions which were determined to reassert the lost power position of the Reich by military means even before the Versailles Peace Treaty had been drafted. But in mobilizing nationalist resentment the main purpose the conservative right was pursuing was the strengthening of its own domestic position.

The provisions of the Weimar constitution contributed equally little to the instability of the Republic. The much criticized system of proportional representation certainly encouraged the proliferation of small parties and splinter groups. But the primary responsibility for the creeping constitutional crisis which took hold from 1920 and became finally irreversible with the formation of the presidential cabinets from 1930 lay, along with the declared anti-republicanism of the bourgeois right, in the increasingly unbridgeable differences between the bourgeois centre and the SPD (Social Democratic Party). These proved to be temporarily surmountable only in the area of foreign policy. This effectively meant that only coalition governments, which were internally very fragile, could be formed. The decisive factor in this was the weakness of the bourgeois forces in Germany, which, together with the moderate sections of the working class, were the only basis on which a new order could have been constructed. These were internally divided, destabilized by the widespread fear of threatening social decline and characterized by a growing moral indifference. The dissolution of the bourgeoisie as a cohesive class and as the bearer of the democratic traditions inherited from classical liberalism and the Enlightenment made bourgeois groups increasingly susceptible from the mid-nineteenth century to anti-socialist resentment, political irrationalism and a stifling form of nationalism. The following selection of essays starts therefore with an analysis of this complex.

The parties of the bourgeois centre which participated in the establishment of the Weimar Republic sought to extricate themselves from responsibility for it from as early as the signing of the Versailles Peace Treaty. But, despite conforming to the hybrid nationalism of the period, they were rapidly marginalized. The erosion of basic liberal values and the sharpening conflict of interests within the bourgeois parties of the centre as a result of the economic stagnation of the Weimar years were decisive factors in this process.[1] The general anti-liberal trend of the time was most forcefully reflected in the mentality of younger intellectuals and academics, though it was also evident among other groups of the younger generation. These saw themselves effectively excluded from political participation and their vociferous opposition to the established parties contributed decisively to the paralysing of the parliamentary system of Weimar. In this sense the generational conflict of the period formed part of the general crisis of democracy in Weimar Germany and the second essay examines the conflict in this context.

The following essay deals with the immobility of the labour movement. Due to the weakness of the liberal centre, from the birth of the Republic, the Social Democratic Party became the main upholder of parliamentary democracy. The SPD effectively committed itself finally to the parliamentary system when it joined the Reichstag Inter-Party Committee of 1917. But it did not embrace it unconditionally or irrevocably. This was demonstrated by the debates which continued within the party throughout the Weimar era and was even clearly evident in its conflict with the USPD (Independent Social Democratic Party of Germany) in 1919. The reluctance of the SPD leadership to enter coalitions with the bourgeois parties was reinforced by the uncompromising stance adopted by the DVP (German People's Party) in particular. The DVP persisted in its intransigence despite the fact that Gustav Stresemann, its leader for many years, realized by no later than 1924 that a stabilization of the parliamentary system was only possible through a coalition compromise based on the common ground with the SPD. During the revolutionary phase in 1919–20 the social democratic leaders made some serious and irreversible mistakes. These were the result of both the excessive emphasis placed in the party leadership on the principle of strict adherence to legality and of the political indecisiveness of the leaders of the MSPD (Majority Social Democratic Party of Germany). But, apart from this, the organized labour movement was also confronted by fundamental structural problems over which it had little control. In contrast to the favourable conditions which the economic growth of the pre-war era had created for the movement, the limited expansion rate of the gross national product after 1918 led to an intensification of the conflict about its social distribution. The simultaneous process of industrial modernization meant that the working class had stopped growing as a proportion of the overall employed population. The rising 'new middle class', that is, the white-collar sector which was steadily growing in importance, increasingly stressed its independence from traditional labour and largely remained aloof from socialist organizations.

In addition to this weakening of the organized labour movement by structural factors, the SPD and the Free Trade Unions suffered from the specific handicap that their corps of officials as well as their memberships were becoming progressively over-aged. This phenomenon was not by any means confined to the SPD and affected the bourgeois parties equally. Nevertheless it contributed to the relative immobility which characterized the response of the reformist labour organizations to the rise of the Nazi movement. It also explains why the SPD tended to seek refuge in parliamentary opposition rather than risk being tainted with the uncomfortable compromises inherent in coalitionist politics, which tended anyway to contravene the traditional party programme.

The fourth essay, 'Class War or Co-determination', tackles the question of the role of economic power in the Weimar Republic. The unbridgeable differences with the KPD (Communist Party) forced the SPD further on to the defensive. Precisely for this reason, the social policy which the state pursued assumed a crucial significance for the inner stability of the

parliamentary system; this was especially because the much feared drift of
sections of the industrial working class to the radical left could only be
prevented if social peace was secured. The spectacular growth of the
organized labour movement from 1917 rapidly went into reverse from 1920
in line with the general trend throughout western Europe at the time. This
quantitative weakening of organized labour in the post-revolutionary period
hit the bargaining power of the trade unions particularly severely. It was
offset to some degree, however, by advances achieved in the area of social
legislation and in the institutionalized social machinery of the state. The
social policies pursued in the early period of the Weimar Republic had
largely a compensatory function, given that economic policy continued to
be shaped predominantly in the interests of big industry. This was a result
of the successful rebuttal during the Revolution of the demands raised by
the workers' councils and the unions for a say in economic decision-making
('co-determination'). Social legislation enacted by the state secured the
revolutionary achievements of the eight-hour day and the recognition of
the collective bargaining rights of the trade unions. But with the revaluation
of the Reichsmark in autumn 1923 and the enactment of the Dawes Plan,
which commercialized Germany's reparations debts, heavy industry began
to campaign for the social concessions made during the inflationary period
to be annulled. The unions managed to maintain their position in the iron,
steel and coal sector only by resort to full dependence on the state social
mechanism of compulsory arbitration. Given the imbalance between the
social partners, the notion of free collective bargaining was largely fictitious
anyway, and in heavy industry both sides willingly shifted responsibility for
wage decisions to the state arbitrator. This ultimately proved too great a
strain on the cabinet. The demands raised by the ADGB (General Federation of German Trade Unions) for an expansion of workers' participation
in economic decision-making within the firm, its Programme for Economic
Democracy and the willingness of the unions to take on responsibilities in
the overall economy implied in the WTB Plan for employment creation,
issued by the ADGB in 1932, represented a workable basis for overcoming
the imbalance between employers and workers. But this approach met no
concrete response until after 1945.

Big industry played a decisive role in the destruction of the Weimar
Republic and indirectly in its replacement by the Nazi dictatorship. This
lay not so much in the rather insignificant financial support it gave the
NSDAP (National Socialist German Workers' Party) and even less in the
temporary political support for the Nazis which came from some circles of
heavy industry. But the conscious destruction by heavy industrial interests
of the social compromise achieved in the revolutionary phase of 1919–20
decisively weakened the inner ability of the Republic to resist the onslaught
on it from the nationalist right. The substantial political influence wielded

by heavy industry through its multifarious political contacts was fatal in this regard and was way out of proportion to the declining economic importance of heavy industry. Its position was reinforced, however, by the fact that its political co-operation was indispensable in meeting Germany's reparations obligations. The political pressure brought to bear by the industrial interest groups played a major role in the collapse of the Grand Coalition in spring 1930 and thus in toppling the last government of the Weimar Republic based on a parliamentary majority. The insistence of heavy industry that free collective bargaining be largely eliminated also undermined the authority of the Brüning government. Brüning broke with the SPD under pressure from the DVP and this made the transition to a presidential cabinet system unavoidable.

The two essays on the Brüning era – on the relationship between bureaucracy and state in this period and on the political isolation of Brüning – examine the failure of the attempt by Chancellor Brüning to stabilize government as a system freed from party political control and based on the bureaucracy, in the context of his expectation that a successful outcome to the reparations negotiations was imminent. In contrast to traditional interpretations, Brüning's policies are not seen as having been aimed at tackling the economic crisis but rather as a strategy to use the crisis to achieve certain longer-term political goals. Recent historical studies have claimed that the crisis-laden economic development of the Weimar Republic was largely due to overgenerous concessions made on the wages front for political reasons and to an excessive level of social welfare provision. It is argued that these contributed to the chronic shortage of investment capital and to excessively high production costs. This interpretation has been put forward most forcefully by Knut Borchardt,[2] who bases his argument particularly on the disproportionate level of wage costs during this period. But, as against this, it should be noted that effective wages were generally higher than those achieved by collective bargaining and, in terms of the rise in labour productivity, were certainly not exorbitant, which would indicate that the unions did not in fact pursue full equalization. The growth of the white-collar sector as a proportion of the employed population in comparison to blue-collar workers led to wage costs being higher than in the Wilhelmine period and had a far greater influence on the rise in general wage costs than the limited successes achieved by trade union activity. In a properly functioning system of industrial relations, the pressure from the workforce to maintain wage levels would have curtailed the persistence of economically unviable production and forced the pace of modernization. But this occurred to only a very limited degree in the raw materials sector during the Weimar period. In fact, it was precisely in heavy industry, which substantially shaped the industrial relations and social policy climate of the time, that the investment policies pursued by employers contributed greatly to the relative stagnation of the Weimar economy. Their market expectations were over-optimistic and their assessments of their competitiveness faulty; furthermore, structural overcapacity was created through rationalisation and exports were consciously subsidized at the expense of domestic consumers.

Whether the state social mechanisms established during the Weimer Republic were economically tenable can only be judged in conjunction with the closely related question of the economic and financial policies pursued by Brüning during the economic crisis. Borchardt defends Brüning by arguing that for both political and economic reasons there was no alternative to the deflationary policy he rigorously pursued.[3] But Brüning persisted in his policy of deflation at all costs, despite the fact that with the banking crisis of 1931 the public fear of inflation which had lingered since the early 1920s had been largely dispelled. This was because his primary aim was a political one of achieving a definitive end to reparations, and this took clear priority over any boosting of the economy through employment creation and credit formation. But the chancellor's inflexible financial policy finally alienated the bourgeois right completely, as they could not see the ultimate aim of his strategy. In preparing the ground for his plans to reform the constitutional structure of the Reich, Brüning also prepared the instrument which his successor, Franz von Papen, was to use to replace the social democratic coalition government in Prussia with a commissarial regime.

Both Brüning and the right-wing bourgeois politicians who succeeded him believed that the growth of the NSDAP was only a transitory phenomenon and that it would lose its significance once the parliamentary system had been transformed in an authoritarian direction. Despite a similar process that had occurred in fascist Italy, they failed to realize that Hitler and the national socialist movement, which was increasingly centred on Hitler's person, would not allow themselves to be torn apart in a bourgeois coalition of the right. This failure was a result of the conservative 'taming' concept which presumed that Hitler would ultimately have to submit to the logic of reality and would thus end up dependent on bourgeois expertise. The definitive break with the SPD and the Free Trade Unions, which was seen as the prerequisite for tying Hitler into the system, in fact made the conservatives totally dependent on him.

Ideologically the NSDAP was linked mainly with the traditions of German imperialism and the anti-semitic völkisch movement of the Wilhelmine period. But the explosive political potential of the Nazi movement lay in the manner in which it unscrupulously manipulated and mobilized repressed social resentments while simultaneously avoiding tying its hands politically. The party profited from the disillusionment of large sections of the bourgeois electorate with the Weimar parliamentary system, which was blamed for the process of social restratification under way at the time at the expense of the 'old middle class' (*Mittelstand*). The Nazi Party's sympathizers included a substantial proportion of younger voters who felt alienated in the 'old men's Republic' of Weimar. No force in the Weimar Republic benefited more than national socialism from the generational conflict which emerged in the second half of the 1920s.

The content of Nazi ideology did not differ substantially from that of the traditional bourgeois right. But the NSDAP was geared exclusively to achieving electoral successes. Its campaign strategy, which presented the party as the radical alternative to the 'system' of the Weimar era and gave the impression of being an unstoppable and growing movement, was far superior to that of the bourgeois nationalist forces. The Führer cult, the successful infiltration of the numerous associations on which the traditional parties of the bourgeois centre and right (with the exception of the Catholic Centre Party) had relied and a campaigning approach meticulously geared to appeal to variable electoral interests secured it a growing section of the electorate. But this growing support was among an increasingly volatile electorate.[4]

The debate on the extent to which the development of the Nazi movement and the Third Reich were determined by Adolf Hitler alone has continued among historians. The argument centres on whether the actions of the Nazi regime were simply the implementation of a programme decided upon at an early stage[5] or were more the product of a complex interaction between the dictator and the power structures of the regime which, due to the failure to institutionalize them, developed their own momenta. The plethora of institutions and rulers in the Third Reich was not simply the product of a calculating dictator acting to protect his own position. The effect of the intense rivalries which emerged was necessarily to progressively radicalize the regime's development. But Hitler, who consistently encouraged this process, not only benefited from it but was also its prisoner. Although many recent studies have examined this theme, the basic case as put in the two articles reprinted here, 'Continuity and Change' and 'Hitler's Position in the Nazi System', retains its validity.[6] As opposed to recent trends in studies of Hitler,[7] the author remains firmly convinced that it is utterly misleading to portray Hitler as a 'revolutionary' character or as a clever statesman and to attribute to him a master plan which he only revealed in stages and which went beyond the politics of allocating and manipulating power. Hitler's visionary political goals certainly indicate an extraordinary tactical flair, but they were increasingly divorced from reality. In the carrying out of these policies, the diligence of his subordinates put him under intense psychological pressure to proceed with the immediate implementation of what hitherto had been vague long-term ideological aims.

The institutional interpretation of the national socialist system[8] given in these essays indicates that responsibility for the crimes of the Third Reich was shared by an extended spectrum of people and encourages an examination of their wider social causes. From this perspective, an analysis of the various strands of the German resistance to Hitler acquires a fundamental importance because it reveals what the possible alternatives to the Nazi dictatorship were. The socialist and communist resistance based on the banned organizations of the labour movement was confined to their former activists and therefore remained largely isolated. Quite a few socialists realized the hopelessness of a resistance movement based on the suppressed labour organizations and decided to link up with the national conservative conspirators who planned the coup of July 1944. In the end, the socialists involved played a major part in organizing the coup attempt, and this is shown in detail in the article '20 July 1944 and the German Labour Movement'. The fact that the Weimar Republic had been completely discredited created an apparent legitimacy for the Nazi regime. This made the position of the opposition extremely difficult because, unlike the resistance in the rest of western Europe, it had no usurped constitutional base to seek to restore. This explains the comprehensive planning by the national conservative resistance for a social and political 'new order'. They proposed a 'third way' between parliamentary democracy and fascist dictatorship and some of their ideas were certainly utopian. The essay 'German Society and the Resistance to Hitler' does not concentrate on the German resistance movement's chances of success or on its weaknesses and mistakes. It examines instead its importance as the only social force capable of providing an alternative to the Nazi regime.

The crimes of the Nazis culminated in the genocide of the European Jews symbolized by the name Auschwitz. It is commonly supposed that Hitler was determined from the start to exterminate the Jews of Europe in the event of war. The essay entitled 'The Realization of the Unthinkable', however, illustrates the complex process which began with the segregation and expropriation of the Jewish population and led to their deportation and extermination without a systematically calculated programme or a formal order from Hitler being required. In fact, it is exactly the cloud of self-deception, secrecy and anti-semitic incitement in which the extermination process occurred that helps to explain why no substantial protests came from the military and administrative elites, which had, after all, never been Nazified completely. The most frightening aspect is not the fanatical anti-semitism of those who carried out the genocide, but rather the acceptance and toleration of it, indeed the approval and support for it, which came from the leading officials in all areas of the regime.

It was precisely this problem of guilt through failure to intervene in a major historical event made up of individual trivial components which Hannah Arendt raised in her report on the trial of Adolf Eichmann in Jerusalem. The final essay in this volume takes issue with Arendt's specific interpretation of the Holocaust. Despite factual errors and some erroneous interpretations of minor points, she anticipated the direction modern analyses have taken. When her *Eichmann in Jerusalem* was first published, it was subjected to the fiercest criticism both in and outside Israel. The singularity of the Nazi genocide of the Jews distinguishes it from all previous anti-Jewish pogroms. A major question is whether this makes impossible a comparison with other acts of collective crime in history. Hannah Arendt answered this by suggesting that the crime committed by the Nazis against the Jewish people was equally directed against humanity generally. The most extreme form of inhuman violence conceivable was encountered in the Holocaust, which also encompasses the Nazi crimes of violence committed against other peoples, races and religions, as well as against political opponents, alleged 'antisocials' and finally the sick and the old, who, as the fascists viewed people as an economic resource, had become superfluous. Hannah Arendt's discovery of the 'banality of evil' is a warning against believing that genocidal crimes only occur in a charismatically charged atmosphere and dressed in ideology.

In this volume, key problem areas of German history in the period of the two world wars are examined. These include the structural weaknesses of Weimar democracy and the underlying reasons why these ended in a radical fascist dictatorship rather than in an ordinary authoritarian regime. The author attempts to explain why resistance to the rule of crime and terror did not emerge earlier and was not more comprehensive, and also why it remained confined to marginal political and social circles. The NSDAP finally achieved its breakthrough as a mass movement, putting itself forward with the help of the conservative cliques around Hindenburg and von Papen as the saviour of Germany from communism. It achieved this with the promise of bringing the socialist sections of the working class over to the nationalist camp but then proceeded rapidly to dispense with the shackles of bourgeois cabinet government. But the book makes it clear that the political and moral will of German society to resist the destruction of the constitutional rule of law and pluralist foundations of the Republic had already crumbled long before this occurred.

The crisis of German society was a result of the refusal to accept that the military defeat of 1918 was a reality, of the illusion that the failed 'national awakening' of 1914 could be successfully re-enacted under national socialist leadership and of the dream that a classless society free of internal conflict could be realized under the auspices of the right. These factors explain why the democratic socialists had no chance in the long run of stabilizing the republican system and why the national conservatives only began to try to distance themselves from Hitler when his position of power had already become unshakeable. The opposition within the social elites, and not just in the politically indoctrinated population, was therefore hopelessly isolated from the start. This remained the case despite the widespread criticism of the regime's policies evident from 1941. Such criticism, however, normally excluded the person of Hitler, who had become the symbol of national identity, and never crystallized into political resistance.

In 1986 a heated controversy erupted among West German historians – known as the *Historikerstreit*[9] – as to whether or not it would be appropriate to finally lay the history of Nazism to rest or at least to treat it like any other period of German and European history. The call for the history of national socialism to be 'historicized' was a concealed attempt on the part of some of those involved to relativize the crimes of the Nazi regime – which were unique in their sheer scale – and particularly to put them on a par with the crimes of Stalinism. These attempts, however, failed to convince either public or historiographical opinion in West Germany.

In fact, the question of the singularity or comparability of the Nazi regime was wrongly framed. A central issue in the study of the Nazi epoch concerns the complete collapse of inherited moral conventions in an advanced western society which unleashed unparalleled destructive energies. Everything would tend to indicate that events of this kind will not repeat themselves in the same form and particularly not on the same scale. But the example of Nazism, which is singular in this regard at least, teaches us to be alert to the vital necessity of protecting the institutional foundations of society and the state, because it was the destruction of these that made the escalation of crime which characterized the Third Reich possible in the first place. While the ideological justifications which such regimes construct for themselves often appear interchangeable, the conditions under which individuals and entire societies become implicated in a collective guilt are certainly comparable. The history of national socialism is a unique and vivid example of how easily the patina of social civilization can crumble, as well as how trivial the mechanisms can be through which this occurs; together these factors can lead to inhumanity and the cynical use of violence being given free rein. There was no inner logic of any kind determining that German historical development should lead from Weimar to Auschwitz. But that this fall could take place in little more than two decades and drag the whole of Europe with it in its wake is a lesson to us never to become complacent about inner threats to freedom.

1

The Decline of the Bürgertum in Late Nineteenth- and Early Twentieth-Century Germany

It is probably impossible to define accurately what constituted the bourgeois era and which criteria transformed the concept of Bürgertum from its original function – describing the social rank of those urban groups outside the feudal structure – into a comprehensive definition of a specific type of social behaviour, mentality, way of life and cultural habits. If the term 'Bürgertum' is taken to refer not merely to the middle class in the technical sense, such as exists in all societies, but rather to a specific socio-cultural phenomenon, then an attempt to elucidate it for a later historical period should help to clarify or at least to correct our picture of it. The following essay is an attempt to do this. It is based on the hypothesis that both the political and the social development of Germany from the late nineteenth century were marked by the progressive disintegration of the bourgeois way of life and the decline of the bourgeois ethos.

The basic contention of this hypothesis is that the Bürgertum, particularly in the nineteenth century, constituted both objectively and subjectively and despite much internal differentiation a uniform social formation with a specific system of values;[1] this uniformity, though admittedly developed primarily in reaction to other classes, gradually diminished and the Bürgertum as a specific social formation dissolved. An important question which arises in conjunction with this is when exactly the political and cultural forms of association specific to the Bürgertum underwent this change. The same goes for the socio-cultural patterns of consciousness which shaped it. If a change in values or an abandonment of previously accepted values can be established which demonstrate that the Bürgertum as a social formation declined not only as a class, but also as the bearer of a specific culture, this would contribute to a more exact definition of the criteria delineating the concept 'bourgeois' as outlined above.[2]

In analysing this it is necessary to differentiate between objective socio-cultural factors and their effects on consciousness and organizational forms, given that there was a certain lapse of time before such effects became apparent. The process of rapid social restratification which occurred during the imperialist period formed the background to the crisis in bourgeois consciousness which became increasingly pronounced from the turn of the century.[3] This was expressed in intensified internal migration and particularly in the growth of the urban population, the steady advance of urbanization, changes in the structures of social mobility and the disintegration of a previously homogeneous bourgeois establishment.[4] This process of social restratification was evidenced in the composition of residential areas, which now began to show a greater social mix, and in the local government structure, where the hitherto sacrosanct position of the old bourgeois establishment began to be challenged. In the same context, the socially dominant position enjoyed by the sections of the upper middle strata shaped by the classical bourgeois ethos and the newly emergent business-class groups came under increasing threat, not least from the new and partly Jewish financial aristocracy. The increasing social differentiation within the middle classes which accompanied the emergence of the white-collar stratum was reflected in the fragmentation of middle-class organizations. While continuing to share a common bourgeois interest in containing social democracy, these were otherwise divided internally along socially antagonistic lines.[5]

The major socio-economic changes briefly sketched here were interpreted by bourgeois society primarily as a cultural crisis. But they also precipitated a widespread self-criticism within bourgeois society which developed some pointedly anti-bourgeois strands. Such was the case with the youth movement which emerged as a protest against bourgeois obsessions with security,[6] the often sectarian reform movements accompanying this, the rise of 'vitalism' and the growing trend towards irrationalism. These phenomena were, however, essentially internal to bourgeois society and, as partial deviations from it, served to confirm bourgeois structures as a whole. Pariahs could be tolerated so long as they did not seriously threaten these structures. This characterized the manner in which assimilated Jews were accepted and also the outsiders of the Monte Verita movement, the followers of naturism, the anthroposophists and other neo-religious movements which still await a systematic analysis.[7] Rebellion against the bourgeois virtue of security, contemptuously dismissed as 'Spiessertum' (petit bourgeois), and against the overwhelmingly materialist bourgeois mentality informed the basic outlook of large numbers of *fin de siècle* intellectuals. It was closely related to the relativization of values which affected all areas and rapidly gave rise to the replacement of traditional value patterns by voluntaristic norms.[8]

The First World War gave an added impetus to these sentiments, which, through the call for a fundamental renewal of society, took hold particularly among the activist section of the younger generation. There was a widespread feeling that the war would put an end to the era of bourgeois prosperity and security once and for all. This converged with the extreme ideological conflict which emerged between the war and post-war generation on the one hand and the social elites still tied to the values of Wilhelmine society on the other.[9] In the agitation of the extreme right, polemics against the 'redundant' Bürgertum formed an integral part of the general attack on the 'senility' of the Weimar Republic. This was the case, for example, with the polemics of Gregor Strasser and Joseph Goebbels.[10] The conviction of being aligned uncompromisingly against the elites of Weimar society and their bourgeois values was also central to the outlook of the bündisch youth. While this movement originally rejected politics, it also sought a totally reconstructed society based on new models of community.[11] Parallel to this and with a broad support in intellectual circles which should not be underestimated, neo-conservative thinking aimed to reverse the effects of the revolution of 1789 and to abolish not only liberal political forms but also the bourgeois individualism which had given risen to them.[12]

It became fashionable among the younger generation of Weimar to be anti-bourgeois. The same was true of the neo-conservative writers behind the Stahlhelm who acted as the harbingers of a new conservatism in political ideas. In the latter years of the Weimar Republic they found an outstanding mouthpiece in Zehrer's periodical *Die Tat*.[13] Similar feelings were also evident on the reformist left. These were expressed by Theodor Haubach when he spoke of the barriers erected by the Republic against the forces of the younger generation.[14] But the generational conflict concealed a new outlook on life which, although it regarded itself as anti-bourgeois, could in fact only have developed from specifically bourgeois premises. The example of the Freikorps, which were recruited almost exclusively from the Bürgertum, is a case in point. They believed that they were developing a heroic military culture counter to that of bourgeois society, which they denounced as symptomatic of national disintegration. Ernst von Salomon was a typical representative of this counter-culture. It developed from a deep-seated revulsion at the satiated society of the nineteenth century.[15] Von Salomon typified the glorification of violence in politics which, as Hitler astutely noted, could elicit a positive response from wide sections of the Bürgertum. The abandonment of bourgeois convictions and values was epitomized in the rejection of an ordered, institutionalized approach to regulating conflict and in the flight to an aestheticized myth of violence;[16] these were dialectically tied, however, to a rigid adherence to what were specifically bourgeois notions of order.

The disintegration of specifically bourgeois social forms may be seen most clearly in the political field. There can be little argument but that the Verein represented the form of cultural and political organization that was characteristic of bourgois society and closely tied to the bourgeois concept

of 'public life'.[17] In contrast to pre-constitutional forms of political organization, such as clubs, reading rooms, secret societies and salons representative of an earlier transitional phase, the Verein was a form of association
which in both its internal organization and outward purpose was intrinsically
oriented to the public domain and produced public opinion. Its basic
defining characteristic was its open accessibility to all people of a like mind.
Following the consolidation of the constitutional system and the transition
to parliamentary forms, it was not uncommon for political parties to adopt
the organizational form of the Verein at first. In the conservative camp this
occurred belatedly and was soon superseded by a form of organization
geared towards mass integration and dominated by organized interest
groups.[18] This was also true of the majority of bourgeois associations,
though these progressed sooner to transitional forms.

A significant turning-point came with the decline of the Verein as the
preferred form of political and associative organization from the turn of the
century, or at least the abandonment of its specifically public aspects. This
process had been under way since the 1870s but became more marked
during and particularly after the First World War. It is hardly surprising
that this was most evident among the groups on the right wing of the
bourgeois spectrum. The names adopted by such organizations were
extremely vague: the Reichshammerbund, the Dürerbund, the Germanic
Order, the Thule Society, the June Club, the Herrenklub, the Wednesday
Society and the National Club of 1919. These organizations were legion
and there were such large areas of overlap between them that a detailed
listing would have little meaning. They were characterized by their return
to pre-liberal forms of association. The Verein principles of free recruitment
and voluntary membership that was available to all those interested were
discarded in favour of co-opted membership, ritual practices and secrecy.
The so-called ring movement of ever expanding networks of contacts linking
the leadership circles of society was without doubt characteristic of the
structure of hitherto bourgeois society as it went into decline. This is
despite the fact that the movement also existed in aristocratic circles and
even among sections of the political left, as epitomized by organizations
such as the ISK (International Socialist Fighting League) or the circle
around the *Neue Blätter für den Sozialismus*.[19]

The socio-political significance of the overwhelmingly neo-conservative
ring movement of the 1920s can hardly be overstated. Many of the prominent figures in it were also involved in the political party structure. But this
network of personal cross-contacts linking the elites embraced the entire
political system and functioned both as an umbrella organization and as a
substitute for the bourgeois party system as this went into decline.[20] The
parties of the left were an exception to this, being at best only loosely
connected with it through individual right-wing outsiders. The bündisch

movement paralleled the ring. Its form of organization was equally fundamentally opposed to bourgeois principles of association and was based on
the fiction of a closed, spiritually homogeneous community. This was the
case with organizations of the militant right generally, from the Freikorps
and their successor organizations to such right-wing groupings – now almost
forgotten – as Eugen Kogon's Bund Kreuz und Adler[21] and other similar
associations of an explicitly political nature.[22]

Taken together, these circles formed an anti-republican, counter-public
opinion which, while working deliberately to undermine the dominance of
political parties in general, were essentially aligned in support of the parties
of the right. They constituted in effect the new 'Front' which Hans Zehrer
passionately advocated as the united force to replace the particularism of
the party state.[23] They also signalled the retreat of the Bürgertum to an
elitist defensive position. By exerting their influence indirectly, they hoped
to be able to manipulate the 'mass society' they despised to suit their
purposes and to fundamentally restructure it in the long run. To understand
this fully it is necessary to look in some detail at how bourgeois interest
organizations, closed circles of elites like the ring movement and the new
mass organizations, whose primary function was to indoctrinate and mobilize
the masses outside the parliamentary arena, were interconnected and overlapped with one another.

The parliamentarization of politics and the eventual concession of equal
suffrage in Prussia confronted the Pan-German League with a new situation. The dominance of politics by traditional establishment circles through
the exertion of indirect influence on the political system and a commercially
determined control of the press was no longer assured. The League therefore set about creating auxiliary organizations of a party political nature to
mobilize and rally 'the masses'. This change of strategy was summed up
simply by *Justizrat* Class: 'What have we got to offer the lower orders?'[24]
To accommodate the exigencies of a democratized political system, the
League founded the Deutschvölkischer Schutz- und Trutz-Bund in co-
operation with the Germanic Order and the Thule Society. The express
aim was to rally the masses by mobilizing the weapon of anti-semitism and
thus wean them from the influence of the dreaded socialist movement. The
DAP/NSDAP was to emerge from an identical context and it is significant
in this regard that Anton Drexler was an agent of the Thule Society.[25]

The same type of organizational cross-connections characterized the
emergence of the DHV (German National Association of Commercial
Employees). It too started as an auxiliary organization of the Pan-German
League and the Christian-Social Party, with anti-semitism again a major
feature. While this anti-semitism was originally directed against the Jewish
entrepreneurs dominating the wholesale trade, it lost its social momentum
with the rise of large business houses and the expansion of the white-collar

sector. Trade unionist concepts grew to dominance within the DHV almost in direct proportion as anti-semitism lost its mass appeal.[26] This explains the apparent paradox that the DHV was to prove almost totally immune to national socialist attempts to assimilate it after 1931.[27] The programme of the DHV in its early years had been directed towards achieving self-employed status for commercial employees, which rapidly proved an illusory aim. It is significant that the association sought to compensate for the loss of status implicit in admitting this by developing an educational organization of its own.

The Hanseatic Publishing House (Hanseatische Verlagsanstalt) was the first notable example of book publishing aimed almost entirely at a specific audience, in this case the membership of the DHV.[28] It was not completely accidental that prominent personalities in the DHV leadership, including Max Habermann and Hans Bechly, were booksellers by trade. They thus represented a middle stratum between the Bildungsbürgertum – the aloof, educated bourgeois elite – and the emerging groups of white-collar workers. The DHV's contacts with the Dürerbund, in which Eugen Diederichs and Wilhelm Stapel played leading roles, provided the impetus for it to establish its own publishing enterprise before developing a book club tailored specifically to its own membership. This was to develop into the most powerful publishing group in the Weimar Republic after the Hugenberg concern. What was remarkable about it was that the market at which it was aimed was not the general public but a closed public defined by its specific völkisch nationalist outlook.

The background to this development was the major transformation of the book trade brought about by falling production costs, the decline of lending libraries and contraction in the traditional quality bourgeois market. Mass production of popular trivial literature which undermined the classic bourgeois book trade also played a part. The old bourgeois publishing interest represented by the Commercial Association of the Book Trade (Börsenverein des deutschen Buchhandels) lost the monopoly of the market it had previously enjoyed. The competition began as a campaign against Jewish 'filth and trash' and was given a gloss of cultural nationalism by the Dürerbund. Wartime conditions and not least the formation of army libraries at the front led to the rapid rise of the book clubs. In the conditions of accelerating inflation during the early 1920s and with the general failure of the traditional German book trade and its fixed prices system, these clubs were also a way of securing control of particular sections of the market.[29] The old bourgeois ethos was thus undermined in two ways. Firstly, the liberal myth at the heart of the way it was organized – that, in being aimed at the educated, book publishing reached a limited though not restricted public – was exploded. Secondly, the spread of popular libraries, the emergence of middle-class associations as producers on the book market and the guarantee of specific audiences where material was tailored to suit particular socio-political points of view had the effect of fragmenting the traditional concept of enlightenment and undermining its claim to universal validity.[30]

Book publishing was integrated into the capitalist market and politicized in a single process. This process saw the end of the monopoly previously enjoyed in this area by the bourgeois educational elite and reflected the cultural crisis confronting this Bildungsbürgertum. It also meant that publishing was becoming increasingly subject to political manipulation and suffused with political irrationalism. This was all a part of the general disintegration of bourgeois rationalism and the break-up of the previously homogeneous liberal educational ethos. The process of radical democratization dissolved the previous unity of the bourgeois interest. In attempting to bring the masses outside the educated or property-owning middle classes under their influence and keep them apart from the socialist labour movement, the bourgeois associations had to make major concessions to populist prejudices. In this context anti-semitism and integrative nationalism assumed a central importance.[31]

This tendency had been fully apparent as early as the stock market crisis of 1873 when it was reflected in the emergence of the Berlin movement, the foundation of anti-semitic parties and the rapid spread of intellectual anti-semitism in bourgeois circles.[32] Recent studies have shown that the traditional Bildungsbürgertum was not among the social groups most attracted by these movements. On the contrary, the anti-semitic associations were recruited mainly from intellectuals left behind by the general rise in prosperity and prestige and from the rising urban commercial middle classes. The latter were particularly amenable to anti-semitism following the economic recession which took hold from 1873, and they blamed Jewish influence in the economy and in cultural life for the ruin they faced.[33] These strata had only superficially absorbed the values of classic idealism. Anti-semitism in its new racist form and a German nationalism based on Germanic mythology had a pseudo-religious character; they functioned as ideological compensation for the social decline these strata feared and the permanent insecurity which hung over them.[34]

The immense popularity of Houston Stewart Chamberlain's anti-semitic creed lay less in his criticism of the Jews than in the myth it gave rise to that, on the example of the Jewish race, the Germans could arise again as a nation, transcending class antagonisms and narrow interest group rivalries. The retreat to sentiment and impulse which had characterized the era of German idealism was thus revived. But it lacked the ethical content of that idealism and was shaped instead by the decisionist irrationalism coming to characterize the bourgeois populist movements in general. This was to find its most extensive organizational expression in the Fatherland Party.[35]

The progressive abandonment of the bourgeois liberal values of the early nineteenth century can be clearly traced in the development of the Wagner Societies.[36] What had originally been bourgeois patronage clubs formed to help finance the Bayreuth Festival gradually developed into an ideological movement centrally controlled by the editorial board of the *Bayreuther Blätter* and committed to a cult of Wagner and the anti-semitic völkish ideology associated with him. The educated elite in the narrow sense remained aloof from this movement. It was dominated rather by the rising business classes of the cities then emerging as commercial centres. There was a considerable overlap of membership and numerous personal contacts connecting the Wagner Societies to the anti-semitic movement and its associated anti-vivisectionist and animal rights movements. Similar cross-connections existed with the Christian-Social Reich Party and the various elements of the reform movement. The latter was an early manifestation of the trend towards forming pseudo-religious sects, groups, leagues and private societies which was current throughout Germany at the turn of the century.[37] What had begun as a movement to develop the cultural aspects of national formation within the classical liberal tradition following the foundation of the Reich had thus changed as early as the 1870s into a militantly backward-looking tendency, which was anti-parliamentarian and anti-capitalist and hostile to enlightenment and rationalist thought. It was fertile soil for the Wagner cult and for the spread of Schopenhauer's and Nietzsche's critiques of modern culture as vulgarized and distorted by their followers. The neo-conservative ring movement of the 1920s was thus anticipated not only in the Wagner Societies but also in the various contemporary movements advocating changes in lifestyle, behaviour and ideals.

It is difficult to grasp the sheer extent and multiplicity of organizations that emerged from the late 1890s mobilizing large sections of the middle classes. What they had in common was their advocacy of fundamental cultural change and their hostility to liberal and enlightenment traditions. They were also similar in their attempts to shape themselves as closed ideological societies. They were partly of an avant-garde sectarian character and partly intended as broader cultural movements for an inner renewal of society. Völkisch ideas came increasingly to the fore in the outlook of such groups. This was exemplified by the Mitgart-Bund, the rural settlement movement, the League of St George founded by Fidus and the anti-semitic Hammerbund. Taken together, the trend towards ideologically closed societies led to the demise of the classic bourgeois Verein. The pseudo-religious undercurrent common to such movements was reflected in the way they organized themselves as 'communities' and in the profane sacral forms they adapted, as impressively exemplified by Fidus's designs for temple buildings.[38]

The retreat to a new 'inner life' and the conscious identification with the romantic heritage was often purely sectarian. But numerous attempts were also made to create a mass populist base for the cultural reform movement. This was epitomized by the ethical idealism institutionalized in the Society for Ethical Culture (1892), the Dürerbund (1902) and the Monist League (1906), to mention only the most important. Ferdinand Avenarius, the influential ideologue of the Dürerbund and publisher of the *Kunstwart*, declared in 1903 that the interests of the movement demanded an organizational expression: 'We represent valid interests too, a strong public interest of vital importance . . . let us organize ourselves and let our weight count where decisions are made'.[39] With an indirect membership of 300,000, the Dürerbund was one of the largest associations of this kind. Of much greater importance than the size of its membership, however, were the numerous cross-connections which linked it with other similar cultural organizations and the publishing and educational activities which it developed. These included contacts with the DHV, the Wandervogel and, later, with the Bündische Jugend, the Deutscher Werkbund, an array of adult educational institutions, patriotic county associations and athletic clubs. Avenarius's objective of an 'expressive culture' was directed against the threat of mass society, big city culture[40] and consumerism; it sought a return to national cultural values which, it was alleged, would socially reintegrate the middle classes and parts of the lower classes into the nation by aesthetic means.

Although the educated bourgeois elite played an important role in the Dürerbund, the membership of this movement was composed primarily of members of the rising middle class. Elementary and secondary school teachers dominated it while university professors were comparatively under-represented.[41] The membership of the Dürerbund was made up of those elements from the educational system equivalent to the social groups to which the DHV appealed. The contrast with the strictly bourgeois Vereine of the mid-nineteenth century was clear. This could be seen in the willingness of the Dürerbund to use modern propaganda and organizational techniques. It was also reflected in its conviction that the social divide separating capital from labour could be superseded by a cultural mobilization of the lower middle class and as far as possible the working class too.[42] The various associations of the bourgeois reform movement contributed to the creation of an overall and specifically anti-modernist subculture. They were hostile to the rule of big business which they denounced as Jewish and were critical of the ongoing process of urbanization and the threat of mass society which they equated with moral decline and the loss of national cultural traditions. These groups ranged from those advocating a new occultism or propagating the idea of education as a means to social integration to those campaigning for a return to nature, for naturalist body culture, community sport, liberation from the dictates of fashion, agrarian communes and rural settlement, for comprehensive land reform in Dam-aschke's sense or Sylvio Gsell's movement for communal land as well as those who enthused about the new 'science' of racial hygiene and propagation.

Fundamental to the bourgeois ethos had been the idea that education and property delineated a person from the 'raw' lower orders. The DHV was a prime example of an organization whose originally dominant aim of securing the social status of its members gradually gave way to a populist strategy which nurtured the illusion that class tensions could be resolved if the masses were rallied on a nationalist basis to achieve a new 'national community' based on a common cultural identity. The comprehensive public education programme launched by the DHV had this as its explicit aim, though commercial motives certainly played some part. It involved publishing concerns with close ties to the DHV, including the Hanseatic Publishing House and Eugen Diederichs' press. The programme was given an added impetus and achieved a greater social power under the conditions of world war.[43] In one sense it was a contemporary version of the inte-grationist role which bourgeois public education had played in the idealist era, except that this time it had a pronouncedly conservative outlook which rejected the liberal tradition, was easily assimilated into the neo-conservative movement and later found its ultimate expression in the völkisch nationalist camp of the Weimar Republic. The social groups dominating the member-ship of this movement came from the middle classes. But its attacks on cultural crudity and the relativization of values meant that it decisively rejected the self-contained bourgeois outlook of the nineteenth century.

An essential contributory factor to this process of internal differentiation and re-formation within the bourgeoisie was the insecurity of status which spread rapidly among broad sections of the established bourgeois upper stratum from 1918 as it too began to show signs of disintegration in the wake of the inflationary upheavals. The feeling that industrial 'mass society' had robbed them of their original position in society was strongly reinforced by the events of the November Revolution. Even before the end of the war, Friedrich Meinecke pointed to the 'relative decline in the influence of the Bürgertum'. Later he commented that 'the academically trained bourgeoisie, once on the offensive against the old ruling classes, then united with them in a kind of joint rule and partly fused with them, now feels itself on the defensive against all those social groups produced in the transition from an agrarian to an industrial state – the broad masses of industrial and white-collar workers'.[44] Insecurity of status henceforth became a basic feature in the consciousness of the upper middle class. This included professors, higher civil servants and members of the commercial strata squeezed by competition from big business, department stores and supermarket chains.[45]

The divide within the bourgeoisie, which largely coincided with the conflict between old and new middle-class interests, was also reflected in the field of representative associations. Characteristic of this was the disaffiliation of senior civil servants from the DBB (German Federation of Civil Servants) to found the RhB (Reich Federation of Higher Civil Servants) and the open opposition of this new association to the progressive equalization of civil servants' salaries at the expense of senior officials.[46] State Secretary Hans Schäffer went as far as to warn Brüning of the unrest spreading among senior civil servants who could no longer afford to maintain housemaids.[47] For tradesmen and the commercial middle class, who regarded themselves as the main victims of economic rationalization and depression, there was the added element of conflict with the large industrial and agricultural associations. The breaking up of the middle classes into rival interests which this gave rise to has been described in detail by Larry Jones.[48] The declining influence of the old bourgeois establishment could also be seen in the area of elective local government. While the influence of the bourgeois parties in this area should not be overestimated, it is significant that the large number of seats held by independent voters' associations until the early 1930s came increasingly under the control of the organizations of the new middle classes, not least the DHV. It also appears that the proportion of independent entrepreneurs and businessmen in the chambers of industry and commerce and other institutions representing the middle class declined in relation to that of salaried managers.

A systematic examination of the literature available on individual professional groups and branches of business would provide a more accurate picture of this process. The relative decline in the social status of the upper middle class can, however, be illustrated by the changes which occurred in the social and economic position of the Jewish section of the population, as detailed data are available on this.[49] By the 1920s at the latest the younger generation could no longer be certain of inheriting the social position of its parents. This explains why so many children of Jewish families in this class chose to opt for academic or artistic careers. Zionism and the Palestine movement were also at least partly a product of the social psychology of the Jewish population in a situation where its younger generation was rejecting the thoroughly bourgeois mores of the old Jewish middle class. The tenacity with which many from the German upper middle class clung, formally at least, to the lifestyle associated with economic independence should not be underestimated. Nevertheless, its circumstances would appear to have been generally similar to those of the Jewish upper middle class. This was illustrated by the increasing trend towards self-criticism among bourgeois intellectuals. It was most pronounced in the work of Ernst Jünger, whose heroic nationalism Leopold Schwarzschild described as being rooted in an 'extreme hatred of bourgeois values' and as the very 'antithesis of heroism'.[50] The stylized figure of the 'worker' propounded by Jünger was the exact opposite of the bourgeois citizen whose culture, grown sterile and displaced by the new political realities, and sense of the *juste milieu* now belonged to history.[51]

What appears in the case of Jünger and similarly minded neo-conservatives as individual rebellions against the bourgeois way of life occurred in a milder form as a general trend throughout the Bürgertum as it became increasingly insecure in its inherited role of cultural leadership. Fear of the working class remained a consistent element in its political outlook and was to culminate in a rigid and virtually hysterical anti-bolshevism.[52] But the feeling of having been both superseded and betrayed was even more acute and was expressed in a growing antipathy to party and interest group politics in general and particularly their republican form. Even before the First World War, an extreme aversion to the party political system and its parliamentary functions had taken hold in the bourgeois reform movement, the most activist section of the Bürgertum. This is not to deny that the spectrum of leagues and mass organizations sketched above, from the völkisch, nationalist and neo-conservative groups to the DHV, was tied by numerous personal contacts to the bourgeois party system.[53]

By the time of the Weimar Republic, however, the focus of bourgeois organizational life had shifted decisively to the extra-parliamentary arena. This was exemplified by the emergence of the 'Young German Order'. Its social composition and political outlook had an emphatically bourgeois flavour.[54] Its peculiar and atavistic organizational form, which appeared to employ the terminology of the Teutonic Order, was borrowed from the bündisch youth movement and the Freikorps. It differed from the paramilitary and patriotic associations of the political right, which were still strongly influenced by Wilhelmine nationalism, in its republican orientation and dissociation from paramilitary elements. Its transformation from being a consciously extra-parliamentary ideological movement to a political party was symptomatic of the general trend in bourgeois politics. The formation of the State Party (Staatspartei) through a fusion of the order with the People's National Conservative Association (Volksnationale Reichsvereinigung) and the DDP (German Democratic Party) in 1930 was, however, largely a failure.[55] The order was the most explicit example of a league-type organization being absorbed by the political system. The labour camp movement first propagated by Arthur Mahraun on the other hand believed the 'national community' could only be achieved through an inner regeneration of the nation.[56] As with the DHV, the Young German Order represented a complete break with the bourgeois political traditions of the nineteenth century. The return to corporatist models of organization, typical of both associations and increasingly advocated in contemporary political literature,[57] signalled the defensive abandonment by the Bürgertum of the political and social leadership function it had previously exercised with such apparent self-confidence.

The Young German Order too was a product of the 'ideas of 1914'. It held to the vision of a new order embracing the whole of society; this would supersede divisions of interest and the class struggle of the proletariat and produce a harmonious corporatist order in which the Bürgertum would again occupy its traditional position and exercise its function as the leading cultural stratum of society.[58] The concept of a 'national awakening', propagated during the First World War and taken up with increased vigour after Germany's defeat, had its forerunner in the ideology adopted by the bourgeois reform movements since they first appeared at the end of the nineteenth century. In an atmosphere where the feeling of imminent apocalyptic crisis was widespread, it must have been received as an all-embracing solution, appearing as it did to bring unity to the otherwise fragmented world of the middle-class ideological organizations which had developed below the bourgeois parties. The myth of a new force capable of integrating society and imbuing it with common values, often including calls for a leader figure, was henceforth to be a decisive force in bourgeois politics. Apart from the extreme left of the DDP, already essentially isolated from 1919, this was true of all the bourgeois parties with the exception of the Centre Party, though it too conformed to the trend after 1929.[59] The increasing drift towards authoritarian constitutional attitudes corresponded to this trend.[60]

The accelerating fragmentation of bourgeois politics as a result of the inflationary crisis, however, makes generalizations difficult. The decline of the liberal parties to the benefit at first of interest-based parties and then of the NSDAP corresponded to the growing disorientation among the old middle class.[61] The NSDAP, which had been formed as an anti-bourgeois movement, emerged paradoxically as the most important rallying force precisely for those members of the old middle class who had either not been fully integrated by the DNVP (German National People's Party) or were disillusioned with it. On the other hand the NSDAP at first held little attraction for the growing numbers of white-collar employees who later rallied to it only to a limited extent. Bourgeois establishment figures held back from joining the NSDAP at first due to social inhibitions, though this changed in the early 1930s.[62] Of considerable importance in the emergence of the NSDAP as a mass movement, however, was its successful assimilation at local level of the generally non-political bourgeois associations which had continued in the traditions of the nineteenth-century Vereine.[63] This process was reflected in the way the NSDAP replaced the old free electors' associations on municipal and local government bodies virtually at a stroke. The same occurred in the Protestant church elections of 1932.[64]

The breakthrough of the NSDAP as a mass movement from 1929 took place as the bourgeois party spectrum gradually disintegrated and as those sections of the bourgeois electorate which the DNVP could not hope to contain in the long run swung to the right. As a party of protest, the NSDAP profited principally from the growing gulf between modern and traditional sectors of society. Following its major breakthrough into the farming electorate, the party gradually succeeded in winning the support of those elements of the middle class which were already caught in social decline or threatened by it.[65] It would, however, be wrong to infer from this that bourgeois values and attitudes had totally disintegrated. Hitler and Nazi propaganda in general conspicuously avoided identifying with bourgeois interests, though from 1927 the party did opt decisively for the maintenance of the capitalist system despite repeated propagandistic declarations to the contrary on specific issues. But, by stressing anti-bolshevism, adopting the mythology of 'national awakening' and committing itself to a return to a politically and economically stable order, it did appeal to the political frustration prevalent among sections of the old middle class. The call to re-establish the professional civil service is an example of how the NSDAP consciously exploited the longing in bourgeois circles for security or for the re-establishment of lost privileges.[66]

But the popular interpretation of national socialism as the destroyer of the Bürgertum – usually accompanied by apt quotes from Hermann Rauschning's *Conversations with Hitler*[67] – is basically incorrect. The policies pursued by the NSDAP to benefit the middle classes were certainly to prove as unsuccessful as its programme of rural resettlement.[68] But to claim that the bourgeois social position was destabilized would be just as wrong, and in terms of ideology the Nazi regime often in fact linked directly into nineteenth-century bourgeois national traditions. The domestic lifestyle adopted by party satraps imitated upper middle class ostentation even if the social divide between them and the cultivated Bürgertum remained unbridgeable. The destruction of traditional bourgeois values therefore did not begin under the Nazis. It was a process which had already been long under way. Phenomena such as the growth in moral indifference had arisen as a consequence of the priority given to maintaining one's social status.[69] This helps to explain the absence of bourgeois resistance to national socialist political practice despite the utter incompatibility of Nazism with bourgeois concepts of public order. But it also helps to explain how bourgeois society could suppress the qualms it may have felt at the criminal consequences which this had to have. It also explains the willingness widespread in bourgeois society to subscribe to the fiction that a bourgeois order had been re-established by referring to the new regime's formal adherence to the rule of law and to the curbing of the more radical elements of the national socialist movement.[70] It seems only logical, therefore, that after the collapse of the Third Reich the same bourgeois forces would again offer themselves as the guarantors of the new political order and in this way seek to restore their position in areas such as the civil service code, the universities, the education system and also in the economic sector.

Attempts to explain the national socialist seizure of power using the usual hackneyed phrases of 'panic in the middle class', 'extremism of the centre' or 'capitulation' by the Bürgertum[71] fail to take adequate account of the complex background of events against which the NSDAP emerged as a mass movement and was summoned to lead the government of the Reich. It would be more appropriate to speak of Weimar as the unviable bourgeois republic abandoned by large sections of the bourgeoisie. The lack of moral inhibitions which pervaded bourgeois circles and which was to reach new heights during the Third Reich was only the culmination of a development which had started long before the First World War. This was also the case with the growth in ideological self-delusion which Fritz Stern has described in his notable work.[72] It is questionable whether the crisis which afflicted the German parliamentary system, though it was by no means restricted to Germany, can be attributed primarily to the relative weakness of bourgeois liberalism. The authoritarian character of German society, so often blamed for so much, and the absence of a pragmatic approach to politics certainly contributed to the virtual total failure to emerge of opposition to the imposition of fascist political structures. The divide between modern and outmoded social groups, accentuated by wartime defeat, hyperinflation, economic stagnation and economic crisis, also affected the bourgeois centre, which was no longer a socially or politically homogeneous group. The 'third estate' in fact collapsed into antagonistic camps and divergent interest and professional groups characterized by mutually contradictory interests.[73] The fact that the old middle class and particularly the educated elite reacted with bitterness and resentment to the rise of the white-collar sector and to the emergence of new professional groups in business, trade and industry as well as in public and private sector services hardly demands a detailed explanation. The principles of classical education had already lost their former importance by the end of the nineteenth century. A flight to elitist and often esoteric behaviour had begun as early as the 1870s and by the turn of the century had developed into a general phenomenon, the common denominator of which was a rejection of enlightenment and liberal traditions and values. This was facilitated by the development of new educational structures and new forms of access to education. It was reinforced by the numerous attempts undertaken to popularize idealized versions of traditional themes so as to recruit the rising lower middle class as a potential ally, as was the aim of the Dürerbund. The leading elements in this movement were briefly united in the campaigns for changes in lifestyle and habits. This *Lebensreform* movement, which collapsed again into numerous sects in the 1920s,[74] was not in the main composed of elements from the traditional bourgeois elites but drew its members principally from the newly emergent sections of the middle class. Their social resentments were expressed through nationalism and völkisch anti-semitism. The older idealistic religion of education was no longer an adequate compensation for the social insecurity which they felt. This movement first made its appearance in the form of Wagnerianism and, especially in the intellectual and artistic arena, led to the end of the romantic and idealist view of the world.

In 1932 Theodor Geiger, on the basis of available social statistics and his analysis of the mentalities of various social groups, warned not only against applying the term 'middle class' too generally, but also against attempting to subsume the old and new middle classes in the term 'Bürgertum'.[75] In particular, he attacked what he regarded as the misleading term 'bourgeois' as being of little use in the changed social conditions of the 1920s except as a type of criterium for describing outward behaviour or lifestyle. He particularly rejected the notion that the new and old middle classes were united by a common 'bourgeois' outlook or behaviour. Instead, he argued, 'even if that were true of parts of the older generation of both strata, or even if what is meant by it is a single "bourgeois" type of behaviour as opposed to an umbrella term for two different mentalities, it would still only be a relic in today's conditions. The younger generation in all sections of the population today has completely lost any sense of bourgeois feelings or concepts. "Bourgeois" for us of the older generation still denoted a way of life we understood while rejecting it for ourselves ... For the youngest generation today "bourgeois" simply has no relevance whatsoever, has no role even from an oppositional interest, has in fact no meaning at all.' That went as much for academics as it did for white-collar employees and business people. 'The younger generation at the turn of the century rebelled against its parents' generation and way of life; the younger generation of the second quarter of the century appears to be content to simply wait for the previous generation to die off.'[76]

In fact the social basis of the Bürgertum as a relatively homogeneous socio-cultural class had been destroyed by the end of the Weimar era, as were the values and way of life associated with it. Despite strenuous efforts, the educational tradition was not capable of integrating society in its interest and itself collapsed rapidly under völkisch and nationalist pressures. The new cult of the 'aesthetic disciplines', the elitist and politically presumptuous reinterpretation of the idealist tradition into a general critique of so-called mass society and the triumphant assertion of a mythology of leadership and national harmony over relativized values were all part of this same process. The dream of a socially harmonious 'national community' was hardly any substitute for a culturally and economically secure bourgeois society. Political irrationalism was largely a product of the sense of general crisis already dominating bourgeois society at the end of the nineteenth century. Driven by an urge to assert itself as a 'class', the fragmented Bürgertum became easy prey to being manipulated through its resentments.

This development was probably inevitable. All western countries appeared to undergo a fundamental internal crisis as the liberal tradition declined and the legitimacy of liberal parliamentarism was challenged. In Germany this crisis occurred earlier and in a sharper form than in France or Britain, though comparatively late in relation to the states of east and central Europe, and thus released incomparably greater destructive forces. Given its structure as an advanced industrial society, these forces could not be contained within an authoritarian dictatorship. This was possibly partly due to the weakness of the bourgeois strata which, dominated by regressive concepts of political order, became politically 'unattached' in a parliamentary republic which they generally regarded as incapable of catering for their interests. In the resistance movement against Hitler they were represented most notably by Carl Goerdeler. The demand for 'decency and order' central to his outlook was a classic bourgeois formula. Under the conditions at the time, this was hardly a sufficient basis to secure broad support for the *coup d'état* of July 1944.[77] Such was the tragedy of bourgeois politics as reflected in the conditions of the Third Reich.

2

Generational Conflict and Youth Rebellion in the Weimar Republic

The events of 1968 at many western universities gave added impetus to research in the social sciences into the question of intergenerational conflict.[1] In the years following the appearance of Ronald Inglehart's book, *The Silent Revolution*, a school of political and social scientists has been devoted to in-depth research into the role of generational change in patterns of political participation and opposition.[2] Using comprehensive statistical data, this school has attempted to construct a transnational comparative analysis of the role of generational factors in the formation of political consciousness. The central contention of the Inglehart thesis is that in 'affluent societies' a propensity to emphasize 'non-material values' tends to accompany the process of generational change, and thus to increase the rebellious potential of the young.[3]

Historians by comparison have, with few exceptions, largely ignored the role of intergenerational tensions and conflicts. Robert Wohl's pioneering work, *The Generation of 1914* (1979), is the first, through its comprehensive analysis, to deal with the inter-war years and compare developments in Britain, France, Germany and Italy.[4] He concludes that an ideology specific to youth, though exacerbated by the experiences of World War I, had already developed in these countries before 1914. It reflected deep tensions which had arisen between the adult population and sections of the rising generation. Wohl interprets this self-assertiveness of the 'generation of 1914' and the virtual open revolt of the younger age groups which followed it as a product primarily of bourgeois intellectuals and writers. He is inclined to view the generational conflict of the Weimar years as a rebellious stance taken only by particular social groups and confined to a purely literary and intellectual level, rather than as a phenomenon characterizing contemporary society as a whole.[5]

With all respect for Wohl's methodically rigorous and carefully constructed analysis, there is much evidence to suggest that generational conflict, in Weimar Germany at least, was a phenomenon that embraced more than only a few social groups and substantially influenced the shaping of the political process at the time. A careful analysis of the socio-economic and socio-cultural aspects of this phenomenon may contribute to uncovering some of the deeper causes of the structural crisis affecting the Weimar political system. It would therefore seem worthwhile to pay particular attention to these aspects, while also emphasizing that the public debate on the generational question and its manipulation by extreme right-wing political movements and comparative studies, especially in Italy and France, have played a major role in forming the changing public consciousness in Germany today.

The rather mechanistic method employed by the Inglehart school and its tendency to explain events by means of monocausal theories are not of great use in analysing the Weimar Republic. This is quite apart from the fact that the emphasis placed on 'non-material values' by the younger generation of the Weimar Republic can hardly be due to its having been socialized in a period of economic abundance. The wave of youth protest which reached its climax in the post-1928 period had developed within a society which had been under severe economic stress since 1914 and had stagnated economically since the inflationary era of the early 1920s. Of much more use are the propositions which Karl Mannheim put forward in his contemporary analysis of the generational problem.[6] He differentiated between 'generational standpoint', 'generational context' and 'generational unity' and underlined the extent to which generational conflicts relate to the total socio-cultural framework within which they occur. They represent varied reactions by different groups to the challenges of commonly experienced changes in social conditions. In certain circumstances those members of a given generation who tend to respond actively to socio-cultural change develop a common basic mentality which transcends that determined by both social interest and traditional political loyalties.

A 'generation' in this sense is not a group definable simply in terms of the numbers of persons in a certain age-group and is thus not a statistically quantifiable whole. It is rather a social group whose subjective identity is formed mainly by a shared consciousness of being different from its parents, from its fathers' generation. In normal situations the process of generational change is an unremarkable occurrence when studied, other than in specific individual cases or in terms of the father–son, or, rather, the parent–child conflict within the individual family. During periods of major social and political change and particularly of radical revolutionary change, which thoroughly restructure social consciousness, the individual generational conflict tends to develop into a phenomenon affecting society as a whole. This is because the manner in which the rising generation is socialized politically – which is regarded as the main factor informing the social outlook it will have as an adult generation – takes place under social conditions fundamentally different from those experienced by the preceding generation. The First World War was such a watershed. The outlook of those whose political views had been formed before 1914 appears generally to have been different from that of those who grew up in the grey conditions of the war and post-war years.

This intergenerational tension was considerably aggravated by the socio-cultural effects of the rapid social and technological changes produced during the period of intensive industrialization. It was reinforced by the rising generation's novel experience of independence. This phenomenon was not purely coincidental. The increasingly technical nature of industrial society and its ever more radical division of labour forced a lengthening of the time-span required for the individual's basic education and training in work skills. Increased life expectancy reinforced tensions between the world of youth and that of adulthood. Technological change disrupted the handing on from father to son of traditional skills which, given the changing nature of work and the new types of training required, were more and more irrelevant. The internal migration which accompanied industrialization led to young people separating from their families at an earlier age. Public education and apprenticeship diminished the role of the family as the dominant element in the socialization process.[7]

As well as the rapid growth in internal migration, of special importance for Germany was the clear over-representation of younger age-groups in the populations of the emerging urban centres; this was further aggravated by the demographic factor of a disproportionate population growth rate from the early 1870s which led to a marked reduction in the average age of the general population.[8] This development affected the industrial working class particularly. It also had important consequences for the organized labour movement, which, while developing some new forms of politics, was also confronted by a new type of militancy among younger and mostly unorganized workers. This was expressed socially in the apprentice problem, the basis from which the socialist youth movement in Germany emerged around the turn of the century.[9] The distrust with which the officials of the SPD and Free Trade Unions greeted the demands of working-class youth for a political say was symptomatic of this. The Law of Association (*Reichsvereinsgesetz*) of 1908 enabled them largely to domesticate their rebellious youth. This movement had been tending towards political radicalism of both the left and right and to an activism regarded with great suspicion by the SPD party hierarchy.

But the emergence of a youth problem in late Wilhelmine society was reflected primarily in the rise of the bourgeois youth movement. It was also reflected in the new trend whereby political parties realized that they had to appeal to the younger generation and in the consequent establishment of political youth organizations. These included groups such as the Young

Germany League, which was established with an eye to future military recruitment and achieved a membership of about 750,000 by 1914.[10] The 'competition among the parties for the loyalty of the young' often referred to at the time was evident from the turn of the century.[11] The beginnings of a concern for the special needs of youth and the first legislative attempts to protect the interests of the young further demonstrated the extent to which youth had become an important social factor and was recognized as such by public opinion.[12] The breakthrough achieved by the educational reform movement, which had roots going back to the early nineteenth century, was part of this; it advocated education geared towards the development of the individual instead of to mere social conformism and the instilling of traditional values.

The bourgeois youth movement was a specifically German phenomenon with roots in the deeply idealistic tendencies which pervaded the middle classes as a legacy of the bourgeois enlightenment tradition. It reflected the growing tendency among the young generation to break with the social and political behavioural norms of late Wilhelmine society. It unmistakably formed part of the same context which produced other such contemporary movements as the *Lebensreform*, vitalist philosophy, neo-Kantianism, Nietzschian anti-modernism with its indirect revival of Rousseau's cult of nature and the so-called youth style, which took its name from Fidus's magazine, *Die Jugend*. The youth movement was composed mostly of private secondary school pupils and university students from upper middle class backgrounds and was to remain confined to a socially esoteric movement. It rejected Wilhelmine obsessions with security of status and the absolute belief in progress which dominated a bourgeois civilization it regarded as over-mechanistic. It disavowed the authoritarian and militarist tendencies of the period and their emphasis on individualist values. In these ways it undoubtedly had an emancipatory function even if it was also in part a movement of escapism from contemporary social realities.[13]

The demand articulated by the Hohen Meissner Programme for a common goal of autonomy for youth from the adult world and, under Heinrich Wyneken's influence, even for an autonomous youth culture, indicates that a totally new generational consciousness was emerging. Influenced by anti-modernist critiques and the agitation for lifestyle reforms, the outlook that emerged foresaw a 'revolution' by the younger generation that would create a new society in which interest group politics and materialist values would be replaced by a community shaped by idealistic values and life-affirming philosophy. This recourse to the German 'soul' reflected the cultural conflict taking place within the bourgeois enlightenment ethos and was expressed in the philosophical writings of Dilthey, Simmel and Natorp and in the sociology of Toennies and Max Weber. At the root of this lay the blatant contrast between the traditional but formalized catalogue of idealist shibboleths and the reality of the bourgeoisie's capitulation to material and military criteria of status.[14]

While the outbreak of the world war in 1914 and the experiences of the following years at the front gave an impetus to this movement, it also broke it in many ways. Young men motivated by the ideals of the youth movement to volunteer for the war sought to maintain their common identity through the 'front line hikers movement' (*Feldwandervogel*). But they experienced a reality which had nothing in common with the 'lofty' human ideals propagated by the ideologues of the 'ideas of 1914'. The much read book by Walter Flex, *Der Wanderer zwischen beiden Welten* ('Traveller between Two Worlds'), vividly expressed the deep identity crisis of the generation which experienced war at the front, had turned its back on the shallow untruth of Wilhelminism and had found that its longing for a community experience transcending social or military rank had been anything but fulfilled by its experiences in the field. The later heroization of the 'war experience' in the writings of Ernst Jünger, Franz Schauwecker and many others did not at all correspond to the sobering and depressing reality of the trenches of World War I.[15]

The war raised expectations among the younger generation across Europe that a fundamental social and cultural transformation was imminent. The 'social harmony' preached by wartime propaganda, the avowals of 'Prussian Socialism' and the apparent imminence of a genuine 'national community' were not to be fulfilled, however. The younger generation reacted to this not only with bitterness and disillusionment but equally with the conviction that it was now its task to bring about a fundamental renewal of society.[16] This kind of idea was widespread. It was reflected in Moeller van den Bruck's book *Recht der jungen Völker* ('The Rights of Young Nations') as well as in neo-conservative writing generally where the myth of youth was usually given a wide berth.[17]

The apolitical attitude which had dominated the youth movement in the pre-war years gave way to a strong sense of political commitment in a movement now led by a younger age-group and spread over a broader political spectrum. These young people welcomed the collapse of November 1918 as an opportunity for a new start. In the 'dream-world of the armistice period', as Ernst Troeltsch called this phase,[18] a rejection of pre-war society converged with euphoric expectations for the future. The move to the land and the establishment of communes in the countryside[19] were attempts to realize some of the classic aims of the youth movement. Groups of the most diverse complexion advocated such aims at the time using almost identical language. These ranged from the Anarchist Youth, the Communist Youth Movement, the socialist Hofgeismar Circle and the social-liberal Leuchtenburg Circle to the Free German Youth and the völkisch groups of the right. The concept of the nation as an organic people was held up as an alternative to the abstract principle of the state and the idea of a federally structured Reich to that of the narrower Prussian-centred German national state.[20]

What all of these ideas had in common was that they largely ignored the social and economic realities of industrial society. Very much in keeping with German political traditions and neo-romantic ideas, they postulated the ideal of a society free of conflict. The varying degrees of intensity with which the legitimacy of political parties was contested and the general view that they represented merely sectional interests was symptomatic of this. In 1921 Harald Schultz-Hencke, a member of the Free German Youth, published an article which attracted much attention at the time with its claim that the 'young generation would dispense with political parties'. 'The party of the future', according to this article, would 'rally all those already united by a common feeling, who want not just for themselves but for the whole community.'[21] This was the start of the myth that it was the younger generation which would dispense with the Weimar party state and shape the future of Germany. It was also the context of Hans Zehrer's remark as editor of *Die Tat* in 1928 that if the 'young front' could succeed in forcing the political parties to a truce, their final capitulation would be assured.[22]

After the failure of merger attempts in the early 1920s, the bündisch youth movement broke up into a myriad of individualistic smaller groupings. The great majority of them were hostile to the parliamentary system. Many members of the immediate post-war generation joined the Freikorps for the opportunity it offered them to play an active role in events.[23] The Akademische Freischaren took an active part in the fighting in Upper Silesia. Some nationalistic youth groups came to play a more constructive role in the political system. This trend was exemplified by the Young German Order. It defended the Republic and the principle of accommodation with the western powers, but it also advocated that 'mechanistic parliamentarism' be replaced by a leadership-centred, elitist structure based on an ideology of national community.[24] Only a minority within the order inclined to the radical völkisch camp, though völkisch and anti-semitic strands had played some role in the pre-war movements. The majority of middle-class bourgeois youth organizations, such as the Deutsche Freischar, were basically apolitical.

The sections of the younger generation which were organized in the youth wings of the political parties or, like the Leuchtenberg Circle,[25] which developed a positive attitude to the Republic were largely isolated or marginalized by the official party bureaucracies, which remained the exclusive preserves of the older generation. There were many reasons for this and they are certainly not simply reducible to youthful immaturity. In all sections of society the war experience had given rise to exaggerated

hopes of sweeping social change after the war. Young workers, who formed
the main driving force behind the mass strike movements from 1917, were
no exception to this. They differed from older workers not only in that
they lacked experience of trade union practices and did not understand the
importance of persevering, long-term organizational work in securing the
interests of wage earners. They were searching for new perspectives and
values and wanted to achieve an immediate equality between capital and
labour instead of the mere gradualism offered by traditional trade unionism.
They conceived of socialist society as an immediately realizable aim. They
broke with the economistic quietism and organizational fetishism which
dominated the thinking of the social democratic hierarchy. The anthropological element of socialism was for them a necessary and obtainable
demand.[26]

Hardly surprisingly, the rigid party structures of the SPD and KPD had
great difficulty in attempting to integrate these youthful impulses and the
activist voluntarism which went with them. The separate organization of
the Young Socialists was a constant source of conflict within the SPD.
Neither the left-wing 'Hanoverians' nor the Hofgeismar Circle, a group
very strongly influenced by the ideas of the youth movement, could be
contained within the party.[27] The party executive reacted with deep distrust
to the emergence of the Reichsbanner and the Iron Front, both of which
exercised a strong pull on young people with republican leanings. Younger
members of the SPD gravitated towards either the left- or right-wing
oppositions which formed against the quietist politics pursued by the party
leadership. Many of them left the party after the disillusioning experience
of the Leipzig Conference of 1931 and went to the SAPD (Socialist
Workers' Party of Germany). The younger members of the KPD found
themselves similarly in opposition to the bureaucratic rigidity of the Communist Party machine and dominated the radical splinter groups which split
from it. This was despite the fact that the KPD, in comparison to the SPD,
had considerably greater success in integrating its younger members through
the Roter Frontkämpferbund, the KJVD (German Communist Youth
Association) and other organizations with a special appeal for young
people.[28]

Significantly, both the right and left wings of the youth opposition in the
SPD agreed on the basic point that the internal democracy of the party
had been reduced to a farce by progressive bureaucratization and the
control exercised over the party by its full-time paid officials. In fact, the
opportunities for younger members to participate in a meaningful sense in
the party or to pursue political careers were extremely limited. This was
obvious from the elderliness of most members of the party executive and
of the Reichstag parliamentary party; when a limited attempt was made in
1931 to rejuvenate the party leadership by co-opting some younger members

on to it, preference was given to long-serving officials with no real contact with the younger generation. This neglect of the young meant the general membership was becoming extremely aged. Under-25-year-olds were represented in the party two and a half times less than in the general population.[29]

Ageing was a universal characteristic of the leadership strata of the Weimar Republic. Theodor Haubach was fully justified when he complained of 'the barriers that have been erected in Germany between the political bodies of the state and youth'.[30] From 1928, and following Walter Lambach's revolt, attempts were made to prevent the collapse of the parties of the bourgeois centre by involving the younger generation more actively. The amalgamation of the Young German Order and the DDP to form the German State Party and the foundation of the People's National Conservative Association (Volkskonservative Vereinigung) were belated attempts of this kind to win the younger generation back to the Republic.[31] But even the generation returning from the war had never really been integrated. Their expectations, nourished by the experience of war, had been thoroughly dashed; they regarded themselves largely as a 'lost generation' powerless to shape their destinies. The immediate post-war generation was the group most imbued with war veteran mythology, and this was accentuated by romanticism and nationalism. It abandoned its political apathy from 1928 but, with few exceptions, was rarely willing to identify with the Republic.

It was in this context that Ernst Niekisch spoke of the 'irreverence of modern youth' as the 'reappearance in a new guise of the bankruptcy of the older generation'.[32] Utmann von Elterlein pointed to what he regarded as the gulf separating 'the people of the late nineteenth century' from those of the 'beginning of the twentieth century': they were so foreign to each other that one could easily doubt that they even belonged to the same people.[33] Ernst Günther Gründel spoke of the 'final bankruptcy of the entire world of the older generation'.[34] Gregor Strasser exploited the myth of the 'young generation' for the NSDAP. His main accusation against the representatives of the Republic – 'that these are the same old figures they were before the war and the revolution, before the convulsion and the new awakening' – expressed what an entire generation thought.[35] The latent anti-parliamentarism in the socialist movement was rooted in similar sentiments; there was a refusal to identify with the republican present, and calls for a 'surge' forward to socialism were constantly raised; on the whole democracy was generally seen at best as a transitionary step towards it.[36]

This outlook transcended political party affiliation and reflected the tendency which soon emerged for the political forces of the 'Weimar system' to return to the ideological positions they had occupied before the war. This made them incapable of offering worthwhile prospects for young people to work for. Goebbels's contemptuous aside, the 'old men's Republic', struck home at this central weakness of the Weimar elites.[37] Calls for the 'younger generation' to become a political force thus reflected a general trend, particularly among bourgeois youth where the myth of youth also served to relativize the left–right divide in politics; the phenomenon of 'national bolshevism' exemplified this. The advocacy of a voluntary labour service and the labour camp movement of the final years of the Republic were also partly attempts to mobilize the younger generation as a force transcending rigid class divides.[38]

These ideas were advocated most notably by the circle around the magazine *Die Tat*. When a tendency towards reintegrating into the parties of the centre became apparent among parts of the younger generation in 1930, Hans Zehrer issued the call, 'Youth Front Beware! Stay Outside!'[39] Behind this was the idea, widespread in any event, that those elements of the war generation which had remained active, together with the post-war generation, would form a 'third front' to establish the new society on which they placed their hopes. This would occur without reference to the infighting of party politics and the pressures of interest group conflicts. The neo-conservative intellectuals who popularized this objective were not thinking in terms of the NSDAP, though its age structure and deliberate adoption of youth mythology in its propaganda projected an extremely youth-oriented movement. Although Gründel called the NSDAP the first 'positive expression of the war experience' by the young generation,[40] even he saw it as representing only a transitionary phase. This was because it did not break radically enough with the shackles of a party-type movement. The *Tat* circle did not expect the 'third' or, as it was sometimes called, the 'fourth front' of the young generation to finally come to fruition until the 1940s.[41]

The notion developed by these circles of a 'cultural' revolution in which the 'young generation' would come into its own differentiated them qualitatively from national socialism. While they rejected the idea of actually organizing the 'third front' they proposed, the NSDAP did not hesitate both to claim the mythology of youth as its own and simultaneously to mobilize the young using the most modern organizational techniques. Despite apparent ideological similarities, even the extreme völkisch elements in the youth movement differed from the NSDAP in the emphasis on the cultural in their value concepts. It is revealing that the majority of bündisch youth leaders remained aloof from national socialism and that many of them were later to be found in the anti-Hitler resistance.[42]

But the protest movement among bourgeois youth also contributed substantially to creating the atmosphere of national expectation on the crest of which Adolf Hitler was to ride to power. Without a doubt, the tendency to use highly emotionalized language and the strongly irrationalist flavour of the ideas dominant in the youth movement contributed to the inability of a political movement opposed to the NSDAP taking form. The bündisch movement on its own only accounted for 2.1 per cent of all organized youth; but it exercised a powerful influence on the youth organizations of the churches as well as on sections of the socialist youth movement. It represented an important element of the rising generation of intellectual elites; its emergence is therefore indicative to a certain extent of the outlook prevalent among the active sections of the younger generation. It contributed decisively to the collapse of the authority of the republican system. At the same time it was also, despite ideological similarities, at least latently antipathetic to the later authoritarian presidential cabinets which preceded Hitler. But von Papen's intention of raising the voting age was certainly not a solution to the deep-seated crisis of confidence in the political system which indirectly benefited the NSDAP.[43]

It was characteristic of Weimar society that the debate on what part youth should play in it was a topical issue, seriously discussed in virtually all forums. The humanities, contemporary literature and poetry and especially pedagogics and psychology repeatedly tackled the question of relations between the generations.[44] This leitmotiv of Weimar culture was, as some critics have pointed out, something of a fashion, but it was also more than that: it reflected the deep anxiety in society and the political system to establish a balanced relationship with the younger generation. Despite the numerous attempts made through youth legislation, criminal law reform and educational and social policy to respond to the needs of the rising generation more sympathetically than before, these could not have bridged the gulf which had emerged between the Republic and its youth and which in the final analysis was a legacy of the First World War.

It is certainly valid to ask whether, if the Republic had been a success itself, it would have been more successful in integrating its young people. In addition, the youth problem was possibly only a relatively minor factor among the host of causes at the root of the structural crises and final failure of the Republic. But the apparently almost insurmountable obstacles which prevented democracy taking root in Germany are clearly reflected in the generational conflict of the time. It provides a key to undertanding the roots of the fundamental crisis of the social order in the imperialist period. The psychological effects of the First World War reinforced the process of societal change which it had unleashed and caused a deep break with tradition. Following the failure of the November Revolution and the foundation of the Republic to encroach on the position of the traditional elites in German society, this found a belated expression in the generational problem of the 1920s.

The rebelliousness of specific generations and generational conflicts are the products of situations shaped by epochal social conflict. In Germany these began in the era of the *Kaiserreich*, were barely suppressed during the First World War and re-emerged in the 1920s, accentuated by the political and economic conditions which characterized the Weimar Republic and militated against it achieving stability. It was thus not simply a matter of a change of values taking place in the ideological domain. In the case of Weimar, novel forces arising from the social and psychological effects of the war considerably aggravated this effect. It finally led to the political system losing its legitimacy. The mythology of youth revolution directly benefited the NSDAP in its breakthrough as a mass movement.

Destabilizing effects of a similar kind were also apparent in the period after World War II, even if these were not of a comparable intensity. The Extra-Parliamentary Opposition (APO) and the student movement in the Federal Republic were products of the disparities in the conditions under which different generations were socialized.[45] There is much evidence to suggest that changes in mentality are a feature of processes of generational change in highly mobile industrial societies and should be given particular attention. When political systems experience obvious difficulties convincing the rising generation of their basic norms, they are already in the grip of a deep-seated crisis of legitimacy. Such a crisis can be contained by force; but under democratic conditions it is essential that opportunities for political and social participation be broadened. These must include the younger generation, even if the price of this is decreased efficiency and some risks in the field of foreign policy. It could of course be argued that the increased internal and external political problems which this would produce would only be a further obstacle to integrating the young generation. The Weimar experience, however, would tend to support the view that this would be a disastrous approach to adopt.

3

Social Democracy on the Defensive:

The Immobility of the SPD and the Rise of National Socialism

How the NSDAP could have emerged as a mass movement and Hitler's dictatorship was established are questions which have been analysed thoroughly in the growing literature of recent years on the history of the Weimar Republic. These studies have concentrated primarily on two areas: the institutional weaknesses of the parliamentary system and the social composition of NSDAP membership and support. Particular attention has been focused in these studies on examining in greater depth both the old and the new middle classes[1] as well as the role of social policy and the part played by the socio-economic structures of the Republic in shaping its political system.[2] But apart from some regional analyses, since Richard Hunt's excellent study[3] no attempt has been made to critically examine how the socialist labour movement reacted to the rise of fascism. The studies by Erich Matthias and Siegfried Bahne of the politics of the SPD and KPD in the final years of the Weimar Republic[4] and Hannes Heer's work on the role played by the Free Trade Unions during the Nazi takeover give a detailed picture of the weak resistance offered by socialists and communists to the attempts to establish either a fascist dictatorship or one shaped by more traditional authoritarian forces.[5] The underlying causes of why the advances which had been achieved so painstakingly by the labour movement were abandoned with so little fight need a more thorough examination. This would also help us to understand why the bourgeois democratic system as a whole failed.

During the presidential cabinets of the early 1930s the SPD emerged as the only consistent defender of the democratic constitution and parliamentary system. Large sections of the population placed their hopes on its determination and will to resist. Its existence as a political force was dependent on the Republic surviving. The Weimar Republic could survive only as long as there was a willingness in the bourgeois camp to seek an accommodation with the social democratic section of the working class. But by attacking the social institutions of the Republic during the economic crisis, heavy industry directly undermined its political foundations. The attempts under Heinrich Brüning to restructure the constitution in an authoritarian direction had the effect of isolating the SPD politically[6] and, in von Papen's 'New State', the elimination of organized labour formed a central element. The forced resignation of the Prussian government and the Gleichschaltung (co-ordination) of Prussia with the Reich on 20 July 1932 saw the democratic labour movement gripped by a deep-seated political paralysis. The political neutralization of the SPD which the Prussian coup achieved removed the last barrier to a national socialist dictatorship. The elimination of the labour movement was an absolute requirement for the triumph of fascism.

Why the SPD did not resist more resolutely and effectively cannot be explained solely by the complexities of the domestic political situation of 1932. The stance adopted by the SPD and ADGB on 20 July has been carefully examined by historians. It is incontestable that a mass rising against von Papen had not the least chance of success given the balance of political forces at the time. Perhaps some attempt at mass resistance would have at least offered a clear sign of labour's will to fight. But the SPD, for internal reasons, was simply incapable of mobilizing a mass opposition outside parliament against the imposition of a dictatorship from the right. The party executive, the ADGB leadership and the SPD members of the Prussian government remained totally passive while von Papen prepared the Gleichschaltung of Prussia, despite the many accurate warnings and predictions of what he planned. When the crisis of 20 July came, the SPD executive avoided taking a clear position, stating this to be the sole prerogative of the Prussian SPD ministers. The coup had a devastating psychological effect on the organized labour movement and particularly on the Reichsbanner and the Iron Front. The débâcle of 20 July exposed the total ineffectiveness of the SPD's legalistic strategy for confronting fascism. When Prussia was abandoned without a fight, the political balance shifted fundamentally to the detriment of labour.

After this disastrous defeat, which set the party back to its 1918 position, the SPD leadership tried to recover its balance by calling on its members to 'secure the elections!' It simultaneously instructed the Reichsbanner and the Iron Front to prepare for an imminent confrontation with the Nazis. The position the leadership adopted provoked a severe crisis of confidence within the party. The party hierarchy sought to control this by questionable disciplinary means. The increasing resignation in the party's leadership circles combined with widespread disorientation among the mass of its supporters; the political isolation of the party further weakened its ability to act decisively despite the continued readiness of many of its members to make whatever sacrifices were necessary and to remain loyal to their ideals. Repeated declarations that there was a 'chance for a restoration of democracy by democratic means' as long as 'the fighting organizations of labour remained intact, were not under immediate threat and retained the trust of the masses' were, however, pure self-delusion.[7] The paralysis gripping the party made it incapable of acting decisively or coherently in spite of the militancy of many individual members; by failing to give its formal protests political substance, the SPD abandoned one position after another in the Republic it had substantially helped to form. Following the Enabling Act, the SPD, purely in the hope of securing its continued organizational existence, finally even abandoned its hitherto uncompromising hostility to the fascist regime. Otto Wels's courageous speech in the Reichstag on 23 March took a clear stand against the Nazis' extortionist tactics; but his references to Bismarck's Socialist Laws show how mistaken the party leadership was even at this stage in what it expected the future to bring.

The passivity with which the labour movement met the threat of fascist dictatorship was without a doubt due in large measure to the striking failure of the SPD and, even more, of the trade union leaderships. Although a severe critic of the SPD, Walter Löwenheim could write in his introduction to the pamphlet *Neu Beginnen!* that the national socialist seizure of power had struck the labour movement 'like a bolt from the blue'.[8] This was certainly true of the mass of workers, who were insufficiently prepared for it. But the party leadership was well informed. Of relevance here is Konrad Heiden's statement that the history of national socialism was the history of its constant underestimation. The social democratic and not just the bourgeois liberal press polemicized more against Hugenberg as the 'economic dictator' in the Cabinet of National Concentration than against Hitler. The SPD's total misjudgement of the situation in 1933 was a product of both its general outlook and political perspective as well as its organizational and political composition.[9]

The immobility of the SPD in the face of ascendant fascism cannot be isolated from the general crisis of European democracy in the inter-war period. Similar symptoms of weariness and paralysis were evident in the parties of the bourgeois centre. The general political and cultural backwardness of German society was a major factor limiting the extent to which German labour could break free from the fetters of its own traditions and take on the task of democratizing society under the difficult conditions of the inter-war era. Nevertheless, it is important to try to establish what factors internal to German labour contributed to its defeat. As regards the SPD, these arose from the party's traditional outlook, which prevented it from developing new forms of political attack with which to confront the Nazis. They were accentuated by the outdated political strategy for tackling critical situations which both the right and left wings of the party shared despite their otherwise divergent aims. The defensiveness which, as will be shown, characterized social democratic politics in this period pervaded all sections of the party, whether of a reformist or revolutionary orientation.

One of the most blatant weaknesses of social democratic politics in the late Weimar era was the lack of a coherent long-term political perspective. Its relationship to parliamentary democracy was also never fully clarified. While it is beyond doubt that the party, including the right wing of the USPD which reunited with it in 1922, was fundamentally committed to the constitutional system, its original hopes of transforming the Republic founded at Weimar into a true social democracy gave way to a more ambiguous attitude following the fierce social and political conflicts of 1919. The defeat of the labour movement after the Kapp Putsch and the loss by the Weimar Coalition partners of their parliamentary majority in June 1920 signalled the start of the social democrats' retreat from their original enthusiasm for what they now often called this 'bourgeois' Republic. When the Görlitz Programme was adopted by the SPD in September 1921, it no longer corresponded either to the actual situation in which the party found itself or to the outlook of its supporters.[10] Ambivalence towards the constitutional system reached its height during the period of bourgeois block governments. While calls were made by the SPD for the public administration and the judiciary to be republicanized and democratized,[11] no positive relationship to parliamentary democracy emerged.

The rather defensive attitude to democratic constitutionalism already evident at Görlitz was more pronounced in the debates at the 1927 SPD conference in Kiel. In his main speech Rudolf Hilferding attacked disparaging references to 'formal' or 'bourgeois' democracy; democracy, he said, had 'always been' a working-class issue, both historically and sociologically.[12] But this was merely a conclusion he drew from a justification for coalitionism based on an economic analysis, and hardly had inspirational force. Hilferding's plea that the SPD continue its participation in the Prussian coalition government and seek eventually to participate in a Reich government reduced this affirmation of democracy to a question of tactics. The line of argument was completely defensive: 'We must tell the people', Ulrich declared, 'that we are determined to defend the Republic with everything we've got, because we regard it as a more promising arena in which to realize our social policies and socialist goals than a monarchy' – as if this had been a serious alternative. Paul Löbe argued along similarly sterile lines that, with the establishment of the democratic Republic, the SPD had 'won an important beach-head in its march from capitalist democracy to a socialist people's state'. The Republic therefore had to 'be defended as further advance [would] otherwise be impossible'.[13] Equally circumspect, Hilferding argued that 'if the democratic framework is destroyed we will be thrown on the defensive and have no choice' but to resort to violence. No one could wish for such a scenario as there was 'no more serious obstacle to the realization of socialism' than civil war.[14] The entire debate was laced with much historical reference and self-criticism; Scheidemann believed this should have been avoided for the sake of maintaining a public image of party unity. But it was also characteristic of the debate that the issue of the threat to the Republic took second place to the desire to distance the party from the forces to the left of it.

Gustav Radbruch complained that the party 'regarded democracy purely as a ladder to socialism to be discarded as soon as socialism was achieved' rather than as 'that important half of its programme already realized and constantly in need of being realized anew'.[15] This accurately described the ambivalent attitudes in the SPD towards parliamentary democracy; it was seen as a relatively unattractive transitionary phase which had to be defended for tactical reasons. Many voices were raised on both the left and right wings of the SPD criticizing this basic weakness in the social democratic position and calling for a turn-round in the party's uninspiring politics. Democracy had to be positively asserted rather than merely defended and existing democratic freedoms expanded instead of merely preserved. In a sharp polemic against the party leadership, Hanns Müller declared that the SPD's lack of 'attractiveness and effectiveness' was a result of its not having done enough to instil a positive democratic consciousness in the people. Workers had become used to judging the achievements of day-to-day politics against the yardstick of the movement's most general long-term goals. A proper schooling in democracy and the development of a realistic political consciousness had been totally neglected.[16]

It is understandable that, particularly after its experiences in 1923, the party showed little interest in expending itself in further bourgeois coalitions. But it is remarkable that, although the necessity of maintaining a pragmatic attitude to coalition was never questioned, few in the party ever argued positively in favour of governmental participation as a means of achieving its goals. The SPD press gave the impression that participation in bourgeois coalitions was a temporary expedient which served firstly to defend working-class interests and secondly to deflect political crises which threatened the continued growth of the party. This mentality was epitomized by the *Vorwärts* of 6 December 1925, which declared that the SPD had never forced its way into government and had only participated in cabinet when 'the extreme need of the people demanded this sacrifice of it'.[17] Its relation-ship to democracy was thus reduced to a question of whether the party could not better serve the interests of the working class in opposition, as a 'negative party of government' as Paul Levi put it.[18]

This attitude was also a reflection of the SPD's growing political isolation, which was expressed in the urge to return to the oppositional role it had occupied before 1914. The tendency to seek refuge in pre-war political models and concepts was evident in all political parties at the time. It was exacerbated in the SPD, however, by the hope that this would relieve the pressure on it from the KPD and from its own left wing. In addition, the mass of its supporters seemed to respect it more when it pursued oppositionist politics rather than played an active part in government.[19] The SPD could not be expected to overcome its former role as a subculture in the Wilhelmine empire at a stroke; indeed, many elements of its social isolation were purposely perpetuated so as to maintain the militant appeal of socialist institutions.[20] But this mentality had to lead to the SPD never getting beyond a purely legalistic defence of the democratic order when confronting the conservative right and the NSDAP. It could offer its supporters no alternative to deforming the constitutional order by means of the presidential cabinet system. This problem was to re-emerge in the resistance movement under the Third Reich. Advocates of a parliamentary democratic system were in a decided minority in the resistance. There appeared to be little point in fighting for a constitutional system which had proved cumbersome and fraught with conflict and in whose future no one had believed.[21]

But many proposals were put forward for an alternative to the excessively formal concept of democracy dominant in the SPD and among Weimar democrats in general. These were reflected in numerous calls for greater popular participation, both within party political structures and outside them. The debate on this topic which took place within various wings of the SPD, particularly among younger party intellectuals, has still not completely exhausted itself to this day. The issue that sparked it off was the bureaucratic and sometimes authoritarian methods employed by the party executive to assert its control over the party organization. The low level of internal party democracy and involvement of party supporters was sharply criticized by both the left- and right-wing opposition groups in the party. Both wings agreed that the party apparatus needed to be decentralized and its rigid structures loosened, that a 'democracy of the component organizations'[22] was required to reduce its oligarchical tendencies and bureaucratic sterility. Calls of this kind usually arose in reaction to the bureaucratic attempts made to discipline the left and the party youth movement, though they also went beyond this. The left took USPD organizational ideas as its point of reference, but in the discussion that developed a new emphasis emerged which anticipated the anti-authoritarian currents that have been evident in the Federal Republic since 1968. The central concerns were that the level of participation within the party be increased, that political debate in the party press be enlivened and that the party be more open at its lower levels to actively involving party sympathizers. In raising these demands, the left was supported by the advocates of a resolute socialist reformism on the right. There was a crisis of internal democracy in the SPD which lay hidden behind what Theodor Haubach called the antiquated democratic rituals of party life. He condemned the 'uselessness of a stereotyped, stage-managed assembly democracy' which only served to further undermine internal party participation.[23]

The organizational ideas of the left were certainly immature and to some extent even contradictory. In the case of the ISK, for example, Leninist principles were mixed with latently fascist ones.[24] The desire for modern leadership methods, which would also have entailed a greater emphasis on plebiscitary extra-parliamentary forms of politics, united left- and right-wing critics of the executive. Helmut Wagner, expelled from the party in September 1931 as a supporter of the revolutionary left, declared that the central problem facing the SPD was the need to find 'a proletarian solution to the "leadership question" and a dynamic unity of organizational work and mass struggle'.[25] This was not incompatible with demanding a strengthening of internal party democracy; but it lacked credibility in that it could offer no way of ensuring that outsiders or unsavoury individuals did not capture leadership positions. The bureaucratic leadership methods of the party executive, which were concealed by a wealth of ostensibly democratic procedure, effectively prevented an active solidarity beyond that passed on by tradition developing within the party. This could have facilitated the constructive interaction of the sharply divergent strands of thinking which existed within the party. All groups advocating a greater political activism were pursuing the same goal in their polemics against the party's leadership methods. Julius Leber, Carlo Mierendorff, Theodor Haubach, the 'Class Struggle' group, the Young Socialists and often even the SAJ (Socialist Working-Class Youth) were all equally convinced that the executive's leadership methods effectively depoliticized ordinary party members. Haubach remarked sarcastically that the SPD was 'excellently administered but not led at all'[26] and Julius Leber spoke in similar tones.

The spirited activism on the right- and left-wing extremes of the SPD sought to liberate the party from its defensive stagnation by having it adopt a more dynamic concept of democracy and increase its attractiveness, particularly to the younger generation. But these forces remained isolated. Democracy as a mechanism for regulating the distribution of offices and positions had no attractive power of any kind. This was why the demands were raised for the party to adopt new political, agitational and organizational methods. The great majority of party officials rejected such ideas as idealistic theorizing. In 1928 Paul Levi commented prophetically that 'the SPD is almost the only place where democracy has a home today' and if 'it died out there . . . fascism will be its grinning heir'.[27] During the final phase of the Republic the SPD did in fact stand virtually alone in defence of the democratic Republic. But it lacked the inner conviction necessary to put up a serious fight on its behalf. The party leadership began to realize that the ambivalent attitude to the Republic it had maintained over the years could no longer be justified. But the indifference of the mass of the people to the existing system could not be transformed overnight. The effects of this neglect were made all the more acute during the period of the presidential cabinets when the SPD no longer had any political room to manoeuvre and was not in a position to openly challenge the increasingly anti-parliamentary tendencies of the Brüning government.

The SPD reacted helplessly to the emergent threat of a conservative–NSDAP alliance. This was partly due to its mistaken defensive strategy, which was ultimately a product of the prognosis outlined by Friedrich Engels in his famous preface to Marx's *Class Struggles in France*.[28] At the 1929 party conference in Magdeburg, Otto Wels declared that the SPD would not hesitate to assert its 'right to resort to dictatorship' if democracy was threatened with destruction by the KPD, the Stahlhelm or the NSDAP.[29] But this declaration was just a reformist variant of the left's demand that the instrument of proletarian dictatorship be used in the event of an attack on democracy by the bourgeoisie. Wels's statement turned Engels's tactical advice on its head in that he attempted to justify with legalistic arguments the exceptional measures the SPD would have to resort to in a civil war. This demonstrated the absence of any real determination on the part of the SPD leadership to fight counter-revolution with revolutionary means. The left wanted the SPD to adopt the strategy of the Austrian social democrats; but in its enthusiasm for their Linz Programme of 1926 it failed to recognize the misreading of the political situation on which this was based. The position advocated by the left was in fact identical to that proposed by the party leadership, except for its more radical form.

The Linz Programme threatened to impose a dictatorship in the event of an attempted counter-revolution by the bourgeoisie. It is still hotly debated whether the programme was a tactical mistake which made it easier for Seipel to isolate and finally defeat the socialists.[30] But this obscures the basic problem that the programme itself was based on a false political perspective. In 1890 Engels envisaged a situation where the bourgeoisie would attempt by counter-revolutionary means to prevent the democratic take-over of power by the proletariat at a time when the latter already had the support of the majority of the population and of substantial parts of the army. In such a scenario, time was on the side of the proletariat. But in 1930 the labour movement, quite apart from the split within its own ranks, did not have the support of the majority of the population and had no reason to expect any rapid improvement in its position. Engels's concept related to Bismarckian plans to stage a *coup d'état* in the event of the democratic triumph of social democracy. It had little relevance to the situation of the late 1920s and early 1930s, where the conservatives and then the fascists gradually succeeded, by exploiting constitutional loopholes and by other pseudo-legal means, in destroying the basis of democratic labour and forcing it to resort to revolutionary – that is, non-legal – defensive measures, which in turn provided the excuse for finally extinguishing it. Hitler's pseudo-legal road to power, which built on precedents established by the presidential governments, as well as that of Dollfuss, presented the labour movement with an almost insoluble dilemma. Either it deployed its forces before a counter-revolutionary dictatorship had been established and thus risked expending them, or else, by holding back for a more opportune moment, risked missing its chance to stage an effective resistance. Otto Bauer studied the situation in Germany thoroughly and made a very accurate analysis of it. But this did not prevent his making the same mistake in confronting Dollfuss as had been made in Germany. The moment to stage an act of revolutionary resistance which had some chance of success was allowed to pass: the revolt of February 1934 was ill-prepared, uncoordinated and carried out at the politically least opportune moment.[31]

The objective was to resort to violence to counter an all-out attack on democracy and possibly to develop this into a struggle to establish a socialist democracy. This strategy was based on the belief that the working class had no need for revolutionary action as long as the democratic framework for working-class political advance was intact and was not threatened by a counter-revolution. The threat to impose a revolutionary dictatorship was, significantly, also to be used in the event of a communist putsch. The intention in this eventuality was not to seize power but rather to reassert the rule of law. This line of argument sustained the illusions of the socialists' supporters that the strength of the movement had remained intact. It thus served to justify party policy against criticism from the left and to block attempts to radically change existing party tactics. It also made it easier to concentrate party activity on confrontation with the KPD and in comparison to play down the threat to the Republic from the conservative right. This political tunnel vision, which was reciprocated on the communist side, was not restricted to the party hierarchy or pragmatic reformist circles alone.

The party's lack of political flexibility was closely related to its organizational structure. The process of bureaucratization which had been evident even before 1914 had accelerated alarmingly after the end of the war. This was not least due to the rapid organizational growth of the party. There are no reliable data by which to measure the size of the party bureaucracy accurately. Richard Hunt has estimated that it had about twenty to thirty thousand salaried officials. If the functionaries of the trade union organizations traditionally associated with it are added to this, the extent of bureaucratic influence in the party's structures becomes obvious.[32] It was particularly evident in the higher echelons of the party apparatus, the parliamentary party and the delegations to annual conferences, where the proportion of full-time officials was astonishingly high and aggravated the self-importance which was increasingly a feature of such congresses. The conservative mentality which dominated the party apparatus and led to its outlook becoming more and more apolitical was sharply criticized even at the time.[33]

The progressive bureaucratization of the SPD and its rigid adherence to traditional perspectives had the combined effect of reducing debate and limiting the turnover of personnel in elective positions within the party. This was demonstrated most clearly by the manner in which internal dissent was suppressed, especially when it came from the left. Open criticism of long-serving party leaders was regarded almost as a felony. Paul Levi spoke of a pogromist mood against the left opposition. If the party hierarchy had had its way, Levi, who had been expelled from the KPD in 1921, would have suffered the same fate in the SPD.[34] Valid criticisms of the party apparatus were often dismissed with the argument that these only served to damage the party's public image. Over-representation of the party leadership at annual conferences had the effect of containing the party opposition, and this was often further reinforced by manipulative devices. The left, supported in this by intellectuals on the right of the party, sought in vain for local party branches and youth organizations to be given greater autonomy, for the system of delegation to annual conferences to be changed to allow for greater representation from strands differing from executive policy and for debate to be promoted in party journals. Motions to this effect were generally denounced as pro-communist by speakers from the executive and these were applauded by the silent majority of officials who, out of ingrained habits of loyalty to their leaders, uncritically supported all resolutions tabled by the executive. The tendency to suppress debate between divergent strands in the party or to manipulate it to the benefit of the executive and the general aversion to theoretical discussion – a legacy of the traditional antipathy to intellectuals – encouraged the growth of 'intellectual mediocrity and drilled routine', as Leber remarked bitterly.[35]

The phenomena described here were characteristic above all of the situation in the party in the final phase of the Weimar Republic. The dismal results produced by the policies pursued by the party, compounded by the political pressure on its constituency from the KPD, increased the insecurity of the SPD leadership. It sought to compensate by rigorously attacking the left opposition in the party. The irritation with which the party hierarchy reacted to criticism, the attempts to neutralize oppositional groups by organizational manipulation and the spirit of intolerance which was spreading rapidly in particular among veteran officials and older members, pointed to a deep crisis in the party. Part of the background to this was the disillusioning contrast between the optimism which had accompanied the party's rise to power and spectacular growth in 1918 on the one hand and the stagnation which had set in from 1920 on the other. This was reflected in party membership trends. The SPD succeeded in recovering its full membership strength relatively quickly after the losses of the war years and in expanding it to 1.2 million by 1921 and 1.26 million by 1923 following the return to the party of the USPD rump. But the period of bourgeois bloc government saw a substantial decline, with membership sinking to nearly 0.8 million before it rose again between 1929 and the summer of 1932 to stabilize at around 1 million. War casualties and the stagnation in the population growth rate were only a minor factor in this. Defection of members to the KPD also played only a limited role; the proportion of former social democrats in the KPD in 1927 – before the dramatic rise in KPD membership to over 300,000 – was only 30.2 per cent.[36] Nor was the stagnation in SPD membership a result of its development from a member-centred to a primarily electoral organization, though the size of its membership and its electoral support did not correspond; they even diverged sharply in terms of social composition.[37] In the late Weimar Republic substantial membership fluctuation became a marked feature of the SPD as of other parties, but in comparison with them it maintained a high level of membership stability. This contrasted with the extreme levels of fluctuation in membership experienced by the KPD and NSDAP.

Stagnation in SPD membership was probably mainly due to the rapid process of social restratification which occurred during the Weimar Republic. Along with the rise of the service sector and the growth in white-collar employment, the most notable demographic trend was the stagnation in the number of blue-collar workers as a proportion of the total employed population.[38] The numbers of blue-collar employees in large and medium-scale industrial concerns in particular were falling and declined to about 30 per cent of the workforce.[39] Given that a high proportion of the party's overall membership (76.9 per cent in 1930) was made up of workers, most of whom were skilled industrial workers, this retrogressive trend was bound to vitally affect the party. The party failed to make inroads among white-collar workers, however, and become a force in this sector, despite the growth in the lower middle class proportion of its membership to 21.2 per cent.[40] This was reflected in the sharp decline in the membership of the AfA, the social democratic white-collar workers' union. From 650,000 members in 1923, when it could compete successfully with other middle-class organizations, it had fallen to 203,000 by 1931, and these were largely full-time officials in party and trade union structures or employees of local government offices controlled by the SPD.[41]

This turn-about in trends in relation to the pre-war era was even more pronounced in the party's electoral support than in its membership. Although short of its own expectations, the MSPD's remarkably favourable result of 37.9 per cent in the elections to the National Assembly in 1919 was never to be achieved again. Its best subsequent performance was the 29.8 per cent it won in the Reichstag elections of 1928. The very unsatisfactory vote of 20.4 per cent in the November 1932 elections was partly caused by the swing among SPD supporters to the KPD, but also showed that the oppositional stance of the SPD was no longer the electoral advantage it had been previously. Apart from the swing of November 1932, this steady electoral decline only partly benefited the KPD. The combined socialist vote sank from 45.5 to 37.3 per cent.[42] In addition to the decline in its actual influence, the psychological effect on the SPD of repeated failure at the polls can hardly be overstated. The entire strategy and organizational work of the party presumed continuous growth. This dream was shattered with the June 1920 elections, but it took a certain period of time before the party leadership began to realize the full consequences of this. The conclusive research of Emil Lederer and Theodor Geiger, which established the changed spectrum of potential SPD recruits, sparked off a lively debate within the party from 1927.[43]

The remarkable stability of the party's membership in comparison to its electoral support had a psychologically negative effect in that it reinforced the tendency of party officials to devote their energies to internal organizational work, thereby ignoring the political crisis which was gripping the party. In so far as they regarded the old traditional membership as the party's solid and reliable base, the willingness to innovate was bound to decline and the political isolation of the party and apolitical mentality of its activists bound to increase. It is not surprising therefore that attempts to transform the SPD from a class-based party of the industrial proletariat, and especially of the skilled workers, into a broad-based popular party failed utterly during the fourteen years of the Weimar Republic. Although the necessity for such a transformation had been recognized in theory at Görlitz in 1921 and even at Heidelberg in 1925, the SPD did not succeed in decisively increasing the non-proletarian proportion of its electoral support relative to the pre-war era, when this had represented about 25 per cent of the total. The very early period of the Republic represented a brief exception to this. SPD electoral support among the middle classes and farmers increased by 10 per cent at most, though it lost this again during the economic crisis.[44] The dilemma for the SPD was that when it pursued a moderate course its attractiveness to fringe middle-class elements grew but it lost an almost equal number of voters to the competing parties on the left − first the USPD and then the KPD. This brought home the fact that changes in overall trends could not be achieved in short periods of time by changes in party policy alone. The abandoning of specifically Marxist elements of its programme or indeed ideological factors in general did not substantially affect the extent to which the SPD was attractive to non-proletarian voters. The strong influence of the reformist trade unions probably shaped the party's proletarian image more than the attempts by the left to revive Marxist ideas and reinforce the proletarian base of the party.

The party did not continue its efforts to win over non-proletarian supporters to any serious extent following its early setbacks. The increasing success of the parties of the right and the NSDAP in attracting the middle classes was watched with a sense of resignation. The tendency in trade unionism was to revert to the traditional politics of class isolation. The attempts to socially integrate the working class outside the party sphere which had been vigorously pursued in the early years of the Republic under the catchword of joint employer–union 'working associations' (*Arbeitsgemeinschaft*) were discontinued.[45] Priority was generally given to intensifying recruitment among the traditional working class. Big successes were registered in this area among agricultural labourers (with a certain time-lag in relation to the pre-war situation), though attempts by the party to achieve inroads into the Centre Party's working-class support had only limited success. From a tactical point of view, these campaigns only further weakened the SPD's political position in the party system. Comparative regional analyses could furnish more concrete conclusions in this regard.[46] On the whole, however, it would appear that the party successfully established durable roots only among very small groups of the non-proletarian electorate.

A decisive weakness in the SPD's approach to recruitment was its serious underestimation of the social-revolutionary energy at the root of the KPD's mass support. After the revolution, the SPD leadership tended to morally dismiss even the individual communist and this deep antipathy to communism also lay at the root of its deep suspicion of its own left wing. Winning back the support of the communist-oriented section of the working class was regarded not only as hopeless but as undesirable and there was little readiness to consider political concessions in this area. The belief persisted, despite its limited validity, that KPD sympathizers were mostly floating voters, many of whom had previously supported the right. The extremely high proportion of KPD supporters among the unemployed and the comparatively low percentage of industrial workers among its membership aroused a certain social resentment among SPD supporters towards the type of working-class support attracted by the KPD. The presumption that the KPD was doomed to collapse encouraged the SPD members in their inclination to focus on the long-term development of socialism, in the course of which the unity of the labour movement would be automatically restored when the KPD finally disappeared. The permanent leadership crises in the KPD, usually induced by outside interference, were regarded by SPD members as confirmation of the correctness of their own leadership's methods. A political confrontation with the KPD was regarded as superfluous: 'Confidence in the individual and his worth', according to Wels, speaking at the SPD annual conference in Magdeburg in 1929, was one of the many characteristics which differentiated the SPD from the communists.[47] The KPD's calls for a united front with the social democrats, quite apart from the tactical motives behind them, were rejected out of hand by the SPD hierarchy.

A significant opportunity to recruit supporters from outside the working class was presented by the Reichsbanner, which was organized and financed largely by the SPD. But, as Karl Rohe has shown,[48] this opportunity was not really exploited. Numerous organizational considerations played a role in this. At the SPD annual conference at Kiel in 1927 Otto Wels declared that it was time to establish the 'debit and credit' with regard to the Reichsbanner; party recruitment among young workers had been neglected due to over-concentration on the Reichsbanner.[49] An undercurrent of distrust shaped the attitude of many party officials towards the extra-parliamentary activities of the Reichsbanner and there was a constant fear that it could develop into a political party competing with the SPD. The Reichsbanner, and later the Iron Front, adopted a questionable outward style which, however much it corresponded to the political norms of the Weimar Republic, was distasteful to the average party or trade union official. These were used to thinking solely in parliamentary and trade union terms rather than the new forms developed by the Reichsbanner. In so far as extra-parliamentary means were considered at all after the experience of the general strike against the Kapp Putsch, it was solely in terms of traditional labour organizations.

The stagnation in membership and declining electoral support of the SPD was aggravated by the political inflexibility of the party's leading officials. By rigidly adhering to traditional mechanisms of co-option, the average age of the members of leading party bodies and the parliamentary party progressively increased, as Richard Hunt demonstrated in some detail.[50] This ageing process in the party executive was not fully apparent from the statistics as, with the death of some executive members and its expansion following reunification with the USPD rump, some younger members came on to the executive as replacements, though virtually all of these were long-serving career officials. The average age among members of the party executive in 1890 had been 39.6 years; during the Weimar period it was between 50 and 55 years. Promotion to office was effectively by acclamation; only once was a member voted off the party executive, and he, significantly, was a representative of the left. Only in 1931 and following a chorus of criticism at the excessive age of party leaders were some youth representatives taken on to the executive, and they were all known opponents of the political outlook of the SAJ and Young Socialists.[51]

There are little accurate data available on the age structure of the party apparatus. The vigorous criticisms voiced at the expected costs needed to cover party pensions and the fact that the promotion prospects of party officials were determined by age seniority would make it safe to assume that the vast majority of party positions were occupied by officials who had been schooled politically in the Wilhelmine era. The situation in the SPD Reichstag party was not much better. The seventh legislative period was the only one during which the proportion of deputies under 30 years of age was over 5 per cent of the total. The age of the average SPD Reichstag deputy – it fluctuated around 50 – was higher than that for most of the bourgeois parties. If the length of time for which the average SPD deputy held his seat is examined, the picture is even more negative. It was considerably greater than that of the other parties; almost 25 per cent of SPD Reichstag members held their seats for more than 10 years compared with 10 per cent in the other parties. The number of newcomers in the entire Weimar period was extremely small. The tendency, already evident in the pre-war era, for party members to nominate Reichstag deputies respected for their service to the organization and regardless of their political affiliations continued after 1918 and reinforced the isolation of the parliamentary party from the party supporters. Apart from the structurally debilitating ageing process within the party leadership stratum, this factor had the effect of considerably impeding the rise of politically talented and popular leaders from the party's second ranks into leading positions.

There was a direct relationship between ageing among the party's leading stratum and the relatively high average age of party members. The party executive at first sought to ignore this problem, dismissing statistical analyses of it as a waste of time. Nevertheless, following some regional studies, a survey of party members' ages in 320 local branches was undertaken. This sample was extensive enough to permit accurate generalizations regarding the whole membership.[52] It gave a very unfavourable picture of the situation as it was in 1930: the average age of party members was 42.5 years and the proportion of members under 20 was only 1.2 per cent. The proportion of members between 20 and 25 was about two and a half times less than the same group in the general population and the proportion of members between 25 and 30 was about half the figure which could have been expected in a membership structure which corresponded to that of the general public. The 40–60 age-group on the other hand was conspicuously over-represented in the party. The negative age structure of the party bureaucracy and leadership thus reflected an even more marked ageing among the membership.

For a party whose objective was to see its final goals achieved within generations, the apparent lack of interest among the young towards the SPD had a profound psychological effect. The party leadership tried to play down the growing criticisms being voiced of the ageing of its leaders and suppress the agitation from its younger ranks. But its assurances that the mass of working-class youth still stood loyally by the party and that young people were joining it in increasingly large numbers could not prevent this issue from becoming a central theme of internal party debates. This problem was not limited to the SPD, and it affected the bourgeois parties too in a hardly less worrying form. It was a product of the general inability of the Weimar party system to integrate the generation which was born too late to have been shaped by political experiences during the Wilhelmine era or First World War. But the situation was particularly unfavourable for the SPD. Compared with Weimar Germany's youth population of 19 million, the SAJ counted only about 56,000 members in 1931 while in 1923 it had had 105,000. In addition, the Red Falcons had 150,000 members in 1929. The Red Youth Front, whose membership partly coincided with that of the communist youth organization, the KJVD, which comprised about 20,000 members in 1931, had a membership of approximately 25,000.[53] The Free Trade Unions' youth sections had a little over 1,250,000 members. Allowing for overlapping membership, the total number of young people organized in the Workers' Sports Associations came to about half a million. These figures are particularly low when compared with those for the bourgeois youth organizations. Protestant youth groups had a total of over 1.5 million members and Catholic groups had over 1.3 million; the youth organizations of the various right-wing movements had about 250,000 members and the Hitler Youth about 40,000.[54]

The failure of the SPD and trade unions to attract the young to any serious extent reflected the lack of sympathy among older SPD officials – going back to the nineteenth century – for the needs and mentality of working-class youth. Most young people in the party tended to the left and Haubach believed that a majority of them had supported the USPD at the beginning of the Weimar Republic.[55] Efforts to intensify youth work and to allow younger members to participate in party work, and not just at the lower levels, were repeatedly brought to nought by the executive's policy of containing the influence of left-wing youth organizations in the party by organizational and disciplinary means, particularly the Young Socialists, and of forcing oppositional younger elements to conform to the party line. Following attempts to curtail the influence of the Young Socialists by raising the maximum age for SAJ membership, its separate organization was finally dissolved. This move was motivated by the close affinity of Young Socialist groups to the ISK, the Rote Kämpfer and later to the SAPD. The main reason for suppressing them, however, was their fierce attacks on official party policy. The numerous disciplinary measures taken against organizations and individuals of the party's youth sections have been comprehensively described; they reached a macabre high point in the executive's attempt to use its remaining authority in its confrontation with the Berlin youth organizations to ban the SAJ from re-establishing itself underground following the national socialist take-over.[56]

The party's endeavours to intensify its youth work in the late 1920s were not totally without success. Theodor Haubach stated with some satisfaction that 'regeneration of the age structure' of the SPD had made considerable progress.[57] But for the party leadership the generation problem continued to be viewed primarily from a disciplinary point of view; it was hoped that intensified educational efforts would keep the party youth from radicalism and from taking political initiatives of its own. Erich Nölting admonished the Young Socialists at the annual conference in Leipzig in 1931 not to 'confuse Karl Marx's sociological lectures for politics' and told them that their political error lay in their 'cult of yesteryear', that is, the Marxist tradition. This reprimand illustrated the complete inability of the party leadership to understand the political attitudes of younger members. It was reminiscent of the fatal objections to a political role for working-class youth raised by the party centre before 1914.[58]

The hopes of the younger members of the SPD that the Leipzig congress would see the adoption of a conciliatory stance towards the aspirations of the party youth movement and that Erich Ollenhauer would emerge as a forceful representative of the younger generation were completely dashed. Mierendorff reported that Ollenhauer's speech lacked any perspective, was delivered in schoolmasterly fashion and had 'a beard down to its knees'.[59] The Young Socialists were not allowed separate representation at the conference and, largely due to Wels's clever chairmanship, even their former representatives were not given a chance to speak. The youth question, despite the fact that its relevance to the problem of fascism had been clearly established since the elections of September 1930, was played down at the conference and dealt with as a mere organizational problem. Young people were said to lack political sense and maturity and the Young Socialists specifically were accused of political failure. The political criticisms raised by the party youth were not addressed. Instead, the situation was represented, as it had previously been in the party press, as one where youth, given its susceptibility to radical ideology, was the actual problem in the party and was responsible for allowing destructive external influences to slip into the party and threaten its unity.[60] The assertiveness of the Young Socialists was met with disciplinary measures and the dissolution of the Young Socialist groups. The party's young members were declared incapable of making political decisions. Ollenhauer stated indirectly that the SPD had left its youthful phase behind it and had entered an era of protracted positional warfare.

The Leipzig congress did not break through the 'barrier which exists in Germany between the political bodies of the state and the younger generation'[61] but rather reinforced it. It was regarded as a political catastrophe by both right- and left-wing opposition groups. Many younger members went over definitively to the SAPD as they doubted that the party would be able to assert itself against ascendant fascism with the methods and tactics it employed. But those who, like Carlo Mierendorff, remained loyal to the party now began demanding that it take a clear swing to the left and that the executive resign. The youth issue was no longer just an internal question of regenerating the SPD but had become an indicator of the capacity of democratic groups generally to resist the fascist menace.

The unattractiveness of the SPD and most bourgeois parties to young people contrasted with the extraordinarily high attraction which the NSDAP and, to a lesser extent, the KPD exercised over the younger generation. There were many reasons for this. The classic youth movement had advocated the abandonment of politics; while the younger generation of the Weimar era was quite highly political, it rejected traditional forms of political mobilization and the political style of the Republic, which came across to it, sometimes understandably, as a monopoly of the establishment. The thinking of active young people was strongly irrational and emotionally flavoured. They spoke a different language from the preceding generation. In an article on the character of German fascist youth, Emil Henk analysed this question. This section of youth, he wrote, though 'passionately active and politically assertive', could not be won over by rational arguments but 'only by the sole effective forces of belief in and enthusiasm for a vision of genuine and meaningful socialism'.[62] The younger generation in general was characterized by its inclination to militancy and radicalism, to reject traditional forms of organization and to idealize the community ideal and by its urge for action and change; these traits were common across the board, regardless of political persuasion. The socio-psychological origins of this phenomenon, with its appeals to the youth experience and to a philosophy of life, cannot be examined in detail here. It was primarily a reaction to modern industrial society with its levelling and collectivist tendencies; it contained a fundamentally critical view of modern civilization which had some socialist elements. This generation's energies and indubitable idealism, however unrealistic, were not necessarily only capable of benefiting the forces of fascism and anti-republicanism.

Nevertheless, the Republic left this younger generation largely to its own devices. It was a Republic of the older generation and it was generally oriented, paradoxically, to pre-war conditions. These became the yardstick by which all economic or foreign policy matters were judged.[63] This trend was nowhere more clearly evident than in the SPD. Its officials held rigidly to pre-war tactics and agitational methods and stressed the continuity of party tradition. But the younger generation operated on different premises which were rooted in its own experiences. It did not share the older generation's feeling of satisfaction at the achievements of the party since the annulling of the Socialist Laws, which had the effect of casting the otherwise disappointing results of social democratic politics in the Weimar era in a somewhat better light. Younger people had experienced the November Revolution not as a success but as a defeat. They refused to judge the party's politics against the yardstick of the past. Their yardstick was their own all too hazy visions for the future. Neither did they share the petit bourgeois and paternalistic catalogue of virtues espoused by the party elders who encouraged them to busy themselves with organizational work while refusing them any measure of political responsibility.

The generational conflict so often spoken of in the Weimar Republic had its origins in the conflicting experiences and value systems of the generation moulded in the Wilhelmine era and the First World War and the younger generation which had its first political experiences in the everyday dullness of post-war life. It was accentuated by the fact that the November Revolution did not destroy the conceptual social and political norms of the Wilhelmine era and that the Republic continued largely in the mould of the economic and bureaucratic structures of the pre-war era despite the fundamental upheaval in society which had taken place. These antagonistic elements were at the root of the rebelliousness of Weimar's young generation. The NSDAP and the KPD successfully exploited these to their own advantage. Both parties were historically younger than the competing bourgeois and socialist parites, their age structures approximating to that of the SPD of 1890. Numerous leading KPD officials had been active in the pre-war labour youth movement. The KPD also profited greatly from the political disorientation of unemployed youth denied the experience of work by the international economic crisis. The militant and radically oppositionist stance adopted by the KPD corresponded to their own outlook. The other side of this coin was the extreme fluctuation in its younger membership, which in large measure was a direct result of the inflexibility and bureaucratic character of the Communist Party structure.

The NSDAP was equally successful in exploiting the youth cult which existed across the board in the Weimar Republic and was by no means confined to the political right. It was adept at manipulating the anti-modernist resentments and the 'community' syndrome so popular in youth culture and at portraying itself as the party of youth. Neo-conservative thinking had paved the way for it in this regard. The question which faced the SPD was what methods to use to counter this. Theodor Haubach recommended that greater regard be paid to the political sensitivities of young people and that greater emphasis be placed on outward forms: 'our movement must come to realize that ceremony, authority and disciplined leadership are not by any means undemocratic and certainly not unsocialist'.[64] Mierendorff advocated a more resolute use of graphic symbolism and effective propaganda techniques. The success of the Iron Front and the effectiveness of the three-arrow symbol proved that this could achieve results; but what was worrying about this was that it meant more or less adopting a version of fascist stylistic forms.

There was no shortage of imagination or of attempts to give SPD propaganda a new look, and the design of posters and recruiting leaflets shows that the artistic and stylistic development of the party, in this area at least, was not neglected. But the real problem was a deeper one. The SPD in the Weimar Republic no longer exuded the charisma transcending mere political rationality which had characterized it in its early days. Paul Levi pointed this out as early as 1924. He argued that the exclusively rational appeal of SPD propaganda, the realist pragmatism of its leadership and its almost classic liberal belief that political and social conflict were open to rational solutions were in the last resort a recipe for failure. Marx and Engels as well as classic social democracy had regarded the eschatological element and the power of elemental moral outrage as decisively important factors alongside the 'sharp logical weapon' of Marxist theory. This power totally transcended the rational and was the driving force behind all 'great historical movements'. It was 'the force which had made the social democratic movement great, which had rallied thousands upon thousands of people to it and which even in the caricature of it represented by contemporary communism continued to retain its power'. Political movement and conflict was anything but a purely intellectual process: 'Perhaps experience will show us yet', he added prophetically, 'that there is something more powerful than the ability to be clever.'[65]

In his 1935 study on the defeat of the labour movement in the face of fascism, Ernst Bloch focused on Levi's self-critical assessment and summed it up succinctly: 'Nazis speak deceptively, but of people – communists speak the truth, but of things.'[66] This statement could be just as accurately applied to the pragmatic and realist mentality of the SPD. Bloch saw the reason for the triumph of fascism as lying in its successful mobilization of deeply traditional attitudes and modes of consciousness and explained this as an 'expression of the unsimultaneous nature' of social conflict. In fact, the mass-effectiveness of fascism lay in its ability to mobilize the resentments and fears of declining social status, which were widespread in society, against the relentless completion of industrial society with its levelling and rationalizing effects. The youth rebellion, whether expressed politically in demands for a class community or a national community, was very much part of this picture. The fascist movement, which despite its categorical anti-modernism made full use, in its propaganda for example, of the most modern technical innovations, thrived parasitically on the process of social restratification which had been under way since the turn of the century, particularly among the middle classes. The labour movement, oriented to the realities of political life, underestimated the significance of residual social groups and mentalities. As the 'other side of the completed liberal structure', as Ernst Bloch put it,[67] it was helpless when confronted by the force of political irrationalism. This was especially true of the SPD's reformism, which was absorbed in the detail of day-to-day politics.

It would be wrong, however, to conclude in retrospect that had a more radical and revolutionary propaganda replaced the party's reformist practice, things would have developed in a fundamentally different direction. The example of the Austrian socialists, who were not operating under pressure from a strong Communist Party and who, in contrast to the German SPD, had a clear left-wing orientation, shows that a greater emphasis on class politics was by no means an answer to the dilemma of socialism's inherent weakness in facing the nationalist and fascist offensive. Inflexibility and bureaucratic paralysis were just as evident in the KPD during this period. The subservience of its party hierarchy to Comintern strategy meant that its ordinary members were constantly confronted with having to defend policies that bore little relationship to the real world. In other European countries too the labour movement was forced on the defensive, but, while partially successful in containing the crisis of parliamentary democracy, was incapable of structurally mastering it. The deeper cause for the crisis in the labour movement in Europe generally lay in the loss of its original character as a movement. This was a process related to the fundamental changes which had taken place in the structure of society since the imperialist epoch. The social democratic movement in the Weimar period had an impressive network of organizations of the most diverse kind at its disposal, encompassing all areas of social and political life. The multifarious activities of the party and of its full-time and voluntary officials did not converge and form a concerted political force. The momentum was diffused and the negative effects of organizational rivalries began to develop beyond control.

What united the opposition groups of right and left within the SPD despite their otherwise sharp ideological differences was their concern to infuse political life back into the party and revive its original character as a movement. As the party executive fortified its position and attempted to stifle the chorus of criticism levelled at the party's passivity, numerous oppositional social democrats left the SPD, believing productive political activity no longer possible within it. The party executive exacerbated this trend by initiating expulsion proceedings against representatives of the left and effectively provoking the foundation of the SAPD. It was characteristic of the last phase of the Republic that virtually all activist elements in the German labour movement left the SPD and KPD and reorganized themselves in splinter groups around the two large party structures: the KPO (Communist Party Opposition), the ISK, the Rote Kämpfer, the SAPD and a number of smaller formations, several of which were later absorbed by the SAPD.[68] Determined reformist socialists such as Carlo Mierendorff, Theodor Haubach and Julius Leber persisted in oppositional politics within the SPD.

It was not totally a coincidence that among the best areas of recruitment for these oppositionist socialist groupings was the SPD youth organizations and in particular the Young Socialists. Despite the factional disputes which soon erupted within the SAPD and rapidly absorbed its political energies, basic unanimity remained on the aim, which was – as Anna Siemsen summed it up – to 'loosen up and blast open the rigid and paralysed big parties'.[69] In organizational terms these attempts to regenerate socialist politics were doomed to fail. Their historical importance lies rather in the fact that they prepared the ground intellectually for the underground resistance movement against the Nazi regime. This was partly a result of their rejection of the belief that the triumph of socialism was an inevitability, a belief which lay at the root of much of the paralysis affecting the socialist movement. In his pamphlet *Neu Beginnen!* Walter Löwenheim settled accounts with both the old SPD executive and the KPD. He concluded from the debate on basic aims that had raged for years within the SPD that socialist revolution and a socialist transformation of society were not 'historically inevitable', but rather contained a 'large element of historical chance' which it was in the power of man to exploit.[70] He called for a return to the accountability of autonomous individuals for their actions and for the will of socialism to be liberated from dependency on historical determinism.

In the conditions of 1931–2 these attempts to reactivate the socialist movement were necessarily destined to be only diagnoses and not actual cures for the problem. Their warnings that a fascist take-over had to be prevented at all costs as its rule would not be a short-lived episode but would entail the long-term emasculation of the labour movement went largely unheeded. The SPD was no longer capable of sounding an offensive against the mutilation of the constitution by the presidential governments. The KPD concealed its powerlessness behind a campaign against the alleged 'social-fascism' of the SPD. Too closely tied to the parliamentary system as it drifted towards its doom, the SPD lacked the room to manoeuvre necessary to accommodate the attempts being made to revive, rejuvenate and democratize the party's structures and thus to implant a democratic consciousness more firmly in the broad mass of the people. This would have necessarily entailed its adopting the role of a consistently oppositional party, but, given the inherent weaknesses of the Weimar democratic system, would only have facilitated the enemies of the Republic in seizing and monopolizing power. By ensuring the relative stability of the parliamentary system, including in the period in which it pursued a 'tolerationist' policy, the SPD was predestined to share its fate. Its very persistence in holding to obsolete traditions and to its historical perspective enabled it to immunize the mass of the working class against the irrational and fascist tendencies of the time. Relative political inflexibility was the price it paid for this. If the party had not held to this line, despite the minimal chance of its being a success given the situation of economic stagnation and the extreme pressure from employers on the unions, the Republic would certainly have collapsed much earlier, probably in the second half of the 1920s.

In spite of the inherent weaknesses of the politics it pursued during the Weimar era, which in many ways were a consequence of its political isolation in the Bismarckian and Wilhelmine Reich, the SPD made important progress towards transforming itself from a purely class-based party into a democratic popular party. The historical conditions and the shortness of the period which preceded the onset of the economic crisis prevented this trend from coming to full fruition. The SPD attempted to fulfil a double function. It sought to defend the parliamentary democracy it had helped to found against the pressures on it from the right, which were gathering momentum from an early stage, while simultaneously attempting to improve the social conditions of the working classes. This was too much of a burden for it to bear. It is possible to identify a range of tactical mistakes made by the SPD in the coalitionist strategy it pursued. But it must be emphasized that it was prepared to share responsibility for unpopular decisions. These included policies which threatened its electoral base but which its sense of national duty dictated that it support. Blame for the destruction of the constitutional order which followed the toppling of the Grand Coalition in March 1930 rests squarely with the bourgeois conservative groups which inaugurated and implemented the policies of the presidential cabinets. The political exclusion of the social democratic labour movement for which they shared responsibility inexorably paved the way for Hitler's victory.

4

Class War or Co-determination:

On the Control of Economic Power in the Weimar Republic

The holding of this series of public lectures in memory of Hugo Sinzheimer, the pioneer of modern labour law in Germany, should help to diminish the reserve felt in the trade union and labour movement towards universities and colleges and replace it with a spirit of co-operation. It also demonstrates that there is a desire to bring the creative era of German labour law associated with Sinzheimer's name back to public notice and, to use Thilo Ramm's phrase,[1] to overcome the 'mental dissociation' from this formative period of German social development which exists at present. It is fitting therefore that a social historian has been asked to become involved in this process of active commemoration and for this I would like to express my thanks. Hugo Sinzheimer's outlook and political commitment create a rich heritage for the social historian seeking to deepen his or her knowledge of the social history of the Weimar Republic. It is an equally rich legacy for legal scholars involved with labour and social law who are continuing his work both directly and indirectly.

As the Weimar Republic was being established, Hugo Sinzheimer sided unequivocally with the Social Democratic Party. He resolutely opposed all those who advocated that the parliamentary democratic system be replaced by a dictatorship of workers' councils. He wished to see the parliamentary system complemented by democratic institutions of economic administration. During the political debates which preceded the summoning of the National Assembly in Weimar, Sinzheimer, as a spokesman for the MSPD, took a clear stance against the attempts by the workers' council movement to establish itself in place of the state and the system of law which it embodied.

Otto Kahn-Freund pointed out that Sinzheimer's concept of the state was deeply rooted in German tradition as it presumed a friction between state and society. Among the most fruitful results of his academic and political work was that he turned this friction into a positive element, using it to reinforce the principle of the autonomy of the economic and social areas. He was a pioneer of the idea of economic councils and the provision for them in Article 165 of the Weimar constitution was drafted by him.[2] Sinzheimer demonstrated that a purely 'political democracy' in public life would never be sufficient. He believed it was essential that political democracy be complemented by a comprehensive system of social democracy. Even in the most complete system of political democracy, he argued, 'the possibility of dangerous tensions emerging between the political order and the system of social relations as it developed' would continue to exist.[3] This statement of Sinzheimer's from 1919 reflected his basic optimism that the democratic forces of the Weimar National Assembly would succeed in infusing the new constitution with real life and in fending off the conservative nationalists then only beginning to rally against it. His ideas presumed a level of political development where the democratic principle governed all areas of life and where democracy meant more than simply a form of government, a mechanism for channelling the public political will and a free judiciary. But far from this vision being realized, the bitter reality was that the overwhelming majority of the bureaucratic, military and economic elites of Weimar refused to accept the social consequences of democracy and destroyed the foundations of the Republic by attacking its social achievements.

It is precisely for this reason that Sinzheimer's study of the relationship between political and social democracy, and hence of the connection between political autonomy and socio-economic partnership, is of central importance to any accurate assessment of the internal development of the Weimar Republic. But it has proved to have a wider significance too. It can serve as a test case for the whole question of whether the parliamentary system *per se* can function at all in a highly industrialized society if it is not accompanied by institutional arrangements which prevent parliament and government being powerless in the face of socio-economic forces and dominant economic interests. Looked at from this viewpoint, the experiences of the Weimar Republic in the area of social policy in particular take on a major importance. The question is whether the specific form which industrial relations took in the Weimar Republic, where the state was forced to act as a perpetual arbitrator,[4] was not bound to place an excessive strain on the Republic's parliamentary institutions given the absence of any other framework for mediating social conflict. In this context it is important to understand the central position which social policy in its widest sense occupied in the Weimar Republic. In no other field of domestic or foreign policy were lasting positive achievements and total failures, successes and defeats, accumulated to such a degree. The historiography of the Weimar Republic has only in recent years begun to examine these issues to any great extent. This has led to an overall reassessment of this period of German history, and its relevance to today's situation has become increasingly apparent.

When the Federal Republic was being established and consolidated, the Weimar period was regarded above all as its precursor but also as its negative image, and it was examined primarily from a constitutional and institutional perspective. The relatively positive picture of it that pertained at that time gradually gave way to a substantially less favourable one in the 1960s. The element of continuity from the Republic to the Third Reich was emphasized more, and its outward and internal structures were analysed from a standpoint that sought to explain how the breakthrough of the NSDAP as a mass movement had become possible. A more pessimistic view emerged of the Republic's chances of survival as well as of its achievements. This balance sheet deteriorated further when comparisons began to be made with the development of the Federal Republic since 1949.

Since the 1960s on the other hand, the social history of the Weimaer Republic and comparative studies of it have received greater attention. The originally excessive concentration on studying the origins of national socialism is gradually giving way to a more structuralist historical analysis, superseding by degrees the previous narrow emphasis on theories of comparative fascism. This has led to the history of the Weimar Republic being viewed in the broader context of the restoration of bourgeois capitalist Europe after the First World War.[5] The crisis-prone period of inter-war development is being studied in terms of the structural changes which took place in the capitalist economic system. These confronted the labour and trade union movement in all European industrial countries with problems of a totally new type. Some historians use the concept of 'organized capitalism' coined by Rudolf Hilferding to describe the socio-economic transformation of modern industrial society which occurred in this period[6] and to place a greater emphasis on the similarities between the socio-economic structures of the inter- and post-war eras.

In establishing the elements of historical continuity between Weimar and the political system of the Federal Republic, the most important area is that of social policy.[7] All major aspects of the social structures of the West German state were developed or already institutionalized during the Weimar era. With only minor exceptions, this is the case with the corpus of legislation covering collective bargaining, contracts of employment, the system of unemployment insurance, occupational safety and hours of work as well as industrial relations within the plant. Weimar social policy was to remain a skeleton, however. This was exemplified by the failure of the much heralded Code of Labour Law to become a reality.[8] The system of economic self-regulation and self-administration foreseen in the provision for a National Economic Council in Article 165 of the Weimar constitution never materialized. This would have involved a tiered system of workers' and economic councils. On the other hand, however, a wealth of social policy initiatives of lasting importance were implemented. If one compares what was achieved in this area during the fourteen crisis-laden years of the Weimar Republic in very unfavourable economic circumstances with similar measures introduced during the more than two and a half decades of the Federal Republic's development, the balance sheet for Weimar is a strikingly positive one. A period of dismantling the social and welfare state provisions of the Republic only began with Franz von Papen's presidential cabinet of 1932.

Social policy moved more and more to the centre of internal political conflict in Weimar and in many ways came to be the touchstone of the viability of the democratic republican system. The Republic as we know did not fall to a frontal attack by the forces of counter-revolution. Kapp's defeat in 1920 was only the first of a series of abortive attempts by right-wing circles to establish the dictatorship they openly craved. Despite the symptoms of deep crisis which accompanied it in its early years and the violent convulsions of the inflationary period, the Republic succeeded in substantially consolidating itself politically following the external normaliz-ation brought by the Dawes Plan. But from as early as 1920 and with the collapse of the liberal centre, the political balance was increasingly weighted to the right. As a result, democratic republican positions were progressively surrendered to traditional interests in the state bureaucracy and in society which were vigorously reasserting their influence. But as long as the forma-tion of government coalitions between the SPD on the one hand and the bourgeois parties of the centre, including the DVP, on the other remained possible in principle – thus bridging the class divide at the political level of government – the growth of anti-republican groupings on the extreme left and right did not pose a fundamental threat to the constitutional system, though this was now in virtual permanent retreat. In this context, it is evident that the NSDAP, despite its temporarily spectacular electoral suc-cesses, would have been destroyed by severe internal crisis had not the court elites in Hindenburg's entourage succeeded by deceptive manipulation in establishing Hitler in the Chancellery just as the momentum of national socialism as a mass movement had already clearly passed its peak and gone into decline.[9]

The break-up of the Grand Coalition in March 1930 can thus be seen as a decisive turning-point in the internal development of the Republic. Chancellor Hermann Müller resigned because the trade union wing of the SPD in the Reichstag opposed a continuation of the coalition and also because he did not want to be party to any dismantling of unemployment benefits. That was a tactical mistake. If the government had fallen following

an open parliamentary battle, the responsibility of the DVP for the governmental crisis would have been clear for all to see. That the social democratic
coalition would be toppled was predetermined anyway, though it was
planned that this would not happen until after the Young Plan had been
adopted. This was because the right had no intention of being associated
with the plan's unpopularity and preferred instead to have an SPD chancellor bear the odium of concluding an agreement on the country's foreign
debts. The Reich president and the cartel of large-scale agricultural and
heavy industrial interests had long been agreed on establishing a government
based on a right-wing coalition. Strengthened by the extra-parliamentary
'right-opposition' in whose service Brüning, as Hindenburg's chancellor,
had effectively placed himself, these forces believed that this must wait
until after the economic crisis in Germany's foreign relations had been
resolved by the successful conclusion of the reparations negotiations, which
had been under way since 1928. Once in power, they planned to proceed
with dismantling the social institutions of the state so as to appease heavy
industry. Major constitutional changes in an authoritarian direction, as
advocated, for example, by the Bund zur Erneuerung des Reiches, were
therefore far from mere utopian aims.[10]

Having seen many of the considerable political advances in social policy
achieved in November 1918 reversed during the inflation years – including
the eight-hour day, which had been a major point of prestige for both
employers and workers – the SPD as well as the Free and Christian Trade
Unions had come to regard the retention of the state system of social
security as the minimum position they could accept politically. The freedom
to manoeuvre of ADGB union leaders was tightly restricted by the unrestrained agitation of the communists against them. But just as the economy
had begun to enjoy a certain level of stability, influential business circles
began pressing for a total revision of the social security system. Heavy
industry identified this institution with parliamentarism *per se*. The interests
of the mining and steel industries had come to dominate the RdI (Reich
Federation of German Industry) and other substantial leading economic
organizations. This had been brought about mainly through price control
arrangements, such as the AVI (Working Association of the Iron Processing
Industry) agreement, which had enabled these sectors to bring the tool-
making industry under their control. This development was to have drastic
political consequences.[11] In contrast to the 'new' industries, a tendency
emerged for the heavy industrial sector to attempt to tackle the alleged
'primary costs' crisis by ruthlessly cutting wages and increasing working
hours. This crisis had arisen as a result of the collapse of world market
prices, progressive cartelization to facilitate mass production and relatively
high wage costs, and despite the radical rationalizations under way.[12]

Exponents of heavy industry openly advocated a return to pre-1913 wage costs and social security charges without reference to the levels of rationalization in production or the increased cost of living reached since then. This policy was directed ultimately at reversing the achievements of the 1918 Revolution. These circles were well aware that this could not be realized within the framework of a parliamentary system.

The dissolution of the Weimar Republic was certainly not solely a result of such individual, isolated factors. But it cannot be disputed that the socio-political basis of the Republic's authority and political vitality was destroyed as this social conflict escalated from 1924 and reached a temporary peak in the dispute in the Ruhr steel industry in 1928.[13] The NSDAP was the delighted heir to a political constellation where the KPD slandered social democrats as 'social fascists' while the parties of the right refused to draw distinctions between democratic socialists and Leninists. There were certainly many social democrats too who harboured grave misgivings about the Republic. This was the context of Gustav Radbruch's complaint that many in the SPD still viewed democracy merely as a 'ladder to socialism' while failing to grasp its vital importance to the development of the working class.[14] But the fate of the Republic was only finally sealed when the belief gained ground that the SPD could be permanently excluded from political power and the Free and Christian trade unions neutralized. Adam Stegerwald's attempt to revive the Central Working Association of employers and unions (ZAG) in 1931 in a context of escalating international economic crisis failed not only because of the stance adopted by the employers. They were not prepared to seriously consider Brüning's proposed linkage of wage decreases to price reductions, and preferred instead to see the situation as an opportunity to assert the autonomy of the economy from the state which they had long demanded. On the other side, the individual unions in the ADGB believed that there were simply no further concessions they could convince their members to accept and that they had to insist on wage decreases being made conditional on the prior imposition of wage reductions. These developments reflected the change in the balance of power between employers and trade unions which had occurred since the establishment of the Central Working Association in December 1918. When it was established, it had been in the interests of industry to seek to bolster its position by reaching agreement with moderate unions which had a vested interest in economic stability and in this way deflect the strong trends of the time towards greater state economic planning and contain the radicalization spreading among workers. This balance of forces shifted decisively in the employers' favour during the period of economic stabilization. While the ADGB vigorously opposed Chancellor Brüning at first, it rapidly became dependent on government as the international crisis deepened and the phenomenon of mass unemployment emerged.[15] The politics pursued by the trade unions after the 1918 Revolution must be judged in the light of these developments.

Following the revolutionary upheaval of November 1918, Carl Legien decided on behalf of the General Commission to adhere to the agreement which had established the Central Working Association. Even at the time there was an intense debate as to whether this decision contributed to the fatal political isolation of the Free Trade Unions in the period of acute social tension and widespread industrial unrest which followed.[16] The major concern of the ADGB leadership was to hold on to what had been achieved by the agreement; this included the recognition by heavy industry of both collective bargaining and the exclusive right of trade unions to negotiate on behalf of workers. The excessive hope which the ADGB placed in the industrial co-operation it sought in all sectors of the economy was well expressed in Hans von Raumer's description of the agreement as the 'Magna Carta of the trade unions'.[17] The ADGB leadership believed that the exclusive negotiating rights and the at least temporary suppression of 'yellow' unions (those committed to harmonious relations with the employers) which the agreement achieved were important successes in their own right. It also saw these as a means to eliminate the power of the workers' council movement. The Majority SPD for its part hoped that the energies of this movement could be diverted away from political questions into the sphere of economic participation.[18] One of the ADGB's chief motives in seeking the agreement with the employers was to extend trade union influence into the area of the economy as a whole, though this would necessarily entail the unions tying their hands with respect to the radical demands of their members, notably on the issue of socialization. This strategy is only understandable in terms of Carl Legien's conviction that it was pointless trying to advance by such means of direct confrontation as strikes and other extra-parliamentary actions; he believed in a strategy of militant co-operation, of loyally collaborating with the employers but on the basis of an increasingly powerful and united trade union apparatus. In this his thinking was representative of the overwhelming majority of German trade union leaders. Legien operated on the premise that the trade unions, in partnership with the MSPD but as an independent force, would be able to gradually change existing society in a socialist direction by occupying important positions in the economy. The willingness of the trade unions to co-operate constructively with the authorities during the war had substantially increased their influence, despite repeated setbacks and the stubborn intransigence of heavy industry. A similar tactical outlook also governed the ADGB leadership during the negotiations on the formation of the Central Working Association. In this case, however, the employers' strategy had the specific objective of excluding the state from any involvement in the economy. Legien's long-term strategy was to enforce the effective co-determination of the trade union movement in overall economic planning, prices policy and foreign trade questions.

But these ideas had not yet fully matured. Legien had addressed the issue of co-determination by the unions in the context of collective bargaining as early as 1902.[19] Participation in economic decision-making was a natural corollary of the path pursued by the unions in collective bargaining since the turn of the century, of gradually replacing industrial conflicts by organized agreements. Given the situation of sustained blockade, widespread hunger and civil unrest, the ADGB leadership in 1918 understandably overestimated the importance of planning and dirigist measures as opposed to the free play of economic forces. These were in fact to rapidly reassert themselves as soon as the conditions for capitalist reproduction had been fully restored. Even before the collapse of the Wilhelmine regime, large-scale industry was able to wrest considerable concessions on pricing policy from the government, which established its extremely favourable strategic position in the post-war economy.[20]

An important precondition for the success of the Legien strategy was that trade union strength would continue to grow, as indeed union leaders believed it would. The ADGB was at first successful in substantially expanding its membership compared to its pre-war level. But the general trend in union membership from the beginning of the 1920s was retrogressive. There was a certain time-lag before the political retreat signalled by the June 1920 elections took effect in this area. It was caused by a combination of factors, which included tactical mistakes by the ADGB in the socialization debate, the tendency towards stagnation in the numbers of industrial workers and the corresponding rise in the services sector as well as the crippling damage inflicted on the unions by the inflation. In addition, the trade unions reacted to the widespread radical strike movements of 1918–19 by trying to deflect the exaggerated demands being made for improved working conditions and higher wages. This led to them occasionally running the risk of appearing as agents of the employers. Given the situation they were in and the logic of the Legien strategy, they also found themselves at a loss when dealing with the government or acting in the newly created economic regulatory bodies supporting the demands of the employers' associations: they believed they had little alternative but to support the employers' demands for increased subventions, higher prices and lower taxation. The last was justified as compensation for the allegedly uneconomic 'political' concessions which the government had been obliged to make in the areas of wage norms and working conditions.[21] The trade union side thus had a certain hand in creating the fiction of the 'political wage'.

During the inflation the centre of political decision-making in the social area shifted to the Ministries of the Economy and Labour. The vision of self-regulation by employers and unions in industry, which had played such a major role in the formation of the ZAG, gave way to an increasingly tense atmosphere between the social parties. The events which immediately followed the Kapp Putsch showed clearly that the ADGB was neither determined enough nor in a position to force its will on the government. Legien's nine-point programme with its revival of the socialization issue and its ultimatum-like demands could not change the situation that had now emerged. This was shaped by the stiffening resolve of the employers' associations to hold their ground, by the stagnation in the government's programme of social reform and by the continually weakening position of the trade unions due to the raging inflation. In some sectors, particularly the mining industry, employers and unions proved unable to reach long-term compromise agreements through collective bargaining. In this situation the state arbitration machinery, which had originally been established to oversee the critical phase of demobilization, was perpetuated as a semi-permanent institution. This occurred just as the currency was successfully restabilized.

The forced retreat of the unions to a defensive position was in line with the general trend throughout the industrial countries of Europe at the time. In Germany this was accentuated by the inflationary crisis that financially weakened the unions, on top of which they suffered damage as a result of the effects of widespread rationalizations and the retrogressive trend in union membership. Partial socialization, in the coal industry for example, would not only have had little practical meaning but would have brought little amelioration. A policy of using the workers' council movement to make inroads into traditional social and administrative power structures would certainly have made psychological sense, but this would have run counter to the historical instincts of the unions. There was basically no alternative to the strategy pursued by the ADGB. One of the chief weaknesses of union tradition in Germany was its concentration on the area of social policy. This had been reinforced by its experiences in the wartime economy. 'The politics of trade unionism', Legien repeatedly declared, 'is social policy.'[22] The unions were interested in economic policy only in so far as it had immediate social consequences, however much they sought the right to participate in economic decision-making, for example through the ZAG. They were more interested in asserting control over the functioning of the economy than in tackling purely economic problems which by their nature related to the problems of particular sectors or firms. This corresponded to the distinction that was typically drawn between economic and social policy in the Weimar Republic. These were generally entrusted to ministers with divergent perspectives and priorities. Given the relative economic stagnation during the period under review here and the function of an economic policy in which the main factor was the reparations issue, social policy had a largely compensatory function. Its role was to ameliorate the socially damaging consequences of economic and financial policy decisions. Heinrich Brauns, who as a long-standing minister for labour played a major part in creating the social and welfare machinery of the Weimar Republic, was fully alive to this fact.[23]

The unions were inclined to regard wage bargaining as an autonomous sphere and to call for maintenance programmes by the state where declining profitability or restructuring crises produced social distress. A related factor was the increasing tendency of the unions to resort to compulsory arbitration even though it could only weaken their position in the long run. This development was facilitated by the interest of the employers' associations in seeing the responsibility for unpopular wage decisions being deflected from them to a public institution. Preller's argument that compulsory wage controls were an anomaly in politically organized social relations is probably incontestable;[24] but it is equally beyond doubt that relative social stability could be guaranteed only if the state intervened authoritatively in the wage bargaining process. The function of the state was largely a restraining one and to that extent the opposition voiced against it was unfounded.[25] A decisive factor in the essentially positive attitude adopted by the unions towards compulsory arbitration, despite their reservations, was their fear that industrial action would only give new impetus to communist and syndicalist agitators.

The relatively strong position of the communist Revolutionary Trade Union Opposition (RGO) and anarcho-syndicalist unions in specific industries was to some extent a direct result of the failure of the Free Trade Unions to fully integrate the works councils at the start.[26] This was partly a result of the neglect of shop-floor organization by the unions themselves, which contradicted somewhat the energetic support they had given to the establishment of workers' committees during World War I. These committees were the first institutionalized form of workers' participation at the shop-floor level. The reserve the unions showed the works councils which replaced them after the war was not solely in reaction to the intention of certain MSPD circles to politically neutralize the councils by transferring certain trade union tasks to them. There was also the fear that if workers' shop-floor representatives were given too far-reaching a role, this would undermine the exclusive negotiating rights which the official unions had won after a long struggle to represent workers' interests in wage negotiations with employers. The unions were accustomed to centralized decision-making and believed that effective advance in the area of social control was possible only through socialization measures at the macroeconomic level. This thinking was decisive in influencing the belief of trade union officials that works councils should be restricted to the regulation of purely social matters.[27] Given the vacillating attitude of the unions, the resolute opposition of the employers ensured that the final draft of the Works Council Law effectively excluded workers' immediate representatives from participating in economic decision-making at the factory or company level. The idea of shop-floor participation could not make any progress in these circumstances and it was to survive only in mutilated form in the bitterly contested Works Council Law of 1920.[28]

The Programme for Economic Democracy, which was drafted by Fritz Naphtali at the direction of the ADGB and presented in 1928, not surprisingly recommended that the role of works councils 'both in the social and economic sphere should be only a subordinate one' and that their role in supervising or implementing measures at the level above that of the immediate factory floor should be restricted.[29] That interest in workers' participation at the shop-floor level remained relatively slight was certainly in part a result of the ambivalence of the works councils' function as outlined in the Works Council Law; as well as a statutory right to represent workers' rights, this included a provision obliging councils to equally uphold management's rights with respect to the workforce. Employers also took every step imaginable to limit the jurisdiction of the works councils as guaranteed by the law. In the case of workers' rights to representation on company boards, they attempted to circumvent clear statutory provisions by creating special intermediate boards of management.[30] No thorough examination has yet been undertaken of the role played by workers' company board representatives or by the few directors for labour affairs appointed during this period.

The deeper reason for the relatively low value placed on shop-floor participation was the centralist mentality which traditionally distinguished German trade unionism from its west European counterparts. This was clearly reflected in Naphtali's statements on the question of works councils: 'As long as a system of economic management above factory level and influenced by the unions does not exist, economic participation by works councils can only be a purely private enterprise and cannot be considered part of the working-class struggle to establish a system of managing the economy which is independent of individual factories.' Shop-floor democracy was deliberately ignored and received only scant mention in Naphtali's treatise: economic democracy would only come about 'when a public institution is established above the level of the factory which treats individual factories as social formations subservient to it'.[31] Statements like this reveal both the social inferiority felt towards entrepreneurial management at the factory level and the indifference with which economic decisions at this level were regarded. The same appears to apply to attitudes to worker participation at the level of the firm, though the ADGB did demand that committees of works councils' conveners be formed at company level.[32] The reason for this reluctance to become involved in these areas also lies in the structure of the class conflict of the time. Employers were particularly insistent that social policy be regulated at plant level and, especially after the demise of the ZAG, vigorously promoted the idea of the self-contained 'factory community'.[33] Continual attempts were made by the employers to shift the focus of wage bargaining to the factory or firm level, where it was generally easier for them to assert their position than by dealing with the workers' representative union centres. But the indifference of the unions to shop-floor participation had another serious failing which was rarely recognized then. By neglecting this area, communications between the trade unions' official structures and their members were weakened. What could have been a great opportunity to expand trade union rights in the area of economic co-determination was thus not exploited.

The concept of 'economic democracy' was the most modern trade union programme in existence in Europe at the time.[34] It was an offensive programme for the future developed from the lessons learned since 1918. It was well suited to rally a membership which to some extent had become disillusioned and was numerically in decline. It was also a determined attempt by the unions to get beyond the defensive position they had been in since the beginning of the period of economic stabilization. Rudolf Kuda has distinguished two stages in the development of the programme, a defensive one and a more offensive one.[35] The latter was clearly in evidence at the Hamburg trade union congress of September 1928. This in part reflected the extreme optimism which briefly prevailed after the collapse of the bourgeois bloc and the formation of the social democratic coalition government led by Hermann Müller.

Naphtali's plan set out in stages a process of democratization within an overall perspective of an advance to socialism. Prominent among these was the establishment of economic control bodies with equal representation for employers and unions along the lines of the regional economic institutions already operating in the mining industry. Economic democracy thus became a means towards socialization and in the process the term 'socialization' came to embrace a wide range of possible measures. Even if there had been a willingness among employers to co-operate in such a programme, it could not, quite apart from its ultimately maximalist character, have advanced the cause of economic co-determination. Michael Schneider has described the Programme for Economic Democracy in this respect as ultimately an alternative model economic system rather than a reconciliatory one.[36] It offered very little scope for practical co-operation between employers and unions. This interpretation, with its strong anti-capitalist perspective, is argued with a current political purpose in mind which has little relevance to the conditions of the late 1920s. The programme in fact contained little in the way of a concrete strategy by which it might have been realized. The discussion in it of the idea that, once the structure of economic democracy was in place, private ownership of the means of production could be abolished and the new structures made to serve as the framework of an overall socialist system shows the speculative nature of the entire concept, which in the last resort was the work of intellectuals rather than pragmatists. The programme had virtually nothing to say on economic policy in the narrower sense. In this area it limited itself to demanding for the unions extensive participatory rights, which tended towards a monopoly, and emphasizing that the needs of society in general had to take precedence over the utilitarian interests of capitalism. Its separation of the needs of private enterprises from the area of overall economic policy, which was very much in the German idealist tradition, comes across as arbitrary and as confusing content with form.

The transformation of society which it advocated was conceived overwhelmingly as a product of intervention by the state. The concept of autonomous self-regulatory structures first put forward by Moellendorf and Wissell in 1919 reappears in the proposal that the state should have the power to grant rights of sovereignty to economically autonomous bodies. The notion that the unions could first achieve certain objectives in specific sectors and then expand them to the state as a whole with the help of legislation was totally absent. The transformation of society envisaged was conceived largely by thinking backwards from the point of view of the end result it sought. Its reliance on the state apparatus as the means by which the process of transformation would be carried out was a fundamental weakness in the overall concept. In this sense at least, the concept behind the programme was not very Marxist. There is also an interesting tendency in the programme to assume that permanent social change could be achieved by the state simply incorporating trade union aims on to the statute book.

Critics of the concept of economic democracy are therefore not totally wrong when they point to the similarity of the thinking behind it to the politics pursued by the ADGB during the period of General von Schleicher's chancellorship and in the early days of national socialist rule.[37] During the negotiations held in late 1932 with representatives of other organizations, including the NSDAP, Leipart toyed with the idea of eventually severing all connections between the unions and the SPD. This idea was taken up again following the national socialist seizure of power.[38] The notion that it would be possible to exert influence directly on the government, circumventing the political parties, underlay this thinking. The Programme for Economic Democracy implicitly contained the basis for such thinking. Naphtali's pamphlet significantly made no mention of how the individual objectives of the programme were to be realized politically or how the projected economic structure was supposed to relate to the political system. The somewhat apolitical nature of the individual components of the concept of economic democracy was also evident in the idea of democracy which emerges from it.[39]

As the economic crisis took effect, drastically curtailing the possibilities for effective trade union activity and making strike action virtually impossible, the need to develop a constructive approach to economic policy was recognized by certain leading figures in the ADGB. This represented the first step towards overcoming the traditional separation of social and economic policy. It is what gives such historic importance to the WTB Plan which Wladimir Woytinsky, Fritz Baade and Fritz Tarnow presented to the ADGB executive on 23 December 1931 and which was adopted as official policy by the Free Trade Unions in April 1932.[40] The SPD executive and even Naphtali and Hilferding had argued vociferously but in vain against this proposed job creation programme. They believed it would only serve to fuel the inflationary process. The criticism of the WTB Plan by certain SPD circles essentially accepted liberal economists' diagnosis of the economic crisis as a 'rationalization' process, even if from different premises. Such a perspective made an interventionist strategy to solve it appear pointless. The historic importance of the WTB Plan lay precisely in its discarding of fatalistic attitudes to economic crisis, and in this respect the ADGB was in the vanguard of the international trade union movement.[41]

There was no direct connection between the WTB Plan and the Programme for Economic Democracy. Baade had been involved in developing the programme and Tarnow had taken part in the discussions preceding it. On the question of job creation, Fritz Naphtali totally opposed the approach proposed in the WTB Plan. Apart from his rigid insistence that there was no alternative to deflation to tackle the crisis, he was almost certainly also influenced by a concern that the WTB Plan would lead trade union politics into a novel and risky course that would render obsolete the whole concept of 'economic democracy' which he and his fellow authors had developed in the programme published in 1928. Naphtali's programme, for all its detailed proposals, dealt with questions of economic control only in the broadest sense. It covered all conceivable areas of social policy and included a thorough treatment of education policy – one of its most useful elements – but it lacked an economic perspective in the narrower sense. To exaggerate slightly, it was essentially a programme to 'administer' the economy rather than to shape it. The 'economy' to be democratized and socialized comes across as a static autonomous object. There were no proposals for stimulating economic growth, increasing investment activity or expanding production and the problem of the complete absence on the trade union side of any personnel with the economic training necessary to take on management tasks was totally ignored.

Compared with the Programme for Economic Democracy, the WTB

Plan represented a fundamentally new departure. By proposing that the unions seek to actively influence state policy on economic growth, it broke through the fatal division which had traditionally separated social and economic policy. With its concept of an active role in economic policy for the unions, the principle of co-determination, or workers' participation, in the process of regulating production took on a different meaning from the one it had in Naphtali's programme. There the concept of economic 'self-administration' had been given characteristic priority; this was also the case with its perspective on co-determination at the factory level, the sectoral level and at the level of the overall economy. Naphtali wanted to see these functions restricted to the official trade union organizations, which to him were the product of the working class's arduous struggle for emancipation. To him the works councils, as statutorily instituted bodies, were inherently unsuited to such tasks. But how could one seriously claim to be pursuing an active economic policy or even to be influencing economic decisions if one continued to hold that the central focus of workers' co-determination at plant level should be primarily on social and personnel issues and not questions of economics or production?

The idea of workers' co-determination made only limited and fragmentary progress under Weimar conditions and failed to have any substantial influence on the climate and substance of social relations at the time. This can only be understood against the background of the escalating social conflict, which was relentlessly provoked by influential groups, particularly in large-scale industry, in the vain belief that they could force a return to pre-war conditions. The whole system of free collective bargaining was destroyed due to their intransigence and their misreading of the economic situation generally. Following the dissolution of the ZAG, the unions believed that there was now no other way forward in the area of institutionalized co-determination than through legislation. Also, the Ministry of Labour had been intervening on a statutory basis in organized industrial relations with ever greater frequency since its involvement in the demobilization of the army. In fact, even the system of tiered structures of economic self-regulation originally planned was essentially undermined from the start by the economic and financial policies pursued by the state. Given these circumstances, the question of workers' participation at plant level was understandably of only secondary importance to the unions. Many even regarded it as a disruptive issue in the context of the participatory role they sought in the overall economy. This corresponded with their excessive reliance on the role they believed the state bureaucracy could play, which was also evident in Fritz Naphtali's work.

Forms of co-determination which went beyond securing social rights at the workplace and were directed at achieving equal participation for workers in the production process were largely conceived by the Free Trade Unions and the SPD from the perspective of establishing socialist control over a still capitalist economy. Treating co-determination at factory and above factory level as an element in a strategy for changing the overall structures of society tended to ignore the emancipatory aspect of workers' participation and its potential for mass involvement. It was this aspect which the left liberal Friedrich Naumann had in mind when at the turn of the century he called for 'some form of participation by public officials and workers in the management' of modern large-scale enterprises. His concept of 'industrial parliamentarism', however much it overestimated the extent to which social conflict could be harmonized, was not conceived primarily from the point of view of satisfying workers' material needs but arose rather from his view that a new form of 'servility of the masses' could only be averted if social relations at the workplace were democratized. For him the central issue was one of human rights: 'Can human rights be upheld in the industrial era? This is the central problem in regulating social relations in industry.'[42]

Under Weimar conditions, the Free Trade Unions in particular were motivated in their thinking chiefly by the belief that the challenge presented by the increasingly consolidated forces of the employers could only be controlled within a structured and disciplinary apparatus. This took the form of autonomous administrative bodies to regulate the economy, which were organized as effectively and hence as bureaucratically as possible and regarded by the unions as embryo institutions of a future socialist state. This type of thinking was without a doubt the product of Marxist theories of class relations and of the labour movement's experience as an excluded oppositional force in the Wilhelmine system. But it obscured the autonomous aspect central to any functional idea of workers' co-determination. This went way beyond the aims of merely controlling economic power and securing workers' material interests. It was in fact the basis for a truly creative and active system of workers' participation in the modern industrial system.

Workers' participation, which must lead ultimately to parity in representation, is not a magic formula for solving social conflict. Nor does it in any way mean that collective bargaining, an active trade union wages policy or the strike weapon can be dispensed with. Experiences with parity co-determination in the coal and steel industries, which has its origins in developments during the Weimar Republic, must be judged in their historical context. The lowest point was reached with the open attack by heavy industry on the social institutions which formed the foundations of the Weimar Republic. It may honestly be stated that if the social system of the Federal Republic, which in many ways is a direct inheritance from Weimar, is to remain functional in the long term, effective economic co-determination by workers is as essential to it as the institution of free collective bargaining and the principle of the socially institutionalized state. In this context, it should be remembered that the pioneer of a socially progressive liberalism in Germany, Friedrich Naumann, was among the first to present the issue of workers' participation, in large-scale enterprises particularly, as a basic human challenge of the future; furthermore, he was also prominently involved in ensuring that the constitution of the Weimar Republic, with its assertion of the 'duties of property', introduced into the democratic constitutional tradition of Germany the principle of property's obligations within a socially institutionalized state. This framework is an essential precondition for a successful system of economic co-determination.[43]

State and Bureaucracy in the Brüning Era

The role played by bureaucratic structures in the political decision-making process and their function in ensuring continuity during periods of change in the political system are regular themes of historical research. This is particularly the case with studies on the part played by the Prussian state bureaucracy in the formation of the German constitution in the nineteenth and twentieth centuries. The central role of the bureaucracy in the development of the Prussian state did not start with the Reform era of the early nineteenth century. The entire early constitutional history of Germany is simply incomprehensible without reference to the part played in it by enlightened state officials.[1] Rheinhard Koselleck has shown conclusively how right up to the 1848 period it was the Prussian civil administration, strongly influenced by the great representative figures of the Reform period, which forced the pace of bourgeois social emancipation. The Prussian bourgeoisie was still too dominated by guild notions of social status to be the driving force in this process. The reforms introduced by Stein and Hardenberg were implemented incompletely or in a reactionary form and failed finally with the onset of the Restoration. But the memory of the bureaucracy's function as a 'political class' and as a type of substitute legislature remained at the centre of the political outlook of broad sections of the German bourgeois class.[2]

Despite the increasing dominance of conservative restorationist thinking in the Prussian civil service from the period of Friedrich Wilhelm IV, and notably in the Bismark era, large sections of the population continued to hold public officials in uncritically high esteem. The growth in the power of the senior civil service in Germany did not provoke the emergence of any movements hostile to bureaucratic power. Max Weber's sharp attacks on the bureaucratic stagnation of the Wilhelmine political system were long to remain an isolated occurrence.[3] The repressive policies pursued by the state during the *Kulturkampf* and the Socialist Laws certainly had some effect on this mentality. Distrust of state officials was to persist particularly in the SPD and the Centre Party. The SPD campaigned for the reform and democratization of the civil service, which it saw as a conservative weapon of state. But while it continued to formally adhere to the demand in its programme that public officials be elected – a legacy of 1848 radicalism – in practice this hostility to the administrative structures of the state gradually lessened. The emerging governmental bureaucracy of the Reich even had a certain common interest with the political and trade union wings of the labour movement. Wilhelmine social policy and institutions were shaped to a large degree by the civil service, and the social democrats found themselves increasingly having to defend these against reactionary attempts by heavy industry and landed interests to dismantle them.[4] The SPD tended to lay the blame for the political defects of the *Kaiserreich* on its ruling circles rather than on the civil service.

The Reich and Prussian bureaucracies played a crucial role in establishing the war-economy system during World War I. This system was later severely curtailed by the Army Supreme Command (OHL) and was distrusted by heavy industry. The major new departure was in the area of social policy. Initiatives by the administrative leaders of the system established to manage the war economy led to the political integration of the Free Trade Unions. State socialist schemes such as those developed by Wichard von Moellendorff and Walter Rathenau were almost entirely the products of ideas which had been developed within the bureaucracy. In the late autumn of 1918 heavy industry moved towards a co-operative arrangement with the unions which resulted in the foundation of the Central Working Association (ZAG). It was motivated in changing its line at least partly by the hope of averting a state-capitalist alliance of the bureaucracy and the unions, of which it had such an exaggerated fear at the time.[5]

Despite its increasing atrophy and the extent to which it was implicated in the discredited regime, the traditional civil service survived the collapse of the Wilhelmine system without any serious loss of prestige. That the self-confidence of the administration survived the Revolution of November 1918 unbroken has been well established.[6] The First World War had reinforced the belief that in critical situations the bureaucracy was the one stabilizing force which could guarantee the continuity of the state. Bourgeois state secretaries continued to occupy powerful positions under the Government of People's Deputies and the Majority SPD promptly recognized the status of the professional civil service, not least in the extensive rights guaranteed it in the Weimar constitution. These developments, along with the refusal of the new government to interfere in any substantial way with the existing structures and composition of the bureaucracy, were symptomatic of the high esteem in which the civil service was held and of the widespread view of it as an indispensable instrument of politics. Even the workers' councils, with few exceptions, stopped short of interfering with the civil service. While they attempted to assert some control over it, the idea of actually taking over its tasks was rarely considered. This enabled the bureaucracy, mostly by manipulating financial mechanisms, to contain and finally to eliminate the influence of the workers' and soldiers' councils in their field.[7]

The self-confidence of public officials and the political influence they exercised was also evident in the unusually rapid emergence of civil servants' professional associations in this period. After the November Revolution of 1918 and still influenced by the wartime propaganda slogans of the common national interest of all classes, these were able at first to unite the divergent political and class interests of their members in a common front.[8] The power wielded by the civil servants' associations made itself felt even before the National Assembly met. Friedrich Ebert's attempt to reconcile the civil service with the republican system by conceding far-reaching institutional guarantees to civil servants had a decisive influence on the Weimar parliamentary system from the start. This was not a result solely of the overcautious approach of the Weimar Coalition to republicanizing the public administration. In no area was a clean break made with the traditional idea that the civil service fulfilled a role of state which was above political parties. In this view the concept of 'interests of state' was seen as the antithesis of 'party political interests'.

The view of the civil service as representing the interests of the state was shared by all political forces outside the extreme left. This was not diminished by the fact that both social and liberal democrats could hardly have failed to realize that this ideal was contradicted by the reality of a higher civil service which had remained substantially anti-republican and monarchist. On this basis, the parties of the centre and the right could operate self-confidently in the knowledge that they had substantial political support within the governmental bureaucracies of both Reich and the Länder.[9] The civil service was tacitly accepted as a politically neutral force. This was given mute expression in the failure of the parties of the Weimar Coalition to resolutely oppose demands for the formation of cabinets composed of state officials or to attack the principle of including allegedly 'non-political' experts in cabinets, even though such practices considerably reduced the power of political parties in the governmental system. After the formation of the Cuno cabinet, the appointment to cabinet positions of 'experts' who either did not belong to a political party or held only a minor position in one ceased to be a matter of serious contention.

The mentality which this expressed ultimately contributed to the progressive undermining of the parliamentary system. The failure to republicanize the public service, which historians have seen as critical,[10] is only fully comprehensible in this context. The implicit retreat to Prussian bureaucratic state traditions formed a framework in which more or less explicitly anti-republican politics were given a political base and legitimacy. Certain sovereign rights were withdrawn from the Reichstag, such as the prerogative tacitly granted President von Hindenburg to nominate a person in his personal confidence as army minister. This was a product of the myth that the continuity of state had to be safeguarded against the change-able aims of parliament and parties by being vested in the bureaucratic apparatus of the state. There was a growing trend to retain state secretaries from one coalition to the next and even, as explicitly demanded by Arnold Köttgen, to accept that the continuity of government affairs would be best assured by instituting permanent state secretaries.[11] This finally reached the stage where ministerial positions were widely regarded as administrative appointments transcending party politics. This was given dramatic expression when the members of von Papen's cabinet publicly resigned their party memberships on their appointment as ministers.[12]

The presidential cabinets of the early 1930s were accompanied by con-certed attempts to replace the parliamentary system with a system of constitutional rule by the administration. Ideas in this direction had been maturing over a long period. They were the products of the traditional view of the bureaucracy as representative of the common interest which accompanied the widespread criticism of political parties for their alleged inability to handle 'questions of state'. This tendency was expressed ideo-logically in the campaign mounted by the political right and conservative legal theorists for the maintenance of a professional civil service and against the republicanization of the public administration. Calls to protect the status of professional civil servants were motivated by more than merely a concern to defend the privileges and salary and career structures enjoyed by public officials. They aimed ultimately to free the state bureaucracy from control by parliament and political parties. This objective pervaded the writings of Arnold Köttgen, the constitutional lawyer. In this he was representative of a broad school of contemporary thinking, one of the most gifted and influential spokesmen of which was Carl Schmitt.[13]

Demands that the civil service be divested of its party political features[14] and reconstructed as an elite political 'corps' concerned solely with duties of national sovereignty stood in odd contrast to the actual role increasingly played by the civil servants' associations and the governmental bureaucracies of the Reich and the Länder. The power of the state bureaucracy grew as cabinets rapidly succeeded one another, compounding the progressive ero-sion of the parliamentary decision-making process. The result of this was that the governmental bureaucracy gained a decisive influence in political affairs, which was particularly marked after the parliamentary function of striking compromises began to shift from the Reichstag to ministerial offices. Direct interaction between the governmental bureaucracy and vested interest groups developed as the Reichstag was excluded from the political process. One of the greatest levers with which the governmental bureaucracy could assert its power was financial policy, which, with the growing budgetary problem from 1929, came to dominate virtually all areas of policy.[15]

The politically motivated attempts to establish the administration as an autonomous force made considerable progress during Brüning's period in government. In his important work, *Württemberg und die deutsche Staatskrise*, still indispensable to any assessment of Brüning, Waldemar Besson singled out the growth of bureaucratic power at all levels of government as the decisive development of this era. Besson has provided us with the most vivid and impressive description of the bureaucratic solidarity which developed between the civil services of the Reich and the Länder as a result of the Reich cabinet's policy of cut-backs and Brüning's repeated appeals for 'pragmatism' and 'political responsibility'. Besson characterized Brüning's manner of government as effecting a progressive 'bureaucratization of politics'.[16] This showed itself in two ways. On the one hand the relationship between the governmental bureaucracy and the Reich and Länder parliaments shifted clearly in the former's favour. Brüning actively encouraged this transfer of political decision-making power to groups of senior civil servants in a number of ways. He relied increasingly on the Reichsrat as opposed to the Reichstag for political support for his government's measures and later reinforced this tendency by introducing blatantly unconstitutional bodies such as the Economic Advisory Council (Wirtschaftsbeirat). His dependency on the Reichsrat increased the power of the bureaucracies of the Länder. The authority granted to Länder governments and municipal executives by the Dietramzell Emergency Decree to implement cut-backs in expenditure without having to secure the consent of Länder or municipal parliaments as required by the constitution gave the bureaucracies at these levels a virtual free hand in relation to party political groups.[17]

The government's deflationary policy was closely linked with the whole process of accumulating emergency decrees and had a similar effect. The fact that rule by emergency decree proved to be a means of circumventing the Reichstag played an important part in this. Brüning's break with the Reichstag in the summer of 1930 did not occur abruptly. The Reichstag continued to play a legislative role even after the September 1930 elections, though this was largely restricted to legislation of a secondary nature. Apart from the temporary obstructionism of the NSDAP and DNVP, the Reichstag was generally quite willing to adapt to the limited role the government wished it to play and to come to terms with a system of semi-parliamentarianism in which all matters of political consequence would be dealt with by presidential emergency decrees.[18] The transition to a presidential system represented by the formation of the Brüning cabinet was not recognized at first for the decisive watershed in domestic politics which it was. Even the protagonists of a presidential system were initially unsure as to how far they could go in using Article 48 without being accused of breaching the constitution. It was to take a certain period of time before they grasped the opportunities for political power which the system presented.[19]

The steady gathering of bureaucratic momentum was reflected in the rising numbers and scope of the decrees promulgated. This development was a direct consequence of the belief that legislation by the Reichstag had to be pre-empted by decisive action, since initiatives from the Reichstag would inevitably involve compromise solutions which were objectively and financially untenable, as Brüning repeatedly stressed.[20] Rule by emergency decree was increasingly resorted to until it virtually became the norm. The bureaucratic momentum which this produced resulted in legislative *faits accomplis* free of the diluting influences of interest group pressure and party political compromise. The bureaucratic element in Brüning's politics lay precisely in the manner in which the government consciously isolated itself from the pressures of divergent social and political interests and ignored the need for political backing for its measures. This, however, made it more and more dependent on the president's office, which gradually acquired a virtual right of veto over the legislative initiatives of the government.[21] Waldemar Besson showed that this narrowing of the cabinet's political base represented a 'depoliticization' of governmental work and that this was the basis for the emergence of the governmental bureaucracy of the Reich and the Länder as the substantial power at the centre of the system. But the growing politicization of the the bureaucracy in its turn ultimately had to negate the policies pursued by Brüning. The political system based on an alliance between the chancellor and the higher civil service at central government and Länder level was undermined by the fact that the 'bureau-cratization of politics' was negated by the 'politicization of the bureaucracy' – as Besson put it poignantly.[22]

Whether a 'bureaucratization of politics' was an actual aim of the strategy pursued by Brüning needs closer examination. There can be no doubt that to achieve his ends Brüning exploited the sense of common purpose widespread among civil servants. This extolled 'objectivity' as a virtue and believed that it was the duty of the civil service to bolster the central state and its authority against the rising forces of radicalism. But, if personalities such as Otto Braun or Eugen Bolz were prepared to serve the chancellor's policies to the point of virtually abdicating from political responsibility themselves, they did so from motives which were emphatically different from those of the chancellor. They were totally unaware of what Brüning's ultimate aims were. It is sometimes claimed that Brüning was inclined retrospectively to represent measures which were essentially forced on him by the exigencies of the financial crisis as integral elements of his medium- and long-term political strategy. Since the appearance of his memoirs, however, it can no longer be disputed that he was intent from the start on implementing drastic financial cuts to serve both the reparations strategy and the reform of the Reich's structure towards a unitary state which he regarded as politically necessary. The apparently simply bureaucratic policy of rule by emergency decree thus concealed a highly ambitious programme of reform which, despite some bureaucratic elements, was shaped primarily by fundamentally political priorities. These were based on some erroneous political judgements and it was these which sometimes gave rise to the impression that the chancellor's outlook was essentially apolitical.[23]

A study of the relationship between the state and the bureaucracy during the Brüning era therefore cannot be restricted to tracing the bureaucratic elements in the policies he pursued. In developing Besson's analysis further, it is essential firstly to examine Brüning's relationship with civil servants and the state bureaucracy in general and secondly to clarify what effects the policies he pursued had on the civil servants themselves. This context raises the question of what general political consequences the measures implemented by the Brüning cabinet had on the areas of civil service pay, personnel policy in the public sector, administrative reform and the legal status of public officials. Brüning's civil service policy, though it was only substantially implemented following the government's adoption of a broad programme of rigorous deflation, formed an integral part of both his long-term socio-political goals and the constitutional reforms he hoped to implement in the shorter term.

An important question which must be asked first, however, is to what extent the chancellor was acting under outside political pressures in the manner in which he ruthlessly cut civil servants' pay and extensively rationalized the administrative apparatus. These pressures arose partly from the political composition of parliament which confronted him on assuming office and partly from the influence exercised by industry and unions alike. They were necessarily further aggravated by the financial and economic policies which his government then pursued. Brüning ascribes a sense of political purpose to himself in his memoirs, not only in the reparations and disarmament fields but also with regard to his plans for domestic political reform; this is not evident to anything like the same extent from the records of cabinet meetings, which reveal him more often as vacillating and indecisive. These plans allegedly included a return to a constitutional monarchy, a reduction in the federalist powers of the Länder and a curbing of the influence of parliamentary bodies. It is very plausible to argue that Brüning, as befitted his innately dogmatic and unwavering nature, tended to use political measures which the financial crisis forced upon him to advance his own political aims, that this was why he increasingly isolated himself from the competing political forces with which he was confronted and that this process ultimately made his fall inevitable.

Brüning regularly displayed a public image of dogmatic and unwavering adherence to principle and of holding rigidly to positions once they were adopted. This fits in well with an interpretation of his approach to government as essentially a bureaucratic one. But a bureaucratic style of leadership cannot be imputed to Brüning, as that would contradict the extremely personalized understanding of political processes which characterized him as well as his obsessive overestimation of the importance of intrigue. Despite his pronounced Prussianism and Spartan lifestyle, Brüning was anything but the bureaucratic type. He had begun his career as a trade union official and his short spell in the Prussian Ministry of Social Welfare was certainly sufficient to make him an admirer of the Prussian administrative tradition. But he acquired only a superficial knowledge of the administration, the problems of personnel management policy which large civil service structures involved and the relationship of secondary administrative bodies to central authorities. The bureaucratic ways of modern administrative structures remained basically foreign to him. Brüning was a finance politician, and the specific problems associated with civil service pay, which as part of the government's general wage reduction policy continually occupied the cabinet, were remote to him. He always avoided taking clear stances on individual problems, tending instead to leave these to the ministers for labour and finance and the governmental civil servants directly concerned.

A more substantial influence in shaping his political world view than his quite superficial involvement with the administrative structures of the state was his military experiences in the First World War. Like many bourgeois conservative politicians, he idealized the Prussian administrative tradition and viewed it from a conservative Prussian reformist perspective. He often praised the objectivity and practical experience of civil servants and contrasted these with what he saw as the largely tactically motivated behaviour of political parties. He was also inclined to give greater weight to the judgements of higher civil servants than to those of politicians with long years of experience; in a strange reversal of the usual attitude towards bureaucrats, he often accused the latter of a lack of decisiveness compared with civil servants and a dangerous tendency to compromise.[24] But statements by him to this effect, which obviously arose from his excessive reverence for Prussian tradition, were not thought out and corresponded with the general syndrome of ascribing to the civil service the function 'of state' described at the start of this article. They should not be read as implying any particular regard on Brüning's part for civil servants themselves. Given his backward-looking social philosophy, which rejected the social consequences of industrialization as much as the phenomenon of the bureaucratized state, it is hardly surprising that Brüning was totally unable to grasp the full complexity of modern administration.

It was characteristic of Brüning that he should display an intense reserve towards what he saw as the 'tidal wave' of bureaucracy which had arisen during the Weimar Republic, particularly at the municipal level. He regarded the very extensive cuts in staffing levels which had been carried out in Prussia on the basis of the Staff Reductions Decree as completely inadequate. It appears that in civil service questions Brüning was strongly influenced by Adam Stegerwald, whose prejudices against civil servants, despite all his denials, were clearly evident from his contributions during the debates on civil service pay reform.[25] Brüning, like Stegerwald, considered the 1927 Salary Reform Act as fundamentally flawed, though he does not appear to have taken a public stance on it at the time it was enacted. As chancellor he worked resolutely within cabinet for its repeal.[26] In his memoirs he boasted how he had forced cabinet to accept a regulation in the area of civil service salary legislation whereby in future every third position falling vacant due to resignation or retirement should not be refilled.[27] His principal aim in this area was to rigorously reduce the size of the civil service, which he regarded as far too large in comparison, for example, with that of France. In this he was at one with Parker Gilbert, the Allied reparations agent, who was fond of refuting Germany's alleged inability to pay by referring to what he regarded as the inadmissibly high sums spent on public administration in Germany.

Brüning judged problems of public administration primarily from the perspective of the higher civil service. To him it was self-evident that civil servants should put their personal interests completely aside where those of the state were involved. He could accept that this would necessitate the public purse assuming certain social welfare responsibilities towards public officials, but saw these in terms of a Frederickan state paternalist perspective which had little relevance in the modern world. As chancellor he showed little sympathy for the wretched position of lower- and even medium-ranking civil servants. He also had an extremely negative opinion of the civil servants' associations, despite the fact that the Centre Party had important ties with them. He basically regarded their activities as incompatible with the special duties of civil servants. For him, the principle of representation of social interest did not apply to civil servants.[28] It was characteristic of his attitude that during the negotiations to save the insolvent Civil Service Bank he could declare that the entire civil servants' support system would have to be abolished.[29]

The psychological prerequisites for a durable co-operative relationship between Brüning and the representatives of the civil servants' associations were absent therefore from the start of his chancellorship, in spite of the fact that the associations were originally very loyally disposed to him and largely agreed with his programme for government and his plans to curtail parliamentary influences. At his increasingly infrequent meetings with the civil servants' leaders, he came across as unmotivated and made little impression. He had no interest in the details of his salary reduction measures. His response to the associations' repeated pleas to defend civil servants against what they regarded as the unsubstantiated polemics of trade unions and employers' organizations was at best half-hearted. Given the marked hostility to civil servants among large sections of public opinion, Brüning believed that he could afford to ignore the political pressure brought to bear by the civil servants' associations, though he must have been aware of the extraordinary extent of their parliamentary connections.[30] He attempted to keep the differences which emerged between the government and the civil servants' associations from the public. It was typical of him in this regard that he refused permission to the ADB (General Federation of German Civil Servants) to publish what was an objectively accurate and quite unhostile communiqué following a particular meeting with the combined associations.[31]

When the co-operative attitude of the civil servants' associations turned to open criticism of the government, Brüning reacted with extreme irritation and felt that he had been personally betrayed. The civil servants' magazines finally accused Brüning of being an enemy of the professional civil servant, which was not objectively accurate. But it is true that statements from him clearly supporting the civil servants' case had been noticeably lacking. Brüning probably never even considered what cumulative effects his salary reductions and cut-backs in administrative expenditure had in changing the legal status quo of civil servants. He brushed aside the complaints of the civil servants' associations about the drastic nature of the salary reductions by arguing that prompt payment of salaries could not be guaranteed otherwise. This unquestionably oversimplified the problems at hand.[32] Fundamentally Brüning was not prepared to recognize the leaders of the major civil servants' association as representative of the mass of public servants. He repeatedly appealed for sacrifices from each individual and appears to have indulged the illusion for some time that the great majority of civil servants were willing to put requirements of state above all else. That in so doing he undermined the position of the generally moderate civil servants' leaders within their associations by adding to the memberships' growing disillusionment and embitterment appears hardly to have occurred to him.

The increasingly tense relationship between the Brüning cabinet and the civil servants did not result solely from the accumulated savings measures proposed by the government, but was also partly a product of the manner in which these were implemented. Brüning was regularly accused of being untrustworthy. This arose from his tactic of denying to the last minute that any further salary cuts were in the offing so as to keep the associations at bay. Frequent breaches of faith by the government destroyed the trust of the civil servants' representatives. After repeatedly meeting with a deaf ear in the Chancellery, they began to turn directly to the president's office and there add to the complaints gradually mounting against the chancellor.[33]

Despite the differences between them on detail, the main civil servants' associations, including, with some reservations, even the ADB, had been prepared initially to loyally support the chancellor's policies and accept the unavoidable consequences for them of the government's deflation policy. But Brüning failed to use the considerable level of support which his government had enjoyed among substantial sections of the civil service to broaden his political base. When finally even the civil servants joined the united front of organizations opposed to the continuation of the Brüning administration and the original hostility which had existed between civil servants' associations and trade unions began to give way to a growing recognition that they shared a common interest, this – along with the growing political radicalization of civil servants – represented a catastrophic failure for Brüning's domestic policies.

However much the chancellor was later to complain of the chronic deterioration of relations between the government and its civil servants,[34] it was at least in part a direct result of the distrust which Brüning's devious style of governing produced almost automatically. This was evident not only in his manner of dealing with representatives of parties and interest groups, but also in his relationship with the inner circle which prepared decisions for cabinet. Brüning never felt bound by the authority of experts in any particular field. He preferred to place his reliance instead on a relatively small circle of governmental officials with whom he got on well and who were unhesitatingly loyal to him. He was wont to discuss political measures directly with the government official concerned without consulting even the competent cabinet minister. State Secretary Hans Schäffer reported how Hermann Dietrich, the minister for finance to whom he was directly responsible, once vigorously reprimanded him for not telling him anything of the plans for an Austro-German Customs Union with which he had been entrusted. Schäffer replied that Brüning had instructed him not to report anything of the matter to the minister for finance.[35] Brüning concealed his strategic political aims even from his closest associates. A common complaint in his entourage was that no one knew what the aims of the 'boss' actually were.[36] In addition, Brüning often drew on outsiders for advice. In his memoirs he stated that when drafting the emergency decrees he had often consulted Privy Councillor Kugeler, whom he knew from his period in the Prussian Ministry of Social Welfare.[37]

Brüning's style of government was thus certainly not intrinsically bureaucratic. But his tendency to regard all important questions as exclusively his prerogative and to reach definitive decisions on them within the confines of his small immediate circle effectively increased the power of the higher civil service. In this context, the task of minimizing the influence of outside forces on the cabinet was transferred to the bureaucratic domain. It is clear from surviving records that senior civil servants in the Chancellery shielded

Brüning from the influence of organizations, political parties and Länder governments much more than he would have liked. This is also revealing of the self-confidence with which these senior officials consciously exercised their power. The excessive burden of work on the executive which arose from the incessant and increasingly difficult tasks imposed on it as it struggled to close budgetary gaps led to an extraordinary concentration of power in the hands of a small circle of state secretaries, notably Hermann Pünder and Hans Schäffer. Pünder's diary entries betray the near euphoric sense of power which pervaded the higher civil service at this time as it accumulated ever greater authority in a political framework shaped by the government's rigid adherence to deflation as a policy.[38] One result of this was that leading governmental civil servants rather than government ministers became the prime targets for lobbyists working on behalf of the main interest groups.

To a certain extent therefore, Brüning grew more and more dependent on the governmental bureaucracy but, despite this, he never lost sight of his primary political objectives. He was determined to achieve the ending of reparations, to secure Germany's economic superiority during the process of managing the economic crisis and to fundamentally restructure the Reich to achieve a more centralized state. These aims necessitated a rigorous deflationary programme, which in turn entailed a major contraction in the state's budget. In so far as he concealed or played down his strategic aims, however, he risked the means he employed to achieve them taking on a momentum of their own and preventing the success of the strategy as a whole. But the emphasis he placed on 'pragmatism' as a principle as well as the demand, which he elevated to a virtual article of faith, that the budget be balanced and his dogmatic insistence on stabilizing the currency – allegedly necessitated by foreign policy considerations – favoured precisely such a development. This was particularly evident in the case of the public administration. The bureaucratic momentum which the policy of saving at any price produced in this area was given added impetus by the recourse to emergency decrees and the state's refusal to consider further lending, particularly at the municipal level. This led to an almost uncontrollable wave of cut-backs in expenditure and rationalization measures. Their cumulative effect on those who had to bear the brunt of them was excessively harsh and the consequences in terms of tax revenue lost were incalculable, even by the experts. Typically, these measures hit hardest at public service employees, always first in the state's line of fire, as well as the masses of the unemployed. Their political cost was often out of all proportion to any financial savings they accomplished.

The major cuts made in civil servants' pay and in the structures of the public service during the Brüning era were not solely a consequence of the devastating financial and economic crisis rocking Germany at the time. The pressure from influential business circles as well as trade unions for a contraction in staffing costs at the Reich, Länder and municipal levels predated this. The Staff Reductions Decree of 27 October 1923 and the other savings measures which had followed it had, for example, produced a substantial reduction in public payroll costs.[39] On the other hand, the civil service pay reform which Heinrich Köhler introduced in 1927, and which was later to be criticized by Brüning, had brought major increases in civil service salaries which had risen only modestly since 1923. Despite massive protests from Adam Stegerwald and the unions, this Salaries Bill achieved widespread support in the Reichstag, due in no small measure to the influence wielded there by the civil servants' lobby.[40] The primary political motive behind the Salaries Bill had been to compensate civil servants for social policy reforms introduced or planned in the areas of reduced working hours and unemployment insurance, which would have benefited other sectors.

The Salary Reform and Unemployment Insurance Acts had only been possible on the basis of an over-optimistic and, as rapidly became clear, unrealistic assessment of the Reich's financial strength. The two areas were bound to clash when it became financially impossible to cover both following the onset of the economic crisis and the rapid growth in mass unemployment. The normal response when faced by imminent financial crisis was to increase taxation revenue. But this option was neither psychologically nor politically open to the Grand Coalition government, which, believing that concessions on reparations payments were imminent following its ratification of the Young Plan, held out the prospect of tax reductions. This produced a three-sided conflict which was to tear the Republic apart. Once the cabinet prematurely promised tax reductions to stimulate private investment, it became politically impossible to introduce increases in turnover and income tax. To close the budgetary gaps which had been produced primarily by the subventions the Reich Treasury was forced to pay to cover the strains on the unemployment insurance system, Chancellor Hermann Müller proposed the introduction of a *Reichshilfe* (Reich contribution) from each securely employed worker. This was in reality a concealed tax increase which entailed a salary cut for civil servants, public service employees and those with secure jobs in the private sector.[41] The imposition of this levy meant that those income groups not threatened with unemployment or covered by the social security system were to pay the cost of restoring the solvency of the unemployment insurance system.

The original idea of a small decrease in the salaries of those securely employed was understandably very popular with ordinary workers across the spectrum, including large sections of the Centre Party's following. It appeared a just solution in a situation where wages had fallen markedly since 1927 while civil servants had enjoyed considerable salary increases.

During the debates on the Salaries Bill, these increases had been specifically defended as necessary to bring civil service pay back into line with the then favourable trends in wages.[42] Even the civil servants' associations did not dispute the logic of this way of thinking, which was so widely endorsed by public opinion. The DBB declared that it was prepared in principle to make some concessions. The RhB, however, made its agreement to the proposed levy conditional on the differentials established in the Salaries Act between lower, medium and higher grades in the service being amended in their favour, which in reality meant that they sought to be exempted from the salary cut.[43]

The politically explosive element in the emergency levy issue, though, was primarily its potential to dangerously upset the increasingly tenuous balance of interests within the DVP. The DVP had supported the Salaries Act with the one reservation that it was excessively egalitarian in the manner in which it affected different groups of civil servants. This, however, did not prevent it from claiming the credit for the success of the reform and exploiting it politically.[44] The intertwining of DVP and RhB leaderships in the person of Scholz and the strong influence exercised by civil service interests in the party made it difficult for the DVP to make concessions on the emergency levy issue. This was further aggravated by the DVP industrial wing's adamance in rejecting the proposed salary decreases because they were designed to help fund the social security system, despite the fact that it had continually called for savings in the public budget identical to those demanded by the Business Party (Wirtschaftspartei). Hermann Müller was finally forced to drop his proposal for an emergency levy because of the bitter resistance mounted against it by the DVP.[45]

The last parliamentary cabinet in the Weimar Republic based on a Reichstag majority finally broke up over the issue of proposed increases in the social security contributions paid by workers and employers. The idea of an emergency levy had originally been proposed precisely so as to restore the solvency of the insurance system. The rejection of Brüning's compromise proposal by the trade union wing of the SPD parliamentary party forced the cabinet's resignation, though Brüning had at first hoped that this would not happen until the autumn. As in 1923, the SPD again proved unable to convince public opinion of where responsibility for the resignation of the government lay, which in this case was unquestionably with the DVP. The stubborn position adopted by the DVP on the emergency levy issue prevented a politically workable compromise in the decisive area of budgetary control, the central issue of which was finding a means to finance the social security system.[46]

By mid-April, following massive political pressure from the president, including threats to dissolve the Reichstag, Brüning had succeeded in finding a majority for the contentious budgetary measures which had caused the break-up of the Grand Coalition. But during the preparatory work on the financial estimates for 1930 which began soon after, it rapidly became apparent that these measures would not be sufficient to close the financial gaps which emerged when the actual tax intake for the year lagged behind the projected figures. Brüning had originally hoped to be able to manage by raising income tax on childless and single people and by a range of other minor savings measures. But, as early as 24 May, he intimated to State Secretary Schäffer that it would probably be impossible to avoid reducing civil servants' salaries.[47] Added to this was the demand presented in an ultimatum by the Business Party, on whose support the cabinet was reliant, that public service salaries be cut. The Centre Party too returned to the idea that public service employees should be included in any programme of cut-backs. At its executive council meeting of 17 May a motion was passed directing the party 'to seek the implementation of the emergency levy and to establish contact with Chancellor Dr Brüning, as the cabinet must lead on this issue'.[48] The Centre Party was acting under pressure from the SPD, which on 10 April had introduced a bill in the Reichstag providing for an emergency levy of 10 per cent of income tax on incomes in excess of 8,000 RM.[49]

As the civil service issue again came to the fore, the coalition of political forces which had brought about Hermann Müller's fall began to reassemble. At the cabinet meeting of 27 May 1930 the opposing sides clashed openly. The minister for labour, Adam Stegerwald, declared that any further cuts in unemployment benefit payments would have to be conditional on salary reductions being implemented simultaneously, as he had no intention of being singled out as the only minister responsible for cut-backs. Bredt demanded that civil service salaries be reduced, arguing openly that the 1927 Salaries Act had been a mistake. Treviranus stated in his usual exaggerated manner that public service employees had to be included in any programme of salary reductions as the measures proposed by the cabinet to rationalize the public administration, such as centralizing head offices, were hopelessly inadequate. The chancellor said that repeal of the Salaries Act was worth pursuing in its own right. He had wanted to lay the basis for this beforehand by introducing a spending reductions bill which would have produced substantial administrative savings. The gaps in the budget, however, demanded that countermeasures be taken immediately. In reply the minister for finance, Moldenhauer, who knew that the stance he was adopting would be resisted by his party in the Reichstag, declared that salary reductions would have to be preceded by wage cuts. Brüning avoided taking any side in the conflict: he pointed out that it was essential that the option of salary reductions be at least kept in mind, but did not take any definite position himself.[50]

Brüning had hoped to be able to get the budget adopted either by parliamentary majority or by means of an enabling act. But he was now confronted by a wide range of divergent positions. The demand from the Business Party, presented as an ultimatum, that the Salaries Act be repealed, was supported in principle by the army minister and the president's court. But the constitutionality of such a move, of which Brüning himself was dubious, would certainly have been challenged. The dominant attitude in cabinet was that a repeal of the Salaries Act would entail an attack on the 'established incremental rights' of civil servants and that there was no hope of securing the two-thirds parliamentary majority which such a constitutional change would require. The president's representatives thought similarly.[51] Moldenhauer's idea of turning the emergency levy on those in secure employment, now referred to as the 'Reichshilfe der Personen des öffentlichen Dienstes' (Reich Aid Programme by the People of the Public Service), into a permanent salary cut, was thus rejected.[52] The only alternative, if the increases in income tax demanded by the SPD and resolutely opposed by the bourgeois parties were to be avoided, was a temporary reduction in public sector salaries.

Despite Moldenhauer's personal willingness to compromise on this, the emergency levy idea even in amended form was rejected outright by the DVP. Moldenhauer now had little option but to demand corresponding decreases in general wage and price levels as well and a linking of civil service salary cuts with the Spending Reductions Bill proposed by Brüning. He also made the Reichshilfe programme conditional on the sickness benefit fund being reformed, thus accommodating one of the principal demands of the DVP's industrial backers.[53] Moldenhauer was essentially trying to delay a final decision. He was also adopting Brüning's tactic of burying the emergency levy issue in a basket of parallel measures so as to neutralize it politically. The chancellor had also to take the interests of his own party into account. Against Moldenhauer's express opposition, von Guérard argued for the inclusion of company directors' fees as he rightly feared that civil servants in the Centre Party would vigorously oppose any punitive measures restricted solely to public service employees. Except for the income tax increases which he intended to impose on childless and single people, Brüning had wanted to avoid such a move, but now began to think in terms of a general increase in income tax on all those in secure employment outside the public service.

Addressing his remarks principally to the DVP, Brüning told the cabinet that it was essential that agreement be reached between the coalition parties, as otherwise the Reichstag would proceed to impose some general taxation measure along the lines of the income tax supplementary levy proposed by Breitscheid.[54] This he wanted to avoid at all costs. He was fearful that industrial interests would bring all their weight to bear against any measure which would lead to a contraction in private investment and encourage the flight of capital already making itself felt. It would also have run counter to his line in reparations policy; his major purpose was to drastically squeeze public expenditure without actually weakening Germany economically through excessive demands on the business sector and thus giving the impression that Germany was unable to meet the reparations payments demanded of her. The interim budgetary plan adopted by the cabinet on 5 June, which included the controversial Reichshilfe levy on employees of both the public and private sectors, was considered by Brüning as a purely temporary measure. Although his chief aim in the medium term was the establishment of a right-of-centre coalition government, he did not want to burn all his bridges to the SPD; he still hoped that the social democrats would eventually both realize the necessity for and be prepared to support the 'entirely new structuring of the financial system of the Reich, the Länder and the municipalities which would require amending the constitution' and which he believed he would be able to implement by late autumn.[55] The chancellor also hoped that he would be successful in getting social demo-cratic agreement to his planned Spending Reductions Bill, which would have considerably limited the competence of the Reichstag in expenditure decisions.[56] These tactical considerations with regard to the SPD were the reason why he could not drop the Reichshilfe scheme proposed in the interim budgetary plan to cover cuts in the unemployment benefits system and why he had to try to resolve the budgetary problem without recourse to the uncompromising solutions demanded by the right.

It soon emerged, however, that the DVP had meanwhile resolved, under pressure from its industrial wing, to use the opportunity presented by the budgetary impasse to press home an attack on the established system of collective bargaining. Although the DVP's demands for decreases in wage and price levels corresponded to the chancellor's own basic position, Steger-wald refused to give in to the pressure from heavy industry for statutory wage cuts. This also marked the limit for Brüning if he did not want to endanger his medium-term budgetary strategy. The Labour Court ruling at Bad Oeynhaus on 10 June granting wage reductions of 7.5 per cent in the north-west regional iron and steel industry to be met by corresponding price decreases whetted the appetite of the major industrialists' organiza-tions, which now began demanding wage cuts across the board.[57] Brüning's hopes that direct negotiations between employers and unions would lead to a revival of the Central Working Association (ZAG) and to voluntary wage and price decreases rapidly collapsed. Negotiations held by the RdI and the VdA (Federation of German Employers' Associations) with the three trade union federations broke down without any narrowing of the gap between their respective positions. On 13 June the employers' side rejected as 'unacceptable' an offer from the unions intimating their willingness to accept wage cuts on condition that price decreases were implemented first, though they also demanded that a general emergency levy be imposed on all sections of the population not directly affected by unemployment and that existing levels of unemployment benefit payments be maintained.[58] All hopes for agreement being reached outside the parliamentary and governmental arena were now shattered.

On 16 June a meeting of the DVP parliamentary party rejected the notion of an emergency levy and increased its pressure on the cabinet by deciding to withdraw Moldenhauer from it, a move which he in turn attempted in vain to pre-empt by offering his resignation on 18 June.[59] On 24 June the cabinet was confronted with an ultimatum in the form of 'guidelines' drawn up by the DVP parliamentary party following the intense internal party meetings held between 16 and 18 June. These proposed, as an alternative to the cabinet's interim budgetary plan, a reduction in central government's current expenditure, a 5 per cent decrease in revenue transfers to the Länder and the introduction of a poll tax to eliminate the need to meet the shortfall this would create at local level through increased property taxes or rates. To these were added the usual demands for further cuts in unemployment benefit payments, taxation of public enterprises and the other traditional demands of the major industrialists' organizations. The DVP ultimatum was largely in line with RdI and VdA demands. It ended by stating that there could be no question of new sources of revenue being tapped and particularly rejected any 'one-sided burdening of particular strata and professions'.[60]

During the negotiations which followed, Scholz stated categorically that the DVP also rejected the latest variant of the emergency levy suggested by the new minister for finance, Hermann Dietrich. Dietrich proposed a measure restricted to public service employees, and its provisions for taxing higher income groups were in fact more deceptive than real. Scholz nevertheless stressed that the DVP was particularly opposed to any levy on income tax. He indicated that a compromise on the Reichshilfe issue was conceivable only if 'the civil servants' associations agreed voluntarily to make such a sacrifice' – a statement that revealed the sharp antagonisms which existed between the DVP's industrial wing and the civil servants' lobby among its supporters.[61]

The cabinet could see no alternative to the Reichshilfe. The only compromise solution discussed proposed salary reductions in the public service and an increase of about 5 per cent income tax on higher salaries. There were differences in cabinet as to how high the proposed salary reductions should be. Curtius regarded 2.25 per cent as a maximum and Treviranus argued for a 3 per cent ceiling. Brüning was in favour of a 2.5 per cent limit on the basis – typical of his reasoning – that the final figure would probably settle at nearer 4 per cent. Differences of opinion continued to be voiced on the question of whether or not widows and orphans should be exempted, whether double-taxation could be avoided and whether higher civil servants should be totally or only partly excluded from the programme of salary cuts. The DVP's ultimatum was opposed most vociferously by Stegerwald and Dietrich, and was totally inadequate anyway to cover the gap in the budget. But they were also worried about the political consequences if they accommodated the DVP's demands on the income tax levy. Dietrich stated that if the DVP's proposal were adopted, civil servants would gain the impression that they were being singled out unfairly for 'special treatment'. Dietrich knew well that the compromise reached on this question was nothing other than a cosmetic exercise. State Secretary Schäffer had already warned Brüning against 'penalizing civil servants' and pointed out that a 5 per cent income tax levy would be largely buff as in percentage terms it would bear no relation to the actual salary decrease it would entail.[62]

It was obvious that in this situation Brüning's original intention of forcing the adoption of his plan in this area by means of an enabling act was no longer viable, given that the DVP would withdraw its support unless the cabinet abandoned the Reichshilfe programme. Brüning calculated that at this stage an enabling bill would secure at best only 139 votes in the Reichstag, which would effectively represent a vote of no confidence in his government. In addition, as he explained in cabinet, he did not want to 'use up' the potential of an enabling act at this stage, as it would be needed for other political measures by autumn at the latest. This is worth noting, because it shows that up to the early summer of 1930 Brüning was totally undecided on whether he should seek to implement his political programme solely on the basis of presidentially sanctioned emergency decrees. But when conflicting party interests prevented the adoption of the budget, he believed that he had no option but to do so.[63]

Brüning decided at first to introduce his budgetary plans into the Reichstag via the Reichsrat, in the hope that he still might be able to persuade the DVP to change its stance. This was why he took on board the DVP's poll tax proposal and retrospectively incorporated a provision for a municipal poll tax into the government's estimates.[64] In its final draft the budgetary bill attempted to conciliate both the SPD and DVP with a compromise formula typical of Brüning. The 'Reichshilfe der Personen des öffentlichen Dienstes', due to come into force on 31 March 1931, provided for salary cuts of 2.5 per cent. Salaries of less than 2,000 RM per annum and salary earners paying social security contributions were exempted. The 5 per cent income tax levy was imposed only on salaries of over 8,000 RM. This far from socially equitable formula was repeated in the bill's poll tax provisions, though they were an optional measure in municipalities. The poll tax took the form of a tax on each head of population. The sliding scale demanded by the Centre Party, the DDP and the SPD was left out entirely at first and was only reintroduced in the emergency decree which subsequently appeared.[65] The tax was structured in the 'didactic' sense sought by the DVP and the Business Party to keep expenditure on unemployment welfare programmes at local level as low as possible and to prevent further increases in property taxes and rates, and particularly in taxes on business. As Dietrich rightly pointed out, however, the actual financial returns it produced were unimpressive. It was a classic case of burdens inequitably distributed. Only the unemployed were exempted from having to pay the poll tax, while workers now had to pay both it and the increased unemployment security contribution introduced in the budget.[66]

When presenting his budgetary programme in the Reichsrat on 28 June, Brüning declared that the government was determined at all costs that it be implemented in its entirety without any changes and that its schedule be punctually adhered to. It was also well known that he intended if necessary to resort to Section 48 of the Weimar constitution to ensure this.[67] But, as Landsberg was later to argue when presenting the SPD's case for rescinding the emergency decrees,[68] the chancellor himself was inconsistent in this as the poll tax had only been added to the budget when it already lay before the Reichstag. Brüning must have been aware that, although the SPD was prepared to tolerate the Reichshilfe scheme in the budget and allow it through, it could not accept the poll tax provisions. Indeed, the SPD continued to offer talks with the government on the poll tax right up to the end. Brüning dismissed these approaches with the abrupt argument that any such talks would undermine support for the government among the parties of the right and he was explicitly supported in this stand in cabinet by Joseph Wirth, the minister for the interior.[69] The SPD had introduced an alternative proposal to the poll tax in the form of a salaries and pensions reductions bill which provided for maximum limits for salaries, pensions and supplementary earnings, including taxable secondary sources of personal income. At the cabinet meeting of 16 July such an approach was rejected by a majority of the government as a threat to the professional civil service and, as the minister for justice suggested, because it was probably unconstitutional.[70] Brüning too was critical of the idea, despite the fact that his government was shortly afterwards to adopt just such a policy of cuts in pensions and state maintenance payments. The idea of cutting pensions did, however, meet with sympathy within the Centre Party. It decided nevertheless to delay raising the issue of a pensions bill until after the Reichstag had passed the general provisions of the budget, thus effectively postponing the enactment of a pensions law until the autumn.[71]

Rudolf Breitscheid told Esser that the poll tax provisions, which had been introduced only after the first reading of the Finance Bill had been completed and after the SPD had allowed the Reichshilfe programme through during the vote on the first section of the budget, were totally unacceptable to the social democrats. Nevertheless, he persisted in his attempts to mediate with the government. Brüning rejected any further talks, though it was abundantly clear by this stage that the DNVP would vote against the budget. The negotiations which preceded the government's defeat in the Reichstag clearly demonstrated the key parliamentary position again occupied by the DVP as, without its support, there was no hope that elements of the DNVP could be won over to the government's side. The DVP for its part had made the poll tax a *conditio sine qua non* of its support for the budget and was also successful at first in preventing the sliding scale sought by the DDP and the Centre Party from being included in it.[72] Brüning's tactics had proved a complete failure; he now resorted to the systematic use of presidentially sanctioned emergency decrees which he had intimated so often and, after securing the sanction of the Reichstag, he dissolved parliament on 18 July and induced the president to enact the Finance Bill by decree on 26 July on the basis of Article 48 of the constitution. This implemented the budget, only slightly modified by additional provisions covering unemployment insurance and the 1930 budgetary statement.[73] As with the collapse of the Grand Coalition, the substantial point at issue had once again been the contentious linking of the civil service pay issue with the crisis in the social security system. A compromise with the SPD would still have been possible, and both Pünder and Schäffer believed that the only solution to the political crisis which now emerged lay in the inclusion of the SPD.[74]

Brüning was determined to forge ahead with his programme of what he regarded as essential basic economies in public spending. This necessarily implied drastic reductions in the public administration, even though it meant aggravating his conflict with the Reichstag. He hoped, however, that the escalation in the economic crisis predicted for the autumn would have a sobering effect on parliament and induce it to comply with his plans. His final aim was clear: by means of substantial cuts in public expenditure, comprehensive wage and price reductions and simultaneous measures to stimulate private investment activity, he wanted to create the preconditions for firmly placing ultimate control of all finances and financial policy in the hands of central government. This he hoped would exclude the possibility of future surrenders such as he believed the Young Plan had been. Following the completion of reparations payments, which he expected to bring about within two to three years, he intended to secure a free hand for Germany in foreign trade relations and bring about a balance of payments surplus on the basis of a 20 per cent devaluation of the Reichsmark and the economic recovery and stability which Germany would have achieved by then. He saw this as laying the foundations for the recovery of Germany as a major power. The economic crisis – which Brüning blamed first and foremost on the vicious cycle of reparations payments and the disruption of the international economic and currency systems which this caused –

was to serve as the means to realize this grand plan. 'The first country prepared to implement all the unpopular domestic measures necessary', he later explained in outlining his strategy at that time, 'will rise to the top.'[75]

These unpopular measures included cutting the costs of the public service through salary decreases and reductions in staffing levels. Brüning's standard argument in support of this policy was to refer to the lower budgets allocated for personnel costs in comparable industrial countries such as France; in this he had the backing of industry and also at first of the unions. He regularly pointed out that German civil servants' salaries continued to be higher than those of their French counterparts.[76] The economic crisis had consequences that had been totally unforeseen and forced all countries affected by it to make drastic cuts in their public service payrolls. As comparative figures for neighbouring European countries show, salary reductions carried out in Germany were as extensive as anywhere else.[77] But, quite apart from the provisions in the Weimar constitution guaranteeing special rights to civil servants, which in retrospect can be seen to have been a mistake,[78] the civil service salary issue in Germany was fraught with other particularly intractable problems. The statutory reduction in staffing levels implemented in 1923 and the regularly renewed ban on promotion considerably reduced civil servants' advancement prospects and, except for in the municipal sector, pruned the civil service as a body to such an extent that when savings measures were introduced there was little room left for them to be implemented with any flexibility. Also, compared with their pre-war levels – a standard method of comparison used in virtually all sectors of the economy and financial policy during the Weimar Republic – civil servants' salaries did not rise excessively. Higher civil servants in particular suffered a marked decline in social status as a result of the great inflation. Given the general situation of widespread economic distress at the time, complaints by higher civil servants that they could no longer afford maidservants[79] may seem somewhat grotesque, but they illustrate how susceptible medium-level and higher civil servants in particular had become to extreme feelings of resentment. This was further exacerbated by the widespread public hostility to civil servants which, while understandable in conditions of mass unemployment, could have been considerably tempered had governments dealt with the situation more tactfully. Brüning disregarded the many warnings he received in this regard, not least from the civil servants' advisory committees of the Centre Party.[80]

Even State Secretary Hans Schäffer, otherwise quite sympathetic to the SPD,[81] rejected the notion that continuous salary cuts were an adequate answer to the problem. Surprisingly, he was supported in this view by Paul Silverberg, who as early as September 1930 remarked that great caution should be exercised in dealing with civil servants' salaries and conditions.[82] In a letter to Warburg, a leading banker with whom he was friendly,

Schäffer warned against a public caricaturing of civil servants, who were a 'financially and socially disenfranchised group' providing an 'excellent breeding ground for all types of radical movements'. It was not the salary of the individual civil servant which was too large but the total expenditure resulting from an excess of uncoordinated 'independent units of government' and an inordinate subdivision of the administrative and judicial systems into independent offices at the lowest local levels.[83] The principal issue confronting the Brüning government was therefore whether it could succeed in going beyond a purely schematically conceived programme of cut-backs across the board to the broader question of the reform – so long overdue – of public administration at central government level, in the Länder and particularly at municipal level.

As early as July 1930 the escalating financial crisis forced the cabinet to adopt a range of cumulative savings measures in the area of public administration. The seriousness of the crisis dissipated the arguments which had surrounded the Finance Bill. Against stiff opposition in cabinet, Stegerwald proposed cutting pensions and maintenance payments, pointing out that the cost to the government of state pensions was now 4 billion RM in comparison to 1.9 billion before the war. As was clear even from the debates in cabinet, the grounds on which the planned reduction in state pensions would be opposed was that legally this was 'confiscation' and represented a 'dangerous attack on the professional civil service'.[84] But the government really had no alternative since the policy of wage and price decreases that was being implemented simultaneously would otherwise have been difficult to justify to the public. In addition, the catastrophic results of the September 1930 Reichstag elections meant that a budget could be passed only if the social democrats agreed to abstain, and they were adamant from the start that state pensions had to be reduced. The minister for finance too felt that he had no option but to seek a further cut in public service salaries and wanted these implemented by 1 April 1931 at the latest. But his insistence on introducing a sliding scale of pay cuts – from 5 per cent on all salaries up to the level of governmental councillor, to 10 per cent for governmental councillors and higher civil servants and up to 30 per cent on ministerial salaries – was vigorously opposed in cabinet. Treviranus, though, supported this proposal and pointed out that a 5 per cent cut across the board would result in the lowest-paid groups paying proportionally most given the different tax bands involved.[85] Brüning took the side of the higher civil servants and the sliding scale was abandoned. However, for the sake of appearances, cabinet agreed to reduce ministerial salaries by 20 per cent and cut back on Reichstag deputies' allowances.[86]

The Salary Reductions Bill passed by cabinet at the end of October and finally set to take effect from 1 January 1931 – though later put back to 1 February out of consideration for middle-class traders dependent on earnings over the Christmas period – was innovatory from the constitutional point of view in that it statutorily obliged Länder governments and municipal executives, as well as the Länder parliaments and elected municipal councils themselves, to legislate reductions in salaries, allowances and pensions in line with those being introduced at Reich level. It also circumvented the normal chain of authority between the Reich and its regional and local units. Another directive, drawn up in conjunction with this bill and designed to limit personnel costs in the public administration,[87] which in particular reinforced the privileged position of those civil servants on special allowances, was also included in the first comprehensive Presidential Decree for the Protection of the Economy and the Public Finances promulgated on 1 December 1930.[88] The Reichshilfe scheme was introduced ostensibly as a temporary expedient and, taking the form of a 'salary cut' of 6 per cent, was initially due to expire on 31 January 1934. The income tax levies on higher earners and single people were set for considerably shorter durations.

Brüning was well aware that, given the stance adopted by the DNVP, the emergency decree would require the passive toleration of the social democrats to pass the Reichstag. Although he could rely on the support of Otto Braun, the Prussian prime minister, he tried to pressurize the SPD by threatening to dissolve the ruling coalition in Prussia if the social democrats refused their support in the Reichstag.[89] But his greatest problem were the Länder and municipalities. The constitutionality of extending government ordinances to the Länder was open to dispute in its own right, and there was no precedent for imposing salary cuts on municipalities. There was no provision for national authority over salaries at municipal level similar to that in the national and Länder salary legislation which formed the legal basis for the salary cuts at those levels.[90] The Länder, however, offered no opposition. Indeed, the savings measures had been drawn up in close liaison with the Prussian authorities. The salary cuts would naturally have a much greater effect on the finances of the Länder than on those of the Reich. Far from protesting at the obvious encroachments on their autonomy, the Länder, particularly as the economic crisis deepened over the winter and assumed a more permanent character, demanded that the Reich proceed with even more decrees of a similar nature. This was partly to provide a legal basis for salary reductions in public services at Länder level and partly to deflect responsibility for cutbacks in public spending from themselves.[91]

A further dramatic deterioration in the public finances forced the government to consider further and more thoroughgoing cut-backs in the spring. The Länder were particularly severely affected as the decline in tax revenues which occurred at the same time as the escalating costs of funding the unemployment insurance system produced a desperate financial situation. Finance Minister Dietrich resisted the salary cuts demanded categorically by Reichsbank President Luther. Dietrich argued that the savings these would produce for the Reich – in contrast to whatever benefits they would bring to the Länder and municipalities – would be relatively small and would not be worth the growing unrest they would add within the civil servants' associations.[92] He suggested instead increasing turnover tax to 1.5 per cent, which Brüning, however, rejected. But by now the chancellor too was against any further impositions restricted to public service employees and thought in terms of a general levy on the employed. This later emerged in the form of the Crisis Levy. For domestic political reasons, prominent among which was Brüning's decision to wait until after the SPD's annual conference so as not to cause any undue trouble for the social democrats, the Second Emergency Decree for the Protection of the Economy and the Public Finances was not promulgated until 5 June 1931.[93] It provided for reductions in salaries and pensions on a sliding scale from 4 to 8 per cent, savings in child benefits and cuts in disability and wounded war veterans' pensions. In addition, the decree obliged the Länder and municipalities to reduce the salaries and wages of their civil servants, clerical staff and workers, at least to the levels of central government employees.

In addition to measures which directly affected salaries, a wide range of other cut-backs were implemented. A detailed description of these would go beyond the bounds of this analysis. A law was introduced, for example, changing the civil servants' legal contract of employment to rule out special claims for salary increases or maintenance allowances on the basis of past or future special duties.[94] Similarly, the privileged position of employees on retainers was reinforced and consideration was given to raising the retirement age to sixty-eight, though this would have necessitated considerable changes in promotion practices within the public service. Both central government and the Länder also cut back on such side benefits of public service employment as disturbance payments, housing, travel, out-of-town allowances and the like. Attempts were made to encourage married female civil servants to resign and to discourage double-income families.[95] The Prussian government considered reclassifying teachers, whose pay accounted for a considerable proportion of the Land's budget, to a lower grade on the civil service scale. As a law to this effect would have required an amendment to the constitution, Severing voiced the possibility of having it enacted by referendum if necessary, though he added that such a move would be conditional on large salaries in the private sector being included in the general programme of cut-backs.[96] Several Länder took the step of abolishing the emeritus status of university teachers.[97] These developments revealed the particular vulnerability of the educational sector to programmes of expenditure cuts which were carried out more or less schematically.

By the summer of 1931 at the latest the immense difficulties produced by the deflationary policy rigorously pursued by Brüning with the support of

Reichsbank President Luther had become blatant. In the Länder opposition steadily mounted to the pressure exercised by central government on them through the reductions in revenue transfers from the central treasury. This forced them to cut civil servants' salaries below, and without reference to, those of central government employees. There was a danger, as an urgent message from Baden warned the chancellor,[98] that this would lead to a growth in radicalism among civil servants. In addition, constitutional difficulties arose regarding the legal rights of civil servants in the Länder and the accountability of Länder governments and municipal executives to their respective parliamentary assemblies. To deal with these difficulties, Brüning promulgated the so-called Dietramzell Emergency Decree of 24 August 1931, which empowered the Länder to reduce civil servants' salaries by decree without having to obtain the consent of Länder parliaments or municipal assemblies. He could justify this by referring to the fact that the Länder governments had specifically sought powers of this type. But contrary to what they had wanted, the effect of the decree was that the Länder governments were forced by the curtailment of financial support from central government to resort to drastic cuts in civil servants' pay.[99] This necessarily led to the emergence throughout Germany of a widely divergent range of schemes for paying civil servants.

Several of the Länder reacted to what appeared to be a desperate financial situation by offering to institute measures towards a Reichsreform (reform of the structure of the Reich) and to reduce staff costs by establishing joint administrative structures with other Länder. This was perfectly in line with Brüning's objective of dismantling federalist structures, at least north of the river Main, and of achieving a fusion of Prussia and the Reich through the absorption of the north German Länder by Prussia.[100] Nevertheless, Brüning rejected these offers from the Länder as well as their demands that central government institute further cuts in civil service salaries in line with their own. He argued that the Länder should wait until they had exhausted all available possibilities in the area of spending cuts at Länder level before meeting again to discuss further measures at Reich level. He let it be known that he was acting on the basis of 'very definite ideas'. The establishment of a joint public administration with Prussia was useless to him as long as the Prussian parliament continued in existence. Equally, the savings it was hoped a Reichsreform would produce would only become clear at a later date. What was more immediately important to him therefore was to minimize friction rather than save money. 'There is only one major issue involved in the relations between the Reich and Prussia', he said. He wanted to wait for the Länder to go bankrupt so as to be in a stronger position to proceed with the Reichsreform. He expected the parliaments of the Länder to prove incapable of implementing the necessary salary reductions and hoped that the exponents of Länder autonomy would finally be forced to agree out of necessity to the dismantling of regional parliamentarism which he sought.[101]

Leaving aside the ethics of such a tactical manipulation of the financial crisis to achieve political ends, Brüning's strategy failed, except in the case of several small north German Länder. This was because he underestimated the efforts the Prussian government in particular would make to tackle the financial crisis. The Prussian prime minister was willing to try virtually anything to reduce the enormous discrepancy which existed between the situation of the masses of unemployed largely dependent on unemployment relief and the relatively comfortable position of numerous groups of public servants, above all local government officials. But the policy of expenditure cut-backs pursued by the Prussian minister for finance, Höpker-Aschoff, and his outspoken intervention in the debate on the Reichsreform caused major differences within the Prussian cabinet and led to his resignation on 12 October.[102] On the question of further reductions in public pensions and a structured reduction in the public pay bill, the Prussian government was determined to proceed with decisive measures regardless of central government. These included a plan to enforce a general ban on incremental salary increases by emergency decree if necessary.

Dietrich, the minister for finance in the Reich government, had lost faith in salary cuts across the board. He adopted instead the Prussian approach and in September 1931 presented a proposal to cabinet suggesting a ban on increments for two years as well as further reductions in pensions. Dietrich was only half-hearted about the measure but felt himself bound by the agreement with the Prussian government. The proposal, however, met with intense opposition in cabinet. The postal minister regarded any postponement of increments as intolerable. Groener and Wirth warned of the dangerous psychological consequences of such a measure in repelling young people and offending older people.[103] In fact, in addition to the differences in the regulations covering civil service salaries in Prussia and the Reich and especially the less favourable scales in the latter,[104] such a measure would have confronted every single civil servant with the prospect of never reaching the top of the scale and ending up on a lower pension than they had calculated. Similarly heated disputes with the Army Ministry erupted on the issue of pension reductions. Following protracted negotiations, when Brüning sided with the Army Ministry – which had the support of the president's office – Wehrmacht officials and Prussian police officers were excluded from the regulation's provisions.[105] Disputes of this kind became more and more common. They demonstrate the extent to which pressure from the civil servants' associations and from individual professional organizations had increased and how fears of encouraging radical sentiment among civil servants were gaining ground inside the cabinet too.[106]

The halt on increments was finally abandoned and the regulation covering pensions adopted with suitable exemption clauses. Brüning's reaction to the finance minister's final draft, which he had apparently not cleared with him beforehand, was quite typical. During the cabinet meeting of 24 September Brüning and Stegerwald declared that, given the 'deflationary policy which will have to be pursued in the immediate future', the government would again be confronted in October with the need to make 'decisive cuts which will have to include salary policy in the civil service'. It would thus be inopportune to hit civil servants at this stage. Dietrich reacted to this announcement with unusual bitterness, declaring that he would 'only co-operate with a general reduction in civil servants' salaries if similar cuts were made across the board, affecting not only civil servants, but workers and other wage and salary earners as well. He was not prepared to countenance any measures singling out civil servants.' In this he was not being totally consistent, as the salary proposals he presented were in fact restricted to the public service. Nevertheless, this represented yet another attempt to get round a direct salary cut. Dietrich's behaviour resulted from his realization that the vicious circle of shrinkage in incomes and taxation made no economic or financial sense. He had told Schäffer in early August that further deflationary measures would ruin everything and that there could therefore be no question of any further reductions in wages and salaries.[107]

Even if only to justify the policy of continuous wage decreases, Stegerwald meanwhile committed himself to even more drastic measures to cut expenditure in the public service. He argued that Germany could simply no longer afford the luxury of an excessively costly public administration. Rationalization of public administration had to be enforced, he told the cabinet meeting of 2 October 1931, by means of either a Reichstag resolution or a plebiscite. Both ideas were unrealistic and were aparently intended purely rhetorically to prepare the ground for his proposal that whatever measures were necessary should be drafted 'on the basis of emergency legislation yet to be created'. This, he claimed, would be the only guarantee against the 'threat of dictatorship'. The time had come, the labour minister declared, 'for the government to choose between loyalty to the constitution and loyalty to the state and the people'. The plan to force through a dismantling of the public administration by circumventing the constitution if necessary could not have been put more clearly. Stegerwald also voiced the idea of purposely using financial collapse in the Länder as an instrument to enforce a rationalization of the public administration. Several financial crises could be expected during 1932 in the Länder and municipalities. 'Dismantling the excessively large administration will then be a simple matter,' he concluded.[108]

Brüning avoided commenting directly on Stegerwald's argument and limited his remarks to the characteristic statement that it was advisable to wait for the psychologically most opportune moment before taking drastic measures. There can be no doubt, however, as is obvious from a range of comparable statements he made, that he fully supported Stegerwald's line.[109] It was suggested that the 1927 Salaries Act simply be repealed, but this would have been of little benefit since, as the postal minister pointed out, the salaries of some groups of civil servants had already declined to the level they had been at in 1924.[110] What was clear, though, was that a comprehensive reform of salary regulations which would have left higher civil servants relatively better off – as sought by Treviranus – had no chance of being accepted under existing conditions. In early December 1931 Brüning again raised the issue of the need for a definitive solution to the problem, but he added that it would never be possible to achieve this through the Reichstag. This meant that for the time being there was no alternative to reductions across the board in civil servants' salaries.[111]

The 'clean sweep' finally came on 8 December with the publication of the Fourth Decree for the Protection of the Economy and the Public Finances which indeed, in comparison with the decree issued the previous October, did have a considerably greater impact on the civil service.[112] As well as further reductions in pensions and allowances and other lesser expenditures, it included a 9 per cent cut in basic salary rates. Despite the banking crisis, the fall in the value of sterling and the catastrophic situation on the labour market, Brüning held rigidly to the course he had embarked upon. He was intent on reducing general levels of prices and costs throughout the German economy, with the exception of the agricultural sector. He was prepared to take the risk that some of these measures, such as increases in turnover and property taxes, would weaken the economy. Central to this policy was an insistence on cutting the budget for public expenditure and, hence, on further reductions in personnel costs, including state pensions, retirement allowances and maintenance payments. When this intensification of government policy produced an unprecedented wave of opposition within the president's entourage in late autumn 1931, Brüning declared emphatically that the reparations situation left him with no choice but to proceed with the programme of expenditure cuts he had initiated, especially in the area of civil service pay, as this was regarded by the creditor powers as a yardstick of Germany's economic and financial capabilities.[113]

In his chancellor's speech of 13 October 1931 Brüning again stressed the importance of bringing domestic policy priorities into line with the changing balances in international politics.[114] He was convinced that foreign policy requirements dictated another period of austerity. He repeatedly warned his cabinet members not to allow the facts regarding Germany's financial difficulties to leak out as this would make it impossible to pursue a successful foreign policy.[115] When viewing statements of this kind, it must be understood that even Brüning himself was beginning to doubt the economic and political wisdom of the deflationary line he was pursuing. Many of his closest associates admitted that the deflationary policy could no longer be adhered to and urged that the reparations problem be sorted out without further delay. The rigid adherence to deflation was widely condemned by public opinion, with the civil servants' associations, among others, arguing against it primarily on the basis of purchasing power theories.[116] Brüning became noticeably more unsure of himself. 'This deflationary contraction must be stopped at some point,' he told Schäfer. If pursued beyond a certain point, he said, deflatoin could rebound into inflation.[117] In reply to Vögler, a supporter of cost reductions who believed that economic recovery would follow 'if we could combine 1913 social security and taxation rates with wartime cost levels', the chancellor said that it would be impossible to reduce wages 'without increasing pressure on the public purse'.[118] In response to the deteriorating situation precipitated by the devaluation of sterling Brüning openly admitted that it was hopeless continually trying to keep pace with the budget deficit: 'It is quite obvious that if economic contraction continues it will be impossible to balance the budget in the long run.' He made this statement shortly before the introduction of the drastic deflationary measures of the Fourth Emergency Decree.[119]

That Brüning – and the same went for Reichsbank President Luther – held rigidly to his programme of wage, salary and price reductions even though he realized the retarding effect his savings policies were having on economic recovery was without doubt a consequence of his strategy of using the crisis as a means to effect a general realignment in both domestic and foreign policy. This was clearly revealed in the dispute which arose between these two politicians and the economist Ernst Wagemann, who had called for a comprehensive programme of measures to stimulate credit formation. Brüning, who in early 1932 attempted to prevent him from delivering a speech scheduled by the Society for Money and Credit Reform, argued against Wagemann's position primarily on the basis of the exigencies of the reparations situation. In this he indirectly revealed the political priorities of his economic policy. Wagemann created the impression, he said, that means other than deflationary ones existed 'to improve our situation and increase our competitiveness'. Wagemann's publications would, he feared, 'disrupt the reparations programme' as the French would accuse the Germans of duplicity if they got the impression that measures to stimulate economic recovery had been deliberately delayed until recognition of Germany's inability to pay had been secured at Basel.[120]

But Brüning also regarded Wagemann as a threat to his domestic programme for rationalizing the public administration and for reducing social security costs. The unions would immediately exploit an expansion in credit to demand a comprehensive job creation programme. Luther's reaction was identical. At first he considered formally refuting Wagemann's claims in public as they could do fatal damage to the government's programme. All proposals for reforming the public administration would be thwarted if the idea gained ground that the crisis could be resolved by means other than deflation. The working class would move to block any further reductions in the welfare system. Schäffer, who kept notes of these discussions,[121] warned Luther that if he took such a public stance he would cause a 'rebellion among the workers' and advised him to confine himself to statements on currency questions.

But deflation had by now become a central dogma in the government's foreign and domestic policies. Both Brüning and Luther regarded the economic crisis as a unique historical opportunity to slim down the public administration. They thus applied to the machinery of state the contemporary notion that the economic crisis was a natural rationalization process. The idea that it was possible to restore the civil service to the role of a small elite entrusted with the essential affairs of state and to replace the mass of lower and medium civil service ranks with ordinary employees played a part in this thinking. Brüning considered returning to the principle of honorary officials carrying out the duties of local government. But such a restructuring would have undermined the material position of large groups of civil servants and in any case was incompatible with the steadily growing social and planning functions of the modern industrial state. The policy of salary reductions and administrative contraction pursued by the government was no answer to the administrative reforms which were undoubtedly long overdue but which could hardly be implemented in the middle of an economic crisis. Although many of the large centralized bureaucracies such as the post office, the national railways and the customs service, as well as those of the Länder, began increasingly to form joint administrative units at local level, it is significant that Brüning repeatedly intervened in this process to advise caution for fear of the negative reaction it might provoke from the electorate. He accused the Prussian government of having initiated their rationalization programme at an inopportune time and of thereby having aggravated the voters unnecessarily.[122]

It is revealing that Brüning was particularly irritated by the relatively successful savings policies implemented by the Prussian government, especially under Finance Minister Klepper, though Klepper's public statement that Brüning's economic policies were causing a contraction in tax revenues played a certain part in this.[123] The chancellor's distrust of the Prussian government was repeatedly made clear. One gets the impression that Brüning did not want Prussia to be successful in its budgetary programme as that would have changed the conditions for the fusion of Prussia and the Reich which he was planning – a plan given concrete expression in his proposal to transfer particular Prussian ministries to the central government.[124] The creation of a joint public administration with the smaller north German Länder appeared imminent. The Brüning government's policy with regard to the civil service was at least partly designed to precipitate the Reichsreform towards a unitary state; the more rapid financial recovery expected for the central government administration was an important element. In the wave of protests which was likely to ensue in the Länder when public officials there could no longer be paid, Brüning saw a useful lever with which to neutralize the political forces opposed to his plans for a unitary state structure. Similar thinking lay behind the 'taming' strategy he adopted towards the formation of coalition governments with the NSDAP in the Länder.[125]

The basic weakness in Brüning's overall economic and financial policy also affected his policy towards the civil service: the rigorous foreign policy rationale of his austerity policies proved an excessive strain. Given the situation of mass unemployment, decisive cuts in the pay of civil servants, government employees and public service workers were unavoidable, though the argument used to justify them – that these categories enjoyed the privilege of secure employment – actually only applied to civil servants proper. The civil servants' associations had made their agreement, or rather their passive acquiescence, to salary cuts conditional on the implementation of corresponding price reductions. But Brüning's aim of achieving a general reduction in cost levels by lowering wage and price levels and thus improving the economy's export capability proved to be only partly realizable, despite increased intervention by the state. Although a notable decrease in the cost of living was registered, this was not as large as the fall in salary and wage levels. The situation was compounded by the government's maintenance of price supports for farm produce to stimulate agricultural recovery; this indicated that it could hardly have been hoping to see any major decline in general food prices, which was the decisive economic factor for the mass of ordinary people.[126]

The psychological effects the salary cuts had on public service employees was of greater importance than the decline in their real incomes. Continuous reductions in pay accompanied by the government's blatantly dishonest assurances that no further decreases in pay were being considered tended to confirm the suspicion that the notoriously secure salaries of civil servants were now under threat. It is essential to remember the effects which the savings policies Brüning forced on the Länder had on the great mass of public service employees in Germany. The desperate financial situation at the Länder level set in motion a process of contraction which inevitably developed along the line of least resistance and led to an epidemic of expenditure cuts in which all political perspective was lost. The higher echelons of the Länder bureaucracies, granted virtually unconditional power by the emergency decrees, gave full vent to their partly latent and partly open resentment of those parliamentary groups which they had always held responsible for excessively lavish public spending when in power by unleashing a veritable tidal wave of cut-backs in staffing costs and general public expenditure.[127] The fixation on cutting expenditure which now erupted everywhere was implemented with bureaucratic thoroughness: in the sections of the population most immediately affected this aroused feelings of insecurity and reinforced public perceptions of the social injustice of the measures being implemented. The trend, supported by Brüning though opposed by Dietrich, of forcing salary levels in Länder and municipal administrations below those to which Reich civil servants' salaries had been reduced also aggravated separatist tendencies in the Länder.[128]

Brüning's salaries policy was repeatedly attacked, particularly by the DDB and the ADB, for the socially inequitable manner in which it was applied. There can be no doubt but that the groups which suffered most in the crisis were the blue-collar workers and the lower salaried sections of the public service. This relative disadvantage was blatantly apparent in the salary cuts of up to 23 per cent borne by civil servants on top of the abolition of their special allowances and the Crisis Levy imposed on them. The inadequacy of the sliding scales meant that lower- and medium-level civil servants suffered most. This was particularly the case with the regulation of child benefits.[129] Although even Brüning complained that higher civil servants had not been sufficiently exempted, all in all they succeeded in maintaining their relatively privileged position due to the structures of the tax system, while the full impact of the cut-backs fell most heavily on the lower-income groups. In addition, the cabinet had felt obliged to exempt certain groups of civil servants from the full rigour of the cuts, notably the police, the army and the judges of the national and disciplinary courts.[130] Some expenditure cuts, such as the lowering of the pensions of wounded war veterans, widows and orphans, bore no financial relationship to the bitterness they caused.

Furthermore, Brüning could not prevent the impression that public service employees had been singled out for particularly harsh treatment from gaining ground. This was mainly due to the fact that the government, for political reasons, treated people with private sources of income with a great deal more consideration. Under the incessant pressure of the financial crisis – though also to conciliate the SPD, whose passive 'toleration' was essential if the policy of rule by emergency decree was to be continued given the political balance in the Reichstag – the cabinet was forced to complement the Crisis Levy on public servants' pay with levies on general income tax. These, however, were much more modest in comparison and took considerably longer to take effect. To appease public opinion it was decided to introduce a special tax on company directors' retainers; Brüning also sought to reduce the maximum levels of state pensions, though this would have needed a two-thirds majority in the Reichstag as it required an amendment to the constitution.[131] But these were largely cosmetic exercises. The government's taxation policy continued to be generous in its treatment of agrarian interests and industrialist groups and thus remained largely under the control of the political forces behind the DVP and the Business Party. The consideration lavished on DVP interests, despite the fact that that party was effectively siding more and more with the opposition rather than with the government, was a major factor contributing to the confusion in the government's taxation and pay policies. If Brüning had accepted the solution of a general increase in income tax proposed by the SPD in July 1930, the internal inconsistencies of his financial policy would not have been so pronounced.[132]

The programme of expenditure reductions was carried out mainly at the expense of the weakest groups in society and of the internal homogeneity and public standing of the public administration. The raising of the retirement age, delays in filling promotional vacancies, the trend towards contraction in pay scales, the various bans on recruitment, the abolition of posts and the privileged treatment of civil servants on retainers all had negative effects on staffing policy and planning, especially with regard to the age structure in the public service. In terms of the overall economy, these measures led to a further rise in youth unemployment; Groener in particular, as army minister, repeatedly warned the cabinet about the dangerous political consequences of this.[133] A situation in which there were numerous unemployed secondary school leavers and university graduates, including many young trained teachers and solicitors, greatly enlarged the potential pool of NSDAP supporters. It was not purely coincidental that within the civil service resistance to salary reductions was most intense in the Army Ministry and the president's entourage. This was illustrated by General von Schleicher's comment to State Secretary Schäffer that civil servants had to cease being used as political pawns and that the policy of progressively lowering civil servants' salaries was one of Brüning's biggest political mistakes.[134] Even though the civil service issue was not a direct cause for the fall of Brüning's government, it certainly contributed to the deterioration in the chancellor's personal relationship with Hindenburg in so far as the president grew increasingly apprehensive as to whether Brüning's directives on salaries were at all compatible with the provisions for rule by emergency decree laid down in Article 48 of the constitution.

The fact that at the birth of the Republic the traditional institution of the professional civil service had been strengthened rather than weakened by the inclusion in the constitution of provisions guaranteeing its status and the strong position in which the civil servants' associations had emerged militated both legally and politically against the Brüning government's salaries policy from the start.[135] What had been welcomed during the prewar era of 'national rallying' of the parties of the centre and the right as a stabilizing factor guaranteeing continuity in the state proved in the economic crisis to be an unexpectedly difficult obstacle to any attempt to dismantle what was seen as the atrophied administrative apparatus and to hold in check the civil servants' assertion of their interests as a group. Even after the Salaries Bill had been enacted in 1927 the civil servants' associations complained that their salary conditions had fallen behind 1913 levels and lodged a claim for restitution. The vigorous attempts by the parties of the Weimar Coalition to republicanize the public service were wantonly attacked by the parties of the right as a recipe for a 'card-carrying civil service', which only served to reinforce latent anti party political and anti-parliamentary resentments.[136] The regular calls for a professional 'non-political' civil service strengthened the position of the civil servants' associations, who then skilfully used them in the parliamentary arena itself to further their interests. This was clearly demonstrated by the central role played by the salaries question in both the dissolution of the Grand Coalition and the evolution of the Brüning government into an openly presidential regime.

As with the legislative instruments of Article 48 of the constitution, attempts during the Weimar Republic to restructure the legal status of civil servants within the terms of the constitutional guarantees they enjoyed failed, in spite of several attempts. The Civil Service Act of 1873 remained the legal framework, supplemented by the Civil Service Acts of the various Länder and particularly that of Prussia. The urgent need for a unitary legal status for civil servants throughout the Reich was never tackled, even in the Brüning era, despite the fact that the necessary preparatory work had been completed. This was finally to be used by the Nazi minister for the interior, Wilhelm Frick, as the basis for the German Civil Servants' Act of 1937, the last constitutional reform promulgated during the Third Reich.[137] Even measures unconnected with financial problems which could have contributed to a unitary legal code for civil servants, such as the Civil Servants' Representation Act and the Public Service Disciplinary Act, made no headway.[138] Rather than tackling the long overdue need for a unitary system covering salary and career structures, Brüning's deliberately uncoordinated measures to reduce expenditure had the effect of increasing the discrepancies in the legal codes covering the various civil service systems of the Reich, the *Länder* and the municipalities.

At the centre of the dispute was the question as to how the pledge to secure the 'established incremental privileges of civil servants' (*die wohlerworbene Rechte der Beamten*) contained in Article 129 of the Weimar constitution should be conceptually and practically realized. Despite the provisory clauses in the Salaries Acts, the attitude most dominant in legal interpretations until well into the economic crisis was that these incremental privileges included standards of pay and particularly of pensions, which were regarded as a deferred element of salary. This helps to explain the reluctance of the Brüning cabinet to consider the idea of a straightforward cut in civil servants' salaries. This legal aspect played such a considerable role that at first the only idea discussed by the cabinet was the introduction of a temporary emergency levy or short-term solidarity contribution by public service employees. The idea occasionally mooted to employ the fiction that a part of civil servants' salaries was being temporarily withheld, to be repaid later, is only comprehensible in this context.[139] During the Grand Coalition's period in government Brüning had been among those who had argued that an emergency levy would be unconstitutional and would therefore require a two-thirds majority in the Reichstag.[140] The proposal originally put forward by the SPD, and later exploited to great success by the NSDAP, to restrict salaries and pensions to a maximum of 12,000 RM and 6,000 RM respectively was repeatedly rejected in cabinet as unconstitutional.

Doubts as to the constitutionality of implementing salary reductions by emergency decree were only finally removed by a Reichsgericht ruling of 10 July 1931.[141] Although this ruling did not completely endorse the theory which was advanced by Carl Schmitt in support of the government's position[142] that the constitution's provisions covering professional civil servants were purely an 'institutional guarantee', it did allow for salary reductions on the basis of the Salaries Acts' provisory clauses. Salary cuts could therefore be introduced by simple legislation. Up to this point the Brüning cabinet had been acting just within the bounds of what was legally permissible and subsequently it was to remain a matter of dispute as to whether the emergency decree provisions of Article 48 were applicable to the area of civil service pay or whether this was solely the prerogative of the Reichstag. Salary reductions where the relevant regulations did not include a provisory clause, as was often the case with contracts covering municipal officials, were the subject of particularly intense legal speculation.[143]

It would go beyond the bounds of this analysis to attempt to detail the legal matters at issue in the area of civil servants' status and pay, complicated as they were by the fact that, due to the lack of legislative regulations in this area, the legal situation was governed to a large extent by rulings in individual cases by the highest courts, which by their nature are difficult to generalize. Carl Schmitt's theory of the 'institutional guarantee' largely reduced the state's obligation to merely maintaining the security of civil servants' career and pension structures. It precipitated a wide-ranging constitutional debate which centred increasingly on the character of the civil servant's contract.[144] Whereas the Reichsfinanzhof tended towards Carl Schmitt's position on civil servants' pay, the Reichsgericht took a middle position: while a civil servant's pay represented 'a subjective, established and legally valid claim to the full status of an established incremental right', certain reductions were permissible on the basis of provisory clauses when they did not affect the security of civil servants' 'income as defining their social standing'.[145] This certainly put an effective legal limit, difficult to assess exactly, to any further salary reductions.

The fact that the originally widespread legal reservations about both material measures and the jurisdiction of the Reichstag dropped more and more into the background illustrates the extent to which the Weimar constitution fell into abeyance and the presidential cabinet system, developing rapidly under the conditions of the financial crisis, grew in self-confidence. Following the ruling by the Reichsgericht, the government rushed to draft a Law Altering Civil Servants' Legal Standing and to prepare a stricter definition of civil servants' status. This was to be based on the formal issuing of a certificate of appointment, so as to limit the basis for claims to rights of appointment or salary increments apparently possible under existing civil service law.[146] But the position regarding reductions in pensions remained unclear and this occasioned the presidential Chancellery to warn against attempting to proceed in this area with measures not clearly covered by the provisions of Article 48 of the constitution.[147] If the limits of deflationary policy as it affected the area of public service pay had not already been obvious, it can be safely assumed that Brüning's and Steger-wald's considerably more ambitious plans in other areas would not have secured the blessing of the courts. The changing attitudes of the leading members in both Brüning cabinets towards expanding the system of rule by emergency decree is an indication of how completely the authoritarian mode of presidential government had triumphed.

The attitude of government officials as a whole cannot be deduced from the relatively compliant behaviour of the courts and of public lawyers. The cuts in salary and the numerous accompanying measures affecting their career prospects and concrete employment conditions as well as their material situation were regarded by civil servants, with the exception of relatively small groups of senior officials, as an attack on their incremental rights. The agitation by the parties of the right, originally directed against the SPD and the Centre Party for their alleged undermining of the professional civil service, was now turned against Brüning, despite his government's formal commitment to maintain the status of the professional civil service. This led to an increase among civil servants in support for the parties of the right, especially as they effectively combined their attack with a sharp polemic against disciplinary measures taken against civil servants whose open support for the 'National Opposition' (the DNVP and the NSDAP) had led to flagrant breaches of their duty to political neutrality in office. The attempts by the government to exploit civil servants' sense of loyalty, its mistaken belief that there was no limit to the demands it could make on public officials' 'sense of duty to the state' and the manner in which it pushed their willingness to accept sacrifices to the extreme finally led to open conflict between the civil servants' associations and Brüning's presidential cabinet in June 1931.

One of the most catastrophic effects of Brüning's deflationary policy was the political radicalization of civil servants who increasingly believed that only a fundamental change in the political system could bring any improvement in their situation. In the absence of detailed examinations it is difficult to make an accurate assessment of the susceptibility of civil servants at this time to the propaganda of the NSDAP and also to some extent of the KPD. The rise of communist civil servants' associations and the success of communist propaganda among civil servants were noted with alarm by both the ministry of the interior and the Prussian government.[148] Advances by the NSDAP among medium-level and higher civil servants was much more marked, however, particularly among finance, postal and customs officials; this last group was almost totally under national socialist influence by early 1932.[149] Yet the chancellor tended to ignore the reports on these developments coming to him from all quarters as he did not want to jeopardize the NSDAP–Centre Party coalitions he wished to see emerge in the Länder by enforcing measures preventing civil servants from canvassing for the NSDAP. He turned a deaf ear to appeals in this regard from the Länder, and especially to the call by the Prussian government to enforce at Reich level the measures it had adopted in Prussia.[150] Due to Brüning's lack of interest and his delaying tactics, measures drafted particularly by Groener and Wirth along Prussian lines with the support of the leading civil servants' bodies were never implemented.[151] This produced a growing sense of helplessness at national socialist infiltration of the public administration. Incidents became ever more frequent in which republican-minded civil servants were disciplined by national socialist superiors or were obliged to make financial contributions to the NSDAP by threats that they would otherwise lose their positions following the impending change of regime.[152]

The signs of political disintegration within the public service were not solely or perhaps even mainly a result of the disastrous civil service policy pursued during the Brüning era. At the same time, the accusation that Brüning, in contrast to the Prussian government, failed to take virtually any steps to contain the growth of NSDAP influence among civil servants still carries much weight. His 'taming' concept and his aim of keeping open the possibility of a broad coalition of the right played a crucial role in this. But the thorough collapse of confidence among civil servants in the presidential regime was an even more important factor, for without this the agitation by the extreme right would hardly have achieved such major successes among them. The destruction of civil servants' traditional sense of loyalty to the government and its transfer to the parties of the extreme right could have at least been partly avoided, as the positive reaction by civil servants' associations to the sympathetic policy adopted by Chancellor Schleicher was later to show.[153] The crisis revealed that the traditional assumptions that the interests of the bureaucracy were identical to those of the state and that civil servants identified first and foremost with the 'political requirements of state' were no longer valid. On the contrary, civil servants were merely an interest group like any other, even if better organized than most. The adherence to the myth that the public official was always willing to make sacrifices in the interests of the state illustrates the esoteric political outlook of Brüning and of the conservative bureaucratic groupings which supported his regime. But, to the extent that this outlook also sought a weakening in the authority of the state, it undermined and finally destroyed the psychological and political preconditions for the destabilized Republic to be restabilized along authoritarian, state-administrative lines.

Brüning's policy towards the civil service – the financial elements of which were to be perpetuated by the national socialist regime[154] – had a deeply unsettling effect on public officials; it played a decisive part in paralysing their will to resist the destruction of legal norms by the Nazi regime and facilitated the process by which they sought to accommodate the new system following the Nazi seizure of power, even to the extent of disowning the traditions of Prussian public administration. This end result, while certainly not intended by Brüning, was in large measure a consequence of his political expediency and of the extreme tensions induced by his deflationary programme. Brüning held rigidly to his deflationary policy despite being fully conscious of its negative effects on the economy in order to secure the long-term economic and political power position of the Reich. But, in addition, the worst effects of the policy of expenditure cuts across the board, which was technocratically applied from above, had to be felt by those very areas of the state infrastructure – particularly the educational system – which were most capable of being used to check the rise of the radical forces of the extreme right and left, which were destroying the public structures of the state.

Brüning equally failed to realize that state intervention in the material structure of the public service was a vital tool of social policy. If at the start of his chancellorship social policy in the narrow sense and policy towards the civil service were regarded as areas of spending where the costs of one could be offset by savings in the other, both were to suffer considerable contraction when deflationary policies and expenditure cuts in direct social spending and in the public service together produced a growing financial burden on the lowest-income groups. The situation induced by state measures to depress wages and salaries led inexorably to the dismantling of the system of collective bargaining, which was later officially sanctioned by von Papen, and hence to a progressive decline in the power of broad sections of the population to assert their social interests. Administrative reforms, which were long overdue in themselves and required an overall concept of the long-term aims being pursued, needed to be patiently planned and carefully executed in a series of individual stages. But these had had to be abandoned precisely because of the sweeping nature of the expenditure cuts which were undertaken.

In this way, Brüning's concept of comprehensive reform on the domestic front cancelled itself out as heterogeneous political aims conflicted with one another. An opportunity was squandered to prepare the ground for a thorough and constructive reform of the public administration and to create a legal basis for the public service suited to the conditions of a highly industrialized state. The consequences of this are nakedly apparent today. But it is difficult to avoid the conclusion that the fatal consequences of the policies pursued by the presidential cabinets have hardly been grasped in the Federal Republic. Instead of the structural reforms long overdue in the public service, political pressures and growing budgetary deficits have recently led to its superficial shortcomings being tackled with precisely the kind of measures which during the Brüning era contributed so decisively to escalating social and political tensions.

6

Heinrich Brüning as Chancellor:

The Failure of a Politically Isolated Strategy

Brüning's political isolation as chancellor

The debate on Heinrich Brüning's politics as chancellor, given new impetus since the publication of his memoirs,[1] shows the limits of historical interpretations based on the actions of particular individuals. The final crisis of the Weimar Republic, together with the progressive destruction of its parliamentary system and the political neutralization of the SPD, occurred during the era of the presidential cabinets and are not explicable solely by reference to the actions of individual politicians; they merely executed the carefully planned designs of certain dominant social interests. These plans were expressed ever more forcefully as the international economic crisis escalated.

In Brüning's case, however, an analysis of his personal motives and aims is important because, as chancellor, he pursued what in many ways was his own independent line and adhered to it with remarkable rigidity, despite the mounting political resistance which in the end he was unable to control. Even his political associates had only a vague picture of what this strategy entailed. Brüning's posthumously published memoirs altered little in the overall picture which specialists had already formed of this era.[2] They nevertheless attracted great attention because the apparently honest picture they presented of the chancellor's political aims differed in several major respects from what contemporaries, including political supporters and close associates of the chancellor, had believed these were. This creates a major historical problem in interpreting the Brüning era, for how could leading political figures of the time have been so mistaken in their judgements of him? This was as true of associates of the chancellor like Alfred Hugenberg and Ernst Scholz as it was of opponents like Otto Braun and Rudolf Hilferding.

Political situations arise in which leading actors gain a freedom to manoeuvre, albeit only an apparent one, because the major trends and forces in society are balanced in a temporary stalemate. Heinrich Brüning's chancellorship was only possible because the Republic had reached such an impasse. While the republican forces had lost the initiative and lacked the will to reassert their position, the parties and forces of the right did not yet consider the time ripe to proceed to monopolize power. Brüning became chancellor during this transitionary phase. He firmly believed that there was a realistic political course he could pursue which would enable him to realize the 'comprehensive solution' he envisaged, revive Bismarck's adroit diplomacy in both domestic and foreign politics, control the political forces opposed to him and force them to concur with his strategy. But this was an exercise in self-delusion and his politics progressively lost touch with reality.

Despite his complicated tactical manoeuvrings and the lip service he paid to domestic and foreign policy realities, Brüning's political strategy ultimately amounted to a policy of 'going it alone'. He refused to reveal the overall context that shaped his political strategy and prevented any discussion of its premises or aims, even among his closest associates. This reinforced both the dogmatic tendency of his politics and his increasingly doctrinaire refusal to accept political realities which contradicted his plans. He often tried to explain away such contradictions, particularly where domestic issues were concerned. This is why he was later totally unable to understand why he had failed politically, other than in terms of devious intrigues and duplicitous manoeuvres by certain opponents.[3] His memoirs betray a clear desire to portray the politics he pursued as the product of a systematically thought-out system, as a type of 'grand design'. This may help to explain the psychological element in his behaviour. He presents himself during his period as chancellor as a statesman toppled just as his final goals were within grasp. He fell, he claims, only because President von Hindenburg and his entourage failed to understand what he was attempting to achieve. This was despite the fact that it was he who had finally solved the reparations issue and was the only one who could have carried out the major domestic reforms so urgently needed and have crowned them with a return to a constitutional monarchy. All the careful preparations he had made were wantonly squandered by his successors.

Any attempt to distinguish between the picture which Brüning later drew of his aims as chancellor and what they actually were at the time would be fraught with difficulties even if reliable editions of his memoirs and correspondence were available. Several factual discrepancies can, however, be clarified. The plan which he claims to have had for re-establishing the monarchy, for example, cannot possibly have existed in the form described in the memoirs.[4] But this does not help explain how Brüning's aims were so 'misunderstood' by contemporaries. He had a general tendency when dealing with people, whether speaking or in writing, to use tactical ploys to disguise his real political intentions and this militates against any attempt to clearly separate his contemporary motives from the retrospective explanations he offers in his memoirs and letters.

Brüning was later rarely prepared to admit that his policies had had to change constantly in response to the deepening economic and political crises, which were of a kind and severity never experienced before. He could not accept that he had to some extent been more a prisoner of events than in control of them. What the ex-chancellor sought to portray in his memoirs as a coherent long-term political strategy actually comes across to the historian as an extraordinarily flexible system of tactical stopgap measures. He hoped, in his characteristically doctrinaire way, that he would solve the central political problems facing Germany in a matter of a few years. For him, these were the reparations question and, connected to it, the issue of disarmament. He also aimed to fundamentally restructure the German economic and financial systems, reform the political structure of the Reich, establish a new system of municipal financing, initiate certain constitutional reforms and reconstruct the parliamentary system along Bismarckian lines. He was skilled at concealing these ambitious aims or at only initimating to others the logic which in his mind bound them together in a coherent whole. In fact he did achieve a solution to the reparations problem, but only at a cost in domestic politics which was far too high by any standards. Brüning could not grasp even in retrospect that the room to manoeuvre which he had appeared to have and which had in reality been continually contracting was totally dependent on the extent to which he was both prepared to serve and could succeed in serving the interests of particular ascendant groups. Due to the international as well as domestic balance of political forces, these groups could not risk being publicly identified with the political decisions they wanted implemented at this stage.

During Brüning's period as chancellor the government and the state bureaucracy which carried out its decisions attempted to assert their independence of social and political forces.[5] The resultant balancing act appeared to have some success at first. But it ended with the government being completely dependent on the dominant elites in society and the constitutional framework of the state being totally undermined. This was reflected in the development of government towards a pure presidential system, which reached its peak in early 1932, and also in the esoteric style of the Brüning regime. Part of the problem was the chancellor's sometimes pathological belief that important decisions should be reached only within small groups of trusted advisers and then presented as accomplished facts to the relevant constitutional bodies, whether the cabinet, the Reichstag or the Reichsrat. Brüning's chancellorship witnessed a protracted and thorough erosion of the democratic decision-making process. There were certainly precedents for this, notably during Hans Luther's period as chancellor. Brüning's inclination to 'go it alone' and to exclude not only the Reichstag but finally even the Reichsrat from any political say was illustrated by the establishment during his chancellorship of semi-constitutional bodies, such as the Economic Advisory Council, as well as in his repeated attempts to legitimize decisions through conferences with party leaders or Länder premiers and in the establishment of the 'Finance Circle' within the cabinet. Cabinet colleagues frequently discovered that they had not been fully informed on important decisions before these were taken and were often confronted with *faits accomplis*. This happened, for example, to Dietrich, the minister for finance, on the issue of the Austro-German Customs Union.[6] During the summer of 1931 the feeling that they were totally in the dark regarding Brüning's real aims rapidly gained ground among his immediate associates.[7]

It was not in Brüning's nature to seek popular support for his political position. His public statements centred mainly on calls to persevere through difficult times and reminiscences of the First World War. They were strained and lacked the conviction that might have given some credibility to the sacrifices he demanded of the nation. He avoided as far as possible clearly stating his political intentions. On the reparations issue, where his strongest arguments undoubtedly lay, he repeatedly shrank from clearly explaining the logic of his position. Even his supporters could not understand why he stalled on the reparations problem and delayed resolving it. It was understandable therefore that the general public only grasped particular aspects of his policy at any given time. By refusing to draw even his government partners into his confidence and by leaving them ignorant of the long-term aims of his strategy, he fell victim to the distrust he had himself sown and which finally spread to the president's office too, thus eroding his last bastion of support.

The increasing marginalization of the Reichstag was underscored when the parties of the 'National Opposition' dramatically withdrew from it on 9 February 1931 in protest at the adoption of a motion reforming order of business procedures. While this had a positive effect on the House's ability to function,[8] it offered only an illusory respite to the government. This was because the growing irrelevance of party politics which it signified led to direct pressure on the cabinet from organized interest groups rising proportionally as the importance of parliamentary connections declined. As a rule, Brüning avoided dealing directly with such groups for he feared, not without reason, that this would lead to concessions being made on the rigorous financial policy he was pursuing. His characteristic response to such advances was to refer them to the ministers directly responsible, despite the fact that the system of rule by emergency decree had left these with little authority to act autonomously. Brüning had little sympathy for those who argued that he ought to make some concessions, even if only verbal ones, to the leaders of the main interest groups so as to enable them to dispel the mounting unrest in their ranks. Typical of this was the manner in which he dealt with the civil servants' associations. These had been particularly hard hit by the government's deflationary policy of salary cuts and rationalization measures in the public administration.[9]

Brüning's repeated appeals for sacrifices in the national interest could not deflect the pressure from the main social interest groups in the long term, though these had at first generally tended to accept in principle the need for the deflationary policy the government was pursuing. This had been true even of the trade unions, but the failure of Brüning's economic strategy to produce results, along with the escalating economic crisis and the disastrous growth in mass unemployment, forced them increasingly into a polemical confrontation with the government, although there was no practical alternative to it. Brüning's rather half-hearted attempts to revive the idea of a Central Working Association of employers and unions (ZAG) failed. So too had his previous attempts to contain the smouldering conflict between heavy industry and the Free Trade Unions by forming an Economic Advisory Council consisting of representatives of both.[10] Large landed interests, in a strong position from the start given the unequivocal support they enjoyed from the president, ignored the chancellor's weak appeals for restraint. Instead, they forced him to pursue an agricultural policy which directly contradicted the logic of his wage and price reduction measures. Despite Brüning's concessionary attitude towards it, the large landed interest finally turned against him completely. The agricultural lobby accused him of 'agricultural bolshevism' because of his plans to use insolvent East Elbian estates for his land resettlement programme, and this confirmed Hindenburg in his determination to break with the chancellor at the first available opportunity.[11]

The large landed interest played a major role in toppling Brüning. But this should not detract from the fact that lobbying by associations representing bourgeois interests, as well as the increasing tendency of interest groups to sidestep both the Chancellery and government ministries and concentrate their efforts directly on the president's office, were equally important in contributing to Hindenburg's growing lack of faith in the chancellor's policies. Brüning's precarious balancing act and his propensity to deflect political pressure by making promises he could not keep in the end of the day satisfied no one. He underestimated the danger to his position represented by the growing alienation of the major interest groups from his government. In his memoirs he commented bitterly that 'the agitation by representatives of various interests continued remorselessly as if nothing had changed . . . While the Reichstag gradually and quite willingly surrendered many of its prerogatives, the interest group lobbyists whipped popular anger up to a pitch.'[12] He failed to recognize the direct connection that existed between the marginalization of the Reichstag and the decline in the influence of political parties on the one hand and the increasing power of lobby groups in the non-parliamentary area of politics on the other.

It is therefore an oversimplification to argue that President von Hindenburg, by dropping Brüning, bore the main responsibility for his fall. The Reichstag majority prepared to passively tolerate the government was certainly no longer in a position to play any role in bringing him down. Brüning fell because he was not prepared to co-operate in reconstructing the government on the more firmly right-wing basis sought by the president as he feared the negative effects this would have on foreign policy, in particular the weakening of the German position at the forthcoming Lausanne Conference. Brüning attempted to stabilize his cabinet by introducing prominent right-wing figures after Warmbold and Groener resigned. But this move failed after bourgeois interest groups, which were no longer prepared to support the government and sought a fundamental change of course, brought their pressure to bear. In a speech to the Reichstag Foreign Affairs Committee in May 1932 Brüning personally appealed for his government not to be toppled 'a hundred yards before its goal'. By this he did not mean an end to the economic crisis, but the final abolition of reparations and a decisive breakthrough in the disarmament negotiations.[13] Brüning resigned when he realized that the president was determined to form a new cabinet after the Lausanne Conference with Brüning as foreign minister. What actually happened was thus precisely what Brüning had hoped to be able to prevent: rather than securing his presidential cabinet and forming the basis for him to proceed with a comprehensive programme of domestic political reforms, the decisive success in foreign policy now in sight in fact signalled the end of his transitional government and its replacement by a regime controlled by a clique around the president. This clique openly plotted the introduction of an authoritarian system, was dismissive of the Reichstag and naïvely believed it could win over the popular support then enjoyed by the NSDAP by enacting some of its policies – thereby breaking Alfred Hugenberg's notorious intransigence and bringing the DNVP in behind the regime.

Brüning's policies and the reparations question

Many of Brüning's contemporaries believed that while a resolution to the economic crisis may not have been his main priority, he certainly concentrated much of his attention on this question. This impression arose because of his budgetary policy, which was generally regarded by both public opinion and the economic thinking then dominant as the correct path to economic recovery. The measures he introduced to depress wage and price levels were open to being misinterpreted as an intention to stimulate increased economic activity. Brüning's supporters have repeatedly claimed that the chancellor was acting in accordance with contemporary economic thinking.[14] But this claim needs to be qualified as Brüning personally met and talked to J. M. Keynes and was constantly publicly called upon to increase mass spending power, a thoroughly popular idea at the time. He dismissed demands for an artificial stimulation of credit with political rather than economic arguments. There are indications that he deliberately intended his policies to deepen the economic crisis as he hoped that this would enable Germany to get over the worst of the crisis before other comparable industrial states.[15]

As against earlier interpretations of Brüning's economic and financial policy, there is a widespread consensus today that the chancellor was more interested in 'deliberately deepening the crisis' than in defeating it.[16] One of the main reasons for this was that he saw the economic crisis as a direct product of the reparations system, and hence of the vicious cycle of financing reparations payments which had arisen round the USA, its western creditors and, as the debtor nation, the German Reich. Consequently he believed that the economic crisis could not be tackled effectively until the reparations issue was resolved and the international currency system reorganized. From the start, therefore, he regarded measures to tackle the crisis as secondary to solving the reparations question. He hoped he could achieve this on the basis of successfully managing the domestic budget through a policy of rigorous deflation.

It is often presumed that Brüning's almost dogmatic adherence to the principle of deflation arose from his experience of the hyperinflation in Germany after World War I. Although memories of the inflationary era played an important part in the consciousness of business and political people, this factor should not be overrated in assessing Brüning's own position. In the early 1920s he had held that the only way the Reichsmark could be restabilized was if the reparations problem was solved and had claimed that reparations payments were the principal cause of the inflation.[17] Germany was prevented by the Young Plan from devaluing the Mark below its 1923 rate. But it was not on account of such treaty obligations that he refused to sanction a devaluation in October 1931. This was forcefully demanded at the time, particularly by the export-dependent sections of heavy industry, following the drop in the value of sterling.[18] He was determined to reserve this interventionist instrument for a strategically more favourable moment. His intention was to apply a 20 per cent devaluation of the Mark once the economic crisis had passed. The idea of using devaluation as a strategic instrument was constantly in his mind and he was later to propose that the Mark be devalued by 40 per cent.[19] He was also quite willing to exempt certain sectors of the economy, notably agriculture, from his general policy of deflation.

Brüning's combination of devaluation abroad and deflation at home shows quite clearly that he was acting on the basis not so much of theoretical economic dogmas as of his own strategic aim: he foresaw using the ending of reparations as an instrument to secure long-term trading advantages and thus to reassert Germany's former position in the world market. From this perspective, it is hardly surprising that Brüning sought to take advantage of the economic crisis to further German interests. This entailed a two-pronged approach. On the one hand, he hoped the international effects of the crisis would convince the western powers that the schedule of repayments set out in the Young Plan was unviable from an economic and financial point of view. On the other, he was convinced that the financial and economic restructuring of the German economy which his deflationary policy would produce, and which he regarded as essential anyway if reparations were to be finally abolished, would leave Germany in a very favourable position economically at the end of the crisis. His aim was to re-establish a starting position for Germany equivalent to what it had been in 1913. 'The first country prepared to implement all the unpopular domestic measures necessary', he told Hitler when revealing his plan to him on 6 October 1930,[20] 'will rise to the top.' 'Those countries', he added, referring to the crisis, 'which are affected by it last would also be the last to take the countermeasures necessary to deal with it and would thus fall behind.' What lay behind this was his basic belief that he could use economic policy measures as a means to reverse the Versailles Peace Treaty in a series of stages and thus realize one of his chief strategic aims.

Brüning believed that the depression would not be overcome before the end of 1933. From some of his individual statements it would seem that he did not expect any real upswing in the economy before 1935.[21] He was fully aware that the economic and financial policy he was pursuing not only demanded considerable 'domestic sacrifices' but was also bound to have long-term effects on Germany's trading partners and thus generally deepen the crisis internationally. In early 1932 he told the Reichstag Foreign Affairs Committee that his government's financial policy would have 'automatic consequences for the whole world economy'.[22] But it seems that he did not give sufficient consideration to the fact that, given Germany's dependency on foreign trade, the increasing of tariffs by Germany's trading partners had to have a detrimental effect on the chances of success of his declared aim of reducing wage and price levels in Germany.

As the economic crisis continued to escalate, Brüning showed some signs of beginning to doubt whether his policy of trimming public expenditure while simultaneously depressing wage and price levels could be adhered to indefinitely. In conversation with State Secretary Hans Schäffer he expressed his fear that there could be a point where deflation would rebound into inflation.[23] But he pushed such thoughts from his mind. The polemical tone of his attacks on those who advocated an artificial stimulation of credit[24] was probably a subconscious product of the personal doubts he harboured about the correctness of his financial policy, though he naturally never revealed these in public. He dismissed the clamour for comprehensive job creation programmes on the basis that they would run counter to his strategy on the reparations issue and would prevent a future upswing in the economy.[25] The key to understanding Brüning's deflationary measures and his rigid adherence to the principle of balancing budgets lies not so much in his orthodox views on financial policy as in the foreign policy aims he was attempting to realize above and beyond a simple resolution of the reparations question.

Brüning's medium-term aim was to reduce the Reich's economic dependence by a programme of comprehensive cuts in public expenditure at all levels, including the Länder and municipalities. He believed this would also serve to reverse what he saw as the habits and omissions of a decade of mistaken financial policies. From this basis, Germany, despite her military weakness, would be in a position to take a firm stand in negotiations with the former victor powers.[26] Brüning's thinking thus converged increasingly with the illusion widespread on the right at the time that the establishment of economic autarchy in Germany was both feasible and desirable.

Any proper assessment of Brüning's political strategy must appreciate the overall context in which he himself saw it. In this, economic 'reassertion' was closely tied to the abolition of reparations and fundamental changes in the domestic political structure. These centred above all on the need for a dramatic reduction in the size of the public administration, a curtailment of the parliamentary powers of the Länder and Reichsreform in favour of a centralized unitary state. The domestic and foreign policy objectives pursued by the presidential cabinets he led were thus inextricably linked and were seen as such by the forces behind them. His now notorious insistence that Centre Party support for ratification of the Young Plan be made conditional on a balanced budget, which he only very reluctantly dropped at the time, was clearly a product of this outlook, which had its roots in the early 1920s.[27] It would be misleading therefore to presume that the chancellor regarded financial austerity measures as ends in themselves or that the strategy he pursued, however much it was in line with the anti-parliamentarian and semi-authoritarian tendencies of the period after the bourgeois bloc cabinets, was basically an apolitical and 'pragmatic' one. Such an interpretation would lead to the conclusion that Brüning deliberately ignored the major interest groups in society and acted purely out of loyalty to a formal concept of the interests of state.[28] But this confuses two questions. The chancellor drove himself into political isolation by recklessly pursuing overambitious political aims while successfully concealing the actual motives which lay behind his politics. These aims have become clear since the appearance of his memoirs.

The experience of World War I and of Germany's military defeat had a profound influence on the generation of politicians to which Brüning belonged. Their attitudes towards domestic politics and foreign relations were inextricably interlinked in a single syndrome. Brüning first made his name as a finance politician, but his views on financial policy were closely tied from the start to the reparations question. Together with the inflation problem, this was the central issue of German financial policy throughout the Weimar Republic, though in retrospect the reparations payments actually made appear quite small. An article on the 'Reconstruction of our German Finances' published by Brüning in 1921[29] is a clear example of his attitude. He argued that the Versailles Treaty had to be destroyed if the finances of Europe as a whole were to be restabilized. It would be pointless to restructure Germany's financial system and devalue its currency in advance of this, he claimed, as this would only precipitate another inflationary crisis.[30] Brüning believed that Germany's financial recovery required ruthless cuts in public spending and he therefore criticized the expansion which had occurred in the administrative structures and public services during the war and pre-war period.

Brüning was convinced that the German economy could not survive in the foreseeable future without foreign loans and that these were also needed to meet reparations payments. But he regarded borrowing by the state as a purely temporary expedient. He called in particular for foreign credit not to be used to cover public spending as this would destroy Germany's room to manoeuvre on the reparations issue. But statements by Brüning on the question of borrowing were not always consistent. While he sometimes advocated the prompt repayment of interest on foreign loans as a lever to secure concessions from the creditor nations on reparations, at other times he used Germany's loans problem to stall progress in the disarmament negotiations.[31] Brüning believed that to solve the reparations problem it was essential that the often thoughtless resort to foreign loans to cover budget deficits be replaced by a firm financial policy. He also believed that the extent of Germany's real financial resources had to be clarified. During the negotiation of the Young Plan, Brüning had been deeply affected by the extent of Germany's financial dependence it revealed. The ease with which the Reichstag tended to approve increases in expenditure and the loose attitude to public spending common among municipalities, he told a Centre Party meeting on 8 August 1930,[32] had produced a situation where 'at a time of acute shortage debts are looming everywhere of such a magnitude that they effectively robbed us of any room to manoeuvre at Paris last year'.

A similar line of argument pervaded virtually every statement Brüning made on financial policy. He regularly quoted comments made by Parker Gilbert, the reparations agent, to support these. At the plenary session of the Reichsrat on 4 November 1930, for example, he stressed that the 'legislative programme' he was presenting – that is, the financial and economic measures enacted the following month by emergency decree[33] – were an immediate and 'essential precondition of foreign policy'. The programme of financial legislation was, he said, designed specifically to increase the 'versatility and freedom of our foreign policy'.[34] At the final meeting of this Reichsrat session, Curtius, in seconding the motion approving the chancellor's programme, remarked that the interdependence of domestic and foreign policy was even closer and more immediate at a time of ferment and tension than at other times.[35] Brüning repeatedly appealed to the patriotism of Länder governments, political parties and the general population, asking them to 'persevere' with his financial programme until the 'complete solution' of the reparations problem for which he was striving had been achieved.

But this tactic proved to be double-edged. The public – and even some leading politicians who otherwise fully supported him, such as Eugen Bolz, the state president of Württemberg[36] – could not understand why the chancellor continued to postpone a final resolution of the reparations question. This attitude began to spread among his closest associates as well. State Secretary von Bülow, commenting in April 1932 on Brüning's approach to the reparations issue,[37] declared that 'no one has any idea what the chancellor is really after'. The lack of communication between the chancellor and public opinion was a result of Brüning's desire to wait until a suitable moment after the American presidential elections before commenting on Germany's ability to pay. This was so as not to be forced prematurely into having to accept provisional piecemeal solutions to the reparations problem, which in his view would block the way to a complete resolution of the issue. He could not state this publicly and therefore took the risk of being regarded as 'spineless' by the public and particularly by the parties of the right.

To a certain extent Brüning manoeuvred himself into this no-win position. The cabinet did nothing to disabuse the public of the belief that the reparations payments inflicted on Germany were the root of the economic crisis. The government's rigid adherence to a policy of deflation and expenditure cuts led to increased public calls for a 'resolution of the reparations issue'. Even the unions inclined to the dubious belief that economic recovery would result if the western Allies conceded ground on reparations. The emergency decree of 6 June 1931 was intended to lay the financial basis for the definitive breakthrough on the reparations issue Brüning hoped to achieve at his forthcoming meeting at Chequers. The pressure brought to bear on the cabinet by the parties of the right, acting through the president's court, finally forced Brüning to attempt to deflect the latent opposition to this decree on the domestic front by making his so-called tribute speech.[38] This speech occurred directly as a result of urgings by the DVP. State Secretary Schäffer, one of the chancellor's closest advisers, shared the DVP's belief that a public statement setting out the limits of Germany's ability to pay would have 'the same effect at home' – deflecting pressure from the government – as a postponement of payments would have brought. Brüning hoped it would dispel the growing 'wave of right-wing radicalism' and effectively neutralize the loud demands that DNVP ministers be included in the cabinet.[39] But the 'tribute speech' only fanned suspicions that the increasingly oppressive cuts in public expenditure, particularly in unemployment assistance and civil servants' pay, were to cover the cost of reparations payments. The nationalist tone of the speech brought the government a brief respite at home, but its effect in London and particularly in Paris was a hardening of diplomatic attitudes towards Germany. The main outcome of the 'tribute speech', however, was that the foreign policy victory for Brüning represented by the Hoover Moratorium on reparations payments was nearly lost on public opinion in Germany.

Brüning was plagued by the reasonable fear that if the financial system collapsed Germany would have little option but to concede to what he regarded as France's intolerable demands. One of his main arguments against a cabinet of the right partly controlled by the Nazis was the threat that the DNVP and NSDAP might attempt to reach a hasty deal on reparations to gain short-term popularity and thereby throw away the chance of a final solution to the problem.[40] He was equally worried that the balance of payments difficulties which had arisen since the banking crisis of summer 1931 would become public knowledge and weaken Germany's negotiating position. Referring to the extreme problems in bridging the budgetary gap, Brüning told the cabinet meeting of 12 April 1932 that 'if these things leak out, foreign policy will become impossible. I am making it everyone's duty to act publicly in such a manner as to enable us to survive through next winter as well. That is the only way we can ensure that they don't get the feeling abroad that we have no option but to accept any conditions they choose to impose on us.'[41]

But even before the Lausanne Conference, Brüning's tactic of arguing that foreign policy had to take priority, and of thus excusing the government's passivity in the face of mass unemployment and increasing radicalization on the domestic front, was beginning to rebound on the chancellor. His deflationary policy was partly intended as a means towards comprehensive reforms at home. These were, in particular, a reduction in the state's administrative costs, a dismantling of the social security system and a strengthening of the middle classes. But his foreign policy objectives increasingly dominated his actions and absorbed all his time and concentration almost directly in proportion as domestic resistance to his policies grew. This concentration on foreign policy requirements led him to fatally neglect central political problems on the home front. He was firmly convinced that a solution to the reparations question had to be achieved before he could tackle these. A solution to the reparations issue would, he believed, decisively strengthen his political position at home and ease resistance to the programme of reform he planned to implement. The foreign policy success of which he dreamed was not, however, to produce the watershed in domestic politics he planned. This is to say nothing of the fact that his successor, Franz von Papen, received the credit for the abolition of reparations which had been just in sight as the Brüning government had fallen.

As long as Germany's financial dependence did not permit an open break with the western powers, which Hitler eventually carried out by withdrawing Germany from the League of Nations,[42] any policy other than that pursued by Brüning of loyally adhering to Germany's treaty obligations would have been dangerously irresponsible. This was made abundantly clear when Germany's attempt to go it alone on the issue of an Austro-German Customs Union provoked the withdrawal of French credit, which precipitated the collapse of the Austrian Kreditanstalt and the resultant banking crisis in Germany. This ruled out a dominant role in government for the parties of the right, particularly the DNVP as led by Alfred Hugenberg. Groups otherwise sympathetic to the militant right, including the RdI, backed this view. While they opposed the Young Plan, they could not countenance an open break with the western powers at this stage because of the consequences it would have for the banking system and foreign trade. Brüning's foreign policy strengthened his political position in that it made him 'indispensable' until the abolition of reparations had been achieved and France had been financially weakened by the economic crisis. But this had to change once his foreign policy gamble proved a success. The political balance within Germany during the later years of the Weimar Republic determined that Brüning would be toppled as soon as it appeared that Germany's interests in the reparations and disarmament areas had been secured and that the amalgam of large landed interests and courtier groups in the president's entourage which opposed him could proceed to monopolize political power without risking Germany's international position.[43] In 1930 the fall of the Müller cabinet once it had secured a temporary resolution of the reparations issue – in its case the successful enactment of the Young Plan – had been just as inevitable.

Brüning's domestic policies must be seen in this foreign policy context.

His prime domestic objective was to reverse what he regarded as disastrous developments in the past, especially of the period since the war. These included the growth of the public bureaucracy, the unregulated development of relations between the Reich and the Länder and, connected to this, the need for constitutional reform, though his ideas in this area remained rather sketchy. He regarded the financial reforms implemented by Erzberger as unavoidable at the time, given the obligations imposed by reparations. But he also criticized them for their negative effects on financial management in the Länder and municipalities and called incessantly for a definitive stabilization of the Reich's finances. That, he had declared, must be the ultimate aim of all financial policy. Success in this area would decide 'whether the present form of parliamentarism in Germany can survive or not'.[44] He made similar statements during the campaign for the Reichstag election of September 1930, which was called following the president's dissolution of parliament in July. The use at his instigation of Article 48 of the constitution to achieve this was not, he asserted, part of a fight against parliamentary democracy but was rather part of his 'fight to save parliament'.[45]

The emergence of the presidential system of government

Brüning's attitude to parliamentary democracy is still the subject of intense debate. The publishers of his memoirs claimed that the English parliamentary tradition had been the main influence on him and Werner Conze described him as a committed adherent of the parliamentary democratic system.[46] The memoirs themselves, however, reveal a certain preference for the political system of fascist Italy. Brüning was certainly influenced by the strong affinity with the Italian system – verging on an idealization of Mussolini – prevalent in neo-conservative circles at the time. His understanding of parliamentarism was probably largely shaped by what he regarded as the model constitutional system of the Bismarck era. But he did not put forward specific institutional proposals for changes in this area.

A member of the Reichstag from 1924, Brüning was one of the leading parliamentary figures of the Weimar Republic. His memoirs nevertheless betray an extreme lack of enthusiasm for the institutions of the National Assembly and the Reichstag. He once commented that in the last resort it is possible to govern and to achieve lasting results under any constitution or electoral system 'once certain traditions of responsibility for the general good remain alive in both the people and the government . . . As a type of constitutional 'depositum fidei', these are a more powerful defence against the misuse of governmental power than any formal constitutional ground rules.'[47] This encapsulates virtually completely the anti-parliamentary mentality so widespread among right-wing circles in the Weimar Republic. The same attitude was also evident in his recurring argument that a 'tried and trusted administration' is of much greater importance in governing than a constitution and that it was the civil servants rather than the parliamentarians who had saved Germany from catastrophe in 1918–19.[48]

Brüning was fond of describing his own aim as to 'restructure parliament and the democratic system to make them more effective'.[49] What exactly he meant by this would require a detailed examination of contemporary statements by him. There is considerable evidence, however, that he thought that parliament should act primarily as a check on the executive and that it was out of the question that the Reichstag maintain its sovereignty during periods of crisis. This was why he was such an adamant defender of Article 48 of the constitution.[50] His principal aim was to restrict the Reichstag's authority in financial questions purely to the annual budget. During his period as chancellor, he definitely treated the Reichstag's prerogative to initiate legislation as a highly questionable one. His demand that spending proposals be prohibited unless adequately covered by financial provisions, which he finally had adopted by having the order of business procedures of the Reichstag amended,[51] was partly designed to limit the length of parliamentary sittings. He hoped to persuade the Reichstag to restrict motions of no confidence to budgetary issues, to limit debate on the chancellor's speech and to accept a political position for the head of state 'stronger than that in the Bismarckian constitution'.[52] These proposals were similar to the draft constitutional legislation which the DVP had introduced in December 1928 to limit the provisions of Article 54 but which had failed to secure a majority in the Reichstag. In resubmitting them in 1930, Brüning exploited the fact that a majority in the Reichstag wanted to remove the weapon of motions of no confidence from the right-wing opposition. These had been constantly used, particularly by the NSDAP and the KPD to try to discredit the SPD among its supporters.[53]

The emergence of the presidential system of government during the Brüning era was by no means an inevitable or preordained process. But the use of the full powers of Article 48 in the formation of the Brüning cabinet already marked a clear departure from the norms which had still operated under the Grand Coalition. In March 1930 Brüning had believed that a fundamental change in political direction was essential but wanted to wait until the autumn before precipitating the fall of the Grand Coalition. Tactical considerations were the main reason for this, including fears that a new election might be called.[54] The process of forming the new cabinet went unusually smoothly, but its subsequent development towards a presidential system by no means followed a straight path. In mid-April Brüning succeeded in getting sufficient Reichstag support to pass the contentious emergency budget proposals which had brought down the Grand Coalition.

This was only possible, however, by threatening to dissolve parliament otherwise. The East Elbian landed elite had a particular interest in not endangering the government's Eastern Aid (*Osthilfe*) programme and Brüning exploited this by deliberately making implementation of the programme conditional on the budget being adopted; this played a central role in securing the majority he needed.[55] But during the preparatory work on the financial estimates for 1930 it became clear that new budgetary gaps would emerge due to the fall in tax revenues.

The fall of Hermann Müller's government had been an indirect result of the DVP's refusal to countenance the idea of an emergency levy on those in secure employment. This opposition had forced Chancellor Müller to abandon the proposal. The glaring social injustice of the resulting budget led the Free Trade Unions in turn to insist that the SPD-led government resign. With the inclusion of the 'Reichshilfe der Personen des öffentlichen Dienstes' in the budgetary plan of 5 June 1930, the party political line-up of March re-formed. The DVP rejected the Reichshilfe programme with an ultimatum demanding the introduction instead of a municipal poll tax which would both avoid the need for any increases in rates and simultaneously force municipalities to limit their escalating expenditure on unemployment relief.[56] The DVP, which effectively withdrew Finance Minister Moldenhauer from the cabinet because of his public identification with the government's budgetary programme, was acting under pressure from the RdI and the VdA, key groups of the heavy industry lobby.[57] These were determined to use the economic crisis to force through a thorough dismantling of the social security system, and particularly of state funding of the unemployment insurance system.

A detailed examination of the budgetary plan would go beyond the bounds of this essay. The decisive issue when it came before parliament, however, was that the SPD could not accept the proposal it contained for a poll tax. This was introduced only during the second reading of the Finance Bill. While rejecting the poll tax proposal, the social democrats repeatedly indicated their basic willingness to reach a compromise on the budget. Brüning had included the poll tax so as not to give the parties of the right any excuse to vote against the government. But this meant consciously risking provoking the opposition of the SPD. His strategy failed because of the intransigence of the DNVP. Although Brüning had indicated his intention to force through his budgetary programme by emergency decree under Article 48 if parliament rejected it – which was what in fact happened several days later – his advisers believed at first that the crisis would be resolved by a cabinet reshuffle. The resort to a pure presidential system was thus by no means an option which had been clearly decided upon in advance.[58] Brüning had originally considered demanding that the Reichstag pass an enabling act to allow the adoption of a budget. But he backed down from this because he believed that, as the economic crisis was expected to deepen, he had to retain this weapon for the autumn when he would need it to force through basic financial reforms which could no longer be deferred, including reductions in expenditure on the public service and in civil servants' pay.

The transition to a presidential regime only finally occurred following the governmental crisis which arose when a constitutional majority of the Reichstag rescinded the emergency legislation. Parliament was thereupon dissolved and the emergency legislation re-enacted virtually unchanged by a presidential decree on 26 July 1930. The constitutionality of substantially re-enacting by decree an emergency law rejected by the Reichstag was highly debatable, yet the government secured a court ruling endorsing the legality of its actions.[59] Apart from the clearly conservative and authoritarian mentality which this ruling reflected, it also represented a decisive blow to the authority of parliament.

The disastrous outcome of the September 1930 elections, in line with the trend already evident in the municipal and Landtag elections held during 1929, forced the Brüning cabinet further down the parth of presidential government. This was because both the negotiations aimed at stopping Hitler by making concessions to the NSDAP in Prussia and the efforts to overcome Hugenberg's intransigent refusal to join the government failed. With a minority cabinet, Brüning became totally dependent on the SPD's willingness to tolerate government policies and on the support of President von Hindenburg. The government's base in the parties of the centre, which had originally participated in the cabinet, grew increasingly narrow. Apart from the Centre Party and DVP, which had failed to make any inroads into the electoral support of the DNVP, and some even smaller groups, the government's only reliable partner was the State Party. The DVP increasingly opposed government proposals and the Business Party withdrew from government altogether in December 1930. These were precisely the groups Brüning had been trying to placate when he abandoned all attempts to conciliate the SPD in June 1930.

The withdrawal of the DNVP and the NSDAP (the 'National Opposition') from the Reichstag in February 1931 reduced the role of the House to that of a rump parliament. But the effective marginalization of parliament was already well advanced and was reflected in the ever decreasing number of days on which it met.[60] The important question is to what extent Brüning had consciously sought this development. The government certainly had not originally planned on totally excluding the Reichstag from the political process. But it sought to base its position increasingly on support in the Reichsrat, even if this was originally intended as a provisional measure only. This development was particularly evident in the political preparations which preceded the promulgation by decree of the financial and economic reforms of December 1930. Brüning personally chaired the plenary session of the Reichsrat which dealt with these, referring explicitly to the exemplary role which the Reichsrat had for the Reichstag.[61] But this could not alter the fact that the government was no longer able to muster a permanent majority in the Reichstag, except for legislation of a purely technical nature, and for defeating motions from the opposition to repeal the emergency laws.

The fact that meetings of the Reichsrat committee were confidential made it easier for the cabinet to achieve a consensus between the various Land and party interests represented in it. The practice in the Reichsrat of treating emergency decrees as comprehensive pieces of legislation and the fact that the order of business determined that a bill could only be rejected in full and not in part had the additional effect of suppressing reservations about individual elements of such legislation.[62] Waldemar Besson described the Reichsrat in this connection as acting as a 'substitute legislature'.[63] What motivated Brüning to force the Reichsrat into this position of parliamentary arbiter and to use it as a means of circumventing unfavourable motions in the Reichstag[64] is in need of closer examination. There is some evidence that the government had in mind the constitutional situation which had pertained during the First World War. At that time the Reichsrat had in fact performed the role of substitute legislature and been responsible for financial and economic matters in particular. But it would appear to have been symptomatic that as the Reichstag was increasingly marginalized so the role of the Reichsrat too was gradually reduced. This was particularly so as the gathering momentum acquired by the state bureaucracy as a direct result of the political stalemate led to a decrease in the number of judicial decrees requiring any parliamentary ratification and hence to a decline in the functional role of the Reichsrat.[65] The directing committee of the Reichsrat recorded many formal complaints against this development, claiming that the government was in breach of its duty to report to it as stipulated in Article 67 of the constitution.

The presidential system which emerged under Brüning developed at first as a type of alternative legislature. This was a result of Brüning's determination, regardless of parliamentary balances, to exclude the Reichstag from a say in his programme of financial reforms. He was determined not to endanger the reform programme as a whole by having to engage in political compromises. It was typical of him that he sought to win acceptance for his ideas in cabinet by arguing that if this course were not adopted the Reichstag would proceed to enact much more extreme measures that would be totally unacceptable.[66] At first he tried to gain political support for his government by establishing direct links between his ministries and the various institutions of political life. An informal process developed around the preparation of emergency decrees by the cabinet. This involved meetings with party leaders, consultation with the Reichsrat and occasionally also with the committees of the Reichstag, conferences with Länder governments and the creation of institutions not envisaged by the constitution, such as the Economic Advisory Council. It produced a type of secondary system for legitimizing government action, which tended to require an ever greater recourse to Article 48 and to neutralize the constitutional misgivings to which this had originally given rise.[67]

The rigidity with which Brüning adhered to his programme for a total restructuring of foreign policy once he had embarked upon it automatically led to the system of rule by emergency decree at home continually expanding and gradually shedding its original character as a provisional expedient. This was particularly apparent in the numerous individual decrees covering the most diverse matters, which were now promulgated without expiry dates, as well as those providing for emergency powers for individual ministries and Länder governments. These decrees were increasingly treated as indistinguishable from normal legislation, as, for example, when they were used to amend standing law.[68] Similarly, while not constitutionally obliged to do so, the cabinet tended more and more to forgo even consulting the Reichsrat as had been originally intended. The end result was that legislative authority was effectively transferred to the bureaucracies of the Reich and the Länder. While this corresponded to the chancellor's own personal preferences, in the long run it gave a *carte blanche* to bureaucratic prerogative in the area of legislation. The same trend was reflected in the escalating numbers of Reich commissars appointed during the Brüning era even though no constitutional provision of any kind existed for such appointments.

It was in the logic of this development that the autonomy of the Länder could not remain unaffected and that similar trends towards bureaucratic rationality and a disregard for representative bodies would make themselves felt at that level. This explains the apparent contradiction between Brüning's original attempt to use the Länder, as organized in the Reichsrat, as a base from which to launch his attack on the competence of the Reichstag and his subsequent confrontation with them when he emerged as an opponent of federalism. His rigid deflationary policy included sharp reductions in the financial subsidies paid to the Länder by central government, the object being to force comprehensive cut-backs in the administrative structures of the Länder and municipalities. The latter had certainly relied to an inordinate degree on subsidies from the Reich and had been excessive in their expenditure programmes. This was reflected, for example, in the considerably better pay enjoyed by local government officials compared with their opposite numbers in the Länder and Reich civil services. With the Dietramzell Emergency Decree of 24 August 1931, the chancellor cut deep into the political autonomy of the Länder. The concealed aim of this move was to use the excuse of clearing financial bottlenecks as a lever to bring about the Reichsreform that he planned.[69] But the progress in reforming the structure of the Reich which this was meant to produce was not to come about, partly because the Länder asserted their autonomy by uniting to deal with their financial difficulties; this only further reinforced the chancellor's hostility to them.

The inconsistency of this policy was also demonstrated by Brüning's belief that he could neutralize and destroy the NSDAP by drawing it into coalition governments at Länder level. This was why he insisted on an NSDAP–Centre Party coalition being formed in Hessen while simultaneously planning to undermine the autonomy of the Länder and 'nationalize' the Prussian police and judicial systems if the NSDAP came to power there.[70] But the NSDAP did not fall into the trap Brüning had laid to lure it into a limited passive 'toleration' of his policies. His efforts to keep open the possibility of co-operation with the NSDAP prevented the Länder governments from taking decisive steps against the violent excesses of the SA and the infiltration of the public administration by NSDAP members.[71] However unequivocal his hostility to national socialism may have been, his attempt to make tactical political capital by exploiting the existence of the NSDAP was a disastrous mistake. He failed to realize that the policy of 'tolerating' his regime which the SPD and the Free Trade Unions had adopted was primarily forced on them by their fear of the consequences if the NSDAP came to power. The conflict with Hindenburg and Schleicher and the downfall of Groener – caused by the ban on the SA, which was imposed far too late to have any political effect – may have been the issue which finally toppled the Brüning government. But in the last resort the government fell as a direct result of the chancellor's own prevarication and of his belief that he could postpone having to make clear and unequivocal political choices.

The failure of Brüning's policy of going it alone

The presidential election of early 1932 did not reflect the central confrontation in German politics at the time, but it demonstrated in several ways the extent to which the cabinet was functioning in a political vacuum. Brüning had supported the candidacy of Hindenburg even before he had had any reason to fear that Hitler would emerge as a contender. From late autumn 1931, however, he became increasingly concerned at the prospect of a national socialist challenge for the presidency and this reinforced his determination to draw the NSDAP in some form into the cabinet.[72] The ensuing negotiations to secure parliamentary approval for an extension of the president's tenure of office was a desperate attempt to persuade the

Reichstag, which had virtually ceased to function anyway, to formally con-nive in the elimination of the last vestiges of its authority. But this scheme was as illusory as his calculations that in the not too distant future he would be able to muster the two-thirds constitutional majority he needed for his Reichsreform and for his first tentative steps to reintroduce the monarchy. Memories of the national unity propaganda of the First World War probably played a role in his thinking here, but this would need to be examined separately in detail.

Brüning's politics from late autumn 1931 are reminiscent of a juggler who has lost his balance wrestling to restore control while playing a full hand. His extensive plans to reform the German constitution may only have assumed the proportions of a relatively systematic and coherent programme in the process of writing his memoirs in 1935; in the concrete political situation in which he had been involved they were little more than attempts to rationalize and intellectually justify individual stopgap measures he was forced by circumstances to implement.[73] But even apart from this, his manner of government was characterized by an overstretching of political resources. This resulted directly from his ruthless subordination of financial and economic policy and steps to counter the economic crisis to the exigencies of his foreign policy objectives. This was most clearly evident in his vacillating attitude to the SPD: appealing to alleged 'national interest', he effectively demanded of the party that in support of the regime it set aside its programme and leave itself dangerously exposed, without offering it any clear guarantee that the status quo in social policy would be main-tained. On the contrary, it would seem that he cold-bloodedly set about attempting to split the SPD, which was a policy that would undoubtedly have ultimately antagonized the right as well. Morsey has pointed out that Brüning deliberately used the economic crisis to realize his aims and was quite prepared to make the parties of the centre – including the Centre Party, which formed the backbone of his support – bear the full responsi-bility for the consequences of the policies he had implemented: 'In this way the parties of the right were to have been spared being implicated; they would therefore be in a position, once the crisis had been overcome, to assume governmental control in a Germany which had been strengthened politically and militarily, revived financially, rationalized economically and simultaneously de-parliamentarized, but which would nevertheless have remained a state with an effective constitutional and legal framework.'[74] This pointed characterization requires little embellishment.

Brüning could continue to rely on 'tolerationist' majorities in the Reichs-tag despite the mounting inconsistencies of his deflationary policy and the increasingly disastrous consequences of the economic crisis and mass unemployment. But this was due only to a limited extent to his undoubted gift for tactical politicking. A more substantial reason was the apparently insoluble deadlock in domestic politics brought about by the rise of the Nazi movement and the growth in KPD support which caused such deep anxiety among the SPD and the Free Trade Unions. This was not by any means the only reason. There was a widespread 'faith in the state' among middle-class circles which applauded any development towards an authoritarian system and a diminution in the power of political parties. The chancellor consciously appealed to this and used it to further his position. But, by emasculating the authority of parliamentary institutions, the direct influence of powerful interest groups on government and their freedom from public control was increased. This fact was studiously ignored. It was symptomatic of the political balance in Germany at the time that Brüning had less reason to fear a rebellion from the supporters of the parliamentary system and the Weimar constitution than he had from his opponents on the right. These attacked him for not having broken decisively enough with the party system and regarded even the indirect involvement of the SPD through its 'toleration' of the government as intolerable. Brüning believed he was in full control of the situation. But the reins were bound to begin slipping from his hands the nearer he appeared to come to achieving his goal of a government coalition of the right and a thorough reconstruction of the constitutional system. In so far as he himself was a prisoner of the 'myth' that the Versailles Treaty and the November Revolution could be reversed, he was preparing the ground for Hitler and the conservative right, including the socially reactionary elements of heavy industry. It rings a little hollow therefore, even in retrospect and considering what followed, when Brüning complains in his memoirs that his successors merely carried out the policies he had prepared, but, unlike him, could only do so by destroying the constitution.[75] Breaking the spirit of the constitution and replacing it with formal legalisms was his doing. This contributed to the final destruction of the Weimar Republic just as surely as the systematic escalation of the economic crisis, which he deliberately engineered, produced the atmosphere of utter hopelessness which rebounded in the profound political irrationalism which Hitler could exploit more effectively than any other.

7

National Socialism:

Continuity and Change

Explanations of the national socialist variety of fascism have so far fallen into two categories; one starting from a consideration of the fascist mass movement, the other interpreting the specific features of the national socialist governmental system. Particularly during the immediate aftermath of World War II, stress was laid on the ideological forebears of national socialism[1] and on attempts, starting in the late thirties, to provide a socio-logical explanation, which paid especial attention to the radicalization of the lower middle classes during the Weimar Republic.[2] This line of research belongs to the first type of interpretation and usually assumes that the mobilization of people to the fascist cause during the pre-1933 campaign decisively shaped the policies of the national socialist regime. As against this, almost all Marxist and neo-Marxist theories of fascism start from the realities of fascist dictatorship, conceived, with variations, as the reign of 'finance capitalism'.[3] To a greater or lesser degree, these theories fail, like the original Comintern theory of fascism, in that they take insufficient account of the social causes and the specific manifestations of fascist mass parties.[4] This is also true of the totalitarian dictatorship theory[5] that evolved as early as the war years and was disseminated mainly by German refugees, deriving some indirect support from attempted interpretations by conserva-tive teachers of constitutional law within the Third Reich.[6] Its various forms[7] are pre-eminently based on the national socialist regime, stressing its monolithic and terrorist aspects.[8] Elsewhere a mirror-image reverse of the Comintern theory of fascism, it shares with it the presupposition of a rationally structured government apparatus and of an effective centre of political decision.

Initially, the concept of totalitarian dictatorship served a useful purpose. By replacing the earlier, mainly ideological derivation of national socialism, it provided a starting-point for a comparative study of fascist movements[9] and systems, despite the drawback that parallels drawn (more markedly under the influence of the Cold War) between fascist and bolshevist regimes tended to obscure the specific elements of fascist policies and government. Historical researchers have in consequence largely abandoned this concept as a hindrance to the understanding of the national socialist regime's antagonistic power structure.[10] Quite apart from this aspect, however, the weakness of such a theoretical starting-point was that it gave a somewhat inadequate answer to the question as to which factors were instrumental in the NSDAP's success as a mass movement. The concept of totalitarianism as a definite rational government by a single party was reduced to an ideological syndrome, by which it was assumed that the chief attraction of national socialist propaganda was essentially to be found in the authoritarian and totalitarian disposition of the population groups to whom it was addressed.[11]

Special emphasis was, however, laid on the plebiscitary and charismatic elements of Hitler's leadership; the 'leadership principle' and the part played by the centralized party structure were made to appear as the trademarks of national socialist policy. This theory does, it is true, overcome the difficulty that national socialist *Weltanschauung* was neither consistent nor particular original: rather it was an eclectic conglomeration of völkisch concepts indistinguishable from the programmes of out-and-out nationalist organizations and parties of the imperialist period, or from the ideas of ring-wing bourgeois parties during the Weimar era. The interpretation of national socialism as a machiavellian technique, tailored to Hitler's personality, for seizing and exercising power may have lent credibility to conservative apologists who have presented national socialism essentially as 'Hitlerism', characterized partly by its ruthlessness in the choice and application of political methods and partly by Hitler's own destructive fanaticism.[12]

The totalitarian dictatorship theory may indirectly have taken over a function similar to that of the Comintern analysis of fascism, which started from the premise that the national socialist regime relied on the effective suppression of the greatest possible number of the people and should therefore be regarded as a specific manifestation of domination by a capitalist elite. Such a view also served to strengthen the hypothesis of a growing resistance among the mass of the people under the leadership of the Communist Party.[13] The KPD's obstinate attachment to the slogan of 'social fascism' and its continued struggle against the SPD as the main enemy, even after Hitler's seizure of power, was thereby quietly relegated to the background.[14] At the same time, the totalitarianism theory, with its emphasis on the machiavellian and demagogic nature of the Hitler regime, favoured the conspiracy of silence about the conservative's share of responsibility in the eventual victory of national socialism.[15]

Moreover, the totalitarian theory, by equating bolshevism and national socialism, has stood in the way of a proper undertanding of the structural features peculiar to fascist parties. It is undoubtedly true that both Mussolini and Hitler, in developing their own movements, took socialist party movements for their model; the Austrian Christlich-Soziale Partei, too, served Hitler as a pattern. Attempts were also made by the national socialists to take over some structural elements of the Communist Party, such as the system of blocks and cells. The main difference between the NSDAP and the existing parliamentary parties consisted in the substitution of the leadership principle for the principle of democratic procedure within the party. At the same time, however, its organizational structure differed widely from the communist principle of democratic centralism which, by preventing the formation of splinter groups among the lower echelons and insisting on their commitment to party decisions, ensured strict obedience to the central leadership. In communist parties, elections and internal discussions about central issues nevertheless continued to exist at all party levels, including, despite the cult of Stalin, collective decisions as to leadership.

The form of the NSDAP, which evolved in the later twenties under the influence of the central Munich leadership, presented a completely new type of party, fundamentally different both from the communist and from the traditional democratic parliamentary parties. Simulating, with increasing success, the pattern of nineteenth-century socialist party movements, it deliberately moulded itself into a 'negative' people's party. It neither saw itself as a traditional parliamentary party which would give its followers some kind of share in directing the party's own ideological development, nor did it see its function as the fighting of electoral campaigns, despite its ever increasing success in this field after 1926. The NSDAP was in essence a political propaganda organization. Party officials and members limited their efforts to making propaganda, to obtaining the means for propaganda and to representing the party in public, if only by sporting its badge. Since the party's policies were in all essentials established by the central office and the party press, and since any discussion of party matters was regarded as obsolete and a lapse into the despised 'parliamentarianism', the NSDAP was, as it were, held together from outside, by its own propaganda and, more and more, by a systematically built up Führer cult.[16] Similarly, the aestheticization of politics, a characteristic of fascist movements, served the purpose of externalizing the party; as by the cult of uniforms, the adoption of the völkisch salute, the observance of rituals such as consecration of banners and standards, the hoisting of flags at party rallies and meetings, the development of a peculiar and intentionally spectacular ceremonial and the predilection for paramilitary demonstrations.[17]

A significant feature of the organizational structure of the NSDAP is the virtual absence of any internal mechanism of integration. Hitler's first accession to power in 1920, with the fusion of the DAP and the NSDAP, was accomplished by means of propaganda meetings rather than by the intervention of the official party leadership; the executive committee was faced with his ultimatum, sanctioned by the acclaim of party audiences at public meetings, as a *fait accompli*. The leadership principle which replaced the statutory executive was not exclusive to the NSDAP; it took its model from the Alldeutscher Verband and völkisch groups such as the Deutschvöl-kischer Schutz- und Trutzbund. In the NSDAP, however, it reached an acme of refinement, dispensing with all responsible, even merely advisory, bodies. More and more, NSDAP party rallies lost any other function than to cheer the leader. Whereas at first some motion or another might have been introduced at local or regional level or sporadic political discussion might have taken place, the party rally eventually became no more than a propaganda platform, a medium for the acclamation of the Führer: even in internal party committees, exchange of political views dwindled. Leadership conferences, which had still retained some importance in the latter half of the twenties, either vanished altogether or were transformed into demonstrations or gatherings whose sole purpose was to receive orders from above. When, in 1928, Hermann Dinter demanded an advisory council for Hitler, party headquarters in Munich saw to it that the motion was unanimously rejected. The Senate Hall in the Brown House was never put to its proper use. Despite honest endeavours by the Reich Chancellery,[18] Hitler's often repeated promise to institute a senate or some similar body to elect a leader was never kept.

The intensification of the leadership principle resulted in the absence of any institutional means available to the NSDAP for dealing with conflicts of interest within the party. Such conflicts were, however, inherent in the principle of imposing on party officials a duplicated control – as to their function and by means of discipline – and were further aggravated by the fact that, apart from occasional interference by instructors from head-quarters, there was no effective supervision of section leaders, who were usually appointed from above. Obviously, such a mass organization, bolstered up by an ever growing bureaucracy and engaged almost exclusively in propaganda activities,[19] was totally unable to cope with the exercise of control and guidance urgently needed after the national socialist seizure of power.

It follows that the NSDAP, as a political mass organization within the national socialist regime, became almost devoid of political function and restricted to welfare and training activities; the party as a whole never achieved the role of a central control agency, effectively overseeing both administration and social institutions and directing their policies. Such a theoretical presupposition of totalitarian dictatorship was in line with the Third Reich's self-image rather than with its reality. On the other hand, the political style evolved in the Movement phase and the specific organizational pattern of a dynamic party exclusively devoted to propaganda activities decisively influenced both the process of political decision-making and the internal structure of the national socialist regime. To this extent, the tension between the elements surviving from the Movement phase and the political requirements of the System phase of national socialism is of basic importance to any adequate description of the political process within the Third Reich. In consequence, modern comparative fascism theory has introduced an essential criterion in differentiating between the Movement phase and the System phase.[20]

In the main, the model of totalitarian dictatorship evolved from the attempt to explain the relative stability and effectiveness of fascist governments. In the case of the Third Reich, as opposed, say, to the Spanish Falange, successfully subdued by authoritarian groups led by General Franco, the question why the Nazi regime could not curb its plethora of objectives and so achieve lasting stability of the system is at least of equal importance. Surely, Hitler's personal charisma and the role of Nazi ideology can hardly suffice as the sole explanation. The process of cumulative radicalization, hampering any creative reform by the regime, exposing it to early disintegration and eventually to inevitable dissolution from within, cannot simply be ascribed to the effect of ideological factors. The latter may rather be correlated with the regime's specific inability to adjust itself to interim priorities and to find constructive solutions for existing social and political conflicts of interest.[21]

The explanation of the national socialist regime's relative stability is that, during the Seizure of Power phase, Hitler had been obliged to make far-reaching concessions to the conservative elite controlling the army, economy and administration, thereby frustrating those elements in the Nazi movement who pressed for total seizure of all social and political institutions. Although indirectly annulled as time went by, these concessions acted as a brake, enabling the regime to consolidate itself with remarkable success before the movement's destructive forces, geared to disintegrate the system of government, could bring about a final overstretching and overtaxing of available resources and the economic bases of power. The root of these forces lay in the movement's own apolitical and millennial dynamics and also in the antagonistic interests among the various groups in the national socialist leadership. Nevertheless, it was this structure which allowed an unprecedented short-term mobilization of all available political energies to achieve particular political ends, especially in foreign and military policy areas, although the price paid was an epidemic of split political responsibility, an unbounded and increasing antagonism between all power groups and institutions having any say in the political process, and a growing irrationality in political decision-making, which was completely subordinated to the rivalries among the national socialist leadership elite.[22] In this respect the regime failed to overcome the shortcomings of the Movement phase; the relative stabilization, achieved in 1933–4 with the dismantling of the national socialist 'revolution', was in fact nullified by the customary quarrels and conflicts which, exacerbated by the Second World War, again broke out within the national socialist movement. The leadership rivalries during the last weeks of the Third Reich were a characteristic expression of this development, arising from the inner logic of fascist policies.[23]

Central to contemporary historical research is the elucidation of the social and political causes of the NSDAP's breakthrough as a mass movement. Marxist interpretations tend to underrate the fact that substantial big business support for the NSDAP, if indeed there was any, occurred only after the September 1930 elections,[24] when it had managed to become the second largest parliamentary party with 18.3 per cent of the vote. Consequently, tentative 'agent' theories miss the point of the problem. Contrary to current belief, the NSDAP's rise was by no means uninterrupted. Anton Drexler's Deutsche Arbeiterpartei, set up with the support of the völkisch organizations and the Bavarian Reichswehr, had at first been an insignificant splinter group; it achieved regional importance after the early twenties as the NSDAP under Hitler's leadership. The rise of the party was linked with the nationalist restoration countermovement following the defeat of the Munich Soviet Republic, within the counter-revolutionary climate of the Bavarian capital, marked by the illegal activities of the subsequently disbanded Freikorps and Heimwehr organizations.[25]

In the crisis year of 1923 the NSDAP, absorbing the nationalist völkisch groups in Munich and some parts of Bavaria, was able to enlist 55,000 more members and to extend its organizational activities to Württemberg, Baden and northern Germany. As it became involved in plots to overthrow the government, engineered by authoritarian Bavarian groups associated with Captain Ehrhardt and Erich Ludendorff, Hitler attempted to enforce his leadership by staging the Beer Hall Putsch. Following the failure of the march on the Feldherrenhalle, Hitler's arrest and sentence and the proscription of the party, NSDAP membership suffered a sharp decline.[26] The North German NSDAP and surrogate organizations, such as Alfred Rosenberg's Grossdeutsche Volksgemeinschaft and Julius Streicher's Franconian Deutsche Arbeiterpartei, ensured continuity of the organization, although competition arose from von Graefe's Deutschvölkische Freiheitspartei, which was for a time joined by part of the successor organizations to form the Nationalsozialistische Freiheitspartei.[27] Hitler's adroit move in re-establishing the NSDAP and driving Ludendorff into political isolation by supporting his hopeless candidature for the Reich presidency in 1925 enabled him to assume unquestioned leadership of the party. In this he was assisted by the Führer mythology, built up to a peak of elaboration, particularly by Hermann Essler, during Hitler's imprisonment in Landsberg Fortress. To obtain control, Hitler had to grant independence for a time to a federation of Gauleiter in north-west Germany who, however, never managed to dislodge the power monopoly of the Munich branch and, although they deprecated the opportunism of the Munich leadership, lacked the ideological consistency to prevail against it.[28]

Despite continued legal harassment, the NSDAP made remarkable strides during the 1925 through 1928 phase, membership rising from 27,000 to 108,000. Electoral success, however, did not keep pace: during the May 1928 Reichstag elections, the NSDAP suffered a crushing defeat, obtaining only 2.6 per cent of the vote. For a time the party was proscribed and, in Prussia, Hitler was forbidden to speak until 1928; that these prohibitions were lifted must be taken in conjunction with the general opinion that the party had lost all parliamentary influence. The contradiction between a flourishing of the organization and a lack of electoral success during the decisive phase of consolidation is explicable by the absorption into the party at that time of the potential adherents of their former competitors, the völkisch associations and especially the Deutschvölkische Freiheitspartei.[29] Extreme racial anti-semitism, with its implied resentment of capitalism, and the uncompromising anti-parliamentarianism of national socialist propaganda ensured a monopoly for the NSDAP within the völkisch movement. No genuine mass basis, however, could be gained in this way; what was needed was the penetration of large sectors of the bourgeois-conservative electorate.[30]

From the end of 1928 onward, however, that is, even before the devastating effects of the world economic crisis had been felt in Germany, the NSDAP enjoyed rapid growth, culminating in considerable success in the local elections of 1929 and thereafter in the breakthrough of September 1930. Evidently this turning-point was not preceded by any basic change in national socialist propaganda, as Dietrich Orlow has suggested, but thereafter national socialist propaganda was intensified in rural areas and middle-sized towns. This does not mean a deliberate break with an alleged 'urban plan'.[31] NSDAP invasion of the bourgeois centre and right-wing parties – the Zentrum alone was almost totally immune to fascist infiltration – presupposes the beginnings of doubt among bourgeois middle-of-the-road voters as to the efficiency of their political representation, particularly in relation to the protection of middle-class and agrarian interests. One indication of this process is the growing importance of parties, such as the Wirtschaftspartei, standing for bourgeois middle-class interests; this led to splinter groups, particularly among the conservative organizations, and to a multiplication of parties in general. The political undermining of the centre and right-wing parties must be seen in the light of increasing anti-parliamentarian tendencies during the phase of bourgeois party coalition governments.

Recent publications, including Jeremy Noakes's excellent study,[32] point out that during this phase, the NSDAP, here and there allied to the DNVP and DVP, succeeded in invading the political infrastructure of the bourgeois parties at the local level (the Zentrum again excepted), at the same time obtaining a decisive influence over bourgeois and agrarian pressure groups. This applied to every kind of middle-class organization, as well as to the Reichslandbund. With the memory of November 1918 in mind, Walther Darré's 'agrarian political apparatus' had originally been set up to forestall a possible agricultural boycott and the ensuing collapse of food supplies in the event of a revolutionary take-over by the NSDAP. By this strategic move, coupled with preliminary 'packing' of local groups followed by propaganda pressure on their central leadership, the agrarian organizations were successfully subverted.[33]

Through their growing influence in bourgeois and agrarian bodies and local tie-ups with the DNVP, the national socialists were assured not only of increasingly favourable treatment by the right-wing nationalist press but also of a measure of respect from bourgeois groups, previously repelled by the political rowdiness of the party and particularly the SA. Hitler's about-turn after Landsberg towards strict legality, in the formal sense, and his far-reaching concessions to capitalist notions did not mean that party propaganda ceased at the same time to use pseudo-socialist slogans to win over marginal groups from the SPD. Under the pretext that a united front was needed to combat the 'Marxist' parties, strenuous efforts were later made to secure all vital key positions for NSDAP officials.

The conquest of the bourgeois infrastructrue, at the end of the national socialist phase of consolidation, simultaneously linked with the perfecting of both the national socialist propaganda machine and the vast local and regional bureaucratic organization of the party, was one of the most important social preconditions for its seemingly irresistible momentum up to mid-1932.

Moreover, the NSDAP's undoubted attraction for younger people was an important socio-psychological factor.[34] At that time Ludwig Kaas was appointed leader of the Zentrum, the DNVP's chairmanship passed from Westarp to Hugenberg, opposition to Stresemann's policies was increasing on the DVP right wing and later on the DDP was transformed into the Deutsche Staatspartei. In this way, all the bourgeois parties were displaying a tendency towards the strengthening of traditional ideological alignments, whereas attempts at revision in the intermediate parties – Volkskonservative, Jungdeutscher Orden and Christlich-Sozialer Volksdienst – met with no success. The rift between the generations was thereby widened: the high-level political leadership of the Weimar Republic, including the social democrats, were striving to regain their respective pre-war political positions; while the younger generation in all political camps, to whom the

Kaiser's era and the world war meant only post-war privations and inflation, endeavoured to create new political styles and structures. Young people were thirsting for a new political perspective, offering something more than a return to 1913: the desire for a new German future was, however, systematically and with growing success exploited by the NSDAP to recruit young members and voters. The unfavourable age structure of the SPD and the bourgeois parties (except the Zentrum, which drew its support from the broad spectrum of Catholic organizations) clearly showed their lack of political attraction for the younger generation,[35] whereas the age structure of the NSDAP, and to some extent that of the KPD, showed a decided tendency towards a decreasing age level. Whilst the traditional bourgeois youth movement had already become outdated,[36] the NSDAP profited from the need of large sectors of bourgeois youth for political integration and commitment to forward-looking policies.

Up to the summer of 1932 the NSDAP drew roughly a third of its gains in voting strength from former DNVP and DVP voters, another third from young voters and the remainder from those who had previously abstained.[37] Nevertheless, its influence on working-class youth was limited; possibly it was only effective on young trainees, unable to begin their working life because of mass unemployment, and therefore never having been exposed to trade union influence, whether independent or Christian. Although the NSDAP had succeeded in transforming itself into a mass movement, it could not achieve an overall landslide; both Catholic areas and urban centres displayed a marked immunity to national socialist propaganda.[38] The consequences of the world economic crisis exacerbated the situation. Not only mass unemployment but also the social disorientation of middle-class groups, aggravated by the crisis and the lowering of wages and incomes, particularly affected employees, minor officials and small traders. The comparatively passive acceptance by social democrats and the Zentrum of Brüning's deflationary policies reinforced these socio-psychological effects and the desire for a fundamental change of direction in German politics. At the same time, the anti-Marxist propaganda by right-wing parties, clearly shown by William Sheriden Allen,[39] coupled with the growing polarization among the parties and the increase in communist voting strength, acted in favour of the NSDAP, which, for instance, now attacked the von Papen government's capitalism and the SPD's passive, and therefore pro-capitalist, attitude during the crisis. By this means it was to a large extent able to mobilize in its own favour the resentment among non-socialists against capitalism, revived by the economic crisis, and at the same time gain the sympathies of part of the army and a number of industrial magnates. These men, fearing a serious threat to the capitalist structure from recently intensified left-wing demands for nationalization, intended to use the NSDAP as auxiliaries on this particular front, even though in other respects they had strong reservations about it and fully supported von Papen's idea of a 'new state'.

Impressed by its extraordinarily rapid growth after 1928, the public viewed the NSDAP as an irresistible force. Propaganda manoeuvres deliberately stressed this aspect; incessant skirmishing kept all party members constantly on the move and the NSDAP seemed to be everywhere at once.[40] By innumerable individual actions, meetings, rallies, and also by systematic provocation of terrorist incidents, the party leadership achieved an approximate imitation of traditional socialist party movements. Even during the Regime phase, mass rallies, processions and well-rehearsed public appearances by the Führer were used to give an impression of a party based on mass support, an impression confirmed by the plebiscites of 12 November 1933 and 19 August 1934.[41] As a consequence, the mass-movement nature of the NSDAP and the plebiscitary foundation of Hitler's rule have been greatly overestimated, even up to the present day.

Closer analysis of the membership and voting patterns, however, puts a different complexion on the matter. Prior to 30 January 1933 sharp fluctuations in membership occurred; this to a lesser extent was also true of the KPD. Out of 239,000 members joining before 14 September 1930, only 44 per cent were still in the party by early 1935; at that time the membership was 2,494,000, but another 1,506,000 had already left the party.[42] Even though the statistical data available permit no absolutely precise deductions to be made, it is virtually certain that the NSDAP could not permanently assimilate its mass following to any significant extent, apart from a small, predominantly middle-class hard core. From this it is reasonable to conclude that the mass-movement aspect of the NSDAP was a transient phenomenon, for the millionfold membership of the Regime phase can scarcely be ascribed to actual political mobilization, but rather to the need to conform. What is known of the violent fluctuations within the corps of political leaders,[43] too, suggests that the organization's mass character was preserved only by the petrifaction of the largely depoliticized party apparatus and by massive political pressure.

Researches so far carried out, especially Heberle's and Stoltenberg's studies of Schleswig-Holstein,[44] throw some doubt upon Seymour Martin Lipset's argument that in the main national socialism represented a revolt by formerly liberal sectors of the middle class.[45] Rather, the NSDAP succeeded in penetrating various fields of voting potential, without, however, effecting more than a temporary capture. Agrarian voters, the mainstay of the party's electoral success in September 1930, had for the greater part already defected by the November 1932 elections. The false impression of a popular movement was given by the fact that various social and professional groups – not industrial workers nor the stalwarts among the

Zentrum voters – joined the NSDAP for a time, only to fall off again fairly rapidly. Confirmation for this may be seen in the NSDAP's internal crisis at the end of 1932, especially in the decreasing commitment among members.[46] Under the influence of the economic crisis, a simultaneous bandwagon effect masked this tendency, and is sufficient, quite apart from exploitation of anti-communist tendencies and political pressure, to explain, if not diminish, the electoral success of 5 March 1933.

In view of the NSDAP's internal inconsistency and its inability to mobilize little more than a third of the electorate, Hitler's appointment (as a result of von Papen's intrigues against Schleicher) as chancellor of a Cabinet of National Concentration, assumed major importance. Whereas Gregor Strasser had urged the adoption of a constructive policy, Hitler's obstinacy in demanding vital key positions in a presidential government now reaped its political reward. Whether Hitler sensed that, in view of the cracks within the national socialist movement, a partial success would be tantamount to defeat is a matter which might repay closer investigation. In any event, it should be emphasized that the national socialist share in the governments of Brunswick and Thuringia had led to disillusion among the electors and a fall in voting strength.[47] To that extent, Brüning's tactics of allowing the NSDAP to fritter away its strength in various Länder coalitions are shown to have been correct in principle, however problematical a Zentrum–NSDAP coalition might have been.[48] Apart from this, however, the NSDAP – as has been repeatedly stressed – would have suffered considerable losses in any further electoral campaign. Goebbels was quite aware that the party's success depended on the maintenance of its propaganda dynamic: his sceptical feeling that the NSDAP would, in electoral terms, 'kill itself with winning',[49] since no outward success in the form of any responsible share of government was forthcoming, throws some light on the critical situation before the turning-point engineered by von Papen came at the end of December 1932.

Seldom has any party been so unprepared for political power as was the NSDAP on 30 January 1933.[50] Basically, their objectives did not go beyond a political power monopoly. Some sporadic groundwork, it is true, had been carried out at central and Gau headquarters as a preliminary to a possible achievement of power. It had not progressed very far and was primarily concerned with measures to safeguard power once it had been obtained. Draft legislation for a prospective national socialist government, such as there was, had been produced by outsiders.[51] In addition, the Nazi leadership had envisaged the setting up of a comprehensive indoctrination machinery, which was to be realized only imperfectly in the Ministry for Public Enlightenment and Propaganda.[52] No model for the construction of a state was contained in the Boxheim documents, they merely sketched extensive measures for eliminating political adversaries and dealt with a transition period before national socialist rule should have become stable. The institutional form of such rule was visualized in contradictory terms. Opinions were united on the necessity of removing the parliamentary system; middle-class tradesmen and skilled workers in particular welcomed endeavours at that time to replace parliamentarianism by corporate order. Nowhere, however, not even in the leadership circles closest to Hitler, were there any clear ideas as to the nature of a national socialist state. Hitler had referred in *Mein Kampf* to the transfer of the national socialist party organization to the state, but without going into details.[53] How this could be put into practice remained to be seen. The party, almost exclusively bent on propaganda, had adopted a political style in which all options remained open and decisions were dealt with *ad hoc*.

Moreover, the quasi-legal seizure of power, achieved on 30 January 1933, had come as a complete surprise. The party as a whole had always believed that its accession to power would in some way be linked with the suppression of a communist rising and would therefore be revolutionary Presidential government politics had offered the alternative of a pseudo-legal seizure of power through the existing constitution and by strategic use of the parliamentary system for the party's own purposes. A majority within the party regarded the formation of a Cabinet of National Concentration and the elimination of the Reichstag by means of the Enabling Act as preliminaries to the achievement of total power. They expected complete revolutionary change, analogous to the November Revolution of 1918, without, however, any clear idea of its eventual form and aims. When Goebbels called the formation of the government on 30 January 1933 a 'national' and later a 'national socialist' *revolution*, it was not simply a stroke of propaganda to justify the NSDAP's immediate usurpation of power positions supposedly under constitutional safeguard; its aim was also to appease the mass following of the movement. Goebbels remarked that it was extremely difficult to lead the movement out of its previous frenzy into the legality of the national socialist state.[54] He interpreted the process of Gleichschaltung accelerated after March 1933, as a revolutionary act and maintained that 'the German revolution had been carried out from below and not from above'.[55] To the same end, Hitler and Frick repeatedly vowed in the summer of 1933 that the national socialist revolution had been completed, adding the assurance that complete Gleichschaltung of state and society would be introduced by legal means.

Party supporters, however, regarded the seizure of power and the marriage with the apparatus of state – Goebbels spoke of it as the 'last stage of a revolutionary act'[56] – as a further stage in the progress of a revolutionary act and not at all as its termination. Hitler's alliance with the traditional army, civil service and economic elites seemed to them a tactically motivated transition state, beyond which lay the party's undivided mastery. Corroboration for this view was provided by the agreement made prior to the seizure of power that national socialist holders of government appointments should also retain their party appointments.[57] Party veterans (*Alte Kämpfer*) and active members of the SA, in particular, still clung to their expectations of revolution and readiness to fight in its cause; they dreamt of the day when the NSDAP and the SA would comprise virtually the whole of the population and replace the existing social order.[58] In fact, the evolving national socialist system of government was necessarily rather tentative and temporary in nature, characterized as it was by the tension between the old institutions and the superimposed areas of government by party elites. In some national socialist cadres, there still sruvived the utopian idea of a future more radical new order, although without any definite programme for this; the conviction that a truly national socialist state would yet be built was once again revived during World War II. At first, local party organizations imagined that they were carrying out the wishes of the leadership by arbitrary action on their own account: they needed no sophisticated combination of revolutionary measures from below and sanctioning legislation from above, even though, during the process of seizing power, such tactics might have proved highly effective.[59] Except for the SA under Ernst Roehm, the party acquiesced in national disciplinary measures, though sometimes with reluctance.

Only against the background of the myth of the national socialist movement's final victory can the reality of the Third Reich be interpreted. The party, as an organization of the whole people, became more and more politically expendable, to the same degree as its membership rose to several million, before the May 1933 clamp-down on new enrolments. It was, as it were, fixed in its Movement phase structure; in consequence, clashes intensified between the divergent regional, social and economic interests represented in the NSDAP and its affiliated organizations, nor was there any apparent possibility of reconciling these interests. Conflicts first appeared in the field of social Gleichschaltung, although this was a continuation of party policy prior to 30 January. Predictably, party officials at all levels sought compensation for the party's dwindling influence on central decisions and were at pains to build up subsidiary power positions.

In spring 1933 the need for a renewed electoral campaign mounted with vast expenditure of effort, masked the party's atrophy of function. In Prussia, Gleichschaltung had been well prepared and anticipated the total seizure of power elsewhere. This sparked off Gleichschaltung within the Länder, even before the March 1933 elections, and to the party it predominantly appeared as a tactical manoeuvre to facilitate the intended suppression of left-wing parties by means of controlling the police. Moreover, the Reichstag fire gave the national socialists a chance to anticipate the Enabling Act by declaring a state of civil emergency; the emergency decrees of 28 February, despite the qualifications of Goering's[60] implementing ordinance, amounted in effect to such a declaration.[61] While the original strategy had foreseen the act as the starting-point for the acquisition of total power and the elimination of conservative competition, it would now set the seal of legality on national socialist rule. In fact, the aura of legitimacy conferred by the election results had already been used by the government to initiate a mounting stream of ever harsher elimination measures.

Yet again, and for the last time, were the energies of the movement committed to the actions by which first the SPD and the trade unions, and then the bourgeois parties and associations (including the Stahlhelm) were eliminated, and which must be considered as a continuation of an electoral campaign rife with repression and propaganda.[62] For the radical elements of the NSDAP, this heightened activity carried with it the vague hope of a 'second revolution'. Disappointment at the absence of a decisive change and at the waning of NSDAP influence in local and regional sectors was expressed in a growing irritation with governmental bureaucracy. An outlet was, however, provided by the exercise of patronage in official appointments, particularly in local government posts. For the SA, with its growing numbers and insufficient funds, there was on the whole no such outlet, since Roehm, for tactical reasons, strongly objected to simultaneous tenure of party and government positions. Small wonder then that the SA, although its social composition differed little from that of the NSDAP, was the focus of discontent manifesting itself in the call for a 'second revolution'. Under pressure from Goering and Frick, it had bene obliged to surrender its funciton as an auxiliary police force and to a large extent abandon the Commissar system.[63] Apart from the rancorous Bavarians,[64] the SA had no place in the evolving power structure of the regime; Hitler, believing an alliance with the Reichswehr leaders to be essential, was determined to curb Roehm's military ambitions, whose aim was to make the Reichswehr equal or subordinate to the projected SA People's Army. Once Gleischaltung was complete, the SA lost all function in power politics. On 30 June 1934, as a result of intrigues by Himmler and Goering and from fear of a counter-coup by the conservatives, the final blow was delivered, precipitately and at grave risk to the prestige of the regime.[65] In the eyes of the public, the SA's fall opened the way for a stable form of government.

Measures to supplant Länder autonomy and to institute structural reform of the Reich were introduced by the Ministry of the Interior, at first in emulation of Prussia. Though initially ambiguous,[66] their purpose was to end or at least control the overlaps in areas of competence, particularly the usurpation of official positions, which stemmed from the ideology of the Movement phase. At local government level, this was achieved by the introduction of the *Deutsche Gemeindeordnung* (German Municipal Decree) of 1935, with its far-reaching concessions, counterbalanced however by a tightening of the state's supervisory powers. It is common knowledge that no such success was forthcoming at the level of the controversial 'intermediate government' because of opposition among the Gauleiter, who either favoured particularism or were anxious to protect their personal authority. This is not the place for an account of the often quoted defeat – foreseeable at any early stage and finally brought about in 1942 – of the Ministry of the Interior's attempts to build up some kind of rational state structure.[67] Frick's endeavours are known to have foundered not least because of Hitler himself and his characteristic rejection, partly influenced by legal considerations, of the suggestion that a Reich Constitution should replace the Enabling Act. Further, Hitler prevented any attempt to assist him by introducing a legislative senate, or even a senate whose sole function would be to elect the Führer, although this would have been a source of political unification, after the cabinet as an integrating influence had lost all power and fallen into desuetude.[68] The question here is rather how far a perpetuation of specific elements of the Movement phase was responsible for the national socialist regime's metamorphosis, so often described, into an antagonistic and chaotic rivalry of individual power blocs, which it would be an oversimplification to call a dualism of party and state.

For a true internal stabilization of the regime, fundamental reorganization of the NSDAP was a prerequisite, and Hitler was neither ready nor in a position to carry this out. He saw the NSDAP as a driving force on which to rely should the state apparatus fail or oppose him. At one time, the Ministry of the Interior debated whether the party should again become an elite body entrusted with the selection of political leaders. The position of the Gauleiter, answerable only to the Führer, made this impossible. The Law to Safeguard Unity of State and Party (December 1933) granted wide autonomy to the party but deprived it of all real political function. Even before this, Hitler as chancellor had largely neglected the duties of the party leader; the appointment of Rudolf Hess as deputy Führer intensified the incessant rivalry among the NSDAP's top rank. Hess proved quite inadequate as *de facto* head of the party, which promptly split into myriad widely separated power blocs and competing organizations.[69]

While the SS managed to take over a number of functions within the state and so gradually to acquire an all-important position of power in the regime, ultimately monopolizing political control,[70] the NSDAP itself was confined more and more to non-political social work. Significantly, its highest ambition was to supplant the local priest. Consequently, leading party members idealized the institution of the Catholic church.[71] Propaganda duties, hitherto the main task of the party, were now taken over by the Reichs Propaganda Ministry which, in a typical fusion of state and party machinery, assumed direct control over the NSDAP propaganda sections.

Political indoctrination work was still left to the party, but even here it was faced with competition from Alfred Rosenberg and the Deutsche Arbeitsfront.[72] As a result, the party organization *per se* became more and more depoliticized and incapable of integrating divergent community interests. Languishing behind the lines, it might well regret the gradual loss of its vaunted 'common touch' and its growing inability to bridge the gaps – Hess deplored the 'vacuum' between leadership and grass roots.[73]

To curb the prevalent opportunism and increasing bureaucratic inflexibility, the NSDAP would have needed to absorb the independently administered positions of political power as they stood. Instead, the principle of simultaneous tenure of state and party office led to an ever tightening grip on the party by officialdom, the loss of many party functionaries who preferred state to party employment and indirectly to progressive depoliticization. Many foreign observers, impressed by well-organized mass rallies and plebiscitary support for the system, took it for granted that the NSDAP as a political mass organization exerted an authoritative radicalizing influence on decision-making; yet, in fact, it was increasingly condemned to political sterility.[74]

Political importance resided not in the party but rather in high-ranking party officials who used their position as a stepping-stone to the usurpation of public office and functions of state. Only the personal drive of the men concerned determined how far they were able to interfere in local or regional affairs; significantly, party influence at local level varied to a remarkable degree with the political forces involved.[75] Even in the Third Reich, effective political ascendancy depended on holding public office. Party officials, unless they took on some additional state assignment, remained more or less impotent. Notably, Martin Bormann's growing pre-eminence was due far less to his immensely strong personal position within the party than to his success, through the office of deputy Führer and later through the Party Chancellery, in ensuring for himself a monopoly of control over the legislation, although total mastery of the Gauleiter group eluded him. The function of the Party Chancellery as a co-ordinating ministry in competition with the Reich Chancellery gave him a further chance to dominate subsidiary party apparatus – often over the heads of the Gauleiter; despite this, he never quite managed to turn the party into a true channel of executive power.[76]

Similarly, Himmler's power stemmed from the fusion of the offices of Reichsführer SS and chief of German police, although in the latter position he was nominally subordinate to Frick. As Reich commissar for the strengthening of Germandom, he was able to neutralize the authority of the Ministry of the Interior in the annexed and occupied territories up to 1943, when he himself became head of the ministry and could further erode its jurisdiction fo the benefit of the Reichssicherheitshauptamt.[77]

Again, Robert Ley's influence as head of the NSDAP Reich Organization was reinforced by his simultaneous leadership of the Deutsche Arbeitsfront, numerically and financially far and away the strongest mass organization in the Third Reich.

The much discussed enmity between different offices in the Third Reich arose largely because the party organization, while not troubling itself to integrate them politically, lent a veneer of legality to the usurpation of public office by national socialist party officials, a practice which Frick had only temporarily been able to hold in check. Moreover, the party itself exemplified the progressive fragmentation of political competence and responsibility which finally led to the loss of political rationality and the disintegration of the regime. Whilst the NSDAP as a mass organization declined into political sterility, party officials, first and foremost the Gauleiter, persistently created spheres of influence for themselves, so establishing a system of patronage and cliques. The strictly personal concept of politics, absence of respect for institutions, pretensions to the guardianship of the movement's true interests, the party's susceptibility to corruption – these were the contributory causes for the transformation of the national socialist government system into a tangle of personal interdependence, clashing governmental machinery, disputed claims to fields of competence and the unbridled arbitrary rule of each man for himself among the Nazi elite.

One question above all others remains open: how was it possible that remote and fantastic aims should suddenly be brought within easy reach? In reality, the regime's foreign policy ambitions were many and varied, without any clear aims and only linked by the ultimate goal: hindsight alone gives them some air of consistency.[78] In domestic politics, the question is more easily answered. The specific style of leadership, largely based on postponement of decisions and delay in defining fundamental priorities necessarily led to a diminishing sense of reality. The leadership's one-sided attitude was reflected in highly coloured reports and hand-picked information; but impressionistic reportages could never replace hard news as an ingredient in the formation of public opinion.[79] Increasing blindness to reality was the result. Political decision-making was more and more influenced by personal ambitions and official corruption, and took on the irrational guise of non-institutional power struggles between the clients of state and party patronage. In this way, any vestige of political stability was dissipated as soon as it was achieved. In this context, Martin Broszat has referred to the 'negative selection of some elements of *Weltanschauung*' activated by this system.[80]

Wherever massive interests of the various power blocs conflicted, no viable solution was to be found. Any initial attempts towards positive reorganization were sacrificed to an unbridled clash of social interests, clearly to be seen in rival party mechanisms no less than in society at large. Political motive forces, such as the desire on the part of the power blocs to prove themselves politically and so to extend and secure their position, had to take the line of least resistance. This state of affairs was evident in, for example, the treatment of the 'Jewish question'. In each individual case, the common denominator of the competing power blocs was not a midstream compromise, but whatever in any given circumstances was the most radical solution, previously considered as beyond the realms of possibility. To avoid surrendering its overall authority on the 'Jewish question', the Ministry of the Interior consented to drastic discriminatory measures which once and for all showed that the 'rule of law' had been nothing but a painstakingly maintained façade. To prevent Jewish property falling into the hands of the Gau organizations as a result of wild-cat 'Aryanization', Goering, following the November Pogrom (of which he, like Heydrich, disapproved), gave orders for Aryanization by the state; the departments involved hastily busied themselves with supporting legislation, even if only to retain their share of responsibility. The impossible situation created by the material and social dispossession of the Jews caused individual Gauleiter to resort to deportations, regardless of consequences, a move bitterly resisted by the departments concerned. However, the result was not the replacement of deportation by a politically 'acceptable' solution but, on the contrary, the systematic mass murder of the Jews, which no one had previously imagined possible – the most radical solution, and incidentally one which coincided with Hitler's own wishes.[81]

Typical of fascist politics and also of the Movement phase is the use of propaganda slogans, such as *Volksgemeinschaft* (community of the people), to cover up actual social conflicts and to replace political compromise and choice of priorities. While the Movement as such was steadily declining in importance within the regime and no longer initiated any policies, its principle of 'solutions without conflict' was carried over into the sphere of government, now divested of much of its authority. This tendency led to a cumulative radicalization, so that extravagant objectives, far away at first, came nearer to immediate realization. In this way, it provided the possibility of anticipating some of the millennial aims of the Third Reich, such as annihilation of the Jews, eradication of eastern European elites, Himmler's chimerical plans for resettlement and the breeding of a Greater German elite. These efforts were choked by a torrent of crime, blood and mediocrity, and stood revealed in all their inadequacy; nevertheless, they were still impelled by the inhuman consistency of machinery running on, without the slightest relevance to actual political interests and realities. Ample evidence shows that Hitler drew back whenever he met public resistance, such as on euthanasia[82] and the church question.[83] Early in his reign, too, he tended to listen more to the representations of Schacht and civil servants at the Ministry of the Interior than to the radical promptings of his party colleagues. It is not enough, therefore, to cast Hitler as the fanatical instigator. Even the 'Final Solution of the Jewish Question' came to pass only in the uncertain light of the dictator's fanatical propaganda utterances, eagerly seized upon as orders for action by men wishing to prove their diligence, the efficiency of their machinery and their political indispensability. Characteristically, Goering took it upon himself to give the word of command for the Final Solution, although, as in other cases, he gladly left it to others (in this case Himmler) to put it into practice.

In this regard, the search for the elements of continuity and change after the Movement phase must be taken up anew. National socialist dictatorship was based, not on the movement's popular plebiscitary victory but on an alliance of interests between the conservative elites and the fascist party. This equilibrium rapidly gave way to the total exercise of fascist power, but was still propped up by the more or less undisturbed apparatus of government, including the overwhelmingly conservative nationalist civil service, staffed in the main by the same men as before.[84] Initially, too, the autonomy and weapon monopoly of the armed forces was maintained, and the capitalist structure of the economy was kept in being, though politically subordinated. At the same time, the economic sector was rewarded for political good behaviour, by such means as elimination of organized labour and by an armaments boom, enthusiastically welcomed, at least in its beginnings.[85] Fusion of the party and its associated groups (the SA excluded) with the government apparatus seemed at first to ensure internal and external stabilization of the regime. Material assistance in this respect was contributed by the restraining power of the ministerial civil service which was initially able to prevent calamitous errors of judgement in foreign and domestic affairs: but this presented a bitter paradox. The civil service largely succeeded in curbing the plebiscitary role of the mass party and in giving the dictatorship an independent standing as the Führer state[86] by means of subsidiary methods of legitimization. However, its ability to control Hitler and moderate his actions diminished with time. His tendency to pile office on office continually reduced his involvement in individual decisions; proportionately, however, the unbridled forces of the Movement phase, now transformed into uncontrollable and uninhibited power conflicts between independent factions, established a type of cumulative radicalization which annulled the temporary stabilization. The result was an erosion of the apparatus of government and the independence of the army, and increasing inroads into the monopoly of capitalist economy, so that the conservative social foundations of the system itself were threatened even though they had undergone no marked change. A similar process occurred in the field of foreign policy, where excessive and overtaxing demands drove the Reich into a hopeless military situation.

By delaying the revelation of the insoluble contradictions within the regime, the war provided it with some stability, at the same time, however, presenting a threat for the not too distant future. The regime's internal ambiguity, the restlessness caused by constant innovation and the impossibility of pinpointing responsibility prevented consolidation of oppositional forces, both within and outside the party. The people's grievances concerning the regime's many abuses were never moulded into a nationwide criticism of the whole system. As a mythical figure inspiring unity, Hitler could be loyally accepted even by those who utterly despised the rule of party bosses. The confusing coexistence and antagonisms of rival mechanisms and power blocs nurtured the fiction of one rational entity high above the turmoil – the dictator, that is, in the role of Providence – whilst abuses were laid at the door of subordinate leaders. In such a diffuse atmosphere of conflicting power structures, the resistance movement of 20 July could develop without coming to the Gestapo's notice at an early stage. Nevertheless, it too was fatally hampered by the feverishness and instability of the national socialist leadership.[87] The failure of Operation Walküre meant the senseless prolongation of the war in just those last few months of terrible losses. Hitler's order to apply the 'scorched earth' policy to Germany, effectively countermanded by Albert Speer, his curse on the German nation as unworthy of survival and his injunction on posterity to continue the annihilation of the Jews – all this throws light on the falsehood at the core of a gangster regime which had destroyed traditional social and political structures only to proliferate corruption, petit bourgeois mediocrity and a band of criminals of historical proportions, regarded as heroes by shallow moralists. How far the national socialist state had disintegrated from within is reflected in the internecine struggles during the last weeks of the regime: the deposing of Himmler and Goering, the awarding of the Reich presidency to the politically colourless Grand Admiral Doenitz and the turning over of the chancellorship to Goebbels, who evaded the absurd prospect by suicide, while somewhere in Schleswig-Holstein, Doenitz was forming an impotent rump government.[88]

In fascist Italy, the conservative elites had maintained some measure of independence from the fascist government and were able to protect Italy from total destruction and political paralysis by a successful rebellion. Hitler, on the other hand, managed to wield his fatal influence to the last: the national socialist leadership cliques, burdened with guilt, could not free themselves from their traumatic dependence on the dictator, now verging on physical and mental collapse and encapsulated from the outside world within the Führer bunker.[89] Was this the result of the integrating force of the Führer myth, or was that myth only the lie at the heart of a regime now reeling towards total bankruptcy? The Führer myth and the leadership rivalries were interdependent. In combination, they formed an atavistic principle of political rule, entirely consonant with propaganda objectives and allowing maximum tactical flexibility, yet condemned to failure under the conditions of a great modern industrialized state, even when allied to up-to-date forms of bureaucratic rule within the emergent patterns of power competing with the traditional apparatus of government. The destructive dynamics of atavistic leadership rivalries gained extraordinary strength by the total exploitation of the technical and bureaucratic efficiency of rapidly established commissions and organizations. Initially held in check by foreign policy considerations and by the restraining power of a hide-bound civil service, the emergent national socialist leadership groups lost all sense of reality and proportion in the chase after loosely connected aims.

Ever more embroiled in the feverish and confused process of decision-making, the traditional leading elites in the apparatus of government, in the army and the economy, were forced either to join in the cumulative radicalization of the regime or to decline into political oblivion. What ensued was that political decision-making was altogether lowered to the personal level and became progressively more irrational; the unified administrative system was destroyed; communication between divergent leadership factions, and from them to their subordinates, was lost; and feedback mechanism, which might have allowed effective supervision of the increasingly independent power groups, was non-existent. From this stemmed a sense of insecurity as to the success of the regime's domestic policies.

Political energy was, by the same token, dissipated in endless and increasingly obdurate personal squabbles, as well as in actions of dubious value in terms of practical politics, squandering the regime's strength. Such actions included the fateful destruction of European Jewry and of a large proportion of the elite of eastern Europe, Himmler's fanciful resettlement plans and his concept of a 'Greater German Empire of the German Nation', whose end result was envisaged as overlordship by a Germanic elite at some future time. In the same category, too, were Speer's misconceived plans for armaments, with their laborious, but belated, amendments, and the systematic theft of art treasures throughout Europe by Goering and Rosenberg – a mixture of hubris and dilettantism.

The Nazi regime could unleash gigantic energies for short-term priorities. Total mobilization of available resources occurred only at a late stage, and even then only in the face of Hitler's delaying manoeuvres, resulting from his anxiety to avoid an internal political situation like that of late autumn 1918.[90] As in the Movement phase, the existence of the regime depended on the people never being allowed to settle. Certainly this was not consciously intended. The dynamic force of precipitate and overlapping actions, cutting across all previous planning, was quite in keeping with the fascist leaders' way of life and with Hitler's mentality; the irrationality of political decision-making also bore an equal part in the general restlessness. Undoubtedly

Hitler welcomed the flurry of activity brought about by leadership rivalries. It exactly reproduced the pre-1933 NSDAP style of politics and propaganda, and glossed over the lack of internal political integration and thoughtful future planning. Paradoxically, this confused political opponents to the same extent that it kept the people in suspense and neutralized political resistance.

The regime knew well how to perpetuate the crisis atmosphere which had given it birth and how to transmute policies into a series of emergency measures before which internal political differences had to give way. It was incapable of stabilization or of any progress beyond a parasitic erosion of traditional political structures. Hence the chameleon character of the national socialist system; hope of a return to normality persisted, and side by side with the 'prerogative state', the 'normative state', however insignificantly, continued to exist.[91] The inner contradictions of the system – a magnified reflection of the contradictions in the national socialist programme – necessarily led to its internal and external disintegration, while preventing early destruction from within.

Glossing over social tensions, unchanged if not intensified, was a well-tried NSDAP propaganda technique. Terrorist pressure exerted by an ever more bureaucratic police force for an outward show of compliance with the crumbling letter of the law gave the lie to the tenet, stoutly maintained by the inner circle of national socialist leaders, that planned indoctrination would achieve their desired aim: ideological unity and the 'fanatical closing the ranks', called for by Hitler again and again. Significantly, Hitler's subordinate leaders increasingly began to dream of the *Kampfzeit*, when 'genuine idealism' still existed and positive tasks had been assigned to them. Bormann hoped to revive the party, at least after the war, as a self-contained political fighting unit. But the movement was dead; only its elements remained – corruption, rivalry and the supplanting of policy by propaganda. The myth of the 'thousand-year Reich' faded among the ruins of German cities and defeated German armies; political power lay almost entirely in the hands of Himmler and his henchmen, and the Gauleiter as Reich defence commissaries. The goal of total domination over state and society had been attained; the NSDAP had transferred its 'revolutionary legality' to the state; but as the relics of traditional government structures disappeared, so vanished the basis of national socialist dictatorship. In all its ghastly inhumanity, it was now revealed as a gigantic farce upon the stage of world history.

8

Hitler's Position in the Nazi System

Seldom in history was so much power concentrated in the hands of a single person as was the case with Adolf Hitler's role in the Third Reich. His position as Führer and chancellor was unrestrained by institutional rules of any kind. With the death of President von Hindenburg and the amalgamation of the offices of president and chancellor, the final formal authority to which Hitler was judicially accountable was removed. The Enabling Act, which was repeatedly renewed, gave Hitler extraordinary powers as head of government. Its final renewal for an unlimited period by a unilateral declaration of the chancellor in May 1942 abolished the last vestiges of the sovereignty of the Greater German Reichstag. By this stage the Reichstag had long since been reduced to a purely decorative status anyway. By assuming supreme command of the Wehrmacht, Hitler subordinated the last relatively autonomous force within the national socialist system to his immediate control. The cabinet of the Reich held its last meeting in February 1938. But its ministers had long been little more than obedient executors of the chancellor's directives. Hans Lammers fulfilled a co-ordinating role in government as secretary of state and later, from 1937, as minister of the Reich Chancellery. But in the long run he could not uphold even his basic right to report regularly to the chancellor. During the Second World War his very access to the Führer was curtailed by the head of the Party Chancellery, Martin Bormann. Hitler, by withdrawing increasingly from all routine government business and abolishing even formal advisory sessions, effectively prevented any outside controlling influence from being exercised on the decision-making process within his immediate circle.[1]

The type of government which emerged informally under Hitler from 1934 was freed from all previous institutional constraints. It corresponded to the leadership structure that had developed within the NSDAP from 1920 and had secured for Hitler and his group of close associates in the Munich branch absolute power over all decisions in the party. Hitler imposed the Führer principle on the NSDAP in the early 1920s and this stopped the development of collective decision-making processes at any level in the party. It was institutionalized after the party was refounded in 1925 and effectively suppressed all surviving forms of internal consultation. When Arthur Dinter proposed the formation of a leadership council in 1927, the Hitler faction immediately moved to block it. After the party seized power, the idea of creating a 'Senate of the National Socialist Movement' was given repeated consideration. Although a Senate Hall was fitted out for it in the Brown House in Munich and Hitler for a period seemed to endorse the idea, it was never introduced, even in its proposed modified form as a *Führerwahlsenat* – an electoral assembly to ensure an eventual successor to Hitler.[2] Similarly, there was no institutional body with overall control of the party. The title 'Reich Leader of the NSDAP' (*Reichsleiter der NSDAP*) had no substance. The party's annual rallies were set in an atmosphere of intense propagandist fanfare and had as little say in forming party policy after 1933 as they had before the seizure of power. They functioned as organs of acclamation and were a purely decorative element in the regime's stylized image of itself.[3] Conferences of party potentates were summoned quite regularly during the early days of the regime, though only on rare occasions later. But these generally served merely to endorse the political directives issued by Hitler and his informal leadership circle. The conferences of NSDAP officials held after the party rallies, which were never attended by Hitler personally, functioned mainly as an escape valve for party officials to vent their frustrations at their declining political influence. Rudolf Hess, the Führer's deputy, sought to neutralize this discontent with rhetorical pledges.[4] By these means, the authority of the Führer was kept sacrosanct and was reinforced, *legibus absolutus*, by the requirement imposed on ministers, civil servants and army personnel that they take oaths of personal allegiance to Hitler in place of their former oaths of loyalty to the constitution.

While the Führer state was being consolidated, no independent institution existed which might have developed as the focus of a counter-force to Hitler's personal rule. This contrasted with the situation in fascist Italy, where *Il Duce* had to tolerate an independent monarchy, however well disposed it may have been to him. The Wehrmacht was in no position to play such a role. Quite apart from the effects on it of the restructuring of its leadership in Hitler's favour and the emergence of the Waffen-SS in competition with it, it forfeited any political and moral independence it might have had with the opening of the Russian campaign at the latest.[5] Given this situation, Karl Dietrich Bracher assessed Hitler's position in the system as central to it: 'Fundamental to national socialism and its system of rule was that, from the beginning to the bitter end, it stood or fell with this man'.[6] Ernst Roehm was virtually alone among the higher Nazi satraps in maintaining a position relatively independent of Hitler and daring to openly disagree with him. His murder in 1934 left no one of consequence in the diverse Nazi leadership clique who did not subordinate himself totally to Hitler or suppress any doubts he might have felt about the dictator's directives. It was not until the final weeks of the war that Albert Speer dared to rebel against Hitler's insane demolition orders which would have completely destroyed the basis for the continued survival of Germany as a nation if they had been implemented. It was characteristic of the regime that the struggle for succession between Goering, Himmler, Goebbels and Bormann only finally erupted when it was clear that Hitler intended killing himself. His suicide was, of course, portrayed officially as an historic act, with the Führer determined to hold out to the end in the Führer bunker under the Reich Chancellery and to die fighting with a weapon in his hand.

Hitler was uniquely talented in being able to change the minds of politicians and military leaders who had begun to doubt the wisdom of his strategic and diplomatic decisions and – even in the latter years of the Second World War – to imbue them with passionate belief in ultimate victory. This was as true of Field Marshal von Kluge as it was of Field Marshal Rommel, of Armaments Minister Albert Speer as it was of individual Gauleiter who had begun to doubt his leadership. While Hitler's personal charisma played an important part in this, a certain docility and willingness to be convinced were a precondition for it to be effective. It is astonishing how men of otherwise independent judgement completely capitulated under Hitler's hypnotic affect. His ability to focus instinctively on the concerns of the person speaking to him and his habit of persistently trying to convince doubters by persuasion rather than confrontation offer a certain psychological explanation for this. But this does not explain why no one dared to oppose him after it had become blatantly obvious that the Reich was moving towards the precipice. Even the resistance movement of 20 July 1944 vacillated a long time before finally deciding to eliminate Hitler by assassination. Carl Goerdeler remained firmly convinced that an open letter to Hitler from his generals would be enough to convince him of the incorrectness of his policies.[7]

The great majority of the traditional elites of German political society too fell victim to Hitler's charisma even though people in high positions, as distinct from the mass of the population, had access to sources of information which could leave no doubt but that Hitler's military rampage was propelling the entire nation towards total ruin. How this was possible is a central question demanding an explanation. The Führer cult generated with great propagandist displays and intense psychological pressure certainly played a major part in the subjective identification of such circles with the regime.[8] Goebbels was remarkably successful in fixing the attention of the entire nation on Hitler as the leader who embodied the fate of the nation and possessed an energy, insight and commitment allegedly surpassing anything seen before. The Führer myth proved astonishingly stable and became increasingly independent from the prestige of the national socialist movement. German prisoners of war interrogated by American military intelligence on their attitudes to the Nazi regime in early 1945 were very critical of the party, the hierarchy of party bosses and the corruption widespread in the regime. But they significantly excluded Hitler from their catalogue of complaints.[9] The recurrent phrase, 'if the Führer only knew', reflected the dominant mentality which attributed the blatant shortcomings and abuses in the system, the luxurious lifestyles of many Nazi officials and even the crimes of the regime not to Hitler but to his subordinates.[10]

The extreme fixation of broad sections of the population on Hitler was further evident in the temporary sharp rise in the regime's popularity which followed the failed assassination attempt of 20 July 1944. It was also evident in the widespread view that the conservative army generals and not Hitler were responsible for the heavy defeats on the Eastern Front.[11] Many of the regime's upper middle class supporters, such as Albert Speer, as well as numerous senior army officers combined a personal admiration for Hitler with a general indifference to political matters and a relatively critical attitude to the Nazi movement.[12] The liquidation of the SA leadership on 30 June 1934 had a lasting effect in convincing many of the regime's conservative supporters that Hitler, in contrast to what they regarded as the social revolutionary wing of the NSDAP, was basically committed to a moderate line and should be supported against the radical elements in the party. This fatal error of judgement led the Wehrmacht leadership to introduce into the army a personal oath of loyalty to the person of the dictator, without Hitler having to force them to do so. Hitler's radical public speeches were at first often regarded as mere lip-service to the ideals of the Nazi movement rather than as serious statements of intent.

But none of this adequately explains the fixation on the person of Adolf Hitler widespread even among the not expressly Nazi-minded traditional elites of German society. This was particularly remarkable given that his foreign policy went way beyond the national conservatives' traditional programme for reversing the Versailles Treaty and culminated in a war of imperialist aggrandizement, the establishment of the Greater Germanic Empire of the German Nation, the total domination of the continent by the German Reich and a claim to world domination. The internal opposition that formed when it became clear that Hitler intended to militarily destroy Czechoslovakia and risk world war – aims temporarily concealed by the success of the Munich Agreement, which in fact was what made their achievement possible – and again when he decided to invade Poland in August 1939 collapsed after the unexpected and dramatic victories over Poland and France. After the French campaign, Hitler stood at the peak of his popularity at home. Apart from the communist underground movement and the oppositional circles of social democrats, even those who had remained sceptical of the regime up to this point were now convinced of Hitler's military prowess and leadership qualities. With the exception of a small circle around Colonel-General Beck, the military opposition to Hitler only regrouped several years later.

The deteriorating military situation which followed German defeat in the battle of Moscow in winter 1941 and the alleged nature of the war as a fight for basic survival against the bolshevik threat reinforced the loyalty of the mass of the nation to Hitler. It was only when the tide turned at Stalingrad in January 1943 that 'public attitudes' started to change and Goebbels began his desperate attempts to 'boost' the nation's will to carry on. Goebbels's notorious speech in the Berlin Sportpalast with its rhetorical call, 'Do you want total war?', and the ecstatic applause his irresponsible demagogy received showed once again the extent to which many Germans had lost their sense of reality and were only too willing to submit to the euphoria of Nazi pledges of ultimate victory.[13]

There were many reasons for this. It was in the nature of the regime that it prevented people from reflecting soberly on their situation. The conditions of life in the latter years of the war were shaped by the effects of Allied mass bombing, the increasingly excessive demands made on the individual at work and the absorption of personal energies in day-to-day survival. These, combined with the general depoliticization of the population produced by national socialist indoctrination, ensured that criticisms of particular aspects of the regime did not develop into opposition to the regime itself.[14] The Allied demand for an unconditional surrender was cleverly manipulated by Goebbels's propaganda for all it was worth; together with the effects of anti-bolshevik indoctrination, however little it corresponded to the actual experiences of soldiers on the Eastern Front, and the complete lack of access to information, it made the public conscious of being confronted with a desperate situation where survival itself depended on the success of the war effort. One effect of years of Nazi propaganda was that for the average German there was no psychological alternative to loyalty to Hitler short of placing oneself outside the bounds of the nation. Although Hitler no longer made public appearances and spoke more and more rarely on radio, his person had come to symbolize the unity and substance of the nation. This was reinforced by the terrorist nature of the state and the very real danger that comments critical of the regime could lead to incarceration in a concentration camp.

Under the conditions of terrorist dictatorship with its complete control over and manipulation of public opinion there was no way that mass opposition could be mobilized against the suicidal course being pursued by the regime. It was the fate of both the communist and the bourgeois opposition movements that, generally speaking, they were unable to broaden their support beyond the potential of their traditional support bases. With few exceptions, they held no appeal for the younger generation in particular, which had grown up without ever having experienced a political structure other than fascism.[15] Opposition groups had to take into account the power base of the regime within the structures of the state and the NSDAP as well as within such secondary bureaucracies as the SS and the numerous other individual institutions established for various purposes around the state and the party. A basis for opposition to the regime certainly existed in such structures at the centre of the regime, including certain parts of the SS bureaucracy. Discontent and criticism of certain aspects of the regime were also fairly widespread among officials of the NSDAP. The surveys carried out secretly by the Gestapo of attitudes within the system, though not by any means a totally reliable source, provide a wealth of information on the growing tensions which developed within the regime.[16] But this widespread discontent was not articulated politically and was expressed more in apathy and resignation. Criticism was often expressed at incidents of corruption and particularly at the behaviour of party officials, but this was generally lost in the diffuse rivalry between the different sections of the system's power structures. It never cohered into a rejection of the regime as a whole and above all never included the person of Hitler.

Under normal conditions, in a political system under such extreme stress as the Nazi regime was – even given its totalitarian and terrorist character – opposition forces would have had to emerge which would have forced the political leadership to retreat from its grandiose expansionist plans and to secure the political status quo on the domestic front for the sake of the stability of the system. In fact, in January 1933 Hitler's conservative allies had believed that once he had complete political power he would draw back from his more radical aims. The conservative 'taming concept' seemed at first to have been vindicated, even if not in the sense in which Vice-chancellor von Papen and Alfred Hugenberg had expected. In line with political opinion generally, they had believed that Hitler would bankrupt himself politically within a matter of months. During the first phase of the regime Hitler portrayed himself as a moderate statesman, particularly in his conduct of foreign policy, where in the following years he pursued an unexpectedly cautious course. Although the tactical intentions underlying it were not fully understood at the time, for the most part his foreign policy won the critical support of his conservative partners in the DNVP, as, for example, when he concluded the German–Polish Non-Aggression Pact. The suppression of Roehm's alleged putsch attempt seemed further proof of Hitler's determination to block any social revolutionary developments such as were made to seem imminent by the whisper campaign of a 'second revolution'. Hitler intervened to thwart the radical ambitions of the NSDAP and the SA in numerous areas of domestic policy. The government forbade unauthorized interference in the economy by party offices and went to considerable lengths to disband the system of SA and NSDAP commissars which had emerged spontaneously. The NSDAP as led by the unenergetic deputy Führer, Rudolf Hess, did not achieve anything like the influence in the public administration which had been expected, apart from some degree of control at the purely local government level. The party's political officers generally felt they had been passed over in favour of the traditional civil service.[17]

With its propaganda apparatus put at the disposal of the Reich Ministry for Propaganda, the party lost all effective influence on the central decision-making system, despite the Law Securing the Unity of Party and State and the promotion of Rudolf Hess to the rank of minister. Martin Bormann, as Hess's chief of staff, succeeded in securing some influence over legis-lation for the deputy Führer's liaison staff. He created a co-ordinating role for his office between the ministerial level of government and Hitler's immediate staff, in direct competition with the head of department of the Reich Chancellery. But until very late in the war the apparatus built by Bormann was unable to neutralize the influence of the Gauleiter, with whom Hitler maintained direct contact, and was prevented from exerting any control over either Hermann Goering's Four-Year Plan or Heinrich Himmler's multifaceted empire, which soon achieved virtual total autonomy. This is indicative of the relative weakness of the NSDAP as a political organization. Its functions were gradually reduced to carrying out welfare programmes and organizing the Winter Relief after its original purpose had disappeared with the ending of election and plebiscite campaigns. At the insistence of the SD (the SS security service), the NSDAP was forbidden its own internal intelligence organization. Senior Nazi officials could only exercise real political power where they succeeded in combining their positions with public posts or in usurping functions of state.

Many authoritarian conservatives among the traditional ruling elites hoped that the destruction of the SA as a power and the ever decreasing influence of the NSDAP as a mass organization would lead to a smoothly functioning and self-contained state machine. These hopes proved to be illusory. The minister for the interior, Wilhelm Frick, did vastly expand his administrative power base by absorbing the civil services of the Länder into the bureaucracy of the Reich and also greatly rationalized the system, along lines long advocated, by uniting the Prussian administration with that of the Reich, albeit incompletely. But it rapidly became apparent that the Interior Ministry would not be able, despite its greatly increased power, to assert its authority against the Gauleiter, who were securely entrenched in their territorial fiefdoms. As a consequence, both the Reichsreform and the reorganization of the public administration which these measures had been meant to accomplish were never realized. Apart from the rationalization of the local government bureaucracy achieved by the *Deutsche Gemeindeordnung* and the Reich Civil Service Law, which was finally enacted after much dispute in 1937, Frick's plans to comprehensively reform the constitution never got beyond the drafting stage. When he failed to get Hitler's approval for his proposals and lost control of the police to Himmler, who was answerable only on paper to the minister for the interior, Frick realized the hopelessness of implementing his reorganizational plans. These were to have formed the basis for a uniquely national socialist constitution. After Hitler had declined to accept his resignation several times, Frick was finally posted to replace Baron von Neurath as Reich protector in Bohemia and Moravia.[18]

The administrative machinery of state, which had been merely brought into line and 'co-ordinated' with the new regime at first, gradually broke up into a welter of competing institutions. It was swollen by an ever growing number of commissarial bureaucracies which functioned as both public and party offices. This was a fundamental characteristic of the Third Reich, partly instigated by Hitler and partly tolerated passively by him as it developed. The administrative anarchy of the Third Reich so often noted had its origins in the internal structure specific to the NSDAP before it came to power. The party had been conceived exclusively as an organization for electoral mobilization. Any influence exercised by the membership on leadership decisions was at best accidental. The party had no institutionalized internal decision-making structures of any kind. The devolution of power to subordinate party leaders on an *ad hoc* basis and the general tendency to leave such figures a free hand sprang from the party's original need to maximize its effectiveness in competing for popular support.

In stark contrast to communist-type organizations, the NSDAP did not possess a bureaucratically structured hierarchy. Neither was its internal organization modelled on a military chain of command. It was structured to ensure extensive freedom of action for its individual constituent parts but acted simultaneously on the basis of a party programme which was declared 'unalterable' and fanatically adhered to. In practice it was not a hierarchical system at all but a competitive leadership system. This followed the principle of double subordination – disciplinary and political – of each party official[19] while it lacked any system of co-ordinating the political structure with the SA, the SS and its numerous other affiliated organizations and professional associations. The short-term advantages of such a system of 'personal leadership' over a bureaucratic structure are obvious.[20] The rivalries which had perforce to emerge between competing organizations and secondary party leadrs were channelled to produce a tremendous level of political mobilization. This is what was revolutionary in the organizational and propaganda techniques employed by the NSDAP as a specifically fascist-type party.

A memorandum originating within the Party Chancellery in 1942 was extremely critical of the leadership system which characterized Hitler's rule: 'The principle of allowing uncontrolled growth until the strongest had won out is certainly the secret of the movement's almost stupendous development and achievements.' While this had 'definitely been very useful when the party was being built up', it had one major disadvantage. In the long run the movement's energies had to become totally absorbed in internal 'disputes over areas of competency, right down to branch level' and to breed political 'despots' who could not tolerate 'near them any deviations from their opinions'.[21] Practically the only obligation imposed by the organizational structure of the NSDAP on subordinate party leaders was one of unconditional personal loyalty to the dictator. The effect of this, combined with the ban on any expressions of dissent, publicly or privately, was to divert all conflicts of interest into personality clashes and rivalries. This system totally corresponded with the social-Darwinist outlook of Hitler and his immediate clique. Its politically amorphous structure had also suited the Munich branch's interests in preventing any alternative centres of power from developing in the party.[22]

This organizational structure was consciously promoted by Hitler, but it was not merely the by-product of a divide-and-rule tactic, though considerations of this type certainly played a part. If this had been the case, Hitler would have opposed the emergence of bureaucratic power bases which threatened to develop beyond his political control, not least Heinrich Himmler's SS empire. Instead, however, he continually encouraged this process and only intervened reluctantly when his own position seemed under immediate threat. This is what happened at the time of the alleged Roehm Putsch. With the threat of a putsch exaggerated out of all proportion by Himmler and Goering and with the neo-conservative groups behind Vice-chancellor von Papen becoming more active, it appeared that the Reichswehr, armed with the extensive powers of a state of emergency, was about to move to paralyse the Hitler government and prepare the way for an authoritarian military dictatorship. Hitler only agreed very belatedly and after exhaustive attempts at mediation while under massive pressure from the SS, to finally strike at the SA, which he then, however, did 'ruthlessly'.[23]

But Hitler made little attempt to manipulate the rivalries which rapidly emerged between his leading cohorts after the seizure of power. This was in keeping with his practice as party leader of not intervening in internal party conflicts, preferring instead to await their outcome. In this way he could avoid committing himself personally in a manner that could later prove damaging. Thus, in response to Frick's oral complaints about the virtually unchallengeable power exercised by the Reich governors, he determined that he should not be 'put in the position of having to decide' on differences of opinion between governors and the Interior Ministry, except when matters 'of exceptional political importance' were involved.[24] He avoided involvement in similar conflicts in the cabinet, demanding that individual ministers agree a common position among themselves on any particular issue before presenting it to cabinet for ratification. This method of governing meant that contentious questions either became completely taboo, as in the case of the Reichsreform,[25] or were quietly shelved and became the subject of long-running bureaucratic disputes between various government ministries or departments of the party bureaucracy.

Hitler had a habit of postponing or evading decisions on issues of fundamental political importance, apart from certain aspects of foreign policy, for example, which he accorded temporary or permanent priority. This went hand in hand with the practice, also inherited from the party's early days, of establishing new bureaucracies and administrative units to deal with political tasks as they arose without disrupting the existing distribution of areas of competence within the party. The best known example of this was the bureaucracy established to implement the Four-Year Plan, which was created largely from the offices of IG Farben and gradually usurped the authority of the Reich Ministry of Economics.[26] This method of tackling conflict arose from Hitler's deep aversion to civil servants and lawyers, whom he regarded as ineffective and indecisive. As a short-term expedient it could prove comparatively successful, as was notably the case with Albert Speer's relative success in temporarily increasing armaments production capabilities by ignoring all established interests in the field, including the Four-Year Plan.

The exclusive concentration of effort on whatever particular task was regarded as urgent at any one time and the tendency to dispense with having alternative strategies in case the chosen course failed corresponded exactly with the electoral strategy pursued by the NSDAP before coming to power in 1933. For agitational purposes, this had allowed extreme contradictions in policy to coexist in the party's programme and propaganda in the belief that these would not need to be honoured once the party was in power. The concept underlying the *Blitzkrieg* strategy of a short-term exertion of all available resources as opposed to a long-term programme of resource allocation and planning also reflected this specifically fascist method of rule. The Gleichschaltung of the existing structures of state with the new regime from early 1933 did not materially alter this mentality in the party and it continued to characterize national socialist leadership circles. The manner in which authority was exercised and delegated within the party was transferred almost unchanged to the structures of the state, despite the fact that the process of consolidating state power demanded different qualities and skills from those possessed by the Nazi 'party bosses' and propagandists. The chronic inability of the NSDAP to assert its effective control over either existing or newly created bureaucratic systems was a direct result of this.[27]

The dynamics of this system have received much attention and were once described by a leading official of the Reich Chancellery as 'temporarily well-organized chaos'.[28] They were to have some unforeseen political consequences, however. The principle of investing each official with 'complete authority' over his particular area of competence, when combined with the habit of leaving the lines of demarcation between different posts vague or, occasionally, regulated only by private agreement, increasingly destabilized the structures of the state. It also destroyed the internal coherence of the political system – which was anyway integrated in a common purpose only in its propaganda image – in favour of expanding the personal power of particular potentates. The constant conflicts over areas of competence was paralleled by a tendency to renounce competence or to willingly concede it where unpleasant or morally questionable activities were involved. The judiciary, for example, made no attempt whatsoever to assert its authority when instructions were issued for measures against Jews, gypsies or people of Slavic nationality.[29] Thus, on the eve of 9 November 1938 – *Reichskristallnacht* – the chief public prosecutor issued a directive to all subordinate authorities ordering them not to intervene in cases where Jews were taken into protective custody.[30] The Ministry of the Interior always took great pains to ensure that authorizations issued for deportations explicitly absolved it of any competence.[31] In this context, the Gestapo and later the Peoples' Court could encroach more and more on the authority of the regular judiciary. Opponents of the regime and Jews were gradually robbed of any measure of legal protection and came under the direct jurisdiction of the Gestapo. The judicial system was prepared, almost without exception, to abandon the principles of positive law and to adopt a type of qualified law based on the dubious notion of transgressions against the 'healthy feelings of the people'; it willingly subscribed to outrageous legal formulas deduced solely from national socialist ideology.[32]

The absence of any substantial opposition among the conservative elites in the state bureaucracy and judiciary to the mounting arbitrary acts and criminal tendencies of the dominant cliques in the Nazi regime was closely related to the total collapse of liberal and constitutional thinking that had begun taking effect in the Weimar Republic. But this does not sufficiently explain the total lack of resistance with which the traditional structures of the state submitted to the arbitrary rule of the Nazi leaders, particularly as their collaboration with the regime was not by any means purely a result of terrorist pressure. The mechanism by which the old elites became implicated in the regime's criminal policies and were systematically cor-

rupted by them arose primarily from the ever greater willingness of authorities in all areas to keep pace with the progressive radicalization of the regime
so as not to be circumvented or altogether excluded from the system. They
bought their right to continue to exist by perpetually conceding ground on
legal points or on the substance of the rule of law itself. This process had
to lead to a precipitous slope from which there could be no retreat.[33] A
case in point was the manner in which the Wehrmacht effectively forfeited
its moral claim to guardianship of Prussian tradition when it consented to
waging a war of racial extermination against the Soviet Union.

  Why so many people who in general led honest private lives allowed
themselves to be corrupted by the regime cannot be explained simply by
their partial agreement with individual elements of national socialist policy,
especially its anti-bolshevism and also to some extent its anti-semitism.
Members of the traditional elites tended to think of the persecution of the
Jews as the price that had to be paid to distract the Nazi movement from
implementing socially radical measures, such as attacks on the private
property rights and traditional social privileges of the German upper middle
classes. Indeed, even within the resistance movement the 'Jewish question'
became an issue only when persecution was extended to assimilated Jews
and people who were partly Jewish or were married to Jews, and there was
widespread acceptance of the notion that it was essential that the influence
of eastern Jewry on German society be eliminated.[34] The failure of substantial opposition to materialize in broad sections of the army, the economy
and the administration arose partly from the increasing fluidity and chaos
which characterized the entire institutional structure in Germany, both
within the party and outside it. In all areas of the national socialist state,
authority for any particular task tended to be vested in several agencies
and, in the consequent maze of overlapping competencies, competing offices
constantly attempted to usurp each other's functions. This affected even
the highest echelons of the Wehrmacht as well as its whole chain of
command. No Nazi potentate could ever be sure that the position he had
secured for himself would not be usurped in a sudden change in the
distribution of power. Such sudden shifts did not necessarily have to
involve Hitler. Goering, Hitler's designated successor and chairman of the
Ministerial Council for the Defence of the Reich, lost the power he had
amassed piece by piece as his public standing as air minister and head of
the Luftwaffe rapidly declined to near zero-point following the disastrous
outcome of the Battle of Britain and his helplessness in the face of the
Allied bombing offensive against Germany. Goebbels too had temporarily
to fear for his position in Hitler's entourage. This was at least one of his
motives in instigating the pogroms against the Jewish population which
have gone down in history so euphemistically as *Reichskristallnacht*.[35] Even

Heinrich Himmler was finally outmanoeuvred during the final weeks of the war following successful intrigues by Martin Bormann.

The notorious insecurity which pervaded the power structures of the Reich was encouraged by Hitler more out of habit than purposefully and to a large extent was simply a logical consequence of the Nazis' inability to settle into a stable institutional framework once they had achieved power. This insecurity was the source of constant competition for the Führer's favour among the regime's potentates. It led to the top officials of the regime constantly seeking to excel each other in advocating ever more radical policies, though they were always careful to ensure that these were in line with Hitler's ideological tirades and – very importantly – not a threat to the position of other dominant interests in the system. Martin Broszat has described this as a selection mechanism which encouraged the system's negative 'ideological elements' to come to the fore.[36] The cumulative spiral of radicalization which the constant rivalry for positions of power and favour produced thus found its perfect escape-valve in the 'Jewish question'. This was because, particularly after the failure of Schacht's currency policy, the removal of the Jewish section of the population from public office and the professions and later from positions of economic influence did not harm any powerful interests. Similarly, the 'Aryanization' of Jewish property and the proletarianization of German Jewry served to satisfy some otherwise divergent interest groups equally, if not always without conflict.

In any formally functioning political system, regardless of its constitutional form, a balance tends to be achieved between competing interests which takes into account the varied effects of planned political measures on them. In the Third Reich this was to be increasingly less the case. This was a direct consequence of Hitler's refusal to set 'policy guidelines' for clearly defined instructions on which government ministries or party offices could base the 'measures' they had to implement.[37] Numerous orders on matters of detail affecting the administration, the judiciary or personnel policy were regularly issued. But, apart from the businesslike way in which wartime expansion was planned, policy directives on most other central issues were general, unclear and often contradictory.

Planning in a rational and calculating sense that took account of all possible eventualities only existed within individual organizations, which were otherwise uncoordinated with one another. Hitler's manner of operating encouraged this, out of habit, because it suited him and because he believed it heightened his effectiveness. He tended to encourage competing potentates and ministers to take the initiative and he only intervened – generally as a restraining force – when his political priorities seemed endangered or when conflicts came into the open and threatened to compromise the regime's propagandist image of unity of purpose. A manner of government developed, therefore, which was shaped by a host of individual measures implemented by various ministries and authorities without any co-ordination between them. When vital policy aims of the regime were not being realized because no system of setting priorities existed, Hitler would appoint a new plenipotentiary to the area which had been neglected and empower him to take whatever steps were necessary to achieve his task. Even then, however, it was always doubtful whether such an appointee would be in a position to assert the authority vested in him. The regime was thus totally unprepared for dealing with critical situations that arose – as was evident when it sought to deal with the crises in materials supply, the labour market, the currency situation and food supply – and it responded clumsily and often in a totally unsuitable manner to emergencies and bottlenecks which had unwittingly emerged. This method of operating could be very effective in the short term, but the internal frictions it caused led to escalating wastage. This was demonstrated by the relatively low performance achieved by the Four-Year Plan compared with Great Britain's belated rearmament efforts. The tendency of the leadership of the regime to intervene in the activities of its various organizational bureaucracies only in special cases meant that these developed in the most diverse directions. The result of this was often that while draft legislation or regulations were being prepared in one place, plans were already in train in some more influential quarter to supersede them. These symptoms of internal collapse were the cause of many gross miscalculations, not least in technical decisions on armaments, but remained partly concealed by the war effort.

The psychological effects of disorganization were more important, however. Persons in senior positions were rarely consulted on matters of existing or planned measures. The standard practice, not only for security reasons, was for specific tasks to be revealed only to those immediately responsible for implementing them. This produced an extreme gap in communications throughout the middle stratum of the system.[38] As a result, while each authority had a thorough knowledge of the particular problems with which it had to deal, relations even between ministries often tended to be of a casual or *ad hoc* nature. It thus became the exception for policy to be co-ordinated and implemented in a systematic manner. Even the most senior figures were usually badly informed about the actual situation on the domestic front, about diplomatic developments, the military situation and, especially, the measures being taken in the occupied territories.[39]

The Nazi ruling stratum developed a mentality which enabled it to avoid taking cognizance of unpleasant facts. The gap in communications was thereby complemented by a refusal to communicate. This was the context of Albert Speer's insistence after the war that he had not been informed of the 'Final Solution of the Jewish Question'.[40] There was a systematic avoidance of responsibility and no one – with the possible exception of

Martin Bormann, the *éminence grise* of the Nazi system as it collapsed – was prepared to form an overall picture of events. All political thought was channelled into a technocratic fetishism of detail. In this situation, protests against or opposition to disastrous political or military decisions were rarely articulated and then only in exceptional cases. Even more fundamental was that in such an atmosphere protests against brutal or criminal acts, if expressed at all, elicited no response. Progressive collaboration in the systematic destruction of the rule of law and the employment of violence as an instrument of state policy produced an atmosphere of bland resignation and frivolous indifference long before the regime embarked on a calculated policy of extermination of the Jewish and Slavic populations of Europe as well as members of other allegedly inferior races, and executed it with a cynical perfectionism from the start of the invasion of the Soviet Union.

What role did Hitler play in the progressive radicalization of the regime which occurred after the final domestic and foreign policy restraints became irrelevant from September 1939? The dictator had blocked all attempts to fundamentally reform the structures of the state, including Frick's proposals for a comprehensive constitution for the new Greater Germanic Reich.[41] Normal government business was of little interest to him. Unlike Mussolini, Hitler did not bother studying government papers regularly. The basis of Bormann's power, the most bureaucratic of the Nazi leaders, was not least due to his unrivalled knowledge of the daily entries in government and party files; it put him in a perfect position to change or prevent particular measures when necessary. Hitler thoroughly scrutinized the newspaper cuttings presented to him by Dietrich, the head of the press department. He also certainly read the diplomatic correspondence and undoubtedly had the ability when facing important negotiations with foreign statesmen to grasp the essentials of the issues at stake fairly accurately. But apart from this, he concerned himself very little with government business. In most cases he tended to make decisions on the spot after being briefed orally and often without having any knowledge of the situation in the departments concerned. Hitler's manner of governing largely by word of mouth was further aggravated by his tendency to turn night into day and, before 1941, of not leading any daily routine. This often gave his unofficial advisers, whom he had sometimes appointed as 'adjutants' and who usually met him on a casual basis, a more considerable say in government decisions than the relevant heads of departments.

In such a situation it was simply impossible for Hitler, despite his stupendous memory for detail and his ability to grasp the essentials of any issue very rapidly, to really control all the threads of government. Neither had he any interest in asserting such control. After the start of the war he very willingly allowed full legislative powers to be devolved to individual ministries and to the admittedly ineffective Ministerial Council for the

Defence of the Reich, which was chaired by Goering, though with the proviso that the chancellor of the Reich could reappropriate this prerogative when required.[42] This move had the effect of increasing the polycentrism of the system and facilitating the growth of secondary bureaucratic structures.[43] Some of these, like the SS police apparatus, rapidly secured their institutional autonomy from the traditional structures of the state except the Ministry for Finance. Given the territorial expansion of the German empire and the subdivision and multiplication of offices and authorities involved in the administration and governing of the occupied areas, it would be impossible to give an accurate account of the actual developments in any Gau, protectorate or commissariat of the Reich even were this to be attempted systematically. In the East particularly, territorial commissars established an autonomy for themselves which was reminiscent of a neo-feudal system.[44] Hitler, moreover, by assuming supreme command of the Wehrmacht and personally supervising military operations, above all on the Eastern Front, was occupied to such an extent that control of the vast empire of party bureaucracies was bound to slip increasingly from his hands.

A lack of co-ordination was evident even in measures vital to the war effort and ignorance of the overall military and political situation was widespread at the lower and medium levels of the system. But these symptoms also characterized Hitler's immediate circle where the major decisions were made. Under wartime conditions the information gap between ministries in Berlin and the Führer's headquarters assumed astonishing proportions. This was further aggravated by Hitler's increasing refusal to take on board any information which was unpleasant or contradicted his picture of events. He finally issued instructions that he was not to be burdened with news of this kind any longer.[45] Blindness to reality was thus compounded by a refusal to accept reality. The more Hitler confined himself to the Führer bunker, travelled through Germany only by night or with the window-blinds drawn, visited the front increasingly seldom and avoided touring the bombed-out large cities, the more the conferences in his headquarters were marked by a selective assessment of the actual situation; they were in touch with the reality of the situation in Germany and with the military and political situation in the occupied territories only by telephone. The mightiest state territorially which Europe had ever known was run from the ghostly and almost supernatural scenario of the Führer's headquarters. It would be difficult to describe this 'rule' by spasmodic and unsystematic intervention in the political workings of the Third Reich as 'governing'.

On the surface, Hitler's supremacy appeared absolute. His rule was characterized by the decrees which replaced law and which at first required the counter-signature of the head of the Reich Chancellery as well as that of the head of department involved. These were complemented by a range of ordained laws, difficult to define, in the shape of Führer Decrees and Führer Directives; drafted by Bormann, they gave the force of law to often throw-away remarks by the dictator.[46] They reflected the interests of whatever influences were in the ascendant at any particular moment and only very rarely were they the product of a planned and structured policy.

Hitler and his immediate entourage increasingly reverted to the original and fanatically utopian aims of the Nazi movement as their hold on reality slipped and they were gripped by a growing premonition of the military catastrophe facing the Reich. All restraints previously adhered to out of consideration for Germany's allies and the neutral powers and out of fear of possible reprisals by the enemy were abandoned. As the grandiose plans for establishing the Reich as a world power proved more and more illusory and as successive military defeats gradually undermined the euphoric faith in a German victory, the long-term ideological aims of national socialism came ever more to the fore in Hitler's tirades and there was never any shortage of loyal fanatics to diligently convert these into concrete measures and strategies. The more hopeless the actual situation of the crumbling Greater German Reich became, the more Hitler and his followers grew intoxicated with the idea that the radical expectations of the party's campaigning years had been betrayed. They dreamed of an imaginary future where the life and death struggle in which Germany was immersed and which was expected to continue for the unforeseeable future finally produced a triumphant victory for Germany and cleared the way for the realization of 'pure' national socialism.[47]

It is important to state clearly that the policy of the Final Solution, the liquidation of over a million Soviet prisoners of war, the terrible crimes committed against the civilian population of eastern Europe as well as Himmler's fantastic plans to settle the East with German 'stock' could only become political realities in an atmosphere where the highest decisions were taken without rational bureaucratic considerations playing any role whatsoever. The 'Final Solution of the Jewish Question' systematically executed by Himmler was set in motion without any formal order, let alone a written one, being issued by Hitler.[48] This did not arise merely out of a need for secrecy, nor was it the result of shrewd calculation. Implementing such political aims in many ways ran directly counter to the regime's real interests, not least to its desperate efforts to maintain and increase armaments production. It is only against the background of the exclusively propagandist attitude to politics and the extreme informality of the political decision-making procedures which pertained that it is at all conceivable that aims of this kind could have been converted into reality without encountering any substantial opposition. That this was possible was not solely due to Hitler's fanatical disposition. He was given to using the language of naked and ruthless violence not only within his immediate circle but often in official pronouncements too. The potentates of the regime grew as accustomed to this as they did to the absurd codes of honour of the SS and the stylized coded language employed by the regime's killers.

To argue that Hitler did not totally approve the policy of extermination in the East and did not incite his subordinates to execute it, directly or indirectly, is certainly absurd. The bitter truth is that without the intense competition for the Führer's favour which dominated the higher echelons of the regime and the aimless perfectionism which gave the work of its secondary bureaucratic organizations their momentum, Hitler's fanatical racial plans could never have been converted into the staggering reality of the extermination of over five and a half million Jews along with several million Slavs and other victims of the regime. Long-term ideological objectives such as the destruction of the Jewish race in Europe, while actively considered from an early date as general ideas, were never concretized in a political strategy. But how such ultimate ideological aims were transformed into reality is the central problem in understanding the twisted road which led to the Final Solution.[49] Up to the outbreak of war, neither Himmler nor Heydrich thought in terms of systematic liquidation, and the endless speculation on the Madagascar Plan until well into the war, even in Hitler's thinking, clearly demonstrates this. Even Hitler's publicly stated intention to use a world war to destroy Jewry was akin to the vague propagandist threats so typical of him. It would be pointless to speculate to what extent he had developed concrete ideas for realizing it.

Hitler's verbal threat to destroy 'the Jewish race in Europe' does not explain how the actual extermination was set in motion. The outbreak of the Second World War and the military victories in Poland and France considerably reinforced the position of the regime at home and led to both a decline in the active opposition in Germany and a strengthening of the radicalizing trends within the regime. Inhibitions partly motivated by diplomatic considerations continued to play a role until early 1941. But these were discarded one by one as preparations got under way for the campaign against the Soviet Union, which was conceived from the start as an ideological war of extermination.[50] An essential element in this was the anti-bolshevism so central to the thinking of the leading conservative elites; it could now be exploited directly to serve a programme of racial extermination.

The road to Auschwitz, to the systematic extermination of the Jewish population in the territories under German control – ultimately carried out with an unprecedented bureaucratic perfectionism – was a process involving numerous stages of escalation which appear as the systematic realization of a coherent plan only in retrospect. In reality, however, each individual stage was a product of a different set of circumstances, dictated by the changing interests of whichever power groups held the upper hand at any given time. The first euthanasia programmes, which had had to be suspended but which were later revived in a limited and strictly secret form during the war, introduced into the political system the concept of destroying human beings in a machine-like fashion. The catastrophic results of the uncoordinated manner in which both the deportation of the German Jews and the mass ghettoizations in the Generalgouvernement in Poland were carried out were of decisive importance in this process of escalation. The conditions they created were so intolerable that they defied solutions by orthodox methods and bred cynicism and a suppression of all human emotion among the officials of the regime. This paved the way for men of the calibre of Himmler and Heydrich to put to the test their clinically perfectionist approach to solving problems. The measures implemented in occupied Poland – particularly the activities of the Einsatzgruppen – had similar effects. These also developed under their own internal dynamic, gradually transforming into reality the ideological notion that Jews, 'subhumans' and bolsheviks were a single species. But the apparatus of oppression constructed by Himmler fumbled its way forward only slowly. It grew from the systematic execution of Soviet commissars and officers, as well as real and imagined enemies of the regime, before it could reach the stage of the Final Solution of a systematic policy of genocide. In this way, the camps originally established for the 'special treatment' of Soviet officers and commissars who were taken prisoner became the foundations of the extermination camp system. Similarly, the techniques of mass murder employed developed from the euthanasia and T4 programmes.

The 'thought' – that is, Hitler's fanatical proclamations of racial anti-semitism – could not suffice in itself to unleash the systematic extermination of the Jews. The constantly escalating spiral of brutality which immunized the regime's killers in their murderous handiwork and dulled the senses of those who witnessed it was an essential precondition for systematic mass murder to become concrete reality. The fate of Soviet prisoners of war in German hands, less than a third of whom were to survive captivity, played at least as important a role in this, as Christian Streit's remarkable study has decisively demonstrated.[51] After a period as a minor concentration camp, Auschwitz was re-established as an SS-owned 'Labour Camp for Prisoners of War': at first it was intended as the beginnings of 'a major centre for prison-labour armaments works', but, when Soviet prisoners of war were no longer available in sufficient numbers, Auschwitz and Birkenau became a 'turnover centre' for hundreds of thousands of European Jews.

Responsibility for the deaths of several million Russian prisoners of war does not lie exclusively with the various institutions of the SS and the Einsatzgruppen. Army units were regularly involved both directly and indirectly in the process of selecting and executing prisoners; OKW (Armed Forces Supreme Command) and OKH (Army High Command) were responsible for the death by starvation of countless Soviet prisoners of war in their camps. This was not primarily because of a shortage of food, though this was sometimes the case, but because in terms of 'subhuman' theories and the *Lebensraum* mentality Russian lives were considered of no value. The great majority of German front-line generals, with very few exceptions, were either directly implicated in the shocking treatment meted out to Soviet prisoners of war, particularly in the first year and a half of the Russian campaign, or tacitly condoned it. The Wehrmacht generals, most of whom were in full agreement with the ideological premises of the war against Russia, played a major role in this act of genocide, which has been overshadowed and neglected in comparison with the 'Final Solution of the Jewish Question'. The catastrophic fate of Soviet prisoners of war in German hands was not due to any intervention or directive from Hitler. Generally he merely rubber-stamped bureaucratic measures prepared and implemented by the Wehrmacht authorities in collaboration with the SS and police, though these measures were wholly in line with the orders drafted by Hitler for the complete destruction of Leningrad and Moscow and the starvation of their populations.

Like the Final Solution, this example shows that, despite Hitler's unchallenged position of power, his actions were far from being the only cause of the constant escalation in the crimes of the regime. A broad spectrum of military officers, civil servants and technocrats as well as representatives of big industry willingly served a system that was characterized by a cumulative inhumanity and barbaric violence, the full extent of which was only exposed after its fall. There can also be no question that Wehrmacht generals seriously opposed the brutally oppressive and genocidal measures which had to follow from the concept of a war of racial extermination and were 'legitimized' by it. At best, army officers adopted a defensive attitude: they restricted themselves to their own fields of competence, attempted to prevent a collapse of discipline within the ranks or, at least personally, avoided becoming directly implicated in criminal measures. The exponents of a brutal policy of oppression and extermination within the party, the SS and the OKW encountered much less opposition than they had expected from within the army. They found that they could also generally rely on the direct or indirect co-operation of the army in the field when it came to carrying out anti-Jewish measures. Anti-bolshevism, which was closely intertwined with anti-semitism, was a central motive in the willingness of army personnel to abandon basic humanitarian considerations and legal conventions in conducting the war in the East.[52]

The fanatical slogans of Hitler and of a limited group of radical national socialists were constantly echoed in official propaganda and were not restricted to internal meetings. This formed the background to the continuous escalation in the cruelty of the regime's policies. It was this group particularly which sought to suppress the faint-hearted attempts being made to bring the worst perversions committed by officials of the regime before the courts. The regime's criminal policies were not in general carried out by those who encouraged Hitler in his fanatical objectives and who imitated his tirades in front of their own subordinates. This fell rather to the eager and obedient underlings in the system, who could be found even in the highest places and rapidly won the confidence of the clique at the centre of the regime precisely because of their blind loyalty and ruthlessness. Men like Höss, Eichmann and Kaltenbrunner were capable of terrifying perfectionism when it came to realizing schemes for the deportation or extermination of masses of people. They were driven by a variety of motives, including ambition and vanity. Besides fanatical racist anti-semites and anti-communists, the largest single group among those involved in the genocide programmes were obedient executives and technocrats. Such people were cynical to the point of being able to lead extremely petit bourgeois private lives, shielded from their daily crimes.

Virtually all those involved in the mass murder of the Jews clung to the pretext offered them by Himmler and others that their work was a grim necessity arising from a unique situation. This self-justifying delusion was a typical product of the decision-making process within the national socialist system. The Third Reich had no structured framework for resolving political conflicts that was developed on the basis of long-term planning. Instead, conflicts were often aggravated to a point of extreme crisis by groups with an interest in escalating a dispute, and decisions tended to be made as *ad hoc* responses to the vague emergency situations which this gave rise to and which demanded rapid and 'robust' countermeasures. The Roehm crisis of June 1934 was a classic example of this, as were the mesaures adopted after *Reichskristallnacht*; foreign affairs were often conducted in much the same way. This method of operating corresponded totally with Hitler's personal tendency to transform his basically lethargic disposition into one of extreme excitement by outward dramatics. This enabled him, as if 'propelled by fate', to transcend both his own doubts and those of his advisers.

The politics of the NSDAP during its rise to power had consisted mainly of seeking confrontation at virtually any price and profiting from the political dilemmas which were immobilizing the presidential regimes. The Nazi Party was the product and beneficiary of political instability. The mentality which this produced was deeply embedded throughout the Nazi movement and largely remained a major feature of it after the seizure of power. It was temporarily suppressed in the wave of disciplinary measures which party officials who now occupied leading positions in the structures of the

state and who had fallen under the influence of the conservative-oriented
civil service attempted to implement. Hitler's approach to politics, as was
the case with all leading Nazi groups, was geared towards precipitating
crises which could then be exploited for propagandist purposes. This
represented the very essence of Nazi politics. After the NSDAP achieved
power this method of operating continued, even if it no longer applied to
the party's Political Organization, which gradually took a totally passive
role. Apparently insoluble problems were also created by the constant rivalry
for position. This was kept under some control by a continuous process of
provisional stopgap promotions.

Such mechanisms played a central part in the realization of the regime's
criminal policies. These were invariably carried out under the pretext of
tackling exceptional situations, which in fact had been created by the
dynamics of the system. Politics in the Third Reich was in the last resort
nothing other than an endless series of political, military and moral states
of emergency. They were dressed up in a petit bourgeois normality which,
encapsulated in Hitler's lifestyle on the Obersalzberg, was constantly reproduced in the mass media. This meticulously neat world of bourgeois
orderliness and decency also served to create a positive image for Nazi
officials and thus helped them to justify to themselves the destruction of
human norms in the regime's treatment of its opponents.

Neither Hitler's central role as a driving force nor his essentially equal
drive to self-destruction should be underestimated. But it must be recognized that he was only an extreme exponent of the chain reaction of anti-
humanitarian impulses which was unleashed when all institutional, legal
and moral restraints were abolished and, once set in motion, progressively
escalated under its own momentum. He did not always support radicalizing
tendencies in the regime. He successfully opposed Martin Bormann, for
example, by refusing to sanction an attack on the Christian churches as
institutions, and it is known that he reacted very sensitively to changes in
the popular mood. This could be seen in his concern at the possible effects
of food rationing, restrictions in the production of consumer goods and
excessive regulation of the labour market. In particular, Hitler retreated
from radical measures which he feared would provoke determined opposition from important sections of the population. Massive protests by the
churches rather than by individuals from bodies such as the officer corps
would very probably have put severe restraints on the Final Solution and
many of the other barbaric consequences of a war of racial extermination.
Before 1939 Hitler often intervened to dilute radical demands coming from
the party, but during the war this gradually gave way to a ruthless fanaticism.

It is simply too easy therefore to point to Hitler's dominant position as
the primary source of the escalating criminality and destructive arrogance
of national socialist rule. While it is certainly true that the system stood or

fell with this man, such an apparently succinct statement needs to be differentiated and understood in its broader context. Many purely biographical interpretations have been undertaken from various perspectives, but such an approach on its own cannot provide an adequate explanation of Hitler's role. Recent psychological investigations, though very problematic given their exclusive concentration on Hitler's psychological make-up to explain the dynamics which determined the course of the Third Reich,[53] have shown clearly that there is no basis for ascribing either great statesmanship or a type of negative 'historical greatness' to Hitler. They do establish, however, that Hitler withdrew from any part in government business from a very early date and that he was both increasingly out of touch with reality and unprepared to accept truths presented to him.

The mixture of undoubted talent and extreme dilettantism which we see in Hitler, his near neurotic tendency to regard the regime's propaganda image as reality, to confuse fanaticism for efficiency and to refuse to countenance opinions which conflicted with his own was already apparent to some of his most observant supporters at an early date.[54] His behaviour gave people an impression of inner consistency, determination and sense of purpose and this may explain his demagogic charisma. The grandiose error of attributing great statesmanship to Hitler arose from the willingness of his subordinates to unconditionally accept his authority as 'Führer'. This was true not only of the inner circle of top Nazi leaders who were in constant contact with him but also of the majority of the Wehrmacht's generals, who were spurred on by a mixture of personal ambition, anti-bolshevism, an excessive admiration for power and an inherited reverence for established authority.

The clichéd image of Hitler as a genial, machiavellian technician of power cleverly calculating every move had its roots in Hitler's undoubtedly extraordinary talent for tactical manoeuvre and his near psychotic political sensitivity. But this concealed a mediocre and professionally incompetent man who had been driven to the top by the circumstances of the time and who lacked any ability to form normal social relationships. It was typical of Hitler that he tended to avoid conflict with senior figures and only rarely could bring himself to allow such figures to be toppled publicly. In fact, with very few exceptions, he was always very reluctant to have opponents executed who had served the Nazi movement at some stage. In many cases of conflict he went to great lengths to try to persuade critics and doubters of the correctness of his case.

In this way, Hitler's personality certainly played a role in the failure of an effective opposition to him to emerge from within his immediate following. Besides the propensity of large sections of the population to accept the Führer cult systematically promoted by the Goebbels propaganda machine, the willingness of the traditional intellectual elites to bow to the authority of the 'genial' Führer also played a major role in securing his position. This was reflected in the widespread attitude which exempted the Führer from any responsibility for the faults of the regime and contrasted him with the officials heading the party and the SS. The identification of Hitler as the bearer of the state's authority and the representative of the nation sprang from deep-seated attitudes and needs. This proved to be the decisive obstacle to all attempts to politically isolate or outmanoeuvre the dictator which, as Stauffenberg correctly realized, were psychologically essential if he was to be deposed.

During the war Hitler increasingly avoided public appearances and withdrew to the imaginary world of the Führer bunker. But, under wartime conditions, the key psychological strength of his position was further reinforced. The average citizen had no opportunity to distinguish between identification with the nation and the Führer myth. This was the context of the temporary rise in the popularity of the regime following the assassination attempt of July 20, 1944.[55] The psychological reaction to defeat and the collapse of the regime in 1945 was understandably a diametrically opposite one to this. The initial sense of shock gradually gave way to a mentality in which all responsibility for the crimes and mistakes of the regime were placed squarely with Hitler and his immediate associates. These were seen as the embodiment of a 'totalitarian' system which was perceived in static and unpolitical terms; inquiry into its structural origins was avoided. But historians cannot be content with such an interpretation and must try to uncover the mechanisms which set the regime as a whole on a course of almost certain self-destruction.

The Nazi system of rule completely lacked internal coherence and this played an ever greater role in ensuring that no countervailing forces emerged to affect events. Under it, the institutional, legal and social foundations of the political system, at first merely 'co-ordinated' with the new regime, were progressively dismantled and finally destroyed. This necessarily meant that those elements which had at first attempted to avoid implication in, or at least to limit, the violent acts and illegal excesses of the state were gradually corrupted by it. As the dynamic of the regime lay outside institutional channels, no centre survived which might have served as a focus for grievances. A feeling of being unable to effect any change in the course of events gradually spread even among the highest echelons of the state apparatus as well as in the offices of the party.

Experiences since the Second World War have shown that a ruling elite prepared to cynically exercise absolute power and to burn all bridges behind it can maintain its relative political stability for a short time. Such was the situation of the Nazi system in its later stages when it was no longer capable of ensuring its medium-term stability. It began to disintegrate into individual satrapies ruled by Gauleiter and territorial commissars and into isolated chains of command which could only be held together by appeals to the mythical 'will of the Führer' and by the belief that Germany was engulfed in a fight for its very existence as a nation. On the surface, this process of internal disintegration appeared to be a direct result of the extreme press- ures of war on the system. But the tendency had been inherent in the structure of the Nazi movement from the start and only took full effect under conditions of total war, which led to the progressive abandonment of domestic political considerations. This was exemplified by the dismantling of the authority of the Interior Ministry, the establishment of the SS empire with its own internally competitive structures which were unfettered by external control of any kind and the role assumed by the Reich commissars for defence.

But it would be misleading to point out that military defeat was the cause of the regime's destruction without also showing that this defeat was inevitable. The internal dynamics of the regime determined that its resources and military capability would be overstretched precisely because of its early military successes. The accelerating spiral of disastrous strategic decisions in the areas of armaments production, the economy and foreign diplomacy was an inevitable by-product of the irrationalism and declining sense of realism which increasingly pervaded the regime. The Nazi system acted parasitically on the state and social institutions it inherited and destroyed them in the process, without replacing them with durable struc- tures of any kind.

The Nazi regime, by its inherent mixture of brutality and cynical terror and administrative and political dilettantism, mindlessly destroyed the hith- erto accepted social and moral norms as well as their institutional expressions. It abolished the barriers of civilization which stood between society and an atavistic collapse into a social-Darwinist struggle of all against all. Although the regime was internally unstable and doomed to fail, the unprecedented destructive energies released by its thorough deformation of the social and political system were precisely what made it possible in the first place for the 'thousand-year Reich' to establish the tyrannical hegemony over the European continent that was so impressive, albeit only at first sight.

In so far as it is unlikely that a political oddity like Hitler will ever again achieve political power, it is a serious mistake to concentrate study of the Nazi tyranny on an analysis of the role which Hitler occupied in it. Dictators are as dependent on the political circumstances which bring them to power as they in turn influence these. The destructive and profoundly inhuman forces which the Nazi system unleashed at all its levels may well appear again, though under very different political circumstances, with different structures, in a different form and certainly with less forcefulness. This is the context in which the experience of the Third Reich should be analysed thoroughly. The fact that Germany – a civilized and highly developed industrial society – rampaged violently out of control has political implications for us today, and it would be wrong to hide these behind a façade that isolates Hitler as the sole and root cause of it. How Hitler could succeed in securing various degrees of support from considerable sections of the German population must be explained in this context.

9

20 July 1944 and the German Labour Movement

On 30 January 1933 the German labour movement suffered the most crushing defeat of its history. The manner in which this happened was totally unexpected. It was well known that the NSDAP was determined to ruthlessly suppress organized labour once it achieved power, and the violent clashes between the SA and elements of the Roter Frontkämpferbund and the Reichsbanner offered a bitter foretaste of what was to come. But few believed it possible that the political and trade union organizations of the working class could be extinguished at a single blow. It was reckoned that the organizations would be merely banned and the movement driven underground. Even the KPD did not expect that the new regime would bring the machinery of state repression at its disposal so rigorously to bear. Elements in the SPD leadership believed to the last that the party would be able to continue a shadow existence as it had under Bismarck's Socialist Laws. The party's national executive even restated its pledge of strict adherence to legal methods so as not to give the regime any pretext for banning the party.[1]

During the night of the Reichstag fire the KPD, without being formally banned, realized that it could only continue to function from underground. Nevertheless for several months afterwards it still called for mass protests against the regime. This made it easier for the Nazis to destroy the remnants of communist organizations which had not yet adopted conspiratorial methods. Even some elements of the SPD continued until July – against the express opposition of the executive in exile – to believe that some form of effective public existence was still possible. In fact, the SPD was spared the type of persecution to which the KPD was being subjected, mainly for tactical reasons, at least until after the Enabling Act was ratified by the Reichstag. Numerous individual SPD officials were nevertheless arrested and mistreated, and there was no shortage of violent attacks on party institutions and offices.[2]

The reformist ADGB leadership attempted to ensure its continued survival in some form under the new state by publicly dissociating itself from the SPD and supporting moves towards the introduction of corporatist structures. This line, which was vigorously opposed by a range of individual unions affiliated to the ADGB, proved as illusory as the legalistic course of the SPD leadership in the Reich. In April 1933 the Leadership Circle of the United Nations (Führerkreis der vereinigten Gewerkschaften) was formed, with Wilhelm Leuschner and Jakob Kaiser as well as Max Habermann (representing the DHV) playing the leading roles. This effectively fused the three existing trade union federations into a single united union structure, but at the expense of the SPD. Its aim was to pre-empt the threatened destruction of all trade union organization and to reach an accommodation with the new system, including the National Socialist Factory-Cell Organization (NSBO). But it was a tactical move based on a fundamentally erroneous assessment of the nature of national socialism. The collaborationist course of the ADGB culminated in its abject capitulation of 1 May 1933 but failed to prevent the unions from being dissolved, their offices occupied and their property confiscated. Apart from the short reprieve granted the Christian unions, the organized labour movement, with the exception of those groups which had gone underground, was thus effectively destroyed.[3]

While the establishment of the fascist dictatorship merely confirmed the communists in their revolutionary creed, it profoundly shook the belief of most social democrats in the validity of their political assumptions. In the situation that had emerged, their faith in parliamentary democracy had become meaningless. None could now imagine that there was any hope for a return to parliamentary democracy in continental Europe. They had also been forcefully deprived of the classic weapon of democratic socialism: the mobilization of mass protest. The strategy of exploiting the legal framework for revolutionary ends, which had been advocated by Friedrich Engels,[4] was turned on its head. The fact that the repressive measures implemented by the new regime were formally legal meant that the working class was thrown involuntarily into a situation where only illegal revolutionary methods could have any effect. But, given the systematic way in which the dictatorship established itself, there was no possibility of a strategic opportunity to organize such mass resistance as was emerging. The party executive which was elected in April 1933 adopted a collaborationist course not least in the hope of being able to secure the release of imprisoned party officials. It came into almost immediate conflict with the leadership which had begun to take shape in exile and which, as its name 'Sopade' implied, had broken with the home-based SPD by adopting a radically militant and revolutionary programme. The resistance groups which initially emerged in large numbers also broke with the old party. The most important of these, 'Neu Beginnen', established regular contact with the émigré executive in Prague and, along with other groups, kept in touch with it through couriers, at least until the Gestapo succeeded in breaking up the Sopade frontier secretariats.[5]

The party's loss of perspective did not lead to complete passivity, despite the disillusioning effect which the contradictory and indecisive politics pursued by the party after von Papen's Prussian coup of July 1942 had on the majority of SPD supporters. This was a testimony to the vitality of the socialist movement in Germany.[6] But developments following the events of 30 January 1933 caused widespread resignation and bewilderment among the leaders of the SPD. Though in prison he could not be aware of the full gravity of the situation, even Julius Leber believed at first that Hitler should be given a chance to solve the social problems the SPD had been unable to master.[7] Were it not for the brutality with which NSDAP and SA officials wreaked vengeance on their opponents in the labour movement, many of them would possibly have accommodated the new situation, just as the reformist wing of the ADGB had attempted to do. But the severe persecution to which countless labour leaders were subjected reinforced their rejection of the Nazi system. They were further strengthened in this attitude as the popular mood swung clearly against the regime from summer 1933; the swing was more marked from early 1934 when it became clear that the Nazi leadership had no intention of honouring its promises of social change.

Labour leaders certainly saw through Nazi propaganda and its constant suggestion of overwhelming public support for the new system. The results of the work council and later the shop stewards' council elections, which Martin Bormann had to call off in the end,[8] showed that the mass of industrial workers had not by any means fallen for the propaganda slogans of the DAF (German Labour Front). But the effect on the mass of the working population of what Walter Ulbricht called the regime's 'spiritual socialism'[9] should not be underestimated, especially as the ending of mass unemployment, even if only achieved by the forced pace of rearmament, did win over sections of the working class. Younger workers who because of unemployment during the economic crisis had had no experience of trade unionism were particularly susceptible to the regime's social utopian promises. It was also extremely difficult to get reliable information on the attitudes of workers, though the *Reports from Germany* circulated by the Sopade did provide some basis for assessing these.[10]

Socialist resistance groups operating underground generally avoided contact with representatives of the old executive. They regarded these as thoroughly discredited by the policy of tactical collaboration they had pursued before May 1933. Most of the members of the old executive had in any case withdrawn from political activity of any kind. Active resistance was carried out mainly by socialists who before 1933 had been in opposition to the executive and in many cases had left the party altogether and gone over to the breakaway SAPD. Most of these were arrested and the groups they led broken up by the Gestapo by 1935–6 at the latest. While a few of the leading figures succeeded in escaping abroad, many were permanently incarcerated in concentration camps. Representatives of the early social democratic resistance movement rarely formed any links with the national conservative opposition which began to take shape from 1938. Notable exceptions were Carlo Mierendorff and Theodor Haubach who, after initially attempting to reconstruct the Reichsbanner underground, began to take an active interest in developments in conservative circles.

Most leading SPD officials who were arrested after the Nazi seizure of power and dragged from one concentration camp to the next were only released, if at all, after the phase of active socialist resistance had been brought to an end by the increasingly effective Gestapo. Very few groups survived into early 1939 and most of those that did had been drastically reduced.[11]

Others, like Emil Henk, realized at an early stage that the semi-conspiratorial type of resistance carried on by the remnants of the old SPD was pointless and withdrew from any involvement in it, though without ever abandoning their basic opposition to the Nazi regime. While communist resistance groups were generally linked to the KPD underground party organization from the start, oppositional social democrats were reluctant to build up an illegal party organization. This was because by the mid-1930s experience had shown that such structures were highly vulnerable to being uncovered by the Gestapo. They did not believe such an approach had any chance of effectively weakening the regime. They tended instead to maintain loose social contacts with other former social democrats. The trade union group led by Leuschner was one exception to this. It set out to build up an underground embryo trade union organization, though it was confined to a network based on personal contacts among former trade union leaders.[12]

The Gestapo was remarkably well informed about these informal groups and tended largely to tolerate them while ruthlessly suppressing other types of underground activity.[13] They treated such circles of formerly prominent personalities – the resistance of the notables – with astonishing laxity. This was a direct result of the picture they had of the enemy – specifically the political left and in particular the KPD and the network of contacts maintained in Germany by the émigré SPD executive in Prague – and led the Gestapo to underestimate all other forms of resistance. It was also expected that lengthy spells in concentration camps would have a sobering effect and persuade socialists to desist from further oppositional activity. In addition there was the paradoxical situation that the endless rivalries and struggles for power between individuals in prominent political and administrative positions made it very difficult to detect what was actually oppositional activity. It is only for this reason that it was possible for

Leuschner's factory and Leber's coal distribution firm, to name only two examples of many, to develop over years into conspiratorial contact centres. The national conservative resistance escaped detection by the police precisely because it was not professionally organized, did not employ conspiratorial methods and appeared not to affect any sensitive areas of security. It was typical that the Gestapo only became aware of this resistance when it established contacts abroad, as was the case with the Solf Circle.[14] It invariably struck the moment it discovered that contact had been established with the underground KPD, as was demonstrated when Leber and Reichwein were arrested along with the underground Operative Reich Leadership of the KPD just before the assassination attempt of 20 July 1944.[15]

It is noteworthy that social democrats like Wilhelm Leuschner, Theodor Haubach and Julius Leber became involved with the national conservative resistance although they were subject, at least initially, to intense surveillance by the Gestapo. After his release in 1938 – which Werner Best, whom he knew from his period in Darmstadt, possibly helped engineer – Carlo Mierendorff also took this course, establishing contact with Helmuth von Moltke's circle. After putting Leber and Leuschner in touch with each other, he was to become, along with Haubach and Adolf Reichwein as well as Ernst von Harnack, one of the most important representatives of the Kreisau Circle, the origins of which went back to 1940.[16]

But the great majority of social democrats were far too isolated to have any contact with the centres of the resistance movement in Berlin; they kept in close touch with each other at local level and maintained a hostile or at least distant stance to the regime. The circle of former friends from the SPD who grouped around Leber after his release initially avoided political activity. This was not only because they were convinced that there was no possibility of the regime's being toppled from within Germany for the foreseeable future. The deep gulf that separated the social democratic movement from bourgeois political society – despite the SPD's politics of co-operation with the bourgeois centre during the Weimar Republic, it had never been really bridged – was an equally important factor. Those social democrats who were finally to become actively involved in the July plot were generally outsiders who had been on the right wing of the old SPD. They were mostly academics and all came from bourgeois backgrounds. The reformist centre of social democracy was not represented in the conspiracy at all. Similarly, the left bourgeois parties were almost totally unrepresented in the resistance movement generally.[17]

It was typical of the movement behind the July plot that the conspiratorial circle which formed around Colonel-General Beck did not seek any direct contacts with the political wing of the labour movement and that those that were established were to remain relatively tenuous until 1943. This was

also partly because, although the socialists later involved in the July plot –
and especially Julius Leber's circle – built up close relationships with former
party colleagues, they did not originally think in terms of taking a political
initiative themselves but rather were prepared to await developments. The
participation by Mierendorff, Haubach and Reichwein in the early discussions of the Kreisau Circle involved a certain break with the traditional
SPD. This circle concentrated at first on political plans for the aftermath
of a collapse of the national socialist system and did not consider immediate
preparations for a putsch.

Contact with the national conservative resistance was established through
the Christian trade unionists who had been in close contact with Leuschner
since 1933, particularly prominent among whom was Jakob Kaiser.
Relations, though not of a political nature, already existed between
Leuschner and Goerdeler. Leuschner had regarded his imprisonment as
an act of personal vengeance on the part of Robert Ley and, after his
release, he would appear to have harboured certain illusions initially that
trade unions could again become a factor. This was partly because of the
attempts then being made by rival Nazi Party circles to oust Robert Ley from
his position.[18] Leuschner took over the underground Reich Leadership of
the unions after Theodor Leipart's death in 1937. This was more of a
potential than an effective organizational network but did have a certain
base among former members who had maintained contact with one another,
not least because of the many legal claims connected with the dissolved
unions which were still outstanding. It would also appear that Leuschner
was protected by Hermann Göring from the ever suspicious Gestapo which,
typically, moved against Jakob Kaiser the moment they suspected that he
had established contact with the Sopade, possibly via Leuschner.[19] It
remains an open question whether there was any basis for the impression
Emil Henk gained that Leuschner continued to maintain contacts with
high-ranking personalities in the government.[20] It is undeniable, however,
that after his release he enjoyed a certain freedom of movement, albeit
strictly limited by Gestapo supervision. This may have been due to foreign
policy considerations on the part of the regime.

Contact was established between Leuschner and Colonel-General von
Hammerstein through the Christian union leaders Jakob Kaiser and
Theodor Brauer as well as the Cologne trade union group headed by
Bernhard Letterhaus and Nikolaus Gross. This was the beginning of his
relationship with Goerdeler which was only to intensify from 1941. Even
when the participation of the trade union group, which included Max
Habermann as the representative of the DHV,[21] became more permanent,
Leuschner still did not think in terms of taking part in a *coup d'état*. Even
the national conservative circles were not yet by any means decided on
proceeding with an actual coup. Rather, what they were aiming for was the

removal of Hitler and a restructuring of the government on the basis of a temporary military dictatorship. It was only when the military continued to hesitate about taking the type of action explicitly sought by Goerdeler than an independent civilian plot began to take shape in the loose circle of like-minded people with whom he was in contact. Leuschner shared Goerdeler's conviction that the regime could only be toppled by a military *coup d'état*. He continued to believe to the end that the idea of basing it on action by the working class, through a general strike for example, was totally unrealistic.

Leuschner and his political friends, including Hermann Maass, the former general secretary of the German Youth Associations, and Gustav Dahrendorf, had thought at first mainly in terms of a situation re-emerging similar to that of December 1932, when General von Schleicher had experimented with the idea of a government based on an axis which included the trade unions. He wanted to be in a strong position, should an authoritarian system based on the military be established, to demand a key political role for the unions. He continued to believe that the Nazi system could be destroyed by a clean *coup d'état*, the removal of Hitler and a reshuffling of the government.[22] Referring to Germany in 1939 as 'a large prison', Leuschner had pointed to what he considered the hopelessness of attempting to organize resistance on the basis of mass working-class support. But he wanted to be prepared in the case of a successful military coup to establish the united trade union movement he sought.

Julius Leber remained largely uncommitted until late 1943, though he continued to maintain his connections with Leuschner and through him was in occasional contact with the national conservative resistance. Carl Goerdeler in fact initiated the involvement of the trade union circle in the national conservative conspiracy, mainly because he needed them to strengthen his position against the group headed by Ulrich von Hassell and Johannes Popitz. His position in demanding this was considerably strengthened by the response, elicited by the tentative contacts established abroad, that reliance solely on the military would be regarded as inadequate and that the opposition needed a broader base in the population if it wanted to avoid risking being regarded simply as a group of discontented outsiders.[23] But equally important in motivating him was the fact that Popitz and von Hassell had been severely critical of his draft programme, 'Das Ziel' ('The Goal'), and he looked to the trade unionists, who were more likely to sympathize with his constitutional ideas, for support for his position.

The involvement of Leuschner, the Christian union leaders Jakob Kaiser, Bernhard Letterhaus, Nikolaus Gross and Josef Wirmer as well as Max Habermann of the DHV altered the political complexion of the Goerdeler circle to such an extent that it would be more fitting to speak of a Goerdeler–Kaiser–Leuschner Circle. But Leuschner did not reveal the full extent of his contacts with former trade unionists and social democrats and in general only involved Maass, whom he brought as his deputy to meetings of the resistance circle. Later Julius Leber behaved similarly, apparently keeping the circle of social democratic friends who supported him deliberately out of contact with national conservative resistance circles.[24] This was understandable given that socialists were subject to constant surveillance by the Gestapo. By restricting their contacts with their bourgeois partners to a small group of people, many of the social democrats connected with this circle were to escape detection during the wave of persecution which followed the failure of the assassination attempt. This has also made it difficult to assess today the actual extent of the networks of socialists connected with the conspiracy which were developed at the regional level.[25]

The outlook and attitudes of the Goerdeler Circle have mainly survived in the form of Goerdeler's own memoranda and programmatic drafts. These very much bear his personal stamp, though he drew on the advice of a considerable number of people in drafting them. The trade unionists involved limited themselves initially to attempting to reconcile trade union aims with those of their national conservative partners. Leuschner and Kaiser were in agreement that any return to the 'Marxist class unions' of the past had to be avoided and that a future united trade union movement should encompass all people in dependent employment, including white-collar workers and civil servants.[26] They thus adopted the thinking of the Leadership Circle of 1933, though they also took certain elements of the DAF's constitution on board, notably its effectively compulsory membership.[27]

Goerdeler originally thought in terms of maintaining the DAF in its existing form and even later continued to favour maintaining the system of labour trustees instituted by the Nazis. Under the influence of the trade unionists, he included in the group's programme for a social and political new order the idea of a 'German Union' structured very similarly to the DAF. This 'German Union' was to have a monopoly in the representation of all categories of workers and was to be based on compulsory membership. In line with Goerdeler's economic ideas, the united union was entrusted mainly with public service duties, particularly the administration of the unemployment insurance system and the labour exchanges. The role allotted to it in the self-regulating structures planned for the economy and the proposed Reichsständekammer would have given it a position of key social and economic power.[28] This would have been further underscored by the nationalization of basic industries in the raw materials sector, which was adopted on Leuschner's insistence, as well as by the provisions allowing the unions to run economic enterprises of their own.[29] The plans for the future role of the unions were the product of a series of compromises. These included accommodating Goerdeler's determination that the state be excluded from any involvement in industrial relations and that the administration of social welfare be transferred exclusively to workers' representatives. The strong corporatist element which pervaded the constitutional model adopted, and especially its provisions for a structured system of representation for social interests, was a concession to the Christian trade unionists involved, whose thinking was strongly influenced by Catholic Social Principles.[30] Leuschner was probably influenced just as strongly by memories of the war economy system introduced in 1917 and the community economy models proposed by Wissell and Moellendorff.[31]

The 'German Union' idea was in basic conflict with virtually all the aims of the Kreisau Circle. Its centralist and bureaucratic characteristics were diametrically opposed to the view rigidly adhered to by Moltke and Yorck that precisely such 'top-heavy organizations' had to be avoided.[32] It was a testimony to Leuschner's tactical skills that he was able to get the Kreisau Circle to compromise and accept the 'German Union' as a transitionary solution, though Moltke certainly hoped to be able to reverse this eventually. Directives drawn up for the proposed Länder administrators explicitly provided for the union.[33] The Kreisau Circle's ideas favoured in-house unions uniting workers and employers at the factory level which, while similar to the Nazi factory community, had the declared objective of achieving genuinely equal participation for workers and included the principle of profit sharing. But this concept was practicable at best only in small or medium-sized firms and, in addition, would have involved considerable restrictions on workers' mobility and freedom of choice.[34]

The central question of whether the unions of the future would have the right to strike was apparently never resolved. Leuschner appears not to have raised the issue of trade union rights to free collective bargaining with Goerdeler. This would hardly have been compatible with the system of labour trustees favoured by him. The new economic order proposed by the Freiburg economists implicitly excluded the unions from any role and the Kreisau Circle's economic proposals equally were based on premises which ruled out free collective bargaining, positing instead a largely state-centred approach to the regulation of wages.[35] Goerdeler thought that by granting the unions a substantial say in economic decision-making they would exercise considerable restraint on the wages front. It was symptomatic that in line with his economic outlook, which was close to *laissez faire* ideas, he believed that economic growth would require that wages be reduced and working hours increased.[36] In contrast, Leuschner almost certainly believed that the extensive participatory rights granted the unions would guarantee them a sufficient say in influencing wage trends. No definite agreement was ever reached on any of these issues or on the question of a social security system.[37]

The exceptional consideration given the trade unions in the planned new economic order was strongly opposed by the right wing of the resistance, especially by Jens Jessen, Johannes Popitz and Ulrich von Hassell who, not without justification, believed it was excessively weighted in favour of one particular social interest.[38] The fact that a majority of the conspirators finally accepted the idea was a result of the general conviction that class conflict had to be overcome and that a socially equitable order had to be established. Most believed that the establishment of the Nazi dictatorship had come about because the working class had not been sufficiently integrated with the state, despite the extremely divergent views they otherwise held as to how the social question should best be resolved. It was difficult therefore to oppose an accommodation with the unions.

On the other hand, no one could know to what extent workers would welcome the proposed unitary trade union organization. Leuschner's success in getting his ideas largely adopted was not least a result of his constant insistence that he had an extensive network of contacts at the ready which would rapidly re-establish the trade union movement in the event of a successful coup. But both Carlo Mierendorff and Julius Leber were highly doubtful of this. Mierendorff referred derogatively to the individuals Leuschner had in mind to form the leadership of the proposed union as 'half a baker's dozen of toughs'.[39] It is in fact surprising that the personalities Leuschner considered included men like August Winnig, who had long broken with the SPD and were generally regarded as renegades. But it must be remembered that the conspiratorial conditions under which they were working meant that when it came to recruiting people for leading positions there was little choice but to fall back on the existing reservoir of former trade union officials. Indeed, after 1945 the process of re-establishing the trade union movement largely followed this pattern.

Despite the solidarity which emerged between them on the surface, the relationship between Leuschner and the socialists of the Kreisau Circle was not free of tensions and rivalry. Leuschner initially attempted to prevent Goerdeler, who wanted to establish contacts with former social democrats, from involving Leber any more deeply in the work of the group. Leber for his part was distrustful and held back from too close an involvement. He was particularly sceptical of Leuschner's trade union plans. The conflict that had erupted in 1932–3 between the ADGB leadership and the SPD executive on the issue of the unions' party political neutrality, which had never been resolved, was at the root of this.[40]

Leuschner basically held that the creation of a unitary trade union organization made the labour movement's political wing superfluous and that the compromise reached between Goerdeler and the trade union group effectively negated the need for a revival of the SPD. But the fundamental issue was what role political parties would have to play in the structures of the new state. Goerdeler, who in this regard had no major differences with the Kreisau Circle, wanted to minimize the role of political parties as far as possible and prevent the re-establishment of nationally centralized party organizations. He thought that granting them a role in the political process would contradict the principle of self-administrative autonomy which formed the backbone of the type of state he envisaged. He had not totally made up his mind on this issue, however, and for a while considered the idea of allowing for a three-party system in the British mould. Jakob Kaiser thought in terms of creating a broad, socially oriented, populist party across the confessional divide, reminiscent of Adam Stegerwald's Essen Programme of 1920.[41] The basis of this was to be a broad workers' organization along the lines of the British Labour Party. This converged with Habermann's ideas that parties be formed on the basis of professional or social groups.[42]

Leuschner believed that trade union unity was a considerably more effective means to overcome the splits in the labour movement than any ideas of tackling them at the level of party politics. The multiple splintering of the party political system was generally regarded as one of the reasons why the parliamentary system of the Weimar Republic had been unable to function. The trade union group also believed that the Communist Party would not reappear. Only from 1943 was it generally accepted that the old political parties, including the KPD, would re-emerge in the event of a successful coup. The socialists in the Kreisau Circle also sought alternatives to the traditional class-based party political system, however much they were concerned to maintain solidarity among former social democrats.

Helmuth James von Moltke, the guiding spirit of the Kreisau Circle, advocated a fundamental restructuring of society and politics on the basis of 'small communities'. This was basically a conservative version of the workers' councils system and involved a restructuring of the state and society along federalist and decentralized lines.[43] Leading members of the Kreisau Circle, including Father Alfred Delp and Adam von Trott zu Solz, were motivated by a desire for a new social order which would produce fundamental social harmony. Partly influenced by neo-conservative thinking, they were at variance, however, in the importance they attached to the idea of socialism. Count Peter Yorck von Wartenburg in particular hoped that a substantially socialist type of society would be achieved, though one which would leave sufficient space for the development of the individual and hold to the principle of subordinance.

Moltke was concerned from the start to draw workers' representatives into the Kreisau Circle's deliberations. With the involvement of Mierendorff, Haubach, Reichwein and Ernst von Harnack, he was joined by people of a like mind, though as intellectuals of bourgeois background they represented only a fringe element of the labour movement. Of them only Mierendorff had played an active official role in the SPD, in his capacity as Leuschner's press officer in Hesse. Along with Haubach, he had belonged to the circle around the magazine *Neue Blätter für den Sozialismus* which, while it had attracted considerable public attention from 1929, had been outside the official spectrum of SPD opinion.[44] Reichwein had only been a member of the SPD since 1930. As Haubach became increasingly attracted to Christian socialist ideas,[45] Emil Henk, a close confidant of Mierendorff's, remained in the background.

Together with Mierendorff, Moltke continually attempted to win Leuschner over to the ideas advocated by the Kreisau Circle. In this he was to fail completely. Apart from disputes between them on practical issues, they were divided by fundamental differences of political outlook. To the trade union leader accustomed to thinking in the pragmatic terms of organizational power and with little regard for theoretical issues, Moltke's central concept of 'small communities' must have made little sense. It proved possible, however, to prevent a formal breach between the two men. Acting as arbiter, Mierendorff succeeded at least in getting Hermann Maass, Leuschner's close associate, to act as a type of liaison man between them.[46] Moltke regarded Mierendorff, who was killed in an air raid towards the end of 1943, as virtually indispensable, partly because his own ideas were very close to Mierendorff's and partly because of the great respect which the social democrats connected with the conspiracy had for him. Moltke tried to fill the gap left by Mierendorff's death by drawing in Julius Leber, to whom he characteristically gave the undercover name 'Neumann' ('the new man'). But Leber maintained a distinct reserve and avoided too close an involvement. While Moltke expressed his disappointment at this, he never gave up hope of eventually winning him over to the Kreisau Circle's ideas.[47] However much Leber sympathized with Moltke's and Yorck's basic social perspective, he was never comfortable with the more esoteric elements of the Kreisau programme and particularly did not share the belief that the collapse of the Third Reich would be followed by an epochal new start. His pragmatic temperament and democratic Jacobinism contrasted sharply with the contemplative background of much of the Kreisau Circle's original deliberations.[48]

Moltke's attempts to win over Leber occurred at a time when it was becoming clear that Germany was facing military defeat on the Eastern Front. He was realistic enough to realize that any political order inaugurated after the military collapse of the Third Reich would have to take account of the emergence of the Soviet Union as a great power. In his memorandum of December 1943 directed at the British government[49] he pointed, with reference to the establishment of the League of German Officers in Moscow, to the danger of a 'communist-bolshevist development in Germany' and to the threat of a German national bolshevism emerging. He therefore regarded it as absolutely essential that if the post-coup government was not to be in 'a hopeless situation from the start, in constant confrontation with the working class and its communist elements', it would need a very strong left-wing involvement and the support of 'social democratic and trade union circles'. On this point he was strongly supported by Adam von Trott zu Solz and Fritz-Dietlov von der Schulenburg. This position of Moltke's, which has only survived at second hand but is borne out by corresponding statements in his letters to his wife, represented a change of mind on his part. While he had wanted to involve working-class representatives from the beginning, he had originally hoped it would be possible to avoid having to link up with former socialist organizations.

There is considerable evidence to suggest that it was the socialists in the Kreisau Circle, with Mierendorff acting in liaison with Leber, who first drew attention to the possibility of Germany being bolshevized.[50] In these circumstances, the co-operation of SPD representatives assumed an increased importance. But even leaving aside such conclusions, which were drawn from the major changes in the international political balance, both Moltke and Goerdeler wanted to secure social democratic involvement because they believed that – with the Allied insistence on 'unconditional surrender' – it was the only basis on which they could hope to secure enough support among the population for the coup. Again it was the socialists, and particularly Mierendorff, who took the initiative in getting the individual resistance circles to co-operate closely together. This had become vital as it became clear from 1942 that it was no longer sufficient to simply await a German military collapse and the incalculable consequences this would have. Everything possible now had to be done to create a political base for the coup being planned by the military. With regard to the constitutional basis of the government which would follow the coup, the proposals advanced by the Goerdeler and Kreisau Circles were noticeably influenced by one another, despite the very divergent premises from which they had developed.[51]

The decision of late 1943 to draft a common platform for a post-Nazi government had the effect of blurring the differences which had previously separated the two resistance groups occupied with political preparations for the coup. While Goerdeler had been virtually the sole representative of the civilian resistance who was in touch with the military opposition up until then, Leuschner and some of the Christian union leaders, as well as Maass and Leber, now established direct contact with Stauffenberg. The distrust which this provoked in Goerdeler was reflected in the inaccurate assertion in the Kaltenbrunner Reports that 'the underground SPD and the unions had intended using Goerdeler to come to power themselves'.[52] Stauffenberg's immediately positive response to the approaches by the socialists has been well established. But they for their part were plagued by misgivings, as was shown by Maass's reaction to a particular speech by Stauffenberg.[53]

This was also partly why the direct contact between Stauffenberg and Leber which Schulenburg had worked for and finally established only came about at the end of 1943.[54]

An exceptionally close relationship developed spontaneously between the sober and sarcastic-minded General Staff officer and the former Lübeck politician. Leber's military past contributed to overcoming what had at first appeared to be an unbridgeable gulf separating the two personalities. Stauffenberg regarded Leber as a congenial figure and tended if anything to overestimate his political talent. He believed he had found the popular leader who would be able to overcome what he regarded as the tragic schism between the army and the working class which had erupted openly in 1918. Stauffenberg wanted to avoid an old-style purely military putsch at all costs and Leber reinforced him in this conviction. He hoped that in alliance with Leber he would be able to achieve the political integration of the new government with the people after the coup. The two men shared a realistic perspective on the coup's declining chances of achieving international recognition. But most of all they were both insistent on the need for decisive action, including the assassination of Hitler if necessary, which Goerdeler and originally Leuschner too had regarded with extreme scepticism.[55]

Leber's position was one of total support for Stauffenberg. This was in contrast to Leuschner, who was primarily concerned to ensure the reconstruction of the trade union movement in the event of either a military collapse or a change of regime instigated by the military. He also differed from Goerdeler, who believed that Germany needed a fundamentally new constitutional and social structure that went beyond the establishment of a provisional government, which he did not by any means think of purely as a transitionary arrangement.[56] Leber was distinctly sceptical of such long-term planning, in contrast, for example, to Helmuth von Moltke. Moltke, while agreeing to the need for a military coup, was not, or at least not yet, prepared to face up – as a matter of basic principle rather than on any primarily moral grounds – to the political consequences which assassination entailed. For Leber, deposing the Nazi system as soon as possible was much more important than discussing long-term plans for a reordering of society. He argued constantly for an alliance of all available forces and was conscious that émigré elements would have to be accommodated in any future political arrangements.[57]

Leber's position was similar to Mierendorff's in that he regarded it as essential that the provisional government emphasize the socialist elements in its programme and seek to mobilize the widest possible political support in the population. As early as June 1943 and parallel to the third Kreisau conference then meeting, Mierendorff drafted a proclamation calling for the establishment of a mass movement which he labelled 'Socialist Action'.

He had discussed this, at least in idea form, with Moltke and Yorck, but it was to run into opposition from individual members of the Kreisau Circle, including Haubach.[58] While otherwise agreeing with the proposal, Haubach criticized the idea of including communists in the proposed movement's leadership council. Leber was opposed to its emphasis on Christian principles. But both basically agreed on the need to actively involve the general population in the coup to give it the character of a national revolution.

In November 1943 a fundamental disagreement temporarily arose between Moltke and Mierendorff in the context of these plans.[59] This was only superficially resolved and, following Mierendorff's death, was not seriously tackled again. The differences between the two men were apparently connected with Leber's support for Stauffenberg's position and with factional disputes among the socialists at the time. Moltke's fear that backing Stauffenberg would mean sacrificing 'basic principles' very probably referred to the pragmatic approach demanded by Leber, which included proceeding with an assassination attempt on Hitler.[60] Mierendorff for his part attempted to strike a compromise between the Kreisau Circle's perspective – which started from the presumption that the system would collapse completely of its own accord and that the Reich would be militarily defeated – and the consequences if a coup were staged immediately, when the existing political forces of the Third Reich would have to be accommodated. He took it as axiomatic that if a coup were attempted, it would be actively opposed by Nazi-indoctrinated sections of the population.[61]

With the adoption of the plan to create a non-party popular movement, the national conservative resistance effectively abandoned its original perspective. This had been rooted in traditional authoritarian precepts and had envisaged merely a change of government at the top, while the Kreisau concept had foreseen society reconstructing itself on the basis of 'small communities' spontaneously formed at local and regional level. This development was the result of a process which had been initiated by Leber and Mierendorff and had been supported by the other socialists in the Kreisau Circle, though the proposal to include the underground KPD or at least to involve 'non-Muscovite communists'[62] remained a matter of dispute. The leading representatives of the Kreisau Circle, especially Moltke and Yorck, argued for a 'non-party popular movement', which they saw not as a centrally controlled mass organization but rather as an alliance of all responsible forces along the lines of the new political elite drawn from all social classes, as advocated by Moltke.[63] Goerdeler's thinking, coloured by the governmental mentality typical of him, envisaged a mass organization run by the state and established 'from above' following the coup; it would form the basis from which political parties could be formed in the future. The trade union group regarded the proposed democratic mass movement mainly as an instrument of social integration, with Leuschner going a considerable distance to accommodate the Christian union leaders by stressing the Christian element in the movement's proposed programme. This led to vigorous protests from Leber, who made it clear to Leuschner and Kaiser that 'he would not allow important basic principles of the old SPD to be simply thrown overboard, even if this meant jeopardizing the consensus everyone desired'.[64] As against this, however, Leber and Mierendorff saw the proposed popular movement in an explicitly national revolutionary perspective. Both thought in terms of 'a new type of popular front based on all surviving and capable democratic forces'; Mierendorff regarded KPD participation as essential from the start while Leber preferred to leave this question open.

Apart from these disputes over the programmatic perspective of the proposed popular movement, which were not resolved before the assassination attempt went ahead, the issue which now moved to the fore was whether Goerdeler was a suitable choice for the leadership of the government given the changed domestic political situation. The left wing of the Kreisau Circle in particular expressed considerable reservations about Goerdeler, occasionally going as far as lambasting his allegedly 'reactionary' outlook. These were sometimes the result of misunderstandings. The constitutional programme of the Goerdeler Circle did not differ fundamentally from that of the emphasis on the need for federalist structures. There was also a substantial level of agreement on economic policy, but Goerdeler gave considerably greater weight to the maintenance of a private enterprise system. Nevertheless Goerdeler accommodated the trade unionists' demand that the nationalization of basic industries in the raw materials sector be included in the programme and the Kreisau Circle compromised on the trade union question.

It was primarily Goerdeler's decisive rejection of welfare state principles that met with criticism from the Kreisau Circle, which wanted a strong socialist element in any new state structure. In this regard the Kreisau Circle rejected the proposals from its economic advisers, whose ideas were largely identical to those of the Goerdeler Circle. This was hardly surprising given that, just as much as the Freiburg Circle, headed by Constantin von Dietze, which advised Goerdeler, they were influenced by the precepts of classical state liberalism and advocated an end to the Nazi contingency economy and a revival of the 'free play of forces'.[65] Like Goerdeler, this group believed that the unemployment insurance system had failed. They wanted to see the productivity of the economy increased, in the first instance by controls on the regulation of working hours, and hence rejected a return to the eight-hour day. Günter Schmölders proposed a mixed system of private and public enterprise in which the latter would be prevented from retarding the development of the private sector by having imposed on it policies that would maintain lower wage levels and less favourable working conditions. He also thought in terms of having a compulsory labour service to absorb unused labour power rather than any state system of unemployment benefit payments.[66]

Most of the economists advising the national conservative opposition were followers of Walter Eucken. In many ways their proposals were a forerunner of the social market economy pursued in the Federal Republic after 1948.[67] They differed from Goerdeler in that they were committed believers in large-scale production, though they shared his belief in the need for an expansion of anti-trust legislation to maintain the basis of the free market economy. Goerdeler on the other hand regarded the medium-scale independent production unit predominant in Württemberg as the ideal. In this he was close to the views of Fritz-Dietlof von der Schulenburg. Although he was not so unrealistic as to advocate a dismantling of the existing large-city industrial bases, he did think in terms of introducing a licensing system for the siting of large-scale industries so as to limit the growth of industrial concentrations.[68] Schulenburg's radical departure from the principle of the welfare state was an indication of the extent to which the thinking of many of the conspirators ignored the modern world of large-scale industrial production.

But differences of opinion on social and economic policy were far from the central issue at stake in the conflict that arose between Goerdeler on one side and the Kreisau Circle and Stauffenberg's political advisers on the other. It was rather Goerdeler's terminology, so evocative of Manchester liberalism, that was provocative; it brought him accusations – from both the left wing of the Kreisau Circle, as represented by Yorck, and from the right wing of the conspiracy in the person of Ulrich von Hassell – that he was a 'reactionary' and a partisan of large-scale industry, which in this form were not justified.[69] The basic political differences which this signified were further accentuated, however, by the fact that leading members of the Kreisau Circle and also Stauffenberg himself no longer thought it opportune that Goerdeler be made head of government – Moltke even spoke of a 'Kerensky solution'.[70] This was because of Goerdeler's fundamental opposition to any involvement of left-wing socialists or communists.[71]

But Leuschner was not prepared to accede to Stauffenberg's prompting to try to secure the position of chancellor for himself. He was motivated in this decision not only by personal loyalty to Goerdeler but also by the consideration that if he adopted too prominent a role in the transitionary government he would risk prematurely squandering the bargaining position of the labour movement. Given that Leber was equally reluctant, the composition of the cabinet as originally agreed was apparently maintained, with Leuschner as vice-chancellor and Leber as minister for the interior ensuring the socialists an exceptionally strong position. Leuschner brought considerable pressure to bear on Goerdeler in the matter of filling particular positions, such as Haubach's appointment as government press officer. This shows the considerable extent to which Goerdeler's influence declined during the final months before the assassination attempt. It also demonstrates the extent to which Stauffenberg did not consider himself merely the executor of the civilian conspirators' will but had independent views of his own which he sought to realize.[72]

The conflicts which arose over political differences during the final phase of preparations before the coup must be understood against the background of the almost unbearable nervous strain which resulted from the constant postponements of the assassination attempt and the growing threat that the Gestapo would uncover the entire plot. It was also natural that such conflicts would develop once the decision to act had been taken. The emergence of political differences despite the willingness on the part of all concerned to attempt to reach agreement on programmatic issues indicates that the 20 July movement would not have expended its energies in further medium- and long-term planning, which by its very nature had to be largely theoretical, but would have been capable of taking the decisive steps necessary to create a concrete political framework.

Another factor was the psychological pressure exercised by the existence of the 'National Committee for a Free Germany', whose influence the conspirators tended if anything to overestimate.[73] It was this which decided Leber and Reichwein to try to make contact with the communist resistance movement. According to Emil Henk, the communists revealed their readiness to co-operate with the coup at the meeting finally held in early July 1944, though it was hardly in the interests of the Moscow leadership that their hands be tied in an alliance of this kind at such a late period when the military collapse of the Reich was imminent. Following the failure of the assassination attempt, the KPD distanced itself unequivocally from the plot.[74] The political reasoning behind the approach to the communists lay in the attempt it represented to secure their limited co-operation; as the behaviour of the Saefkow group demonstrated, this was not an unrealistic proposition. It was without doubt of benefit to the conspirators to have some idea of how the communists would react. The approach was also motivated by the idea that by involving the communists they could pre-empt any plans the Soviet Union might have had to bolshevize Germany. However problematic this might have been, the meeting with the communists had absolutely nothing to do with the eastern orientation attributed to Stauffenberg by Gisevius.[75]

In assessing the development of the resistance movement which led from the regrouping of late 1940 to the attempted coup of July 1944, one fact which emerges is that the representatives of the organized labour movement, despite their minority position within the circle of conspirators, were remarkably successful in having their views on central programmatic questions adopted. They also exercised a substantial influence on the civilian preparations for the coup. During the final phase they constantly pushed for immediate and decisive action and it was largely by their doing that the various resistance groups which were acting relatively independently of each other beforehand came together to work out a common political platform. The disproportionately large influence exercised by the socialists was not solely due to the fact that men like Leber, Leuschner, Mierendorff and Haubach had had more practical political experience in general than was the case with the majority of their national conservative co-conspirators. What was much more decisive was the gradual realization within the resistance that it would be impossible to secure the political base of the coup if the forces of the working class were excluded.

Whether the mobilization of the industrial working class in the wake of a successful coup for which both Leuschner and Leber hoped, even if in different forms, would have actually occurred had the *coup d'état* not been immediately smashed must remain a matter of speculation. Large sections of even the formerly socialist elements of the working class would probably have reacted hesitantly or even have displayed a certain reserve at the bourgeois character of the provisional government. Nevertheless it was essential that everything possible be attempted to win the working class – the most likely oppositional force – for the new regime as the new government would have neither foreign policy nor military successes to its credit. But the labour representatives in the conspiracy were clear about one thing: that the social democratic underground on its own simply did not have the means to take any effective action, just as the KPD, for all its heroic attempts to create the basis for a mass opposition, never succeeded in extending its influence beyond its immediate membership and largely spent its energies trying to keep its underground network operational.

The political objective of both trade unionists and socialists in the Kreisau Circle dovetailed in many ways with the national conservative concept of a fundamental new start. Only Leber appears to have consciously considered the fact that in the event of a coup coinciding with military collapse, the domestic political considerations on which the alliance with the national conservative elites was based would lose its rationale.[76] But the determination to proceed with the coup despite the apparent increasing unlikelihood of it succeeding transcended all calculations of political interest or strategy. It was rooted in the conviction common to all the conspirators that if there was to be any hope of re-establishing the credibility of politics in Germany, an unconditional stand for humanity and freedom had to be taken against a regime which had gone beyond all bounds in its criminal brutality.

10

German Society and the Resistance to Hitler

Nearly fifty years ago, the attempt of 20 July 1944 to end the Nazi regime's rampage of destruction ended in failure. It is now time to take stock from two perspectives of what this attempted coup involved. On the one hand, the history of the German resistance to Hitler needs to be placed in the overall context of the historiography of the national socialist era as altered and refined by the advances in research and changes in conceptual approaches of recent years. On the other, it needs to be reassessed in terms of its relevance as an integral part of German and European history to present-day politics. When the German opposition to Hitler first became an object of historical interest, it was in the context of attempts to disprove Allied theories of collective guilt and to construct a bridge of historical continuity to span the twelve years of Nazi rule, which were regarded at the time as a catastrophic and unnatural interruption of the historical process by demonically destructive forces. This historiographical context is no longer relevant.

The need to reinforce the historical legitimacy of the democratic order established with the founding of the Federal Republic by referring to the resistance to Nazism has also receded. In the full confidence of the respectability of the new Republic's domestic and international success, the search for historical legitimacy appears to have lost its former urgency. This is in contrast to the German Democratic Republic, for which identification with the tradition of 'anti-fascist struggle' had always been an integral element of its 'national' self-identity and by no means merely a functionalist instrument of propaganda.[1]

Does this mean that the resistance to Hitler has been freed from its 'usefulness' in the political sense and become part of the 'neutral' history of past events? Has it become part of a general and non-controversial consensus from which a regenerated national perspective on German history is emerging? In some general histories it now receives only peripheral mention.[2] In historical research it has lost its previously central position, apart, that is, from secondary studies concentrating on the resistance by the left or on émigré circles. On the other hand, increasing attempts have been made recently to give more attention to the resistance in the schools curriculum, and the introduction of the President's Prize has had the effect of actually intensifying interest in the resistance movement at the local level. Left-wing history workshops have been trying to revive memories of the working-class resistance to Nazism. But these tend to be as excessively idealized as much of the early post-war resistance literature was and have not had much impact on official historiography. The media, as was particularly noticeable at the time of the fortieth anniversary commemorations of the 1944 plot, constantly seek new angles on the subject and recently both the CDU/CSU and, if more circumspectly, the SPD have sought to portray themselves as the political inheritors of the resistance tradition.

It is unanimously accepted that the resistance cannot be judged solely in terms of outward success. Experiences with dictatorships in our own time as well as a more accurate knowledge of the conditions under which the German conspirators worked have shown just how minute the chances were for the regime to be toppled from within. The formula 'conscience in revolt' rightly reminds us that the decision to consciously embark on a course of high treason, with all the issues that involved, demanded deep ethical impulses transcending mere political interest or social motives. But our picture of the resistance should not be limited to a study of its moral dimension. A genuine understanding and balanced assessment of it is only possible if the political motivations and aims of the conspirators are taken into account and considered in the context of both the constantly changing overall situation of the regime and the social and intellectual background to the outlook developed by the resisters, the roots of which go back to the era of the Weimar Republic.

It is as inappropriate, therefore, to idealize the men and women of the resistance as heroes as it is to identify in a purely superficial way with the forces of the 'other Germany'. This can easily lead to a sidestepping of the question of the structural roots in German society which gave rise to the Nazi system. Similarly, the general tendency in the Federal Republic to tacitly taboo the role the communists played in the resistance must be questioned. To attempt to deny the legitimacy of the communist resistance by equating it, as a 'totalitarian' movement, with Nazism fails to recognize the unique nature of the national socialist system and puts political value judgements above analytical criteria. The various forms the resistance took and the many directions within it must be examined as a whole, as a reflection of the actual spectrum of political alternatives to the Nazi system which existed in German society.

The dominant tendency in the past was to interpret the history of the resistance by putting forward an alleged 'other Germany' to counter the national socialist reality.[3] But this picture is contradicted by the actual situation, where the decision to become involved in high treason against the head of the state could coexist with a continued political loyalty in other areas. It was coloured by a great deal of ambivalence, whereby refusal to support the regime merged with tendencies to resist it, and alternative strategies for toppling the regime overlapped with ones which would have substantially maintained the system and ones which sought its total destruction. Similarly, active resistance did not simply follow once an ethically based opposition to the regime had developed, but tended rather to be a result of changed expectations, attitudes and opportunities and of the external and internal development of the regime itself. Indeed, it is precisely these conflicts of loyalty which offer such a rich source of insight for today's younger generation when attempting to understand the nature of the Third Reich.

Even a person who basically rejected national socialism, regardless of his or her individual moral courage, needed some perspective from which the decisive step to resistance could be taken. While communists and socialists were by definition fundamentally and irreconcilably hostile to the NSDAP, there were also numerous other individuals who were opposed to Hitler from the start. Ewald von Kleist-Schmenzin, the traditionalist conservative, is a clear case in point.[4] But, in the early years at least, antipathy to the regime by no means automatically implied actively resisting it. In this phase, bourgeois and conservative circles still mistakenly believed that a moderation of its politics could be achieved if the radical elements of the NSDAP – from which Hitler was amazingly exempted – were brought under control. Before the step to active resistance could be taken, it had to be learned by bitter experience that it would not be enough to modify the regime or its policies by, for example, removing Himmler and Goebbels, restraining the power of the SS or, as was actually done, eliminating the radical leadership of the SA.[5]

The majority of those involved in the national conservative resistance, several of whom held unequivocally Nazi views and most of whom either held senior positions of authority or were members of the officer corps, believed, at least up to the beginning of the war, that they would be able to contain the radicalizing tendencies in the regime. These tendencies were regarded primarily as a threat to the Reich's external security and it was felt they could be contained without having to undertake any major changes in the internal structures of the system. The contingency decision, taken at the time of the international crisis over Czechoslovakia, to arrest Hitler if necessary did not include any intention of changing the regime as such.[6] Similarly, the establishment of foreign contacts directed via the Vatican at

Britain and documented in the X Report, included a proposal to make Hermann Göring chancellor in place of Hitler.[7]

For the KPD, which had already uncompromisingly fought the Weimar system, the establishment of the Nazi regime in 1933 merely meant changing the form of its struggle. This was only fully achieved after the murderous losses incurred when it was still generally believed that the system would rapidly collapse of its own accord. Among social democrats, some elements tried to seek an accommodation with the regime. But, despite numerous warnings from Rudolf Breitscheid and other members of the party, the characteristic attitude adopted in SPD circles was that if a passive stance were taken the party organization would survive the period of open fascist dictatorship intact. Only radical groups such as the 'Neubeginnen' or the Roter Stosstrupp realized the necessity of adapting to conspiratorial methods to resist the regime, but this was foreign to the traditions of German socialism.[8] The churches, and particularly the Catholic youth movement, believed they could survive by simply holding their ground. The illusion that the political situation had remained a basically open one was thus very widespread at first.

What was true of the resistance in its formative phase was also true of its development during the Second World War. Hitler's growth in popularity after the success of the French campaign made the prospect of his removal appear virtually hopeless. The war in the West generally, and the constantly fluid situation it produced in the areas of military and foreign policy, dramatically changed the context for the national conservative opposition. This situation occurred again after the opening of the Eastern Front. The policy of attempting to prevent war became a policy of attempting to contain it or to bring it to an end. Leading military figures who had sympathized with the opposition groups headed by Beck, Hassell, Popitz and Goerdeler up to 1939 now withdrew from any active involvement. By conducting the war in the East as an anti-bolshevik crusade, Hitler won increasing sympathy among army leaders, many of whom, including some later prominent in the military opposition, became enmeshed in the criminal policies implemented in the field.[9] The Allied demand for an unconditional surrender restricted the opposition's psychological room to manoeuvre, however much the majority of them hoped that it would be possible to get around it. Finally, after the Allied invasion at Normandy it became highly debatable whether any attempt to restabilize the military situation could have any hope of success.[10]

The internal political conditions for effective opposition also changed fundamentally. Several factors combined to rule out any possibility of altering the regime simply on the basis of a government reshuffle or the elimination of specific bastions of Nazi power such as the SS or the

Propaganda Ministry: for example, the authority of the traditional government ministries was gradually eroded and simultaneously, as a result of the
system of bureaucratic apparatuses being both individually subordinate to
Hitler and in permanent competition with one another, the exercise of
power was rendered informal. Another factor was the emasculation of the
social homogeneity of the officer corps and of the autonomy of the Wehrmacht leadership deliberately engineered by Hitler.[11] As a result of the
Hitler myth systematically being propagated by Goebbels, no institution –
such as the monarchy in Italy – survived alongside the dictator which could
have functioned to legitimize a government installed by a *coup d'état*.[12]
Stauffenberg's ingenious attempt, with his Walküre plan, to make the army
the stabilizing force behind the new regime after the coup failed not least
because the social homogeneity of the Prussian-German officer corps had
long since been destroyed as a result of the rearmament and war policies
pursued by the Nazi regime.[13]

Both a fundamental rethink and a realization that the national socialist
regime was criminal and inhuman by its very nature were necessary before
it was grasped that, given the structured legality of the regime, only a
'revolutionary' act which went beyond merely eliminating the criminal
elements in the Nazi elite could lead to the fundamental changes required
throughout the entire system. Under the existing conditions, this had to
include the assassination of Hitler. Disregarding the problem of the oath,
to which too much importance was later attached,[14] there was no other way
in which the integrating power of the Führer myth could have been
extinguished. Goerdeler's hope that the mass of the population could
be brought over to the conspirators' side by exposing the crimes and
irresponsibility of the Führer[15] missed the essential point that the loyalty
of the mass of the people to Hitler was based on the irrational need for
national identification. This popular identification with the Führer only
began to show any signs of collapse in the final months of the war and
until then coexisted with a widespread criticism of both the party and the
SS as institutions as well as of particular party and SS members.

In speaking of the 'Nessus shirt' which the conspirators were forced to
wear,[16] Henning von Tresckow defined their situation memorably and
succinctly. Any attempt to destroy the deep bonds of loyalty to Hitler in
the social psychology of the German people had perforce to lead to the
conspirators being regarded as traitors to the nation.[17] This helps to explain
the extreme isolation of active resistance groups, which was due not only
to the Gestapo's relatively effective policing and successful terrorizing of
the population but also, in no small part, to the psychological barriers against
going outside the national community, which were concretely symbolized in
the person of Hitler. It is revealing, therefore, that the only people able to
take the step from being critical of aspects of the national socialist system

to active resistance were either those who, like the communists or left-wing socialists, could resist the Hitler myth on the basis of their own strong ideological or political faiths, or those who had an in-built resistance to the psychological pressure to conform to the Führer cult on the basis of exclusive social background and position, and the inherently self-contained national consciousness or alternative utopia which these involved.

This was reflected in the social composition of the opponents of the regime who opted for active resistance. Following the appearance of Hans Rothfel's book, the view came to be widely held that the resistance circles behind the July 1944 conspiracy included men and women from all social groups and were thus representative of German society as a whole.[18] Helmuth James von Moltke wished to dispel any image of social exclusiveness and sought to involve representatives of the working class in the Kreisau Circle's activities.[19] This was also true of Goerdeler. But the methods of recruitment employed by the national conservative opposition limited its potential base to the upper and upper middle classes and this necessarily gave it a socially exclusive character.[20] The vast majority of those involved in the civilian opposition groups were senior civil servants drawn either from the interior administration and the justice sector or from the diplomatic corps. The trade union leaders involved, such as Wilhelm Leuschner and Jakob Kaiser, and union officials such as Max Habermann and Hermann Maass were in a comparable situation to men like Beck, Goerdeler and von Hassell who had been deprived of their former public positions. Independent lawyers like Josef Wirmer or parliamentarians as represented to some extent by Julius Leber were exceptions. Some intellectuals from between the main social classes, such as Carlo Mierendorff, Theodor Haubach, Adolf Reichwein and, in a certain sense, Father Alfred Delp were also involved.

The prominent role played by members of the aristocracy, particularly in the military opposition, is a further indication of the extent to which the national conservative resistance was based mainly on the remnants of old social classes. These had remained immune to Nazism and had access to pre-political networks of contacts. Professional motives sometimes played an important part in recruitment, particularly for the diplomats and military men involved, and in this connection the extraordinary role played by the elite Infantry Regiment No. 9 as a source of recruits should be remembered.[21] The network was made up largely of family and social contacts rather than any structured conspiratorial organization, such as that developed by the underground KPD on the basis of cells and code-names. Paradoxically, this situation, combined with the critical attitude to the regime widespread in upper-class circles, contributed to the fact that the Gestapo only uncovered many of these resistance circles, such as the Solf Circle and the Abwehr network, relatively late and only became aware of the full extent of the conspiracy weeks after the assassination attempt had been foiled.[22]

From a sociological point of view, the national conservative conspiracy was primarily a resistance movement of top public officials. Their automatic identification with the state as understood in classic German terms explains how the national conservative opposition could presume to act in the interests of the nation without ever considering that some democratic mechanisms to legitimize their actions might be desirable. The plans developed for a new social order by the circles headed by Moltke and Goerdeler were pervaded therefore by the spirit of 'revolution from above', even if the ideas they advocated for autonomously subordinate 'small communities' and their adherence to the principle of self-adminis-trative social structures were directed against the re-emergence of a hierarchical centralized state.[23] The earliest plans for a new social order, such as those discussed in the Abwehr group and in the circle headed by Hassell and Popitz, were based on the premise that the Nazi policy of Gleichschaltung – of 'co-ordinating' all existing social institutions with the regime – and the far-reaching depoliticization of the population achieved by Nazi propaganda had effectively wiped the political slate clean. No one thought in terms of a return to parliamentarism or of a multi-party system re-emerging.

In fact, a brief look at the map of continental Europe at the time would have made it seem obvious that the parliamentary system had been superseded. This was reinforced by the fact that there were virtually no representatives of Weimar politics involved in the national conservative resistance, with the significant exception of the presidential cabinets.[24] The social democrats and trade unionists involved took their cue from the concept underlying the Leadership Circle of the United Unions established in April 1933 and hence largely thought in corporatist terms.[25] Even the socialists in the Kreisau Circle supported the general view that the re-emergence of centralized party organizations and a multi-party system should be prevented or at least severely restricted.[26]

As has been pointed out above, the national conservative resistance only gradually and hesitantly developed from seeking merely to correct abuses in the system and impose alternative strategies on it to the idea of staging a *coup d'état* and establishing a new social order. In this process, the Kreisau Circle acted as the intellectual vanguard. The early plans for a post-Nazi regime were largely derived from the authoritarian experiments of the von Papen and Schleicher periods and from the situation that had emerged in June 1934 at the time of the alleged Roehm Putsch.[27] Only when the social basis of the resistance was broadened were solutions proposed which involved a greater element of popular political participation, though Horthy's Hungarian model and monarchist ideas continued to figure as largely as before.[28] The later schemes for a new social order were largely based on neo-conservative and corporatist ideas from the Weimar period, particularly Spengler's model of a 'Prussian socialism'; Prussian traditions were central in motivating many of the conspirators, including Schulenberg, to join the resistance.[29] These were, however, a source of controversy and were challenged by Yorck and Moltke, who rejected any 'deification of the state' and were clearly aware that the 'lie of the traditional hierarchical state' of which Gustav Radbruch had spoken had been one of the roots of the Nazi Führer state.[30]

The plans for a new social order developed by the national conservative resistance represented an attempt to realize alternatives to the parliamentary system which had not been equally discredited. These included the corporatist model and the principle of self-administrative institutions. There is no doubt that some prominent national socialists, who had retained a sense of respect for the institutions of state and were opposed to the progressive strangulation of the political system under the Nazi regime, thought and attempted to act along similar lines. In the context of plans to restructure the Reich and to reform the administration, there were many areas of agreement between the national conservative conspirators and isolated protagonists of institutional reform within the national socialist ruling elite.[31] Originally the opposition was prepared to retain a range of specifically national socialist institutions, including the German Labour Front, and only to repeal anti-Jewish legislation where it was considered discriminatory. At the same time, it actually welcomed the system of racial apartheid, particularly with regard to Jews who had immigrated from the East since 1918.[32]

The socio-political thinking of the resistance groups behind the July conspiracy was characterized by a deep distrust of what neo-conservative writers had denounced even before 1933 as 'mass democracy', though with some variations and with a playing down of the authoritarian element.[33] The opposition overestimated the political importance of Nazi successes in mass mobilization in the early years of the regime and of the electoral victories of the NSDAP between 1930 and 1933. They regarded these as primarily the result of propagandist indoctrination. For the conspirators, national socialism was not the opposite pole to the Weimar experience but its direct consequence and continuation. The one-party state of the Third Reich appeared to them as the thoroughly logical product of the party-based Weimar state. The conspirators' historical and political point of reference was rather the chance to create a totally new order, which they believed had been wasted in 1918–19. This they saw in terms of the Prussian Reform of 1809 or – with typical refinement – the German uprising of 1813.[34]

On the other hand, the majority of the national conservative resistance, in stark contrast to the core group of the Kreisau Circle, saw no reason to believe that any fundamental social or political transformation was necessary. They were concerned instead to see the 'correct' ideas in national socialism realized. They believed that the national socialist ideal had been perverted by corrupt, ruthless and incompetent rulers, that a 'genuine' national community[35] should be established to replace the chaotic oligarchy of Nazi upstarts and that the German state as a power, and even its hegemony over central Europe, should be rescued from Hitler's irresponsible military adventurism. This was the context of von der Schulenburg's repeated references to the 'Reich of the future'[36] and the central idea that the 'national awakening' had been turned into its opposite by the Nazis. This helps to explain the ambivalent position of many of the conspirators and the large degree of overlap between collaboration and resistance; it could be seen, for example, in Trott's approval of the proposals on India, in von der Schulenburg's later memoranda also intended for Himmler's attention[37] and in the military men's basic loyalty when it came to the prosecution of the war.

Very few of the conspirators wished for the total collapse of the existing political system which both Moltke and Yorck, from their philosophically based understanding of history, regarded as a necessary precondition for a total social and ethical new beginning. They thus limited themselves initially to plans for the society they dreamed of. Despite their deep reservations about assassination and about the arbitrary intervention in the historical process which it entailed, they finally committed themselves to working actively for a coup from 1942. This was after they had become aware of the full extent of the approaching moral, military and political catastrophe which ruled out any idea of passively waiting for events to take their course.[38]

In the conditions of the time, distinctions between criticizing aspects of the regime, being openly hostile to it and actively resisting it were necessarily fluid. It is therefore not very useful, even for the purposes of analysis, to distinguish active resistance as a fundamentally different phenomenon from other forms of resistance or oppositional behaviour.[39] Such an approach might be applicable to the communist resistance, apart from the episode of the Russo–German Non-Aggression Pact, but it becomes problematic as soon as it is applied even to the socialists. Attempts to categorize the oppositional strands within the system along such lines can be very misleading, especially in such borderline cases as Ernst von Weizsäcker and Wilhelm Canaris.[40] The power to define what in the narrow sense constituted actual resistance lay in the end of the day with the Gestapo, which both before and after the attempted coup of July 1944 arbitrarily decided who was to be hounded down and how wide the net should be thrown. This is apart altogether from the obvious case of the wave of arrests following the July coup when the Gestapo launched its 'Operation Thunderstorm' ('Gewitteraktion'), engulfing thousands of potential enemies of the regime and particularly politicians from the Weimar era.[41]

While the extent of the circle of *cognoscenti*, sympathizers and occasional advisers was quite considerable, the number of active conspirators was very small and extremely politically isolated. The dividing-line often cut families down the middle, as in the case of the Schulenburgs. In this it was similar to the situation in the working-class resistance movement, where parents often lived in fear of being denounced by their children who were indoctrinated in the Hitler Youth. One psychological consequence of this was that the members of resistance had scant intellectual regard for outside ideas, despite their numerous foreign contacts and experience abroad, and tended instead to fall back on their own experiences and ideas from the 1920s and early 1930s. This produced the 'introvertism' which so marked their plans for a post-Nazi order when compared with those developed in émigré circles. This isolation in a hostile environment meant that open discussion was generally avoided because of the security risk it involved, even at meetings of like-minded people; it led to serious misunderstandings, such as the false assessment made of Erwin Rommel's stance,[42] and was accompanied by a deep if not always openly expressed distrust of the political maturity of ordinary people.

The plans for a new, post-Nazi order[43] proposed dividing the electorate into manageable local constitutencies. Instead of anonymous party candidates, locally respected citizens, who had risen to prominence through their work on behalf of the local community and through representing the immediate interests of citizens, would stand for election. It was intended that direct elections would take place only at this level and that the system would be otherwise based on representative bodies which were elected indirectly. This would, of course, have led to an oligarchical structure. It was intended to limit ideological and propagandist influences as well as the role of party organizations to a minimum, and politics were to be restricted to the servicing of the immediate needs of the citizen. This was not purely a reaction to the debased plebiscitary politics of the NSDAP. Very similar electoral reforms had been proposed in the early 1930s by Freiherr von Gayl, the minister for the interior in the von Papen government.[44] The national conservative resistance sought a 'de-massing of the masses' in the cultural sense also. This was intertwined with romantic agrarian ideals and the concept of the desirability of at least partly reversing the urbanization of society. It was a matter of dispute, however, whether the results of the Allied bombing offensive could be used to serve this purpose. To this was added an economic policy completely geared to the middle classes and corresponding reforms in the educational area.

The whole gamut of conservative counter-utopias which emerged in these proposals was elaborated upon by the various individuals and tendencies in the national conservative resistance with varying emphases. It illustrates the fundamental dilemma of a political position which in the final analysis regarded the parliamentary system of Weimar in the same light as national socialism. The distortion of the communist resistance movement by Comintern directives meant that its political thinking developed certain similarities to neo-conservative anti-modernism, as evidenced, for example, in Ernst Bloch's contemporary writings. The outlook of the socialists in the resistance was characterized by its marked tendency to converge with national conservative thinking. With its concept of a 'third area' synthesizing western individualism and eastern collectivism and its advocacy of Christian personalism, it was very much in the tradition of the *deutscher Sonderweg*. The Kreisau Circle drew what were in many ways fascinating though ultimately utopian conclusions from these philosophical traditions. Several of these, such as the principle of neighbourly responsibility, the emphasis on religious values as the basis for future transnational structures, the transcending of the traditional nation state through Europeanization[45] and, not least, the references to ecological issues have a renewed relevance in our decade. But none of this can alter the fact that the programme for a new ordering of society proposed by the German resistance had little relevance to the requirements of an advanced industrial society.

It would be wrong to deny that the thinking of the resistance, if not actually backward-looking, contained an explicitly anti-liberal element. This was compounded by a marked social paternalism, even in the case of supporters of a liberal economic system such as Goerdeler. This illustrates the basic ineffectiveness of bourgeois anti-fascism when confronted by the Nazi's success in manipulating substantial elements of German national culture, though it must be remembered that the technocratic element in Nazism certainly had important pseudo-democratic effects. The language used by the opposition also converged with that of the regime in some respects. The panaceas it advanced were to some extent on the same historical plane as the alluring propagandist visions of the regime itself, however little relevance these had to the realities of life in a society in the grip of internal disintegration. Christianity, the principle of a state based on the rule of law and the abolition of corruption in public life were, given the extreme abuses of power in the Third Reich, important and serious aims of the conspirators, who devoted and sacrificed their lives for them. But their concrete proposals for realizing these values appear quite unrealistic, though they certainly intended trying to implement them immediately rather than at some ideal time in the future.[46]

This statement should not be read as detracting in any way from the political morality of the national conservative resistance. It is not an easy matter to admit that national socialism, or at least some of the aims for which it stood, had taken such root in the minds and behaviour of the mass of Germans that any will to resist it could only have been mobilized on the basis of ultimately utopian and deeply religious convictions, while capable pragmatic politicians like Konrad Adenauer or Theodor Heuss[47] resigned themselves to complete passivity or believed there was absolutely nothing that could realistically be done in the situation.

At no time could the circle of conspirators count on winning broad support for their stand among the population. Father Delp's detailed research and Leber's inquiries showed that the mass of the industrial working class remained relatively loyal in its support for the regime.[48] This was influenced by factors such as fear of losing the war and the increased social status within the factory which the regime brought German workers. Attitudinal surveys carried out immediately after the assassination attempt showed a temporary rise in Hitler's personal popularity even in such traditionally 'red' areas as Wedding in Berlin.[49] The communists also learnt by experience that attempts to expand their underground organization beyond the circle of former active members as well as to establish contact with bourgeois and Christian groups were virtually doomed to fail and only increased the threat of detection by the Gestapo.[50] The younger generation especially, at the mercy of indoctrination by the Hitler Youth, represented a potential threat to any attempt to topple the regime. With some exceptions, like the 'White Rose', it took very little part in the resistance.[51]

It was particularly symptomatic of the internal situation in the Third Reich that the broad mass of the middle classes was totally under the sway of national socialist propaganda. Artisans, businessmen, industry and the professions were completely unrepresented in the resistance movement. Goerdeler received some indirect support from Bosch and Krupp, but the extent to which business circles avoided involvement or, like Hermann Abs, played only a peripheral role, is quite striking.[52] Economists like Schmölders and Constantin von Dietze, who were recruited on account of their expertise, advocated social policies hardly distinguishable from those of the regime, however much they denounced it in other respects. The state-oriented liberals among them, whose thinking ran along similar lines to the Kreisau Circle's, tended to become involved only in the meetings which took place within the system; these were organized without Hitler's knowledge by Otto Ohlendorf, as state secretary in the Ministry for the Economy, to plan the post-war economy on the basis of the existing Nazi structures and to draft alternative proposals to counter the post-war plans being developed by the Allies.[53]

The upper middle class members of the resistance, especially Carl Goerdeler, functioned therefore as a type of independent bourgeois element without any basis of support in their own class. This helps to explain the almost complete rejection of liberal traditions by these circles and the persistent attempts to seek a return of the monarchy. But, given the lack of interest of the Hohenzollern heirs, this proved to be a totally utopian aim, though it retained an importance through the part it played in indirectly legitimizing the authoritarian form of government sought. Adopting Herm- ann Rauschning's critique, Hitler was viewed primarily as the destroyer of the German Bürgertum, the traditional middle class.[54] But in fact it would be more accurate to describe him as the incarnation of Germany's middle classes as they denied their own traditions, because no serious impulses to resist Nazism existed among them. As in the pre-1848 period and in 1848 itself, it was again the senior public administrators who stepped in as the guardians of the national interest.

The reality of this was reflected in the plans for a new order drafted by the national conservative resistance. They postulated a substantially state-centred structure in which the executive authority would assert the interests of the state over those of society. This would be largely independent of conflicting social interests, which were supposed to harmoniously resolve their differences in corporately structured institutions representing all professions and interests. While formally stressing the principle of the rule of law but allowing for only a limited 'participation by all classes of the people',[55] it was inevitable that powerful interests would eventually assert their dominance in such a system, though a majority of the conspirators would of course never have intended this. The national conservative oppo- sition finally realized that any attempted coup would have to have a broad base in the population to ensure its success and establish its legitimacy. This realization was prompted not least by the changed form of the communist resistance when it established the 'National Committee for a Free Germany'.[56] The 'non-party popular movement', so hotly disputed in the final months before the assassination attempt, was meant to serve this funciton and represented a neo-conservative alternative to the international tendency of the time towards all-party governments and party-bloc sys- tems.[57] But it is significant that the planning of the coup never got beyond the preparatory stage where such controversial elements of its programme were involved.

The social isolation of all strands of the resistance movement was at least one of the reasons why it spent so much of its time drafting proposals for radically new social and political institutions to replace the Nazi regime. At first glance one would think the obvious course would have been to return to the Weimar constitution which, formally at least, had by no means been fully abandoned, even if the continuity with it in constitutional law had ended with Hindenburg's death. It would also have been conceivable for planning to have been limited to pragmatic measures essential to stabilizing the government installed by the coup and to its immediate tasks. Psychologi- cally, however, this was out of the question for, to be able to function, the resistance actually needed a vision of a fundamentally new order of society derived to a certain extent from the mythology of 'national awakening' of the early 1930s.

In the relatively depoliticized atmosphere of the Third Reich, the planning of the coup took on a markedly technocratic character with little reference to either interest groups or the latent party divisions within society. This is indicative of the extent to which the Nazi dictatorship's early years of success were experienced as a definitive break with Weimar conditions, even by those circles critical of it. The only foundations on which a political alternative to Hitler could have been constructed were the concepts of order and the political values inherited from the anti-republican strands of the social elites of the Weimar period. Communist and left-wing socialist programmes, including their diluted versions of the national committee or democratic bloc ideas, would not have evoked any substantial response, even in the working class.

Countess Marion Yorck, who participated in the Kreisau movement, made the pertinent remark that Claus Schenk von Stauffenberg would not have proceeded with the assassination attempt if the planning of the coup, despite its concentration on military precision and its ultimate reliance on the weapon of a military state of emergency, had not been backed up by a comprehensive alternative concept to Hitler.[58] This characterized the military wing of the conspiracy in general, where the initiative came mainly from younger officeres of the General Staff rather than from the generals involved in conducting the war. But, with all respect for their convictions and for what they did, these men lacked a revolutionary quality. They were still profoundly influenced by the trauma of the November Revolution of 1918. The deep fear that the coup and the inevitable loss of the war would produce a similarly uncontrollable situation to that at the end of the First World War was one of the strongest forces impelling the civilian wing of the conspiracy to draft comprehensive plans for a post-Nazi order. These plans would certainly have helped to politically legitimize the *coup d'état* and remove the odium of having been carried out purely to serve specific military and social interests – as Nazi propaganda and even Winston Churchill, in his fatal Commons speech, later claimed.[59]

The thinking behind the July 1944 conspiracy was confined within the intellectual and political horizons of the ideology of a *deutscher Sonderweg*. To this extent, it belongs to the historical epoch which came to an end with the collapse of national socialism and the fascist movements in May 1945, though several offshoots continued to have some relevance until the decisive turning-point in German domestic politics of 1948–9. The thinking of the resistance did not exert any serious practical political influence on the foundation of democracy in West Germany. The survivors saw themselves rather as isolated from this process or, as in the case of Theodor

Steltzer and Paulus van Husen, in opposition to the actual developments which led to the multi-party democracy of Bonn.[60] The communist resistance groups were largely excluded from developments in East Germany, even if to a lesser extent than the bourgeois democratic representatives of the resistance there. In both German states, West and East, the political initiative reverted to political elites, however divergent, which had been to the fore in the Weimar era. The claims to continuity with the traditions of the resistance raised in both states reinterpreted these traditions to suit the exigencies of their respective parliamentary or people's democratic outlook. This represented a profound distortion of both the intentions of the opposition of the Third Reich period and the conditions which had forced on it the form it had taken. It was also part of the more general suppression of inquiry into the deeper social causes which had given rise to the Nazi dictatorship.

From a greater distance and with more open access to information and witnesses' reports from the time, however fragmentary these are, it is precisely the self-contained intellectual outlook and political ethos of the national conservative resistance that are so striking; they do not lend themselves to being forced into any strait-jacket of hackneyed clichés which accompany commemoration ceremonies in the safety of less dangerous times. It was neither the democrats, the republican parties nor the churches as institutions which sought to save Germany from Hitler or to avert the impending political, military and, most of all, the moral catastrophe precipitated by the uncontrolled rampage of the Hitler regime in its later phase. On the contrary, it was a group of people – largely outsiders – who, ejected from the community of the nation after 20 July 1944, took the decision to attempt a coup under incredibly difficult conditions and finally in the knowledge of its utter hopelessness. They took a stand against the rule of absolute inhumanity personified by Hitler while the great majority of the nation and its elites stood passively by.

The actions of the conspirators of July 1944 – as of the many others who opposed the regime in their own ways, whether by giving refuge to Jews, helping Soviet prisoners of war, spreading knowledge of the regime's crimes or protesting against the euthanasia programme or the systematic destruction of people – continues to challenge us in a way that has not been made redundant by Germany's return to liberal democracy. Helmuth James von Moltke once remarked that in the last resort it was a question of re-establishing the image of humanity 'in the hearts of our fellow citizens'.[61] The call for an inner renewal based on the individual, social and moral identity of people as a precondition of freedom and social justice, for a deepening of neighbourly commitment and of relations between people, for a greater willingness to shoulder responsibility and for more individual initiative in a society marked by the growth of anonymous structures has not lost any of its validity today.

The cultural and social crisis of the 1920s and 1930s, which the national conservative resistance regarded as the principal cause of national socialism but of which it too was a product, has yet to be confronted intellectually and politically in the Federal Republic. There are many indications today that after a period of inner suppression, arguments and positions which were a product of the crisis of consciousness of the inter-war period are again being adopted, even though the history of the German resistance clearly reveals their inherent ambiguities. It is to be hoped that, instead of superficially reaffirming latter-day prejudices or opinions, the renewed historical interest in the German opposition to Hitler will demonstrate a readiness to confront the deeper political and historical roots which made its defeat inevitable.

11

The Realization of the Unthinkable:

The 'Final Solution of the Jewish Question' in the Third Reich*

The history of the Holocaust defies simple explanations. Since the pioneering account by Gerald Reitlinger, which appeared in English in 1953,[1]
researchers from many countries have produced detailed analyses of the
persecution and liquidation of European Jewry.[2] The actual course of events
has now been largely established, and the description of the deportations
and exterminations is not subject to dispute among serious researchers;[3] at
most, there is marginal controversy about the exact number of victims,[4]
although this does not affect the overall assessment. Nevertheless, the
horror of that culmination of inhumanity outstrips the capacity of historians
to imagine and describe it. How could the unimaginable utopian dream, the
extermination of more than 5 million European Jews, become unspeakable
reality,[5] and with such appalling efficiency? Propaganda alone – the savage
tirades of hate directed against Jewish fellow citizens and minority groups
by Hitler, Goebbels, Streicher, the SS paper *Schwarze Korps* and the press
– cannot explain why the many people who were directly or indirectly
involved in the destruction of the Jews did not find some way to withhold
their co-operation. References to manipulation by terror or to the compul-
sion to obey orders are also inadequate. The real problem in providing a
historical explanation of the Holocaust lies in understanding the overall
political and psychological structure that gave rise to it. Human nature
shrinks from the depiction of the immeasurable barbarity that attended the
activities of the SS Einsatzgruppen and the use of factory methods to
destroy human life in Auschwitz, Chelmno, Belzec, Sobibor, Treblinka and
Majdanek. This is also true in an objective sense. When the subjugation
and ill-treatment of human beings drives them to the edge of existence,
reducing them to naked and hopeless desperation, then the last quasi-moral
mechanisms governing human relations collapse in ruins. To the liquidators,
but also to those who merely happened to come into contact with the

* Translated by Alan Kramer and Louise Willmot.

business of murder, the victims had ceased to be human beings; they were classed lower than the most common criminals, whose individual identity was still recognized.[6]

In the immediate post-war years it was widely believed that the Final Solution was carried out by a very limited circle – by the sworn order of the SS, or indeed by an even smaller group consisting of the Death's Head Divisions, who provided the guards for the concentration camps.[7] However, recent research has tended to contradict this theory. Although the 'technical' implementation of the Final Solution was carried out by relatively small staffs, it would not have been possible without the co-operation of relatively large groups of officials. The claim that the Wehrmacht was entirely or even largely uninvolved has been exposed as untrue. It has been established that the OKW and the OKH actively participated in the preparation of criminal orders, and that Army units repeatedly provided essential support in the Soviet Union and other occupied countries in eastern, south-eastern and western Europe. Officials of the Reich railways and the Reichsbank, the diplomatic service, the civilian administrations in the occupied territories, the German and non-German police forces – all these contributed actively to the Holocaust in some form. The crucial question is why they were not aware of what they were doing, or why they were able to suppress with such strange consistency such knowledge as dawned upon them.[8]

An essential element in the explanation of the Holocaust was the removal of the inhibitions of the Einsatzgruppen, of the concentration camp guards involved in the extermination process, and indeed of all those who implemented the Final Solution. This loss of inhibition is not necessarily linked to anti-semitic and racial–biological indoctrination of the persecutors and the onlookers; we know, for example, that many of the officials responsible for the Final Solution were not primarily anti-semitic. Technocratic and subordinate attitudes could be as important as blind racialism or the mere parroting of national socialist anti-Jewish clichés. The motivation of each individual must therefore be assessed separately. In this connection, Hannah Arendt has spoken of 'the banality of evil';[9] at a certain level, the destruction of human life – under orders to do so – was perceived as a skilled job like any other. It lay below the threshold of social and, ultimately, moral behaviour towards individual human beings.

The example of Rudolf Höss (camp commandant of Auschwitz) has frequently been used to illustrate the divided morality of the SS thugs: he was able to combine the everyday business of organizing mass murder with scrupulous respect in the private sphere for all those secondary virtues incorporated in the apparently moral concepts of 'German order' and hygiene.[10] The speeches of Heinrich Himmler in October 1943 and January, May and June 1944 also contain the double standard that maintains that adherence to 'decent' practices – the forbidding of sadism, the avoidance of personal gain and the acceptance of 'personal responsibility' – can be used to justify criminal deeds.

This dichotomy between criminal acts and hypocritical and frequently cynical pseudo-morality was fundamental to the entire system, not just to Heinrich Himmler and the SS. True responsibility based upon ethics was eliminated, being replaced by a formalized canon of values devoid of any real content. Traditional concepts such as 'doing one's duty', 'loyalty', 'honour' and 'serving one's country' withered into execrable phrases, used repeatedly to justify the actions of the regime, as self-justification by its representatives, and to compel loyalty.[11]

There is no doubt that the liquidations that followed the deportation of the Jews were implemented with the utmost secrecy; Himmler, Heydrich and the other participants in the planning and realization of the programme knew full well why they kept any knowledge about the annihilation of the Jews from the German population, or more precisely from the pseudo 'public opinion' of the Third Reich.[12] On the one hand, the destruction of the Jews was described as a vital task in world history; on the other, it was to be kept secret from the world. The idea that traces of these crimes could be obliterated by opening up the mass graves and attempting to burn the bodies before the arrival of the Red Army was both absurd and utterly grotesque. This psychological reaction reveals that the veneer of ideological bigotry that covered the awareness of guilt was really very thin.[13]

The victories of the Red Army and the looming prospect of military defeat began to destroy the Nazi dream-world of cynical power politics and megalomaniac schemes for the future. At the same time, pangs of remorse over the crimes they had committed, or something approaching a moral conscience, began to be felt. Himmler's speech in Poznań on 13 October 1943, and his subsequent attempts to spread knowledge of the Final Solution – and thus the burden of responsibility for it – more widely, were symptomatic of this.[14] However, the diffused nature of decision-making in the Third Reich made it impossible to say afterwards that responsibilities had been delegated according to a set plan. The accused at the Nuremberg Trial of Major War Criminals were often not even willing to admit their knowledge. In many cases they shifted responsibility to the Führer and, except for Goering and perhaps Speer,[15] argued that they were merely carrying out orders. The flight from responsibility and the suppression of knowledge of criminal actions did not begin in 1945, however.

Despite a considerable degree of agreement among historians about the deportation and extermination process, opinions differ in analysing the causes of the Holocaust and are sometimes diametrically opposed to one another. In view of the vital importance of the subject in world history, this is not surprising. Many historians still believe that Hitler had envisaged the actual physical extermination of the Jews from the beginning and had set himself to achieve this as a long-term objective.[16] However, the carefully recorded statements of the future dictator on the subject do not provide conclusive proof of such an intention. Moreover, verbal expressions of this nature are not uncommon, being typical of radical anti-semitic wishful thinking since the late nineteenth century.[17] In fact, Hitler's actual instructions for action during the 1920s are rather more restrained.

Hatred of the Jews are indisputably fundamental to Hitler's *Weltanschauung*; opinions conflict, however, about how much influence he exerted on the detailed moves to force Jews out of German social and economic life and to deprive them of legal rights. There is a consensus of opinion that Hitler approved the cumulative intensification of persecution and that his attitude served as its legitimating authority. This does not mean that he actually initiated each step. As in many other aspects of domestic policy, he intervened only in isolated instances, frequently after receiving information from unofficial sources.[18] This is illustrated by his criticism of the sentence passed on one Markus Luftgas, which he thought too lenient; on Hitler's intervention, the sentence of imprisonment for hoarding food was replaced by the death penalty. However, there was a series of cases that demanded that he decide between rival, competing strategies. In these, he shrank away from making definitive, unambiguous commitments, and proved to be dependent on changing personal influences. Whenever he was confronted with a choice between two courses of action, he would favour the less extreme solution rather than play the part of revolutionary agitator.[19] The development of the Nuremberg Laws, for example, reveals that in the sections relating to 'Aryans' Hitler did not follow the party radicals but tended to support compromises, even if his attitude did not always remain firm.

From the intentionalist point of view there appears to have been an escalation in the measures of persecution against the Jews consistent with the interplay between the pressures of extremist groups in the Nazi Party and the subsequent moves of the regime. However, it cannot be said that the illegal 'spontaneous' attacks on Jewish citizens, and the subsequent judicial measures to destroy the social and professional position of the Jewish community, were co-ordinated. The party had made extremely radical legislative proposals in spring 1933, but its initiatives were largely blocked by bureaucrats in the higher civil service (although those involved in the administration of justice were more prepared to conform). External economic and foreign policy considerations played a significant, but not decisive, role. The friction between the ministerial bureaucracy and the lower and middle-ranking party apparatus also slowed the pace of persecution. Thus, even those measures that satisfied the conventional demands of conservative groups for racial separation were considerably delayed and were mostly put into effect only after November 1938.

Many ordinary Germans gained the impression that the anti-semitic outrages that had accompanied the process of Gleichschaltung (Nazification of state and society) after March 1933 were declining, and that calm would return once the government took vigorous action to prevent 'spontaneous' attacks. This was certainly an illusion. The rabble-rousing tirades of the NSDAP, led by Julius Streicher's semi-pornographic paper *Der Stürmer*, influenced the political climate sufficiently to make people refrain from public contacts with Jews. They did not, however, generate the desired pogrom atmosphere, as was clearly proved in 1938. Radical anti-semitism gained its real political impact from the fact that the Political Organization of the NSDAP, which had previously been restricted more or less to welfare work, was increasingly diverted into the political arena. The higher civil service, still predominantly conservative despite efforts to Nazify it, endeavoured to make concessions to the NSDAP in the sphere of anti-semitism whilst evading party claims to control the administration, except in the municipal sector. It failed to perceive that it thereby opened the door to the abandonment of legal moderation in the conduct of state affairs and of the principle that the state should be under the rule of law. In Jewish affairs in particular, policy was set on a twisted road, which had no limits and no end.

After the Nazi seizure of power, those groups in the NSDAP that originated in the extreme völkisch movement – including the vast majority of the *'Alte Kämpfer'* – did not become socially integrated. Many of them remained unemployed, while others failed to obtain posts commensurate with the services they believed they had rendered the movement. The social advancement that they had hoped for usually failed to materialize. This potential for protest was increasingly diverted into the sphere of Jewish policy. Many extremists in the NSDAP, influenced by envy and greed as well as by a feeling that they had been excluded from attractive positions within the higher civil service, grew even more determined to act decisively and independently in the 'Jewish question'. The pressures exerted by the militant wing of the party on the state apparatus were most effective when they were in harmony with the official ideology. It was against Hitler's mentality openly to oppose these endeavours – with which he was in any case instinctively in sympathy – although he privately agreed to measures that counteracted them. Hitler was thus decisively responsible for the escalation of persecution. The initiative rarely came directly from him, however. He was not concerned with detailed moves to achieve the desired 'solution of the Jewish question'. This was connected not least with his visionary concept of politics, in which anti-semitism was less a question of concrete political measures than of a fanatical ideological approach. Consequently, the regime failed to develop a coherent strategy until

Heydrich took control of Jewish policy into his own hands.

The genesis of the 'Nuremberg Laws' reveals the mixture of improvisation and programmatic commitments that guided the policies of national socialism. The militant wing of the NSDAP had long demanded a general ban on mixed marriages as well as the dissolution of existing ones. Preparations for legislation of this kind had begun immediately after the seizure of power, although the various departments concerned had not progressed beyond drafting various legislative proposals, for fear that anything more might undermine the legalist course. The same fate befell the plans announced by Secretary of State Pfundtner, which envisaged the creation of a special right of citizenship linked with the requirement to document 'Aryan' descent. In this case, the scheme was shelved partly because of the extreme demands of the NSDAP, which was pressing for the general adoption of its own much stricter rules on 'Aryan' descent; these excluded persons with one Jewish great-grandparent from membership of the party. The Reich Ministry of the Interior was also anxious to avoid serious repercussions for the German minorities in Poland, especially in Upper Silesia.

In the summer of 1935 there emerged the beginnings of a compromise between radical party circles and civil servants in the Ministry of the Interior, at least to the extent that the civil servants agreed to make certain concessions on the issues of mixed marriages and the restriction of the Jews' right to citizenship, on condition that attacks on Jewish businesses ceased and that there should be no compulsory confiscation of Jewish property. This compromise provided the background to Hitler's decision, on the occasion of the Nuremberg party rally, to use legislation to regularize the 'Jewish question' as a 'unique secular solution'. Hitler had originally summoned the Reichstag and the diplomatic corps to Nuremberg in order to make a solemn government declaration, using the Abyssinian conflict to announce Germany's own revisionist demands in foreign affairs. On the recommendation of Baron von Neurath, this plan was dropped on the evening of 13 September. As the passing of the Reich Flag Law was hardly sufficient to justify the special session of the Reichstag, the inner circle of party leaders decided to introduce a Judengesetz (Jewish law) to the Reichstag instead, mainly in the hope of improving the acutely strained relations between the party and the ministerial bureaucracy. There were no concrete suggestions about the substance of this legislation, and, in the night-long deliberations that followed, Hitler vacillated over which precise policy he should propose.

On the same night, the experts on Jewish affairs and citizenship in the Reich Ministry of the Interior were ordered to Nuremberg and instructed there and then to submit drafts for a Reich citizenship law and a law on mixed marriages. They were therefore unable to refer to the preliminary work that had been done within the various government departments. This explains why Gürtner, the Reich minister of justice, first learned about the 'Nuremberg Laws' only when they were announced. In the main, the laws did not really represent a qualitatively new stage of national socialist Jewish policy. They contained little more than sweeping stipulations that could be interpreted in various ways. In the prescribed language of the regime, the laws offered German Jewry the opportunity to establish itself as a 'national minority'. Despite their discriminatory language, they did not go beyond a programme of segregating the Jews from the rest of the population, and were actually regarded as an acceptable 'legal solution' by many of those people most affected by them. Only after the issue of provisions for the precise application of the laws, which mostly occurred at a much later stage, were they used as an instrument for the further, systematic persecution of the Jewish people.

The Reich Citizenship Law excluded Jews from the right to Reich citizenship, which was due to be created as an addition to mere nationality status. Loss of Reich citizenship had no concrete significance, apart from the loss of the right to vote; the issue of whether the Jews should be deprived of German nationality and placed under Alien Law, as the NSDAP had intended, was thus sidestepped. Furthermore, the experts in the Reich Ministry of the Interior succeeded in making both the Reich Citizenship Law and the Law for the Protection of German Blood and German Honour applicable only to full Jews and to those half-Jews who belonged to the Jewish religious community and did not live in mixed marriages. They thus did not fulfil the more extreme proposals of the NSDAP to include 'Grade 1 and Grade 2 persons of mixed descent'. On the other hand, the First Ordinance to the Reich Citizenship Law prohibited Jews from holding public posts, replacing the emergency regulations on the civil service which had been in force since 7 April 1933.

In fact, the new Reich Citizenship Law never had any practical significance. Certainly, Hitler did approve the Law on Provisional Citizenship in March 1938 after the *Anschluss* (annexation of Austria), thereby granting the population of Austria the right to vote. However, he forbade further preliminary work on the implementation of the law when serious disagreements arose between the Ministry of the Interior and the Office of the Führer's deputy over the racial and political criteria to be applied to each citizen. The idea of submitting every German to a formal 'tribunal' hearing before an official *Reichsbürgerbrief* (Deed of Reich Citizenship) could be issued actually raised serious doubts about Wilhelm Frick's grasp on reality.

The Law for the Protection of German Blood and German Honour was seen as particularly odious outside Germany because of its discrimination against the Jews. On closer inspection, however, it cannot be regarded as a victory by the NSDAP over the more moderate ministerial bureaucracy.

The Jews were prohibited from raising the Reich flag, but this only confirmed the status quo and at least protected them from being attacked for failing to honour the swastika. The law contained the ban on mixed marriages that was already *de facto* in effect, but refrained from decreeing that all existing mixed marriages were automatically dissolved, as party militants had demanded. It also made *Rassenschande* (sexual intercourse between 'Aryans' and 'non-Aryans'), a category of offence developed by Nazi lawyers, into an offence punishable by law. Although in early summer 1935 Hitler had suspended the ban on the employment of 'Aryan' domestic servants under the age of forty-five by Jews, he now gave in to pressure from high-ranking party officials and permitted the inclusion of this provision. In an attempt to find a precedent for it, Gerhard Wagner, the head of the Reich Medical Association and one of the leading rabble-rousers, had gone back to fifteenth-century regulations governing the employment of domestic servants; copies of these regulations were preserved in the NSDAP central archive. On the issue of the legal definition of the status of Jews, on the other hand, Hitler inclined towards accommodating the concern of the jurists in the Ministry of the Interior about the introduction of legislative measures that they regarded as too extreme. Although the provision stipulating that the law should apply only to full Jews was deleted, Hitler proposed that a press notice should be issued that would make this limited application clear.

It is therefore not surprising that the Nuremberg Laws produced an angry response from the NSDAP. Goebbels had the radio broadcast of the Reichstag session cut short before the bills were read out and instructed the party's press and officials not to discuss the laws until the provisions for their implementation had been decided upon. At a secret Führer conference in Munich on 24 September, Hitler adopted the position of the experts from the Ministry of the Interior: using the argument of Bernhard Lösener, the official responsible for racial affairs in the ministry, he spoke in favour of a more restricted legal definition of Jewishness and warned against creating a group of people who had nothing to lose. This meant that half-Jews who were not members of the Jewish religious community, and 'Grade 2 persons of mixed descent', would not be affected by the law. However, Martin Bormann persuaded Hitler to issue secret instructions that paragraph 6 of the First Ordinance to the Reich Citizenship Law, which would have ruled out any introduction of more sweeping regulations governing entry to public institutions, including the German Labour Front, and which he had just signed, was not to be applied.

Bormann was thus compensated for his defeat over the actual drafting of the Reich Citizenship Law. He also got his way on another issue later. The draft Law on the Acquisition and Loss of German Nationality, which had been prepared in early 1939 with the assistance of Hans Globke, contained a provision to strip the offspring of racially mixed marriages of their German nationality (instead, they were allowed a right of abode as long as they were permanent residents). This clause later provided a stepping-stone for the Eleventh and Twelfth Ordinances to the Reich Citizenship Law, which were issued in 1943 and indirectly sanctioned the deportation of the Jewish population. However, there was never a definitive regulation of the legal status of the Jews – the government departments opposed it for a variety of reasons and adopted delaying tactics, whilst Hitler showed no personal interest in legal regularization.[20]

On this issue it would seem that Hitler cannot be regarded as one of the extremists; instead, he tended to compromise between the position of the various departments and the demands of party officialdom. Specifically, his regard for public opinion made him recognize the merits of a policy of exempting from persecution those sections of the Jewish population that were largely assimilated, at least for the time being. He remained susceptible to arguments of this nature, although there can be no doubt that in principle he wanted to see persons of mixed blood removed from the German 'blood union'. Characteristically, as late as 1942 he decided against the deportation of the partners in 'privileged mixed marriages', who had previously been exempted from persecution, and also of people of mixed descent (*Mischlinge*) in general.[21]

Hitler's conduct can be interpreted in various ways. Some historians believe that his decisions were determined by his conviction that the 'Jewish question' would be 'solved', possibly during a war, and that he acted throughout in pursuit of a plan that had long been decided. In this case, caution and tactical considerations – and even sometimes simple convenience – must be considered as determining factors in shaping his policies. This pattern of conduct is said to apply in particular to the field of foreign policy.[22] It was second nature to Hitler to make his decisions only when the situation seemed over-ripe, but it is certainly an exaggeration to claim that he waited upon events with the sure-footedness of a sleep-walker, as the propaganda would have us believe. Equally, he was not always, and not unconditionally, afraid to make decisions. His immediate and instinctive perception of impending dangers was rooted in a deep psychological insecurity, masked by a mixture of megalomania, joviality, harshness, determination and, not least, endless tirades of rhetoric. Ultimately, he would respond with restless activity and a flood of decisions, thus 'taking the bull by the horns'.[23]

As far as I can see, no such reactions have been documented in the Jewish question. None of the measures to restrict and then to deny Jews their civil and economic rights, and to make them into social pariahs, were directly attributable to initiatives of the Führer himself. This is true of the boycott campaign of April 1933; of the Nuremberg Laws (abhorrent though they were, their significance in the persecution of the Jews has often been exaggerated);[24] of the pogrom of November 1938, which was unleashed by Goebbels;[25] and of the subsequent 'Aryanization policy' promoted by Hermann Goering.[26]

To state these facts is not to claim that the events occurred without Hitler's approval and even encouragement. Nevertheless, given the ideological framework and the existence of machinery to trigger off 'spontaneous' anti-semitic outrages, they were first conceived by the rival satraps around Hitler, who were unscrupulously determined to outdo one another in implementing national socialist policies, and thus to please the Führer. Only in retrospect have these measures acquired the appearance of being part of a systematic and cynical escalation of persecution. This can be demonstrated, for example, in the case of Goebbels. After the failure of his attempts to generate a pogrom atmosphere among the population in connection with the boycott campaign, he adopted the policy of legal measures against the Jewish community.[27] It is not likely that this change was the result of a tactical decision taken after consultation with Hitler. The Führer cared little for legal actions; he probably agreed to this course because it suited his objectives in foreign policy. However, it is also true that Hitler had little patience for the struggles of the rival departments as they strove to obtain, or to maintain, leadership in the Jewish question; he was instinctively in sympathy with the strong-arm methods favoured by the militant groups in the NSDAP, though he sometimes found it necessary to bypass them.[28] Nor did Hitler interest himself in the detailed implementation of the anti-semitic programme; his few interventions do not reveal any practical plan. The propaganda aspect was of paramount importance for him, in this as in other issues. His conduct after the unsuccessful boycott campaign of 1 April 1933 reveals this clearly. He had approved Goebbels's initiative, had probably entrusted Streicher with the task of carrying out the boycott, and had defended the measures in the face of cabinet criticism by claiming that there had been no other way to appease 'the anger of the people'.[29] Nevertheless, he was careful to distance himself from these events in public. He was fascinated by the idea, put forward by Goebbels at this time, of using German Jews as hostages for obtaining the good conduct of the western powers in their foreign policy dealings with the Reich. This notion, which Goebbels had originally used as a propaganda expedient, was taken up by Hitler as a serious strategic argument. In later years it became a recurring leitmotiv in his public pronouncements.[30]

Hitler's threat to take bitter revenge on 'world Jewry' in the event of war, and to destroy German Jewry in retaliation, was thus made in the context of exerting propaganda pressure. Many authors have nevertheless deduced from these utterances that Hitler was firmly resolved to wage an all-out campaign of genocide against international Jewry. The repetition of this threat has been interpreted as the decision that set in motion the systematic extermination of those Jews in German hands.[31] There is absolutely no doubt that Hitler's own ideas did indeed involve the physical destruction of the Jews, but they also involved the destruction of other entire populations. He did not hesitate to demand the liquidation of large groups of Slavs, and expressly ordered that the besieged population of Leningrad should be left to starve to death.[32]

In the case of the Final Solution, Hitler maintained the taboo on public discussion of the issue until the very end. In this he was more consistent than Himmler, who spoke openly of the systematic liquidation of the Jews in the speeches mentioned above. This fact has led David Irving to assert that Hitler was not fully informed about the extermination programme before 7 October 1943 – and even then only informally – although it had been in full swing for over eighteen months by that date.[33] In one respect Irving is correct: the actual measures for implementing this monstrous scheme never were discussed, either officially or privately, in the Führer's headquarters. Hitler always kept carefully within the confines of the prescribed phraseology – to the effect that 'the Jews are, *en bloc*, being mobilized for the appropriate labour duties', as Bormann put it in a confidential directive to high-ranking party officials on 11 July 1943 in an attempt to counter rumours about the 'special treatment' of the deported Jews.[34] Himmler's use of this camouflage language – at its most striking in the reports of the SS statistician Richard Korherr[35] – reveals that the observance of secrecy and the use of prescribed terminology extended even to the internal correspondence of the Führer's headquarters.

Hitler nevertheless continued to express his extreme radicalist and anti-semitic opinions, which were nothing short of paranoid, in countless unofficial and official statements. Phrases typical of the language of *Der Stürmer* occur with great frequency: the Jews are described as a 'bacillus', as carriers of disease, and as dangerous vermin which must be destroyed. This terminology, which he shared with the militant anti-semitic wing of the party and the SS, remains constant throughout and did not become more extreme in response to the Holocaust. Typically, it remained within the framework of propagandistic metaphor. With the exception of his comment to a Slovak diplomat at the beginning of 1939 that 'Now we are going to destroy the Jews',[36] there are no known statements by Hitler that refer directly to the policy of genocide.

There are, however, some recorded remarks that appear at first sight to refer to the issue. The 'Table Talk' of 25 October 1941 contains Hitler's observation: 'By the way, it is no bad thing that we are rumoured to have a plan for the destruction of the Jews.'[37] The remark was made before the policy of genocide was systematically implemented (which began to occur only in March 1942 after preliminary steps had been taken in autumn

1941), so the comment must be interpreted in the context of proposals to settle the Jews in the Russian marshlands. Hitler wound up his remarks with the observation: 'Terror is salutary.' This was a reference to the liquidation programme of the Einsatzgruppen, which led to, but is not identical with, the subsequent Final Solution.[38] It is therefore not correct to infer from the passage quoted that Hitler was actually alluding to the policy of the Holocaust. A similar picture emerges from the 'Table Talks' of 23 and 27 January 1942 and also from a note by Goebbels on 14 February 1942: 'The Führer once more expressed his determination to clean up the Jews in Europe pitilessly.'[39] These comments amounted to massive threats against the Jews and emphatic support for the deportation programme, but did not constitute admission of an actual intention to commit genocide.

It is also worth recalling Hitler's conversations with Marshall Antonescu and Admiral Horthy in mid-April 1943, when he evaded the straightforward comments of his Hungarian guests by resorting to standard anti-semitic rhetoric.[40] His reaction has been described by Martin Broszat, who emphasizes Hitler's ability to distort the facts and turn them upside down whenever he was faced with the reality of criminal actions.[41] The apparently reliable record of Hitler's reaction to the reproaches of Frau von Schirach[42] also reveals how he deliberately avoided any mention of the true facts, indicating an instinctively defensive attitude.[43] The statement that comes nearest to an admission of genocide is Hitler's secret speech to Wehrmacht officers and generals on 26 May 1944, in which he explained, in apologetic tones, 'By removing the Jews, I eliminated the possibility of any kind of revolutionary nucleus or germ cell being formed. Of course, you could say to me: Yes, could you not have solved the problem in a simpler way – or not simpler, for everything else would have been more complicated – but in a more humane way?' This justification is strikingly similar to remarks made by Himmler only a short time before. Significantly, it is once more only the policy of deporting the Jews that is being admitted, not the policy of mass liquidation; the reference to an allegedly 'more humane' solution should be regarded as a possibly subconscious allusion to the liquidation. In any case, his ambiguous statements reveal that Hitler himself felt a compulsive need for self-justification, psychologically balanced as always by aggressive accusations directed against the alleged enemy. This was especially apparent after the subject was taken up in Allied news reports.[44]

The controversy provoked by David Irving over the question of how far Hitler was informed about the actual measures taken to implement the Final Solution – and this is the only point of real dispute – cannot easily be decided by examining the ambiguous statements of the Führer.[45] The question of whether or not Hitler was thoroughly briefed on the state of the genocide programme during Globocnik's visit to Führer headquarters on 7 October 1942 is not conclusive either.[46] Gerald Fleming, who disputes

Irving's interpretation from beginning to end, nevertheless concludes that, despite the violent threats and prophecies in his speeches, Hitler used calculated cunning to disguise his own *personal* responsibility for events, especially for the implementation of the policies of destruction that he had nurtured for so long. In contrast to Irving, Fleming emphasizes that Hitler himself arranged the use of the camouflage language that was used whenever the policies of genocide were discussed.

Such an interpretation – also made by others[47] – seems to be both plausible and consistent with the evidence. However, it also raises a number of difficulties. Even within Hitler's closest circle of trusted friends, there is no sign that he was ever prepared to abandon his usual metaphors in his references to the 'Jewish question'. If such behaviour had been based only on machiavellian cunning, there would have been no reason not to speak directly when the perpetrators were discussing events among themselves. There is not a single reliable piece of evidence that this ever happened. Himmler's speeches, in which he revealed the policy of the Final Solution, contain only passing references to a 'military' order by Hitler; he may well have been referring specifically to Hitler's speech of August 1939.[48] In so far as the implementation of the measures of liquidation rested on an order, rather than merely a 'wish of the Führer',[49] that order was the Commissar Order (*Kommissarbefehl*) of 1941 and Hitler's instructions on how it was to be carried out.[50]

In fact, we must conclude from these observations that Hitler gave no formal order to carry out the Final Solution of the 'European Jewish question'. Krausnick still believes that Hitler gave a secret order to exterminate the Jews in March 1941 at the latest, in connection with his intention to 'have the political commissars of the Red Army shot'.[51] However, it is crucial to distinguish between the partial destruction of the Jews of eastern Europe, based on the Commissar Order, and the systematic policy of the Final Solution, in spite of the fact that the latter developed from the former. As will be shown in a different context, preparations for the systematic implementation of the Final Solution were begun only in late autumn of 1941 and were not based on a written order. There are also many internal reasons for believing that Hitler never gave such an order orally, either.

The exclusively metaphoric language in which the Führer discussed the 'Jewish problem', as well as his general reluctance to take decisions that might have caused public opposition and perhaps have had to be withdrawn, make it unlikely that he would have come to a binding decision. Remarkably, even in early 1942 Hitler considered reactivating the abandoned Madagascar Plan.[52] If one attributes such behaviour to a desire to dissemble even among his closest friends, then it would simply be evidence of the extent to which he shrank from referring openly to the factory-style destruction of human life. His conduct in this and other matters, however, appears to be due less to an extreme intellectual cynicism than to an ability to dissociate himself completely from reality.[53]

Hitler's speech to the Reichstag on 30 January 1939 is cited more than any other as evidence of his early intention to destroy the Jews systematically: 'Today I shall once more be a prophet. If the international Jewish financiers inside and outside Europe should again succeed in plunging the nations into another world war, then the result will not be the bolshevization of the world and thus a victory for Jewry, but the annihilation of the Jewish race in Europe'.[54] This argument, repeated in the speeches of 30 January 1941, 30 January 1942, 30 September 1942 and 8 November 1942,[55] is complemented by Goering's report at the infamous meeting at the Reich Air Ministry on 12 November 1938, in which he quoted Hitler: 'If the German Reich comes into conflict with foreign powers in the foreseeable future, it goes without saying that in Germany too our main concern will be to settle accounts with the Jews.'[56] Although at first sight the connection with the subsequent genocide policy may appear to be evident, the political motive behind this statement is in fact ambivalent. Such threats were intended primarily to exert pressure on the western nations, particularly Britain and the United States. They are thus connected with the hostage argument, which had surfaced as early as 1923: in that year the radical anti-semite Hermann Esser had argued that, in the event of a French invasion, one German Jews should be shot for every French soldier who stepped on to German soil. Andreas Hillgruber has concluded that such statements revealed the radical, racial–ideological objectives of the regime in the coming war. This is to overstate their significance, although the potential for a 'war of racial destruction' that is discernible in them is not disputed.[57]

Hitler considered the 'Jewish question' from a visionary political perspective that did not reflect the real situation. The struggle against Jewry was for him an almost metaphysical objective; as his 'Political Testament' reveals, it eventually took on a chiliastic dimension.[58] Hitler had always sympathized with 'spontaneous' attacks on Jews. They reflected his belief that anti-semitic opinions could be used both for mass mobilization and for the integration of the party's supporters. A campaign of extermination, implemented with extreme secrecy and with an increasingly bad conscience (as in the case of Himmler), was not completely compatible with this concept. Time and time again Hitler argued – quite incorrectly – that it was the Jewish element in the population, and especially the Jewish elites, who were mobilizing resistance to national socialism and opposing the triumph of the 'anti-semitic idea' in the world. The alleged need to 'remove' the Jews from German territory and to fight Jewry on the principle of 'an eye for an eye, a tooth for a tooth' can always be traced back to the chiliastic component of Hitler's otherwise fragile personal philosophy. By contrast, the spurious justifications of the Einsatzgruppen for the murder of the Jewish population – ranging from housing shortages and the danger of insanitary conditions through to partisan warfare[59] – reflect their need to justify a crime that went beyond the causal connection of racial–biological anti-semitism.

Throughout his career Hitler, out of a mixture of instinct and vanity, avoided any attempt to confront his ideological dream-world with political and social reality. He felt strongly that the inner consistency of his *Weltanschauung*, or of the 'National Socialist Idea' as he described it with typical formalism, would be damaged if confronted with the complexity of the real world. Even during the *Kampfzeit* (the period before 1933; lit. 'time of struggle') he had adopted the habit of simply ignoring inconvenient realities. The refusal to accept disagreeable information increasingly became a dominant feature of his style of government. J. P. Stern has emphasized that Hitler's popularity was based on the fact that he turned his private sphere into a public one.[60] Political success and almost unlimited power enabled him to turn his subjective opinions on issues more and more into objective yardsticks for decision-making. Anti-semitic imagery spared him the need to reflect on the true consequences of his prophecies of the 'destruction of the Jewish race in Europe', a tendency that was reinforced after the invasion of the Soviet Union had committed him to an 'all or nothing' strategy. There was no middle ground between Hitler's daily work, crammed with military and armament production details, and the construct of ideas that formed his ideology and that bore no relation to reality. His passion for architectural planning was just another way of escaping into a dream-world once his supremacy as a military commander was threatened by unacknowledged defeats. Hitler's escape into the illusory world of film and opera formed part of the same syndrome.[61]

When confronted with the actual consequences of the destruction of the Jews, Hitler reacted in exactly the same way as his subordinates, by attempting not to be aware of the facts or suppressing his knowledge. Only in this way could he give free rein to his anti-semitic tirades and his threats to destroy the Jews physically whilst simultaneously avoiding nearly all direct identification with the policy of genocide that was actually being implemented. The collective repression of disagreeable facts and criminal actions is an inevitable adjunct of any kind of political irrationalism; under national socialism, the mechanism of repression was perfected. In 'good' years it was moderated by foreign policy considerations and by Hitler's instinctive perception of how the population would react. Above all else, he feared public alienation from the regime, and it is no coincidence that he vowed repeatedly that the events of 9 November 1918 would never be repeated.[62] However, as the war took its course this last corrective disintegrated, and the criminal and destructive energies that lay at the root of

Hitler's personality ultimately prevailed over tactical and political considerations.

The fact that the Final Solution tied down large quantities of materials, including vital transport capacity, and critically diminished the labour force that was so desperately needed, ought to have suggested the need for a modification of the deportation and murder programme. When Hitler was confronted with this problem, he usually responded evasively. In cases where he sensed a possible loss of prestige, as in the deportation of Jews from Berlin to Riga,[63] he ordered that the measures be delayed. However, the Führer did not stop Himmler and his thugs. As before 1939, he felt bound to stand by the party and the SS, institutions whose members took literally the 'grand' historical perspective presented them by Hitler. On the 'church question', Hitler was able to restrain Martin Bormann; on the 'Jewish question', he was the slave of his own public prophecies. Any retreat would have made him lose credibility in his own eyes, when his supreme guiding principle was to avoid any such development. At its root was his manic idea that, as bearer of the 'National Socialist Idea', he must not allow himself to contradict his own previous statements.[64]

The realization of the Final Solution became psychologically possible before Hitler's phrase concerning the 'destruction of the Jewish race in Europe' was adopted as a direct maxim for action, particularly by Himmler. Hitler, it must be conceded, was the ideological and political author of the Final Solution. However, it was translated from an apparently utopian programme into a concrete strategy partly because of the problems he created for himself, and partly because of the ambitions of Heinrich Himmler and his SS to achieve the millennium in the Führer's own lifetime and thus to provide special proof of the indispensability of the SS within the national socialist power structure.[65] Himmler's statements indicate that he intended to fulfil in one single, 'masterful', self-sacrificial act something that had actually been intended as a timeless programme.[66] He thus directed a large part of his energies towards a programme that, for Hitler, had only a low priority in comparison with the conduct of the war.

Himmler and Heydrich thus played a decisive role in implementing the Final Solution. Nevertheless, it must be stressed that a purely personalized interpretation would prevent full understanding of the issue. The eventual step towards mass destruction occurred at the end of a complex political process. During this process, internal antagonisms within the system gradually blocked all alternative options, so that the physical liquidation of the Jews ultimately appeared to be the only way out.

At this point it is necessary to recall the various stages of the national socialist persecution of the Jews. It was certainly not carried out according to a carefully prepared plan; Karl A. Schleunes has justifiably spoken of a 'trial and error' method.[67] Only in 1941 did Heydrich succeed in eliminating rival contenders for control of the 'Jewish question'. Previously there had been constant infighting between departments and party offices determined to safeguard their own authority in the field. This infighting resulted in a continuous escalation in the persecution of the Jews. Seen from the perspective of the subsequent policy of genocide, the numerous individual moves against the Jewish community would appear to have been logical steps in one coherent plan. However, it would be inappropriate to seek any such degree of rationality in the motives of the men who initiated the specific measures.

It would also be an entirely improper simplification of this process to trace it back to ideological factors alone. Anti-Jewish initiatives gained their momentum because they were associated with other interests. A desire to enhance their own prestige and to extend their authority was an important motive for many national socialists, especially the Gauleiter; their rival attempts to declare 'their' districts 'Jew-free' play a conspicuous role in the genesis of the Holocaust. Straightforward economic interests were usually involved as well: in the case of the Gauleiter,[68] in the case of Goebbels in relation to the pogrom of November 1938;[69] in the anti-semitic outrages in Austria directly after the *Anschluss*;[70] in the case of the Reich Security Head Office (RSHA), especially with regard to the attempts to establish an SS economic empire;[71] in industrial and banking circles as the 'spontaneous' and legalized 'Aryanization' measures and the exploitation of the labour of concentration camp prisoners offered advantages to many;[72] and among the commercial middle class which, especially in the early years of the regime, tried hard to intensify the repressive measures against their Jewish competitors.[73] The list could be extended at will: direct and indirect, legal and illegal gains at the expense of Jewish wealth and property were part of daily life in the Third Reich, which can accurately be described as a system of officially promoted corruption in this as in other respects.[74] It is scarcely surprising that Speer's construction department showed no reluctance to make use of Jewish dwellings in Berlin, and that Nazi officials at every level were prepared to claim Jewish property for their own private use without embarrassment.[75]

Another mechanism, equally effective in radicalizing the persecution of the Jews, was provided by the Judenreferate (sections for Jewish affairs) which were established in each government department after 1933. These sections felt the need to justify their existence by introducing cumulative anti-Jewish legislation. Numerous shameful restrictions were imposed on German Jews by means of administrative decrees that were usually both defamatory and economically superfluous. Moreover, they were issued openly; every citizen could have found out about the inhuman treatment of his Jewish fellow citizens by reading the *Reichsgesetzblatt* (Official Gazette).[76] No less shocking is the willingness of the authorities to enforce this legislation down to the last detail, although their own primary motivation was not anti-semitic.[77]

The anti-semitism of the conservative nationalist civil service elite, although more moderate than that of the NSDAP, prevented them from resisting anti-semitic infringements even when they involved blatant violations of the law. The same is true of the Wehrmacht, the public administration and the courts. The majority of those involved in the legal profession were willing to adapt the administration of justice to the dominant ideology of anti-semitism, even before the legal basis for such behaviour had been created.[78] They contented themselves with the illusion that the regime would go no further than the complete segregation of the Jewish section of the population.[79]

In contrast to the conduct of a large proportion of the German upper class, anti-semitic feeling was less easily mobilized in the population as a whole. The boycott of April 1933 had been a complete failure in this respect. Similarly, the pogroms of November 1938 were greeted with overwhelming disapproval among the population.[80] There were scarcely any anti-semitic outbursts of the kind characteristic of eastern European countries; only in Vienna after 18 March 1938 did anti-semitic outrages occur that had a comparatively broad basis of popular support. Anti-semitic resentment was traditionally directed more against non-assimilated Jews. It took years of systematic propaganda to transfer the stereotyped image of the east European Jew to the entire Jewish population and to indoctrinate the younger generation in particular with anti-semitism.[81]

The strategy of exerting pressure on German Jewry by unleashing popular resentment thus proved to have been ill-conceived. Goebbels soon turned instead to the systematic 'legal' elimination of the Jews from public life, a course of action that was to be justified by the fiction that their alleged preponderance in certain professions had to be rectified and a programme for racial segregation implemented.[82] Accordingly, the attacks of the storm troopers and NSDAP were gradually supplanted by 'legal' procedures; this was not so much the result of a deliberate strategy linking 'spontaneous' with legal actions, but was due rather to the fact that the Nazis had no clearly thought-out conception of how they should proceed in the 'Jewish question'.[83] At any rate, it had quickly become apparent that toleration of 'spontaneous' actions by party hotheads did not bring a 'solution' of the 'Jewish question' any closer. All the leading Nazi officials concerned with the issue – Heinrich Himmler, Reinhard Heydrich, Hermann Göring, Martin Bormann and Wilhelm Frick – were convinced until after the outbreak of the Second World War that a systematic policy of compulsory emigration offered the only real 'solution'.[84]

However, the exclusion of Jews from public and social life, begun in 1933 and increased until 1939 though with varying degrees of intensity,

must also be accounted a failure from this point of view; it was simultaneously an incentive and a handicap for those Jews who wanted to
emigrate. The regime's reluctance even to make the financial terms of
emigration tolerable – the Reich Flight Tax (*Reichsfluchtsteuer*) introduced
for quite different reasons by Brüning was retained[85] – resulted in a
relative decline in the number of emigrants. After the introduction of the
Nuremberg Laws, which despite their discriminatory provisions were seen
by many German Jews as providing a definitive statement of their legal
position, Jewish emigration declined significantly.[86] Even more significant
were the steps that undermined the economic position of the Jewish community. A series of measures was enacted to exclude them from professions
in the public service, to withdraw legal protection from them, to discriminate
against them economically and to confiscate Jewish businesses by means of
'Aryanization' (a process that began long before November 1938). Such
campaigns ensured that those Jews who remained, who were often older
members of the community, frequently did not have enough money to
leave; the emigration rate was correspondingly reduced.[87] The reluctance
of the potential host countries to accept large numbers of Jews, so fateful
in the light of later developments, also made emigration more difficult.[88]

The expropriation, proletarianization and ostracization of the Jewish
minority cut their social contacts with the majority of the population and
forced them to seek refuge in the anonymity of the cities. The well-intended
efforts of Bernhard Lösener, the official responsible for racial affairs in the
Reich Ministry of the Interior, to exempt half-Jews and Jews living in so-
called 'privileged mixed marriages',[89] actually heightened the isolation of
the Jews. The segregation and extreme social isolation of the Jewish community were vital in ensuring that the majority of Germans – with the
exception of genuine opposition groups – remained indifferent to their
fate.[90] Gestapo terror helped to complete the social ostracization of the
Jews.

The intensified persecution of the Jews after 1938 was unquestionably
connected with the foreign policy successes of the regime, which made
caution in its dealings with foreign powers appear less necessary and also
led to a more robust style in other areas of national socialist politics. The
Anschluss with Austria resulted in a marked radicalization, especially as
regards 'Aryanization'. This policy had long been demanded by groups
within the party but it had been postponed, not least owing to the influence
of Schacht, because of its negative effects on the economy and particularly
on armaments production.[91] Subsequently, the important phases of radicalization were first tried out in the 'colonial territories' and then transferred
to the Old Reich. The annexation of Austria, and by analogy all subsequent
territorial extension of German rule, ensured that the size of the emigration
problem grew constantly. Eichmann's successes in establishing the Office

for Jewish Emigration in Vienna, and subsequently the Reich Central Office for Jewish Emigration within the RSHA in 1939, were thus cancelled out.

The creation of Jewish ghettos, first mentioned during the conference at the Reich Air Ministry on 12 November 1938, and the transformation of the 'Jewish question' into a police problem, resulted in a transfer of authority for the Jewish question to the RSHA, despite Goering's official responsibility for it. Both Himmler and Heydrich had, for different reasons, disapproved of the orchestration of the *Kristallnacht* pogrom by Goebbels; characteristically, the participants then reached agreement on the most radical line imaginable. All sides were thus saved from any loss of prestige by this approach, which was possible because no established interests stood in its way.[92]

The RSHA remained committed to the emigration programme even after the outbreak of the Second World War had drastically curtailed the opportunities for Jews to emigrate. Because of their powerful position in the occupied Polish territories, and also Himmler's personal position as Reich commissar for the strengthening of Germandom (*Reichskommissar für die Festigung Deutschen Volkstums*), the SS were able to take almost complete control of initiatives in the 'Jewish question'. It was crucially significant that the fate of the vastly increased numbers of Jews in German hands became inextricably linked with Himmler's scheme for the resettlement of ethnic Germans in the East, which culminated in the *Generalplan Ost* (resettlement programme for eastern Europe). As Reich commissar for the strengthening of Germandom, Himmler ordered on 30 October 1939 that the Jewish population of those Polish territories that had been annexed by the Reich should be deported to the Generalgouvernement, a policy that was to be implemented side by side with the creation of Jewish ghettos.[93] A preliminary decree by Heydrich on 21 September had already distinguished between a long-term 'ultimate objective', which was to be kept top secret, and the intermediate stage of 'forced expulsion'.[94] The primary motive was revealed in the executory provisions of Himmler's decree for the Reichsgau Wartheland: 'The purging and protection of the new German areas' was designed to provide housing and employment prospects for the ethnic German settlers (*Volksdeutsche*).[95] There is no doubt that the resettlement programme agreed to in the Nazi–Soviet Non-Aggression Pact, whereby ethnic Germans living in the Soviet Union were to be settled mainly in the Wartheland, provided the impetus for the large-scale deportation programme, which affected Poles as well as Jews.[96]

Although there was as yet no thought of systematic mass annihilation, a qualitatively new situation was created by ghettoization and the system of enforced labour for Jews, which was ordered at the same time.[97] These measures were crucially significant, although they were hampered by the opposition of the Generalgouverneur, Hans Frank, by the preparation and waging of war in the West, and by sheer organizational chaos. Methods that were later extended to the Old Reich were first tested in the General-gouvernement; moreover, the deportation programme encouraged the Gauleiter of the Reich to send 'their' Jews to the Generalgouvernement. Hans Frank staunchly resisted further mass deportations of Jews, as demanded by Gauleiter Greiser in particular; he argued that the Lodz ghetto had become a transit camp for deported Jews and that intolerable conditions prevailed there.[98] This brought the deportation programme to a temporary halt.[99]

The debates of late 1939 and early 1940 reveal that there was as yet no single, comprehensive programme of persecution. In March 1940 Frank stressed that the deportation of Jews from the Old Reich could be achieved only after the war.[100] One new feature was the fact that emigration, including forced emigration, was no longer regarded as the only 'solution', because there were now more than 3 million Jews under German rule.[101] The various departments concerned therefore produced schemes for the creation of a 'Jewish reservation'. The Ostministerium (Ministry for the Occupied Eastern Territories) suggested that such a 'reservation' should be created along the German–Soviet demarcation line.[102] This potential solution, which was supported by Hitler, was taken up eagerly by Eichmann, who was responsible for the deportation programme. The Nisco Project and similar attempts failed not so much because of the objections of Frank but because of catastrophically inept organization. On 24 March 1940 Goering responded by prohibiting further deportations from the Old Reich.[103]

It is certain that the reservation plans were not intended for implemen-tation until after the war. On 25 June 1940 the representative of the Reich Association of Jews in Germany was informed of a plan to settle vast numbers of Jews in some as yet undesignated colonial reservation area; at this stage Eichmann still favoured an extensive programme of emigration to Palestine.[104] The scheme was to involve the Jewish communities of the Old Reich, Austria, the Protectorate (Bohemia and Moravia), the Generalgouvernement, Scandinavia and western Europe, including Britain. However, the scheme was developed more rapidly than had been antici-pated, especially after the defeat of France made the end of the war seem very near. On 12 June 1940 *Legationsrat* (legation councillor) Karl Rademacher of the German Foreign Ministry submitted the Madagascar Plan.[105] Even if Britain had agreed to it – which was most unlikely – the Madagascar project was actually completely unsuitable as a 'European solution to the Jewish question', quite apart from the fact that a rapid reduction of the population was anticipated due to the harshness of the climate and to the effects of severe overcrowding. Nevertheless, the project was taken up by Eichmann and the RSHA. Subsequently, Eichmann distinguished between a 'short-term plan' – i.e. an intermediate solution in the form of concentrating the Jewish population in certain parts of the Generalgouvernement – and a 'long-term plan' of deportation to Madagascar. Once the Russian campaign had begun these considerations receded into the background; however, not until 10 February 1941 did Rademacher report that the war against the Soviet Union had offered the possibility of using other territories for the Final Solution and that, on the instruction of the Führer, the Madagascar Plan could be dropped. There is no basis for the argument that the Madagascar project had the subjective function of concealing the regime's intention to annihilate the Jews.[106]

The resumption of deportations to the Generalgouvernement and the deportation of 7,500 Jews from Baden and the Saarpfalz to France[107] were carried out as temporary measures and following pressure from the local Gauleiter. Heydrich's 'third short-term plan' of 8 February restricted to 250,000 the numbers to be deported from the annexed Polish territories; however, this total was not achieved and deportations were halted once more.[108] These facts indicate that the 'territorial final solution', a programme demanded by Heydrich as early as June 1940 and that gradually replaced the now unworkable emigration scheme, was to be achieved only after the war. Considerable efforts were made to exploit Jewish forced labour in the Reich instead, something that had hitherto been imperilled bureaucratic friction.[109] Hitler intervened in this issue to reject any repatriation of Jewish labour from the East to the Reich for such purposes, a decision that was connected with his reluctance to revoke decisions once they had been made.[110]

The attack on the Soviet Union on 22 June 1941, and the dazzling early successes of the German armies, influenced the planning process in the RSHA. The Commissar Order, and the deliberate use of the Einsatzgruppen to liquidate Jewish population groups in the occupied areas, signalled the start of a new phase.[111] Initially, however, the belief that a 'solution' of the 'Jewish question' could be implemented only after the war was retained. In summer 1941 the Nazi leadership expected the Soviet Union to be defeated in a matter of weeks, and at latest by autumn of that year, although they accepted that skirmishes might continue in the Asiatic regions of the Soviet Union.[112] It was taken for granted that Britain would have been forced to yield by this time.[113]

Only against this background is a correct interpretation possible of the authorization given by Goering to Heydrich on 31 July 1941 in which Heydrich was instructed 'to present for my early consideration an overall draft plan describing the organizational, technical and material requirements for carrying out the Final Solution which we seek'.[114] The authorization, drafted by Eichmann and submitted to Goering for his signature,[115] is not connected with any preceding order from Hitler, although the existence of such an order has often been suspected. Its context is clearly that of the strategy pursued until that point, which was not yet directed towards systematic extermination. Its aim was a 'solution' that would no longer be implemented under the cover of war in the East.

At the same time, the Einsatzgruppen were carrying out their massacres. These were based on the Commissar Order, unlike the systematic policy of the Final Solution that followed. There can be no doubt that Hitler approved and supported these measures, although it is a matter for conjecture how far he took notice of actual events.[116] Approximately 1.4 million Jews were murdered in these extensive operations, which were carried out on the pretext of securing the rear area of the battle zone; Hitler had from the outset declared the campaign against the Soviet Union to be a war of annihilation. Nevertheless, it is almost inexplicable that the leaders and members of the Einsatzgruppen lent themselves to this unimaginably barbarous slaughter and that the Army – with few exceptions – either stood by, weapons at the ready, or in many cases gave active support to the Einsatzgruppen.[117] In the framework of national socialist propaganda against 'subhumanity', the Russian Jews, like the Polish Jews before them, were classed as the lowest of the low. The massacres also provided an opportunity to rid the German-occupied territories of a part of the Jewish population, which had by then increased beyond any 'manageable' size. The fact that the killings were carried out on oral orders only, and that the Einsatzgruppen were careful to avoid giving only racial reasons for them in their reports, [118] indicates that the decision to liquidate the entire Jewish population had not yet fully matured.

A decisive turning-point was necessary before leading officials would adopt a course of action that had been unthinkable only a short time before. Certainly, everything was propelling events towards a violent 'solution' of the 'Jewish problem' which the Nazis had created for themselves. The logistic prerequisites for the mass movement of populations were completely lacking. Conditions in the improvised ghettos were appalling, and appeared completely unacceptable to the German sense of order. In summer 1940 Greiser had already described conditions in the Lodz ghetto as untenable from the 'point of view of nutrition and the control of epidemics'.[119] On 16 July 1941 SS-*Sturmbannführer* Höppner drew attention to the catastrophic conditions in the ghetto which, as a transit camp for the Jews transported from the Old Reich, was permanently overcrowded. Besides, it was the only ghetto within the Reich and was regarded by Greiser as an intolerable burden. Höppner added in his letter to Eichmann that 'it should be seriously considered whether it might not be the most humane solution to dispose of those Jews who are unfit for work by some quick-acting means. At any rate this would be more agreeable than letting them starve'.[120]

Martin Broszat has emphasized the symptomatic significance of this reaction.[121] It is not an isolated one. The idea that it would ultimately be more 'humane' to finish off the victims quickly had already emerged in 1940; it was frequently prompted by the sight of countless trains standing at stations in the biting cold, with their captive Jewish passengers deprived even of drinking water during the dreadful journey to the Generalgouvernement. The war in the East provided even more reasons for such arguments. The indescribably cruel treatment of the civilian population caused few protests and produced instead a fatal blunting of moral feeling among the Germans. The partial liquidation of transports of Jews from the Old Reich and the annexed territories was a desperate new step. It could not be justified as part of the destruction of bolshevik resistance cells. A pseudo-moral justification was needed as a precondition for the systematic implementation of the Final Solution. Inhumanity had first to be declared as 'humanity' before it could be put into technocratic practice,[122] with moral inhibitions thereafter reduced to a minimum. Then, once the necessary bureaucratic apparatus had been created, a programme could be set in motion that was applicable to all deportees, including women and children.

The operations of the Einsatzgruppen served as the link that enabled the exception – premeditated liquidation – to become the general rule. The immediate liquidation of groups of German Jews deported to the Reichskommissariat Ostland, to Riga, Kovno and Minsk, did not proceed smoothly. Moreover, like the killings begun with the assistance of the 'euthanasia' experts in Chelmno in December 1941, they also encountered opposition, which led to the suspension of further transports.[123] Even if only for this reason, the change in the Jewish policy of the RSHA was by no means abrupt. One indication of such a change was that Jewish emigration from German-occupied areas of continental Europe was halted, although it had previously been explicitly supported. The head of the Gestapo, Müller, announced the prohibition of further Jewish emigration on 23 October 1941. Only ten days previously, Heydrich had actually approved a proposal by the under-secretary of state, Martin Luther, that Spanish Jews resident in France should be included in the Spanish cabinet's plan to send 'their' Jews to Spanish Morocco. A few days later his decision was revoked on the grounds that these Jews would then be too far outside the German sphere of influence to be included in the Final Solution to be implemented after the war.[12]

The reference to a 'post-war solution' reveals that at this point the decision for systematic genocide had not yet been reached. On 16 December 1941 Frank stated that 3.5 million Jews in the Generalgouvernement could not be liquidated, but that 'action will have to be taken that will lead to successful destruction, in connection with the major measures which are to be discussed at Reich level'.[125] This was a reference to the impending Wannsee Conference, which is usually equated with the immediate launch of the genocide campaign throughout Europe. However, the 'operations' mentioned by Heydrich in connection with the 'evacuation of the Jews to the East' were presented simply as opportunities to gain practical experience 'in view of the coming Final Solution of the Jewish question'. The liquidation of those Jews who were deemed unfit for work was implied, and the subsequent destruction of the 'remaining stock' explicitly disclosed.[126] The psychological bridge between the emigration and reservation 'solutions' and the Holocaust itself was created by the fiction of *Arbeitseinsatz* (labour mobilization); reference was also still made to the chimerical 'territorial final solution', which was now to be achieved east of the Urals. On the other hand, the formulation that 'certain preparatory work for the Final Solution' should be carried out 'in the areas concerned', i.e. the Generalgouvernement, signified the beginning of selective liquidations. These started early in 1942 and from spring onwards acquired the character of a planned and systematic programme. Even then, however, it was implemented with varying degrees of intensity; initially the measures were mainly improvised and some operations had to be countermanded.[127] It is important to note that the programme of annihilation thus retained its character as a temporary measure taken during the wartime state of emergency. The inclusion in the programme of the Jews in the occupied countries and satellite states[128] originally occurred within the framework of a long-term 'labour mobilization' programme; however, even the most elementary requirements for the fulfilment of such a scheme were lacking.[129]

One further development was important for the implementation of the Final Solution. Since autumn 1941 Auschwitz-Birkenau had been expanded into an enormous 'prisoner and munitions centre', mainly for the 'utilization' of Soviet prisoners of war.[130] The selection of Soviet prisoners, and the brutal treatment inflicted upon them, reflected Himmler's own belief that there were unlimited human reserves in the East.[131] However, the turn of the tide in the war, and the appalling death-rate among the prisoners, meant that fewer human reserves than anticipated were available and that they were urgently needed to fill gaps in the labour market in the Reich itself.[132] Scarcely a week after the Wannsee Conference, Himmler issued his instruction to 'equip' the SS concentration camps primarily with German Jews.[133] Birkenau camp, where the technology of gassing had been developed with Soviet prisoners of war as the victims,[134] was not to be part of a comprehensive programme for genocide. The *Generalplan Ost* stood in the background, preventing any attempt to fall back on interim territorial 'solutions' to the 'Jewish question' in the occupied territory of the Soviet Union. The programme of annihilation was now implemented with astonishing speed and in several waves. This operation (later named 'Reinhard' after Reinhard Heydrich, assassinated in Prague in May 1942) formed the direct link between the Einsatzgruppen and the factory techniques of the Final Solution. The systematic destruction of the ghettos was followed by the withdrawal of Jewish labour from war industries; Jewish workers were also removed from the SS enterprises in the Lublin region, which then collapsed.[135]

The use of gas vans as a transitional stage in the development of factory methods to destroy human life had begun because of a desire to prevent undesirable side-effects on the SS men caused by the semi-public shootings at Vilna and elsewhere.[136] The fiction that only those Jews who were unfit for work were to be killed remained psychologically important. The selection process on the ramp at Birkenau helped Himmler's thugs to preserve this fiction. It was only a short step from this way of thinking to 'orderly' destruction, which could be justified on the grounds that organized killing was more practical and 'humane' than death from starvation or epidemics in the ghettos and camps.[137] The horrific conditions produced by the brutal and inhumane treatment of the deported Jews were actually exploited by Goebbels to justify the deadly theory of 'subhumanity'.[138] More importantly, people who under normal circumstances would have been roused to anger by the treatment of the Jews became indifferent, and their feelings of compassion were dulled. How many had the personal courage to see the whole truth behind the chain of cruelties, rather than putting the blame on occasional abuses?

After all, work camps of all kinds – voluntary labour service, compulsory labour and ultimately the practice of working people to death – were the civilian counterpart of military service, which sent millions to the slaughter. Everywhere in occupied Europe, even in the Reich itself, the labour camp became part of ordinary life. The atomization of the family, the destruction of traditional social structures, the sending of all age-groups and professions to labour camps, training camps, education camps – these were everyday features of the Third Reich. The network of concentration camps and prisoner-of-war camps appeared to be part of this second civilization, offering an extreme example of the exercise of power over human beings.[139]

The transfer of people within this labyrinthine network of camps was nothing unusual. However, the concentration of Jewish citizens in labour camps became an increasingly important transitional stage on the path to the Final Solution. The circumstances in which deportations occurred sometimes excited public criticism, but in general people chose to believe the fiction of the 'mobilization of labour'; moreover, the removal of Jews to transit camps ensured that their fate was decided out of sight of their fellow citizens. Even in the occupied areas, resistance to the 'mobilization' of Jewish labour occurred only rarely. Within the concentration camps, it had long been the practice to work people literally to death. The concept that arose as a result – that of 'destruction by labour' – was one of the most effective pieces of cynicism in national socialist ideology. The inscription on the gates of Auschwitz – '*Arbeit macht frei*' ('freedom through work') – reveals that cynicism; it illuminates the entire master-race mentality, which degraded human beings into mere numbers and had no respect even for the dead. This attitude first manifested itself in the 'euthanasia' programme.[140]

The fiction of mobilizing Jewish labour was used by the perpetrators of the Final Solution as a psychological justification for their actions. It is symptomatic that fanatical anti-semites such as Hans Frank and Wilhelm Kube began to protest against the systematic implementation of the extermination programme when it was turned against the reserves of indispensable Jewish labour in the Eastern regions.[141] When the liquidations were not justified by the pretence that they were measures to combat partisans and to weaken 'Jewish–bolshevik' potential, as was the case with the Einsatzgruppen, then they were frequently accounted for by the need to make space for fresh transports. There were phases during which the pace of the extermination programme was slowed, to permit the temporary exploitation of the prisoners by means of forced labour. Many Jews saw this as their only chance of survival.[142]

The use of bureaucratic and technocratic methods to destroy human life also served to suppress quasi-moral inhibitions.[143] The original motive behind the development of technical methods of killing such as carbon monoxide and *Zyklon B* had been to avoid unrest among the general public. However, it was rapidly transformed into a problem of killing-capacity. The decisive preliminary stages of the systematic policy of the Final Solution were thus accompanied by the efforts of the RSHA to learn about these technical possibilities; the instructions given to Eichmann and Höss in autumn 1941 were of this nature.[144]

The Holocaust was not based upon a programme that had been developed over a long period. It was founded upon improvised measures that were rooted in earlier stages of planning and also escalated them. Once it had been set in motion, the extermination of those people who were deemed unfit for work developed a dynamic of its own. The bureaucratic machinery created by Eichmann and Heydrich functioned more or less automatically; it was thus symptomatic that Eichmann consciously circumvented Himmler's order, at the end of 1944, to stop the Final Solution.[145] There was no need for external ideological impulses to keep the process of extermination going. Protests from those parties interested in saving the Jewish workforce – the Wehrmacht, the armaments industry, SS-owned factories in the concentration camps and the administration of the Generalgouvernement – proved largely ineffective.[146]

The widespread assumption that the systematic policy of genocide rested on a clear directive from Hitler[147] is based on a misunderstanding of the decision-making process in the Führer's headquarters. If such an order had been given, even if only orally, then those in high office around Hitler must have known about it; they had no motive to deny the existence of such a directive in their personal records and testimonies after 1945.[148] Gerald Fleming has made a comprehensive search for traces of such an order from the Führer. All he can prove is that at the middle level of command there was talk of it in one form of another; however, Hitler's express approval of criminal orders and his intensification of the fight against partisans seem to be the only concrete basis for these opinions.[149]

In fact, the idea that Hitler set the genocide policy in motion by means of a direct instruction can be completely rejected. Such an order would have compromised the fiction of the 'mobilization of labour', which included the theory of 'destruction by labour'. This could not have been in the Führer's interests, especially as he would then have had to choose between the destruction of human lives and the mobilization of labour demanded by the war economy. Hitler consistently avoided making such a choice.[150] This situation made it particularly difficult for the parties opposed to the extermination process to marshal their arguments: first, there was no one to whom they could appeal, and secondly, even if there were, they would have had to break through the taboo that surrounded the Final Solution. Thus it was that Generalgouverneur Hans Frank saw no possibility of appealing to Hitler over the withdrawal of urgently needed Jewish workers.[151]

The absence of any direct order for extermination also explains how almost all those in an influential position were able to suppress their awareness of the fact of genocide. Albert Speer provides the most striking example of this tendency.[152] Hitler's dominant position at the centre of all the national socialist elites reinforced such behaviour, because his conduct was exactly the same as theirs: he took care not to allow conversation to turn to events in the concentration camps. This gave rise to the widespread impression that Heinrich Himmler was the driving force. In terms of ideological motivation this was not the case, for Hitler was always the advocate of radicalization.[153]

The utopian dream of exterminating the Jews could become reality only in the half-light of unclear orders and ideological fanaticism. Then, despite all opposing interests, the process developed its own internal dynamic. It is therefore impossible to assign sole responsibility for events to Hitler, Himmler, Heydrich, Bormann, the SS and the activists in the German Foreign Ministry. Many leading national socialists tended to stay out of events as much as possible, although they had actively supported the deportation programme. The willingness with which the Ministries of Justice and the Interior gave up to the Security Service (SD) and the Gestapo their jurisdiction over the deportations, which they had initially defended strenuously, is a striking example of a general endeavour among officials to divest themselves of any responsibility whilst accepting that the events themselves were inevitable.[154]

Adolf Eichmann offers a spectacular example of the mechanism of compartmentalized responsibility, which in his case was combined with bureaucratic perfectionism and submissiveness to the demands of the authoritarian state. As he testified in Jerusalem, his authority extended only as far as the gates of Auschwitz-Birkenau; he was just responsible for carrying out the deportations.[155] This fragmenting of responsibilities was a typical feature of the regime. It had its roots in the organization of the NSDAP, which had been imposed by Hitler and his followers during the 1920s.[156] The relative efficiency of the national socialist system was based precisely upon Hitler's principle of conferring unlimited powers for specific tasks and allowing political co-ordination between institutions only where it was unavoidable. Any institutionalized communication between the lower levels of government was systematically prevented. Responsibilities were thus segmented. In the various war crimes trials, the former satraps of the regime always pleaded that they had merely followed orders and been cogs in the machine. No one was prepared to accept overall responsibility or to consider the political consequences of the individual decisions that they made. Non-communication and collective suppression of knowledge complemented each other and, when these mechanisms failed, they were replaced by a vague awareness that involvement in the escalation of crime had gone too far for any opposition to be possible.[157]

If these psychological mechanisms prevented the national socialist elite from facing up to the escalation of criminality and drawing the necessary conclusions, then we can more easily accept that most ordinary Germans were reluctant to believe rumours and incomplete information. It is significant, in this respect, that the truth about the Holocaust was accepted only with hesitation and reluctance even by western public opinion and Allied governments.[158] In so far as German civilians must bear a share of moral responsibility, this does not lie in the fact that they did not protest against the Holocaust, particularly in view of its all-pervasive activity; instead, it is to be found in the passive acceptance of the exclusion of the Jewish population, which prepared the way for the Final Solution. An awareness of increasing injustice definitely did exist, as can be seen in the reaction of public opinion to the revelations about the Katyn massacre.[159]

Ideological factors – the effects of anti-semitic propaganda and the authoritarian element in traditional German political culture – are not sufficient in themselves to explain how the Holocaust became reality. The political and bureaucratic mechanisms that permitted the idea of mass extermination to be realized could also have occurred under different social conditions. The ultimately atavistic structure of the national socialist regime, coupled with the effective power of newly established bureaucracies, proved to be the decisive factor in the selection of negative 'elements of *Weltan-schauung*'[160] and in the overwhelming loss of reality that was epitomized by Hitler's mentality.[161] The genesis of the Holocaust offers a deterrent example of the way in which otherwise normal individuals can be led astray when they live in a permanent state of emergency, when legal and institutional structures collapse and when criminal deeds are publicly justified as national achievements. The Holocaust is a warning against racial phobias and social resentment of minority groups; but it is also a reminder that the manipulation and deformation of public and private morality are a constant threat even in advanced industrial societies.

12

Hannah Arendt and the Eichmann Trial

When the state of Israel began legal proceedings on 23 May 1960 against former SS Colonel Adolf Eichmann, kidnapped several days previously in Argentina by a commando unit of the Israeli security forces and brought to Haifa, it attracted worldwide attention. This was not so much because of the circumstances of Eichmann's arrest and the illegality in international law of his kidnapping, though these were to have an ultimately inconclusive diplomatic sequel.[1] It was rather because of Adolf Eichmann himself, whom international public opinion regarded as the main figure responsible for carrying out the 'Final Solution of the Jewish Question' in Europe. His capture seemed to offer a chance to finally dispel the darkness which had continued to surround the events which had led to the factory-like murder of over 5 million Jewish people. The Eichmann trial attracted more attention than any other post-war prosecution of a leading representative of the Nazi extermination machine since the Nuremberg Trials.

The trial itself, which opened on 11 April 1961 before a special tribunal of the Jerusalem District Court, continued for several months. Judgement was delivered on 11 December 1961 and was ratified by the Court of Appeal on 29 May 1962. The extent of the documentary evidence presented by the prosecution and the large number of historical witnesses questioned made the case the biggest since the Nuremberg Trials. Israel claimed the right, on behalf of the victims, to be the competent judge of the case, particularly as, apart from Argentina, no state – including West Germany – applied for an extradition. There were suggestions that Eichmann should be tried by an international court. But, as no international forum existed which was competent to try a genocide case, Israel's claim to judge him was accepted internationally.[2]

Among the many international observers at the trial in Jerusalem was Hannah Arendt. She had been assigned by the respected American weekly magazine the *New Yorker*. When she took up her appointment to report on the trial, which had been constantly delayed, she thought merely in terms of writing an article about it. In the end, however, this grew to a series of five successive essays. In 1963 she expanded these into a book, *Eichmann in Jerusalem*. The international controversy which her articles in the *New Yorker* had provoked reached a new pitch when the book appeared.[3]

The wealth of source material available at the trial led her to go beyond merely reporting the events in the court. Instead, she proposed a theory of her own to counter the interpretation of the Final Solution put forward by the prosecution and in the judgements delivered by the courts. She also commented on some contentious aspects of the organizing of the trial itself and on some elements which were certainly deserving of criticism. But her intention was not to attempt a systematic account of the Holocaust.

Responding to her critics, who accused her of having produced an incomplete account short on detail, she argued that her primary purpose had been to produce an account of the trial and not a systematic description of the Holocaust itself. But her work is unmistakably an attempt at an overall interpretation of the Holocaust set against the background of a trial which she believed had been conducted on totally wrong premises.

From the professional historian's point of view and concern for a precise and comprehensive analysis of the available sources, Hannah Arendt's *Eichmann in Jerusalem* can be faulted in several respects. It contains many statements which are obviously not sufficiently thought through. Some of its conclusions betray an inadequate knowledge of the material available in the early 1960s. Its treatment of the historical events involved, besides making some use of Gerald Reitlinger's older work, was based primarily on the account by Raul Hilberg of the extermination of the European Jews which had appeared in 1961.[4] Although she was very critical of Hilberg's overall interpretation,[5] his conclusions were very similar to her own on critical points. She also sometimes betrayed a journalistic approach in her evaluation of information whose authenticity could only be established by careful historical analysis and to a great extent by a further examination of the original sources.[6] But neither was it her intention nor was she professionally qualified to produce a historically satisfactory account.

The understandable interest of international public opinion in the Eichmann trial bore no relation to any new information which emerged on the implementation of the Final Solution. While the trial, and particularly the testimony of survivors, once again revealed the terrible conditions under which the murder of the European Jews had taken place, anyone who had been expecting it to produce decisive new clues as to how it had come about was to be disappointed. This fact shaped the character of Hannah Arendt's analysis as she concentrated instead on describing Eichmann's psychology and character and in the process uncovered the simple but horrific truth that the Holocaust had not been the result of a systematically executed political plan. The defendant was generally regarded as the central figure in the organization of the mass murder of the European Jews. But he proved to be a servile bureaucraft who, except on a few occasions, had never displayed any initiative of his own and was totally devoid of the demonic characteristics and ideological fanaticism which everyone had expected of him. The impression arose that Eichmann either had a very bad memory or was purposely remaining silent about events of which he was not directly accused.

Eichmann was in fact quite willing to tell what he knew on all issues of importance. The agreement elicited from him to face trial in Israel included a statement that he would attempt 'to give expression, without any embroidery, to the facts relating to my last years of service in Germany, so that a true picture of the events may be transmitted to future generations'.[7] He was also well aware that he was facing a certain death sentence. The prosecutor's approach of attempting to establish that Eichmann was wilfully lying or was deliberately concealing facts was thus fundamentally flawed. There is every reason to believe that Eichmann actually told the truth, not least out of vanity, though, as Hannah Arendt also complained, his faulty memory hindered him considerably in this. On all important historical points, Eichmann's testimony was not distorted due to any intention on his part, but only by the manner in which it was treated by the investigating and prosecuting authorities. They confronted him with over two thousand documents in evidence, including some witnesses' statements which do not appear to have been totally reliable. More importantly, they confronted him with a fixed picture of events which he often just agreed with so as not to endanger his credibility. The chance which the trial had appeared to offer to elucidate what had actually happened was thrown away by this tailoring of Eichmann's testimony to make it suit a preordained picture of events.

The prosecuting authorities could simply not believe that the Nazi regime's extermination machine had been anything but systematically organized. In fact it had been characterized by constant internal rivalries and a singularly obscure chain of command. Hannah Arendt rightly pointed out that the prosecution's attempt to pin additional responsibility on Eichmann for the deportations in occupied Russia and Poland – which the court finally accepted – was wholly misguided. The judges, however, did not accept some of the more exaggerated claims, such as Musmanno's argument that Eichmann had received his orders directly from Hitler. The prosecution was psychologically unable to grasp that even Eichmann had only indirect knowledge of many important events. It overestimated the power of the Department IV B4 which he headed. Rudolf Höss's well-known statement that the extermination process had been set in motion by an order from Hitler of 1 July 1941, despite evidence to the contrary, was apparently the basis for Eichmann making a similar claim. As opposed to this, Dieter Wisliceny's testimony at Nuremberg and an analysis of its context, which admittedly was only carried out later, tended to date the transition to systematic mass extermination closer to early 1942.[8] Eichmann's descriptions of his visits to Minsk and Riga in October 1941 offer further evidence to support this. But, during cross examination, the prosecution used these merely to entangle Eichmann in contradictory statements and to accuse him of deliberately lying because his account did not conform to their incorrect view that the systematic liquidation of the European Jews had already been decided upon at this date.

Hannah Arendt came close to realizing this but still presumed that an order to this effect had been issued by Hitler in May or June 1941. This corresponded with the view current among historians at the time that on 31 July 1941 Heydrich, at his own urging, had been entrusted by Göring with the execution of the 'Final Solution of the Jewish Question' precisely on the basis of such an order from Hitler. Arendt doubted that a definite decision to proceed with the Final Solution had been reached as early as 1939, but she did speak of an order issued in September 1939 for the systematic liquidation of the Polish Jews.[9] The German resettlement policy in Poland, which she briefly described, did not yet involve a systematic extermination of the Jewish population, though it gave rise to some massacres. She deduced from this that the territorial contingency plans, which, like the Nisco Project and the Madagascar Plan, were quite absurd and would ultimately have resulted in the physical destruction of the Jews anyway, were fictitious from the start, even in the minds of SS planners.

On this issue historians have become less certain. Intensive studies of the fragmentary sources available leave no doubt that the activities of the Einsatzgruppen after the start of the Russian campaign were aimed at exterminating the native Jewish population as far as possible. But their original orders had not explicitly envisaged this. The transition to a policy of systematically liquidating all Jews in the territories under German control and the authorizing of Adolf Eichmann with the comprehensive deportation programme necessary for this occurred in early 1942. This followed the uncoordinated massacres which had taken place in October 1941 and culminated with the Wannsee Conference, where the technical aspects of implementing such a policy were clarified with the various departments involved. The change of policy started when Jewish emigration was halted in late autumn 1941, as Hannah Arendt also mentions. Everything seems to indicate that no formal order for the implementation of the Final Solution programme across Europe was ever issued by Hitler. It remains a matter of contention whether Himmler and Heydrich, as most experts presume, proceeded on the basis of an oral directive from the dictator, or whether Hitler only indirectly precipitated this development and never himself went beyond the official terminology which referred only to the 'deportation' of the Jews. This is, of course, quite apart from his visionary-like ideological pronouncements which could only have been interpreted as incitements to mass murder.[10] Hitler's personal responsibility cannot be diminished. While he may have been unaware of some of the details of the Final Solution, he constructed the ideological and political framework which gave it what Hannah Arendt aptly described as the character of an automatic process. This was as immune to moral protest as it was to interventions motivated by sectional interests. But it was also symptomatic that Hitler did not want to be seen to be the originator of what he well knew were highly unpopular mass murders, though this did not prevent him giving free rein to his visionary hatred of the Jews.

As an account of the events which led to Auschwitz – the name which symbolizes the totality of the mass murder of the Jews – Hannah Arendt's interpretation is incomplete, sometimes contradictory and not sufficiently critical in its use of sources. But her work represents a challenge to historians to make a deeper analysis of the atmosphere which prevailed within the structures of the Nazi system and to clarify the extraordinary diffusion of authority which allowed such singularly horrific crimes as the Final Solution to be committed without meeting any substantial resistance. She accomplished this by the manner in which she described Eichmann's mentality so that it remains relevant today. This in itself is enough to justify republishing her *Eichmann in Jerusalem*, which has been the cause of such contention. Indeed, her thorough analysis of the Holocaust has if anything increased in relevance, especially given the wave of genocidal crimes committed in the decades which have passed since its original publication.

Some of the problems thrown up by Hannah Arendt's account have not been adequately analysed to this day. These include the contentious question of the extent to which the German and other European peoples implicated in the process of deportation and extermination were aware of what was taking place. Hannah Arendt's expositions of the psychological effects of the manipulative terror exercised by totalitarian systems, of the blunting of moral awareness and of the role of pseudo-justifications for crime offer an indispensable key to understanding how numerous Germans – including holders of the highest positions in the Nazi system – could claim with apparently genuine conviction that they had known nothing of the systematic extermination of the European Jews even though the veil of secrecy surrounding it had been far from watertight. Hannah Arendt presumed that the intention to proceed with Final Solution, and the facts relating to its implementation, were well known in leading party circles from as early as 1941. She also makes clear the function which keeping knowledge of it secret played and not least the manner in which the constant use of official jargon prevented recourse to moral judgements. Adolf Eichmann was an outstanding example of this.

One of the most shocking aspects of the factory-like mass murder of the

Jews was that, except within the relatively small group involved in the actual killings, the fact that what was taking place was a crime was subconsciously suppressed in a systematic manner by those who knew about it. This was an integral feature of national socialist rule and pervaded the entire system, including the highest positions. It is undeniable that the German population knew that a grim fate awaited the Jews, who were generally rounded up for deportation in full public view. Rumours of mass liquidations also circulated and soldiers on leave from the front brought details of what they had seen or heard. The opinion surveys carried out by the SD reported that news of the Katyn murders had elicited many comments to the effect that the German treatment of the Jews had not been much different. Nevertheless, the systematic nature of the mass exterminations remained generally unknown. Attempts to get accurate information were fraught with risks and, given the official taboo on the subject, even persons in high places were not always able to get reliable information on what was taking place or who was responsible. It is significant that the national conservative opposition was only scantily informed of what was happening and only became aware relatively late in the war of the true extent of the massacre of the Jews. Only Helmuth von Moltke, using his Abwehr contacts, succeeded in getting precise details. One result of the system of non-communication which had been deliberately fostered between the various offices of the regime was that no institution existed to which protests could have been addressed. When Hans Frank intervened to secure Jewish labour for the Generalgouvernement in Poland, the Führer referred him to Himmler, Frank's arch enemy, as the competent authority to approach about the matter.

It was easier for left-wing opponents of the regime, who believed Hitler was capable of anything, to credit that such horrific crimes were being committed than it was for those who had originally sympathized with the regime and supported its national aims. At the end of the day the ordinary man in the street was more prepared to believe reports of these atrocities, which were also broadcast by foreign radio stations, than were people in official positions. The reflex 'not to believe such things possible' and the attitude that such incidents were regrettable but basically isolated atrocities by SS thugs helped to obscure the full extent of what was taking place. At the time it was understandably very difficult to form a clear picture. Psychologically, people were used to thinking in terms of emergency situations and to suspect Allied propaganda of exaggerating atrocity stories. The gradual assimilation of the regime's systematic anti-semitic indoctrination destroyed any basis for feelings of solidarity towards the Jewish victims. As Hannah Arendt correctly pointed out, however, even without knowledge of the extermination camps a widespread if imprecise feeling of guilt pervaded German society. But the suppression of discomforting information was not purely an individual subjective response. The Nazi regime was virtually based on a reflex mechanism of collectively suppressing disturbing or ominous knowledge. To this can be added the moral indifference among the nation's functional elites long before 1933. Adolf Eichmann was a classic example of how values such as obedience and subordination were instrumental in justifying murder.

In attending Eichmann's trial, Hannah Arendt seized the opportunity presented by the *New Yorker* posting to study at first hand the motivations which underlay Nazi crimes, especially as she had not had any direct involvement with the Nuremberg Trials at the time they were held. Her interest was primarily a theoretical one; 'to study this evil directly in its entire awful nothingness and not through the medium of the printed word'.[11] This was her basic motivation and she later encapsulated it in the subtitle of her book, 'A Report on the Banality of Evil'. It was not a new discovery for her. In her earlier book, *The Origins of Totalitarianism*, published in 1951, she had already established that what was singular about the Final Solution, which undoubtedly had precedents in the 'administrative mass murders' of imperialist colonial policies, was that it took place devoid of a moral dimension, had no apparent cause and fulfilled no recognizable, practical objective. In this work she described how the national socialist extermination machine had been able to function absolutely free of sentiment and how murder had been transformed into a mechanical routine operation that was unamenable to conscientious protest.

Besides her desire to examine the validity of these general ideas in the specific case of Adolf Eichmann, she also believed at the start that the trial would be of historical importance in demonstrating 'the horrific extent to which the Jews collaborated in the organization of their own destruction'.[12] While her choice of words was certainly exaggerated, what it expressed was not simply an offhand opinion. Even before she had thoroughly studied the sources, she had referred in private to the role the Jewish Councils and Jewish groups had played in assisting the organization of the Holocaust. Her opinions in this area were to emerge as the central issue in the bitter controversy which her publications provoked. Many of her critics accused her in effect, if not directly, of Jewish masochism and, in the case of Gershom Scholem, the Jewish religious philosopher,[13] of a lack of sympathy for the Jewish people.

For Hannah Arendt, reference to the responsibility borne by the leaders of Jewish organizations was not purely a moral question. She was convinced that only by being able to admit the responsibility which they had shared for the catastrophe of the European Jews was there any possibility for a new and constructive political start to be made, not least by the Jewish people itself.[14] For her, Nazi genocide had a relevance in general human terms. The sight of a highly mechanised and bureaucratized world where genocide and the extermination of entire groups of people who were regarded as 'superfluous' could become a normal occurrence, without evoking any protest or public moral outrage, made her an outspoken critic of the attitude that once the guilty – or at least those who could be caught – had been prosecuted, it was possible to simply return to life as it had been before or, as in the case of the dominant Zionist forces in Israel, to consciously use the experience of the Holocaust to legitimize a state.

When Hannah Arendt took up her post reporting the trial, she believed that the Israeli decision to prosecute Eichmann was unavoidable, though in principle she agreed with the call by her friend, Karl Jaspers, that Eichmann be tried by an international court. She did not directly disagree with Jasper's objections regarding the illegality of kidnapping Eichmann and his point that judicial 'embarrassments' arising from this could be expected at the trial. But she made it clear in the manner in which she portrayed Shalom Schwartzbard in her report that she would have preferred a more objective method of establishing guilt to have been chosen. In addition, she recognized Israel's right to speak if not for the entire international Jewish community at least for the victims of the Holocaust. She did not regard the criticisms levelled at the trial's legalistic aspects as very relevant to the substantial point at issue. She was rather more concerned by the fact that Eichmann's affidavit declaring that he had been brought voluntarily to Israel appeared to have been signed only after he had arrived there.[15] This reinforced her suspicion that the trial was intended to serve certain political purposes.

She went as far as to claim that the Israeli prime minister, Ben Gurion, had linked the trial to political deals aimed at strengthening Israel's position against the Arab world and pressurizing West Germany into continuing financial concessions after the set compensation had been paid. She also claimed that the prosecution had deliberately precluded treatment of certain aspects of the Final Solution. But this accusation, which would require access to the official records for verification, does not affect her central point. This is even more true of her criticisms of the way in which the trial was organized. She was particularly critical of the behaviour of the Israeli chief attorney, Gideon Hausner, and could not conceal her very definite resentment of him. She accused him firstly of being ignorant of the facts. This was justified to the extent that Hausner was inclined to base his arguments on a fixed picture of the Final Solution which even at the time was highly questionable given the documents and witnesses' testimony available. Hausner remained adamant that Eichmann had been central to the extermination process, had played the controlling role in it and was the main person responsible for the extermination of the European Jews. Hannah Arendt felt that his insistent attempts to establish Eichmann's direct involvement in extremely brutal individual acts of murder and his attempt to portray him as a criminal pervert were especially absurd.

Hannah Arendt realized that the prosecution had trapped itself from the start in an untenable position. They saw in Eichmann the actual initiator of the Final Solution rather than the archetypal administrative mass murderer that he was. This opinion was totally contradicted by the available evidence. Only in the case of the murder of the Hungarian Jews did Eichmann show any initiative and even then it was of a purely bureaucratic nature. He would admit to his own part in events but to nothing beyond that. The prosecution's constant attempts to establish that he was lying missed the point that the accused only hesitated to give information or became unsure when his memory failed. To a certain extent he was an expert witness only because he had been fed with the comprehensive documentary evidence before the court. But, by attempting to associate Eichmann directly with individual acts of sadism, the prosecution distracted attention from the central fact that he was an archetypal office desk criminal incapable of feeling remorse for his deeds. Hannah Arendt made similar criticisms of the hearings before the Court of Appeal, which to a certain extent resorted to the same arguments the prosecution had used. She ascribed a high degree of intelligence and an honest desire to be objective to the judges of the Special Tribunal, however.

Her main criticism of the trial was levelled at its tendency to portray the Holocaust as an integral part of the history of anti-semitism, as many Israeli politicians were also wont to do. In her opinion this made the Holocaust appear as a necessary and inevitable stage in Jewish history. In her study *The Origins of Totalitarianism* she had already decisively rejected the idea of an 'eternal anti-semitism'. She argued that the road to the Final Solution was not comprehensible in terms of the continuity of anti-semitic strands but was primarily the result of the inherent need of a totalitarian regime to develop an enemy figure. The Jews, who had never really been integrated as a group into German society, were most suited to this role. She put great emphasis on the totally different context which had given rise to anti-semitism and the function it had fulfilled in preceding eras compared with the new phenomenon it had become in the twentieth century.[16] She also stressed that the assimilated Jews had been characterized by an innate aversion to power, even when they had enjoyed a relatively advantageous economic position, and had not taken full advantage of the avenues of influence which had been open to them. She denied that there was any conflict of interest between Jews and the majority of the population in twentieth-century society. In fact, the relative preponderance of Jews in particular professions had declined markedly from after the First World War at the latest.[17] In this context she referred to 'inexperience of hatred of the Jews' as a characteristic of the twentieth century. By this she meant that anti-semitism as an 'objective hatred of Jews' had lost its basis in reality and been transformed into a purely ideological phenomenon. She saw this as part of the general transformation in the nature of anti-semitism which had occurred from the late nineteenth century and which she believed formed the moral basis of the later genocide by the Nazis. The very existence of assimilated Jews, who rejected their 'Jewishness' and had themselves baptized, changed the 'crime' of being a Jew into a 'vice' which could no longer be dealt with by punishment but only by extermination.[18] Her line of argument on his question contained a certain element of self-criticism in its insinuation that the willingness to assimilate had itself played a part in transforming the nature of anti-semitism.

Hannah Arendt did not regard the fate suffered by the Jews under the Nazis as unique and singular compared with what other repressed groups suffered. Instead, she saw it as the archetype of complete disenfranchise-ment and dehumanization of the individual. To her, the fact that the Jews who were persecuted by national socialism were 'led to the slaughter' regardless of their personal situation or their complete innocence was the central issue. Their extermination was not the product of an anti-semitism defined by any material considerations or calculations of utility. It was a consequence solely of the fact that the Jewish enemy-image established by the totalitarian rulers took on a momentum of its own which bore no relationship to reality and in which those carrying it out communicated with each other only in a coded language. She underestimated the quite signifi-cant effect which the self-interested motives of certain middle-class groups had had in the escalation of the persecution of the Jews before 1939, and particularly in their exclusion from economic influence. Nevertheless, she described with extraordinary clarity the atmosphere of total moral indiffer-ence in which the Final Solution policy was executed.

Hannah Arendt realized that a precondition for the extermination policy finally carried out was that the persecuted group had first to be completely excluded socially and legally from everyday society. This insight was first articulated in her study of totalitarianism, where she commented that the right to life only came into question after the victims had been totally disenfranchised.[19] She used the term 'outcast' to describe the situation of a group of the population which had been systematically deprived of its rights. She drew a parallel in this regard with the manner in which a deportee is gradually stripped of his citizenship and, along with his home-land, loses his legal existence as a person. These she regarded as the indispensable basis of human existence. For her, this human experience had by no means ended with the collapse of the Third Reich. The emergence of a permanent stratum of 'displaced persons', which as a mass phenomenon was initially a product of totalitarian rule, appeared to her to be a central characteristic of the post-war era. She regarded the denial of citizenship as a modern fate, which by its nature carried with it the threat of a new genocide. The expulsion of the Palestinian Arabs appeared to her to be an evil omen that the vicious circle that had begun with mutual exclusion would continue. But she also saw in the phenomenon of denied citizenship the negation of history and the symbol of a thoroughly new political and social era that was dawning. Her passionate defence of the Diaspora against the Zionist position, which was inclined to deny non-Israeli Jews any historical role, was for her part of the same context.[20]

Hannah Arendt passionately rejected the Zionist view that anti-semitism was an insurmountable historical continuum that justified the Jewish settlement of Palestine. She predicted that this would merely involve an exchange of positions, particularly as she was convinced that the religious claim to a special role for the Jewish people had lost its binding power. She also predicted that the insularism adopted by Zionism in relation to the non-Jewish world would ultimately lead to a traditional nationalism or at worst to its next stage of development, an aggressive imperialism. In this same context she regarded the failure to laicize the Jewish state as the most crucial mistake made during the foundation of Israel. She feared that the Yishuv, the organized community of Jews who had emigrated to Palestine and settled there permanently before the foundation of Israel, would be forced into a confrontational position with regard to its Arab neighbours similar to the Nazi regime's stance towards the Jews. She did not hesitate to impute fascist tendencies to the Israeli political system.

From this perspective, Hannah Arendt believed that the prosecution in the Eichmann case made a serious error in recapitulating the entire history of anti-semitism and thus pushing the central issue of the 'unprecedentedness' of the systematic nature of the Nazi genocide to the background.[21] To her, the singularity of the Holocaust lay in its total lack of a moral dimension and hence its exclusively technocratic nature. But in this she was demanding too much of the competence of the court, and this would have been true of whatever court had been involved. For even she was unable to resolve the conundrum that the case to be established with regard to Eichmann was in a certain sense simply not amenable to legal justice given his lack of any feelings of remorse. The alternative basis on which she proposed that he be judged was overwhelmingly regarded by her critics as an unacceptable insult to the court, especially as she raised it in the same context as the issue of the legality of the case. What she wished to establish, as she had concluded in her correspondence with Karl Jaspers,[22] was that the central issue was not that a crime against 'humanity' had been committed but a crime against 'mankind' *per se*. She agreed with the necessity for a death sentence but wanted to see it founded not on the individual guilt of the accused but on the supra-personal basis that Eichmann had placed himself beyond the bounds of human society by actively participating in genocide.

In referring to the inadequacy of the Israeli law of 1950 for punishing Nazis and their accomplices, Hannah Arendt touched on the fundamental difficulty of attempting 'to encompass political matters with legal concepts' and to deal with the legacy of the Third Reich by judicial means.[23] The West German war crimes trials, which had finally begun after inordinate delays and were often to end with shockingly light sentences, were censured by her for operating on the basis of the normal criminal code, including arraignment for murder, instead of a retrospective law allowing for the trial of deeds which had been legal under the conditions of the Third Reich. The dilemma at the centre of the German trials, as in the Eichmann case, was that in general 'malice' was not involved. This was quite apart from the recurrent problem of having to establish the truth of events which had occurred in the distant past and in the diffuse reality of what had become a permanent emergency situation. A retrospective law governing genocide would hardly have changed this situation. To that extent her otherwise justified criticism of the tardy prosecution of war crimes cases in West Germany detracted from the thorough analysis she presented of the legal and political problems involved in the Eichmann trial.[24]

But it was Hannah Arendt's description of Eichmann's role rather than her views on the legal aspects of the trial which provoked the storm of outrage in Jewish public opinion. Her concern to present as accurate and objective an analysis as possible of what had motivated Eichmann contrasted fundamentally with the bulk of contemporary reportage, which clung rigidly to the cliché of Eichmann as the sinister *éminence grise* behind the Final Solution and, as with Hausner, portrayed him as an obdurate liar.[25] Her criticisms of the court and her wish to be as objective as possible led many to feel that she was becoming partial in the case. But she was very far from harbouring any sympathy for Eichmann. Motivated rather by a principled concern for the truth, she established that the determining motive in Eichmann's case, apart from personal ambition, lay in his misguided concept of devotion to duty and his slavishly bureaucratic sense of obedience. With this discovery, she anticipated the recurring experience of independent researchers and the prosecuting authorities in the West German trials of participants in the Final Solution. These were staged in rapid succession following the Einsatzgruppen trial at Ulm. Eichmann had led an unsuccessful life until he achieved a certain level of satisfaction working for the regime – in his case a posting with the RSHA in 1939 – without ever losing his extremely subservient attitude. In retrospect, this seems to have virtually defined the type of person entrusted with carrying out the crimes of the Nazi regime. Equally characteristic was that Eichmann's involvement had not been motivated primarily by anti-semitism. He had established relations with Zionist organizations and at his trial he even sought to defend himself with the grotesque argument that, in his capacity as head of the

Jewish Emigration Bureaux in Vienna and Prague and later as head of the Central Emigration Bureau in Berlin, he had in fact indirectly contributed to lowering the number of Jews later deported to extermination camps.

Hannah Arendt was already convinced, with good reason, of the personal and moral mediocrity of the defendant after she had read the reports from Argentina published before the trial.[26] This led her to the conclusion, later encapsulated in the subtitle of her book, that evil is 'banal'. The more it became clear to her that Eichmann had functioned as only one mechanical link in the Nazi system's machinery of extermination, the more she saw her earlier observation confirmed that the criminal character of such a system was ultimately the product of a mosaic of what were individually trivial elements. In her earlier study of totalitarianism, and using the impressionistic deductive method peculiar to her, she had already brought some of the essential elements of the national socialist system to light. These have since been considerably developed by historians. Among them was her observation that the dictatorship was by no means shaped by Hitler's demonic will-power but that, on the contrary, the regime's intrinsic need to maintain its 'movement'-based structure in a constantly mobilized state was the basic force in the continual radicalization of the objectives and brutality which characterized it. This led her to remark that Hitler was 'simply a vital function of the movement'.[27] Her exaggerated claim that totalitarian systems inherently tended to shed their talented servants and replace them with charlatans and fools sprang from the same thinking.

In her book *The Origins of Totalitarianism* Hannah Arendt correctly emphasized the absence of hierarchy as a structural characteristic of the Third Reich. In her study of Eichmann she described the complementary effect which the regime's subsidiary bureaucratic apparatuses had on this, though without recognizing the dialectic dynamic produced by the constant disputes over areas of competence, well described by Eichmann, which contributed immensely to the progressive radicalization of the measures taken against the Jews. With this discovery, she concretized her earlier analysis whereby she had described the tendency within totalitarian systems to condition all groups in society by constant indoctrination and terror in such a way that they became equally suited to playing the role of either executioner or victim. The mechanism employed to achieve this, she wrote, was the incessant increase in terror, which immobilized people as if 'they and their spontaneity were only obstacles in the way of national and historical processes'.[28] Written in the context of the Stalinist purges, this theory, in some respects exaggerated, arose from her analysis of the relationship between executioners and victims. Her critics generally missed the point she was attempting to make. She was trying to establish the nature of extreme borderline situations, where the liquidation of innocent people occurred without provoking a murmur of dissent or rebellion.

The similarity in the mentality of executioners and victims first posited by Hannah Arendt has been confirmed by a range of studies.[29] What was involved was a specific type of social psychological phenomenon, which emerged under the extreme conditions of the concentration and extermination camps and was a product, in the final analysis, of the basic human need to maintain the semblance of social relationships even under conditions of utter disenfranchisement and depersonalization. This explains both the passivity with which the victims went to their deaths, however much they had already been reduced beyond the limits of human endurance, as well as the co-operation in the process, however forced, of the *Kapos* and *Sonderkommandos*. The intricate functional hierarchy which existed between camp guards and prisoners was also part of this. The role of ensuring that events proceeded in an orderly fashion, which was forced on Jewish community leaders and organizations at the other end of the process, operated on a different level. Without any doubt, a thoroughly functionalist division of labour developed between local SS offices and the Jewish Councils which were operating under extreme psychological duress. Hannah Arendt feared that Eichmann would use this collaborationist relationship in his defence and thereby give a new impetus to the anti-semitic argument.[30] She believed that only by thoroughly explaining the complex involved in this was there a chance to prevent the emergence of an anti-semitic interpretation of the Holocaust in the future.

Hannah Arendt forthrightly claimed that, were it not for the co-operation of Jewish officials, the Final Solution could not have been realized to the extent it was. This touched on a taboo area which to the present day has not been fully clarified. The mention of it is still understandably regarded by those who survived the catastrophe as insensitive and arrogant. It is undeniable that a large degree of forced co-operation existed between the Jewish Councils and the Reichsvereinigung der deutschen Juden – the compulsory Federation of German Jews established by German diktat – on the one hand and the offices of the SS on the other. It is also undeniable that this co-operation considerably facilitated the deportation measures for which Eichmann was primarily responsible.[31] One of the reasons for this was that the Jewish minorities, not only in eastern Europe, saw themselves surrounded by a virulent anti-semitism which made the very idea of mass escapes appear hopeless from the start. Similarly, an organized refusal on a large scale to obey the orders of the police or the SS authorities functioning in the East would undoubtedly have precipitated horrific reprisals. But it would have considerably disrupted the programme of mass liquidation and necessitated a manifold increase in the number of personnel engaged in it. Moreover, it would have robbed the regime of yet another of the pretexts for its policy.

It has been equally well established that organized resistance to the Final

Solution came almost exclusively from political groups of the left and not from the rabbis as a body. Hannah Arendt totally rejected the fashionable theory of the east European Jews' alleged ghetto mentality, which Raul Hilberg had used to explain this phenomenon.[32] She regarded the claim that the passivity of Jewish officials resulted from a specifically Jewish mentality as a negative argument serving only to perpetuate anti-semitism. In fact there is no evidence to show that east European Jews acted in any substantially different way from other elements of the population. In her *Origins of Totalitarianism* Hannah Arendt had pointed out the conditions which help explain what had led the victims to co-operate in their own destruction. Her critics naturally did not miss the opportunity to point to an inconsistency in this regard on her part.[33] It is difficult but not impossible to accept how, in the incredibly horrific conditions in the ghettos, the SS were able to get certain groups of Jewish officials to act pliantly. The Jewish population was neither morally nor politically prepared for the liquidation measures with which they were confronted. These were carried out, more-over, in a strangely diffuse situation where recurrent sparks of hope of the possibility of survival precluded totally accepting that one was faced with certain extermination.[34]

It would have been helpful if Hannah Arendt had distinguished more sharply between the various stages in the tacit co-operation that developed between Jewish organizations and the Nazi rulers.[35] That a co-operative relationship was established between the Gestapo and Zionist organizations in the period up to 1936 is as indisputable as the fact that a negative identity of aims existed between both sides. A complete separation of the Jews from the general population was unquestionably a central requirement for the Nazis to be able to implement their anti-Jewish programme without provoking substantial resistance from the majority of the population. The Zionist groups indirectly abetted this process initially. It would also not be difficult to establish that a certain affinity, rooted in the general thinking of the time, existed between the ideological attitudes mobilized by the Nazis and those present in the Zionist movement. Despite the unequivocal position adopted by the Central Association of German Citizens of the Jewish Faith before 1933 that national socialism represented a mortal threat to the Jews, the representative body which can be regarded as its successor generally hoped until 1938 that it would be possible to establish a *modus vivendi* with the regime. But this had no substantial influence on the course of events, as the main reasons why Jewish emigration was brought to a halt had more to do with the shortage of currency and the unwillingness of countries where the Jews sought refuge to grant them entry.

The Reichsvereinigung der deutschen Juden, forced to co-operate with Eichmann's office, was in a no-win situation from the start and this was equally true of the other comparable Jewish organizations in western Europe. Hannah Arendt would have helped her case had she referred to the work done to provide welfare services by such organizations, in which she herself had been involved during her period in Paris. Characteristically exaggerating her argument, however, she dismissed this institution so typical of Jewish community life as nothing but a waste of time in that it represented a basic willingness to accommodate to circumstances and an attitude limited to day-to-day survival, which prevented the Jewish population from taking measures, even if at a great price, to meet the looming threat of liquidation before it was too late. This was also the conclusion reached by radical Zionists.

But Hannah Arendt was not always consistent in her approach to Zionism. While she clearly sympathized with the early kibbuzim movement, she simultaneously accused it of adopting a siege position and not developing any future-oriented concept for solving the problems inherent in establishing a Jewish settlement in Palestine. She suspected the Zionists who favoured an offensive concept, including military and terrorist methods, of reverting to a backward nationalism. During the latter years of the war she argued for the establishment of a Jewish military formation in the framework of the Allied alliance, which was not a very realistic proposal. But, at the same time, she accused the Zionists in Palestine of exploiting the war situation purely to enhance their own positions. There is no evidence in any of her writings that she had any clear perspective on the question of Palestine. For a while after the war she explicitly supported the Ichkud party and called for a joint Jewish–Arab arrangement in Palestine under international supervision. On the other hand, she also regarded a federation of Arabs and Jews as unimaginable.[36]

These issues were not central, however, to her study of Eichmann. The problem of Jewish resistance is also not dealt with systematically. Israeli historians in particular have been collecting data on this area over the last decades which show that passivity was by no means always and everywhere the norm. But resistance was nevertheless restricted to small isolated groups and, as in the case of the Warsaw uprising, was organized primarily by representatives of the political left and occasionally by Zionist youth groups.[37] All the same, Hannah Arendt regarded Hausner's routine question as to why there had been no resistance as 'frightful' and 'foolish'. She drew a distinction between the Jewish masses and the Jewish officials, of whom she demanded retrospectively that they should have refused to co-operate in any way. Given the situation in the ghettos, that would certainly have been unrealistic. The Theresienstadt camp, largely ignored by the prosecution, was a different matter, however. The judges too were critical of the court's failure to use the studies available on it, which, as Hannah

Arendt correctly remarked, showed that a smoothly functioning system of collaboration with the SS had existed and that co-operation had been widespread, even in the selection process.[38]

The radicalism of her condemnations of Jewish leadership groups – including those outside the areas controlled by the Nazis – for their readiness to co-operate up to a point was not dissimilar to the harshness with which she judged the German opposition to Hitler. With good reason, she emphasized the ambivalence which pervaded large sections of the national conservative resistance on the Jewish question, though her information on the attitudes of Helmuth James von Moltke and Adam von Trott zu Solz as well as the general outlook of the Kreisau Circle was very sketchy. She dismissed the plans of the Kreisau Circle as 'fantasy' and Carl Goerdeler's reform proposals as 'stupid and ridiculous' and did not neglect to mention his questionable idea of establishing a state for the Jews in Canada. She attributed a basic level of agreement with certain aims of the Nazis to the bourgeois conservative resistance generally.[39] Her opinions in this area were based on the critical analyses published by Henry Paechter and George K. Romoser.[40] For the German edition of her book, Hannah Arendt modified these statements somewhat following the personal intervention of several individuals, including Emil Henk. But it still contains the wildly inaccurate statement that communists joined the NSDAP in huge numbers and totally unjustifiably disparages the communist resistance movement.[41]

Since the 1960s West German analyses of the resistance have in fact developed a substantially more critical interpretation, diverging from the largely heroic and uncritical picture which had pertained up to then.[42] Hannah Arendt's pronouncedly polemical account, which even Jaspers opposed, did, however, point out the difficulties of the situation in which the national conservative resistance was forced to operate, as well as its basic political outlook. But she did not adequately explain the deeper reasons why a general will to resist the regime did not develop. As in her interpretation of the collaboration of many Jewish officials, she made the absence of a willingness on the part of individuals to sacrifice their lives the yardstick of her judgement. The categorical way in which she put her case not only provoked intense hostility to her, it also revealed the essential conundrum in Hannah Arendt's position in that she formed her judgements on the basis of an essentially metapolitical perspective. But this way of viewing events was as apolitical as the outlook of those she criticized, whether Jewish notables, German resistance fighters or the non-Nazis who held high positions in the Third Reich whom she accused of lacking political realism.

Hannah Arendt tended to argue both in private and in public with pointed sarcasm and an unusual tenacity. This brought her accusations, particularly with regard to her Eichmann study, of being arrogant, of indulging in rhetoric and of being tactless and insensitive towards the victims of Nazism.[43] Many contemporaries found the relentlessness of her frontal assaults on comfortable myths destructive. The severity of her criticism and the unsparing way in which she argued seemed inappropriate given the deeply tragic nature of the subject with which she was dealing. Very few recognized that to review horrific events without collapsing into moralizing plaintiveness or merely provoking instincts of revulsion by presenting a catalogue of abhorrent scenes of deeply inhuman perversity entailed resorting to irony and sarcasm to conceal the deep emotional involvement which lay behind them.

Hannah Arendt did not anticipate the full extent and bitterness of the polemical attacks on her which her Eichmann articles aroused. This is in need of some explanation. She was not exactly gentle in dealing with opponents herself and this must have been as obvious to her as the fact that by pronouncing Jewish 'collaboration' in the Holocaust she was touching on an extremely sensitive complex of historical problems. She had also openly attacked the Israeli authorities and not least Ben Gurion and Golda Meir in person. She was nevertheless totally taken aback by the general rejection her book encountered. When she returned from a journey abroad she was met by an insurmountable quantity of hostile mail, followed by numerous mostly polemical magazine articles and public attacks on her position. In a foreword to the first German edition of her Eichmann study she later wrote, not without cause, of a campaign organized largely by Jewish groups to silence her – from her point of view by grossly distorting her intentions and twisting her arguments. Pressure, indeed, was brought to bear on the media from various quarters and this led in many cases to the few people prepared to support her being prevented from doing so publicly and Arendt herself only on rare occasions being given the opportunity to answer her critics. She was challenged to withdraw her book from circulation and an attempt was made to stop the appearance of its German edition.[44]

Criticism of the Eichmann book was not restricted to pro-Zionist groups. Hannah Arendt was soon confronted by a wall of rejection and had to suffer the depressing experience of seeing even old Jewish friends turn their backs on her. These very probably included Kurt Blumenfeld, with whom she had had a close intellectual relationship since the early 1930s. He had put her in contact with the Zionist organizations in Berlin through whose efforts she had then secured a job with the *Allyah* youth in Paris. It also destroyed her working relationship with the Leo Baeck Institute in New York, which in 1958 had published her book on Rahel Varnhagen. Only very few of her friends publicly supported her. She was deeply upset when Gershom Scholem, whose writings she had edited, turned against her because, she claimed, of misleading information he had received about

the contents of her Eichmann book.[45] Although the attempt to silence her
failed, Hannah Arendt now found herself isolated from all those Jewish
groups with which she had worked over many years and without whose
help she would hardly have been able either morally or materially to have
survived the bitter experience of exile in Paris and later in New York.

In spite of her deep upset, Hannah Arendt was courageous and sturdy
enough not to display her angry feelings in public.[46] When it is considered
that it was precisely in the concept of 'Loneliness' – not in terms of being
on one's own, but rather in the sense of being denied dialogue – that she
saw the most extreme form of human distress, it can be understood to
what extent the 'Eichmann Controversy', as this utterly one-sided media
campaign soon became known, represented such a deep disruption of her
life despite her outward professional success – and this although the
contentious book represented in many ways only a logical development of
her earlier thinking and contained in concise form many known facts and
previously widely accepted ideas. In West Germany too rejection was the
norm, and where supportive voices were raised they came mostly from the
wrong quarter. Many insights and challenges which the book contained
came too early for a general public unprepared for such shocks. The rigid
picture which had emerged of the Nazi system under the influence of the
theory of totalitarian dictatorship had first to lose its dominant position in
academic thinking before her interpretation of the Final Solution could
become a respectable subject for discussion. It is ironic that Hannah Arendt
herself had unwittingly helped to foster this theory even though her account
of the 'origins of totalitarianism' diverged in many crucial points from what
in the meantime had become a dogmatic explanation of the nature of
political systems.[47]

Only a few of those who thought like her realized that her 'Report on
the Banality of Evil' contained a piece of hidden self-criticism. This was
admittedly the case with virtually everything Hannah Arendt ever wrote. It
was very closely connected with the problem of German-Jewish identity
with which she constantly saw herself challenged. To assess this, it is
necessary to retrace her outlook and her career. Hannah Arendt was the
daughter of a respected middle-class Jewish family which was intimately
involved in German culture and felt part of it. She studied at university in
Marburg, Heidelberg and Freiburg and from there moved on to Frankfurt
and Berlin before arriving via Paris in the USA. There, after the hard years
of exile, she succeeded in working her way up to become a world-renowned
publicist. Her study of philosophy at Marburg and Heidelberg, her youthful
love for Martin Heidegger, which never totally faded, her close relationship
with Benno von Wiese and her lifelong association with Karl Jaspers were
to remain of abiding importance to her. Her intense involvement with
German philosophy in those years had a much stronger influence in shaping

her thinking than is betrayed by her published works, which were written overwhelmingly for circulation in the English-speaking world.[48]

The dialectical argumentation typical of Hannah Arendt was a product of her intense involvement with early existential philosophy.[49] The anti-historicist tenor which was not only encountered in Heidegger and Jaspers but which pervaded the humanities generally and stood militantly opposed to the relativization of values then on the ascent was also characteristic of Hannah Arendt's philosophical and publicist work. From this basis she was able to break free from the tradition of positivist specializationism and to combine the experiences of different epochs intellectually, very much in the enlightenment mode. This enabled her to produce fascinating insights into universal phenomena, though not without occasionally becoming entangled in overwrought intellectual constructions. Basically she was unmethodical and resorted instead to an impressionistic sensitivity to establish associations and to combine these in an overall view constructed from ontological elements. Her tendency when analysing a subject to approach it from its extremes misled her to overestimate the internal coherence of totalitarian dictatorships, as David Riesman pointed out to her in friendly criticism.[50] To a certain extent she was herself a victim of what she called the 'inexorable logic of deductionist thinking'[51] which she incorrectly ascribed to totalitarian dictatorships.

The intellectual attractiveness justifiably attributed to her was certainly in part based on the constant attempts, characteristic of her thinking, to link together apparently incompatible phenomena in dialectical relationships and to combine a basically pessimistic outlook on life, fashioned by the cultural criticism of the 1920s, with a *vita activa*, with a fundamentally lively and open approach to life. This was noticeably present in the tension between her 'Jewishness', which subjectively she felt very strongly, and her deep association with the markedly idealist and romantic traditions of German culture. During her formative period at Heidelberg, her study of Rahel Varnhagen von Ense led her to attempt to clarify the nature of her cultural identity. As an assimilated Jewess living in an environment of latent anti-semitism, this had to involve an attempt to analyse the position occupied by the Jews in European bourgeois society.

When she left Germany in 1933, Hannah Arendt had not completed the manuscript on Rahel on which she had been working. It would possibly never have been published had the Leo Baeck Institute in New York not suggested to her in 1956 that the nearly forgotten manuscript be included in its series of publications. It was typical of her way of thinking, which was oriented towards future configurations rather than reflections on the past, that she felt the task of preparing this book for publication more as a chore and passed the job of putting her disorderly manuscript into shape over to Lotte Köhler, who in the following years was to become one of her closest friends. The fear of being too personal may explain the almost businesslike handling of the subject in the book. But, despite the fact that its subject had little in common with her later interests and concerns, this work represents a statement of Hannah Arendt's basic intellectual outlook and is a key to understanding her later works of historical and political interpretation.

In examining the life of Rahel Varnhagen – or rather, the repeated failures of an unusually talented Jewess determined on complete assimilation into Prussian society – Hannah Arendt was confronted with the problem of whether and to what extent assimilation was possible and what psychological consequences were associated with it. The study may have been originally intended more as an examination of the role of the female intellectual in general. Nevertheless, the approach she adopted in her interpretation of Rahel Varnhagen's life gives the book a marked autobiographical flavour. The language of the book, which in many ways approaches the style of a novel and is by no means a philosophical work, unmistakably betrays the influence of Friedrich Gundolf, whose lectures Hannah Arendt had attended at Heidelberg. The book's poetic elements, which in no sense only arise in references from Rahel, indicate the extent to which the author identified with her subject. Her description of Rahel's fate as 'the chosen insecurity of a life of self-exposition' anticipated her own existence just as she did when, in criticizing her heroine, she stated her determination – it was to remain an abiding principle for her throughout her life – that she would avoid the basic error which had prevented Rahel 'from perceiving her private misfortune within its broader social context'.[52]

In this developmental novel written in the poetic language of the romantic era Hannah Arendt described the role of even the assimilated Jew as essentially that of an outsider in a society, with the alternatives only of being either a pariah or a parvenu, a role which she had not yet herself experienced to any great degree. That she thought the former alternative superior is evident from her almost casual remark that only the pariah has the ability to sense 'true realities', has access to the false bottom of human existence. This also explains her critically justifying Rahel for remaining both a Jewess *and* a pariah. 'Only by holding fast to both did she find a place in the history of European mankind.' This was the reason why Rahel's 'rebellious heart' had been able to produce such a perceptive talent and thus to break through the small-minded fetters of her genteel high-society environment. By retaining her identity, which was forced upon her, as a pariah within the parvenu role of the 'inescapably Jewish' assimilated Jew, the 'vista' was 'opened' to her 'through which the pariah, as an outcast, can survey life as a whole'. This was 'the same path which leads him [the pariah] to the "great love for free thought"'.[53]

This rationalization was certainly not a final resolution of the German-

Jewish crisis of identity with which Hannah Arendt, like many German Jews of her generation, was confronted. The refuge she found in her first Jewish marriage with Günther Stern (the writer Günther Anders) represented a stage on the way to her positively identifying with her Jewishness and indirectly freed her from her intimate relations with Martin Heidegger and Benno von Wiese. Hannah Arendt was only confronted with the reality of Jewish community life when she went to Berlin and worked for the Jewish welfare service, without at the time being aware that this was the first step in her escape to Paris.

During this period she resolved morally and intellectually that under no circumstances would she seek to become a parvenu and thus abandon her own tension-laden identity, which she was aware did not offer any security of socially belonging. In the book on Rahel she gave clear expression to her conviction that it was impossible to solve the Jewish question on a 'personal' basis as this entailed denying the existence of the unassimilated Jews, the majority of whom did not belong to the upper middle classes but existed rather on the verge of proletarianization. Denying them meant suppressing one's own roots and living a lie and in addition also inherently entailed accommodating anti-semitism.[54]

Hannah Arendt opted to be a pariah, to turn the role of outsider into a positive force so as to be able to maintain an inner distance to things, to assert the 'freedom of the mind'. During her period in Paris she separated from Günther Stern and also made contact with representatives of the European left, including Bert Brecht and Walter Benjamin. It was also the beginning of her indissoluble relationship with Heinrich Blücher, who, though critical of Stalinist politics (he was a party colleague of Heinrich Brandler and joined the KPO), maintained his faith in communism. But her involvement with socialist issues did not leave any deep traces in her thinking. She remained a child of German existential philosophy and its markedly elitist and apolitical outlook. The examination of the social side of Jewish life as well as of the social problems of post-industrial society that she had intended to pursue failed to materialize, and her knowledge of Karl Marx, including his earlier works, which had been shaped by Hegelian ideas and formed the anthropological basis of his theory, remained superficial.[55] The restriction of her theoretical work to political philosophy in the narrow sense, fully in the tradition of Montesquieu and of Greek philosophy as interpreted ontologically, was marked by its total eschewal of the social aspect. She reduced this to the empirically unsound notion of the 'mob', which she described as a phenomenon transcending class divisions. Despite the fact that she lived in the poorest conditions, which were only to improve in the late 1950s, she remained in every inch of her person a bourgeois. That she felt the basic contradiction of this may explain why she pilloried Jewish affluence as a false solution to social oppression with such unjustified trenchancy. Her identification with being an outsider did not lead her to cut herself off from people who shared her opinions, but it did involve a certain distancing of herself from others and an increasing tendency towards a pronounced non-conformism. This and, not least, its upshot in her opposition to McCarthyism and her support for the rebelling students of the 1960s lent her a progressive image. But her protests against the racial desegregation enforced against parents' wishes after the events at Little Rock[56] showed clearly that her non-conformism stopped short at the social barrier to the lower class; she did not permit it to challenge her pronouncedly elitist conservative views on democracy and politics, which set up the concept of authority as a counter to that of power and posited a concept of individual freedom based on the model of the ancient *polis*. In this sense she remained a conservative in values who judged her political environment from the point of view of ethical standards and who characteristically only studied Max Weber's *Economy and Society* for the first time late in her life. This ultimately moral perspective, free from the restrictions of practical politics, helps to explain the sharp disagreements – occasionally coupled with grotesque misjudgements – which she had with Konrad Adenauer's chancellor-democracy. They were also present in the Eichmann book and gave rise in West Germany to the totally unfounded suspicion that she sympathized with the political left.[57]

The role of outsider which was forced upon her, together with her consideration for Heinrich Blücher – for whom she maintained a remarkably old-fashioned wifely concern which did not at all fit in with her otherwise emancipated position – may have been among the reasons why she avoided taking up one of the many secure posts at America's outstanding universities constantly being offered to her, and thus to her establishing a school of philosophy of her own. Her unpredictable professional life with its various teaching, lecturing and publishing duties and its consequences in what was at first a poverty-ridden lifestyle and from the early 1950s an affluent one in New York – which did not exclude a high degree of material and aesthetic enjoyment – also certainly served to stop her from sliding into the role of a parvenu. At any rate she sought to avoid a formal bourgeois lifestyle and thus prevent what she called the 'bourgeois world of nothing-ness'[58] from entering her sphere of independent thought. She allowed only a small circle of close friends to participate in this life and apparently remained somewhat cool towards public acclaim, tending rather to withdraw out of a mixture of personal shyness and a feeling of intellectual superiority.

In any event Hannah Arendt seized the opportunity presented to her by the role of perpetual 'exponent', which was forced on her by the circumstances of her life and which characterized the function of the intellectual in modern society in general, and used it positively. Her role as an outsider was born when she recognized the anti-semitism rising sharply in the latter years of the Weimar Republic. It was reinforced by her existence as an expatriate intellectual – she only took out American citizenship in 1951 – and was reflected in the ambivalence of her attitude towards Jewish organizations in the USA. In the early post-war years she gradually loosened her connections with Zionist groups. She regarded herself as consciously representing the Jewish Diaspora and regularly referred to the immense cultural achievements which had been produced precisely by the transitionary situation in which Jews who had broken free of older religious binds but had not yet been fully assimilated found themselves. Equally, she was pronouncedly sceptical of the emergence of a Hebraic Jewish national culture, she herself never having mastered Hebrew. She saw in it a reversal to what she regarded as outmoded nineteenth-century nationalism and in this regard did not shy from comparing the conditions laid down for Israeli citizenship with the Nuremberg Laws of 1935.[59]

While Hannah Arendt strongly identified with the Jewish people and stressed her Jewish origins, she felt no connection to Judaism as a religion and, by marrying Heinrich Blücher, a non-Jew, she evaded integration into the narrower Jewish society in the USA. She did not totally exclude the possibility of returning to West Germany but this was ruled out by Blücher's categorical refusal to consider the idea. Hannah Arendt was thus an individual without any real homeland, however much she praised liberal American society as exemplary. Against this background, the sharpness of the polemics with which she was wont to argue her case is understandable, particularly as this was combined with an intellectual fluency which constantly questioned its own assumptions. It also explains her contradictory attitude towards Israel. While in response to Gershom Scholem she described her Jewishness as one of the 'indisputably central facts of my life', this did not lead her to feel any special relationship to Israel as a collective formation. She believed that, with the dissolution of the original biblical tradition, Israel had no call on her love.[60] But her criticisms of what she considered the politically dangerous tendencies of the Israeli government concealed a personal loyalty and emotional involvement. Her differences with it became irreconcilable when Israel claimed not to be just a nation among others but sought to divide itself strictly from the non-Jewish world and demand a blind subservience from the Jewish Diaspora to its interests as a state. She reminded her opponents of the origins of the Zionist movement and of how these had not been characterized by any such exclusivist demands.

The conflict over Hannah Arendt's Eichmann book concealed a more fundamental dispute over how the past should be dealt with and resolved. She regarded this as a particularly essential task for the Jewish side. She doggedly opposed all attempts to establish Jewish history as a continuity in which the Jews were permanently victims and had a special fate. This way of thinking, she believed, indirectly justified anti-semitism. This was why she emphasized in her study of Eichmann that the Final Solution was not simply a problem concerning the relationship between Jews and non-Jews but was a 'crime against mankind, committed against the Jewish people', which actually and potentially had been equally directed against gypsies and members of the Slavic nations and had also encompassed 'antisocial' and 'superfluous' sections of the population. She admitted at the same time, though many of her opponents overlooked this, that she was basically unable to adequately explain the reasons why open resistance had not occurred.[61]

Her personal answer lay in her identification with 'rebelliousness' and with the morally based refusal of an individual to comply. This is why she placed such importance on the episode of a certain Sergeant Anton Schmidt, who had sacrificed his life opposing a mass liquidation.[62] She saw in the appeal to moral rigour a force which could bridge the tension between historical determinism – represented by the totalitarian system in its full manifestation which she dated for Germany to 1941–2 – and the responsibility of the individual who was reliant solely on his or her conscience. Her adherence to what has been called 'German subjectiveness' comes across unmistakably in this.[63] At the very minimum she insisted that responsible behaviour demanded that a person be scrupulously accountable, not least in the situation of the Final Solution.

She required of the individual what she herself tried to practise: to dare to leap into the realm of freedom, the basis for which had been laid by existential philosophy, to break all ties with the past, with the pressures of spent involvements and their ideological disguises, and to dare to make a genuine new start.[64] She believed that this was too much to expect of people *en masse*, but insisted on it in those who had assumed any kind of political responsibility, even if only as members of the Jewish Councils. Her work, moreover, was not restricted solely to appeals to conscience and to outlining the opportunity which existed for succeeding generations to break free of the fetters of a past which had outlived itself. In the last decade of her life she concentrated her efforts increasingly on attempting to develop a theory of politics which would again liberate the *vita activa*, the human creative will, and make it easier for the individual to accept freedom and authority as great, mutually reliant elements and so reject theories of power based on the state and so-called *Realpolitik*. In a world where the realization is constantly growing that the comprehensive social, ecological, security and demographic problems facing it can no longer be tackled from a purely realist or pragmatic political perspective, interest in the 'Jewish rebel' trained in the spirit of 'German philosophy', which Hannah Arendt always was, is bound to rise, particularly among the younger generation to whom she always addressed herself first and foremost – and despite the fact that she was never really to finally resolve the conundrums at the centre of her work.

Notes

APSR   *American Political Science Review*

AfS   *Archiv für Sozialgeschichte*

APZ   *Aus Politik und Zeitgeschichte*

BA   Bundesarchiv (Federal Archives), Koblenz

GHH   Gütehoffnungshütte (steel company)

GuG   *Geschichte und Gesellschaft*

HZ   *Historische Zeitschrift*

IfZ   Institut für Zeitgeschichte (Institute for Contemporary History), Munich

IMG   *Der Prozess gegen die Hauptkriegsverbrecher vor dem Internationalen Militärgerichtshof. Nürnberg, 14 Oktober 1945–1 Oktober 1946*

JMH   *Journal of Modern History*

MCWS   *Marxism, Communism and Western Society*

PVS   *Politische Vierteljahresschrift*

RGB1   *Reichsgesetzblatt* (German Statutes Gazette)

VfZ   *Vierteljahreshefte für Zeitgeschichte*

Introduction

1 Cf. the recent thorough account by Larry E. Jones, *German Liberalism and the Dissolution of the Weimar Party System 1918–1933* (Chapel Hill, 1988).
2 Knut Borchardt, 'Zwangslagen und Handlungsspielräume in der grossen Wirtschaftskrise der frühen dreissiger Jahre', in idem, *Wachstum, Krisen, Handlungsspielräume der Wirtschaftspolitik* (Göttingen, 1982), pp. 165–82.

3 See his later contribution: Knut Borchardt, 'A Decade of Debate About Brüning's Economic Policy', in Jurgen Baron von Kruedener (ed.), *Economic Crisis and Political Collapse: The Weimar Republic 1924–1933*, German Historial Perspectives Series, general eds, G. A. Ritter, W. Pols, A. J. Nicholls, vol. V (New York, Oxford and Munich, 1990), pp. 99–152.

4 Thomas Childers, 'The Limits of National Socialist Mobilization', in idem (ed.), *The Formation of the Nazi Constituency 1919–1935* (London, 1986), pp. 232–59, idem, *The Nazi Voter: The Social Foundations of Fascism in Germany, 1919–1933* (Chapel Hill, 1983), and Richard F. Hamilton, *Who Voted for Hitler?* (Princeton, 1982), contain meticulous analyses of NSDAP electoral support.

5 Thus Eberhard Jäckel, latterly in idem, *Hitlers Herrschaft. Vollzug einer Weltanschauung* (Stuttgart, 1986).

6 For a review of the latest literature on this issue, see Ian Kershaw, *The Nazi Dictatorship: Problems and Perspectives of Interpretation* (London, 1985).

7 Cf. Rainer Zitelmann, *Hitler. Selbstverständnis eines Revolutionärs* (Hamburg and New York, 1987).

8 See Timothy W. Mason, 'Intention and Explanation: A Current Controversy about the Interpretation of National Socialism', in Gerhard Hirschfeld and Lothar Kettenacker (eds), *Der 'Führerstaat': Mythos und Realität. Studien zur Struktur und Politik des Dritten Reiches* (Stuttgart, 1981), pp. 23–42.

9 See the documentary volume, *'Historikerstreit'. Die Dokumentation der Kontroverse um die Einzigartigkeit der nationalsozialistischen Judenvernichtung* (Munich, 1987, and succeeding edns). See latterly the authoritative study by Charles S. Maier, *The Unmasterable Past: History, Holocaust and German National Identity* (Cambridge, 1988).

Chapter 1 The Decline of the Bürgertum in Late Nineteenth- and Early Twentieth-Century Germany

1 From the extensive literature on this subject, cf. especially Lutz Haltern, 'Bürgerliche Gesellschaft – Theorie und Geschichte', *Neue Politische Literatur*, 19 (1974), pp. 472–88; 20 (1975), pp. 45–59, and idem, *Die bürgerliche Gesellschaft* (Darmstadt, 1985); M. Riedel, 'Bürger, Staatsbürger, Bürgertum', in O. Brunner, R. Koselleck and W. Conze (eds), *Geschichtliche Grundbegriffe*, vol. 1 (Stuttgart, 1972), pp. 672–725; Peter Stearns, 'The Middle Class: Toward a Precise Definition', *Comparative Studies in Society and History*, 21 (1979), pp. 377–96.

2 Cf. Jürgen Kocka, 'Bürgerliche Gesellschaft und die Grenzen der Bürgerlichkeit', in G. A. Ritter and J. Kocka (eds), *Deutsche Sozialgeschichte*, II: *1870–1914*, 3rd edn (Munich, 1982), pp. 62ff; Rudolf Vierhaus (ed.), *Bürger und Bürgerlichkeit im Zeitalter der Aufklärung* (Heidelberg, 1981). The term 'Bürgerlichkeit' (bourgeois) has various contradictory connotations and is not a wholly satisfactory one. Taking similar lines to Stephen Strasser, Jürgen Kocka has argued that 'bourgeois', beyond its original class-specific function, 'defined the practices and intellectual climates of entire societies', with the principles of rationalism and liberal discourse evolving from the basis of equality

before the law. But this appears to confuse concepts of very varied kinds and to equate liberalism with bourgeois in a not very convincing way. See J. Kocka (ed.), *Bürger und Bürgerlichkeit im 19. Jahrhunder5* (Göttingen, 1987), pp. 16f.

3 On this, see Fritz Stern, *The Politics of Cultural Despair: A Study in the Rise of the Germanic Ideology* (Berkeley, 1961), pp. 27ff; Klaus Vondung, 'Zur Lage der Gebildeten in der wilhelminishen Zeit', in idem (ed.), *Das wilhelminische Bildungsbürgertum* (Göttingen, 1976), pp. 20–33, 175ff.

4 This cannot be dealt with in detail here. Cf. Karl-Erich Born, 'Der soziale und wirtschaftliche Strukturwandel Deutschlands am Ende des 19. Jahrhunderts', *Vierteljahresschrift für Sozial- und Wirtschaftsgeschichte*, 60 (1963), pp. 361–76 (also in H.-U. Wehler [ed.], *Moderne Deutsche Sozialgeschichte*, 5th edn [Cologne, 1975], pp. 271–84); H.-U. Wehler, *Das Deutsche Kaiserreich 1871–1918* (Göttingen, 1972), pp. 30f; Wolfgang J. Mommsen, 'Wandlungen der liberalen Idee im Zeitalter des Imperialismus', in idem, *Der europäische Imperialismus* (Göttingen, 1979), pp. 178f. No comprehensive studies for Germany have as yet appeared; cf., however, H. Henning, *Das westdeutsche Bürgertum in der Epoche der Hochindustrialisierung 1860–1914. Soziales Verhalten und soziale Strukturen*, 1: *Das Bildungsbürgertum in den preussischen Westprovinzen* (Wiesbaden, 1972).

5 Cf. D. Stegmann, *Die Erben Bismarcks. Parteien und Verbände in der Spätphase des wilhelminischen Deutschland* (Cologne, 1970); Hans-Jürgen Pühle, 'Parteien und Interessenverbände 1890–1914', in Michael Stürmer (ed.), *Das kaiserliche Deutschland. Gesellschaft und Politik 1871–1918*, 2nd edn (Darmstadt, 1975), pp. 340–73; Thomas Nipperdey, 'Interessenverbände und Parteien in Deutschland vor dem Ersten Weltkrieg', in Wehler, *Moderne Deutsche Sozialgeschichte*, pp. 369–88; also W. Rüegg and Otto Neuloh (eds), *Zur soziologischen Theorie und Analyse des 19. Jahrhunderts* (Göttingen, 1971), especially the contributions by Kaelble, Pühle and Winkler.

6 Cf. especially Ulrich Aufmuth, *Die deutsche Wandervogelbewegung unter soziologischem Aspect* (Göttingen, 1979); J. Müller, *Die deutsche Jugendbewegung als Hauptrichtung neokonservativer Reform* (Zurich, 1971); Peter D. Stachura, *The German Youth Movement 1900–1945: An Interpretative and Documentary History* (London, 1981).

7 Cf. Werner E. Mosse and Arnold Paucker (eds), *Juden im wilhelminischen Deutschland: 1890–1914* (Tübingen, 1976); *Monte verita, Berg der Wahrheit. Lokale Anthropologie als Beitrag zur Wiederentdeckung einer neuzeitlichen sakralen Topographie, Ausstellung der Akademie der Künste Berlin, 25. März–6. Mai 1979* (Milan, 1978); Janos Frecot, Johann Friedrich Geist and Diethart Kerbs, *Fidus 1868–1948. Zur ästhetischen Praxis bürgerlicher Fluchtbewegungen* (Munich, 1972), as well as Jost Hermand, *Der Schein des schönen Lebens* (Frankfurt, 1972), pp. 55–127; Hermann Lübbe, *Politische Philosophie in Deutschland. Studien zu ihrer Geschichte* (Basel, 1963), pp. 142ff.

8 Cf. Lübbe, *Politische Philosophie*, pp. 226f.

9 Cf. Hans Mommsen, 'Generational Conflict and Youth Rebellion in the Weimar Republic', in this volume, pp. 32f.; Willibald Karl, *Jugend, Gesellschaft und Politik im Zeitraum des Ersten Weltkrieges* (Munich, 1973), pp. 156ff; Robert Wohl, *The Generation of 1914* (Cambridge, Mass., 1979).

10   See Gregor Strasser, 'Macht Platz, ihr Alten!', in idem, *Kampf um Deutschland.*
     Reden und Aufsätze eines Nationalsozialisten (Munich, 1932), and Joseph Goeb-
     bels, *Die zweite Revolution. Briefe an Zeitgenossen* (Zwickau, 1926), pp. 5ff.

11   Cf. Barbara Stambolis, *Der Mythos der jungen Generation. Ein Beitrag zur polit-
     ischen Kultur der Weimarer Republik* (Bochum, 1982), pp. 27ff; Theodor
     Wilhelm, 'Der geschichtliche Ort der deutschen Jugendbewegung', in W. Kindt
     (ed.), *Grundschriften der deutschen Jugendbewegung* (Cologne, 1963), pp. 50ff; cf.
     also Walter Z. Laqueur, *Young Germany: A History of the German Youth Movement*
     (London and New York, 1962).

12   Hermann Lebovics, *Social Conservatism and the Middle Classes in Germany,
     1914–1933* (Princeton, 1969), pp. 164f; Walter Struve, *Elites against Democracy:
     Leadership Ideals in Bourgeois Political Thought in Germany 1890–1933* (Princeton,
     1973), pp. 253f; Joachim Petzold, *Wegbereiter des deutschen Faschismus. Die
     Jungkonservativen in der Weimarer Republik* (Cologne, 1978), pp. 211f. and pas-
     sim.

13   See Klaus Fritzsche, *Politische Romantik und Gegenrevolution. Fluchtwege in der
     Krise der bürgerlichen Gesellschaft: Das Beispiel des Tat-Kreises* (Frankfurt a.M.,
     1976); Kurt Sontheimer, 'Der Tat-Kreis', *VfZ*, 7 (1959), pp. 229ff.

14   Theodor Haubach, 'Die Generationenfrage und der Sozialismus', in idem,
     *Soziologische Studien zur Politik, Wirtschaft und Kultur der Gegenwart. Alfred Weber
     gewidmet* (Berlin, 1930). cf. Martin Martiny, 'Sozialdemokratie und junge
     Generation am Ende der Weimarer Republik', in Wolfgang Luthardt (ed.),
     *Sozialdemokratische Arbeiterbewegung und Weimarer Republik. Materialen zur
     gesellschaftlichen Entwicklung*, vol. 2 (Frankfurt a.M., 1978), pp. 56ff.

15   Cf. James M. Diehl, *Paramilitary Politics in Weimar Germany* (London and
     Bloomington, 1977). Karl Heinz Bohrer, *Die Ästhetik des Schreckens: Die pessi-
     mistische Romantik und Ernst Jüngers Frühwerk* (Munich, 1978).

16   Cf. Peter H. Merkl, 'Approaches to Political Violence: The Stormtroopers
     1925–1933', in W. J. Mommsen and G. Hirschfeld (eds), *Social Protest, Violence
     and Terror in Nineteenth and Twentieth Century Europe* (London, 1982), pp. 367ff.

17   Essential on this is Jürgen Habermas, *Strukturwandel der Öffentlichkeit. Untersu-
     chungen zu einer Kategorie der bürgerlichen Gesellschaft*, 2nd edn (Neuwied, 1962),
     esp. pp. 58ff.

18   Cf. Thomas Nipperdey, *Die Organisation der deutschen Parteien vor 1918*
     (Düsseldorf, 1961).

19   On the George Circle, which anticipated these in its structure, cf. Lebovics,
     Social Conservatism, pp. 80ff; H. N. Fügen, 'Der George-Kreis in der "dritten
     Generation"', in W. Rothe, *Die deutsche Literatur in der Weimarer Republik*
     (Stuttgart, 1974), pp. 334–58. On the ISK, see Werner Link, *Die Geschichte
     des Internationalen Jugendbundes (IJB) und des Internationalen Sozialistischen
     Kampfbundes (ISK). Ein Beitrag zur Geschichte der Arbeiterbewegung in der Weimarer
     Republik und im Dritten Reich* (Meisenheim, 1964), pp. 103ff; on the *Neue
     Blätter*, see Martin Martiny, 'Die Entstehung und politische Bedeutung der
     Neuen Blätter für den Sozialismus und ihres Freundeskreises', *VfZ*, 25 (1977),
     pp. 373ff.

20   A systematic analysis of this has yet to appear. The manner in which the

network of personal cross-contacts functioned is very clear from the account by Heidrun Holzbach, *Das 'System Hugenberg'. Die Organisation bürgerlicher Sammlungspolitik vor dem Aufstieg der NSDAP* (Stuttgart, 1981), pp. 138ff and 192ff. Though restricted to an examination of the Young Conservative element, see also Petzold, *Wegbereiter des deutschen Faschismus*, pp. 111ff.

21 Klaus Breuning, *Die Vision des Reiches. Deutscher Katholizismus zwischen Demokratie und Diktatur (1929–1934)* (Munich, 1969), pp. 225f.

22 Cf. Felix Raabe, *Die bündische Jugend. Ein Beitrag zur Geschichte der Weimarer Republik* (Stuttgart, 1961). On the Freikorps movement in general, Diehl, *Paramilitary Politics*.

23 Hans Zehrer, 'Ein Vorschlag der Verbände', *Die Tat*, 20 (1928), p. 125; cf. Mommsen, 'Generational Conflict', pp. 35f.

24 Uwe Lohalm, *Völkischer Radikalismus. Die Geschichte des Deutschvölkischen Schutz- und Trutzbundes 1919–1933* (Hamburg, 1970), p. 53.

25 Cf. George Franz-Willing, *Die Hitlerbewegung. Der Ursprung 1919–1922* (Hamburg, 1962), pp. 62f; cf. Albrecht Tyrell (ed.), *Führer befiehl. Selbstzeugnisse aus der Kampfzeit der NSDAP* (Düsseldorf, 1969), pp. 20f; R. H. Phelps, 'Anton Drexler – der Gründer der NSDAP', *Deutsche Rundschau*, 87 (1961), pp. 1134f.

26 Iris Hamel, *Völkischer Verband und nationale Gewerkschaft. Der Deutschnationale Handlungsgehilfenverband 1893–1933* (Frankfurt, 1967); cf. Larry Eugene Jones, 'Between the Fronts: The German National Union of Commercial Employees from 1928 to 1933', *JMH*, 48 (1976), pp. 462–82.

27 See Thomas Childers, *The Nazi Voter: The Social Foundation of Fascism in Germany, 1919–1933* (Chapel Hill, 1983), pp. 233ff.

28 See Gary D. Stark, *Entrepreneurs of Ideology: Neoconservative Publishers in Germany, 1890–1933* (Chapel Hill, 1981), pp. 22ff.

29 Cf. ibid., pp. 140ff; Gerhard Kratzsch, *Kunstwart und Dürerbund. Ein Beitrag zur Geschichte der Gebildeten im Zeitalter des Imperialismus* (Göttingen, 1969), pp. 369ff. Cf. further Günter Ehni and Frank Weissbach, *Buchgemeinschaften in Deutschland* (Hamburg, 1967); Roland A. Fullerton, 'Creating a Mass Book Market in Germany: The Story of the "Colporteur Novel" 1870–1890', *Journal of Social History*, 10 (1977), pp. 265–83; Helmut Hiller and Wolfgang Strau, *Der deutsche Buchhandel*, 5th edn (Hamburg, 1975).

30 Cf. also Heinz-Joachim Heydorn and Gernot Koneffke, *Studien zur Sozialgeschichte und Philosophie der Bildung*, II: *Aspekte des 19. Jahrhunderts in Deutschland* (Munich, 1973), pp. 179ff.

31 On Stapel, cf. Heide Gerstenberger, *Der revolutionäre Konservatismus. Ein Beitrag zur Analyse des Liberalismus* (Berlin, 1969), pp. 59ff; Heinrich Kessler, *Wilhelm Stapel als politischer Publizist* (Nuremberg, 1967); see also the recent dissertation on the Hanseatic Publishing House by Siegfried Lokatis (Ruhr University, Bochum).

32 Cf. Peter Pulzer, *The Rise of Political Anti-Semitism in Germany and Austria* (London, 1965; revised 1988); Paul W. Massing, *Vorgeschichte des politischen Antisemitismus* (Frankfurt, 1959); Richard S. Lewy, *The Downfall of the Antisemitic Political Parties in Imperial Germany* (New Haven, 1975). Cf. also Walter Boehlich (ed.), *Der Berliner Antisemitismus-Streit* (Frankfurt a.M., 1965).

33   Cf. Stern, *Politics of Cultural Despair*, pp. 62ff; Shulamit Volkov, 'The Social
     and Political Function of Late 19th Century Antisemitism: The Case of the
     Small Handcraft Masters', in H.-U. Wehler, *Sozialgeschichte Heute* (Göttingen,
     1974), pp. 416–31, as well as the study by Volkov, 'Kontinuität und Diskontinu-
     ität im deutschen Antisemitismus', *VfZ*, 33 (1985), pp. 231ff.

34   Cf. Volkov, 'Kontinuität und Diskontinuität', pp. 227f; further Uriel Tal,
     *Christians and Jews in Germany: Religion, Politics and Ideology in the Second
     Reich 1870–1914* (Ithaca, 1977); see also Shulamit Volkov, 'Antisemitism as a
     Cultural Code: Reflections on the History and Historiography of Antisemitism
     in Imperial Germany', *Leo Baeck Institute Yearbook*, 13 (1978), pp. 25–46.

35   Cf. Holzbach, *Das 'System Hugenberg'*, pp. 61ff, and Karl Wortmann, 'Gesch-
     ichte der deutschen Vaterlandspartei' (Ph.D. thesis, Halle, 1926). Cf. also
     Stegmann, *Die Erben Bismarcks*, and idem, 'Zwischen Depression und Manipu-
     lation: Konservative Machteliten und Arbeiter- und Angestelltenbewegung
     1910–1918', *AfS*, 12 (1972).

36   Veit Veltzke, *Vom Patron zum Paladin. Wagnervereinigungen im Kaiserreich von
     der Reichsgründung bis zur Jahrhundertwende* (Bochum, 1987).

37   See Wolfgang Krabbe, *Gesellschaftsveränderung durch Lebensreform* (Göttingen,
     1974); cf. Kratzsch, *Kunstwart und Dürerbund*, pp. 30f, 36ff; Janos Frecot,
     'Die Lebensreformbewegung', in Vondung, *Wilhelminisches Bildungsbürgertum*,
     pp. 138–52, 196ff; Nelson Edmundson, 'The Revolution', *JMH*, 28 (1966),
     pp. 161–80.

38   Frecot, Geist and Kerbs, *Fidus 1868–1948*, pp. 232ff, 246f.

39   Kratzsch, *Kunstwart und Dürerbund*, pp. 28, 151, 336, 362.

40   Ibid., pp. 151f; cf. Klaus Bergmann, *Agrarromantik und Grossstadtfeindlichkeit*
     (Meisenheim, 1970).

41   Kratsch, *Kunstwart und Dürerbund*, pp. 337f.

42   Hamel, *Völkischer Verband*, pp. 57ff.

43   Kratzsch, *Kunstwart und Dürerbund*, pp. 370f.

44   Friedrich Meinecke, *Politische Schriften und Reden* [= *Werke*, vol. II] (Darmstadt,
     1958), p. 388. Cf. Eike-Wolfgang Kornhass, 'Zwischen Kulturkritik und
     Machtverherrlichung: Kurt Riezler', in Vondung (ed.), *Wilhelminisches Bildungs-
     bürgertum*; Fritz Ringer, *The Decline of the German Mandarins: The German
     Academic Community 1890–1935* (Cambridge, Mass., 1969).

45   Fritz Stern, 'The Political Consequences of the Unpolitical German', in idem,
     The Failure of Illiberalism: Essays on the Political Culture of Modern Germany
     (London, 1972), pp. 3ff; Heinrich-August Winkler, 'Der rückversicherte Mit-
     telstand: Die Interessenverbände von Handwerk und Kleinhandel im deutschen
     Kaiserreich', in Rüegg and Neuloh, *Zur soziologischen Theorie*, pp. 163–79.

46   See Hans Fenske, 'Beamtenpolitik in der Weimarer Republik', *Verwaltungs-
     archiv*, 64 (1973), pp. 117–35; Andreas Kunz, 'Stand versus Klasse. Beamten-
     schaft und Gewerkschaften im Konflikt um den Beamtenabbau 1923/24', in
     GuG, 8 (1982), pp. 55–86. Cf. also Lothar Döhn, *Politik und Interesse. Die
     Interessenstruktur der Deutschen Volkspartei* (Meisenheim, 1970), pp. 272ff.

47   Cf. Hans Mommsen, 'Die Stellung der Beamtenschaft in Reich, Ländern und
     Gemeinden in der Ära Brüning', *VfZ*, 21 (1973), pp. 160ff.

48 Larry E. Jones, '"The Dying Middle": Weimar Germany and the Fragmentation of Bourgeois Politics', *Central European History*, 5 (1972), pp. 23–54.

49 Cf. Hans Mommsen, 'Zur Frage des Einflusses deutscher Juden auf die deutsche Wirtschaft in der Zeit der Weimarer Republik', in *Gutachten des Instituts für Zeitgeschichte*, vol. 2 (Stuttgart, 1966), pp. 366ff.

50 Leopold Schwarzschild, 'Heroismus aus Langeweile', in idem, *Die letzten Jahre vor Hitler*, ed. by Valerie Schwarzschild (Hamburg, 1966), p. 35; cf. Hans Peter Schwarz, *Der konservative Anarchist. Politik und Zeitkritik Ernst Jüngers* (Freiburg, 1967), pp. 71ff.

51 Schwarz, *Konservativer Anarchist*, pp. 88ff; cf. also Thomas Koebner, 'Die Erwartung der Katastrophe; Zur Geschichtsprophetie des "neuen Konservativismus"', in idem (ed.), *Weimars Ende. Prognosen und Diagnosen in der deutschen Literatur und politischen Publizistik 1940–1933* (Frankfurt, 1982), pp. 354ff.

52 A systematic study of this has yet to appear. Cf., for example, Günter Plum, *Gesellschaftstruktur und politisches Bewusstsein in einer katholischen Region 1928–1933. Untersuchung am Beispiel des Regierungsbezirks Aachen* (Stuttgart, 1972), pp. 154ff.

53 Hans Mommsen, 'Die nationalsozialistische Machtergreifung und die deutsche Gesellschaft', in Wolfgang Michalka (ed.), *Die nationalsozialistische Machtergreifung* (Paderborn, 1984), pp. 32f.

54 Cf. Alexander Kessler, *Der Jungdeutsche Orden in den Jahren der Entscheidung*, II: *1931–1933* (Munich, 1976), pp. 32ff.

55 See Larry E. Jones, 'Sammlung oder Zersplitterung? Die Bestrebungen zur Bildung einer neuen Mittelpartei in der Endphase der Weimarer Republik', *VfZ*, 25 (1977), pp. 265–304.

56 On the labour camp movement, cf. Karl Bühler, 'Die pädagogische Problematik des freiwilligen Arbeitsdienstes' (Ph.D. thesis, Aachen, 1978); cf. also Walter Greiff, *Das Boberhaus in Löwenberg/Schlesien 1933–1937. Selbstbehauptung einer nonkonformen Gruppe* (Sigmaringen, 1985), pp. 17ff.

57 See especially Klaus-Jörg Siegfried, *Universalismus und Faschismus. Das Gesellschaftsbild Othmar Spanns. Zur politischen Funktion seiner Gesellschaftslehre und Ständestaatskonzeption* (Vienna, 1974), and also Martin Schneller, *Zwischen Romantik und Faschismus. Der Beitrag Othmar Spanns zum Konservatismus in der Weimarer Republik* [= *Kieler Historische Studien*, vol. 12] (Stuttgart, 1971), pp. 43ff.

58 On the Young German Order, cf. especially Kessler, *Jungdeutscher Orden in den Jahren der Entscheidung*, I: *1928–1930*, II: *1931–1933* (Munich, 1975, 1976).

59 On the Centre Party, see Rudolf Morsey, *Der Untergang des politischen Katholizismus* (Stuttgart, 1977).

60 Cf. Mommsen, 'Nationalsozialistische Machtergreifung', pp. 38f.

61 See Childers, *The Nazi Voter*, pp. 228f, 234ff; for a somewhat different interpretation, see Jürgen Falter, 'Radikalisierung des Mittelstandes oder Mobilisierung der Unpolitischen?', in Peter Steinbach (ed.), *Probleme politischer Emanzipation im Modernisierungsprozess* (Stuttgart, 1982), pp. 438ff.

62 Cf. Michael H. Kater, *The Nazi Party: A Social Profile of Members and Leaders*

1919–1945 (Cambridge, Mass., 1983), pp. 62ff; Richard F. Hamilton, *Who Voted for Hitler?* (Princeton, 1982), pp. 413ff.; Geoffrey Pridham, *The Nazi Movement in Bavaria 1923–1933* (New York, 1973), pp. 144f.

63   Cf. Rudy Koshar, 'Two "Nazisms": The Social Context of Nazi Mobilization in Marburg and Tübingen', *Social History*, 7 (1982), pp. 27–42; see idem, *Organizational Life and Nazism: A Study of Mobilization in Marburg an der Lahn* (Michigan, 1985).

64   See Klaus Scholder, *Die Kirchen und das Dritte Reich*, I: *Vorgeschichte und Zeit der Illusionen* (Frankfurt, 1977), pp. 248f, 255ff.

65   Besides the literature quoted in notes 61 and 62, cf. also Hans Mommsen, 'Zur Verschränkung traditioneller und faschistischer Führungsgruppen in Deutschland beim Übergang von der Bewegungs- zur Systemphase', in Wolfgang Schieder (ed.), *Faschismus als soziale Bewegung. Deutschland und Italien im Vergleich*, 2nd edn (Göttingen, 1983), pp. 157–81, and Mathilde Jamin, *Zwischen den Klassen. Zur Sozialstruktur der SA-Führerschaft* (Wuppertal, 1984), pp. 372ff.

66   Cf. Hans Mommsen, *Beamtentum im Dritten Reich. Mit ausgewählten Quellen zur nationalsozialistischen Beamtenpolitik* (Stuttgart, 1966), pp. 46ff.

67   Cf. Theodor Schieder, *Hermann Rasuchnings 'Gespräche mit Hitler' als Geschichtsquelle* [= *Rheinisch-Westfälische Akademie der Wissenschaften, Vorträge G 178*] (Opladen, 1972), p. 47. The authenticity of Rauschning's book, moreover, is no longer accepted today.

68   Cf. the overview in David Schoenbaum, *Die braune Revolution. Eine Sozialgeschichte des Dritten Reiches*, new edn (Cologne, 1980), pp. 170ff, 222f.

69   Cf. Rainer C. Baum, *The Holocaust and the German Elite: Genocide and National Suicide in Germany 1871–1945* (Totowa and London, 1981), pp. 24ff, 66ff; cf. pp. 99f.

70   Symptomatic of this was the reaction in these circles to the events of 30 June 1934 (see Mathilde Jamin, 'Das Ende der "Machtergreifung": Der 30. Juni 1934 und seine Wahrnehmung in der Bevölkerung', in Michalka, *Nationalsozialistische Machtergreifung*, pp. 196–207), and to the pogroms of 9/10 November 1938 (see William Sheridan Allen, 'Die deutsche Öffentlichkeit und die "Reichskristallnacht" – Konflikte zwischen Werthierarchie und Propaganda im Dritten Reich', in D. Peukert and J. Reulecke (eds), *Die Reihen fast geschlossen. Beiträge zur Geschichte des Alltags unterm Nationalsozialismus* [Wuppertal, 1981], pp. 397–412).

71   Cf. Heinrich-August Winkler, *Mittelstand, Demokratie und Nationalsozialismus. Die politische Entwicklung von Handwerk und Kleinhandel in der Weimarer Republik* (Cologne, 1972), pp. 31f, 157ff; Adelheid von Saldern, *Mittelstand im Dritten Reich. Handwerker, Einzelhändler, Bauern* (Frankfurt, 1979), pp. 13f, 26ff.

72   Stern, *Politics of Cultural Despair*, pp. 267ff, and idem, 'The Collapse of Weimar', in idem, *Failure of Illiberalism*, pp. 193ff.

73   Theodor Geiger, *Die soziale Schichtung des deutschen Volkes. Soziographischer Versuch auf statistischer Grundlage*, 2nd edn (Stuttgart, 1967), pp. 124f, 130. Cf. also Hans Speier, *Die Angestellten vor dem Nationalsozialismus* [= *Kritische Studien zur Geschichtswissenschaft*, vol. 26] (Göttingen, 1977), pp. 102ff.

74 Cf. Ulrich Linse, *Barfüssige Propheten. Erlöser der zwanziger Jahre* (Berlin, 1983), esp. pp. 234f.

75 Geiger, *Soziale Schichtung*, pp. 100, 131.

76 Ibid., p. 131.

77 Cf. Hans Mommsen, 'German Society and the Resistance to Hitler', in this volume, pp. 214f.

Chapter 2 Generational Conflict and Youth Rebellion in the Weimar Republic

1   See Lewis S. Feuer, *The Conflict of Generations: The Character and Significance of Student Movements* (New York, 1969); John R. Gillis, *Youth and History: Tradition and Change in European Age Relations, 1770 to the Present* (New York, 1981; German edn, *Geschichte der Jugend. Tradition und Wandel im Verhältnis der Altersgruppen und Generationen*, Weinheim, 1980).

2   Ronald Inglehart, *The Silent Revolution: Changing Values and Changing Political Styles among Western Publics* (Princeton, 1977); idem, 'The Silent Revolution in Europe: Intergenerational Change in Post-Industrial Societies', *APSR*, 65 (1971), pp. 991ff. Further Stephen F. Szabo, 'West Germany and Changing Security Perspectives', in idem (ed.), *The Successor Generation: International Perspectives of Postwar Europeans* (London, 1982); Peter Kmieciak, *Wertestrukturen und Wertewandel in der Bundesrepublik Deutschland* (Göttingen, 1976); Joachim Matthes (ed.), *Sozialer Wandel in Westeuropa* (Frankfurt a.M., 1979).

3   Inglehart, *Silent Revolution*, p. 285.

4   Robert Wohl, *The Generation of 1914* (Cambridge, Mass., 1979). On the historiography, see Hans Jaeger, 'Generationen in der Geschichte. Überlegungen zu einer umstrittenen Konzeption', *GuG*, vol. 3 (1977), no. 4, pp. 429ff.

5   Wohl, *Generation*, pp. 205, 208f.

6   Karl Mannheim, 'Das Problem der Generationen', in L. v. Friedeburg (ed.), *Jugend in der modernen Gesellschaft* (Cologne and Berlin, 1965); also in Mannheim, *Wissenssoziologie*; originally published in *Kölner Vierteljahrshefte*, 7 (1928–9), nos 2–3.

7   Cf. Friedrich Tenbruck, *Jugend und Gesellschaft: Soziologische Perspektiven*, 2nd edn (Freiburg, 1965); Gillis, *Geschichte der Jugend*, pp. 109ff; Wohl, *Generation*, pp. 206ff.

8   See Klaus Tenfelde, 'Grossstadtjugend in Deutschland vor 1914', *Vierteljahresschrift für Sozial- und Wirtschaftsgeschichte*, 69 (1982), pp. 195ff.

9   Cf. Alex Hall, 'Youth in Rebellion: The Beginnings of the Socialist Youth Movement in Wilhelmine Germany', in Richard J. Evans (ed.), *Society and Politics in Wilhelmine Germany* (London, 1978), pp. 442ff.

10 Cf. Peter D. Stachura, *The German Youth Movement 1900–1945: An Interpretative and Documentary History* (London, 1981), pp. 69ff, 77ff.

11 Cf. Thomas Nipperdey, 'Jugend und Politik um 1900', in Walter Rüegg (ed.), *Kulturkritik und Jugendkult* (Frankfurt a.M., 1974), pp. 87ff.

12 On youth legislation, see, among other studies, Berthold Simonsohn (ed.), *Jugendkriminalität, Strafjustiz und Sozialpädagogik* (Frankfurt a.M., 1969).

13 Ulrich Aufmuth, *Die deutsche Wandervogelbewegung unter soziologischem Aspekt* (Göttingen, 1979).

14 Cf. K. Scemkus, 'Gesellschaftliche Bedingungen zur Entstehung der deutschen Jugendbewegung', in Rüegg, *Kulturkritik*, pp. 44f; Theodor Wilhelm, 'Der geschichtliche Ort der deutschen Jugendbewegung', in W. Kindt (ed.), *Grundschriften der deutschen Jugendbewegung* (Cologne, 1963), pp. 50ff.

15 Cf. Eric C. Leed, *No Man's Land: Combat and Identity in World War One* (Cambridge, 1979), pp. 92ff, 146f.

16 Cf. Willibald Karl, *Jugend, Gesellschaft und Politik im Zeitraum des Ersten Weltkrieges* (Munich, 1973), pp. 156ff.

17 See Joachim Petzold, *Wegbereiter des deutschen Faschismus. Die Jungkonservativen in der Weimarer Republik* (Cologne, 1978), esp. pp. 92ff.

18 Ernst Troeltsch, *Spektator-Briefe. Aufsätze über die deutsche Revolution und die Weltpolitik 1918/22*, new edn (Aalen, 1966), p. 69.

19 Cf. Ulrich Linse, 'Lebensformen der bürgerlichen und proletarischen Jugendbewegung', *Jahrbuch des Archivs der Jugendbewegung*, 10 (1978); idem, *Die Kommune der deutschen Jugendbewegung: Ein Versuch zur Überwindung des Klassenkampfes aus dem Geist der bürgerlichen Utopie* (Munich, 1973).

20 See J. Müller, *Die deutsche Jugendbewegung als Hauptrichtung neokonservativer Reform* (Zurich, 1971); Felix Raabe, *Die bündische Jugend. Ein Beitrag zur Geschichte der Weimarer Republik* (Stuttgart, 1961). On the youth movement in general, see Walter Z. Laqueur, *Young Germany: A History of the German Youth Movement* (London and New York, 1962).

21 Harald Schultz-Hencke, 'Die Überwindung der Parteien durch die Jugend', in Kindt, *Grundschriften*, p. 354; cf. Raabe, *Bündische Jugend*, pp. 108ff.

22 Hans Zehrer, 'Ein Vorschlag der Verbände', *Die Tat*, 20 (1928), p. 125.

23 Cf. James M. Diehl, *Paramilitary Politics in Weimar Germany* (London and Bloomington, 1977).

24 Alexander Kessler, *Der Jungdeutsche Orden in den Jahren der Entscheidung*, I: *1928–1930*, II: 1931–1933 (Munich, 1975, 1976).

25 Cf. F. Borinski et al. (eds), *Jugend im politischen Protest. Der Leuchtenberg-Kreis 1923–1933* (Frankfurt a.M., 1977).

26 Cf. Dick Geary, *European Labour Protest 1848–1939* (London, 1981), pp. 123f, and Tenfelde, 'Grossstadtjugend', pp. 214f.

27 See Martin Martiny, 'Sozialdemokratie und junge Generation am Ende der Weimarer Republik', in Wolfgang Luthardt (ed.), *Sozialdemokratische Arbeiterbewegung und Weimarer Republik. Materialien zur gesellschaftlichen Entwicklung*, vol. 2 (Frankfurt a.M., 1978), pp. 56ff.

28 Cf. Hans Mommsen, 'Social Democracy on the Defensive: The Immobility of the SPD and the Rise of National Socialism', in this volume, pp. 52f.

29 Cf. Richard N. Hunt, *German Social Democracy 1918–1933*, 2nd edn (Chicago, 1970), pp. 106ff; Stachura, *Youth Movement*, pp. 104ff.

30 *Neue Blätter für den Sozialismus*, I (1930), p. 301; cf. Theodor Haubach, 'Die Generationenfrage und der Sozialismus', in idem, *Soziologische Studien zur*

Politik, Wirtschaft und Kultur der Gegenwart. Alfred Weber gewidmet (Berlin, 1930), pp. 106ff.

31 See Larry E. Jones, '"The Dying Middle": Weimar Germany and the Fragmentation of Bourgeois Politics', *Central European History*, 5 (1972), pp. 38ff; idem, 'Sammlung oder Zersplitterung? Die Bestrebungen zur Bildung einer neuen Mittelpartei in der Endphase der Weimarer Republik', *VfZ*, 25 (1977), pp. 265ff.

32 Ernst Niekisch, *Hitler – Ein deutsches Verhängnis*, 1932, reprint 3rd edn (Berlin, 1979), pp. 20ff.

33 Utmann von Elterlein, 'Absage an den Jahrgang 1902', *Die Tat*, 22 (1930), p. 202.

34 Ernst Günther Gründel, *Die Sendung der jungen Generation* (Munich, 1932), p. 39.

35 Gregor Strasser, 'Macht Platz, ihr Alten!', in idem, *Kampf um Deutschland. Reden und Aufsätze eines Nationalsozialisten* (Munich, 1932), p. 171.

36 Cf. Mommsen, 'Social Democracy', pp. 42f.

37 Joseph Goebbels, *Die zweite Revolution. Briefe an Zeitgenossen* (Zwickau, 1926), pp. 5f.

38 Cf. Eugen Rosenstock, *Die Arbeitslager in der Erwachsenenbildung* (Berlin, 1930); Karl Bühler, 'Die pädagogische Problematik des freiwielligen Arbeitsdienstes' (Ph.D. thesis, Aachen, 1978).

39 Hans Zehrer, 'Achtung, junge Front! Draussen bleiben!', *Die Tat*, 21 (1929), pp. 925ff; cf. Klaus Fritzsche, *Politische Romantik und Gegenrevolution. Fluchtwege in der Krise der bürgerlichen Gesellschaft: Das Beispiel des Tat-Kreises* (Frankfurt a.M., 1976).

40 See Gründel, *Sendung*, pp. 420ff.

41 Cf. Leopold Dingräve (pseudonym of Wilhelm Eschmann), *Wo steht die junge Generation?* (Jena, 1931), pp. 13f, 34f, 54; cf. Raabe, *Bündische Jugend*, pp. 109f, 112.

42 Cf. the controversial argument by Michael H. Kater, 'Bürgerliche Jugendbewegung und Hitlerjugend in Deutschland von 1926 bis 1939', *AfS*, 17 (1977), pp. 127–74; Stachura, *Youth Movement*, pp. 65f. Raabe, *Bündische Jugend*, pp. 152ff. Cf. further J. Götz von Olenhusen, 'Die Krise der jungen Generation und der Aufsteig des Nationalsozialismus', *Jahrbuch des Archivs der deutschen Jugendbewegung*, 12 (1980).

43 Cf. the speech by the Reich minister for the interior, Freiherr v. Gayl, at the constitutional commemorations of 11 August 1932, *Schulthess' Europäischer Geschichtskalender*, 73 (1932), p. 139.

44 Cf. Barbara Stambolis, *Der Mythos der jungen Generation. Ein Beitrag zur politischen Kultur der Weimarer Republik* (Bochum, 1982); cf. also Elisabeth Domansky and Ulrich Heinemann, 'Jugend als Generationserfahrung. Das Beispiel der Weimarer Republik', *Sozialwissenschaftliche Informationen für Unterricht und Studium*, 2 (1984), pp. 141f.

45 For a concise overview of the generation question in the Federal Republic, see M. Rainer Lepsius, 'Wahlverhalten, Parteien und politische Spannungen', *PVS*, 14 (1973), pp. 300ff.

Chapter 3 Social Democracy on the Defensive: The Immobility of the SPD and the Rise of National Socialism

1 On this see especially Heinrich-August Winkler, *Mittelstand, Demokratie und Nationalsozialismus. Die politische Entwicklung von Handwerk und Kleinhandel in der Weimarer Republik* (Cologne, 1972).

2 Cf. H. Mommsen, D. Petzina and B. Weisbrod (eds), *Industrielles System und politische Entwicklung in der Weimarer Republik* (Düsseldorf, 1974).

3 Richard N. Hunt, *German Social Democracy 1918–1933*, 2nd edn (Chicago, 1970). The following study is based largely on Hunt's account and attempts to develop it in some points. The process of becoming bourgeois already under way in the SPD before World War I, which Hunt emphasizes alongside the bureaucratization and ageing of the party, is not of great significance in the context of the process of social restratification occurring during the period under examination here.

4 Erich Matthias, 'Die Sozialdemokratische Partei Deutschlands', in idem and Rudolf Morsey (eds), *Das Ende der Parteien 1933* (Düsseldorf, 1960), pp. 101–278; Siegfried Bahne, 'Die Kommunistische Partei Deutschlands', in ibid., pp. 655–739.

5 Hannes Heer, *Burgfrieden oder Klassenkampf? Zur Politik der sozialdemokratischen Gewerkschaften 1930–1933* (Neuwied and Berlin, 1971).

6 Cf. the informative study by Ernst Hamburger, 'Betrachtungen über Heinrich Brünings Memoiren', *Internationale wissenschaftliche Korrespondenz zur Geschichte der deutschen Arbeiterbewegung*, 15 (1972), pp. 28f.

7 *Neue Blätter für den Sozialismus*, III (1932), p. 620.

8 Miles (= Walter Löwenheim), *Neu Beginnen!* (Karlsbad, n.d. [1933]), p. 5.

9 Cf. Wolfram Pyta, *Gegen Hitler und für die Republik. Die Auseinandersetzung der deutschen Sozialdemokratie mit der NSDAP in der Weimarer Republik* (Düsseldorf, 1989), pp. 250ff.

10 Cf. W. Mommsen, *Deutsche Parteiprogramme* (Munich, 1960), pp. 453ff.

11 Cf. Gabriele Hoffmann, 'Sozialdemokratie und Berufsbeamtentum' (Ph.D. thesis, Hamburg, 1970), pp. 227, 231ff.

12 *Protokoll des Sozialdemokratischen Parteitags in Kiel, 1927*, pp. 172f.

13 Ibid., pp. 210, 197.

14 Ibid., p. 173.

15 *Neue Blätter für den Sozialismus*, I (1930), p. 387.

16 Ibid., II (1931), pp. 7f.

17 As quoted in Michael Stürmer, *Koalition und Opposition* [= *Beiträge zur Geschichte des Parlamentarismus und der politischen Parteien*, vol. 37] (Düsseldorf, 1967), p. 137.

18 Cf. Ch. Beradt, *Paul Levi: Ein demokratischer Sozialist in der Weimarer Republik* (Frankfurt a.M., 1969), p. 100.

19 Cf. Hunt, *Social Democracy*, p. 116.

20 For instance, in the creation of its own 'Academy of Labour' and the establishment of an autonomous labour court system.

21 Cf. Hans Mommsen, 'Gesellschaftsbild und Verfassungspläne des deutschen

Widerstands', in Walter Schmitthenner and Hans Buchheim (eds), *Der deutsche Widerstand gegen Hitler. Vier Kritische Studien* (Cologne and Berlin, 1966), pp. 76f.

22 *Die Organisation im Klassenkampf. Die Probleme der politischen Organisation der Arbeiterklasse* (Berlin, n.d. [1931]), p. 67.

23 *Neue Blätter für den Sozialismus*, II (1931), p. 211.

24 On the ISK, see the excellent study by Werner Link, *Die Geschichte des Internationalen Jugendbundes (IJB) und des Internationalen Sozialistischen Kampfbundes (ISK). Ein Beitrag zur Geschichte der Arbeiterbewegung in der Weimarer Republik und im Dritten Reich* (Meisenheim, 1964).

25 *Organisation im Klassenkampf*, p. 105.

26 *Neue Blätter für den Sozialismus*, II (1931), p. 212.

27 Quoted from *Organisation im Klassenkampf*, p. 152.

28 Karl Marx and Friedrich Engels, *Gesammelte Werke*, vol. 22, pp. 509–27. This does not mean to imply that Engels himself would have advocated a defensive position. Nevertheless the scenario he presented had the same effect in that it made the forces of counter-revolution arbiters of when conflict would take place.

29. *Protokoll des Sozialdemokratischen Parteitags in Magdeburg, 1929*, p. 14; cf. H. J. L. Adolf, *Otto Wels und die Politik der deutschen Sozialdemokratie 1894–1939* (Berlin, 1971), p. 231.

30 Cf. N. Leser, *Zwischen Reformismus und Bolschewismus. Der Austromarxismus als Theorie und Praxis* (Vienna, Frankfurt a.M. and Zurich, 1968), pp. 394ff, 398; O. Leichter, *Otto Bauer, Tragödie oder Triumph?* (Vienna, Frankfurt a.M. and Zurich, 1970), pp. 183ff.

31 Cf. O. Leichter, *Zwischen de Diktaturen* (Vienna, 1968), p. 83.

32 Cf. Hunt, *Social Democracy*, pp. 56f.

33 Cf. Julius Leber, *Ein Mann geht seinen Weg* (Berlin, 1952), p. 195. Countless similar statements to this effect can be found in the *Neue Blätter für den Sozialismus* and *Organisation im Klassenkampf*.

34 Cf. Beradt, *Paul Levi*, pp. 76f.

35 Leber, *Ein Mann*, p. 195.

36 Membership figures from Hunt, *Social Democracy*, p. 100; Bahne, 'Kommunistische Partei'.

37 Cf. Hunt, *Social Democracy*, pp. 111ff; Hunt observed a correlation between voter and membership trends at a gap of two years (p. 101).

38 *Statistisches Jahrbuch für das deutsche Reich*, 1937, p. 23; *Statistik des Deutschen Reiches*, vol. 408, pp. 5, 51ff.

39 Unfortunately no reliable analyses of this development on the basis of social statistics have as yet been made. On the basis of the annual reports of the Prussian trade supervision office (*Jahresberichte der Preussischen Gewerbeaufsichtsbeamten*), published by the Ministerium für Handel und Gewerbe (Berlin, 1904ff, which give figures for the numbers of workers employed in industrial plants with over ten or five employees and in mining, salt works and processing plants (appendix, tables IIb and c), a stagnation and even a slight decrease is evident from 1922.

40   Hunt, *Social Democracy*, p. 104.
41   Ibid., pp. 136f.
42   Ibid., p. 112.
43   Cf. Emil Lederer, 'Die Umschichtung des Proletariats', *Die neue Rundschau*, 40 (1929); Theodor Geiger, 'Die Mittelschichten und die Sozialdemokratie', in ibid., vol. 8 (1931).
44   Cf. Hunt, *Social Democracy*, pp. 129f. This central question is in need of more thorough examination.
45   An example of this was the policy pursued by the ADB (General Federation of German Civil Servants), which had sought at first to reverse the split in the DBB (German Federation of Civil Servants) that occurred in 1922 but from 1926 directed the brunt of its polemics against the DBB.
46   Rudolf Heberle, *Landbevölkerung und Nationalsozialismus* [= *Schriftenreihe des Instituts für Zeitgeschichte*, 6] (Stuttgart, 1963); G. Stoltenberg, *Politische Strömungen im schleswig-holsteinischen Landvolk 1918–1933* [= *Beiträge zur Geschichte des Parlamentarismus und der politischen Parteien*, vol. 24] (Düsseldorf, 1962).
47   *Protokoll des Sozialdemokratischen Parteitags in Magdeburg, 1929*, p. 15; cf. Adolf, *Otto Wels*, pp. 224ff, on Wels's rather simplistic attitude to the KPD.
48   K. Rohe, *Das Reichsbanner Schwarz Rot Gold* [= *Beiträge zur Geschichte des Parlamentarismus und der politischen Parteien*, vol. 34] (Düsseldorf, 1966), pp. 314ff, 333f.
49   *Protokoll des Sozialdemokratischen Parteitags in Kiel, 1927*, p. 34.
50   Hunt, *Social Democracy*, pp. 71, 89f, 106ff.
51   Ibid., p. 72.
52   *Jahrbuch der Sozialdemokratischen Partei Deutschlands, 1930*, ed. Vorstand der SPD, pp. 193f; the foregoing and the following are based on a careful statistical analysis carried out by Frau Renate Szameit of Essen.
53   Hunt, *Social Democracy*, p. 110; cf. Detlev J. K. Peukert, *Jugend zwischen Krieg und Krise* (Cologne, 1987), p. 235; Rudolf Kneip, *Jugend der Weimarer Zeit. Handbuch der Jugendverbände* (Frankfurt, 1974); *Statistik des Deutschen Reiches*, vol. 451/II (1933), p. 2210.
54   Cf. A. Klönne, *Hitlerjugend. Die Jugend und ihre Organisation im Dritten Reich* (Hanover and Frankfurt a.M., 1960), pp. 14f; H.-Ch. Brandenburg, *Die Geschichte der HJ* (Cologne, 1968), p. 58. Brandenburg estimates that there were 50,000 Hitler Youth members in 1932; but as against this, cf. ibid., p. 140; H. Pross, *Jugend, Eros, Politik, Geschichte der deutschen Jugendverbände* (Bern, Munich and Vienna, 1964), pp. 469ff.
55   Theodor Haubach, 'Die Generationenfrage und der Sozialismus', in idem, *Soziologische Studien zur Politik, Wirtschaft und Kultur der Gegenwart. Alfred Weber gewidmet* (Berlin, 1930), pp. 106–20.
56   Matthias, 'Sozialdemokratische Partei', pp. 242ff, 190f.
57   Haubach, 'Generationenfrage', p. 112.
58   *Protokoll des Sozialdemokratischen Parteitags in Leipzig, 1931*, p. 215; cf. K. Korn, *Die Arbeiterjugendbewegung. Einführung in ihrer Geschichte* (Berlin, 1922), pp. 121f.
59   *Neue Blätter für den Sozialismus*, II (1931), p. 328.

60 Cf. *Protokoll des Sozialdemokratischen Parteitags in Leipzig, 1931*, pp. 216f, 228f.

61 *Neue Blätter für den Sozialismus*, I (1930), p. 301.

62 Ibid., III (1932), p. 312.

63 It was characteristic of Weimar domestic politics that wages, salaries and taxation levels, though also export and import quotas, were invariably measured against the yardstick of pre-war figures. The trade unions were no exception in this. Employers in particular regarded 1913 as the optimum year which had to be returned to if normal economic conditions were to be re-established. The psychological significance of this in the mental make-up of the Republic deserves a closer examination.

64 *Neue Blätter für den Sozialismus*, II (1931), p. 212.

65 As quoted in Beradt, *Paul Levi*, pp. 96f.

66 Ernst Bloch, 'Der Faschismus als Erscheinungsform der Ungleichzeitigkeit', in E. Nolte (ed.), *Theorien über den Faschismus* (Cologne and Berlin, 1967), p. 197.

67 Ibid., p. 198.

68 Cf. H. Drechsler, *Die Sozialistische Arbeiterpartei Deutschlands (SAPD)* (Meisenheim, 1965), pp. 100ff; K. H. Tjaden, *Struktur und Funktion der KPD-Opposition* (Meisenheim, 1969); Olaf Ihlau, *Die Roten Kämpfer* (Meisenheim, 1969).

69 As quoted in Drechsler, *Sozialistische Arbeiterpartei*, p. 241.

70 Miles, *Neu Beginnen!*, p. 35.

Chapter 4 Class War or Co-determination: On the Control of Economic Power in the Weimar Republic

1 Thilo Ramm (ed.), *Arbeitsrecht und Politik. Quellentexte 1918–1933* (Neuwied, 1966), p. XI.

2 Cf. the excellent introduction by Otto Kahn-Freund in the edition of Hugo Sinzheimer's *Arbeitsrecht und Rechtssoziologie. Gesammelte Aufsätze und Reden*, prepared by him and Thilo Ramm, 2 vols (Frankfurt a.M., 1976), here vol. 1, p. 8.

3 Ibid., p. 326.

4 Cf. Ursula Hüllbüsch, 'Koalitionsfreiheit und Zwangstarif. Die Stellungnahme des Allgemeinen Deutschen Gewerkschaftsbundes zu Tarifvertrag und Schlichtungswesen in der Weimarer Republik', in U. Engelhardt, Volker Sellin and Horst Stuke (eds), *Soziale Bewegungen und politische Verfassung. Beiträge zur Geschichte der modernen Welt* (Stuttgart, 1976), pp. 618f, 650.

5 Cf. on this Charles S. Maier, *Recasting Bourgeois Europe: Stabilization in France, Germany and Italy in the Decade after World War I* (Princeton, 1975).

6 Cf. Heinrich-August Winkler (ed.), *Organisierter Kapitalismus. Voraussetzungen und Anfänge* (Göttingen, 1974), esp. pp. 12ff.

7 The basic text is still Ludwig Preller, *Sozialpolitik in der Weimarer Republik* (Stuttgart, 1949).

8 Cf. Martin Martiny, *Integration oder Konfrontation? Studien zur Geschichte der sozialdemokratischen Rechts- und Verfassungspolitik* (Bonn and Bad Godesberg,

1976), p. 87; Jürgen Wendt, 'Mitbestimmung und Sozialpartnerschaft in der Weimarer Republik', *APZ*, 26 (1969), p. 33; Preller, *Sozialpolitik*, p. 245.

9   Cf. Hans Mommsen, 'Zur Verschränkung traditioneller und faschistischer Führungsgruppen in Deutschland beim Übergang von der Bewegungs–zur Systemphase', in Wolfgang Schieder (ed.), *Faschismus als soziale Bewegung. Deutschland und Italian im Vergleich*, 2nd edn (Göttingen, 1983), pp. 165ff.

10 Cf. Gerhard Schulz, *Aufsteig des Nationalsozialismus. Krise und Revolution in Deutschland* (Frankfurt a.M., Berlin and Vienna, 1975), pp. 539ff.

11 Cf. Ulrich Nocken, 'Inter-Industrial Conflicts and Alliances as exemplified by the AVI Agreement', in H. Mommsen, D. Petzina and B. Weisbrod (eds), *Industrielles System und politische Entwicklung in der Weimarer Republik* (Düsseldorf, 1974), pp. 693ff.

12 On this see B. Weisbrod, *Die Schwerindustrie in der Weimarer Republik. Interessen-politik zwischen Stabilisierung und Krise* (Wuppertal, 1978).

13 See especially the analysis by Ernst Fraenkel, 'Der Ruhreisenstreit 1928–1929 in historisch-politischer Sicht', in Ferdinand A. Hermens and Theodor Schieder (eds), in *Staat, Wirtschaft und Politik in der Weimarer Republik. Festschrift für Heinrich Brüning* (Berlin, 1967), pp. 97–117.

14 *Neue Blätter für den Sozialismus*, I (1930), p. 387.

15 Cf. Ursula Hüllbüsch, 'Die deutsche Gewerkschaften in der Weltwirtschafts-krise', in W. Conze and H. Raupach (eds), *Die Staats- und Wirtschaftskrise des Deutschen Reiches 1929/33* (Stuttgart, 1967), pp. 150ff; Henryk Skrzypczak, 'Die Strategie der Freien Gewerkschaften in der Weimarer Republik', in H. O. Vetter (ed.), *Vom Sozialistengesetz zur Mitbestimmung. Zum 100. Geburtstag von Hans Böckler* (Cologne, 1975), pp. 215f.

16 Cf. Gerhard Brehme, *Die sogenannte Sozialisierungsgesetzgebung der Weimarer Republik* (Berlin [GDR], 1960); for the consequences, cf. Martin Martiny, 'Arbeiterbewegung am Rhein und Ruhr vom Scheitern der Räte- und Sozial-isierungsbewegung bis zum Ende der Weimarer Republik', in Jürgen Reulecke (ed.), *Arbeiterbewegung an Rhein und Ruhr* (Wuppertal, 1974), p. 243f.

17 As quoted in Wendt, 'Mitbestimmung', p. 29.

18 Cf. Martiny, *Integration oder Konfrontation?*, pp. 94ff; Ernst Fraenkel, 'Räte-system und soziale Selbstbestimmung', *APZ*, 14 (1971), pp. 17ff.

19 *Sozialistische Monatshefte*, 1902, p. 29; on the emergence of the concept, cf. Hans J. Teutesberg, *Geschichte der industriellen Mitbestimmung in Deutschland* (Tübingen, 1961), p. 533.

20 Cf. Gerald D. Feldman, 'Economic and Social Problems of the German Demobilization, 1918–19', *JMH*, 47 (1975), pp. 1–23.

21 Cf. Hans Mommsen, 'Sozialpolitik im Ruhrbergbau', in Mommsen, Petzina and Weisbrod, *Industrielles System*, pp. 311f.

22 As quoted in Hein Josef Varain, *Gewerkschaften, Sozialdemokratie und Staat. Die Politik der Generalkommission unter der Führung Carl Legiens (1890–1920)* (Düsseldorf, 1957), p. 47.

23 Heinrich Brauns, 'Neue Wege der Sozialpolitik', in *Deutsche Sozialpolitik 1918 bis 1928. Erinnerungsschrift der Reichsarbeitsministeriums* (Berlin, 1929), p. 11; cf.

Eberhard Pies, 'Sozialpolitik und Zentrum 1924–1928', in Mommsen, Petzina and Weisbrod, *Industrielles System*, p. 263.
24 Preller, *Sozialpolitik*, pp. 231, 498.
25 Cf. Hans-Hermann Hartwich, *Arbeitsmarkt, Verbände und Staat 1918–1933* (Berlin, 1967), p. 305. For an opposite view, Hüllbüsch, 'Koalitionsfreiheit und Zwangstarif', pp. 614f.
26 A thorough examination of this has yet to appear. For the period up to 1923, see Hans-Manfred Bock, *Syndikalismus und Linkskommunismus von 1918–1933* (Meisenheim, 1969); cf. Hans Mommsen, 'Die Bergarbeiterbewegung an der Ruhr 1918–1933', in Reulecke, *Arbeiterbewegung*, pp. 276ff.
27 Cf. Wendt, 'Mitbestimmung', pp. 38f.
28 Cf. Rudolf Kuda, 'Das Konzept der Wirtschaftsdemokratie', in Vetter, *Vom Sozialistengesetz*, pp. 257f, and Michael Schneider, *Unternehmer und Demokratie. Die freien Gewerkschaften in der unternehmerischen Ideologie der Jahre 1918–1933* (Bonn and Bad Godesberg, 1975), p. 47, and also Wendt, 'Mitbestimmung', pp. 36f.
29 *Wirtschaftsdemokratie. Ihr Wesen, Weg und Ziel*, 3rd edn (Berlin, 1928), pp. 151ff.
30 Cf. Preller, *Sozialpolitik*, p. 264.
31 *Wirtschaftsdemokratie*, pp. 152, 144.
32 Cf. Erich Brigl-Matthiass, *Das Betriebsräteproblem* (Berlin and Leipzig, 1926); *Wirtschaftsdemokatie*, pp. 177f.
33 Cf. Wendt, 'Mitbestimmung', pp. 41ff; K. J. Mattheier, 'Werkvereine und wirtschaftsfriedlich-nationale (gelbe) Arbeiterbewegung im Ruhrgebiet', in Reulecke, *Arbeiterbewegung*, pp. 200ff.
34 Cf. Kuda, 'Das Konzept', pp. 253ff; H.-H. Hartwich, 'Wirtschaftsdemokratie und die Theorie vom sozialen Rechtsstaat', in *Probleme der Demokratie Heute*, *PVS*, Sonderheft 2 (1970), p. 300, and also H.-A. Winkler, 'Unternehmer und Wirtschaftsdemokratie in der Weimarer Republik', in ibid., pp. 309f; Martiny, *Integration oder Konfrontation?*, pp. 128ff.
35 Kuda, 'Das Konzept', pp. 261ff.
36 Schneider, *Unternehmer und Demokratie*, pp. 87ff.
37 Cf., for instance, Hannes Heer, *Burgfrieden oder Klassenkampf? Zur Politik der sozialdemokratischen Gewerkschaften 1930–1933* (Neuwied and Berlin, 1971), pp. 18ff.
38 Cf. Gerhard Beier, 'Einheitsgewerkschaft. Zur Geschichte eines organisatorischen Prinzips der deutschen Arbeiterbewegung', *AfS*, 13 (1973), pp. 207ff; idem, 'Zur Entstehung des Führerkreises der vereinigten Gewerkschaften Ende April 1933', in ibid., 15 (1975), pp. 365ff; idem, *Das Lehrstück vom 1. und 2. Mai 1933* (Frankfurt a.M., 1975).
39 Cf., for instance, *Wirtschaftsdemokratie*, pp. 14f.
40 Michael Schneider, *Das Arbeitsbeschaffungsprogramm des ADGB. Zur gewerkschaftlichen Politik in der Endphase der Weimarer Republik* (Bonn, 1975); idem, 'Konjunkturpolitische Vorstellungen der Gewerkschaften in den letzten Jahren der Weimarer Republik', in Mommsen, Petzina and Weisbrod, *Industrielles System*, pp. 229ff.

41 Cf. Robert A. Gates, 'Von der Sozialpolitik zur Wirtschaftspolitik? Das Dilemma der deutschen Sozialdemokratie in der Krise 1929–1933', in Mommsen, Petzina and Weisbrod, *Industrielles System*, pp. 217ff.

42 Friedrich Naumann, *Neudeutsche Wirtschaftspolitik* (Berlin, 1906), pp. 331f, as quoted in Teutesberg, *Geschichte*, p. 485.

43 Cf. Fritz Kübler, '"Eigentum verpflichtet"', *Archiv für die civilistische Praxis*, 159 (1960), pp. 236ff.

Chapter 5   State and Bureaucracy in the Brüning Era

1 Cf. Herbert von Borch, *Obrigkeit und Widerstand. Zur politischen Soziologie des Beamtentums* (Tübingen, 1954); Heinrich Heffter, *Die deutsche Selbstverwaltung im 19. Jahrhundert* (Stuttgart, 1950), pp. 654ff; Werner Conze, 'Staat und Gesellschaft in der frührevolutionären Epoche Deutschlands', in idem, *Staat und Gesellschaft im deutschen Vormärz* (Stuttgart, 1958), pp. 207ff. An example of recourse to older constitutional traditions was Theodor Wilhelm, *Die Idee des Berufsbeamtentums. Ein Beitrag zur Staatslehre des deutschen Frühkonstitutionalismus* (Berlin, 1933).

2 Cf. Reinhard Koselleck, *Preussen zwischen Reform und Revolution. Allgemeines Landrecht, Verwaltung und soziale Bewegung von 1791 bis 1848* (Stuttgart, 1967), pp. 172, 259, 282f.

3 Cf. Wolfgang J. Mommsen, *Max Weber und die deutsche Politik 1890–1920*, 2nd edn (Tübingen, 1974), pp. 180ff.

4 Cf. Gabriele Hoffmann, *Sozialdemokratie und Berufsbeamtentum. Zur Frage nach Wandel und Kontinuität im Verhältnis der Sozialdemokratie zum Berufsbeamtentum in der Weimarer Zeit* (Hamburg, 1972), pp. 25ff; on state social policy, cf. Karl Erich Born, *Staat und Sozialpolitik seit Bismarcks Sturz* (Wiesbaden, 1958).

5 Cf. Gerald D. Feldman, 'German Business between War and Revolution: The Origins of the Stinnes–Legien Agreement', in G. A. Ritter (ed.), *Entstehung und Wandel der modernen Gesellschaft. Festschrift für Hans Rosenberg* (Berlin, 1970), pp. 338f; Gerald D. Feldman, *Army, Industry and Labor in Germany 1914–1918* (Princeton, 1968), pp. 316ff, 522ff.

6 Cf. Hans Fenske, 'Monarchisches Beamtentum und demokratischer Staat. Zum Problem der Bürokratie in der Weimarer Republik', in *Demokratie und Verwaltung. Schriftenreihe der Hochschule Speyer*, vol. 50 (Berlin, 1972), pp. 117ff; idem, 'Beamtenpolitik in der Weimarer Republik', *Verwaltungsarchiv*, 64 (1973), p. 125; F. W. Witt, *Die Hamburger Sozialdemokratie in der Weimarer Republik* (Hanover, 1971), p. 29; on continuity in the bureaucracy, see also Wolfgang Elben, *Das Problem der Kontinuität in der deutschen Revolution* (Düsseldorf, 1965), pp. 31f.

7 Cf. Peter von Oertzen, *Betriebsräte in der Novemberrevolution* (Düsseldorf, 1963), p. 57; A. J. Ryder, *The German Revolution of 1918* (Cambridge, 1967), p. 171.

8 In September 1917 the Council of German Civil Servants' Associations and the Association of German Civil Servants' Clubs formed a national working committee to prepare the amalgamation of all civil servants' associations. This, however, was only finally achieved on 4 December 1918 with the foundation

of the DBB; cf. Dieter Fricke (ed.), *Die bürgerlichen Parteien in Deutschland. Handbuch*, vol. 1 (Leipzig, 1968), p. 423, and Albert Falkenberg, 'Geschichte der Beamtenbewegung', in *ADB: Der erste Gewerkschaftskursus des Allgemeinen Deutschen Beamtenbundes*, Schriftensammlung des ADB, no. 7 (Berlin, 1924); cf. also *Deutscher Beamtenbund. Ursprung, Weg, Ziel* (issued by the Bundesleitung des DBB, Bad Godesberg, 1968).

9   Cf. Fenske, 'Beamtenpolitik', pp. 129ff, and further Lothar Döhn, *Politik und Interesse. Die Interessenstruktur der Deutschen Volkspartei* (Meisenheim, 1970), pp. 272f.

10   Besides the studies by Fenske already quoted, cf. Wolfgang Runge, *Politik und Beamtentum im Parteienstaat. Die Demokratisierung der politischen Beamten in Preussen zwischen 1918 und 1933* (Stuttgart, 1965); Eberhard Pikart, 'Preussische Beamtenpolitik 1918–1933', *VfZ*, 6 (1958), pp. 119–37; Rudolf Morsey, 'Zur Beamtenpolitik des Reiches von Bismarck bis Brüning', in *Demokratie und Verwaltung*, pp. 111ff. As against this, Peter-Christian Witt, 'Reichsfinanzminister und Reichsfinanzverwaltung. Zum Problem des Verhältnisses von politischer Führung und bürokratischer Herrschaft in den Anfangsjahren der Weimarer Republik (1918/19–1924)', *VfZ*, 23 (1975), pp. 1–61, seeks to establish the actual influence exercised by bureaucratic structures using the example of the Ministry for Finance and in the process casts serious doubt on the theory of continuity of personnel, in this area at least, from the imperial era into the Republic.

11   Arnold Köttgen, *Das Berufsbeamtentum und die parlamentarische Demokratie* (Berlin and Leipzig, 1928), pp. 256f; Gerhard Anschütz and Richard Thoma, *Handbuch des deutschen Staatsrechts*, vol. 2 (1932), p. 16.

12   Franz von Papen, *Vom Scheitern einer Demokratie 1930–1933* (Mainz, 1968), p. 212.

13   Cf. Carl Schmitt, *Verfassungslehre*, 3rd edn (Berlin, 1954), p. 272; idem, *Hüter der Verfassung*, 2nd edn (Berlin, 1931), p. 150, and also 'Legalität und Legitimität', in idem, *Verfassungsrechtliche Aufsätze aus den Jahren 1924–1954* (Berlin, 1958), p. 273. On this see Jürgen Fijalkowski, *Die Wendung zum Führerstaat* (Cologne and Opladen, 1958), p. 79; Köttgen, *Berufsbeamtentum*, pp. 267ff; further F. Giese, *Das Berufsbeamtum in deutschen Volksstaat* (Berlin, 1929); G. Jahn, *Das Berufsbeamtentum und die parlamentarische Demokratie* (Berlin, 1929); H. Nawiasky, *Die Stellung des Berufsbeamtentums im parlamentarischen Staat* (Berlin, 1926); *Entwicklung und Reform des Beamtenrechts* [= *Veröffentlichung der Vereinigung deutscher Staatslehrer*, vol. 7] (Berlin and Leipzig, 1932). Cf. Walter Wiese, *Der Staatsdienst in der Bundesrepublik Deutschland. Grundlagen, Probleme, Neuordnung* (Neuwied and Berlin, 1972), pp. 185ff, and Thomas Ellwein and Ralf Zoll, *Berufsbeamtentum. Anspruch und Wirklichkeit* (Düsseldorf, 1973), pp. 37ff.

14   See Karl Dietrich Bracher, *Die Auflösung der Weimarer Republik*, 3rd edn (Villingen, 1960), p. 179; cf. Arnold Brecht, *Das deutsche Beamtentum von heute* (Frankfurt a.M., 1951), pp. 55f.

15   Cf. Martin Vogt, 'Die Stellung der Koalitionsparteien zur Finanzpolitik 1928–1930', in H. Mommsen, D. Petzina and B. Weisbrod (eds), *Industrielles*

System und politische Entwicklung in der Weimarer Republik (Düsseldorf, 1974), pp. 439ff, and Ilse Maurer, *Reichsfinanzen und Grosse Koalition. Zur Geschichte des Reichskabinetts Müller 1928–1930* (Berlin and Frankfurt a.M., 1973). The latently anti-parliamentary consequences of this were demonstrated, for example, by the proposal from the delegation of German experts from Paris on 22 March 1929 that an extra-parliamentary supervisory body be established with an absolute right of veto over Reichstag spending and taxation decisions. Cf. Martin Vogt (ed.), *Die Entstehung des Young-Plans, dargestellt vom Reichsarchiv 1931–1933* (Boppard, 1970), introduction, pp. 40f.

16 Waldemar Besson, *Württemberg und die deutsche Staatskrise 1928–1933. Eine Studie zur Auflösung der Weimarer Republik* (Stuttgart, 1959), pp. 205f, and cf. pp. 152ff, 233.

17 *RGBl*, I (1931), p. 453; cf. Hans Mommsen, 'Die Stellung der Beamtenschaft in Reich, Ländern und Gemeinden in der Ära Brüning'), *VfZ*, 21 (1973), pp. 160ff.

18 Cf. Gerhard Schulz, *Aufstieg des Nationalsozialismus. Krise und Revolution in Deutschland* (Frankfurt a.M., Berlin and Vienna, 1975), pp. 671f.

19 This is abundantly clear from the cabinet minutes. Cf. cabinet meeting of 17 December 1930 (quoted in the following from the microfilm in the Institut für Zeitgeschichte, Munich, as IfZ MA; IfZ MA 151/12), where calls were made to obtain legal advice on this. Cf. State Secretary Hans Schäffer's diary entries (IfZ ED 93, quoted in the following as Schäffer Diary), vol. 19, of 1 March 1932 on visits to Professors Anschütz and Jellinek in Heidelberg re interpretation of Article 48 of the constitution. Cf. also Schulz, *Aufstieg des Nationalsozialismus*, pp. 541f.

20 Cf. Brüning's line of argument in his meeting with cabinet ministers of 3 October 1931 (IfZ MA 149/16, sheet 788.416): if the government did not formulate a new regulation of this by decree, the Reichstag would pass a considerably more radical solution and force the president into the awkward position of having to decide whether to sign such a law.

21 Cf. Schulz, *Aufstieg des Nationalsozialismus*, p. 666; Andreas Dorpalen, *Hindenburg and the Weimar Republic* (Princeton, 1964), pp. 248f.

22 Besson, *Staatskrise*, pp. 241ff. Besson is inclined to overemphasize the bureaucratic elements as particularly characteristic: 'The preponderance of bureaucratic elements . . . justifies speaking of a Brüning era' (p. 355). He refers to the 'bureaucratic style' and the 'bureaucratic solution' of the presidential cabinet system (pp. 188f) and sees this bureaucratization as having arisen primarily from the 'momentum of balancing budgets' which led to a common 'bureaucratic identity' between the Reich and the Länder (p. 215). This was certainly true from the point of view of the Länder, but there can be no doubt that the motivation which lay behind the policy of deflation and hence of the rigid adherence to balancing budgets was primarily political and not bureaucratic. Cf. latterly Schulz, *Aufstieg des Nationalsozialismus*, pp. 546, 857.

23 Cf. Hans Mommsen, 'Betrachtungen zu den Memoiren Heinrich Brünings', *Jahrbuch für die Geschichte Mittel- und Ostdeutschlands*, 22 (1973), pp. 270ff. The apolitical element introduced by Karl Dietrich Bracher and his very

apposite characterization of the Brüning regime should not, however, be misinterpreted as implying that Brüning did not operate on the basis of a very clear scale of political priorities – Bracher, 'Brünings unpolitische Politik und die Auflösung der Weimarer Republik', *VfZ*, 19 (1971).

24 Cf. Heinrich Brüning, *Memoiren 1918–1934* (Stuttgart, 1970), pp. 58, 52f; cf. Claire Nix (ed.), *Heinrich Brüning. Briefe und Gespräche 1934–1945* (Stuttgart, 1974), pp. 532f. Cf. further Rudolf Morsey, 'Brünings Kritik an der Reichsfinanzpolitik 1919–1929', in E. Hassinger, J. H. Müller and Hugo Ott (eds), *Geschichte, Wirtschaft, Gesellschaft. Festschrift für Clemens Bauer* (Berlin, 1974), p. 361.

25 Cf. Helmut J. Schorr, *Adam Stegerwald. Gewerkschaftler und Politiker der ersten deutschen Republik* (Recklinghausen, 1966), pp. 120ff; Josef Deutz, *Adam Stegerwald. Gewerkschaftler, Politiker, Minister 1874–1945* (Cologne, 1952), pp. 127ff; Rudolf Morsey (ed.), *Die Protokolle der Reichstagsfraktion und des Fraktionsvorstandes der Deutschen Zentrumspartei 1926–1933* (Mainz, 1969), p. 147. On Stegerwald's conflict with the DBB, cf. W. Flügel and H. Lenz, *Berufsbeamtentum und Besoldungsreform. Kritische Anmerkungen zur Flugschrift A. Stegerwalds* (Berlin, 1927).

26 Cf. Morsey, *Protokolle*, pp. 148, 152. Brüning adopted a reserved position, viewing the problem from the start in the context of the reparations issue and especially of Parker Gilbert's possible reactions. As chancellor, Brüning avoided reaching any clear decision. See Schäffer Diary, vol. 16, note on the cabinet meeting of 4 December 1931, where the chancellor is quoted as saying: 'At present nothing can be changed. The whole civil servant business was messed up during 1919/1927. It is in need of a clean sweep. That would never get through the Reichstag.'

27 Cf. Brüning, *Memoiren*, pp. 126–9. He boasted that he had forced through staff cuts in the 'toughest fights' of his political career, but there is no proof of any direct interventions by him in this area. Cf. Morsey, 'Brünings Kritik', pp. 371f.

28 Cf. Brüning, *Memoiren*, p. 128, where he speaks of the 'danger of a pure trade union organization of civil servants' emerging; cf. ibid., pp. 52f, 57f. Brüning stated on occasion that the civil servants' organizations would 'all have to be liquidated eventually' (see note 29).

29 Ministerial meeting of 21 March 1932 (IfZ MA 151/15, sheet 789.726): Brüning: A law would have to be introduced 'to prevent civil servants' organizations getting involved in such projects in the future'. They would have to be helped, however, for otherwise the Reichstag would take up the issue and this would end up far more costly to the Reich. Under discussion was the insolvency of the Berlin Civil Servants' Business Club.

30 Cf. Mommsen, 'Stellung der Beamtenschaft', pp. 157ff; cf. the declaration by the RhB of 23 June 1930 and the submission from the DBB to the government of 11 June 1930 (BA R 43 I/2365, p. 13; I/2366, pp. 273ff.). Cf. Schäffer Diary, vol. 8, sheet 130, discussion with Brüning re budget, 24 May 1930: Brüning was not afraid of 'unrest among civil servants as measures against civil servants are popular at present'.

31 Meeting of the civil servants' associations with Brüning of 30 May 1930 (BA R 43 I/2364). Note on the cabinet meeting of the same day and letter from the DBB of 31 May, sheets 101ff. The meeting of 1 June 1931 was similar, with Brüning, in the presence of representatives of the leading associations, declaring, after stressing the severity of the crisis and the unavoidability of further salary cuts, that he 'recognized the danger of radicalization' but would ask that they 'try to get the broad mass of civil servants to understand the difficulties facing the government ... The details released at this meeting must not be used yet however' and should be treated as confidential (BA R 43 I/2369, sheets 225ff).

32 Cf. Brüning's meeting with representatives of the cigvil servants' associations of 27 June 1930 (BA R 43 I/2365, sheets 148ff). Similarly his speech to the national council of the Centre Party on 5 November 1931 (H. Brüning, *Reden und Aufsätze*, ed. by W. Vernekohl with the assistance of R. Morsey [Münster, 1968], p. 81).

33 An example of intended measures being kept secret was the Chancellery's denial, in response to a submission from the DBB of 20 May 1931, that any steps were being considered, despite the fact that the emergency decree promulgated on 5 June had already been drafted (BA R 43 I/2573, sheets 127ff). Typical was the chancellor's reaction to a suggestion from Dietrich on 8 January 1931 that it might be wise to dispel the threat of radicalization among civil servants by arranging an audience for the leading representative associations with the president. He countered that this would only fuel the general hostility to civil servants and that, in addition, the president had to be protected against lobbying by other interest groups; typically, Brüning crossed out the sentence which referred to his own position: 'There are strong suspicions in working-class circles that I am a committed supporter of the civil service' (Dietrich's letter and Brüning's reply [draft] of 31 January [BA R 43 I/2650, sheets 254ff]). Cf. *Deutscher Beamtenbund* 15 (1931), II, p. 155.

34 Cf. Brüning, *Memoiren*, pp. 326, 175f.

35 Schäffer Diary, vol. 11, conversation with Dietrich of 18 June 1931.

36 Ibid., vol. 10, conversation with State Secretary von Bülow of 17 April 1931: 'No one has the slightest idea what the chancellor really wants.'

37 Brüning, *Memoiren*, p. 59. It was thanks to Kugeler that the emergency decrees of 1930/1 were formulated in such a manner that they could have been implemented immediately by the administration.

38 Cf. Hermann Pünder, *Politik in der Reichskanzlei*, ed. by Thilo Vogelsang (Stuttgart, 1961), pp. 57, 74, 78, 81, 100; cf. idem, 'Zusammenarbeit mit Heinrich Brüning in der Reichskanzlei 1930–1932', in Ferdinand A. Hermens and Theodor Schieder (eds), *Staat, Wirtschaft und Politik in der Weimarer Republik. Festschrift für Heinrich Brüning* (Berlin, 1967), pp. 311f.

39 Decree to Reduce the Personnel Costs of the Reich of 27 October 1923, *RGBl*, I (1923), pp. 999–1011; Law Terminating Staff Reductions and Amending the Decree on Personnel Reductions, 7 August 1925, *RGBl*, I (1925), pp. 181ff. According to the Ministry for Finance, of the total number of 1,562,700 employed in the public service, 388,118 had been let go by April 1924, of whom 16 per cent were civil servants, 50 per cent clerical and administrative staff and 32 per

cent workers (cf. *Deutsches Beamtenarchiv* [Berlin, 1924], pp. 603ff); of the total of 589,418 employed in the public service of the Reich in October 1923, 144,198 had been let go by the end of 1924, of whom 13.3 per cent were civil servants, 67.7 per cent clerical and administrative staff and 38.5 per cent workers (*Verhandlungen des Reichstags*, III. Wahlperiode 1924 – hereafter referred to as *Reichstag Proceedings*, III/1924, etc. – appendix to the official minutes of the proceedings, vol. 400, no. 829). But cf. Eckart Sturm, 'Die Entwicklung des öffentlichen Dienstes in Deutschland', in Carl H. Ule (ed.), *Die Entwicklung des öffentlichen Dienstes* (Cologne and Berlin, 1961), pp. 63f.

40 The DBB reported that when the Salaries Bill was passed by 333 to 53 votes with 16 abstentions, only one DVP deputy along with Heinrich Imbusch voted against the proposal, which would suggest that Stegerwald did not vote (*Der Beamtenbund*, vol. 12 [1928], no. 5, supplement p. 2). Cf. Döhn, *Politik und Interesse*, p. 269, and the excellent general account in Gerhard Schulz, *Zwischen Demokratie und Diktatur*, I: *Verfassungspolitik und Reichsreform in der Weimarer Republik* (Berlin, 1963), pp. 549ff.

41 Cf. Helga Timm, *Die deutsche Sozialpolitik und der Bruch der Grossen Koalition im März 1930* (Düsseldorf, 1952), pp. 169ff.

42 Cf. *Der Beamtenbund*, vol. 11 (1927), no. 8; Marx's chancellor's speech of 3 February 1927 (*Reichstag Proceedings*, IV/1928, vol. 428, p. 8791); Josef Bekker (ed.), *Heinrich Köhler: Lebenserinnerungen eines Politikers und Staatsmannes 1878–1949* (Stuttgart, 1964), pp. 250ff.

43 The DBB opposed a 'hidden cut' in salaries and demanded that all sections of the population which could afford it should be included in the measure ('Entschliessung der Bundesleitung des DBB vom 3. März 1930', *Der Beamtenbund*, vol. 14 [1930], no. 18).

44 Döhn, *Politik und Interesse*, pp. 269f.

45 Cf. Schäffer's detailed notes on the cabinet's budgetary discussions of 27 and 28 February 1930 (Schäffer Diary, vol. 8, sheets 60ff). V. Guérard referred to the approval of broad sections of civil servants for the idea of an emergency levy on all in secure employment (sheet 75). Severing suggested that in the event of a dissolution of the Reichstag, the elections should be fought against the parties of the right under the slogan 'Reject the Emergency Levy!' (ibid., sheet 69).

46 Cf. Timm, *Deutsche Sozialpolitik*, pp. 172ff; Vogt, 'Stellung der Koalitionsparteien', pp. 458ff; cf. Morsey, *Protokolle*, pp. 392, 395, 400. On Brüning's timing, cf. ibid., p. 410.

47 Schäffer Diary, vol. 8, sheet 130, conference of 24 May 1930 with Brüning.

48 Morsey, *Protokolle*, p. 447, national council meeting of 17 May 1930.

49 Motion by Breitscheid and comrades of 10 April 1930, *Reichstagsdrucksache* no. 1944; cf. the later modified version of 27 June 1930, *Reichstagsdrucksache*, no. 2241. The former minister for labour, Brauns, was particularly adamant in his support for an emergency levy (*Reichstag Proceedings*, 187th session of 30 June 1930, vol. 341, p. 6025).

50 Cabinet meeting of 27 May 1930 (IfZ MA 151/11); on the stance adopted by the DVP, cf. Döhn, *Politik und Interesse*, pp. 148ff.

51 Cf. Schäffer Diary, vol. 9, notes on the cabinet meeting of 3 June 1930. The

predominant attitude of the courts up to this time had been that the incremental rights of civil servants included the monetary value of their salaries and that paragraph 39 of the Salaries Act and the corresponding clauses in the salaries acts of the Länder were therefore in breach of Article 129 of the Weimar constitution; cf. the commentary by W. Jellinek on the Supreme Court ruling of 10 July 1931 (*Entscheidungen des Reichsgerichts in Zivilsachen*, 134, pp. 1ff), *Juristische Wochenschrift*, 61 (1932), pp. 52f.

52 Cabinet meeting of 27 May: some legal reservations were voiced, however, against the emergency levy. As early as 8 March Brüning warned the Centre Party's national council that in certain circumstances the emergency levy might require a two-thirds majority (Morsey, *Protokolle*, no. 536, p. 408).

53 Cabinet meeting of 3 June 1930; see the note in Schäffer Diary, vol. 9, as well as cabinet meeting of 5 June (IfZ MA 151/12).

54 Cf. Schäffer Diary, vol. 9, note on the cabinet meeting of 5 June 1930; in February Brüning had already rejected an income tax levy, referring to the effect this could have in aggravating the flight of capital (Morsey, *Protokolle*, p. 391).

55 Brüning, *Memoiren*, p. 163.

56 Ibid. Cf. cabinet meeting of 13 June 1930 (IfZ MA 151/12), sheets 783.931ff, and Morsey, 'Brünings Kritik', p. 369.

57 Cf. Ludwig Preller, *Sozialpolitik in der Weimarer Republik* (Stuttgart, 1949), pp. 408f.

58 Cf. the note by the representative of the GHH (Gütehoffnungshütte), Blank, on the presidential and national council meeting of the RdI and the VDA of 13 June 1930 (Archiv der GHH, Paul Reusch Papers). On the pressure which the industrial wing of the DVP brought to bear on the cabinet to reduce wages as a precondition of accepting cuts in civil servants' salaries, cf. Schäffer's discussion with Dietrich of 16 June 1930 (Schäffer Diary, vol. 9).

59 Cf. Döhn, *Politik und Interesse*, pp. 265f, and cabinet meeting of 18 June 1930 (IfZ MA 151/12, sheet 784.062).

60 DVP guidelines of 16 June 1930 with covering letter from Scholz, appended to the minutes of the cabinet meeting of 24 June 1930 (IfZ MA 151/12). On the same day Esser commented during the Centre Party's national council meeting that this concentrated attack on the cabinet was being led by the same industrial wing of the DVP which had been responsible for the fall of the Müller cabinet (Morsey, *Protokolle*, no. 596, p. 457). Brüning commented that this was the same element which had destroyed the attempts to revive the Central Working Association of the early 1920s. Cf. Döhn, *Politik und Interesse*, pp. 266f.

61 Cf. Döhn, *Politik und Interesse*, pp. 268ff, and cabinet minutes of 24 June 1930.

62 Cabinet meeting of 25 June 1930 and Hans Schäffer's notes (Schäffer Diary, vol. 9, pp. 170ff); Schäffer's discussion with Brüning and Dietrich of 24 June 1930 (ibid.).

63 During the cabinet meeting of 24 June, Otto Braun had argued for a general enabling act, though warned that it had to be expected that the SPD would oppose it. This was also Brüning's position, though he abandoned the idea during the cabinet meeting of 25 June (IfZ MA 151/12).

64 *Reichstagsdrucksache* no. 2363 of 15 July 1930, amending motions on the second reading of the draft bill for a Reichshilfe der Personen des öffentlichen Dienstes and one-off extraordinary income tax levies during the financial year 1930. At the meeting of Reichstag party leaders on 12 July (cf. Schäffer Diary, vol. 9) the DVP made the poll tax a condition of its support for the budgetary programme, as it had already done in its ultimatum of 16 June. Cf. also Schäffer's notes on the party leaders' meeting of 8 July 1930 (ibid.).

65 Cf. *RGBl*, I (1930), pp. 210f, 314f. Dietrich in particular argued in favour of a tiered pay-related structure. On the attitude of the Centre Party, see Morsey, *Protokolle*, p. 466 no. 3.

66 Cf. the case made for the poll tax in the Reichstag on 8 July by DVP deputy Cremer (*Reichstag Proceedings*, 194th session, vol. 428, pp. 6227f). The optional poll tax was directed at reducing expenditure on unemployment relief. The same motivation was evident in the internal discussions (see note 64).

67 Cf. C. Horkenbach, *Das Deutsche Reich von 1918 bis heute* (Berlin, 1930), p. 312.

68 *Reichstag Proceedings*, 204th session of 18 July 1930, pp. 6502f; on 15 July (ibid., 200th session, p. 6378) Keil of the SPD had demanded that the poll tax be treated by a separate bill independent of the budget.

69 Cabinet meeting of 16 July 1930 (IfZ MA 151/12); cf. Bracher, *Auflösung*, pp. 338f. Besson's criticism of Bracher (*Staatskrise*, p. 160) fails to take into account that Brüning was by no means decided at this stage on whether or not to opt for a presidential solution but preferred rather to rely on variable majorities in the Reichstag in the medium term. Rudolf Morsey in particular has warned against the tendency to over-rationalize Brüning's political intentions on the basis of the *Memoiren*. Cf. his treatment, *Zur Entstehung, Authentizität und Kritik von Brünings 'Memoiren 1918–1934'* (Opladen, 1975).

70 Cabinet meeting of 16 July 1930; *Reichstagsdrucksache* no. 2214 of 27 June 1930, Breitscheid and comrades. On the Centre Party's positive attitude to this, cf. Morsey, *Protokolle*, no. 609, p. 467.

71 Meeting of the Centre Party Reichstag group of 9 July 1930, Morsey, *Protokolle*, no. 608, p. 466.

72 Centre Party Reichstag group meeting of 16 July, ibid., no. 613, p. 471; *Reichstag Proceedings*, 200th session of 15 July 1930, p. 6377. The SPD demanded a 10 per cent income tax levy in place of the poll tax. Breitscheid's offer of negotiations, 201st session of July 16, pp. 6400ff. On Breitscheid's position, cf. Peter Pistorius, 'Rudolf Breitscheid 1874–1944' (Ph.D. thesis, Cologne, 1970), p. 289.

73 *RGBl*, I (1930), pp. 311ff.

74 Schäffer's discussion with Dietrich on 16 September 1930 (Schäffer Diary, vol. 9, p. 221); discussion with Pünder on 2 September (ibid., p. 201), who held 'that only a government across the complete spectrum from Breitscheid to Treviranus could get on top of the thing'.

75 Brüning, *Memoiren*, p. 195. It is striking that Brüning gave the first clear description of his long-term goals to Hitler, as demonstrated by his discussion of 6 October 1930 with Hitler, Frick and Strasser (ibid.). On this cf. E. Wandel, *Hans Schäffer. Steuermann in wirtschaftlichen und politischen Krisen* (Stuttgart,

1974), pp. 155f. On the devaluation issue, cf. Brüning, *Memoiren*, p. 221, and Nix, *Heinrich Brüning*, p. 33, 476f. Cf. Schulz, *Aufstieg des Nationalsozialismus*, p. 857, whose characterization is very accurate; cf. further Dietmar Keese, 'Die volkswirtschaftlichen Gesamtgrössen für das Deutsche Reich in den Jahren 1925–1936', in W. Conze and H. Raupach (eds), *Die Staats- und Wirtschaftskrise des Deutschen Reiches 1929/33* (Stuttgart, 1967), pp. 40f; Horst Sanmann, 'Deutsche Wirtschafts- und Finanzpolitik in der Ära Brüning', *Hamburger Jahrbuch für Wirtschafts' und Gesellschaftspolitik*, 10 (1965), pp. 115ff; Wilhelm Grotkopp, *Die grosse Krise. Lehren aus der Überwindung der Wirtschaftskrise 1929/32* (Düsseldorf, 1954), pp. 20f.

76 Cf. Schäffer Diary, vol. 12, cabinet meeting with the Prussian government on 31 July 1931; Morsey, *Protokolle*, no. 677, p. 531, meeting of the Reichstag party group and the national council of 14 June 1931.

77 Cf. A. Falkenberg's report on the international civil servants' movement, *Der Beamte*, vol. 4 (1932), no. 3, pp. 181ff.

78 Articles 129–31 of the Weimar constitution were the products of successful lobbying by the DBB. Cf. F. Winters, *Der Deutsche Beamtenbund. Seine Entstehung und seine Entwicklung* (Berlin, 1931), p. 22; Wilhelm Schröder, *Die wohlerworbenen Rechte der Beamten in ihrer politischen und juristischen Bedeutung* (Berlin, 1930), pp. 16ff. Cf. Theodor Eschenburg, *Der Beamte in Partei und Parlament* (Frankfurt a.M., 1952), p. 41.

79 Schäffer's letter to Warburg of 17 September 1930 (IfZ, Hans Schäffer Papers).

80 Letters from the Civil Servants' Advisory Committee of the Lower Silesian Centre Party of 11 May 1931 (BA R 43 I/2369, pp. 19f), warning that this could lead to an 'emasculation of the party structures themselves', and of 17 August 1931 (ibid., 2572, p. 145), where reference is made to a 'disastrous revolutionizing process', the 'politics of desperation' and the danger 'of civil servants being reduced to utter ruin'. Similarly the submission from the Catholic Teachers' Association of 12 May 1931 (ibid., 2369, pp. 20ff).

81 Cf. Wandel, *Hans Schäffer*, p. 28.

82 Note by Schäffer on a discussion with Silverberg on 24 September 1930 (Schäffer Diary, vol. 9). Silverberg recommended increasing turnover tax to 1.5 per cent rather than penalizing civil servants.

83 Letter to Warburg (see note 79).

84 Cabinet meeting of 25 July 1930 (IfZ MA 151/12, sheets 784.425ff).

85 Ministerial discussion of 24 September 1930 (ibid., sheets 784.665f), and meeting of the Reich Ministry of 26 September and of the cabinet of 27 September 1930 (ibid., sheets 784.882ff).

86 Meeting of the Reich Ministry of 26 September 1930.

87 The Law to Reduce Staffing Costs in the Public Service passed by cabinet on 30 October was intended to be permanent; paragraph 12 provided for planned positions in the lower and ordinary services to be filled by contract civil servants or recipients of maintenance allowances up to 31 March 1935. To mollify civil servants it was intended to include a clause specifying that infringements of

their established incremental rights had to comply with the provisions of
this law.

88 *RGB1*, I (1930), pp. 522ff.

89 Ministerial meeting of 30 November 1930 (IfZ MA 151/12, sheet 785.385).

90 Cf. cabinet meeting of 17 December 1930 (ibid.), where the question of
constitutionality was discussed and the ruling by the Bavarian Supreme Court
which found sections of the decree in breach of constitutionally protected
incremental rights of civil servants. Cf. W. Laforet, 'Die wohlerworbenen
Rechte der bayerischen Beamten', *Schriftenreihe des Landesverbands der Bayerischen Staatbeamten eingetragener Verein*, no. 13 (1930); also in BA R 43 I/2555,
sheets 248ff.

91 Cf. the note by Schäffer on his conversation with Hamburg of 6 August 1931
(Schäffer Diary, vol. 13) discussing cuts in civil service salaries by emergency
decree. Cf. the entry for 17 August (ibid.).

92 Note by Schäffer on a discussion with Brüning, Dietrich, Luther and others
of 6 March 1931 (Schäffer Diary, vol. 12, p. 72).

93 *RGB1*, I (1931), pp. 282ff; Schäffer Diary, vol. 12, pp. 138f.

94 The first draft was ready in June 1930 and was intended to accompany the
Spending Reductions Act (see IfZ MA 151/12, sheets 783.995ff); the draft
discussed with and ratified by the Länder was presented to the chancellor by
the minister for the interior on 23 September 1931 but was never dealt with,
as amending the Civil Service Act of 1873 to modify civil servants' existing
conditions 'could not be enforced either wholly or in part by means of
emergency decree' (letter from the minister for the interior of 1 June 1932
[BA R 43 I/2556, sheets 95ff, 152]).

95 Cf. Besson, *Staatskrise*, pp. 220ff, 245.

96 Cf. note by Schäffer of 17 August on a meeting between the Reich and
Prussian cabinets (Schäffer Diary, vol. 13). For the effects on the educational
system, cf. Eugen Löffler, *Das öffentliche Bildungswesen in Deutschland* (Berlin,
1931), esp. pp. 3ff; further, the letter from the Prussian finance minister of
26 October on savings made in the schools system above and beyond those
specified in the Prussian Savings Decree of 12 September 1930 and also
Amtlicher Preussischer Pressedienst of 19 October 1931 (BA R 43 I/2375, sheets
95ff). Cf. also Heinrich Küppers, *Der katholische Lehrerverband in der Über-
gangszeit von der Weimarer Republik zur Hitler-Diktatur* (Mainz, 1975).

97 Besson, *Staatskrise*, p. 245.

98 Note by Schäffer on a meeting with the Länder on 1 September 1931
(Schäffer Diary, vol. 14); ministerial meeting of 8 July 1931 (IfZ MA 149/15).

99 *RGB*, I (1931), p. 453; cf. ministerial meeting of 17 August 1931 (IfZ MA
149/15). Cf. Mommsen, 'Stellung der Beamtenschaft', pp. 161ff. The decree
provoked very bitter opposition from the civil servants' associations, which
contested its constitutionality (submission by the DBB of 3 September 1931
[BA R 43 I/2379, sheets 309ff]; submission by the RhB of 3 December 1931
[ibid., 2572, sheets 336f]; resolution of the DBB of 27/8 October 1931 [ibid.,
2650, sheet 312]). The impression had arisen, this stated, that 'a reform of

the structure of the Reich was to be achieved by precipitating the financial collapse of Länder'.

100 *Memoiren*, pp. 372f, 389f.

101 Schäffer Diary, vol. 14, p. 736; cf. note 98. At the meeting of the Reich and Prussian governments of 11 September (minutes in BA R 43 I/2373, sheets 871ff), Otto Braun, the Prussian premier, was concerned to achieve a uniform approach given the contentious issue of the constitutionality of cuts in salaries at county level, but Brüning avoided a decision on this.

102 *Schulthess' Europäischer Geschichtskalender*, 72 (1931), p. 229; cf. Brüning, *Memoiren*, p. 483, and Otto Braun, *Von Weimar zu Hitler*, 2nd edn (New York, 1940), p. 354.

103 Ministerial meeting of 11 September 1931 (IfZ MA 149/16); appendix: Draft decree on various measures regulating salary matters. Note by Schäffer on the cabinet meeting of 5 October 1931 (Schäffer Diary, vol. 14) and ministerial meeting of 24 September (IfZ MA 149/16, sheets 788.101f).

104 Cf. Dingeldey's letter to Brüning of 15 September 1931 (BA R 43 I/2572, sheets 178ff) referring to the more negative effects of this for Reich civil servants and to the fact that the measure affected only officials on lower incomes. The decree prepared by the Finance Ministry met with fierce opposition from both within and outside the cabinet. Groener pointed to the halt on promotions set for 1 October and warned of the danger of civil servants being attracted to the NSDAP. Stegerwald supported Dingeldey's arguments, while Brüning characteristically held that hasty partial solutions pre-empting the 'programme as a whole' were precisely what were not required, as these would only lead to accusations against the government 'that it appeared always to be attempting to master the situation with savings decrees alone and to lack a coherent overall savings plan'. Dietrich subsequently admitted that he had been negotiating under pressure from the Prussian finance minister (ministerial meeting of 11 September 1931, ibid.). Dietrich's amended proposals also met with determined opposition and doubts as to their constitutionality, including fears that they would put the president in a difficult situation as regards the courts. Meissner declared 'that the president, under pressure from countless letters questioning the constitutionality of the cabinet's proposals, had let it be known that he wished only such items to be included in the new decree which were definitely covered by Article 48 of the constitution (ministerial meeting of 24 September [ibid., sheet 788.132]).

105 On 11 September Groener called the finance minister's proposals an 'extreme measure against the officers of the Wehrmacht' (ministerial meeting, ibid.); cf. ministerial meeting of 29 September, where Dietrich reported on the failure of his talks with the heads of the Army Ministry and Groener threatened to intervene with Hindenburg. The conflict escalated further, with Braun demanding the inclusion of Prussian police officers in the exemption provisions (cf. BA R 43 I/2367, sheets 190ff; I/2572, sheets 372ff, and Besson, *Staatskrise*, p. 248).

106 At the ministerial meeting of 24 September Wirth declared that the effects

of the proposed financial measures were not compatible with the severe harm they would do for civil servants (ibid., sheet 788.102). Cf. Mommsen, 'Stellung der Beamtenschaft, pp. 160f.

107   Ministerial meeting of 24 September 1931 (IfZ MA 149/16, sheet 788.104); Schäffer's note of a conversation with von Krosigk of 31 August 1931 (Schäffer Diary, vol. 13). Cf. Grotkopp, *Grosse Krise*, pp. 75f.

108   Ministerial meeting of 2 October 1931 (IfZ MA 149/16, sheets 788.382ff).

109   Ibid., sheet 788.394; Brüning had already stated that further economic contraction and another programme of economic austerity would be necessary despite the 'vicious cycle' 'produced by constantly attempting to keep pace with the shortfall in revenue' (sheets 788.363ff). He insisted on further savings in wage and salary costs, though he admitted that these had already been reduced 'way below' the cost-of-living index.

110   Ministerial meeting of 28 November 1931 (IfZ MA 149/17, sheet 788.788). On reductions in higher civil servants' salaries, cf. Adolf Bohlen, *Die höheren Beamten nach drei Gehaltskürzungen* (Berlin, 1931), pp. 4ff; due to the extreme variations in the effects produced by the salary cuts, the ADB, in a submission to the government on 18 September 1931, demanded that the provision in the Prussian government's decree of 12 September preventing reductions in excess of 20 per cent by means of a subvention be included in the central government's proposed decree (BA R 43 I/2373, sheets 1095f). This was before the drastic Fourth Decree for the Protection of the Economy and the Public Finances of 8 December 1931 was promulgated. It is virtually impossible to calculate exactly the average reductions in salaries produced by these measures due to the regional variations and constant changes in the statutory regulations covering civil servants' salaries.

111   Cf. ministerial meeting of 4 December 1931 (IfZ MA 149/17, sheets 788.884ff) and Schäffer's note of the same date (Schäffer Diary, vol. 16).

112   *RGB1*, I (1931), pp. 738ff.

113   Cabinet meeting of 5 October 1931 (IfZ MA 149/16). Cf. Brüning's speech to the parliamentary party and national council of the Centre Party of 14 June 1931 (Morsey, *Protokolle*, no. 677, p. 531).

114   *Schulthess' Geschichtskalender*, p. 234.

115   In a conversation with Schäffer on 4 March 1932, Brüning said that 'we absolutely have to hold out until early 1933 even if that means telling lies' (Schäffer Diary, vol. 19, p. 307). Brüning declared in cabinet on 12 April 1932 that 'if these things [the hopeless situation in the national finances] leak out, it will be impossible to pursue a foreign policy. I make it everyone's duty to act publicly in such a way that we will be able to survive through next winter. That is the only way the impression will not be gained abroad that we have no choice but to accept any conditions imposed upon us' (ibid., vol. 20, p. 449); cf. Sanmann, 'Deutsche Wirtschafts- und Finanzpolitik', pp. 134f.

116   Representative for many examples, see DBB executive decision of 27 November 1931 (BA R 43 I/2572, sheets 321ff); *Die deutsche Beamtenschaft zur Wirtschaftslage. Wirtschaftspolitische Forderungen des Deutschen Beamtenbundes*

(Berlin, 1931). Public protests against Brüning's financial policy held jointly by the ADGB, the ADB and the DBB became common, such as that of 3 December 1931 in Berlin (*Der Beamtenbund*, vol.15, no. 92, p. 3).

117   Thus Brüning at the meeting with the Prussian government of 31 July 1931 (Schäffer Diary, vol. 12); cf. ministerial meeting of 2 October 1931 (IfZ MA 149/16, sheet 788.391) and Schäffer's note of it. Brüning was thinking of the collapse in the agricultural market which was manifesting itself despite protective tariffs and reduced interest rates.

118   Schäffer Diary, vol. 12, pp. 511f.

119   Cabinet meeting of 4 December 1931 (IfZ MA 149/17) and Schäffer's note on it (Schäffer Diary, vol. 16).

120   Cf. Ernst Wagemann, *Struktur und Rhythmus der Weltwirtschaft* (Berlin, 1931). Grotkopp, *Grosse Krise*, pp. 34ff, 40ff; Wandel, *Hans Schäffer*, pp. 145ff; Schäffer Diary, vol. 17, entry for 28 January 1932. If the trade unions realized that credit could now be expanded, they would immediately demand a major employment creation programme, rejected by Brüning with the argument that this would only produce greater unemployment in the future (ministerial meeting of 2 October 1931). In answer to Braun's question regarding future inflationary trends, Brüning claimed that 'only deflation could convince the world that Germany could not afford to pay reparations' (meeting of the Centre Party Reichstag group of 25 August 1931, Morsey, *Protokolle*, no. 679, p. 542).

121   Note by Schäffer on a discussion with Luther, the president of the Reichsbank, on 29 January 1932 (Schäffer Diary, vol. 17, pp. 136f).

122   Brüning, *Memoiren*, pp. 481f. Cf. Schäffer's note of a conversation with Brüning on 20 November 1931 (Schäffer Diary, vol. 15), where the chancellor expressed his annoyance at Klepper's claim that the government's economic policy would lead to a drastic decline in taxation revenues.

123   Given that Luther refused the 50 million Reichsmark credit sought by the Prussian government to cover its financial shortfall despite Braun's protests that he could not end his forty-year career in politics with the absurdity of 'introducing measures before an election which are absolutely catastrophic for the governing parties' (Schäffer Diary, vol. 18, pp. 164f), Klepper felt he had little choice but to introduce the 'slaughtering tax'. Brüning gave a diametrically opposite account (*Memoiren*, pp. 483ff); he was angry at Klepper, he told Schäffer on 4 March, because he had claimed publicly in Frankfurt that Brüning had advised him that, given the absence of a subvention to cover the Prussian budget, he should 'stimulate inflation' (Schäffer Diary, vol. 19, p. 319; cf. also vol. 18, pp. 173f, and vol. 17, p. 24). The savings policy forced by Brüning on the Länder did in fact now begin to work against him, threatening to destroy the myth that a further deflation of the economy was unavoidable.

124   Cf. Brüning, *Memoiren*, pp. 568ff. Schäffer's note of a conversation between Brüning and Klepper on 6 January 1931 (Schäffer Diary, vol. 17, pp. 24ff).

125   A thorough elucidation of the various standpoints adopted on the issue of the Reichsreform can be found in Gerhard Schulz, *Zwischen Demokratie und*

Diktatur, II: *Deutschland am Vorabend der Grossen Krise* (Berlin, 1987). Brüning claimed in his memoirs that 'If there had been a government at Reich level completely independent of political parties at this stage, there would have been no need to worry about the situation in the Länder, as the government's financial policy had virtually reached the stage, despite fierce opposition from the new Prussian minister for finance [i.e. Klepper! – author's note] and the Bavarian government, where the Länder governments were to all intents and purposes permanently dependent on aid from the Reich to meet their civil service pay costs. This meant that the Länder could be brought firmly into line whenever they got obstreperous. With these controls in place, the experiment with the Nazis could then have been attempted . . .' (*Memoiren*, pp. 568f).

126 Cf. Brüning's explanation at the ministerial meeting of 27 October 1931 of the new cabinet's economic programme (IfZ MA 149/17, sheets 788.538ff). This was the principal contradiction in Brüning's deflationary strategy. He planned to resolve it by reducing Germany's foreign debts and cancelling the debts of the agricultural sector, but he in fact aggravated it by weakening the capital market. Brüning was later to claim repeatedly that the Young Plan's restrictions on currency equalization prevented him from offsetting the effects of the devaluation of sterling by devaluing the Mark. Brüning had never been an opponent of devaluation out of principle, and was later to consider really drastic devaluations of the German currency. But in late autumn 1931 he rejected out of hand any idea of devaluatoin – which could only have been implemented in agreement with Germany's reparations creditors – as he intended holding out until reparations had been abolished and Germany's foreign debts cleared before using devaluation as an instrument of economic policy. The whole thrust of Brüning's financial policy was to create the conditions for a devaluation of the Mark to stimulate Germany's foreign trade by reducing wages and prices, though the devaluation itself had to be postponed for as long as Germany's reparations creditors were in a position to levy what they assessed as its economic surplus.

127 Cf. Besson, *Staatskrise*, pp. 219ff, 243ff.

128 Cf. Schäffer's notes on discussions with the Länder on 22 August and 1 September 1931 (Schäffer Diary, vols 13 and 14); further the documents reprinted in Besson, *Staatskrise*, pp. 379ff, especially the correspondence between Prime Minister Held and State President Eugen Bolz of March 1931.

129 Cf. Schäffer's criticism of the unsocial effects of abolishing first-child benefits (Schäffer Diary, vol. 10, p. 167); *Die deutsche Beamtenschaft zur Notverordnung vom 5. Juni 1931. Kritik und Forderungen des DBB* (Berlin, 1931), pp. 5f and passim.

130 Cf. ministerial meeting of 11 September 1931 (IfZ MA 149/16, sheet 787.817).

131 Cf. the Draft Decree for Reductions in Private Sector Salaried Incomes and ministerial meeting of 29 September 1931 (IfZ MA 149/16, sheets 788.261ff, 788.245f) at which Joel and Luther expressed strong reservations about the

elements of the decree which involved 'breaking contractual commitments' and involving the commercial court. The Pensions Reductions Act was dropped in the end as it was hoped that more favourable Reichsgericht rulings would be forthcoming which would clear the way for dealing with the matter by simple legislation (cf. ministerial meeting of 15 February 1932 [IfZ MA 151/15, sheet 789.254]).

132   The issue of setting upper limits on salaries and pensions became a highly effective political issue as a result; the SPD's demand for an upper limit of RM 12,000 on all salaries which it put forward in repeated resolutions to the Reichstag was adopted by the NSDAP; cf. the resolution adopted at the conference of National Socialist German Civil Servants' representatives on 20 September 1931 (BA R 43 I/2380, sheets 28ff).

133   See note 103 above; similarly, the Civil Servants' Advisory Council of the Lower Saxon Centre Party warned Brüning that the closing of employment opportunities in the public service for young people would drive them to the NSDAP (letter of 29 March 1932 [BA R 43, I/2629, sheets 54ff]).

134   Discussion with Schleicher of 29 January 1932 (Schäffer Diary, vol. 17, p. 143).

135   Gerhard Anschütz, *Die Verfassung des Deutschen Reiches vom 11. August 1919. Ein Kommentar für Wissenschaft und Praxis*, 8th edn (Berlin, 1928), pp. 339f; cf. H. Heller, 'Das Berufsbeamtentum in der deutschen Demokratie', *Die neue Rundschau*, 41 (1930), pp. 723f; H. Gerber, 'Entwicklung und Reform des Beamtenrechts', *Vollversammlung Deutscher Staatsrechtslehrer*, 7 (Berlin and Leipzig, 1932), pp. 3ff. For an overview of the legal debate, see Runge, *Politik und Beamtentum*, pp. 250ff. Throughout the 1920s between 130 and 150 civil servants sat as deputies in each Reichstag.

136   Cf. Fenske, 'Beamtenpolitik', pp. 121ff; Hans Mommsen, *Beamtentum im Dritten Reich. Mit ausgewählten Quellen zur nationalsozialistischen Beamtenpolitik* (Stuttgart, 1966), p. 23.

137   Mommsen, *Beamtentum*, pp. 193ff, and Jane Caplan, *Government without Administration: State and Civil Service in Weimar and Nazi Germany* (Oxford, 1988).

138   Cf. meeting of the Reich Ministry of 28 January 1931 (IfZ MA 151/12) at which Wirth presented drafts of a Public Service Disciplinary Code and a Civil Servants' Representation Act; these were not dealt with, however.

139   Thus Luther's proposal to Schäffer (Schäffer Diary, vol. 12, p. 70).

140   Morsey, *Protokolle*, p. 408.

141   *Entscheidungen des Reichgerichts in Zivilsachen*, 134, pp. 1ff; this judgement amended the rulings by the Reichsfinanzhof of 15 January and 15 March 1931, which had been largely in line with Carl Schmitt's theory of the 'institutional guarantee'.

142   Cf. Carl Schmitt in *Deutsche-Juristen Zeitung*, 36 (1931), pp. 917ff, and W. Jellinek in *Juristische Wochenschrift*, 61 (1932), pp. 50ff. Cf. Schmitt, *Verfassungslehre*, pp. 170ff.

143   Cf. the memorandum from the president of the Conference of German Towns to the Prussian prime minister of 5 September 1931 (BA R 43, I/2373,

sheets 689ff); meeting of the heads of departments in the Reich chancellery of 11 September 1931 (ibid., sheets 871ff); note by the minister for finance on the draft Emergency Decree Amending Maintenance Regulations of 5 September 1931 (IfZ MA 149/16, sheets 788.144ff) re the constitutionality of the proposed expenditure cuts.

144 This debate culminated with the Conference of German Jurists of 28 and 29 October 1931 (see note 135). The tendency of the majority opinion supporting Carl Schmitt was towards a dismantling of the subjective public rights of state officials and this was to be fully realized under the Third Reich (cf. Mommsen, *Beamtentum*, p. 93).

145 *Entscheidungen des Reichsgerichts in Zivilsachen*, 134, p. 12; cf. ministerial meeting of 17 August 1931 (IfZ MA 149/15, sheet 787.560).

146 BA R 43, I/2556, sheets 96ff; the absence of legal regulations was precisely the reason the authorities did not replace civil service posts with employees as this would have led to 'automatic claims to civil service status'. See also BA R 43, I/2556, sheets 271–310.

147 See note 104 above.

148 Various items in BA R 58/349, 423 and 1128; cf. Runge, *Politik und Beamtentum*, p. 248; Carl Severing, *Mein Lebensweg*, vol. 2 (Cologne, 1950), pp. 275f; Schäffer Diary, vol. 8, pp. 62, 70.

149 Cabinet meeting of 12 April 1932 (IfZ MA 151/15, sheets 789,796ff): 'The terror employed by the national socialists in the civil service has reached such a degree that constitutionally inclined civil servants have been totally intimidated.' Dietrich declared that clear guidelines were urgently needed to tackle the situation. Officials in the customs service were by now totally national socialist, he said. With 90 per cent of his civil servants supporting the Nazis and given the pro-Nazi attitude of the disciplinary authorities, he could 'not do much' without the support of the minister of the interior.

150 Cf. the letter from the state president of Baden of 22 April 1932 and the draft of the Reich Chancellery's reply (BA R 43, I/2557, sheets 20ff); cf. Schulz, *Aufstieg des Nationalsozialismus*, pp. 886f, n. 323. During the debate on the supplementary estimate for the Braunschweig police, Brüning warned against regarding 'the national socialists as representing as great a danger to the state as the communists' (ministerial meeting of 30 October 1930 [IfZ MA 151/12, sheet 785.230]); during the cabinet meeting of 19 December 1930 (ibid., sheet 785.534) he argued for postponing a government position on the issue of banning the NSDAP and rejected the idea of treating the Nazis as the social democrats had been treated in the pre-war era.

151 Cf. Mommsen, 'Stellung der Beamtenschaft', p. 164, and the events documented in BA R 43, I/2557. Given Brüning's tactical policy of turning a blind eye, complaints about the growing influence of the NSDAP on civil servants made little impact (cf. Schäffer Diary, vol. 19, p. 320; cabinet meeting of 12 April 1932). Cf. the polemic against the present author in *Deutscher Beamtenbund*, I pp. 43ff, where the results of the Civil Service Council elections of October 1932 are interpreted as showing a low level of NSDAP influence in the DBB; but this proves nothing either way regarding the indirect

influence exercised by the National Socialist Civil Servants' Committees.
152 The Reich Chancellery, for example, felt obliged to intervene against the disciplinary measures taken by a national socialist manager against a railway engine driver who had canvassed openly for Hindenburg (BA R 43 I/2602, sheets 230ff).
153 Cf. the positive response by the DBB to Schleicher's reference to the 'great tasks facing German civil servants who had received scant thanks for their devoted work in recent years' (*Deutscher Beamtenbund*, vol. 16, 20 December 1932).
154 Brüning's salary cuts were extended at first for one year and then indefinitely by the Decree on Measures in the Areas of Finance, the Economy and the Administration of Justice of 18 March 1933 (*RGBl*, I [1933], p. 109) and the Law Amending and Supplementing Public Finance Regulations of 23 March 1934 (*RGBl*, I [1934], p. 232). The second and third salary reductions introduced by Brüning were repealed in 1948.

Chapter 6   Heinrich Brüning as Chancellor: The Failure of a Politically Isolated Strategy

1 Heinrich Brüning, *Memoiren 1918–1934* (Stuttgart, 1970).
2 Cf. Rudolf Morsey, *Zur Entstehung, Authentizität und Kritik von Brünings 'Memoiren 1918–1934'* (Opladen, 1975), pp. 12f.
3 Cf. Brüning's own account of his resignation, *Memoiren*, pp. 598ff.
4 Cf. Friedrich Freiherr Hiller von Gaertringen, 'Zur Beurteilung des "Monarchismus" in der Weimarer Republik', in G. Jasper (ed.), *Tradition und Reform in der deutschen Politik. Gedenkschrift für Waldemar Besson* (Frankfurt a.M., 1976), pp. 175f.
5 Cf. Waldemar Besson, *Württemberg und die deutsche Staatskrise 1928–1933. Eine Studie zur Auflösung der Weimarer Republik* (Stuttgart, 1959), pp. 249f; Hans Mommsen, 'State and Bureaucracy in the Brüning Era', in this volume, pp. 84ff.
6 Cf. Mommsen, 'State and Bureaucracy', p. 89.
7 Cf. note 37 below.
8 *RGBl*, II (1931), pp. 221ff. The opposition on the right used the excuse of protesting against the reform in the order of business procedures to absent itself from the Reichstag and thus avoid having to vote on the motion from the KPD for an immediate moratorium on all repayments in protest at the Young Plan, although the motion had already been defeated within the Foreign Affairs Committee with the votes of the NSDAP (*Reichstag Proceedings*, V/1931, vol. 444, p. 903).
9 Cf. Hans Mommsen, 'Die Stellung der Beamtenschaft in Reich, Ländern und Gemeinden in der Ära Brüning', *VfZ*, 21 (1973), pp. 157f.
10 The opposition of heavy industry to a revival of the Central Working Association was well expressed by Karl Brandi, the chairman of the Mining Federation, when he remarked to Bernhard, the director of the Danat Bank, on 20 October 1931, 'I only hope the Economic Advisory Council (Privy Council) to the

president which is to be set up will not under any circumstances be on the basis of equal representation [of employers and trade unions – translator's note], i.e. based on the Central Working Association idea' (quoted in Fritz Klein, 'Zur Vorbereitung der faschistischen Diktatur durch die deutsche Grossbourgeoisie [1929–1932]', *Zeitschrift für Geschichtswissenschaft*, 1 (1953), no. 2, p. 901). The Economic Advisory Council was established on 29 October but was to have a short life, ending its work on 23 November shortly after the representatives of the agricultural sector withdrew from it. Cf. Brüning, *Memoiren*, p. 459.

11   Cf. Tilman P. Koops, 'Zielkonflikte der Agrar- und Wirtschaftspolitik in der Ära Brüning', in H. Mommsen, D. Petzina and B. Weisbrod (eds), *Industrielles System und politische Entwicklung in der Weimarer Republik* (Düsseldorf, 1974), pp. 865ff; Henning Köhler, 'Arbeitsbeschaffung, Siedlung und Reparationen in der Schlussphase der Regierung Brüning', *VfZ*, 17 (1969), pp. 276ff.

12   Brüning, *Memoiren*, p. 460.

13   Cf. his speech to the Foreign Affairs Committee of the Reichstag on 24 May 1932 in W. Vernekohl and R. Morsey (eds), *Heinrich Brüning – Reden und Aufsätze eines deutschen Staatsmannes* (Münster, 1968), pp. 182ff, cf. p. 165.

14   Cf. Werner Conze, 'Brüning als Reichskanzler. Eine Zwischenbilanz', *HZ*, 214 (1972), p. 329.

15   Cf. Dietmar Petzina, 'Elemente der Wirtschaftspolitik in der Spätphase der Weimarer Republik', *VfZ*, 21 (1973), pp. 129f; idem, 'Hauptprobleme der deutschen Wirtschaftspolitik 1932/33', *VfZ*, 15 (1967); Rolf E. Lüke, *Von der Stabilisierung zur Krise* (Zurich, 1958); Dietmar Keese, 'Die volkswirt-schaftlichen Gesamtgrössen für das Deutsche Reich in den Jahren 1925–1936', in W. Conze and H. Raupach (eds), *Die Staats- und Wirtschaftskrise des Deutschen Reiches 1929/33* (Stuttgart, 1967), pp. 35ff, and Horst Sanmann, 'Deutsche Wirtschafts- und Finanzpolitik in der Ära Brüning', *Hamburger Jahrbuch für Wirtschafts- und Gesellschaftspolitik*, 10 (1965), pp. 107ff.

16   Cf. Gerhard Schulz, *Aufstieg des Nationalsozialismus. Krise und Revolution in Deutschland* (Frankfurt a.M., Berlin and Vienna, 1975), p. 857: 'A policy to defeat the crisis, regarded as the model alternative course, would thus miss the point not only of the policy which Brüning was actually pursuing, but also of the policies pursued by Germany's diplomatic negotiating partners, particularly the French.'

17   Cf. note 27 and also Rudolf Morsey, 'Brünings Kritik an der Reichsfinanzpolitik 1919–1929', in E. Hassinger, J. H. Müller and Hugo Ott (eds), *Geschichte, Wirtschaft, Gesellschaft. Festschrift für Clemens Bauer* (Berlin, 1974), pp. 359ff.

18   Cf. Heinrich Brüning, 'Ein Brief', *Deutsche Rundschau*, 70 (1947), pp. 1–22; the stance adopted by heavy industry dissipated quickly after it had earlier supported Schacht's express demand for a devaluation of the Mark.

19   'Denkschrift Brünings vom 31. August 1935', in Claire Nix (ed.), *Heinrich Brüning. Briefe und Gespräche 1934–1945* (Stuttgart, 1974), p. 477: 'The final link in the chain of measures planned to revive Germany financially and economically was a devaluation of the Mark in early 1932 by about 20 per cent.'

20 Brüning, *Memoiren*, p. 195.

21 Cf. ibid., p. 192, where he wrote that a steady revival of the economy could be expected only from 1935.

22 Cf. Brüning, 'Ein Brief'; Schulz, *Aufstieg des Nationalsozialismus*, pp. 545f.

23 Cf. Mommsen, 'State and Bureaucracy', p. 108.

24 Cf. ibid., pp. 108f.

25 On this cf. Köhler, 'Arbeitsbeschaffung', pp. 276ff.

26 Cf. his comment to Schäffer: 'I wouldn't go . . . to a reparations conference under any circumstances unless I was sure our finances were absolutely water-tight' (diary entry by Schäffer of 20 November 1931, reprinted in E. Wandel, *Hans Schäffer. Steuermann in wirtschaftlichen und politischen Krisen* [Stuttgart, 1974], p. 319).

27 Cf. anon. (Heinrich Brüning), 'Der Wiederaufbau des deutschen Finanzwesens', *Jahrbuch der christlichen Gewerkschaften für 1921*, n.d. [1921], p. 106: 'Any attempt at a thorough clearing of the Reich's finances is thus pointless as long as the burdens of the Versailles Treaty have to be borne'; Schulz, *Aufstieg des Nationalsozialismus*, pp. 535ff.

28 Cf. Besson, *Staatskrise*, pp. 359ff; Karl Dietrich Bracher's description of Brüning's 'non-political' politics displays a similar tendency (Bracher, 'Brünings unpolitische Politik und das Ende der Weimarer Republik', *VfZ*, 19 [1971], pp. 113ff).

29 Cf. Morsey, 'Brünings Kritik', pp. 359ff.

30 Ibid., p. 363. Rudolf Morsey has correctly pointed to the neglect by historians to date of the apposite publications by Brüning on financial and economic policy.

31 Cf. Schäffer Diary (Institut für Zeitgeschichte, Munich, catalogued as IfZ ED 93), vol. 14, note on a ministerial meeting of 2 October 1931.

32 Vernekohl and Morsey, *Heinrich Brüning*, p. 57.

33 (First) Decree of the Reich President for the Protection of the Economy and the Public Finances, *RGB1*, I (1930), pp. 522ff.

34 *Niederschriften über die Vollsitzungen des Reichsrats*, 44th session, 4 November 1930, p. 524.

35 Ibid., 46th session, 20 November 1930, pp. 566f; Brüning felt forced by reports in the press to deny the misunderstanding that had arisen that the government was prepared to sacrifice policy aims for domestic political considerations.

36 Cf. Besson, *Staatskrise*, pp. 185f.

37 Cf. Schäffer Diary, vol. 10, entry for 17 April 1931.

38 Cf. Wolfgang Helbich, *Die Reparationen in der Ära Brüning. Zur Bedeutung des Young-Plans für die deutschen Probleme 1930–1932* (Berlin, 1962), p. 66.

39 Schäffer Diary, vol. 12, Schäffer's discussion with Brüning and State Secretary Pünder of 6 May 1931, sheets 141f.

40 Cf. H. Mommsen, 'Betrachtung zu den Memoiren Heinrich Brünings', *Jahrbuch für die Geschichte Mittel- und Ostdeutschlands*, 22 (1973), pp. 270ff.

41 Schäffer Diary, vol. 20, cabinet meeting of 12 April 1932, sheet 449.

42 Cf. Christoph M. Kimmich, *Germany and the League of Nations* (Chicago, 1976), pp. 157ff.

43 For a synopsis, see Schulz, *Aufstieg des Nationalsozialismus*, pp. 680ff.

44 Quoted in Morsey, 'Brünings Kritik', pp. 372f n. 78; cf. Heinrich Brüning, 'Finanz- und Steuerpolitik', in Georg Schreiber (ed.), *Politisches Jahrbuch 1927/28. Politik des Deutschen Reiches* (Mönchengladbach, 1928), pp. 720f.

45 Vernekohl and Morsey, *Heinrich Brüning*, p. 64.

46 Cf. Conze, 'Brüning als Reichskanzler', pp. 316, 330ff.

47 Brüning, *Memoiren*, p. 32.

48 Cf. ibid., pp. 31ff; Mommsen, 'Stellung der Beamtenschaft', pp. 158f.

49 Cf. Werner Conze, 'Brünings Politik unter dem Druck der grossen Krise', *HZ*, 199 (1964), pp. 529ff.

50 Cf. Brüning, *Memoiren*, p. 52.

51 Cf. Brüning's speech to the Rhineland Centre Party on 8 August 1930, in Vernekohl and Morsey, *Heinrich Brüning*, pp. 63f; *RGBl*, II (1930), p. 221; Fritz Poetzsch-Heffter, 'Vom Staatsleben unter der Weimarer Verfassung', *Jahrbuch des öffentlichen Rechts der Gegenwart*, 21 (1934), pp. 80f.

52 Brüning, *Memoiren*, p. 373.

53 *Reichstag Proceedings*, IV/1930, Document no. 704, vol. 435; except for the debate on the chancellor's speech and the opening of legislative periods of the Reichstag, the DVP motion proposed that votes of no confidence should require a two-thirds majority to be passed. Brüning planned a further amendment to order of business procedures for the autumn limiting the scope of no-confidence motions (cf. Brüning, *Memoiren*, p. 256).

54 Cf. Rudolf Morsey (ed.), *Die Protokolle der Reichstagfraktion und des Fraktionsvorstandes der Deutschen Zentrumspartei 1926–1933* (Mainz, 1969), p. 410.

55 Cf. Letter from Blank to Reusch of 1 April 1930 (Archiv der GHH, Paul Reusch Papers, 400 101 2024/6), and also Koops, 'Zielkonflikte', pp. 852f.

56 For details cf. Mommsen, 'State and Bureaucracy', pp. 95ff.

57 This was the result of pressure on Scholz and Moldenhauer from the right wing of the DVP, which was substantially controlled by heavy industry. Within the RdI the representatives of heavy industry had a very militant programme adopted – against the opposition of the Federation's leadership and of other more co-operatively inclined sections of industry – which included demands both for legal sanction to pay wages below those set by collective bargaining and for the ruling out of any return to the Central Working Association. On this cf. B. Weisbrod, *Schwerindustrie in der Weimarer Republik. Interessenpolitik zwischen Stabilisierung und Krise* (Wuppertal, 1978).

58 Cf. ibid., pp. 101f; Schäffer Diary, vol. 9, sheet 201.

59 Cf. Poetzsch-Heffter, 'Vom Staatsleben'. p. 134; cf. Gerhard Anschütz, *Die Verfassung des Deutschen Reiches vom 11. August 1919. Ein Kommentar für Wissenschaft und Praxis*, 1933, reprint of the 14th edn (Darmstadt, 1965), p. 295. With its ruling of 5 December 1931, the Supreme Court effectively threw its weight behind the government (cf. Erwin Bumke, 'Der Staatsgerichtshof zu Art. 48 Reichsverfassung', *Deutsche-Juristen Zeitung*, 37 (1932), p. 4.

60 In 1930 it sat on ninety-four days, in 1931 on forty-one and in 1932 on thirteen (Poetzsch-Heffter, 'Vom Staatsleben', p. 101).

61 Cf. *Niederschriften*, 44th session, 4 November 1930, p. 527.

62 On Brüning's use of emergency decrees, cf. Gerhard Schulz, 'Der Artikel 48 in politisch-historischer Sicht', in E. Fraenkel (ed.), *Der Staatsnotstand* (Berlin, 1965), pp. 65ff.

63 Besson, *Staatskrise*, pp. 195ff.

64 Cf. the objection raised by the Reichsrat against Breitscheid's motion proposing levies on the income tax paid by company directors and by the meeting of the Sixth Committee on the income tax levy of 23 March 1931 during the session of 27 March 1931 (*Niederschriften*, 1931, p. 131).

65 Cf. Poetzsch-Heffter, 'Vom Staatsleben', pp. 180ff; Brüning deliberately excluded the Reichsrat from any involvement in the drafting of the decree of 6 June 1931, despite its express request to be allowed to participate (cf. minutes of the plenary session of 27 March 1931, *Niederschriften*, 1931, p. 131, and also Besson, *Staatskrise*, pp. 207f).

66 Mommsen, 'State and Bureaucracy', pp. 94f.

67 Cf. Schulz, *Aufstieg des Nationalsozialismus*, p. 646.

68 Cf. Poetzsch-Heffter, 'Vom Staatsleben', pp. 130ff.

69 Cf. Mommsen, 'Stellung der Beamtenschaft', pp. 160f.

70 Cf. Brüning, *Memoiren*, pp. 585f.

71 Cf. Ilse Maurer and Udo Wengst, *Staat und NSDAP 1930–1932. Quellen zur Ära Brüning*, with an introduction by Gerhard Schulz (Düsseldorf, 1977), esp. pp. XLff, II.

72 Cf. Schulz in ibid., pp. IIIff; Brüning, *Memoiren*, pp. 386ff.

73 Cf. the standard examination of this in Morsey, *Zur Entstehung*, pp. 33ff.

74 Ibid., p. 37.

75 Brüning, *Memoiren*, p. 619.

Chapter 7   National Socialism: Continuity and Change

1 For the study of German self-assessment after 1945, Friedrich Meinecke, *The German Catastrophe* (Cambridge, Mass., 1950) is of fundamental importance. For the conventional interpretation, see William L. Shirer, *The Rise and Fall of the Third Reich* (New York, 1960); and A. J. P. Taylor, *The Course of German History* (London, 1945). Ideological critical analyses are: Martin Broszat, *German National Socialism 1919–1945* (Santa Barbara, 1966), George L. Mosse, *The Crisis of German Ideology* (New York, 1964), Fritz Stern, *The Politics of Cultural Despair: A Study in the Rise of the Germanic Ideology* (Berkeley, 1961). Kurt Sontheimer, *Antidemokratisches Denken in der Weimarer Republik* (Munich, 1962). A good summary is to be found in Karl Dietrich Bracher, *The German Dictatorship*, 4th edn (New York, 1973).

2 Seymour Martin Lipset, 'Der "Faschismus", die Linke, die Rechte und die Mitte', *Kölner Zeitschrift für Soziologie und Sozialpsychologie 11* (1959), Talcott Parsons, 'Some Sociological Aspects of the Fascist Movements 1942', in *Essays in Sociological Theory* (Glencoe, Ill., 1964); Theodor Geiger, *Die soziale Schichtung des deutschen Volkes* (Stuttgart, 1932; 2nd edn, 1967); Ernst Nolte, *Die faschistische Bewegung* (Munich, 1966). Michael Kater, 'Zur Soziographie der frühen NSDAP', *VfZ*, 19 (1971); also Heinrich-August Winkler, *Mittelstand,*

Demokratie und Nationalsozialismus. Die politische Entwicklung von Handwerk und Kleinhandel in der Weimarer Republik (Cologne, 1972).

3 Cf. Irving Fetscher, 'Faschismus und Nationalsozialismus: Zur Kritik des sowjet-marxistischen Faschismusbegriffs', *PVS*, 3 (1962); Theodor Pirker (ed.), *Komintern und Faschismus 1920–1940* (Stuggart, 1965); also Hans Mommsen, 'Antifascism', *MCWS*, 1 (1972), pp. 134–41; Wolfgang Abendroth (ed.), *Faschismus und Kapitalismus* (Frankfurt, 1967); E. Nolte (ed.), *Theorien über den Faschismus*, 2nd edn (Cologne, 1970).

4 Cf. Hans Mommsen, 'National Socialism', *MCWS*, 6 (1973). D. Eichholtz, 'Probleme einer Wirtschaftsgeschichte des Faschismus in Deutschland', *Jahrbuch für Wirtschaftsgeschichte 1963*, pt 3.

5 From the now enormous literature on the subject, the following are the most important: Hans Kohn, 'Communist and Fascist Dictatorship: A Comparative Study', in *Dictatorship in the Modern World* (Minneapolis, 1935); Franz L. Neumann, *Behemoth: The Structure and Practice of National Socialism 1933–1944*, 2nd edn (New York, 1944); Franz L. Neumann, *The Democratic and the Authoritarian State*, ed. by H. Marcuse (Glencoe, Ill., 1957); Sigmund Neumann, *Permanent Revolution*, ed. by Hans Kohn (New York, 1965), C. J. Friedrich and Z. K. Brzezinski, *Totalitarian Dictatorship and Autocracy*, 2nd edn (Cambridge, Mass., 1957). A survey by Bruno Seidel and Siegfried Jenkner, 'Wege der Totalitarismus-Forschung', *Wege der Forschung*, 140 (1968); M. Greiffenhagen et al., *Totalitarismus: Zur Problematik eines politischen Begriffs* (Munich, 1972).

6 Above all, Carl Schmitt, 'Die Wendung zum totalen Staat 1931', in *Positionen und Begriffe* (Hamburg, 1940); Ernst Forsthoff, *Der totale Staat* (Hamburg, 1933); Ulrich Scheuner, 'Die nationale Revolution: Eine staatsrechtliche Untersuchung', *Archiv des öffentlichen Rechts*, new series, 24 (1933–4); and cf. Gerhard Schulz, 'Der Begriff des Totalitarismus und des Nationalsozialismus', in Seidel and Jenkner, 'Wege der Totalitarismus-Forschung', pp. 438ff.

7 It should be remembered here that Hannah Arendt, *The Origins of Totalitarianism* (London and New York, 1951) starts from a different premise in dealing with the ideological and social origins of national socialism, and therefore refers only to a 'so-called totalitarian state'. For more recent discussion, see K. Hildebrand, 'Stufen der Totalitarismus-Forschung', *PVS*, 9 (1968); M. Greiffenhagen, 'Der Totalitarismus-Begriff in der Regimenlehre', in ibid.; Howard D. Mehlinger, *The Study of Totalitarianism: An Inductive Approach* (Washington, DC, 1965); Tim Mason, 'Das Unwesen der Totalitarismustheorien', *Der Politologe*, 7 (1966).

8 Apart from Franz Neumann's *Behemoth*, which is still relevant, Ernst Fraenkel's analysis, *The Dual State* (New York, 1941), is of basic importance and, with Sigmund Neumann, influenced the earlier writings of K. D. Bracher, particularly in Bracher, Wolfgang Sauer and Gerhard Schulz, *Die nationalsozialistische Machtergreifung*, 2nd edn (Cologne, 1962).

9 The initiative for the comparative study of fascism arose from E. Nolte's fundamental study, *Der Faschismus in seiner Epoche* (Munich, 1963; English edn, *The Three Faces of Fascism*, New York, 1966). Cf. Wolfgang Schieder 'Fasch-

ismus und kein Ende?', *Neue Politische Literatur*, vol. 15 (1970), no. 2.

10 David Schoenbaum, *Hitler's Social Revolution*, 2nd edn (Garden City, NY, 1967), p. XIII. A survey of recent tendencies and research problems is to be found in Hans Mommsen et al., 'Faschistische Diktatur in Deutschland', *Politische Bildung*, vol. 5 (1972), no. 1, and in Wolfgang Sauer, 'National Socialism: Totalitarianism or Fascism?', *American Historical Review*, 73 (1967).

11 For socio-political analyses of 'totalitarian' mass movements, see first and foremost Theodor W. Adorno et al., *The Authoritarian Personality* (New York, 1950); Eric Fromm, *Escape from Freedom* (New York, 1941). The wealth of differing versions precludes a summary survey of the psychological and sociological attempts to explain the 'totalitarian' susceptibility of the German middle classes. Besides the linking of socialist and liberal attitudes stemming from the atomization and depoliticization of German society under the influence of a capitalist national state (H. Arendt), there is the widely held conviction that totalitarianism was a pathological extension of radical democracy (J. L. Talmon, *The Origins of Totalitarian Democracy* [New York, 1961]). However, the theory of F. Neumann and S. Neumann, postulating that national socialism destroyed the existing social structure and intentionally kept the mass of the people in a state of constant tension and permanent revolution, has had an even more lasting influence on subsequent research, by stressing that these were the specific totalitarian intentions of Hitler's policies. But national socialism, notwithstanding its dynamic social power, did not effectively level out social differences and structures (except in the anti-aristocrat campaign following 20 July 1944). Instead, it camouflaged them by its community ideologies (see Schoenbaum, *Hitler's Social Revolution*, pp. 275ff).

12 Cf. Hans Buchheim, *Das Dritte Reich* (Munich, 1958), and idem, *Totalitäre Herrschaft* (Munich, 1962). See also Robert C. Tucker, 'Towards a Comparative Politics of Movement-Regimes', *APSR*, 15 (1961), who points out that the party's tendency to abandon sociological and plebiscitary fundamentals in favour of the psycho-pathological character of the Führer was a characteristic of a fascist mass movement rule; he considers 'Hitlerism' to be the appropriate term for this development.

13 See Günther Plum's article, 'Resistance Movements', *MCWS* 7 (1973).

14 On KPD policy, see Siegfried Bahne, 'Die Kommunistische Partei Deutschlands' in Erich Matthias and Rudolf Morsey (eds), *Das Ende der Parteien 1933* (Düsseldorf, 1960).

15 One of K. D. Bracher's great merits is that, in *Die Auflösung der Weimarer Republik*, 4th edn (Villingen, 1964), he brings out the continuity between the presidential cabinets and the Third Reich, and contradicts the widely held belief that January 1933 represented a major break with the past.

16 See in particular Wolfgang Horn, *Führerideologie und Parteiorganisation in der NSDAP 1919–1933* (Düsseldorf, 1972), and also Joseph Nyomarkay, *Charisma and Factionalism in the Nazi Party* (Minneapolis, 1967). Central to the latter's research is the connection between the Führer cult and the party's forming itself into sub-groups.

17 Deliberate fostering of aestheticizing elements as a means of integration distin-

guishes fascist from imperialist movements; see S. J. Woolf (ed.), *European Fascism* (New York, 1969), and W. Laqueur and G. Mosse (eds), *International Fascism 1920–1945* (London, 1969).

18 Cf. the Reich Chancellery draft for the establishment of a senate to elect the leader, June 1941 (BA R 43 II/1213a); and M. Broszat, *Der Staat Hitlers: Grundlegung und Entwicklung seiner inneren Verfassung* (Munich, 1969), pp. 360f.

19 See in particular Jeremy Noakes, *The Nazi Party in Lower Saxony 1921–1933* (Oxford, 1971), pp. 156ff, 164f. Cf. also Geoffrey Pridham, *Hitler's Rise to Power: The Nazi Movement in Bavaria* (New York and London, 1974).

20 Wolfgang Schieder, 'Fascism', *MCWS*, 3 (1972), pp. 282ff.

21 See the authoritative essay by M. Broszat, 'Soziale Motivation und Führerbindung des Nationalsozialismus', *VfZ*, 18 (1970), as distinct from the overemphasis on biographical elements in interpretative models relating to Hitler, found in Eberhard Jäckel, *Hitler's Weltanschauung: A Blueprint for Power* (Middletown, Conn., 1972; German edn, Tübingen, 1969), and the earlier tendency, reintroduced recently by Joachim C. Fest, *Adolf Hitler* (Berlin, 1973), to exaggerate Hitler's role in political decision-making. For criticism of this method, see Edward N. Peterson, *The Limits of Hitler's Power* (Princeton, 1969), pp. 11ff.

22 This is the unanimous conclusion of many recent monographs: A. S. Milward, *The German Economy at War* (London, 1965). Reinhard Bollmus, *Das Amt Rosenberg une seine Gegner* (Stuttgart, 1970); Heinz Höhne, *The Order of the Death's Head: The Story of Hitler's SS* (London, 1969); see also Hans Mommsen, *Beamtentum im Dritten Reich. Mit ausgewählten Quellen zur nationalsozialistischen Beamtenpolitik* (Stuttgart, 1966); and the earlier comments by Robert Koehl, 'Feudal Aspects of National Socialism', *APSR*, 54 (1960).

23 Hugh Trevor-Roper, *The Last Days of Hitler* (London, 1949); Reimer Hansen, *Das Ende des Dritten Reiches* (Stuttgart, 1966).

24 See Henry A. Turner, 'Big Business and the Rise of Hitler', *American Historical Review*, 75 (1969), and idem, *Faschismus und Kapitalismus in Deutschland* (Göttingen, 1972); on the role of industry, see also H. Momsen et al. (eds), *Industrielle Entwicklung und politisches System in der Weimarer Republik* (Düsseldorf, 1964).

25 Werner Maser, *Die Frühgeschichte der NSDAP* (Frankfurt, 1965); Georg Franz-Willing, *Die Hitlerbewegung* (Hamburg, 1962).

26 Henry J. Gordon, *Hitler and the Beer Hall Putsch*, 2nd edn (Oxford, 1973); Ernst Deuerlein, *Der Hitler-Putsch* (Stuttgart, 1962).

27 See in particular Horn, *Führerideologie*, and Dietrich Orlow, *The History of the Nazi Party 1919–1933* (Pittsburgh, 1969).

28 For the national socialist left, see Horn, *Führerideologie*, as well as an earlier study by Reinhard Kühnl, *Die nationalsozialistische Linke 1925–1930* (Meisenheim, 1966), and Noakes, *Nazi Party*, pp. 72ff. Max H. Kele's theory, in *Nazis and Workers* (Pittsburgh, 1973), that Goebbels remained true to his socialist beliefs whereas Gregor Strasser conformed to Hitler's ideas, is without precedent.

29 See Uwe Lohalm, *Völkischer Radikalismus: Die Geschichte des Deutschvölkischen Schutz- und Trutzbundes 1919–1933* (Hamburg, 1970).

30 For the part played by anti-semitism in the political power struggle during the last stages of the Weimar Republic, see the detailed analyses in Werner E. Mosse (ed.), *Entscheidungsjahr 1932. Zur Judenfrage in der Endphase der Weimarer Republik* 2nd edn (Tübingen, 1966).
31 Orlow, *History of the Nazi Party 1919–1933*, pp. 89ff, 95ff, 140ff; cf. Noakes, *Nazi Party*, p. 106.
32 Noakes, *Nazi Party*, pp. 121ff.
33 Ibid., pp. 129ff, Horst Gies, 'NSDAP und landwirtschaftliche Organisationen in der Endphase der Weimarer Republik', *VfZ*, 15 (1967).
34 See Niethammer, 'Faschistische Bewegungen des Zwischenkriegszeit in Europa', in Mommsen et al., 'Faschistische Diktatur', pp. 17–36.
35 See Richard N. Hunt, *German Social Democracy 1918–1933* (New York, 1964); and Hans Mommsen, 'Sozialdemokratie in der Defensive', in idem (ed.), *Sozialdemokratie zwischen Klassenbewegung und Volkspartei* (Frankfurt, 1974).
36 Walter Z. Laqueur, *Young Germany: A History of the German Youth Movement* (London and New York, 1962).
37 See Attila Chanady, 'The Disintegration of the German People's Party 1924–1930', *JMH*, 39 (1967), pp. 65ff; Karl O'Lessker, 'Who Voted for Hitler?', *American Journal of Sociology*, 74 (1968–9), pp. 63–9.
38 See voting analyses in Alfred Milatz, *Wähler und Wahlen in der Weimarer Republik* (Bonn, 1965), pp. 141ff.
39 William Sheridan Allen, *The Nazi Seizure of Power* (Chicago, 1965; revised, New York, 1984).
40 See Z. A. B. Zeman, *Nazi Propaganda*, 2nd edn (London, 1973).
41 Cf. Bracher, Sauer and Schulz, *Nationalsozialistische Machtergreifung*, pp. 95ff, 350ff, and also Bracher, *German Dictatorship*, p. 29.
42 Reichsorganisationsleiter der NSDAP (ed.), *Parteistatistik (Als Manuskript gedruckt:* Munich, 1935), p. 26; Reichsführer SS (ed.), *Der Weg der NSDAP* (Berlin, 1934), p. 91; cf. Niethammer, 'Faschistische Bewegungen', p. 29.
43 On this, see above all Wolfgang Schaefer, *NSDAP* (Frankfurt, 1956), and Hans Gerth, 'The Nazi Party: Its Leadership and Social Composition', *American Journal of Sociology*, 45 (1940), pp. 517ff.
44 Rudolf Heberle, *Landbevölkerung und Nationalsozialismus* (Stuttgart, 1963); Gerhard Stoltenberg, *Politische Strömungen im schleswig-holsteinischen Landvolk* (Düsseldorf, 1962).
45 Cf. also Winkler, *Mittelstand*.
46 Cf. particularly Noakes, *Nazi Party*, pp. 233f.
47 Ibid., pp. 230f.
48 See Josef Becker, 'Brüning, Prälat Kaas und das Problem einer Regierungsbeteiligung der NSDAP 1930–1932', *HZ*, 196 (1963), pp. 74ff, and also Detlef Junker, *Die Deutsche Zentrumspartei und Hitler 1932/33* (Stuttgart, 1969), pp. 86ff.
49 Joseph Goebbels, *Vom Kaiserhof zur Reichskanzlei* (Berlin, 1934), pp. 87, 143.
50 See Peter Diehl-Thiele, *Partei und Staat im Dritten Reich. Untersuchungen zum Verhältnis von NSDAP und innerer Staatsverwaltung 1933–1945* (Munich, 1969), p. 33.

51 Above all Helmut Nicolai, Ernst von Heydebrand und der Lasa, as well as Hans Pfundtner: cf. Mommsen, *Beamtentum*, pp. 28f; Diehl-Thiele, *Partei und Staat*, p. 332, n. 90.

52 Goebbels, *Vom Kaiserhof*, pp. 140, 158; cf. Helmut Heiber, *Joseph Goebbels* (New York, 1972).

53 Adolf Hitler, *Mein Kampf*, 67th edn (Munich, 1933), p. 503.

54 Goebbels, *Vom Kaiserhof*, p. 294.

55 Joseph Goebbels, *Idee und Gestalt des Nationalsozialismus* (Berlin, 1935).

56 Ibid.

57 Goebbels, *Vom Kaiserhof*, p. 261.

58 Cf. Heinrich Bennecke, *Hitler und die SA* (Munich, 1962), and also W. Sauer in Bracher, Sauer and Schulz, *Nationalsozialistische Machtergreifung*, pp. 880ff, pp. 927ff.

59 Cf. K. D. Bracher, 'Stages of Totalitarian "Integration"', in Hajo Holborn (ed.), *Republic to Reich: The Making of the Nazi Revolution* (New York, 1972), p. 115; and Bracher, *German Dictatorship*, p. 206.

60 See Broszat, *Der Staat Hitlers*, pp. 103f.

61 See Hans Mommsen, 'The Political Effects of the Reichstag Fire', in H. A. Turner (ed.), *Nazism and the Third Reich* (New York, 1972), pp. 134f.

62 K. D. Bracher's strongly intentionalistic interpretation, in 'Stages of Totalitarian "Integration"', in my view overrates the degree of central direction involved in spontaneous actions by the SA and party groups.

63 Bracher, Sauer and Schulz, *Nationalsozialistische Machtergreifung*, pp. 460ff.

64 See Diehl-Thiele, *Partei und Staat*, pp. 86ff, and Broszat, *Der Staat Hitlers*, pp. 137ff; Peterson, *Limits of Hitler's Power*, pp. 166ff.

65 See mainly Heinrich Bennecke, *Die Reichswehr und der 'Roehmputsch'* (Munich, 1964). The number of victims is usually overestimated in the relevant literature; there were eighty-eight.

66 The *Reichsstatthaltergesetz* (7 April 1933), the *Neuaufbaugesetz* (30 January 1934) and the measures preceding them were quite inadequately co-ordinated. Cf. Broszat, *Der Staat Hitlers*, pp. 151ff; Diehl-Thiele, *Partei und Staat*, pp. 40ff and 61; also Walter Baum, 'Reichsreform im Dritten Reich', *VgZ*, 3 (1955).

67 Cf. Diehl-Thiele, *Partei und Staat*, pp. 195ff; Mommsen, *Beamtentum*, pp. 117ff.

68 See note 18 above.

69 See Dietrich Orlow, *The History of the Nazi Party 1933–1945* (Pittsburgh, 1973), pp. 102ff, 139ff; Diehl-Thiele, *Partei und Staat*, p. 34.

70 See above all Höhne, *Order of the Death's Head*; Hans Buchheim et al., *Anatomy of the SS-State* (London, 1970).

71 See memorandum of the Gauleiter Weser-Ems (1942) National Archives Microcopy no. T-81, Roll no. R-71, *NSDAP-Parteikanzlei*, pp. 1459f; Orlow, *History of the Nazi Party 1933–1945*, pp. 352f, proves that the memorandum cannot have originated with Röver, but was probably written by his successor, Paul Wegener, and hence reflects the opinions of the Party Chancellery.

72 Orlow, *History of the Nazi Party 1933–1945*, pp. 84ff; Orlow, 'Die Adolf Hitler Schulen', in *VfZ*, 13 (1965); R. Bollmus, *Das Amt Rosenberg*.

73 Speech by Rudolf Hess to the Leader Corps of the NSDAP at the Reichspartei-
    tag in Nuremberg, 16 September 1935 (BA NS 25/item 1183; abstracted in
    Mommsen et al., 'Faschistische Diktatur', pp. 20ff).

74 Cf. Sigmund Neumann, *Permanent Revolution*, pp. 115ff; Franz L. Neumann,
    Democratic and Authoritarian State, p. 249.

75 Apart from W. S. Allen and E. N. Peterson (chaps 4–8), see H.-P. Görgen's
    study, *Düsseldorf und der Nationalsozialismus* (Cologne, 1968). Horst Matzerath,
    Nationalsozialismus und kommkunale Selbstverwaltung (Stuttgart, 1970), has great
    merits, but limits itself to headquarters level. That regional studies are necessary
    and fruitful is shown by Jeremy Noakes's book, already mentioned on several
    occasions.

76 Cf. Orlow, *History of the Nazi Party 1933–1945*, pp. 77ff, 139ff, 339ff, and
    Diehl-Thiele, *Partei und Staat*, pp. 216ff; see also the informative speech by
    Peter Hüttenberger, *Die Gauleiter* (Stuttgart, 1969).

77 Diehl-Thiele, *Partei und Staat*, pp. 197ff.

78 Cf. Klaus Hildebrand, *The Foreign Polich of the Third Reich* (Berkeley, 1973);
    German edn, *Deutsche Aussenpolitik 1933–1945. Kalkül oder Dogma?*, Stuttgart,
    1971); Andreas Hillgruber, *Kontinuität und Diskontinuität in der deutschen Aus-
    senpolitik von Bismarck bis Hitler*, 3rd edn (Düsseldorf, 1971).

79 On the problem of the 'mood' in the Third Reich, see, apart from Heinz
    Boberach, *Meldungen aus dem Reich: Auswahl aus den geheimen Lageberichten des
    Sicherheitsdienstes der SS 1939–1944* (Neuwied, 1965), the investigation by
    Marlis G. Steinert, *Hitler's War and the Germans: Public Mood and Attitude
    during the Second World War* (Athens, Ohio, 1977).

80 M. Broszat, 'Soziale Motivation', p. 405.

81 On national socialist persecution of the Jews, see, as well as the description of
    the Final Solution policy by Raul Hilberg, *The Destruction of the European Jews*
    (Chicago, 1961), the researches by Uwe D. Adam, *Judenpolitik im Dritten Reich*
    (Düsseldorf, 1972), and Karl A. Schleunes, *The Twisted Road to Auschwitz:
    Nazi Policy toward German Jews 1933–1939*, 2nd edn (Urbana, 1990).

82 On euthanasia, see Klaus Dörner, 'Nationalsozialismus und Lebensvernich-
    tung', *VfZ*, 15 (1967), pp. 121–52.

83 See, above all, John S. Conway, *The Nazi Persecution of the Churches* (New
    York, 1968). Günther Lewy, *The Catholic Church and Nazi Germany* (London,
    1954).

84 On the role of the civil service, see Jane Caplan, *Government without Adminis-
    tration: State and Civil Service in Weimar and Nazi Germany* (Oxford, 1988),
    and D. Schoenbaum, *Hitler's Social Revolution*, pp. 193ff.

85 Tim W. Mason, 'Labour in the Third Reich 1933–1939', *Past and Present*, 33
    (1966), pp. 112–41; Hans-Gerd Schumann, *Nationalsozialismus und Gewerk-
    schaftsbewegung* (Frankfurt, 1958); A. Schweitzer, *Big Business in the Third Reich*
    (London, 1964).

86 Typical of this is the commentary by Ernst Rudolf Hubert, *Verfassungsrecht des
    Grossdeutschen Reiches* (Hamburg, 1939); cf. Diehl-Thiele, *Partei und Staat*,
    p. 29, and also Helmut Krausnick et al., *Anatomy of the SS-State* (New York,
    1968), pp. 129, 133.

87 On the resistance movement, see above all Hermann Graml et al., *German Resistance to Hitler* (London, 1970).

88 Cf. R. Hansen, *Das Ende.*

89 See the impressive and still valid report by H. Trevor-Roper, *The Last Days of Hitler*, 1st edn (London, 1947).

90 Cf. Tim W. Mason, 'The Legacy of 1918 for National Socialism', in A. J. Nicholls and E. Matthias (eds), *German Democracy and the Triumph of Hitler* (London, 1971), p. 227.

91 Cf. Fraenkel, *Dual State*, and Buchheim, *Das Dritte Reich*, pp. 133f.

Chapter 8   Hitler's Position in the Nazi System

1 Besides the account by Martin Broszat, *The Hitler State: The Foundations and Development of the Internal Structure of the Third Reich* (London, 1981), see especially the analysis by Lothar Gruchmann, 'Die "Reichsregierung" im Führerstaat. Stellung und Funktion des Kabinetts im nationalsozialistischen Herrschaftssystem', in Günther Doeker and Winfried Steffani (eds), *Klassenjustiz und Pluralismus. Festschrift für Ernst Fraenkel* (Hanover, 1973).

2 Cf. Wolfgang Horn, *Führerideologie und Parteiorganisation in der NSDAP 1919–1933* (Düsseldorf, 1972), p. 268; Broszat, *Hitler State*, pp. 207ff; Alfred Rosenberg too sought a development along these lines.

3 Cf. Hamilton T. Burden, *The Nuremberg Party Rallies 1933–1939* (London, 1967).

4 Cf., for example, the extract from Hess's speech of 16 September 1935 in Hans Mommsen et al., 'Faschistische Diktatur in Deutschland', *Politische Bildung*, vol. 5 (1972), no. 1, pp. 20ff; Hess's speeches at the party's annual rallies may be found in BA NS 26/item 1183.

5 For this cf., besides the account by Klaus-Jürgen Müller, *Das Heer und Hitler. Armee und nationalsozialistisches Regime 1933–1940* (Stuttgart, 1969), the study by Christian Streit, *Keine Kameraden. Die Wehrmacht und die sowjetischen Kriegsgefangenen 1941–1945* (Stuttgart, 1978), esp. pp. 58ff.

6 Karl Dietrich Bracher, *Zeitgeschichtliche Kontroversen. Um Faschismus, Totalitarismus, Demokratie* (Munich, 1976), p. 85.

7 For a synopsis, see Ger van Roon, *Widerstand im Dritten Reich* (Munich, 1979), esp. pp. 146ff.

8 It appears symptomatic that the Führer cult was started by Hitler's closest party colleagues from the Munich days, especially Hess and Esser, and was forced on him to a certain extent; cf. Albrecht Tyrell, *Vom Trommler zum Führer! Der Wandel von Hitlers Selbstverständnis zwischen 1919 und 1924 und die Entwicklung der NSDAP* (Munich, 1975).

9 Cf. Marlis G. Steinert, *Hitlers Krieg und die Deutschen. Stimmung und Haltung der deutschen Bevölkerung im Zweiten Weltkrieg* (Düsseldorf, 1970), pp. 556f.

10 The suggestion by my colleague Winfried Schulze that this attitude had its roots in the German *Kaisermythos* would be worth a detailed examination.

11 Cf. Steinert, *Hitlers Krieg*, pp. 487f.

12 Hans Mommsen, 'Spandauer Tagebücher. Bemerkungen zu den Aufzeich-

nungen Albert Speers im Internationalen Militargefängnis', *PVS*, 17 (1976), pp. 108–14.

13 Cf. Steinert, *Hitlers Krieg*, pp. 334ff; Ernest K. Bramstedt, *Goebbels und die nationalsozialistische Propaganda 1924–1945* (Frankfurt a.M., 1971), pp. 356ff.

14 This is a common thread running through all the attitude reports which refer to dissatisfaction and latent opposition among the population; cf. Martin Broszat et al. (eds), *Bayern in der NS-Zeit*, I: *Soziale Lage und politisches Verhalten der Bevölkerung im Spiegel vertraulicher Berichte* (Munich, 1977), esp. pp. 554f, 595f.

15 My position on this diverges here from the substantially more optimistic assessment by van Roon, *Widerstand*, pp. 39ff; cf. Steinert, *Hitlers Krieg*, p. 589.

16 The material published by Martin Broszat (*Bayern in der NS-Zeit*) is in need of a more differentiated evaluation; the still basic standard work is Heinz Boberach, *Meldungen aus dem Reich. Auswahl aus den geheimen Lageberichten des Sicherheitsdienstes der SS 1939–1944* (Neuwied, 1965).

17 Cf. Hans Mommsen, *Beamtentum im Dritten Reich. Mit ausgewählten Quellen zur nationalsozialistischen Beamtenpolitik* (Stuttgart, 1966), pp. 32ff, and above, note 4.

18 Cf. the basic study on this by Jane Caplan, *Government without Administration: State and Civil Service in Weimar and Nazi Germany* (Oxford, 1988).

19 Cf. Horn, *Führerideologie*, pp. 283ff.

20 Cf. Mommsen, *Beamentum*, pp. 115f.

21 Cf. the memorandum by Paul Wegener of summer 1942 originally attributed to Röver (Dietrich Orlow, *The History of the Nazi Party 1933–1945* [Pittsburgh, 1973], pp. 352f), NSDAP-Parteikanzlei, IfZ (records of the NSDAP Party Chancellery in the Institut für Zeitgeschichte, Munich), sheets 9ff.

22 Horn, *Führerideologie*, pp. 65ff; cf. the basic study by Joseph Myomarkay, *Charisma and Factionalism in the Nazi Party* (Minneapolis, 1967).

23 A conclusive analysis has yet to appear; cf. especially Karl Martin Grass, 'Edgar Jung, Papenkreis und Röhmkrise 1933/34' (Ph.D. thesis, Heidelberg, 1966), esp. pp. 236ff, and further Charles Bloch, *Die SA und die Krise des NS-Regimes 1934* (Frankfurt a.M., 1970), which admittedly suffers from its reliance in part on older, unreliable works.

24 Lammers to Frick on 27 June 1934 (BA R 43 II/495); cf. Peter Diehl-Thiele, *Partei und Staat im Dritten Reich. Untersuchungen zum Verhältnis von NSDAP und innerer Staatsverwaltung 1933–1945* (Munich, 1969), p. 69.

25 Cf. Broszat, *Hitler State*, pp. 112f.

26 For details, see Dietmar Petzina, *Autarkiepolitik im Dritten Reich. Der nationalsozialistische Vierjahresplan* (Stuttgart, 1968).

27 Cf. Hans Mommsen, 'Ausnahmezustand als Herrschaftstechnik des NS-Regimes', in Manfred Funke (ed.), *Deutschland und die Mächte. Materialien zur Aussenpolitik des Dritten Reiches* (Düsseldorf, 1976), pp. 35ff.

28 IfZ, NG-1296, sheet 4.

29 Cf., among others, Hermann Weinkauff, 'Die deutsche Justiz und der Nationalsozialismus. Ein Überblick', in *Die deutsche Justiz und der Nationalsozialismus*, vol. 1 (Stuttgart, 1968), pp. 152ff.

30 Cf. Wolfgang Scheffler, 'Ausgewählte Dokumente zur Geschichte des Novemberpogroms 1938', *APZ, supplement to Parlament*, B 44/78, pp. 3–30.

31 Cf. Hans Mommsen, 'Aufgabenkreis und Verantwortlichkeit des Staatssekretärs der Reichskanzlei Dr Wilhelm Kritzinger', in *Gutachten des Instituts für Zeitgeschichte*, vol. 2 (Stuttgart, 1966).

32 For a particularly clear example of this, see the study by Hans Robinsohn, *Justiz als politische Verfolgung. Die Rechtsprechung in 'Rassenschandefällen' beim Landgericht Hamburg 1936–1943* (Stuttgart, 1977).

33 This was particularly true of the attitude prevalent in the offices which dealt with the exclusion of Jews and other persecuted 'racial' groups from various areas of social life. A typical example was the comment by Johannes Popitz at the heads of department meeting of the Ministry for the Economy on 20 August 1935 that it was essential 'that the government set a certain limit – it doesn't matter where – for the treatment of the Jews, but then makes absolutely sure that this limit is adhered to' (Lösener files, IfZ, F 71/2, note by Lösener of 20 August, sheet 3).

34 Goerdeler's resignation from the post of Lord Mayor of Leipzig in early 1937 following a row over the removal of the Mendelssohn memorial was symptomatic of this moderate anti-semitic attitude which exempted Jews either assimilated by or part of German culture (cf. Gerhard Ritter, *Carl Goerdeler und die deutsche Widerstandsbewegung*, 2nd edn [Munich, 1964], p. 89; all references are to this second German edtion. Cf. Gerhard Ritter, *The German Resistance: Carl Goerdeler's Struggle against Tyranny* [New York, 1958]).

35 Cf. Helmut Heiber, *Joseph Goebbels* (Berlin, 1962), p. 280.

36 Martin Broszat, 'Soziale Motivation und Führerbindung des Nationalsozialismus', *VfZ*, 18 (1970), pp. 392ff.

37 Cf. Edward N. Peterson, *The Limits of Hitler's Power* (Princeton, 1969), pp. 7ff; William Carr, *Hitler: A Study in Personality and Politics* (London, 1978), pp. 40ff; for a dissenting interpretation, Joachim C. Fest, *Hitler* (London, 1974), pp. 536ff, though cf. p. 931.

38 Albert Speer, *Spandauer Tagebücher* (Frankfurt a.M., 1975), is rich in examples illustrating this. An analysis of the disseminators of the various information services in the system would be very useful.

39 This was the case, for example, with the state secretary of the Reich Chancellery, Dr Kritzinger (see note 31).

40 Cf. Albert Speer, 'Entgegnung auf die Ausführung von Professor Erich Goldhagen in *Midstream*, Oktober 1971', July 1972, and 'Ergänzung zu meinen Ausführungen über den Artikel von Professor Erich Goldhagen', July 1973 (IfZ, Archiv ED 99). Cf. note 12.

41 Cf. Broszat, *Hitler State*, pp. 112ff.

42 Cf. Gruchmann, 'Reichsregierung', p. 201.

43 I have introduced this term because the new bureaucratic structures which arose under the Third Reich, such as the Four-Year Plan, the RSHA (Reich Security Head Office) and the Office of the Reich Commissar for the Strengthening of Germandom, cannot be described simply as party authorities or quasi-

party institutions existing alongside the traditional administration of the state; their function was to substantially replace or to act as a means of circumventing the existing mechanisms of state controls.

44 Cf. Robert Koehl, 'Feudal Aspects of National Socialism', *APSR*, 54 (1960), pp. 921–33.
45 A notable example of this was Hitler's policy towards the United States; cf. Hans-Jürgen Schröder, *Deutschland und die Vereinigten Staaten 1933–1939* (Wiesbaden, 1970).
46 Cf. Gruchmann, 'Reichsregierung', pp. 199ff.
47 Cf. Gerhard L. Weinberg (ed.), *Hitler's Secret Book* (New York, 1962).
48 Cf. Martin Broszat, 'Hitler und die Genesis der "Endlösung"', *VfZ*, 25 (1977), pp. 746ff.
49 Cf. Karl A. Schleunes, *The Twisted Road to Auschwitz: Nazi Policy toward German Jews 1933–1939*, 2nd edn (Urbana, 1990).
50 The basic work on this is Andreas Hillgruber, 'Die "Endlösung" und das deutsche Ostimperium als Kernstück des rassenideologischen Programms des Nationalsozialismus', *VfZ*, 20 (1972), pp. 133–53.
51 Cf. Streit, *Keine Kameraden*, pp. 217ff; further Helmut Krausnick, 'Kommissarbefehl und "Gerichtsbarkeitserlass Barbarossa" in neuer Sicht', *VfZ*, 25 (1977), pp. 682–738.
52 Streit, *Keine Kameraden*, pp. 109ff.
53 Cf. Robert G. L. Waite, *The Psychopathic God Adolf Hitler* (New York, 1977), pp. 219ff. I cannot share Waite's far-reaching psychological conclusions, particularly the parallels he draws with German history on p. 244; cf. further Rudolf Binion, *Hitler among the Germans* (New York, 1976). Carr, *Hitler*, pp. 45ff. Cf. Helm Stierlin, *Adolf Hitler: Familienperspektiven* (Frankfurt a.M., 1975), esp. pp. 104ff.
54 In this regard I find a comment attributed to Otto Wagener Pfeffer von Salomon from 1929 worthy of note: Hitler's undoubted and unchallenged position as leader, he said, was the 'great excuse' of his closest party colleagues: 'Woe betide if the momentum of this movement gets steered in a false direction, in other words if the Führer listens to bad advisers or . . . if he himself aims too high! They would go along with him, blindly follow in his tracks, even if it led them into the arms of certain death' (Henry A. Turner [ed.], *Hitler aus nächster Nahe. Aufzeichnungen eines Vertrauten 1929–1932* [Frankfurt a.M., 1978], pp. 29f).
55 Steinert, *Hitlers Krieg*, pp. 109ff.

Chapter 9   20 July 1944 and the German Labour Movement

1 On the politics of the SPD before the Nazi seizure of power, cf. Erich Matthias, 'Die Sozialdemokratische Partei Deutschlands', in idem and Rudolf Morsey (eds), *Das Ende der Parteien 1933* (Düsseldorf, 1960), pp. 127ff; Hagen Schulze, *Anpassung oder Widerstand? Aus den Akten des Parteivorstands der deutschen Sozialdemokratie 1932/33* [= *AfS*, Beiheft 4] (Bonn and Bad Godesberg, 1975), pp. XIXff; for the KPD, see especially, besides the account by Siegfried Bahne

in Matthias and Morsey, *Ende der Parteien*, pp. 656ff, Hermann Weber, *Die Wandlung des deutschen Kommunismus. Die Stalinisierung der KPD in der Weimarer Republik*, vol. 1 (Frankfurt a.M., 1969), pp. 242ff.

2 Cf. Horst Duhnke, *Die KPD von 1933 bis 1945* (Cologne, 1972), pp. 62ff; Klaus Schönhoven, 'Arbeiterbewegung und Nationalsozialismus', in Rudolf Lill and Heinrich Oberreuter (eds), *Machtverfall und Machtergreifung. Aufstieg und Herrschaft des Nationalsozialismus* (Munich, 1983), pp. 223–50; see also Konrad Repgen, 'Ein KPD-Verbot im Jahre 1933', *HZ*, 240 (1985), pp. 90ff; Cf. further the survey in Karl Dietrich Bracher, Wolfgang Sauer and Gerhard Schulz, *Die nationalsozialistische Machtergreifung* (Cologne and Opladen, 1960), pp. 62, 193ff.

3 Cf. Gerhard Beier, 'Zur Entstehung des Führerkreises der vereinigten Gewerkschaften Ende April 1933', *AfS*, 15 (1975), pp. 365ff; idem, *Das Lehrstück vom 1. und 2. Mai 1933* (Frankfurt a.M., 1975). For the historical background to the politics involved, see also Hans Mommsen, 'Die deutschen Gewerkschaften zwischen Anpassung und Widerstand', in idem, *Arbeiterbewegung und nationale Frage* (Göttingen, 1979), pp. 376f. Cf. further the very well documented though rather one-sided account of trade union politics in this period by Hannes Heer, *Burgfrieden oder Klassenkampf? Zur Politik der sozialdemokratischen Gewerkschaften 1930–1933* (Neuwied and Berlin, 1971), pp. 68ff.

4 Cf. Almut Schunck and Hans-Josef Steinberg, 'Mit Wahlen und Waffen. Der Weg der österreichischen Sozialdemokratie in die Niederlage', in W. Huber and J. Schwerdtfeger (eds), *Frieden, Gewalt, Sozialismus. Studien zur Geschichte der sozialistischen Arbeiterbewegung* (Stuttgart, 1976), pp. 464ff; Hans Mommsen, 'Social Democracy on the Defensive: The Immobility of the SPD and the Rise of National Socialism', in this volume, p. 46.

5 Patrik von zur Mühlen, 'Sozialdemokraten gegen Hitler', in Richard Löwenthal and Patrik von zur Mühlen (eds), *Widerstand und Verweigerung in Deutschland 1933–1945* (Berlin, 1982), pp. 59ff; cf. also the survey by Peter Grasmann, *Sozialdemokraten gegen Hitler 1933–1945* (Munich, 1976).

6 Cf. Matthias, 'Sozialdemokratische Partei', p. 144.

7 Cf. Dorothea Beck, *Julius Leber. Sozialdemokrat zwischen Reform und Widerstand* (Berlin, 1983), pp. 143ff.

8 Cf. Hans-Gerd Schumann, *Nationalsozialismus und Gewerkschaftsbewegung. Die Vernichtung der deutschen Gewerkschaften und der Ausbau der 'Deutschen Arbeitsfront'* (Hanover, 1958), p. 128, and also Timothy W. Mason, *Arbeiterklasse und Volksgemeinschaft. Dokumente und Materialien zur deutschen Arbeiterpolitik 1936–1939* (Opladen, 1975), pp. 89f.

9 Cf. Walter Ulbricht, *Die Legende vom 'deutschen Sozialismus'* (Berlin, 1945), pp. 61f.

10 Cf. *Deutschlandberichte der Sozialdemokratischen Partei (Sopade) 1934–1940*, 7 vols (Frankfurt a.M., 1980). These were also published as *Reports from Germany* for international distribution.

11 Cf. von zur Mühlen, 'Sozialdemokraten', pp. 66f; Frank Moraw, *Die Parole der 'Einheit' und die Sozialdemokratie* (Bonn and Bad Godesberg, 1973), p. 53; cf. also Hans Mommsen, 'Aktionsformen und Bedingungen des Widerstands in

der Arbeiterschaft', *Widerstandsbewegungen in Deutschland und Polen während des Zweiten Weltkrieges* [= *Schriftenreihe des Georg-Eckert-Instituts für internationale Schulbuchforschung*, 22/1], 2nd edn (Braunschweig, 1983), pp. 70ff.

12 Cf. Joachim G. Leithäuser, *Wilhelm Leuschner. Ein Leben für die Republik* (Cologne, 1962), pp. 170f, 181ff; Elfriede Nebgen, *Jakob Kaiser. Der Widerstandskämpfer* (Stuttgart, 1967), pp. 39ff. Gerhard Beier's portrayal of the illegal Reich Leadership (*Die illegale Reichsleitung der Gewerkschaften 1933–1941* [Cologne, 1981], pp. 45f) is too optimistic in its assessment of its longer-term organizational cohesiveness.

13 Cf. Moraw, *Parole der 'Einheit'*, pp. 49ff.

14 On the Solf Circle, cf. the survey by Peter Hoffmann, *The History of the German Resistance, 1933–1945*, 3rd edn (London, 1977), pp. 31f.

15 The literature on this topic is unanimous in asserting that this was the result of betrayal by a Gestapo spy. According to information given orally to the author by Theodor Steltzer, however, it would seem more likely that it was the result of a tapped telephone conversation.

16 Cf. Ger van Roon, *Neuordnung im Widerstand. Der Kreisauer Kreis innerhalb der deutschen Widerstandsbewegung* (Munich, 1967), esp. pp. 123ff.

17 Cf. Hans Mommsen, 'Gesellschaftsbild und Verfassungpläne des deutschen Widerstands', in Walter Schmitthenner and Hans Buchheim (eds), *Der deutsche Widerstand gegen Hitler. Vier kritische Studien* (Cologne and Berlin, 1966), pp. 18f; idem, 'German Society and the Resistance to Hitler', in this volume, p. 213.

18 Cf. Mason, *Arbeiterklasse*, pp. 79ff.

19 Cf. Moraw, *Parole der 'Einheit'*, p. 47; Nebgen, *Jakob Kaiser*, pp. 72ff; Mommsen, 'Deutsche Gewerkschaften', p. 377.

20 Emil Henk, *Die Tragödie des 20. Juli 1944*, 2nd edn (Heidelberg, 1946), pp. 43ff.

21 On Habermann, cf. Nebgen, *Jakob Kaiser*, pp. 50ff.

22 Cf. Axel Schildt, *Militärdiktatur und Massenbasis. Die Querfrontkonzeption der Reichswehrführung um General von Schleicher am Ende der Weimarer Republik* (Frankfurt a.M., 1981), pp. 166ff.

23 Cf. Mommsen, 'Gesellschaftsbild', pp. 63f.

24 Cf. Beck, *Julius Leber*, pp. 168f.

25 Cf. Emil Henk's rather sanguine account of the preparations made in Hessen for the coup, *Tragödie des 20. Juli*, pp. 48ff. These were without a doubt an exception. On the other hand, Leuschner's plans regarding the personnel with which he intended staffing the unions were largely uncovered.

26 Cf. *Spiegelbild einer Verschwörung. Die Kaltenbrunner-Berichte an Bormann und Hitler über das Attentat des 20. Juli 1944*, published by the Archiv Peter (Stuttgart, 1961), pp. 496ff; Beier, 'Zur Entstehung des Führerkreises', pp. 385ff; cf. further Leithäuser, *Wilhelm Leuschner*, p. 215.

27 Goerdeler's essay 'Das Ziel' ('The Goal'), in Wilhelm Ritter von Schramm (ed.), *Beck und Goerdeler. Gemeinschaftsdokumente für den Frieden 1941–1944* (Munich, 1965), p. 117.

28 Cf. Gerhard Ritter, *Carl Goerdeler und die deutsche Widerstandsbewegung*, 2nd edn (Munich, 1964), pp. 293f. (All references are to this second German edition. Cf. Gerhard Ritter, *The German Resistance: Carl Goerdeler's Struggle against Tyranny* [New York, 1958]).

29 Günther Schmölders's opinion that the Kreisau Circle would have rejected nationalization of the raw materials sector is inaccurate (idem, *Personalistischer Sozialismus. Die Wirtschaftsordnungskonzeption des Kreisauer Kreises der deutschen Widerstandsbewegung* [Opladen, 1969], pp. 51ff).

30 Ideas in this direction were advocated particularly by Walberberg; cf. Mommsen, 'Gesellschaftsbild', p. 2435, no. 21.

31 Cf. Friedrich Zunkel, *Industrie und Staatssozialismus. Der Kampf um die Wirtschaftsordnung in Deutschland 1914–1918* (Düsseldorf, 1974).

32 Literally, 'hydrocephalic organizations'. Cf. Moltke's letter to Lionel Curtis of 18 April 1942, reprinted in Michael Balfour and Julian Frisby, *Helmuth James von Moltke: A Leader against Hitler* (London, 1972), p. 135.

33 Cf. van Roon, *Neuordnung*, p. 569.

34 Cf. ibid., pp. 429f; Mommsen, 'Gesellschaftsbild', pp. 76ff.

35 Cf. Christine Blumenberg-Lampe, *Das wirtschaftliche Programm der 'Freiburger Kreise'. Entwurf einer freiheitlich-sozialen Nackkriegswirtschaft* (Berlin, 1973); Schmölders, *Personalisticher Sozialismus*, pp. 40ff.

36 Cf. Ritter, *Carl Goerdeler*, pp. 55f. Goerdeler was a decided enemy of the eight-hour day. For the contemporary background to this thinking, cf. Claus-Dieter Krohn, 'Autoritärer Kapitalismus. Wirtschaftskonzeptionen im Übergang von der Weimarer Republik zum Nationalsozialismus', in Dirk Stegmann, Bernd-Jürgen Wendt and Peter Christian Witt (eds), *Industrielle Gesellschaft und politisches System. Beiträge zur politischen Sozialgeschichte* (Bonn, 1978), pp. 120ff.

37 Cf. Ritter, *Carl Goerdeler*, pp. 305f.

38 Cf. ibid., pp. 315f; Mommsen, 'Gesellschaftsbild', p. 62, and the material referred to there.

39 Cf. *Kaltenbrunner-Berichte*, pp. 497f.

40 Ibid., pp. 599f.

41 Cf. Nebgen, *Jakob Kaiser*, p. 166; cf. Larry E. Jones, 'Adam Stegerwald und die Krise des deutschen Parteiensystems', *VfZ*, 27 (1979), pp. 1–29; Mommsen, 'Gesellschaftsbild', pp. 74ff.

42 Cf. Mommsen, 'Gesellschaftsbild', pp. 58f.

43 Cf. van Roon, *Neuordnung*, pp. 390ff; Mommsen, 'Gesellschaftsbild', pp. 52ff.

44 Cf. Martin Martiny, 'Die Entstehung und politische Bedeutung der *Neuen Blätter für den Sozialismus* und ihres Freundeskreises', *VfZ*, 25 (1977), pp. 373–419; van Roon, *Neuordnung*, pp. 123ff; Moraw, *Parole der 'Einheit'*, pp. 13ff; Ursula Schulz (ed.), *Adolf Reichwein. Ein Lebensbild* (Munich 1977), esp. pp. 261f.

45 Cf. Walter Hammer, *Theo Haubach zum Gedächtnis* (Frankfurt a.M., 1955); van Roon, *Neuordnung*, pp. 181ff.

46 Van Roon, *Neuordnung*, pp. 228ff; Balfour and Frisby, *Moltke*, pp. 180, 197, and cf. p. 234.

47 While Moltke's code-name for Leuschner was 'Uncle', he called Leber the 'replacement uncle', which is indicative of the hopes he placed in the social democrats. Cf. Balfour and Frisby, *Moltke*, pp. 285f, 288f.

48 Beck, *Julius Leber*, pp. 177ff.

49 The so-called 'Turkey Essay', reprinted in van Roon, *Neuordnung*, pp. 582ff; cf. ibid., pp. 322.

50 Emil Henk wrote of a meeting of the social democratic members of the Kreisau Circle at Christmas 1942 where it was agreed that any attempt at a coup should be postponed until the Allied invasion, expected around this time, so as to prevent an overpreponderant role for the Soviet Union on the continent; Leuschner is supposed to have only very reluctantly agreed to this position. Cf. *Tragödie des 20. Juli*, pp. 35f.

51 Cf. Mommsen, 'Gesellschaftsbild', pp. 61ff.

52 *Kaltenbrunner-Berichte*, p. 188.

53 Cf. ibid., p. 465.

54 Cf. Beck, *Julius Leber*, pp. 183f.

55 See the material in Mommsen, 'Gesellschaftsbild', pp. 83ff.

56 Cf. Hans Mommsen, 'Verfassungs- und Verwaltungsreformpläne der Widerstandsgruppen des 20. Juli 1944', in Jürgen Schmädeke and Peter Steinbach (eds), *Der Widerstand gegen den Nationalsozialismus. Die deutsche Gesellschaft und der Widerstand gegen Hitler* (Munich, 1985), pp. 570ff.

57 Cf. *Kaltenbrunner-Berichte*, p. 497.

58 Full text in van Roon, *Neuordnung*, p. 589; cf. ibid., p. 260; cf. Mommsen, 'Gesellschaftsbild', p. 80, and also *Kaltenbrunner-Berichte*, p. 501.

59 Cf. Balfour and Frisby, *Moltke*, pp. 285f.

60 Cf. Beck, *Julius Leber*, p. 185.

61 Cf. Eberhard Zeller, *Der Geist der Freiheit. Der zwanzigste Juli*, 4th edn (Munich, 1963), p. 107.

62 Cf. the 'Turkey Essay' (note 49 above).

63 Cf. Mommsen, 'Gesellschaftsbild', p. 79.

64 Cf. *Kaltenbrunner-Berichte*, pp. 234f, 501, and also Mommsen, 'Gesellschaftsbild', p. 82.

65 Cf. Blumenberg-Lampe, *Wirtschaftliches Programm*; Schmölders, *Personalistischer Sozialismus*, esp. pp. 57ff; Mommsen, 'Gesellschaftsbild', pp. 40ff.

66 Cf. Schmölder's essay, 'Wirtschaft und Wirtschaftsführung in einem Europa-Block nach dem Kriege', in idem, *Personalistischer Sozialismus*, pp. 78f, 89f.

67 Cf. ibid., pp. 57ff, and also the study by Ludolf Herbst, *Der totale Krieg und die Ordnung der Wirtschaft. Die Kriegswirtschaft im Spannungsfeld von Politik, Ideologie und Propaganda 1939–1945* (Stuttgart, 1982), which shows that similar ideas were being considered in Otto Ohlendorff's circle.

68 For Schulenberg's ideas on social policy, cf. Hans Mommsen, 'Fritz-Dietlof von der Schulenburg und die preussische Tradition', *VfZ*, 32 (1984), pp. 232f; Ritter, *Carl Goerdeler*, pp. 312f.

69 Cf. Mommsen, 'Gesellschaftsbild', pp. 42f.

70 Cf. Balfour and Frisby, *Moltke*, pp. 207ff, 375 n. 3.

71 Cf. Joachim Kramarz, *Claus Graf Stauffenberg* (Frankfurt a.M., 1965), pp. 172ff;
    Kaltenbrunner-Berichte, pp. 234, 538.
72 For an overall survey, see Mommsen, 'Verfassungs' und Verwaltungsreform-
    pläne', pp. 583ff.
73 Cf. Moltke's memorandum and plans of December 1943 in van Roon, *Neuord-
    nung*, p. 583; Mommsen, 'Gesellschaftsbild', pp. 80f.
74 Cf. Henk, *Tragödie des 20. Juli*, pp. 52f; for the strategy of the KPD Operative
    Leadership cf. Detlev Peukert, *Die KPD im Widerstand. Verfolgung und Unter-
    grundarbeit an Rhein und Ruhr 1933–1945* (Wuppertal, 1980), pp. 415f.
75 Cf. the misleading account in Hans Bernd Gisevius, *Bis zum bitteren Ende*,
    vol. 2 (Hamburg, 1947).
76 Cf. *Kaltenbrunner-Berichte*, pp. 497, 512.

Chapter 10   German Society and the Resistance to Hitler

1 On research on the resistance by East German historians, cf. the literature
   survey in Dieter Lange et al. (eds), 'Forschungen zur deutschen Geschichte
   1933–1945', *Zeitschrift für Geschichtswissenschaft*, 28 (1980), supplement volume
   Analysen und Berichte, pp. 281ff; further Heinz Kühnrich, *Die KPD im Kampf
   gegen die faschistische Diktatur* (Berlin [GDR], 1983), and Klaus Mammach, *Der
   antifaschistische deutsche Widerstand 1933–1939*, 6th edn (Berlin [GDR], 1984).
   Cf. Hans Mommsen, 'Der 20 Juli 1944 aus der historiographischen Sicht des
   geteilten Deutschlands', *Politik und Kultur*, vol. 11 (1984), no. 4, pp. 9–20.
2 For example in Sebastian Haffner, *Anmerkungen zu Hitler* (Munich, 1978),
   pp. 76f, 176f. The Kreisau Circle is not even mentioned by Gordon A. Craig,
   Germany 1866–1945, 3rd edn (Oxford, 1981).
3 Cf. the pioneering study by Hans Rothfels, *Die deutsche Opposition gegen Hitler.
   Eine Würdigung*, 1st edn (Krefeld, 1949, new edns Frankfurt a.M., 1958, and
   Munich, 1969); following in his tracks came Eberhard Zeller, *Der Geist der
   Freiheit. Der zwanzigste Juli*, 4th edn (Munich, 1963); Erich Zimmermann and
   Hans Adolf Jacobsen (eds), *20. Juli 1944*, 3rd edn (Bonn, 1960); *Vollmacht des
   Gewissens*, 2 vols. (published by Europäische Publikation eingetragener Verein,
   Frankfurt a.M., 1960, 1965); John H. McCloy, *Die Verschwörung gegen Hitler.
   Ein Geschenk an die deutsche Zukunft* (Stuttgart, 1963). For an assessment of the
   historiography, see Hans Mommsen, 'Begriff und Problematik des deutschen
   Widerstands gegen Hitler in der zeitgeschichtlichen Forschung', in *Wider-
   standsbewegungen in Deutschland und in Polen während des Zweiten Weltkrieges
   [= Schriftenreihe des Georg-Eckert-Instituts für internationale Schulbuchforschung*,
   22/1], 2nd edn (Braunschweig, 1983), pp. 16–23.
4 Bodo Scheurig, *Ewald von Kleist-Schmenzin. Ein Konservativer gegen Hitler*
   (Oldenburg, 1968). Particularly notable among the early national conservative
   opponents of Hitler were Hans Oster (see Romedio G. Graf von Thun-
   Hohenstein, *Der Verschwörer. General Oster und die Militäropposition* [Berlin,
   1982], pp. 45ff), Adam von Trott zu Solz (see Henry A. Malone, *Der Werdegang*

eines Verschwörers. Adam von Trott zu Solz [Berlin, 1985]) and Helmuth James von Moltke.

5 Heinz Höhne, *Mordsache Röhm. Hitlers Durchbruch zur Alleinherrschaft 1933–34* (Hamburg, 1984), pp. 232ff.

6 Hermann Graml, 'Die aussenpolitischen Vorstellungen es deutschen Widerstands', in Walter Schmitthenner and Hans Buchheim (eds), *Der deutsche Widerstand gegen Hitler. Vier Kritische Studien* (Cologne and Berlin, 1966), pp. 152f. Cf. Klaus-Jürgen Müller, 'Die deutsche Militäropposition gegen Hitler. Zum Problem ihrer Interpretation und Analyse', in idem, *Armee, Politik und Gesellschaft in Deutschland 1933–1945* (Paderborn, 1979), pp. 101ff.

7 Peter Ludlow, 'Papst Pius XII., die britische Regierung und die deutsche Opposition im Winter 1939/40', *VfZ*, 22 (1974), pp. 299–341.

8 Peter Grassmann, *Sozialdemokraten gegen Hitler 1933–1945* (Munich, 1976); Richard Löwenthal and Patrik von zur Mühlen (eds), *Widerstand und Verweigerung in Deutschland 1933–1945* (Berlin, 1982); Hans Mommsen, 'Aktionsformen und Bedingungen des Widerstands in der Arbeiterschaft', in *Widerstandsbewegungen in Deutschland*, pp. 70ff.

9 Christian Streit, *Keine Kameraden. Die Wehrmacht und die sowjetischen Kriegsgefangenen 1941–1945* (Stuttgart, 1978), pp. 33ff.

10 *Spiegelbild einer Verschwörung. Die Kaltenbrunner-Berichte an Bormann und Hitler über das Attentat des 20 Juli 1944*, published by the Archiv Peter (Stuttgart, 1961), p. 111; Christian Müller, *Oberst i.G. Stauffenberg. Eine Biographie* (Düsseldorf, n.d. [1971]), pp. 440ff.

11 On the ever increasing complicity of the army, see Klaus-Jürgen Müller, *Das Heer und Hitler. Armee und nationalsozialistisches Regime 1933–1940* (Stuttgart, 1969), and also Manfred Messerschmidt, *Die Wehrmacht im NS-Staat. Zeit der Indoktrination* (Hamburg, 1969). On the internal disintegration of the governmental system, cf., besides Martin Broszat, *The Hitler State: The Foundations and Development of the Internal Structure of the Third Reich* (London, 1981), especially Lothar Gruchmann, 'Die "Reichsregierung" im Führerstaat. Stellung und Funktion des Kabinetts im nationalsozialistischen Herrschaftssystem', in Günther Doeker and Winfried Steffani (eds), *Klassenjustiz und Pluralismus. Festschrift für Ernst Fraenkel* (Hanover, 1973), pp. 187–223.

12 Ian Kershaw, *The Hitler Myth: Image and Reality in the Third Reich* (Oxford, 1987).

13 Peter Hoffmann, 'Zum Ablauf des Staatsstreichsversuches des 20 Juli 1944 in den Wehrkreisen', *Wehrwissenschaftliche Rundschau*, 14 (1964), pp. 377–97, and also idem, *The History of the German Resistance 1933–1945*, 3rd edn (London, 1977), pp. 417ff.

14 *Vollmacht des Gewissens*, vol. 1; cf. as opposed to this Dieter Ehlers, *Technik und Moral einer Verschwörung. Der Aufstand am 20 Juli 1944* (Bonn, 1964), pp. 59f.

15 Gerhard Ritter, *Carl Goerdeler und die deutsche Widerstandsbewegung*, 2nd edn (Munich, 1964), p. 315. (References are to this second German edition. Cf. Gerhard Ritter, *The German Resistance: Carl Goerdeler's Struggle against Tyranny* [New York, 1958]).

16 Fabian von Schlabrendorff, *Offiziere gegen Hitler*, new edn (Berlin, 1984), p. 129; cf. Bodo Scheurig, *Henning von Tresckow. Eine Biographie*, 4th edn (Oldenburg, 1973), pp. 184f.

17 Stauffenberg was fully aware of this situation; cf. Müller, *Oberst i.G. Stauffenberg*, pp. 346f.

18 Rothfels, *Deutsche Opposition*, pp. 168f.

19 Ger van Roon, *Neuordnung im Widerstand. Der Kreisauer Kreis innerhalb der deutschen Widerstandsbewegung* (Munich, 1967), pp. 226ff.

20 Hans Mommsen, 'Gesellschaftsbild und Verfassungspläne des deutschen Widerstands', in Schmitthenner and Buchheim, *Deutscher Widerstand*, pp. 73ff.

21 Albert Krebs, *Fritz-Dietlof von der Schulenburg. Zwischen Staatsraison und Hochverrat* (Hamburg, 1964), pp. 191ff.

22 Hoffmann, *History of the German Resistance*, pp. 516f.

23 Mommsen, 'Gesellschaftsbild', pp. 119f.

24 It was characteristic of the conspiracy that practical politicians, such as Emil Henk, who functioned as Mierendorff's adviser, and parliamentarians, such as Ludwig Bergsträsser, who was in contact with Leuschner, were not directly involved in it.

25 Gerhard Beier, 'Zur Entstehung des Führerkreises der vereinigten Gewerkschaften Ende April 1933', *AfS*, 15 (1975), pp. 365ff, and also Hans Mommsen, 'Die deutschen Gewerkschaften zwischen Anpassung und Widerstand', in idem, *Arbeiterbewegung und nationale Frage* (Göttingen, 1979), pp. 376ff.

26 Mommsen, 'Gesellschaftsbild', pp. 151f, and also Dorothea Beck, *Julius Leber. Sozialdemokrat zwischen Reform und Widerstand* (Berlin, 1983), pp. 176f.

27 Mommsen, 'Gesellschaftsbild', pp. 131f; it should be remembered in this context that leading military figures such as Beck believed the misinformation being disseminated by Göring and Himmler to be true and operated on the presumption that an SA revolution was imminent and would lead to the proclamation of a military state of emergency.

28 Cf. on this Ritter, *Carl Goerdeler* (Stuttgart, 1954 edn), pp. 308ff.

29 Hans Mommsen, 'Fritz-Dietlof von der Schulenburg und die preussische Tradition', *VfZ*, 32 (1984), pp. 213–39.

30 Moltke's correspondence with Peter Graf Yorck von Wartenburg of summer 1940, published in van Roon, *Neuordnung*, pp. 479ff; cf. pp. 372f.

31 This was the case with the Reich Property Office and the separate training structures for administrative and legal officials which they sought, their plans for a territorial reorganization of the Reich and the creation of a legislative senate. Schulenburg maintained the closest relations with State Secretary Stuckart and Popitz was no different. On this whole issue, cf. Peter Diehl-Thiele, *Partei und Staat im Dritten Reich. Untersuchungen zum Verhältnis von NSDAP und innerer Staatsverwaltung 1933–1945* (Munich, 1969).

32 Christof Dipper, 'Der Widerstand gegen Hitler und die Judenfrage', *GuG*, 9 (1983), pp. 349–80, which is somewhat unbalanced in its evaluation of the material, not taking adequate cognizance of the fact that the majority of national conservatives, very much in the tradition of German conservatism since the Tivoli Programme, advocated de-assimilation of the Jews, with the exception

of native German assimilated Jews. Cf. Mommsen, 'Gesellschaftsbild', p. 130.

33 For example, Edgar Jung, *Die Herrschaft der Minderwertigen, ihr Zerfall und ihre Ablösung durch ein neues Reich*, 2nd edn (Berlin, 1930), pp. 325f. For an overview, see Klaus Fritzsche, *Politische Romantik und Gegenrevolution. Fluchtwege in der Krise der bürgerlichen Gesellschaft: Das Beispiel des Tat-Kreisees* (Frankfurt a.M., 1976), pp. 134ff.

34 Mommsen, 'Gesellschaftsbild', p. 159.

35 Cf. Goerdeler's essay 'Das Ziel' ('The Goal'), in Wilhelm Ritter von Schramm (ed.), *Beck und Goerdeler. Gemeinschaftsdokumente für den Frieden 1941–1944* (Munich, 1965), p. 133, and cf. p. 31. There is a characteristic reference here to a 'non-class national consciousness'.

36 Mommsen, 'Fritz-Dietlof von der Schulenburg', p. 222.

37 Essay of September 1943 on 'Bombing Destruction and Reconstruction', also essays on 'Reform of the Public Administration and the Structure of the Reich' and on social policy (mid-1943) in BA NL 301/2.

38 Mommsen, 'Gesellschaftsbild', pp. 158f. The idea that the Kreisau Circle concentrated exclusively on plans for a new order for the post-Nazi era is still very widespread in the literature on the resistance. See also the documentary material published in Michael Balfour and Julian Frisby, *Helmuth James von Moltke: A Leader against Hitler* (London, 1972).

39 Martin Broszat, 'Resistenz und Widerstand', in Martin Broszat et al.,(eds), *Bayern in der NS-Zeit*, IV: *Herrschaft und Gesellschaft in Konflikt*, pt C (Munich, 1981), pp. 691–709; Peter Hüttenberger, 'Vorüberlegungen zum "Widerstandsbegriff"', in Jürgen Kocka (ed.), *Theorien in der Praxis des Historikers* [= *GuG*, Sonderheft 3] (Göttingen, 1977), pp. 117–34.

40 Rainer A. Blasius, *Für Grossdeutschland – gegen den grossen Krieg. Staatssekretär Ernst Freiherr von Weizsäcker in den Krisen um die Tschechoslowakei und Polen 1938/39* (Cologne, 1981); Heinz Höhne, *Canaris* (London, 1979).

41 Walter Hammer, 'Die "Gewitteraktion" vom 22.8.1944', *Freiheit und Recht, 8/9* (1959), pp. 15ff. According to Hammer, it was originally code-named 'Aktion Gitter' (= 'Operation [Prison] Bars').

42 The evidence in David Irving's book, *On the Trail of the Fox: The Life of Field Marshal Erwin Rommel* (London, 1977), that Rommel was neither initiated into the assassination plot nor decided on whether to support it, is correct.

43 For an analysis, see Mommsen, 'Gesellschaftsbild', pp. 132ff; see also the now partly outdated account by Werner Münchheimer, 'Verfassungs- und Verwaltungsreformbestrebungen der deutschen Opposition gegen Hitler zum 20 Juli 1944', *Europa-Archiv*, 5 (1950), pp. 3188ff.

44 Eberhard Schanbacher, *Parlamentarische Wahlen und Wahlsystem in der Weimarer Republik* (Düsseldorf, 1982), pp. 147f.

45 Cf. Walter Lipgens, *Europa-Föderationspläne der Widerstandsbewegungen 1940–1945* (Munich, 1968).

46 Both the early drafts by Popitz, Hassell, Jessen and Beck for a new social order for the post-Nazi era and the deliberations of the Kreisau and Goerdeler Circles represented long-term plans and did not involve any consideration at all of what measures would be necessary to secure a new government in the

event of the successful overthrow of Hitler. This does not necessarily mean that many of the conspirators would not have radically changed their thinking had a dramatic change in the political situation occurred.

47 On Theodor Heuss, who was in personal contact with many of the conspirators, including Goerdeler, cf. Ralf Dahrendorf and Martin Vogt (eds), *Theodor Heuss. Politiker und Publizist* (Tübingen, 1984), pp. 241, 243f.

48 Mommsen, 'Gesellschaftsbild', p. 75; this has been confirmed by recent studies on the attitude of the working class during the war; Wolfgang Werner, *'Bleib übrig!' Deutsche Arbeiter in der nationalsozialistischen Kriegswirtschaft* (Düsseldorf, 1983); Gustav-Hermann Seebold, *Ein Stahlkonzern im Dritten Reich. Der Bochumer Verein von 1927 bis 1945* (Wuppertal, 1981).

49 Marlis G. Steinert, *Hitlers Krieg und die Deutschen. Stimmung und Haltung der deutschen Bevölkerung im Zweiten Weltkrieg* (Düsseldorf, 1970), pp. 471f.

50 Cf. Emil Henk, *Die Tragödie des 20. Juli 1944*, 2nd edn (Heidelberg, 1946); Detlev Peukert, *Die KPD im Widerstand. Verfolgung und Untergrundarbeit an Rhein und Ruhr 1933–1945* (Wuppertal, 1980); Mommsen, 'Aktionsformen', pp. 70ff.

51 Cf. the (somewhat uncritical) account by Richard Hanser, *Deutschland zuliebe. Die Geschichte der Weissen Rose* (Munich, 1982); Detlev Peukert, *Die Edelweisspiraten. Protestbewegung jugendlicher Arbeiter im Dritten Reich. Eine Dokumentation* (Cologne, 1980). The 'Edelweiss Pirates' were without a doubt uncompromisingly opposed to the entire Nazi system; but it is significant that they were not in any way a product of the traditional organized labour movement. Cf. Detlev Peukert, 'Protest und Widerstand von Jugendlichen im Dritten Reich', in Löwenthal and von zur Mühlen, *Widerstand und Verweigerung*, pp. 177–201.

52 Christiane Blumenberg-Lampe, *Das wirtschaftliche Programm der 'Freiburger Kreise'. Entwurf einer freiheitlich-sozialen Nachkriegswirtschaft* (Berlin, 1973). These proposals rejected the workers' right to strike, for example.

53 Ludolf Herbst, *Der totale Krieg und die Ordnung der Wirtschaft. Die Kriegswirtschaft im Spannungsfeld von Politik, Ideologie und Propaganda 1933–1945* (Stuttgart, 1982), esp. pp. 383ff.

54 Theodor Schieder, *Hermann Rauschnings 'Gespräche mit Hitler' als Geschichtsquelle* (Opladen, 1972).

55 Thus the definition in the autumn 1943 draft of a Law to Restore Orderly Conditions in the State and the Administration of Justice (text in Ulrich von Hassell, *Vom anderen Deutschland. Aus den nachgelassenen Tagebüchern 1938–1944*, 3rd edn [Frankfurt a.M., 1964], p. 337).

56 Cf. Arnold Sywottek, *Deutsche Volksdemokratie. Studien zur politischen Konzeption der KPD 1935–1946* (Düsseldorf, 1971). Further Bodo Scheurig, *Freies Deutschland. Das Nationalkommittee und der Bund Deutscher Offiziere in der Sowjetunion 1943–44*, 2nd edn (Munich, 1961).

57 Cf. Hans Mommsen, 'Verfassungs-und Verwaltungsreformpläne der Widerstandsgruppen des 20 Juli 1944', in Jürgen Schmädeke and Peter Steinbach (eds), *Der Widerstand gegen den Nationalsozialismus. Die deutsche Gesellschaft und der Widerstand gegen Hitler*, 2nd edn (Munich and Zurich, 1986), pp. 570ff.

58 In conversation with the author, Berlin, July 1984.

59   Cf. the regulations issued by Bormann on 23 and 27 July on how the issue
     should be dealt with in speeches, necessitated by a speech by Robert Ley
     condemning the German upper class in its totality (Hans Adolf Jacobsen [ed.],
     'Spiegelbild einer Verschwörung'. Die Opposition gegen Hitler und der Staatsstreich
     vom 20 Juli 1944 in der SD-Berichterstattung, vol. 2 [Stuttgart, 1984], pp. 596f,
     and cf. p. 624).
60   See Theodor Steltzer, Von Deutscher Politik. Aufsätze und Vorträge, ed. by F.
     Minssen (Frankfurt a.M., 1949). idem, Der 20 Juli und die Bewältigung der
     Zukunft. Rede am 20 Juli 1961 in der Johann Wolfgang Goethe-Universität Frank-
     furt (Frankfurt a.M., 1961); on van Husen, cf. van Roon, Neuordnung, pp. 198f.
61   Helmuth James von Moltke, Letzte Briefe, 8th edn (Berlin, 1959), pp. 18f.

Chapter 11   The Realization of the Unthinkable: The 'Final Solution of the Jewish Question' in the Third Reich

1   Gerald Reitlinger, The Final Solution: The Attempt to Exterminate the Jews of
    Europe, 2nd edn (London, 1956); his work was preceded by Leon Poliakov,
    Bréviare de la Haine (Paris, 1951).
2   Konrad Kwiet provides a survey of the vast specialized literature on the
    subject in 'Zur historiographischen Behandlung der Judenverfolgung im Dritten
    Reich', Militärgeschichtliche Mitteilungen, 27 (1980–81), pp. 149–92. West Ger-
    man historians have so far addressed this subject only hesitantly. Apart from
    Wolfgang Scheffler's creditable survey, Judenverfolgung im Dritten Reich
    1933–1945 (Berlin, 1960; 2nd edn, 1979), Helmut Genschel, Die Verdrängung
    der Juden aus der Wirtschaft im Dritten Reich (Göttingen, 1966), and Uwe D.
    Adam, Judenpolitik im Dritten Reich (Düsseldorf, 1972), no comprehensive
    monograph has been published on the Holocaust and its origins. Among West
    German writers, Helmut Krausnick, 'Judenverfolgung', in Hans Buchheim et
    al., Anatomie des SS-Staates, vol. 2 (Olten/Freiburg i.Br., 1965), pp. 283–448,
    still provides the best overall analysis. See also M. Broszat, '"Holocaust" und
    die deutsche Geschichtswissenschaft', VfZ, 27 (1979), pp. 285–98.
3   The literature of the extreme right must therefore be disregarded. See Wolf-
    gang Benz, 'Die Opfer und die Täter. Rechtsextremisten in der Bundesrepub-
    lik', APZ, supplement to Parlament, B 27/80, pp. 29–45; Wolfgang Benz,
    'Judenvernichtung aus Notwehr', VfZ, 29 (1981), pp. 615–17.
4   The Institut für Zeitgeschichte, Munich, is preparing a study: Wolfgang Benz
    (ed.), Die Zahl der jüdischen Opfer des Nationalsozialismus (forthcoming).
5   On the number of Jews murdered, see Raul Hilbert, The Destruction of the
    European Jews, new edn (New York, 1983), p. 767. The figure of 5.1 million
    victims can only be an approximation.
6   See Alexander and Margaret Mitscherlich, Die Unfähigkeit zu trauern. Grund-
    lagen kollektiven Verhaltens, 2nd edn (Munich, 1968), pp. 28–9, 205–6; Pierre
    Aycoberry, The Nazi Question: An Essay on the Interpretation of National Socialism
    (New York, 1981), pp. 182–3. Of survivors' portrayals, one that seems to me
    exemplary is Hermann Langbein, Menschen in Auschwitz (Vienna, 1972).

7 See Martin Broszat, 'Nationalsozialistische Konzentrationslager 1933–1945', in Hans Buchheim et al., *Anatomie des SS-Staates*, vol. 2, 2nd edn (Munich, 1967), pp. 77–8; Hilberg, *Destruction of European Jews*, pp. 572–5.

8 Raul Hilberg investigates this question methodically in *Sonderzüge nach Auschwitz* (Mainz, 1981); see Lawrence D. Stokes, 'The German People and the Destruction of the European Jews', *Central European History*, 6 (1973), pp. 167–91 and particularly pp. 187–9; Marlis G. Steinert, *Hitler's War and the Germans: Public Mood and Attitude during the Second World War* (Athens, Ohio, 1977), pp. 140–2; Christopher Browning, *The Final Solution and the German Foreign Office* (New York, 1978). Christian Streit, *Keine Kameraden. Die Wehrmacht und die sowjetischen Kriegsgefangenen 1941–1945* (Stuttgart, 1978), pp. 109–11; Ian Kershaw, 'Antisemitismus und Volksmeinung. Reaktionen auf die Judenverfolgung', in Martin Broszat et al. (eds), *Bayern in der NS-Zeit*, II: *Herrschaft und Gesellschaft im Konflikt*, pt A (Munich, 1979), pp. 340–2.

9 Hannah Arendt, *Eichmann in Jerusalem. Ein Bericht von der Banalität des Bösen* (Munich, 1964), pp. 188–90, 300. F. A. Krummacher (ed.), *Die Kontroverse. Hannah Arendt, Eichmann und die Juden* (Munich, 1964), documents the spirit in which Arendt's interpretation was received. The older view is found in Robert M. W. Kempner, *Eichmann und Komplizen* (Zurich, 1961).

10 See the introduction to Martin Broszat (ed.), *Kommandant in Auschwitz. Autobiographische Aufzeichnungen von Rudolf Höss* (Stuttgart, 1958), pp. 16–18.

11 See Heinz Höhne, *The Order of the Death's Head: The Story of Hitler's SS* (London, 1969), pp. 146–7, 352–5.

12 Heinrich Himmler on 6 October 1943: 'Perhaps at a much later date one will be able to consider telling the German people more about it [the destruction of the Jews]. I believe it is better that *all of us together* have borne this for our people, have taken the responsibility on ourselves (the responsibility for a deed, *not only for an idea*) and then take the secret with us to the grave.' Quoted in Bradley F. Smith and Agnes Peterson (eds), *Heinrich Himmler, Geheimreden 1933 bis 1945 und andere Ansprachen*, Frankfurt a.M., 1974, pp. 170–1; emphasis added.

13 On attempts to destroy the evidence see Hilberg, *Destruction of European Jews*, pp. 628–9; Adalbert Rückerl (ed.), *Nationalsozialistische Vernightungslager im Spiegel deutscher Strafprozesse* (Munich, 1977), pp. 273–4 and passim.

14 The speech of 6 October is quoted in Smith and Peterson, *Heinrich Himmler*, pp. 162–3; that of 16 December 1943 (extract), ibid., p. 201; that of 26 January 1944, ibid., pp. 201–3; that of 24 May 1944, ibid., p. 203; that of 21 June 1944, ibid., pp. 203–5. Himmler's use of the word 'we' constantly involves the entire SS apparatus in what happened. His statement that 'we' are not justified 'in putting off anything hard or difficult that can be done today' is typical. It is made in connection with his advice that the problem should not be postponed until after Hitler's death (ibid., pp. 202, 204). Himmler's increasing degree of psychological strain was partly responsible for his disclosure of the crime to the higher functionaries and generals (see Höhne, *Order of the Death's Head*, p. 336). It was also related to the fact that he had begun to distance

himself from Hitler inwardly. At the very least, he was aware of the state of Hitler's health and knew that he could not expect the support he normally received from Hitler to last much longer.

15 On Hans Frank's contradictory behaviour during the trial, see Bradley F. Smith, *Der Jahrhundertprozess. Die Motive der Richter von Nürnberg* (Frankfurt, 1977), pp. 214–16; Goering denied, however, that in signing Heydrich's authorization of 31 July 1941 he had been giving notice of any intention to liquidate the Jews. See *Der Prozess gegen die Hauptkriegsverbrecher vor dem Internationalen Militärgerichtshof. Nürnberg, 14 Oktober 1945–1 Oktober 1946* (hereafter cited as *IMG*), vol. 9, pp. 574–6. See also the survey in Hilberg, *Destruction of European Jews*, pp. 684–6. On the problem of Speer, see Erich Goldhagen, 'Albert Speer, Himmler and the Secrecy of the Final Solution', *Midstream* (October, 1971), pp. 43–50; Speer's responses to this, and to W. Malanowsky's position, stated in *Der Spiegel*, 29, no. 46 (October 1975) have not yet been refuted. See my review of the 'Spandau Diaries' in *PVS*, 17 (1976), pp. 108–10; the proof adduced by Matthias Schmidt in *Albert Speer: Das Ende eines Mythos* (Bern, 1972), pp. 232–3, does not refute his defence. Whatever one's doubts about this, it is a fact that the genocide was suppressed. Speer's later justification in *Der Sklavenstaat* (Stuttgart, 1981), pp. 376–8, tends to detract from his credibility.

16 This is the traditional view. It is put most consistently by Eberhard Jäckel, *Hitlers Weltanschauung*, new edn (Stuttgart, 1981), esp. p. 68. Jäckel's thesis that Hitler's attitude became more radical as his *Weltanschauung* developed (pp. 66–7) is not convincing in view of earlier statements by Hitler in a similar tone: see E. Jäckel (ed.), *Hitler. Sämtliche Aufzeichnungen 1905–1923* (Stuttgart, 1980): the connection between anti-semitism and anti-bolshevism is clear from the start. Gerald Fleming, *Hitler and the Final Solution* (London, 1985), and Lucy Dawidowicz, *The War against the Jews: 1933–1945* (New York, 1975), p. 494, follow Jäckel. Fleming's reference to Albrecht Tyrell in Guido Knopp (ed.), *Hitler heute. Gespräche über ein deutsches Trauma* (Aschaffenburg, 1979), does not apply here. With Martin Broszat, 'Soziale Motivation und Führerbindung des Nationalsozialismus', *VfZ*, 18 (1970), pp. 400–2, I emphasize that the propagandist nature of Hitler's statements is inconsistent with any firm intention to translate the metaphor of extermination into reality, despite the fact that he undoubtedly used them as a stylistic device to demonstrate tactical 'moderation', and that he had no psychological inhibitions preventing him from pursuing a policy of annihilation. See Broszat's objections to Jäckel's overemphasis on Hitler's *Weltanschauung* (ibid., pp. 399–401).

17 See Helmut Auerbach, 'Hitlers politische Lehrjahre und die Münchener Gesellschaft 1919–1923', *VfZ*, 25 (1977), pp. 8–10, and the literature cited in his n. 33. Further, Margaret Plewina, *Auf dem Weg zu Hitler. Der 'völkische' Publizist Dietrich Eckart* (Bremen, 1970); George L. Mosse, *Rassismus. Ein Krankheitssymptom der europäischen Geistesgeschichte des 19 und 20 Jahrhunderts* (Königstein, 1978); also the literature cited by Kwiet, 'Judenverfolgung', p. 186; see also Broszat, 'Soziale Motivation', p. 400. The total identification of NS propaganda with Hitler's *Weltanschauung*, frequently found in the literature,

overlooks the correspondence between the anti-semitism of the party and that of the völkisch (racial-nationalist) right, and indeed that of much of the conservative nationalist right as well. This minimizes the extent of racial anti-semitism; see also Werner E. Mosse (ed.), *Entscheidungsjahr 1932. Zur Juden-frage in der Endphase der Weimarer Republik*, 2nd edn (Tübingen, 1966).

18 Hilberg, *Destruction of European Jews*, pp. 293–4.

19 See Hans Mommsen, 'Hitler's Position in the Nazi System', in this volume, esp. pp. 183–6; Karl A. Schleunes, *The Twisted Road to Auschwitz: Nazi Policy toward German Jews 1933–1939*, 2nd edn (Urbana, 1990), pp. 71, 258–60; Adam, *Judenpolitik*, pp. 163–5, 217.

20 On this issue see Adam, *Judenpolitik*, pp. 125–9; the Lösener files, IfZ F 71/2; B. Lösener, 'Als Rassenreferent im Reichsministerium des Innern', *VfZ*, 9 (1961), pp. 264–6.

21 On Hitler's evasions in settling the issues of *'Mischlinge'* and racially mixed marriages, see Adam, *Judenpolitik*, pp. 329–30, and David Irving, *Hitler's War* (London, 1977), p. 391. His position did not mean that Hitler was definitely yielding; it is in fact characteristic of a way of thinking that waits for the development of situations in which individual decisions of this sort are rendered unnecessary.

22 See Klaus Hildebrand, *Deutsche Aussenpolitik 1933–1945. Kalkül oder Dogma?* (Stuttgart, 1971), pp. 26–8; Klaus Hildebrand, 'Innenpolitische Antriebskräfte der nationalsozialistischen Aussenpolitik', in Manfred Funke (ed.), *Hitler, Deutschland und die Mächte* (Düsseldorf, 1976), pp. 237–9 and passim; Hans-Adolf Jacobsen, 'Zur Struktur der NS-Aussenpolitik 1933–1945', in ibid., pp. 172–4; A. Kuhn, *Hitlers aussenpolitisches Programm* (Stuttgart, 1970).

23 See Joachim C. Fest, *Hitler. Eine Biographie* (Frankfurt a.M., 1973), p. 927; Broszat, 'Soziale Motivation', pp. 401–2.

24 On the April boycott, see Genschel, *Verdrängung der Juden*, pp. 43–5. The boycott was announced before Hitler and Goebbels made their decision on 26 March. See Hitler's typical justification of the boycott, ibid., p. 47. Also Karl Dietrich Bracher, Wolfgang Sauer and Gerhard Schulz, *Die nationalsozialistische Machtergreifung*, 2nd edn (Cologne, 1962), pp. 277–8. The *Münchener Neueste Nachrichten* of 15 September commented on the Nuremberg Laws: 'Jews within the borders of the German Reich have been offered the opportunity to become a national minority.' The laws actually sanctioned measures that had already been implemented in many cases; this, together with the language used in Nazi propaganda at this time, implying that there would be no further encroachments, created the impression that a definitive solution had been found.

25 See Hermann Graml, *Der 9 November 1938 – 'Reichskristallnacht'*, 2nd edn (Bonn, 1958), and Adam, *Judenpolitik*, pp. 206–7. It is by no means certain that Hitler approved in advance the extensive pogrom organized by Goebbels. See Wolfgang Scheffler, 'Ausgewählte Dokumente zur Geschichte des Novemberpogroms 1938', *APZ*, B 44/78, pp. 3–30; *IMG*, vol. 20, p. 320; *IMG*, vol. 32, p. 28; *IMG*, vol. 14, pp. 465–6; Klaus Moritz in idem and Ernst Noam (eds), *Justiz und Judenverfolgung*, II: *NS-Verbrechen vor Gericht* (Wiesbaden, 1978), p. 213. According to Schallermeier's affidavit (*IMG*, vol. 42,

pp. 510–12), when Himmler called on Hitler during the night, he received the impression that Hitler 'knew nothing about the course of events', i.e. knew nothing about an extensively organized pogrom as opposed to 'spontaneous' actions.

26 Adam, *Judenpolitik*, comments that 'the chancellor of the Reich in the last analysis determined the course of Jewish policy' (p. 19), while Schleunes, *The Twisted Road*, p. 131, emphasizes that 'Hitler's hand appeared occasionally at crucial moments, but it was usually a vacillating and indecisive one. He did not delegate responsibility for Jewish policy, nor did he keep a close check on it.' On 'Aryanization', see Adam, *Judenpolitik*, pp. 208–10; Genschel, *Verdrängung der Juden*, pp. 180–2.

27 See Schleunes, *The Twisted Road*, pp. 90–1, 97–9.

28 See Mommsen, 'Hitler's Position', pp. 173–4.

29 See Genschel, *Verdrängung der Juden*, pp. 46–8.

30 See Otto D. Kulka, *The Jewish Question in the Third Reich: Its Significance in National Socialist Ideology and Politics*, 2 vols (Jerusalem, 1975), pp. 200–2.

31 Jäckel, *Hitlers Weltanschauung*, pp. 72–4; Krausnick, 'Judenverfolgung', pp. 38–40; Adam, *Judenpolitik*, pp. 25–6. The fact that such expressions were paraphrased in Nazi propaganda after 1933 enabled the public not to take the threat seriously.

32 See, for example, Irving, *Hitler's War*, I pp. 311–12.

33 Ibid., p. 576. On this issue, see M. Broszat, 'Genesis der "Endlösung"', *VfZ*, 25 (1977), pp. 759–61, and Fleming, *Hitler and the Final Solution*, pp. 17–20 and passim.

34 Vertrauliche Informationen der Parteikanzlei, IfZ Db 15.06; see Broszat, 'Genesis der "Endlösung"', pp. 763–5. Any consideration of a 'future total solution' was to be avoided in public discussion. In view of Hitler's deliberate restraint in referring to the mass exterminations, Fleming agrees with Broszat (see pp. 61–3).

35 See Fleming, *Hitler and the Final Solution*, pp. 135–9. There is an obvious inconsistency here. On the one hand, the expression 'special treatment of the Jews' was to be avoided, on Himmler's instructions (ibid., pp. 136–7); on the other, according to Eichmann's statement (ibid., pp. 138–9), Hitler himself broke the prescriptions governing language.

36 'Here we are going to destroy the Jews. The Jews did not cause the ninth of November for nothing. This day will be avenged.' Note by Hewel, 21 January 1939, *Akten zur deutschen auswärtigen Politik*, Series D, vol. IV, p. 170. This remark should be seen in the context of the Reichstag speech shortly afterwards, on 30 January 1939; it is difficult to interpret it as a declaration of intent to liquidate the Jews (see Adam, *Judenpolitik*, p. 235), especially since the term 'Vernichtung' (destruction) was generally used as a metaphor for economic elimination.

37 W. Jochmann (ed.), *Adolf Hitler. Monologe im Führerhauptquartier 1941–1944* (Hamburg, 1980), p. 44. See Broszat, 'Genesis der "Endlösung"', p. 757.

38 See the basic study by Helmut Krausnick and Hans-Heinrich Wilhelm, *Die*

Truppe des Weltanschauungskrieges. Die Einsatzgruppen der Sicherheitspolizei und des SD 1938–1942 (Stuttgart, 1981).

39 Louis P. Lochner (ed.), *The Goebbels Diaries* (London, 1948), p. 48, and Broszat, 'Genesis der "Endlösung"', p. 758.

40 Andreas Hillgruber, *Staatsmänner und Diplomaten bei Hitler*, vol. 2 (Frankfurt, 1970), pp. 232–3, 245, 256–7; talks with Antonescu on 13 April 1943 and with Horthy on 16/17 April 1943.

41 Broszat, 'Genesis der "Endlösung"', pp. 773–4.

42 See Hilberg, *Destruction of European Jews*, p. 652, n. 39, and Henriette von Schirach, *Der Preis der Herrlichkeit* (Wiesbaden, 1956), pp. 187–8.

43 See Helmut Stierlin, *Adolf Hitler. Familienperspectiven* (Frankfurt, 1975), p. 118.

44 Persönlicher Stab des Reichsführer-SS, IfZ MA 316, pp. 4994ff.

45 See Eberhard Jäckel, *Hitlers Weltanschauung*, pp. 77–8, and, following him, Klaus Hildebrand, 'Hitlers "Programm" und seine Realisierung 1939–1942', in Funke, *Hitler*, pp. 78–80.

46 Fleming, *Hitler and the Final Solution*, pp. 63–5; Irving, *Hitler's War*, pp. 391–2. Why should Hitler have broken the normal codes governing language when speaking to Globocnik? See Broszat, 'Genesis der "Endlösung"', p. 760.

47 Fleming, *Hitler and the Final Solution*, p. 20; also Broszat, 'Genesis der "Endlösung"';, pp. 763–4; Krausnick and Wilhelm, *Truppe des Weltanschauungskrieges*, p. 633; William Carr, *Hitler: A Study in Personality and Politics* (London, 1978), pp. 72, 76.

48 Smith and Peterson, *Heinrich Himmler*, p. 202; in the later speeches; Himmler talks of an 'order' (*Befehl*) or 'instruction' (*Auftrag*), which suggests a connection with the Commissar Order.

49 Fleming, *Hitler and the Final Solution*, p. 44, quotes from the record of the interrogation of the *Höherer SS- und Polizeiführer* Jeckeln on 14 December 1945, for the period November 1941, that the liquidation of the Riga ghetto had been 'the Führer's wish'. The testimony of Rudolf-Christoph Freiherr von Gersdorf, quoted by Fleming on p. 53, stands alone; none of the other statements refer to the *European* 'Programme for the Final Solution'. In this they accord with Heydrich's position of May 1942, as testified by Otto Wagner.

50 On the indisputable oral propagation of the Commissar Order see Krausnick and Wilhelm, *Truppe des Weltanschauungskrieges*, pp. 150–1, 348. On Hitler's role, ibid., pp. 114–15.

51 Krausnick, 'Judenverfolgung', p. 361.

52 Henry Picker (ed.), *Hitlers Tischgespräche im Führerhauptquartier*, 2nd edn (Stuttgart, 1977), p. 189: record of 24 July 1942. See Browning, *Final Solution*, pp. 35–7. The sources presented by Browning make it difficult to sustain Leni Yahil's interpretation that, from the start, the Madagascar Plan was merely a cover for the Final Solution, although the plan would itself have meant mass physical destruction; Leni Yahil, 'Madagascar, Phantom of a Solution for the Jewish Question', in Bela Vago and George Mosse (eds), *Jews and Non-Jews in Eastern Europe* (New York, 1974).

53 See Fest, *Hitler*, pp. 925, 927, 931; Broszat, 'Soziale Motivation', pp. 402–3,

407; J. P. Stern, *Hitler: The Führer and the People* (Glasgow, 1975), esp. pp. 83–4.

54 Max Domarus (ed.), *Hitler. Reden und Proklamationen 1932–1945*, vol. 2, pt 1 (Munich, 1965), pp. 1057–8.

55 Ibid., vol. 4, pp. 1663, 1828, 1920, 1937; see Karl Dietrich Bracher, *Die Deutsche Diktatur* (Cologne, 1969), pp. 399–400.

56 *IMG*, vol. 27, pp. 499–500; see Adam, *Judenpolitik*, pp. 209–11.

57 See Andreas Hillgruber, 'Die "Endlösung" und das deutsche Ostimperium als Kernstück des rassenideologischen Programms des Nationalsozialismus', in Funke, *Hitler*, pp. 94–114.

58 *Hitlers Politisches Testament* (Frankfurt, 1981). Incidentally, the self-protective method of expression is maintained even here: 'I have not kept anyone in the dark about the fact that this time millions of European children of the Aryan peoples will not starve, millions of grown men will not die, and hundreds of thousands of women and children will not be burned and bombed to death in the cities, without the real guilty party being made to atone for his guilt, *though by more humane methods*' (emphasis added).

59 On this issue see Krausnick and Wilhelm, *Truppe des Weltanschauungskrieges*, pp. 165–7. Krausnick concludes that there was a corresponding regulation of language. Hilberg, *Destruction of European Jews*, p. 217, by contrast, convincingly points out 'that psychological justifications were an essential part of the killing operations. If a proposed action could not be justified, it did not take place.'

60 Stern, *Hitler*, pp. 23–5.

61 See Fest, *Hitler*, pp. 772–4; Carr, *Hitler*, pp. 135–7.

62 See Tim W. Mason, 'The Legacy of 1918 for National Socialism', in A. J. Nicholls and E. Matthias (eds), *German Democracy and the Triumph of Hitler* (London, 1971), pp. 215–39.

63 See Wilhelm in Krausnick and Wilhelm, *Truppe des Weltanschauungskrieges*, pp. 585–7. Irving, *Hitler's War*, pp. 330–1, concludes from this that Hitler forbade the liquidation, once and for all. Irving's reasoning is faulty, because this solution presupposes a detailed knowledge of plans that Himmler had not yet fully developed, and that Irving denies existed until October 1943. See the explanation in Broszat, 'Genesis der "Endlösung"', pp. 760–1. Broszat suspects that Hitler was not involved at all; Himmler would have anticipated Hitler's antipathy towards campaigns that provoked public protests.

64 See Broszat, 'Soziale Motivation', p. 408.

65 Most of the specialist literature casts doubt on the existence of a comprehensive plan by Hitler; see Hilberg, *Destruction of European Jews*, p. 31; he nevertheless sees a consistent structure in the process of destruction. For my part, I argue that this is an inevitable result of the cumulative radicalization of the system; see Hans Mommsen, 'Hitler's Position', pp. 179–81; see Adam, *Judenpolitik*, p. 357; Schleunes, *The Twisted Road*, p. 2; Yehuda Bauer, *The Holocaust in Historical Perspective* (Canberra, 1978); Yehuda Bauer, 'Genocide: Was it the Nazi Original Plan?', *Annals of the American Academy of Political and Social Science* (July 1980), pp. 34–45.

66 Irving's interpretation (see *Hitler's War*, introduction, pp. XIII–XV) that, while

Hitler explicitly supported and approved the deportation of the Jews 'to the East', he forbade liquidations and postponed a definitive solution until after the war, rests on an inaccurate assessment of Hitler's comments concerning genocide. These were all made in a 'futuristic' context, and present the aim of eliminating the European Jews, and indeed Jews all over the world, as a vision of the future. Unlike Himmler (see note 11 above) or Goebbels (see Hans-Heinrich Wilhelm, 'Wie geheim war die Endlösung?' in *Miscellanea. Festschrift für Helmut Krausnick* [Stuttgart, 1980], pp. 137–9), Hitler never refers to it as a programme directly implemented and in its final stages. This is not inconsistent with greater radicality after Stalingrad as established by Broszat ('Genesis der "Endlösung"', p. 772) and connected with Hitler's attitude, which became increasingly visionary and unrealistic as he confined himself more and more to his bunker. Hitler was intoxicated with the 'idea' of annihilation, but he endeavoured to ignore the reality; here, at least, we must agree with Irving. It is typical that Hitler, who normally had statistical details at his fingertips, used pre-war figures for the proportion of Jews in the population in his conversation with Horthy (see note 40 above).

67   Schleunes, *The Twisted Road*, p. 258.

68   See Genschel, *Verdrängung der Juden*, pp. 240–2, on the 'Aryanization' in Franconia; Peter Hüttenberger's creditable study, *Die Gauleiter* (Stuttgart, 1969), does not include this aspect.

69   See Helmut Heiber, *Joseph Goebbels* (Berlin, 1962), pp. 280–1; Adam, *Judenpolitik*, pp. 206–7.

70   See Gerhard Botz, *Wien vom 'Anschluss' zum Krieg. Nationalsozialistische Machtübernahme und politisch-soziale Umgestaltung am Beispiel der Stadt Wien* (Vienna, 1978), pp. 93–5; Genschel, *Verdrängung der Juden*, pp. 160–2.

71   See Enno Georg, *Die wirtschaftliche Unternehmungen der SS* (Stuttgart, 1963); see also Speer's polemical, but factually accurate, *Sklavenstaat*, pp. 346–8, 381–3.

72   See Hilberg, *Destruction of European Jews*, pp. 166–8, 334–6, 341–2, 586–600. The role of individual banks in the 'Aryanization process' requires more detailed investigation.

73   The basic study is Heinrich Uhlig, *Die Warenhäuser im Dritten Reich* (Cologne, 1965); Genschel, *Verdrängung der Juden*, pp. 67–9.

74   The boundless corruption of the functionaries of the regime, especially over the expropriation of the Jews, contributed to the fact that criticism of the deportation and liquidation was limited to a few individual cases.

75   See Schmidt, *Speer*, pp. 216–18.

76   See the survey in Bruno Blau, *Das Ausnahmerecht für die Juden in den europäischen Ländern*, pt 1: *Deutschland*, 3rd edn (Düsseldorf, 1965).

77   Impressive examples in Paul Sauer (ed.), *Dokumente über die Verfolgung der jüdischen Bürger in Baden-Württemberg durch das nationalsozialistische Regime 1933–1945*, 2 vols (Stuttgart, 1966); *Dokumente zur Geschichte der Frankfurter Juden* (Frankfurt, 1963); Maria Zelzer, *Weg und Schicksal der Stuttgarter Juden* (Stuttgart, 1964).

78   H. Robinsohn, *Justiz als politische Verfolgung. Die Rechtsprechung in 'Rassenschand-*

efällen' beim Landgericht Hamburg 1936–1943 (Stuttgart, 1977); also Ernst Noam and Wolf-Arno Kropat (eds), *Juden vor Gericht 1933–1945* (Wiesbaden, 1975); Bernd Rüthers, *Die unbegrenzte Auslegung. Zum Wandel der Privatrechtsordnung im Nationalsozialismus* (Frankfurt, 1973), pp. 15–77; Ilse Haff, *Justiz im Dritten Reich* (Frankfurt, 1978).

79 See the indications in Hitler's speech of 15 September 1935 (Domarus, *Hitler*, vol. 1, pt 2, p. 537). See also Abraham Margaliot, 'The Reaction of the Jewish Public in Germany to the Nuremberg Laws', *Yad Vashem Studies*, 12 (1977), esp. pp. 85–6. Von Freytag-Loringhoven, a Reichstag member, expressed similar sentiments.

80 See William Sheridan Allen, 'Die deutsche Öffentlichkeit und die "Reichskristallnacht" – Konflikte zwischen Werthierarchie und Propaganda im Dritten Reich', in D. Peukert and J. Reulecke (eds), *Die Reihen fast geschlossen. Beiträge zur Geschichte des Alltags unterm Nationalsozialismus* (Wuppertal, 1981), pp. 397–412. See Botz, *Wien*, pp. 403–4, on the different response to March 1938.

81 See Ian Kershaw, 'The Persecution of the Jews and German Popular Opinion in the Third Reich', *Leo Baeck Year Book*, 26 (1981), pp. 261–89.

82 Schleunes, *The Twisted Road*, pp. 97, 100–2; Krausnick, 'Judenverfolgung', pp. 315–17. See also Hans Mommsen, 'Der nationalsozialistische Polizeistaat und die Judenverfolgung vor 1938', *VfZ*, 10 (1962), pp. 68–70.

83 See the interpretation given by Schleunes, *The Twisted Road*, pp. 71–3; the opposing view is given by Adam, *Judenpolitik*, p. 46, following Sauer in Bracher, Sauer and Schulz, *Nationalsozialistische Machtergreifung*, pp. 870–1, and Bracher, in ibid., p. 54.

84 Schleunes, *The Twisted Road*, pp. 253–5; Krausnick, 'Judenverfolgung', pp. 341–3.

86 See Werner Rosenstock, 'Exodus 1933–1939. Ein Überblick über die jüdische Auswanderung aus Deutschland', in *Deutsches Judentum. Aufstieg und Krise* (Stuttgart, 1963), p. 386; Paul Sauer, *Die Schicksale der jüdischen Bürger Baden-Württembergs während der nationalistische Verfolgungzeit 1933–1945* (Stuttgart, 1969), p. 123; Herbert A. Strauss, 'Jewish Emigration from Germany. Nazi Policies and Jewish Resposnes', *Leo Baeck Year Book*, 25 (1980), pp. 317–39; Hans Lamm, 'Die innere und äussere Entwicklung des deutschen Judentums' (Ph.D. thesis, University of Erlangen, 1951), p. 46.

87 Schleunes, *The Twisted Road*, pp. 212–13.

88 Strauss, 'Jewish Emigration', pp. 351–3; see Bernard Wasserstein, *Britain and the Jews of Europe 1939–1945* (Oxford, 1979), pp. 6–8, 43–5.

89 See Lösener, 'Rassenreferent', pp. 264–6; Sauer, *Schicksale*, p. 103. The number of '*Mischlinge* of the first and second grades' was declining demographically, standing at 84,000 in 1938.

90 Kershaw, 'Persecution', pp. 283–4; Stokes, 'German People', pp. 180–2.

91 Genschel, *Verdrängung der Juden*, pp. 121–2. The flyleaf of Globke's commentary on the Nuremberg Laws (W. Stuckart and H. Globke, *Reichsbürgergesetz, Blutschutzgesetz und Ehegesundheitsgesetz* [Munich, 1936]) announces a forthcoming commentary by Globke on the economic laws concerning the Jews.

When Genschel asked Dr Hans Globke about this, Globke replied that he never intended to write such a commentary. Obviously a law was not passed because it would have resulted in undesirable restrictions of the kind opposed by Schlacht. See Schleunes, *The Twisted Road*, p. 156.

92 See Genschel, *Verdrängung der Juden*, pp. 213–15.

93 See Kurt Pätzold, 'Von der Vertreibung zum Genocid. Zu den Ursachen, Triebkräften und Bedingungen der antijüdischen Politik des faschistischen deutschen Imperialismus', in Dietrich Eichholtz and Kurt Gossweiler (eds), *Faschismusforschung, Positionen, Probleme, Polemik* (Berlin, [GDR], 1980), p. 194; W. Präg and W. Jacobmeyer (eds), *Das Diensttagebuch des deutschen Generalgouverneurs in Polen 1939–1945* (Stuttgart, 1975), pp. 52–3.

94 Pätzold, 'Vertreibung', p. 193.

95 Ibid., pp. 194–5; Martin Broszat, *Nationalsozialistische Polenpolitik* (Stuttgart, 1961), pp. 86–8.

96 See Robert L. Koehl, '*RKFVD*'. *German Settlement and Population Policy, 1939–1945* (Cambridge, Mass., 1957), pp. 49–51, 95–7; Helmut Heiber, 'Der Generalplan Ost', *VfZ*, 6 (1958), pp. 281–3.

97 Pätzold, 'Vertreibung', pp. 196–7; Adam, *Judenpolitik*, pp. 248–50. As Pätzold rightly emphasizes, forced labour was a dominant motive.

98 Pätzold, 'Vertreibung', p. 917; Broszat, 'Genesis der "Endlösung"', pp. 748–50.

99 See Höhne, *Order of the Death's Head*, pp. 279–83. Blaskowitz's intervention with Hitler effected a delay only; the planned measures were eventually frustrated by the opposition of Goering (Broszat, *Polenpolitik*, p. 48).

100 Pätzold, 'Vertreibung', p. 198. Nevertheless, Frank expected to receive between 400,000 and 600,000 Jews into the Generalgouvernement (Präg and Jacobmeyer, *Diensttagesbuch*, p. 131); on 12 July Frank reported the Führer's decision, made at his request, 'that no more Jewish transports to the Generalgouvernement were to take place' (ibid., p. 252).

101 See Heydrich to Ribbentrop on 24 June 1940 (quoted by Pätzold, 'Vertreibung', p. 201): 'The problem *as a whole* – it is already a matter of around 3.5 million Jews in the areas under German jurisdiction *today* – can no longer be solved by emigration. A territorial Final Solution has therefore become necessary.'

102 Adam, *Judenpolitik*, pp. 294–5. Frank too had originally been prepared for such plans, which appeared feasible when the USSR handed over the district of Lublin.

103 Seev Goshen, 'Eichmann und die Nisco-Aktion im October 1939', *VfZ*, 29 (1981), pp. 94–5.

104 See Kulka, *The Jewish Question*, vol. 1, Document 51, pp. 501–3; notes by Dr Eppstein on 25 June 1940 and 3 July 1940 concerning discussions in the RSHA.

105 See Andreas Hillgruber, *Hitlers Strategie. Politik und Kriegsführung 1940–1941* (Frankfurt, 1965), pp. 148–9.

106 See note 52 above; also Pätzold, 'Vertreibung', pp. 201–3.

107 Krausnick, 'Judenverfolgung', pp. 357–8. These deportations – inconsistent

with all medium-term planning – were, symptomatically, done with Hitler's approval.

108 See Adam, *Judenpolitik*, pp. 257–8, 289.

109 Ibid., pp. 185–7.

110 Ibid., p. 290; this decision was to be repeated when it came to the question of using Russian prisoners of war in the Reich; see Streit, *Keine Kameraden*, pp. 192–4.

111 It is of fundamental importance that the generals now offered almost no resistance to Hitler's ideas and, in particular, accepted the equation of bolshevism and Jewishness. See Helmut Krausnick, 'Kommissarbefehl und "Gerichtsbarkeitserlass Barbarossa" in neuer Sicht', *VfZ*, 25 (1977), pp. 716–18; Streit, *Keine Kameraden*, pp. 51–3.

112 An official cessation of hostilities had not been thought of; see Hillgruber, *Hitlers Strategie*, pp. 541–2, 555.

113 This does not, of course, exclude wide-ranging strategic planning; see Hillgruber, *Hitlers Strategie*, pp. 377–9; moreover, Hitler revealed considerable personal uncertainty over the question of England.

114 *IMG*, vol. 26, p. 266; Document 710-PS. Adam's suggestion (*Judenpolitik*, p. 308) – made with reference to Kempner (*Eichmann*, p. 227) – that the authorization was given on Hitler's instructions, is not conclusive.

115 Hilberg, *Destruction of European Jews*, p. 262. Hilberg refers to Eichmann, (see *Ich, Adolf Eichmann* [Leoni, 1980], p. 479), but this procedure is completely plausible, particularly in view of the long-term tendency to give the RSHA full responsibility for the 'Jewish question'.

116 In contrast, Fleming, *Hitler and the Final Solution*, p. 110, points out that instructions were issued that Hitler was to receive 'continual updating on the progress of the Einsatzgruppen. See Krausnick and Wilhelm, *Truppe des Weltanschauungskrieges*, pp. 165–6, 335–6.

117 On the latter, see ibid., pp. 223–5, 232–4.

118 This changed after the systematic Final Solution had been set in motion; see ibid., p. 166.

119 Pätzold, 'Vertreibung', p. 197.

120 Quoted in Hilberg, *Destruction of European Jews*, p. 261.

121 Broszat, 'Genesis der "Endlösung"', p. 749.

122 Himmler's memorandum of May 1940 about the treatment of '*Fremdvölkische*' in the East (ed. *VfZ*, Helmut Krausnick, 5 [1957], pp. 1944–6) still rejects 'the bolshevik method of exterminating a people from inner conviction that it is ungermanic and impossible', but this occurs in the context of a consideration whether 'harshness' would not, in some circumstances, be less cruel.

123 See Broszat, 'Genesis der "Endlösung"', pp. 751–2.

124 Krausnick, 'Judenverfolgung', p. 373; Browning, *Final Solution*, pp. 66–7, 69.

125 Präg and Jacobmeyer, *Diensttagebuch*, pp. 457–8.

126 Wannsee *Protocol* of 20 January 1942, quoted here from W. Jochmann and H. A. Jacobsen, *Ausgewählte Dokumente zur Geschichte des Nationalsozialismus* (Bielefeld, 1966), pp. 2, 3–5. According to Eichmann's testimony, liquidation techniques themselves were discussed at the conference. In view of the

reaction of *Ministerialdirektor* Kritzinger, who was present (see *Gutachten des Instituts für Zeitgeschichte*, vol. 2 [Stuttgart, 1966], p. 381 n. 38), this seems to me unlikely: Eichmann is more likely to be referring to a discussion between the experts involved on the same occasion.

127 See Broszat, 'Genesis der "Endlösung"', pp. 755–6.

128 On the part played by the Foreign Ministry, see Browning, *Final Solution*, pp. 92–4.

129 See Broszat, 'Genesis der "Endlösung"', and Hilberg, *Destruction of European Jews*, pp. 586–600; also Rückerl, *Vernichtungslager*, pp. 13–15.

130 Streit, *Keine Kameraden*, pp. 219–21.

131 See Pätzold, 'Vertreibung', p. 207.

132 Streit, *Keine Kameraden*, pp. 222–3.

133 Broszat, 'Nationalsozialistische Konzentrationslager', pp. 108–9.

134 Streit, *Keine Kameraden*, p. 223.

135 See Speer's description in *Sklavenstaat*, pp. 381–3, and Höhne, *Order of the Death's Head*, p. 401.

136 On *Aktion T4*'s recruitment of personnel and its methods, see Ino Arndt and Wolfgang Sheffler, 'Organisierter Massenmord an Juden in nationalsozialistischen Vernichtungslagern', *VfZ*, 24 (1976), pp. 114–16.

137 See Arendt, *Eichmann*, pp. 135–7, 143–5.

138 See Broszat, 'Genesis der "Endlösung"', p. 755 n. 39.

139 See *Studien zur Geschichte der Konzentrationslager* (Stuttgart, 1970); Broszat, 'Nationalsozialistische Konzentrationslager', pp. 41–3.

140 See Frank Trommler, 'Die "Nationalisierung" der Arbeit', in Reinhold Grün and Jost Hermand, *Arbeit als Thema in der deutschen Literatur vom Mittelalter bis zur Gegenwart* (Königstein, 1979), pp. 102–25.

141 See Fleming, *Hitler and the Final Solution*, pp. 116–19; Hilberg, *Destruction of European Jews*, pp. 253–4; Präg and Jacobmeyer, *Diensttagebuch*, entry for 9 December 1942, p. 588.

142 See Hilberg, *Destruction of European Jews*, p. 343.

143 See Rainer C. Baum's attempt to find a solution, *The Holocaust and the German Elite: Genocide and National Suicide in Germany 1871–1945* (London, 1981), pp. 294–6; cf. pp. 265–7. In addition to the problem of moral indifference, there is also that of the suppression of moral inhibitions, for instance in the deportation of Jewish children.

144 Fleming, *Hitler and the Final Solution*, pp. 93–4, puts forward the view that the Wannsee Conference was postponed because SS-*Sturmbannführer* Lange was unable to attend on 9 December. What seems to have happened is that Heydrich asked Eichmann for information about technical possibilities for mass killings in the late autumn of 1941 (see ibid., p. 73, and Jochen von Lang, *Das Eichmann-Protokoll. Tonbandaufzeichnungen der israelischen Verhöre* [Berlin, 1982], pp. 69–71).

145 Kempner, *Eichmann*, pp. 424–6; Andreas Biss, *Der Stopp der Endlösung* (Stuttgart, 1966), pp. 227–8.

146 Survey in Hilberg, *Destruction of European Jews*, pp. 334–6, 344–5.

147 Adam, *Judenpolitik*, dates the destruction order from Hitler to the period

between September and November 1941 (pp. 311–12). Hilberg, *Destruction of European Jews*, p. 263, surmises that Hitler's decision was made in September, on the basis of information given by Eichmann and Höss, as well as a diary entry by Himmler on 17 November – 'extermination [*Beseitigung*] of the Jews'. Fleming, *Hitler and the Final Solution*, pp. 66–7 and passim, suspects that there was a secret order. Wilhelm (*Truppe des Weltanschauungskrieges*, pp. 630–2) argues that Himmler and Heydrich could not have begun an extensive extermination campaign without Hitler's approval. I, however, concur with Broszat ('Genesis der "Endlösung"'), in seeing a mixture of improvisation and planning as characteristic of the process (see Krausnick and Wilhelm, *Truppe des Weltanschauungskrieges*, p. 635).

148 Christopher Browning's cricitism ('Zur Genesis der "Endlösung". Eine Antwort an Martin Broszat', *VfZ*, 29 [1981], pp. 97–9) rests on the assumption that Hitler instructed Goering, Himmler and Heydrich, in the summer of 1941, 'to prepare a practicable programme for the destruction of the Jews'. He suggests that Goebbels was not necessarily informed, and that Hermann Goering, the only surviving witness, lied at Nuremberg (see *IMG*, vol. 9, pp. 574–6). The testimonies of Höss and Eichmann referring to late summer 1941, on which he relies, are not very specific and also relate to the period before the definitive destruction order which he assumes was given in October/November.

149 Fleming, *Hitler and the Final Solution*, passim. It is indisputable that at no time has there been any doubt that Hitler supported the genocide measures; however, there are different views about the factors that led to the implementation of the policy. For the Führer directive on fighting the partisans, see Walter Hubatsch (ed.), *Hitlers Weisungen für die Kriegsführung 1939–1945* (Frankfurt, 1962), pp. 201–3.

150 On Hitler's equivocation about the deployment of labour, see Speer, *Sklavenstaat*, pp. 367–9.

151 See Präg and Jacobmeyer, *Diensttagebuch*, p. 583; Speer, *Sklavenstaat*, pp. 372–4. Obviously, Frank did not dare to broach this issue in his conversation with Hitler on 9 May 1943.

152 See note 12 above.

153 See Broszat, 'Genesis der "Endlösung"', pp. 758–9 and passim. He justifiably points to the contradictions in Irving's position. However, the systematic transformation of the idea of genocide was the work of the SS bureaucracy.

154 On this see Adam, *Judenpolitik*, pp. 349–51; Hans Mommsen, 'Aufgabenkreis und Verantwortlichkeit des Staatssekretärs der Reichskanzlei' in *Gutachten des Instituts für Zeitgeschichte*, vol. 2 (Stuttgart, 1966), pp. 369–71.

155 See von Lang, *Eichmann-Protokoll*, p. 88: 'with the delivery of the transports to their destination according to the timetable, my responsibilities ended'. On this, see Arendt, *Eichmann*, pp. 258–9.

156 See Albrecht Tyrell, *Vom Trommler zum Führer! Der Wandel von Hitlers Selbstverständnis zwischen 1919 und 1924 und die Entwicklung der NSDAP* (Munich, 1975).

157 Mommsen, 'Hitler's Position', pp. 176–7.

158   See Walter Laqueur, *The Terrible Secret: An Investigation into the Suppression of Information about Hitler's Final Solution* (London, 1980); Wasserstein, *Jews of Europe*; Helen Fein, *Accounting for Genocide: National Responses and Jewish Victimization during the Holocaust* (New York, 1979), esp. pp. 169–71.

159   See Steinert, *Hitler's War*, pp. 143–4; Kershaw, 'Antisemitismus und Volksmeinung', pp. 339–40; Otto D. Kulka, '"Public Opinion" in Nazi Germany: The Final Solution', *The Jerusalem Quarterly*, 26 (1983), pp. 149–51.

160   Broszat, 'Soziale Motivation', pp. 403–5.

161   See Fest, *Hitler*, pp. 925, 927; also Carr, *Hitler*, pp. 6–7.

Chapter 12   Hannah Arendt and the Eichmann Trial

1   See Moshe Pearlman, *The Capture and Trial of Adolf Eichmann* (London, 1963), pp. 62ff.

2   Cf. Pearlman, *Capture*, pp. 70ff; Hannah Arendt bases much of her case on Pearlman's arguments. Cf. Martin Buber, 'Eine Anmerkung', in F. A. Krummacher (ed.), *Die Kontroverse. Hannah Arendt, Eichmann und die Juden* (Munich, 1964), pp. 233f.

3   *Die Kontroverse* contains a generally representative though very limited selection of the polemical attacks on *Eichmann in Jerusalem*.

4   Gerald Reitlinger, *The Final Solution* (London, 1953); Raul Hilberg, *The Destruction of the European Jews* (Chicago, 1961; 2nd edn, 1979, and cf. revised new German edn, *Die Vernichtung der europäischen Juden. Die Gesamtgeschichte des Holocaust*, Munich, 1982). Cf. Hannah Arendt, *Eichmann in Jerusalem: A Report on the Banality of Evil*, revised edn (London, 1977), p. 282.

5   Cf. Hannah Arendt and Karl Jaspers, *Briefwechsel 1926–1969*, ed. by Lotte Köhler and Hans Saner (Munich, 1985), p. 586 (letter to Jaspers of 20 April 1964). Arendt's extreme judgement cannot be condoned.

6   This referred both to the formal agreement between Ben Gurion and Konrad Adenauer as well as to Adenauer's efforts to prevent certain domestic political factors, including the issues of Secretary of State Hans Globke and Friedrich Karl Vialon, from becoming involved in the case. See Arendt, *Eichmann*, pp. 5f, 9ff, 13f; cf. Arendt to Jaspers, 14 March 1965 (*Briefwechsel*, pp. 621f, 821).

7   Full text in Pearlman, *Capture*, p. 58. Cf. Jochen von Lang (ed.), *Eichmann Interrogated: Transcripts from the Archives of the Israeli Police* (London, 1983), p. 4. (For a copy of Eichmann's statement, see the German edition, *Das Eichmann-Protokoll* [Frankfurt a.M., 1984].)

8   Cf. Pearlman, *Capture*, p. 22, also *Trial of the Major War Criminals before the International Military Tribunal, Nuremberg, 14 November 1945–1 October 1946* (Nuremberg, 1947), vol. IV, pp. 355ff. Cf. von Lang, *Eichmann Interrogated*, pp. 264ff, where Avner W. Less tried systematically to establish that a plan for the mass extermination of the Jews had already been drawn up in May 1939.

9   Cf. Arendt, *Eichmann*, pp. 83ff, 93f, 106f, 244.

10   See Hans Mommsen, 'The Realization of the Unthinkable: The "Final Solution of the Jewish Question" in the Third Reich', in this volume, pp. 245f and 250f, as well as the literature referred to there.

11 Letter to Jaspers, 2 December 1960 (*Briefwechsel*, p. 446).

12 Letter to Jaspers, 23 December 1960 (ibid., p. 453).

13 See the correspondence, originally not intended for publication, in Hannah Arendt, *The Jew as Pariah: Jewish Identity and Politics in the Modern Age*, ed. with an introduction by Ron H. Feldman (New York, 1978), pp. 240ff; the original German version of Scholem's letter is in Krummacher, *Die Kontroverse*, pp. 207ff.

14 See the formulation in Hannah Arendt, *Elemente und Ursprünge totaler Herrschaft* (Frankfurt, 1967), p. 9: 'In this historical trap, one does not cease to share responsibility simply because one has become a victim of injustice.' (Cf. Arendt, *The Origins of Totalitarianism* [London and New York, 1951], p. 6: 'The so-called scapegoat necessarily ceases to be the innocent victim . . . and does not simply cease to be co-responsible because it became the victim of the world's injustice and cruelty.')

15 This is contradicted by Pearlman's report, *Capture*, pp. 57f.

16 On this cf. also Shulamit Volkov, 'Kontinuität und Diskontinuität im deutschen Antisemitismus 1878–1945', *VfZ*, 33 (1985), pp. 226ff.

17 See Hans Mommsen, 'Zur Frage des Einflusses deutscher Juden auf die deutsche Wirtschaft in der Zeit der Weimarer Republik', in *Gutachten des Instituts für Zeitgeschichte*, vol. 2 (Stuttgart, 1966), pp. 348–68.

18 Arendt, *Origins*, p. 87, and cf. p. 81.

19 Ibid., pp. 447f.

20 Cf. Hannah Arendt, 'Zionism Reconsidered', in idem, *The Jew as Pariah*, pp. 135ff (or the German edn, 'Der Zionismus aus heutiger Sicht', in idem, *Die verborgene Tradition. Acht Essays* [Frankfurt, 1976], pp. 132, 135f, 151f); further idem, *Origins*, p. 451.

21 Letter to Jaspers, 13 April 1961 (*Briefwechsel*, p. 471).

22 Letter to Jaspers, 23 December 1960 (ibid., pp. 452f).

23 Ibid.

24 Cf. Adalbert Rückerl, *NS-Prozesse. Nach 25 Jahren Strafverfolgung. Möglichkeiten, Grenzen, Ergebnisse* (Karlsruhe, 1971): idem (ed.), *Nationalsozialistische Vernichtungslager im Spiegel deutscher Strafprozesse* (Munich, 1977).

25 A typical example of this is the account of the Eichmann case by Dov B. Schmorak, *Der Prozess Eichmann, dargestellt an Hand der in Nürnberg und Jerusalem vorgelegten Dokumente und der Gerichtsprotokolle* (Vienna, 1964). As opposed to it, Albert Wucher's study, *Eichmanns gab es viele* (Munich, 1961), is still worth reading. Wucher's book, written before the material from the trial was available, described Eichmann as a 'scrupulous tool of unscrupulousness' (p. 23).

26 'Eichmann Tells His Own Damning Story', *Life*, 28 November and 5 December 1960. Cf. Jaspers to Arendt, 14 December 1960 (*Briefwechsel*, pp. 447f).

27 Cf. Arendt, *Origins*, pp. 398ff. Recent research is tending towards a similar interpretation: cf. Hans Mommsen, 'Hitler's Position in the Nazi System', in this volume, pp. 163–88.

28 Arendt, *Elemente*, p. 681; cf. pp. 622, 648 (cf. *Origins*, p. 645).

29 Cf. Falk Pingel, *Häftlinge unter SS-Herrschaft. Widerstand, Selbstbehauptung und Vernichtung im Konzentrationslager* (Hamburg, 1978), pp. 157f, 160ff.

30 Letter to Jaspers, 23 December 1960 (*Briefwechsel*, p. 453).

31 Cf. the account in Hilberg, *Destruction of European Jews*, pp. 700ff, which was similarly attacked by the Jewish side.

32 Cf. *Briefwechsel*, p. 453.

33 See, for example, Krummacher, *Die Kontroverse*, pp. 77, 122.

34 This was the starting-point for Hannah Arendt's criticisms of the Berlin Chief Rabbi and chairman of the Reich Federation, Leo Baeck. The term 'Jewish Führer' used in the (first) English edition (see *Eichmann in Jerusalem: A Report on the Banality of Evil* [New York, 1963], p. 105) understandably provoked a very emotional reaction. Arendt corrected this blunder for the German and the second English editions, though effectively held to her original criticism that Baeck knew of the truth of the exterminations by gas but concealed it.

35 As in her later letter replying to Gershom Scholem (see note 13).

36 For an overall survey, see Elisabeth Young-Bruehl, *Hannah Arendt: For Love of the World* (New Haven and London, 1982), pp. 173ff, 177ff, 182ff; cf. Arendt, 'Der Zionismus', pp. 127ff.

37 Cf. especially Lucien Steinberg, *The Jews against Hitler: Not as a Lamb*, 2nd edn (London, 1978); Konrad Kwiet and Helmut Eschwege, *Selbstbehauptung und Widerstand. Deutsche Juden im Kampf um Existenz und Menschenwürde 1933–1945* (Hamburg, 1984).

38 Hans-Georg Adler, *Theresienstadt 1941–1945. Das Antlitz einer Zwangsgemeinschaft*, 2nd edn (Tübingen, 1960); idem, *Die unheimliche Wahrheit. Theresienstädter Dokumente* (Tübingen, 1959).

39 Cf. the letters to Jaspers of 19 February 1965 and 29 January 1964 (*Briefwechsel*, pp. 618, 580f; cf. also pp. 548ff) and also Arendt, *Eichmann*, pp. 98ff.

40 Sections of the dissertation by George K. Romoser used by Hannah Arendt were published under the title 'The Politics of Uncertainty: The German Resistance Movement', *Social Research*, 31 (1964), pp. 73–93. Henry Paechter, 'Germany Looks in the Mirror of History', *World Politics*, 13 (1961), pp. 633ff. The attitude of the resistance to the 'Jewish question', for long indeed a taboo subject, has – apart from the references to it by the present writer in his study 'Gesellschaftsbild und Verfassungspläne des deutschen Widerstands' in the volume edited by Schmitthenner and Buchheim, also published in the volume issued by Graml (see note 42) – been taken up recently by Christof Dipper in what is, however, a very unbalanced analysis not at all based on a comprehensive examination of the sources available: 'Der deutsche Widerstand und die Juden', *GuG*, 9 (1983), pp. 349–80.

41 Arendt, *Eichmann*, p. 97 (and German edn, p. 133).

42 The change came with the anthology edited by Walter Schmitthenner and Hans Buchheim (eds), *Der deutsche Widerstand gegen Hitler. Vier Kritische Studien*, with contributions by Hermann Graml, Hans Mommsen, Hans-Joachim Reichhardt and Ernst Wolf (Cologne and Berlin, 1966), partly reprinted in Hermann Graml (ed.), *Widerstand im Dritten Reich. Probleme, Ereignisse, Gestalten* (Frankfurt, 1984). For an overview of the latest research on the resistance,

see Jürgen Schmädeke and Peter Steinbach (eds), *Der Widerstand gegen den Nationalsozialismus. Die deutsche Gesellschaft und der Widerstand gegen Hitler* (Munich, 1985).

43 This line of argument is at its most pronounced in Norman Podhoretz, 'Hannah Arendt über Eichmann. Eine Studie über die Perversität der Brillanz', in Krummacher, *Die Kontroverse*, pp. 120, 130f.

44 See Young-Bruehl, *Hannah Arendt*, pp. 348ff.

45 Cf. ibid., p. 332, and also the correspondence with Scholem (see note 13). On the publication of this private exchange of letters, see Arendt to Jaspers, 20 October 1963 (*Briefwechsel*, p. 559).

46 The extent to which she was affected by this wave of animosity was reflected in her correspondence with Jaspers; cf. her letter of 20 July 1963 (*Briefwechsel*, pp. 546f).

47 Cf. the résumé of the debate in Manfred Funke (ed.), *Totalitarismus. Ein Studien-Reader zur Herrschaftsanalyse moderner Diktaturen* (Düsseldorf, 1978); Ernest E. Menzel (ed.), *Totalitarianism Reconsidered* (London, 1981), esp. pp. 44, 152ff.

48 See her comment to Scholem in *The Jew as Pariah*, p. 246.

49 It is regrettable that both Elisabeth Young-Bruehl (*Hannah Arendt*) and Friedrich Georg Friedmann (*Hannah Arendt. Eine deutsche Jüdin im Zeitalter des Totalitarismus* [Munich, 1985]) fail to devote any study to, or even to describe Hannah Arendt's roots in German existential philosophy, though this is absolutely indispensable to an understanding of her intellectual make-up. (Friedmann's biography is limited to paraphrasing Hannah Arendt's most important writings and giving a condensed version of Young-Bruehl's work without adding anything new, apart from some occasional comments distancing himself from the subject.)

50 See the review of *The Origins of Totalitarianism* by David Riesman, *Commentary* (April 1951), pp. 392ff; cf. Young-Bruehl, *Hannah Arendt*, p. 252.

51 Arendt, *Elemente*, p. 691.

52 Arendt, *Rahel Varnhagen. Lebensgeschichte einer deutschen Jüdin aus der Romantik* (Munich, 1962), p. 167.

53 Ibid., pp. 200 and 210.

54 Cf. ibid., p. 205. This conclusion resulted no doubt from a misinterpretation of the comment by Rahel Varnhagen from which Arendt was quoting. Varnhagen was in fact distancing herself from the Jewish lower classes. Cf. Rahel Varnhagen, *Gesammelte Werke*, vol. 2 (reprint, 1983), p. 537.

55 Cf. Hannah Arendt, *Fragwürdige Traditionsbestände im politischen Denken der Gegenwart. Vier Essays* (Frankfurt, 1957), pp. 11ff.

56 See Young-Bruehl, *Hannah Arendt*, pp. 309ff.

57 Cf. *Briefwechsel*, pp. 622, 528ff, 515, 407.

58 See Arendt, *Die verborgene Tradition*, pp. 25f; cf. p. 105. Further Wiebrecht Ries, 'Diese zu Staub gewordene Welt', in Axel von Campenhausen et al. (eds), *Hannah Arendt zum Gedenken* (Hanover, 1977), p. 23.

59 See Arendt, *Eichmann*, p. 7.

60 Hannah Arendt to Gershom Scholem, 20 July 1963, published, among other places, in the *Neue Zürcher Zeitung* (19 October 1963).

61 See Arendt, *The Jew as a Pariah*, pp. 248f.

62 Arendt, *Eichmann*, pp. 230ff.

63 In this context, cf. her essay on Franz Kafka, in Arendt, *Verborgene Tradition*, pp. 62ff, 92ff.

64 See, for one example, Hannah Arendt, *Viva activa oder Vom tätigen Leben* (Munich, 1960), p. 243. The philosophy of a new dawn betrays the clear influence of Heidegger's *Sein und Zeit* (1927) and the similar line of thinking developed by Karl Jaspers.

Glossary

Abwehr	Military Intelligence
Akademische Freischar	Academic militia
Bildungsbürgertum	Bourgeois educated elite
Bund Kreuz und Adler	Cross and Eagle League
Bund zur Erneuerung des Reiches	League to Revivify the Reich
Bündische Jugend	Movement of youth leagues and associations
Bürgertum	Bourgeoisie
Der Kunstwart	'The Culture Sentry'
Deutsche Arbeitsfront	German Labour Front
Deutsche Freischar	German militia
Deutsche Gemeindeordnung	German Municipal Decree
Deutscher Sonderweg	The unique German (historical) road
Deutsche Staatspartei	German State Party
Deutscher Werkbund	German Crafts League
Deutschvölkische Freiheitspartei	German völkisch Freedom Party
Deutschvölkischer Schutz- und Trutzbund	German People's Defence and Offence League
Die Jugend	'Youth'
Die Tat	'The Deed'
Dürerbund	Dürer League
Einsatzgruppen	Nazi execution squads (lit. task units)

Freikorps	Free Corps (volunteer corps)
Gau	Nazi Party administrative region
Gauleiter	Regional Nazi Party leader
Gestapo	Secret State Police
Gleichschaltung	Co-ordination
Grossdeutsche Volksgemeinschaft	Greater German national community
Heimwehr	Local defence militia
Herrenklub	Gentlemen's Club
Justizrat	State Counsel
Kaiserreich	Wilhelmine empire (1870–1918)
Kampfzeit	Period before 1933 (lit. time of struggle)
Kapo	Concentration camp prisoner in charge of a work detachment
Kulturkampf	Cultural conflict (between church and state)
Land/Länder	Federal state/states
Landtag	Federal state parliament
Lebensraum	Living space
Lebensreform	Reform in lifestyles
Luftwaffe	Air force
Nationalsozialistische Freiheitspartei	National Socialist Freedom Party
Neu Beginnen!	'Start Afresh!'
Neue Blätter für den Sozialismus	'New Socialist Press'
Reichsbanner Schwarz-Rot-Gold	Black-Red-Gold Reich Banner (SPD-led republican defence organization)
Reichsfinanzhof	Reich Finance Tribunal
Reichsgericht	High Court of the Reich
Reichshammerbund	Reich Hammer League
Reichshilfe	Reich contribution
Reichslandbund	Reich Land League
Reichsrat	Reich Representation of the Länder

Reichsreform	Reform in the structure of the Reich
Reichssicherheitshauptamt	Reich Security Head Office
Reichsständekammer	Reich Chamber of Corporatist Representation
Reichstag	Parliament of the Reich
Reichsvereinigung der deutschen Juden	Federation of German Jews
Reichsverwaltungsgericht	Reich Administrative Court
Reichswehr	Reich Armed Forces
Rote Kämpfer	Red Fighters
Roter Frontkämpferbund	Red Front Fighters' League
Roter Stosstrupp	Red Shock Troop
Sonderkommando	Special unit
Sopade	Émigré SPD executive, 1933–45
Staatspartei	State Party
Stahlhelm	Steel Helmet (paramilitary veterans' movement)
Verein	Association
Völkisch	Ethnic-racial
Volkskonservative Reichsvereinigung	People's National Conservative Association
Vorwärts	'Forward'
Waffen-SS	SS armed units
Wandervogel	Wanderers (hikers)
Wehrmacht	Armed forces
Weltanschauung	World view
Wirtschaftsbeirat	Economic Advisory Council
Wirtschaftspartei	Business Party
Zentralarbeitsgemeinschaft	Central Working Association

Index

Abs, Hermann   219
Abwehr network   213, 214
ADB (General Federation of
   German Civil Servants)   88,
   89, 111
Adenauer, Konrad   219, 276
ADGB (General Federation of
   German Trade Unions)   4,
   40, 66, 67–8, 69, 70, 72, 74,
   75, 189–90, 191, 198
age structure
   in the KPD   149
   in the NSDAP   149
   in the SPD   3, 34–5, 52–5,
      149
   in the trade unions   3
   of Weimar Republic leaders   35
   and the youth movement   30
agricultural policy under
   Brüning   123, 126
Allen, William Sheriden   149
anti-semitism   227, 240–3
   and bourgeois organizations
      15–16, 17, 18
   and the Final Solution
      227–38
   and Hannah Arendt   262–6
   and the Nazi party   147
   under Nazi rule   174, 182
   see also Jews
APO (Extra-Parliamentary
   Opposition)   38
Arendt, Hannah   8–9, 225,
   254–78

army officers in Nazi Germany
   182
Austria
   Anschluss with   230, 240, 242
   socialists   59
Austro-German Customs Union
   122, 131
Avenarius, Ferdinand   19

Baade, Fritz   75
Bahne, Siegfried   39
Bauer, Otto   47
Bechly, Hans   16
Beer Hall Putsch   146
Ben Gurion, David   261, 271
Besson, Waldemar   83, 84, 85,
   136
Best, Werner   193
Bloch, Ernst   218
Blücher, Heinrich   275, 276, 277
Blumenfeld, Kurt   271
Bolz, Eugen   84, 129
book publishing and bourgeois
   organizations   16–17
Borchardt, Knut   5, 6
Bormann, Martin   156, 162, 163,
   165, 169, 175, 177, 178, 184,
   191, 231, 234, 239, 241, 251
Bracher, Karl Dietrich   164
Brauer, Theodor   194
Braun, Otto   84, 102, 119
Brauns, Heinrich   71
Brecht, Bert   275

Breitscheid, Rudolf   98, 211
Broszat, Martin   157, 175, 235,
   246–7
Bruck, Moeller van den   32
Brüning, Heinrich   5, 6, 21, 40,
   66, 67, 83–140, 242
   attitude to parliamentary
      democracy   132–3
   background   86
   budgetary policies   90–118,
      124–31, 134–6
   and the bureaucratization of
      politics   84–5
   and civil servants   85, 86,
      87–90, 133
   fall from power   123–4
   political isolation as chancellor
      119–24
   style of government   85–6,
      89–90, 133–4, 136–7
   tribute speech   130
bundisch movement   14–15
Bürgertum, decline of   11–27
Business Party and Bruning's
   budgetary measures   93, 94,
   98, 135

Canaris, Wilhelm   216
Catholic Centre Party   7
Catholic church and the
   NSDAP   155
Catholic youth movement   54,
   211
Centre Party   135
   and Bruning's regime   93, 97,
      98, 99, 100, 115, 127, 139
   and the civil service   80
Christian churches under Nazi
   rule   184
Christian trade unions   67, 197,
   201, 204
Churchill, Winston   221
civil service   79–82, 112–17
   and anti-semitism   227, 228,
      229, 241
   associations   81, 87–9, 92, 96,

   108, 110, 112–13, 116–17,
      123
   Bruning's relationship with   85,
      86, 87–90, 133
   and middle-class conflict of
      interests   21
   and the NSDAP   158–9
   salary cuts   87–8, 90, 91–2, 93,
      97, 100–1, 103–4, 105, 110,
      111, 112–14, 135
   staff cuts   87, 100
   under Nazi rule   169
class
   and politics   58–9
   and the resistance movement
      198, 213, 219–20
   see also middle class; working
      class
co-determination (workers'
   participation)   4, 69, 76–8
Code of Labour Law   64
collective bargaining
   dismantling of system of   117
   and the resistance movement
      197
   in the Weimar Republic   4, 5,
      68, 69, 76, 77–8
Comintern theory of facism   141,
   142
Communist Party of Germany see
   KPD
communist resistance movement
   192, 206, 209, 216, 218, 219,
   222, 270
concentration camps   248, 249–50
constitution
   Nazi attempts to reform   170
   Weimar Republic   2, 115, 220
Conze, Werner   132

DAF (German Labour Front)
   191
Dahrendorf, Gustav   195
DAP (German Workers' Party)
   143
Darré, Walther   148
Dawes Plan   4, 65

DDP (German Democratic
    Party) 22, 23, 35, 148
  and Brüning's budgetary
    measures 99
Delp, Father Alfred 199, 213,
    219
democracy
  Bruning's attitude to 132–3
  industrial *see* co-determination
  economic 73–5
  and the Nazi dictatorship 190
  Sinzheimer's views on 63
  and the SPD 42, 43, 44–6,
    47, 67
Deutsche Freischar 33
DHV (German National
    Association of Commerical
    Employees) 15–16, 19, 20,
    21, 22
Diederichs, Eugen 16
Dietrich, Hermann 89, 96, 97,
    102–3, 105, 106, 111, 122
Dietze, Constantin von 204, 219
Dilthey, Wilhelm 31
Dinter, Arthur 164
Dinter, Hermann 144
DNVP (German National People's
    Party) 23, 24, 124, 131, 135
  and Brüning's budgetary
    measures 99, 102
  and Brüning's tribute speech
    130
  and the NSDAP 148, 149
Dollfus, E. 47
Drexler, Anton 15, 146
Dürerbund 16, 19, 25
DVP (German People's Party) 3,
    65, 66, 133, 134, 135
  and Brüning's budgetary
    measures 92, 94–8, 99
  and Brüning's tribute speech
    130
  and the NSDAP 148, 149

East Germany *see* German
    Democratic Republic
Ebert, Friedrich 81

Economic Advisory Council 83,
    122, 123, 137
economic crisis and Bruning's
    budgetary measures 99–100
economic democracy in the
    Weimar Republic 73–5
economic policies in the Weimar
    Republic 5–6
economic power in the Weimar
    Republic 3–5, 62–78
Ehrhardt, Captain 146
Eichmann, Adolt 242–3, 244–5,
    246, 250, 252, 278
  trial of 254–6, 257, 258,
    260–2
Eichmann in Jerusalem (Arendt)
    255, 258
Elterlein, Utmann von 35
Engels, F. 46, 58, 190
Erzberger 132
Esser, Hermann 237
Essler, Hermann 146
Eucken, Walter 205
expenditure cuts under Brüning
    90–118, 128, 129, 130, 135
Extra-Parliamentary Opposition
    (APO) 38

facism, theories of 141–3
Federal Republic of Germany 64,
    65, 118, 208
  and the Weimar Republic 64,
    65
First World War
  and bourgeois society 12–13
  war-economy system 80
  and the youth movement 32,
    37, 38
Fleming, Gerald 235–6, 251
Flex, Walter 32
foreign policy under Brüning
    124, 130, 131, 137
Frank, Hans 243–4, 247, 250,
    251, 259
Free German Youth 32, 33
Free Trade Unions 80, 134
  age of officials 3

and Brüning's regime 134, 138
and the Nazi Party 6, 39
in the Weimar Republic 67,
68, 71, 76, 77, 123
and the WTB Plan 75
and the youth movement 30,
54
Freiburg Circle 204
Freikorps, the 13, 15, 22, 33
Frick, Wilhelm 113, 152, 154,
155, 156, 157, 169–70,
171–2, 177, 230, 241
front line hikers movement 32

Gayl, Freiherr von 217
Geiger, Theodor 26, 50
generational conflict in the
Weimar Republic 7, 13,
28–38, 57
German Democratic Republic
208
German State Party 35
German Union, idea of 196–7
Germanic Order 14, 15
Gestapo 168, 173, 191, 192, 193,
194, 196, 206, 212, 213–14,
216–17, 242
Gilbert, Parker 87, 129
Globke, Hans 231
Goebbels, Joseph 13, 36, 151,
152, 160, 167, 174, 210, 212,
243
and the Jews 233, 240, 241,
243
and the Nuremberg Laws 231
Goerdeler, Carl 27, 165, 194,
195, 196–7, 198–9, 201, 202,
203, 204, 205, 206, 211, 212,
213, 214, 218, 219, 270
Goerdeler Circle 196, 204
Goering, Hermann 154, 158,
159, 160, 161, 165, 169,
171, 174, 178, 194, 211
and the Jews 226, 233, 237,
243, 244, 245–6, 257
Görlitz Programme 42
Grand Coalition 133

break-up of (1930) 65–6, 93
Groener 124, 138
Gross, Nikolaus 194, 195
Gründel, Ernst Gunther 35, 36
Gundolf, Friedrich 274

Habermann, Max 16, 190, 194,
195, 199, 213
Hanseatic Publishing House 16,
20
Harnack, Ernst von 193, 199
Hassell, Ulrich von 195, 198,
205, 211, 213, 214
Haubach, Theodor 13, 35, 44–5,
45, 54–5, 57, 59, 192, 193,
194, 199, 200, 203, 206, 207,
213
Hausner, Gideon 261
heavy industry in the Weimar
Republic 4–5, 5–6, 40,
66–7, 68, 77, 123
Heer, Hannes 39
Heidegger, Martin 272, 273, 275
Heiden, Konrad 41
Henk, Emil 56, 192, 194, 200,
206, 270
Hess, Rudolf 155, 156, 164, 169
Heuss, Theodor 219
Heydrich, Reinhard 158, 180,
226, 229, 239–40, 241, 243,
245, 247, 248, 250, 251, 257
Hilberg, Raul 255, 268
Hilferding, Rudolf 42, 64, 119
Hillgruber, Andreas 237
Himmler, Heinrich 154, 156,
159, 160, 161, 162, 165, 169,
170, 171, 175, 179, 180, 181,
183, 210, 216
and the Final Solution 225–6,
234, 235, 236, 237, 239, 241,
243, 248, 250, 251, 257, 259
Hindenburg, Paul von 9, 65, 82,
112, 120, 123, 124, 138, 163,
220
Historikerstreit 10
Hitler, Adolf
assassination attempt on 166,

186, 193–4, 203, 206, 214
concessions to conservative
    elite 145
and the disintegration of Nazi
    rule 186–8
foreign policy 166, 168, 172
as Führer 163–7, 212, 213
German resistance to 8, 27,
    36, 160, 167–8
and the Jews 158–9, 226–7,
    228, 232–9, 245–6, 250–1,
    257–8
leadership of NSDAP 142,
    146–7, 155, 162
loyalty to 164–7
personality 165, 184–6, 238–9
and Roehm 154
and socialism 143
style of government 163–4,
    175–6, 177, 178–80, 185
suicide 165
and the youth movement 36
Hitler Youth 217, 219
Hofgeismar Circle 34
Hohen Meissner Programme 31
Holocaust, the 1, 8–9
Höpker-Aschoff 105
Höss, Rudolf 250, 256
Hugenberg, Alfred 119, 124,
    131, 135, 168
human rights, Naumann on 77
Hunt, Richard 39, 47, 52
Husen, Paulus van 222

income tax under Bruning 93,
    94, 111
industrial democracy see co-
    determination
industry see heavy industry
    inflation and Brüning's
    policies 125
Inglehart, Ronald 28, 29
intellectuals, bourgeois self-
    criticism by 21–2
interest groups and Brüning's
    policies 123, 124, 127, 140
Iron Front 34, 40, 52, 57

Irving, David 234, 235, 236
ISK (International Socialist
    Fighting League) 14, 45, 54,
    59
Italy, fascist government 160, 164

Jaspers, Karl 261, 264, 270, 272,
    273
Jessen, Jens 198
Jews 224–53
    Aryanization policy 233, 240,
    242
    and bourgeois society 12
    deportation 244–5
    emigration 241–3
    and Hannah Arendt 260–78
    middle class 21
    Nazi genocide of 8–9, 173,
    174–5, 179, 180–1, 182, 183,
    224–7, 233–4, 237, 239–53,
    255–69
    and the NSDAP 158–9, 160,
    161
    and the Nuremberg Laws 227,
    229–33
    see also anti-semitism
Jones, Larry 21
judiciary under Nazi rule 173–4
Jünger, Ernst 21–2, 32

Kaas, Ludwig 148
Kahn-Freund, Otto 62
Kaiser, Jakob 190, 194, 195, 196,
    199, 213
Kämpfer, Rote 54
Kapp Putsch 42, 52, 70
Keynes, J. M. 125
Kleist-Schmenzin, Ewald 210
Kohler, Heinrich 91
Köhler, Lotte 273–4
Korherr, Richard 234
Koselleck, Rheinhard 79
Köttgen, Arnold 82
KPD (Communist Party of
    Germany) 39
    age structure 149
    and civil servants 116

membership 150
and national socialism 142,
    143
and the NSDAP 189
and the resistance movement
    192, 193, 199, 203, 204, 206,
    207, 211, 213
and the SPD 3, 44, 46, 48,
    49, 50, 51–2, 60, 67
and young people 34, 56, 57
KPO (Communist Party
    Opposition) 59
Krausnick 236
Kreisau Circle 193, 194, 197,
    198–9, 200, 201, 203, 204,
    205, 207, 213, 214, 215, 218,
    219, 270
Kube, Wilhelm 250
Kuda, Rudolf 73

labour movement 2–3
    decline of 4, 59
    defeat of 1933 189–90
    and the Nazi takeover 41, 42
    and the resistance to Hitler 8
    and the youth movement 30,
        58
Lambach, Walter 35
Lammers, Hans 163
Länder reform of, under
    Brüning 137–8
Lausanne Conference 124, 130
Law of Association (1908) 30
League of Nations 131
Lebensreform movement 25–6, 31
Leber, Julius 45, 59, 191, 193,
    194, 195, 196, 198, 200, 201,
    202, 204, 205, 206, 213, 219
Lederer, Emil 50
Legien, Carl 68–9, 70
Leipart, Theodor 194
Letterhaus, Bernhard 194, 195
Leuchtenberg Circle 33
Leuschner, Wilhelm 190, 192,
    193, 194, 195, 196, 197, 198,
    199, 200, 201, 202, 204,
    205–6, 207, 213

Levi, Paul 43, 45, 48, 58
Ley, Robert 157, 194
liberalism and the decline of the
    Burgertum 25, 27
Linz Programme (1926) 46
Lipset, Seymour Martin 150
Löbe, Paul 42
local government and the middle
    classes 12, 21
Lösener, Bernhard 231, 242
Löwenheim, Walter 41, 60
Ludendorff, Erich 146
Luftgas, Markus 227
Luther, Hans 121–2
Luther (Reichsbank President)
    103, 104, 108–9

Maass, Hermann 195, 196, 200,
    201, 213
Madagascar Plan 180, 236, 244,
    245, 257
Mahraun, Arthur 22
Mannheim, Karl 29
Marx, Karl 55, 58, 275
Marxist theories of facism 141
Matthias, Erich 39
Meinecke, Friedrich 20
Meir, Golda 271
middle class
    conflict of interests 20–1
    decline of 11–27
    and the fascist movement 58
    and the Nazi party 6–7, 51
    and the resistance movement
        219–20
    self-criticism by intellectuals
        21–2
    social differentiation within 12
    and SPD membership 49
Mierendorff, Carlo 45, 55–6, 57,
    59, 192, 193, 194, 198,
    199–200, 201, 202–3, 204,
    207, 213

Moellendorff, Wichard von 74, 80, 197
Moldenhauer 93, 94, 96, 134
Moltke, Helmuth von 193, 197, 199, 200–1, 202, 203, 205, 213, 214, 215, 216, 222, 259, 270
Monist League 19
Morsey 139
MSPD (Majority Social Democratic Party of Germany) 3, 49, 62, 68, 71, 80
Müller, Hanns 43
Müller, Hermann 65, 73, 91, 92, 93, 134
Munich Agreement 166
Mussolini, Benito 132, 142–3, 177

Naphtali, Fritz 72, 74, 75, 76
national conservative resistance movement 193, 194, 195–6, 203, 205, 207, 210–11, 213–19, 220, 222, 223
National Socialism 141–62
Naumann, Friedrich 77, 78
Neurath, Baron von 170
Niekisch, Ernst 35
Nietzsche, F. 18
Noakes, Jeremy 147
Nölting, Erich 55
November Revolution (1918) 20, 56–7, 81, 140, 152, 221
NSBO (National Socialist Factory-Cell Organization) 190
NSDAP (National Socialist German Workers' Party) 6–7, 143–62
   age structure 149
   and anti-semitism 228, 229, 231, 241
   and bourgeois/right-wing parties 147–8
   and Brüning 110, 138
   campaign strategy 7
   and civil servants 116

disintegration of Nazi system 186–8
emergence of 39, 146–51
Führer cult 7, 160–1, 163–4, 165–6, 185–6
ideology 7
internal crisis in 65
leadership 142, 144, 157
membership 49, 146, 147, 150–1
and the middle class 23–5, 51
Movement phase 145, 154, 155, 158, 159, 161
organization structure 143–5, 170–1
politics of 183–4
propaganda 143, 144, 147, 150, 155, 158, 169
seizure of power 145, 151–7
and the SPD 6, 44, 46
and the state 172–4
withdrawal from Reichstag 135
and young people 35, 36–7, 38, 56, 57, 148–9
Nuremberg Laws 227, 229–32, 242, 277
Nuremberg Trial 226, 260

Ohlendorf, Otto 219
Ollenhauer, Erich 55
Origins of Totalitarianism, The (Arendt) 260, 262, 266, 268
Orlow, Dietrich 147

Paechter, Henry 270
Pan-German League 15
Papen, Franz von 6, 9, 37, 40, 65, 82, 117, 131, 149, 150, 151, 168, 171, 191, 214
party politics and the civil service 81–2
pensions and Brüning's budgetary measures 103, 111, 114
People's National Conservative Association 35
Poland 180, 181
   German border with 1

political democracy 63
Popitz, Johannes 195, 198
presidential system of government
  in the Weimar Republic
  121, 132–8
prices and Brüning's budgetary
  measures 101
Programme for Economic
  Democracy 4, 72, 73–5
property, duties of in the Weimar
  constitution 78
Protestant youth groups 54
Prussia
  and Brüning's administrative
    reforms 104
  bureaucracy 79, 80
  coup (1932) 40
public expenditure see expenditure
  cuts
publishing see book publishing
Pünder, Hermann 90, 99

Radbruch, Gustav 43, 67, 215
Rademacher, Karl 244, 245
Ramm, Thilo 62
Rathenau, Walter 80
Raumer, Hans von 68
Rauschning, Herman 24, 220
reform movement, bourgeois
  19–20, 22, 23
Reich Citizenship Law 229, 230,
  231, 232
Reichsbanner 34, 40, 52
Reichshilfe scheme 95, 96, 97,
  98, 102, 134
Reichsrat 135–6
Reichstag
  and Brüning 132, 133, 135,
    136, 137
  exclusion from political
    process 82–4, 122, 139, 163
Reichstag Inter-Party Committee
  (1917) 3
Reichwein, Adolf 193, 194, 199,
  200, 206, 213
Reitlinger, Gerald 224, 255
reparations payments 99, 121,

  122, 125, 128, 129–30, 131
resistance movement 165, 167–8,
  191–223
  communist 192, 206, 209, 216,
    218, 219, 222, 270
  history of 208–10
  Jewish 267–8, 269
  national conservative 193, 194,
    195–6, 203, 205, 207,
    210–11, 213–19, 220, 222,
    223
  socialist 191–3
RGO (Revolutionary Trade Union
  Opposition) 71
Riesman, David 273
ring movement 14–15
Roehm, Ernst 153, 154, 164–5,
  168, 183
Rohe, Karl 52
Rommel, Erwin 217
Romoser, George K. 270
Rosenberg, Alfred 146, 156, 161
Rothfel, Hans 213

SA (Storm Troopers) 138, 148,
  153, 154, 159, 166, 170, 171,
  189, 210
SAJ (Socialist Working-Class
  Youth) 45, 52, 54
salary cuts under Brüning 87–8,
  90, 91–2, 93, 94, 97, 100–7,
  110, 111, 112–14
Salomon, Ernst von 13
SAPD (Socialist Workers' Party of
  Germany) 34, 54, 55, 59, 60
Schacht, H. 158, 242
Schäffer, Hans 21, 89, 90, 93,
  97, 100–1, 109, 112, 127, 130
Schauwecker, Franz 32
Schirach, Frau von 235
Schleicher, Kurt von 74, 112,
  117, 138, 151, 195, 214
Schleunes, Karl A. 239
Schmidt, Anton 278
Schmitt, Carl 82, 114
Schmölders, Günter 204
Schneider, Michael 73

Scholem, Gershom 260, 271–2, 277
Scholz, Ernst 96, 119
Schopenhauer, A. 18
Schulenburg, Fritz-Dietlov von der 201, 205, 215, 216
Schultz-Hencke, Harald 33
Schwartzbard, Shalom 261
Schwarzschild, Leopold 21
Second World War 163, 166–7, 180
  and the Nazi regime 160
  and the resistance movement 211
Siemsen, Anna 60
Silverberg, Paul 100
Sinzheimer, Hugo 62–3
social democracy 63
Social Democratic Party see SPD
social policies in the Weimar Republic 4, 63, 64–5, 66–7, 70–1
Socialist Laws 79
socialist youth movement 35
Society for Ethical Culture 19
Solf Circle 193, 213
Sopade 190–1, 194
Soviet Union
  deaths of prisoners of war from 181–2
  and the German resistance movement 200
  Nazi invasion of 238
SPD (Social Democratic Party) 2–3, 39–61
  age structure 3, 34–5, 52–5, 149
  and the bourgeois centre 2
  and Brüning's budgetary measures 92, 93, 94, 97, 98, 99, 102, 111, 114, 115, 134
  and Brüning's regime 138, 139, 140
  and the civil service 80
  and coalition governments 65, 66

  and democracy 67
  electoral support 49–50
  and the Kreisau circle 194
  leadership 34–5, 45–6, 58
  membership 48–9, 50
  and the Nazi party 6, 44, 46
  and the NSDAP 154, 189, 190, 190–1
  oppositional politics 59–60
  organizational structure 47–8
  propaganda 57–9
  recruitment 50–2, 59–60
  and the resistance movement 199–200, 201, 209
  Sinzheimer's support of 62
  and trade unions 74, 198
  and the youth movement 30, 34–5, 54–6
Speer, Albert 160, 161, 165, 166, 172, 176, 226, 240, 251
Spengler, oswald 215
SS (Schutzstaffel) 155, 168, 170, 178, 180, 186, 210, 212
  and the Final Solution 225, 226, 249
Stapel, Wilhelm 16
state officials, attitudes to 79–80
State Party (Staatspartei) 22, 135
Stauffenberg, Claus Schenk von 186, 201–2, 203, 205, 206, 212, 221
steel industry in the Weimar Republic 66, 67, 77
Stegerwald, Adam 67, 87, 91, 93, 95, 97, 101, 106, 107, 115, 199
Stelzer, Theodor 221–2
Stern, Fritz 25
Stern, Günther 275
Stern, J. P. 238
Stosstrup, Roter 211
Strasser, Gregor 13, 35, 151
Streicher, Julius 146, 228, 233
Streit, Christian 181
Stresemann, Gustav 3, 148

Tarnow, Fritz 75

Tat, Die (periodical) 13, 33, 36
taxation under Brüning 91, 93,
94–5, 96–8, 109, 111–12, 134
Thule Society 14, 15
Toennies, F. 31
totalitarian dictatorship theory
Hannah Arendt on 258, 266–7
and national socialism 141–3
trade unions
and Brüning's budgetary
measures 95–6
and the DHV 16
in heavy industry 4
and the Nazi takeover 41
and the NSDAP 154, 189–90
and politics 51
and the resistance movement
192, 195, 196–9, 202, 203–4,
207, 213, 214
and wage costs 5
weakening of 4
in the Weimar Republic
67–78, 123
and the youth movement 34
Tresckow, Henning von 212
Treviranus 93, 96, 101, 107
Troeltsch, Ernst 32
Trott zu Solz, Adam von 199,
201, 216, 270

Ulbricht, Walter 191
unemployment
and Brüning's budgetary
measures 112
and the NSDAP 149
and the resistance movement
204–5
in the Weimar Republic 68
USPD (Independent Social
Democratic Party of
Germany) 3, 49, 52, 54

Varnhagen von Ense, Rahel 271,
273–4
Verein, the 13–14, 18, 19, 23
Versailles Peace Treaty 1, 2, 126,
128, 140, 166

violence, political glorification of
13

Wagemann, Ernst 108–9
wages
and Brüning's budgetary
measures 95, 101
in the Weimar Republic 5, 66,
67, 71, 73
see also salary cuts
Wagner, Gerhard 231
Wagner, Helmut 45
Wagner Societies 18
Warmbold 124
Weber, Max 1, 79, 276
Weizsacker, Ernst von 216
Wels, Otto 41, 51, 52, 55
West Germany *see* Federal
Republic of Germany
Wiese, Benno von 272, 275
Winnig, August 198
Wirmer, Josef 195, 213
Wirth, Joseph 98
Wisliceny, Dieter 256
Wissell 197
Wohl, Robert 28
workers' participation *see*
co-determination
working class
decline of 3
and KPD membership 51
and the NSDAP 149
and the resistance movement
198, 207, 219
and SPD membership 49, 50,
61
and the Weimar Republic 39
works councils 71–2, 76, 80–1
Woytinsky, Wladimir 75
WTB Plan 4, 75–6
Wyneken, Heinrich 31

Yorck, Countess Marion 221
Yorck von Wartenburg, Count
Peter 197, 199, 200, 203,
205, 215, 216

Young German Order 22–3, 33, 35
Young Germany League 30–1
young people
  and the bourgeois youth movement 30, 31, 33, 54
  and generational conflict 7, 13, 28–38
  and the Nazi party 36–7, 38, 148–9
  organizations 54
  and the resistance movement 217, 219
  and the SPD 34–5, 53–7, 59–60
Young Plan 66, 91, 99, 125, 126, 127, 128, 131
Young Socialists 45, 52, 54, 55, 60
youth movement and bourgeois society 12–13

ZAG (Central Working Association) 67, 68, 70, 73, 76, 80, 95, 123
Zehrer, Hans 13, 15, 33, 36
Zentrum 148, 149, 151
Zionism 21, 264, 268, 269, 277